($14.95)
23.95

New Readings
on Women
in Old English
Literature

ew Readings on Women in Old English Literature

Edited by Helen Damico and Alexandra Hennessey Olsen

INDIANA UNIVERSITY PRESS

Bloomington and Indianapolis

Manufactured in the United States of America

Library of Congress Cataloging-in-Publication Data

New readings on women in Old English literature /
edited by Helen Damico and Alexandra Hennessey
Olsen.
    p.   cm.
   Includes index.
   ISBN 0-253-33413-6. — ISBN 0-253-20547-6 (pbk.)
   1. English literature—Old English, ca. 450–1100—
History and criticism. 2. Women in literature. 3. Sex
role in literature. I. Damico, Helen. II. Olsen,
Alexandra Hennessey.
PR179.W65N4 1989
829'.09'352042—dc19   88-45459
                                 CIP

1   2   3   4   5   93   92   91   90   89

Contents

III. Language and Difference in Characterization

IV. The "Deconstructed" Stereotype

Preface

The idea for this volume began at the 1980 meeting of the Modern Language Association of America in Houston, Texas, when the editors participated in a special session entitled "Feminine Themes in Old English Literature," arranged by the Division on Old English Language and Literature and chaired by Thomas Cable. Helen Damico presented "The Valkyrie Figure in Old English and Old Norse," source of "The Valkyrie Reflex in Old English Literature," and Alexandra Hennessey Olsen presented "The Rape of Holofernes: *Judith* as a Political Poem." The other two participants were Alain Renoir and Jane Chance. Renoir presented the first draft of "Eve's I.Q. Rating: Two Sexist Views of *Genesis B*," and Chance presented "The Anglo-Saxon Woman as Hero: The Chaste Queen and the Masculine Woman Saint." Chance's contribution to the present volume is "The Structural Unity of *Beowulf*: The Problem of Grendel's Mother." Feminist issues in Old English literature were again the subject of a session at the 1982 meeting of the Medieval Institute at Kalamazoo, Michigan, with Patricia A. Belanoff, Jane Chance, Helen Damico, and Dolores Warwick Frese participating. At these and later conferences, the editors discussed the lack of criticism by both feminists and Anglo-Saxonists on women in the Anglo-Saxon period and concluded that the presentation of an anthology might promote work in a much neglected area of Anglo-Saxon studies. It was in the hope of promoting critical studies on women in Old English literature that the editors prepared this volume of essays, the first and only one of its kind.

The essays are grouped into the four main categories of feminist inquiry: the reconstruction of a female past; the examination of woman's sexuality and her image in folklore and myth; the use of language in differentiating women; and the re-examination of the stereotype. The essays in Part I examine what has been considered negative evidence of women's authority, influence, and image in the Anglo-Saxon period and adjust prevailing misconceptions of these attributes. Those in Part II revise traditional notions on women's sexuality and image, while those in Part III use linguistic analysis for their reappraisals of the women characters. The essays in Part IV deconstruct the stereotype. In so doing, they hope to lay the foundation for subsequent studies that would correct the ideas presented therein.

The collection would not have come into being were it not for the efforts of our contributors, and our thanks first must go to them for their indulgence and generosity. In addition, we thank the SIROW Foundation and the University of Denver Faculty Research Grants for their financial assistance in allowing us individually to pursue research for this volume, and the following journals and publishing houses for their permission to reprint:

Allegorica, for "The Valkyrie Reflex in Old English Literature" by Helen Damico;

The Bodley Head, for "Æthelflæd, Lady of the Mercians," by F. T. Wainwright, which was published by Bowes and Bowes in *The Anglo-Saxons: Studies in Some Aspects of Their History and Culture Presented to Bruce Dickins,* ed. Peter Clemoes;

Medium Ævum, for "The *Ides* of the Cotton Gnomic Poem," by Audrey L. Meaney;

Neuphilologische Mitteilungen, for "*Freoðuwebbe* in Old English Poetry," by Larry M. Sklute (L. John Sklute);

Past and Present, for "The King's Wife in Wessex, 800–1066," by Pauline Stafford; the world copyright for this essay is held by The Past and Present Society, 175 Banbury Road, Oxford, England. This article is reprinted with the permission of the Society and the author from *Past and Present,* no. 91 (May 1981);

Peter Lang Publishing, Inc., for sections from *Speech, Song, and Poetic Craft: The Artistry of the Cynewulf Canon,* by Alexandra Hennessey Olsen;

Religion and Literature, for "*Wulf and Eadwacer*: The Adulterous Woman Reconsidered," by Dolores Warwick Frese, which appeared when the journal was entitled *Notre Dame English Journal*;

The Royal Historical Society, for "The Historical Bearing of Place-Name Studies: The Place of Women in Anglo-Saxon Society," by F. M. Stenton, which appeared in the *Transactions of the Royal Historical Society, Fourth Series,* vol. 25:1–13;

Scandinavian Studies, for "The Politics of Scarcity: Notes on the Sex Ratio in Early Scandinavia," by Carol J. Clover;

The University of Texas Press, for "The Structural Unity of *Beowulf*: The Problem of Grendel's Mother," by Jane Chance (Nitzsche), which appeared in *Texas Studies in Language and Literature;*

The University of Wisconsin Press, for sections of *Beowulf's Wealhtheow and the Valkyrie Tradition,* by Helen Damico;

Edith Whitehurst Williams, for "What's So New about the Sexual Revolution? Some Comments on Anglo-Saxon Attitudes toward Sexuality in Women Based on Four Exeter Book Riddles," which appeared in *Texas Quarterly,* no longer in publication.

Others we wish to thank are at the University of New Mexico: The Women's Studies Program for their support of Helen Damico's SIROW grant; Linda Lewis, Research Librarian for Women's Studies at Zimmerman Library; and Krystan V. Douglas, Leslie Donovan, and Juliette Cunico of the Department of English. At the University of Denver, we thank May Smith, Inter-Library-Loan Librarian at Penrose Library, and Helen Shay, Secretary of the Department of English. We thank also the directors and staff of the English Seminar at the University of Münster for making available their research facilities for Helen Damico while she visited them as a guest professor.

Finally, our thanks must go to our friends and colleagues: Gail Baker, Jess B.

Bessinger, Jr., Michael Fischer, Shirley Nelson Garner, Mary Power, Joyce Rogers, Carolyn Woodward and, in particular, Joan E. Hartman and Raymond P. Tripp, Jr., whose comments and guidance were indispensable in completing this volume.

The abbreviations used for Old English Poetry are those which appear in *A Concordance to the Anglo-Saxon Poetic Records,* ed. J. B. Bessinger, Jr., programmed by Philip H. Smith, Jr. (Ithaca: Cornell University Press, 1978) as, for example, *Beowulf* (Bwf), *Christ* (Chr), *Elene* (Ele), *Judith* (Jud), *Juliana* (Jln), *The Wife's Lament* (WL), and *Wulf and Eadwacer* (WE).

We dedicate our efforts to our sisters—both kin and friend—Kay and Kit, Victoria and Veronica.

MARIJANE OSBORN

The Fates of Women

(FROM FOUR ANGLO-SAXON POEMS)

1

A thief walks dark weathers. A demon in fen dwells
alone. In shadows a woman will seek
her true love with magic, if she does not intend
to perform so brightly among the folk
that some man will offer for her. Ocean is salty.
Flowing across the land are clouds
and floods and streams. Stock in the meadows
are to mate and increase. A star in the sky
shines brightly, as God has bidden it.

2

A leader mounts up and his legion rides;
his men stand fast against the foe.
It is meet that a woman remain by her table;
wandering she will stir up words,
belie good men and be gossiped about
derisively. Often she wrinkles early.
Shame walks in shadow; light shines on the pure.

The deep path of death is the darkest secret.
Holly to the fire—what the dead man has harbored
shall go to his heirs. Glory is best.
The king must pay for his queen with wealth,
with goblets and bracelets, but both must first
be generous with gifts. Grim in combat
must be that lord, and the lady excel,
beloved by her people, in lightness of heart,
in keeping of secrets, courageous in giving
of horses and gold. Gracious with mead
she goes among the companions to meet

the warrior's leader, welcomes him first,
holds out the goblet to his hand,
the cup to her prince. Good council as well
she has for them both in their high home.

The ship shall be nailed, the linden shield
light and well-bound. Her loved one is welcome
to the Frisian wife when his fleet comes in.
His ship is moored and her man is home,
her own husband. She asks him in,
washes his garments, gives him fresh ones,
grants him on land what his love craves.

A wife should be loyal, not wander about
to shame a man—though many will fancy
meeting a stranger, their man at sea.

The sailor long on his voyage should hold out for love,
should wait for what won't be hurried. The wind at last
blows him home, if he lives (unless the sea holds him back
in its long embrace), to the joy of her he's bound to.

3

Often it happens by God's hand
that a man and a woman bring into the world
sons, whom they clothe in the brightest colors,
cuff and coddle, until the time comes
that those young limbs with the passing years
have branched out into a buoyant growth.
The father and mother force and ripen them,
give to them, gear them, and God alone knows
what winter will bring to their burgeoning!

It might even happen that one will meet
in his early manhood a cruel end,
a grim fate—when a grey heath-stalking
wolf devours him! The mother weeps.
But he'll not return. No one can help it.

4

No mother can guess when she gives birth
what waits for her child out in the world.
He she nurtures may come to nothing

but grief—to her own grief, for she must also
endure his hardship at the destined hour.
Often and again she will ache for that boy,
bitterly yearn when he goes forth young
with a wild spirit, a resentful heart . . .
So a mother has no say when she bears a son
over his fate, but can only follow
after him.

> That is the ancient way!

NOTES

The sources from which I have compiled this poem are as follows: Part one is from *Maxims II*, lines 42–49; part two from *Maxims I*, lines 62–66, 78–92, and 95–106; part three from *The Fortunes of Men*, lines 1–14; and part four from *Solomon and Saturn*, lines 372–79 and 384–86. The poems from which these passages were translated may be found in Volumes III and VI of *The Anglo-Saxon Poetic Records*, edited by George Philip Krapp and Elliott Van Kirk Dobbie (New York: Columbia University Press, 1936).

In part two: The fire of line 18 is a funeral pyre, heaped with holly instead of the old king's treasure; the new king will use that wealth to ensure his men's loyalty and as dowry for a queen (lines 20–22). The translation of line 38 about the Frisian wife is based on a comment by C. L. Wrenn; as he reads it, this is the only direct reference to sexual intercourse in Old English poetry. (The "dirty riddles," for example, are oblique, and the passage in "The Wife's Lament" about lovers lying in bed in the morning need not refer specifically to lovemaking.) The last stanza of part two is in the expanded lines that one sometimes encounters in Old English poetry, often marking a passage of special importance.

In part three: "Cuff and coddle" at line 50 is the solution that Peter Ridgewell and I devised for the crux of *tennaþ ond tætaþ* (*Fortunes of Men*, line 4); these are two verbs occurring nowhere else in Old English. *Tennan* may possibly be derived from OE *tān* 'switch,' and *tætan* is cognate with (archaic) Icelandic *teita*, 'to make someone happy, cheer them up.'

New Readings
on Women
in Old English
Literature

HELEN DAMICO AND
ALEXANDRA HENNESSEY OLSEN

Introduction

I thought of Beowulf lying wrapped
in a blanket among his platoon of
drunken thanes in the Gotland billet . . .

Robert Graves, *Goodbye to All That*[1]

OLD ENGLISH LITERATURE IN THE UNIVERSITY CURRICULUM

In a 1979 article, "Bringing the Spirit Back to English Studies," Carolyn Heilbrun recalls the revolutionary response that Graves and his classmate Edmund Blunden had experienced when, freshly returned from battling in the trenches of World War I, they confronted a "classic" of English literature written in a language which their Oxford lecturer assured them had only "linguistic interest," but which they nonetheless were obliged to learn.[2] The remark could only have seemed ironically ludicrous to these young men, still suffering from scarred sensibilities and physical wounds. But happily for them, *Beowulf* became something more than an artifact of declensions, conjugations, and i-mutation. Translating *Beowulf* must have become for them an exercise in immortality. They were able to bridge time and space, to surmount the linguistic barrier, and to make contact with a mind that comprehended, as they did, the horrors of warfare. The attack on pedantry in the teaching of earlier literature which Heilbrun alluded to in recalling this anecdote was also at the root of J. R. R. Tolkien's remarks made in a 1936 address that revolutionized Beowulfian studies. As a way of illustrating his thesis that *Beowulf* was an aesthetically beautiful and humanly meaningful poem, Tolkien related an anecdote about Professor Bosworth's preferred bedtime reading, how the renowned lexicographer read with anticipated pleasure about Beowulf's adventures in a poem which Tolkien defines as "an elaboration of the intensely moving contrast between youth and age, [the] first achievement and final death" of a young Geatish warrior.[3]

Personal responses to *Beowulf* or, in fact, to any other Old English poem are rare, especially ones that suggest that there might be a pleasurable and meaningful interchange between a reader and a literary work. Both Heilbrun and Tolkien are concerned with the marginality of Beowulfian studies (and, for Heilbrun, the concern extended to all of English studies as well) in the university curriculum. The critical approaches of the nineteenth century had almost succeeded in destroying from ennui a poem that physically had survived over nine hundred years of literary vicissitudes.

For Heilbrun and Tolkien, resuscitation lay in a return to the poem for its pleasure and meaning.

Heilbrun further associated the marginality of English literature (and the study of Old English literature is subsumed in the larger context of her argument) with an imbalance and incompleteness of meaning that came about from the exclusion from serious consideration of over half of its readership, the women. She observed that not only were there mistaken analyses of the representations of women in English literature, but that, in addition, there was an acute absence of the works of women writers and critics in the literary canon. For Heilbrun, English studies could never be cured of its malaise until it could correct these misinterpretations and balance and complete the record, for then the literature could be seen whole.

Anglo-Saxon studies[4]—like those in other literary periods—exhibit an imbalance, for they too have tended to center on the work of male scholars and teachers. The list of the names of male scholars whose work has enriched the field is long and distinguished, but there is indisputable evidence of extraordinary scholarly contributions made by women as well. From the pioneer grammarian Elizabeth Elstob to Dorothy Bethurum, a number of women scholars—Nora K. Chadwick, Doris Stenton, and Dorothy Whitelock, to name but a few—have served as models to students and younger scholars in the field. Elstob was surely the first feminist in Anglo-Saxon Studies. Her grammar of Anglo-Saxon—the first of its kind—was written particularly for the enlightenment of women. Nonetheless, women scholars and critics have been a distinct minority. The field has been historically male-dominated, and it has been only within the last fifteen years or so that, at a congress or symposium, there has been an increased number of female scholars as well as male in attendance.

It has also been only within the very recent past that teachers, scholars, and students of Old English have begun to take note of the female characters in the poetry and to develop a balanced assessment of the representations of women—and, hence, of men—in Anglo-Saxon literature. Tolkien's reading of *Beowulf,* for example, despite its brilliance, is biased, although few readers have realized that fact. Responding as a male to male experience, he perceives a poem of two parts which (in broad terms) depicts the hero's rise and fall. This is an acceptable reading, which reflects one of several organizing principles that the narrative allows. But such a two-part division substantially weakens (in fact, almost negates) the thematic importance of the central third of the poem, which in thematic terms is concerned with mothers and their sons, and in which is found the delineation of some vital human female figures and Grendel's Mother. Even when tripartite structurings of the poem have been proposed, they have tended to overlook the significance of the women characters and to center instead on the issue of Beowulf's three great fights with Grendel, Grendel's Mother, and the Dragon. More recently, a three-part structure—one that analyzes the narrative function of the women characters—has been urged by H. L. Rogers, Kathryn Hume, and Jane Chance.[5] Their readings of episodes involving the female characters of *Beowulf* have posited alternative theses that have begun to transform an epic poem heretofore perceived to be about male experience into a work that comments upon female experience as well. These and other interpretations of the poem aim to show women's experience as integral to rather than disengaged from the heroic world. They perceive the women in *Beowulf* as central to the narrative—not ancillary. These perceptions ultimately lead to re-evaluations of the poem and of its literary and cultural milieu.

The work of these critics has been a part of an informal movement that has sprung up in Anglo-Saxon studies which has chosen as its subject the analysis of women and their representation in the literary and documentary records of Anglo-Saxon society. One of the earliest revisionist essays (in 1979) was Sheila C. Dietrich's "An Introduction to Women in Anglo-Saxon Society (ca. 600–1066)." Dietrich enjoined scholars to return to the primary sources and to strip away "accretions of another writer's bias or orientation" in order to attain a more comprehensive understanding of the women in Anglo-Saxon literature. In less than ten years, numerous studies of both article-length (some of which are collected in this volume) and book-length have reexamined women in Anglo-Saxon literature and culture. These works—including Christine E. Fell's *Women in Anglo-Saxon England;* Pauline Stafford's *Queens, Concubines and Dowagers: The King's Wife in the Early Middle Ages;* Jane Chance's *Woman as Hero in Old English Literature;* Helen Damico's *Beowulf's Wealhtheow and the Valkyrie Tradition;* and a large portion of Alexandra Hennessey Olsen's *Speech, Song, and Poetic Craft: The Artistry of the Cynewulf Canon*—are revisionist.[6] They go directly to the primary sources in order to pose "new questions" to "very old records."[7]

As will be readily apparent, the essays collected in this volume are involved in exactly this task. Collectively they also have as their chosen subject the analysis of women as they appear in literary and historical records. They address these overwhelmingly male-authored writings with questions centered on women's concerns, in the hopes of generating a more accurate reading of the texts involved and of promoting a more enlightened understanding of the position, role, and function of women in Anglo-Saxon culture and of the meaning of their experience.

This continued and increasing interest in writing about women in Anglo-Saxon literature and culture parallels to some degree the development of literary criticism on women and their representation in other periods. This general critical inquiry grew out of the feminist social movements which took place in the United States and Europe in the 1960s and which sought the political and social enfranchisement of women. Anglo-Saxonists are late in coming to the re-examination of women in the literary and historical writings that were composed roughly between A.D. 600 and 1200. It has been otherwise with those who study later medieval literature. Joan Ferrante's *Woman as Image in Medieval Literature from the Twelfth Century to Dante,* and what Ferrante sees as the "fusion of male and female characteristics" in medieval writings, for example, was influenced by Heilbrun's work on androgyny.[8] Contemporary feminist literary criticism likewise affected scholars and students who have been working in Old French and Middle English studies, especially those who are examining the work of Christine de Pisan, Margery Kempe, and Julian of Norwich.[9] Most feminist literary criticism in this field likewise has confined its investigations to the late Middle Ages and, in particular, to women authors.[10] Linguistic and historical accessibility may have contributed to this emphasis: the need to learn Old English undoubtedly has presented the primary obstacle to appreciating the literature. But two other hurdles have been equally inhibiting: first, the convention—erroneous though it may be—that *Beowulf,* the major work of the earlier period and thus the work most frequently read and taught in translation, is a poem expounding a warrior ethos of interest only to men, and, second, the lack of named women writers of Old English poems. The essays collected in this volume are devoted to eliminating these obstacles, by bringing to bear on the Old English period the insights of contemporary feminism and by opening up the period to feminist literary inquiry.

We envision that the readers of these essays will be both Anglo-Saxonists, who may not have had the opportunity, the time, nor in some instances the inclination to become familiar with the objectives and methods of feminist literary criticism, and feminists, who have had little, if any, contact with Old English language and literature or with the traditional critical approaches thereto. The following pages, therefore, will offer as an introduction to the essays first what can only be a capsuled review of feminist literary criticism and then a short survey of the critical writings that have been produced on the topic of women in Anglo-Saxon literature and culture.

FEMINISM AND FEMINIST LITERARY CRITICISM

Like all linguistic terms, *feminism* and *feminist literary criticism* are polysemous and contextually related. Feminism is an ideological movement which is based on the principle of empowering women and which, some believe, had its beginnings in John Stuart Mill's petition for women's suffrage presented at the 1866 meeting of the English parliament. The classic statement of feminist principles, however, was Mary Wollstonecraft's *A Vindication of the Rights of Woman,* which antedated Mill's petition by over fifty years (1792). But even before Wollstonecraft, Mary Astell's essays (*A Serious Proposal to the Ladies* [1694 and 1697] and *Some Reflections Upon Marriage* [1700]) called for women's psychological and intellectual emancipation from men. In mid-nineteenth-century America, the classic formulation of women's grievances was Margaret Fuller's (first in 1842, "The Great Lawsuit," and then expanded in 1845, *Woman in the Nineteenth Century*), which was associated with the broader suffrage movement led in part by Susan B. Anthony and Elizabeth Cady Stanton.[11] The publication that gave impetus to the contemporary women's movement was Simone de Beauvoir's *The Second Sex* (1949), regarded by many as the most influential feminist work of this century. Although here, de Beauvoir held that women's equality with men would be achieved as a matter of course through Marxism, she later changed that position.[12] In contemporary America, the term is linked to the Women's Liberation Movement of the 1960s, sometimes referred to as the feminist movement, whose central issues of women's political and cultural discontent were first given public attention in Betty Friedan's 1963 publication, *The Feminine Mystique.*[13]

Feminism advocates women's political, social, and economic equality. The important thrust in the movement is for self-identity and psychological autonomy for women, an objective which underlies the work for reform toward universal equality.

But how to achieve this equality has split the feminists into two groups, the integrationists—who strive for integration into and self-definition within the existing male-dominated social structures—and the separatists—who strive to establish a "countersociety." Like all ideological systems, both positions have the potential of achieving social results which, in turn, might become self-defeating: integrationists, for instance, run the risk of becoming conformists and supporters of the establishment, and separatists, the risk of engaging in a kind of "inverted sexism."[14]

In her "Feminism, Marxism, Method, and the State: An Agenda for Theory," Catharine A. MacKinnon argues for and identifies feminism—previously understood in general as a "collection" of women's complaints on their state—as a theoretical system of inquiry. Its methodology is consciousness-raising, a dialectical system of examination which proceeds connotatively and analytically and which aims to discover and to examine the impact of male dominance on women's experience.[15] For MacKinnon, Marxism and feminism are theories of "power" and its unequal distribution, and they are compatible, in one sense, because they address problems of inequality caused by the oppression of one group of human beings by another. Feminism differs from Marxism in that (1) it has risen from and developed within the social group "whose interest it affirms" and (2) it makes its essential social determination on sexual rather than on class distinctions to demonstrate and explain inequality in society as a whole. Many feminists, however, reject Marxism on the grounds that it is a patriarchal system with male concerns at its center, for it defines work (the determinant of identity) and the distribution of power by male standards and in male language. In the Marxian class hierarchy, women's work still emerges as peripheral, non-continuous, and subordinate.[16] It was the realization of this fundamental Marxian principle that prompted de Beauvoir, the most eminent supporter of Marxist socialism as a means by which women could achieve equality, to abandon it and to identify herself as a feminist. De Beauvoir set the parameters for feminist concerns: to identify and discriminate social, political, psychological, and linguistic injuries (conscious or unconscious) committed against women and to seek redress for these abuses of patriarchal power.[17] The means by which to attain redress allowed for varieties of address and degrees of radicalism, and the need to do so gained support from every section of society, from the marketplace to the classroom.

Critical inquiries into women's writing or woman's image in literature did not begin to appear until the latter half of the 1960s, although (in addition to *The Second Sex*) Virginia Woolf's *A Room of One's Own* had been part of women's (and men's) reading since 1927. Toril Moi marks the beginning of feminist literary criticism with the publication of Kate Millett's *Sexual Politics* in 1969, although of equal importance (if not receiving equal notoriety) were Mary Ellmann's study of the female stereotypes in literature, *Thinking About Women* (published a year earlier) and Katherine M. Rogers's study of misogyny, *The Troublesome Helpmate* (in publication since 1966).[18] All subsequent writings on woman's image and women's writing took the ideas expressed in these works as points of departure for their discussions, culminating about ten years later in publications like *The Madwoman in the Attic* (Sandra Gilbert and Susan Gubar), *Literary Women* (Ellen Moers), and *A Literature of Their Own* (Elaine Showalter). These works have focused on the modern period, from the eighteenth century forward. Collectively, they have (1) challenged the male-centered value system that has selected the traditional literary canon and codified literary history, both of which restrict and/or exclude women writers and their works; (2) attacked and/or distrusted existing literary modes and methodologies, which they see as authoritarian and androcentric; and (3) condemned both authors and critics for their disenfranchisement of the woman character in literature by regarding her either as a stereotype or as an extension of phallocentric fears and desires.[19]

In the broadest terms, feminist literary criticism has been reductively (and unjustly) characterized by its detractors as militant, biased, revisionist, and (especially when written by American literary critics) antitheoretical, with a proclivity toward realism and the perception of literature as an interpretation of life.[20] It holds (as do other schools of criticism) that there is an unbreakable bond between politics, in the broadest sense, and aesthetics,[21] a thesis that cannot be proven but can only be argued by persuasion. Its primary tenet is that critical responses to and evaluations of a given work will depend in large part on the gender of both the author and the critic.[22]

Against the charge of bias (in that they predetermine their subject matter and approach) and revisionism (in that they correct misinterpretations of women's literary representations and work which subordinate and degrade women's experience), feminists rightly argue that bias and revisionism characterize any critical activity that wishes to alter the comprehension and judgment of a particular work or genre. Feminists, on the other hand, are candid enough to warn the reader openly of their ideological stance: they state that underlying their activity—which Showalter describes as "correcting, modifying, supplementing, revising, humanizing, or even attacking male critical practices"—is their commitment to the rehabilitation and empowerment of women in all areas of life.[23] For non-feminists, and for those feminists who have refused the label, this is an unpalatable stance, for it counters a belief that literary studies should be divorced from politics and that objectivity and what Showalter calls "scientism" in literary studies is fundamental to critical activity.[24] Feminist critics hold that there is no such state as critical objectivity nor is there evidence which is non-biased, and that the consciousness of the critic is subject to the "authority of experience."[25] For feminists, all literature and literary criticism are shaped by gender. What had been presented as universal "received opinion" in the interpretation and evaluation of the literary canon and in the recording of literary history had been, in fact, male opinion, prescribed and determined by male experience, and articulated for a community of readers who were predominantly male.[26]

In the fifteen or so years of its history, feminist literary criticism has produced a significant body of work on women writers and the genres they work in, on literary representations of women, and on the process and "difference" in female expression to make visible and to prove true Heilbrun's 1979 charge that discriminatory practices characterize literary studies: "There is no male or female viewpoint. There is only the human viewpoint, which happens always to have been male."[27] In their determination to be "resisting" and "suspicious" readers of male-centered literary representations of women[28] and of androcentric evaluations of women writers, feminist literary critics posit an alternative view which finds gender as a prime force in shaping literature and literary history. This view is perhaps not entirely new in the history of ideas, as Kenneth K. Ruthven points out in his chronological survey of feminist concerns,[29] but nonetheless it is an idea that has taken hold and that will (with persistence and care) lead to the balanced restructuring of literature and literary history.[30]

Feminist literary criticism is a hybrid, a combination of the ideological idea that gender has been a major contributing factor in shaping literature (and, by extension, society and existing schools of thought) and of the diverse critical approaches, which include feminist genre criticism (Miller, Jellinek), archetypal criticism (Pratt), literary historical criticism (Showalter), psychological (Gilbert, Gubar, Gallop) and psycho-linguistic criticism (Kristeva), somatic criticism (Cixous, Irigaray), and structuralist criticism (Kolodny). There are black and lesbian feminist aesthetics; there are marxist-, freudian-, lacanian-, jungian-feminists. There are even (as Showalter has pointed out) theoretical tendencies observable along national lines: "English feminist criticism, essentially Marxist, stresses oppression; French feminist criticism, essentially psychoanalytic, stresses repression; American feminist criticism, essentially textual, stresses expression."[31]

In "Towards a Feminist Poetics" (1979) and later in "Feminist Criticism in the Wilderness" (1981)—as a first step toward the formulation of a feminist theory[32] and as a means by which to make possible a systematic study of the field—Showalter grouped these diverse approaches under two distinct classifications: "*feminist reading* or the *feminist critique*" and "*gynocritics*" (her translation of the French *la gynocritique*).[33] *Feminist reading* or the *feminist critique* is concerned with interpretation and analysis of woman's image in literature and of the role of women in society. Because it posits that woman's image has been distorted by examinations that have been partial and discriminatory, its methods are comparative and interdisciplinary in approach. In this respect, *feminist reading* extends its analysis to include man's image and role, as well as patriarchal creeds and institutions. Most of the literary and socio-historical studies on women in the later medieval period would fall under the category of *feminist reading*. Anthologies of works by women— Katharina M. Wilson's *Medieval Women Writers,* Peter Dronke's *Women in the Middle Ages,* and Eleanor Shipley Duckett's *Women and their Letters in the Early Middle Ages*—and about women—Frances and Joseph Gies's *Women in the Middle Ages,* Rosmarie Thee Morewedge's *The Role of Women in the Middle Ages,* and Susan Mosher Stuard's *Women in Medieval Society*—as well as Ferrante's *Woman as Image* and the other studies mentioned in this introduction,[34] could be classified under *feminist reading* solely on the basis of their subject matter, even though the authors might not declare themselves feminists. They are engaged in interpreting, analyzing, and revising woman's image and functions in literature and in society; they use a variety of critical approaches and methodologies; and they work with a large body of work by both men and women to collect their audience. *Gynocritics,* on the other hand, focuses exclusively on women writers. It eschews male writers and their work and male-centered critical theory and concentrates on the "psychodynamics of female creativity; linguistics and the problem of female language; the trajectory of the individual or collective female literary career; literary history; and, of course, studies of particular writers and works."[35]

French feminist literary criticism, more theoretical than either the British or the

American, concentrates on one branch of gynocritics, linguistics, in its concern with women who write as *women* and with the psychoanalytic and biological influence on women's language. *Écriture féminine* is a dominant school, and its most articulate advocates are Hélène Cixous, Catherine Clément, and Luce Irigaray.[36] The psychoanalytical influence on *écriture féminine* is clear when Cixous and Clément, for example, adapt Freudian terminology to their own purposes: Freud's *hysteric* becomes Cixous and Clément's description of people who "embody incompatible syntheses,"[37] especially women. Cixous argues that a woman "must write her self [i.e., must write with her body]: must write about women and bring women to writing," a polemical point related to the American advocacy of including women authors in the literary canon.[38] Cixous's work is highly individualistic and personal; and, although (as Moi observes), she is an activist in her theory, she refuses to be identified as a feminist because of the term's political associations.[39] Irigaray, another exponent of bio-criticism, asserts that the morphological differences between the female and male sexual organs are the cause for the difference between phallocentric and gynocritic discourse. Cixous and Irigaray argue that women can and should create a somatic-inspired mode of discourse to replace a phallocentric language that acts as if men and masculine values are universal and women and female values are peripheral. Their objective is to discover a woman's language that will liberate women into articulateness, an objective that is Annie Leclerc's as well. Leclerc wants women to "invent a language that is not oppressive, a language that does not leave speechless but that loosens the tongue."[40]

In opposition to Cixous, Irigaray, and Leclerc on the issue of creating a separate female language is Julia Kristeva. Kristeva agrees that language and language structures promote the idea that the male is universal and the female peripheral. She sees this as a reflection of contemporary social power, but thinks that effecting social change will not necessarily resolve the problem of women's marginality. For this, one must re-examine and redefine the production of language.[41] For Kristeva, language is not a system, but a process of signification in continuous flux, which comes about through an interaction between what Kristeva calls "*la sémiotique*" and "*le symbolique*." *La sémiotique* is an "instinctual drive" (*pulsionnel*) to produce language that encompasses non-reductive rhythms and intonations. *Le symbolique* is the employment of the "known" in language—the established signs, syntax, and referents.[42] To attain signification, a speaker (whether male or female) must be in the position of a "questionable subject-in-process," producing language that is a result of the continuous tension created between "the instinctual drive" and the use (and simultaneous challenge) of the "known" in language.[43] Kristeva associates the "semiotic" phase with the "maternal" (a quality that encompasses both male and female) and the "symbolic" with the "patriarchal." She argues that the symbolic has imprisoned both men and women, and has forced even men to suppress those qualities that might be perceived as female. She suggests that a dual-gender language (one that is produced from the processes described above and that is heterogeneous, fluid, and contextual) would free both sexes from the constraints of a patriarchal language perceived as "universal."[44] To invent a separate women's language would simply substitute one type of restraint with another.

Much of British feminist literary criticism concentrates on women's writing as well. But because of the political situation in Britain, it is largely Marxist in orientation, although it tends to incorporate insights drawn from French feminism. Marxist aesthetics, which suggest that the author produces a text that is historically and economically determined, and which claim to be the best available form of critical discourse, have gained a particular influence in Britain because (as David Aers argues) it is compatible with the ideology of modern British politics as reflected in its teaching: "Our 'situated' criticism, our teaching, is inextricably bound up with current attempts to preserve our society in its present form, with its legitimating ideologies, organizations of power, and distribution of resources; or it is bound up with efforts to change it."[45] British work may be typified by the essay "Women's Writing," collectively written by members of the Marxist-Feminist Literature Collective, which analyzes novels by women, giving equal weight to facts of gender, class, and factors of literary production,[46] and drawing upon the theories of Louis Althusser and Pierre Macherey.[47]

American feminist literary criticism is more empirically and politically oriented than either the British or the French. Studies on women's language, for instance, are more systematically ordered; they deal with such topics as identification of linguistic features in women's language, sexist features in social language, or sexism in the language and structure of English, in order to lay the foundation for "re-invent[ing] language," outside the constraints of phallocentric discourse.[48] Like Kristeva (but for different reasons), Showalter argues against women's language, even though there is historical and cultural precedent for such. To invent women's language is non-productive, for it places women's articulateness outside the social context and negates their effectiveness. Feminist energies should be placed on gaining accessibility to language and on demanding (as a right) its use. A woman speaker should not be forced into "silence, euphemism, or circumlocution" (as has been the case in the past) when she talks about female experience.[49]

Much of American feminist literary criticism that has focused on women writers and their work has concentrated its analysis on the restrictive and discriminatory, but subtle, influence of established genres on women's writings and women's representation therein, what feminists call androcentric genres in that they are inherently structured to explore and to promulgate male ideology.[50] Annis Pratt, for example, has contrasted novels by men to novels by Willa Cather, Kate Chopin, and Margaret Atwood to expand the Jungian idea of archetypes and to show the archetypal patterns that influence (and restrict) female authors and characters.[51] Myra Jehlen argues that the novel, whether written by men or women, has a plot structure that traps women, one which promotes the idea of male dominance and which delineates the female characters not as representations of women but as metaphors expressing the emotional life of men. Even novels by women (like George Eliot, writing in the male tradition) depict the experience of the sexes as polarized—men are capable only of public action and women are capable only of emotion and sentiment.[52] And Nancy Reinhardt has argued that we should apply feminist insights and investigations to drama, of which both texts and criticism display male bias. Reinhardt sees tragedy, whether by Sophocles, Euripides, or Shakespeare, as focusing on the *agon* of a male protagonist—a mental and physical struggle which she compares to war—or on a competition involving "alien" or even unsexed female characters who are "one-dimensional" rather than "well-rounded." In the case of Lady Macbeth and Medea, for example, the women's emotional life loses in intensity and effectiveness because they have been presented as unbalanced, a situation that does not occur with a hero like Lear. In comedies like *As You Like It* and *The Way of the World*, traditional female concerns take center stage, but here again, the female is seen only in relation to the male, and she is dependent (for example, she never ventures out alone).[53]

The work of Pratt, Jehlen, and Reinhardt suggests that feminist critical techniques not only can profitably be applied to works written in the present by avowed feminists, but also can illuminate works of the past. Sheila Delany acknowledges that the feminist understanding that gender influences writing has helped her to interpret both Christine de Pisan's *Cité des Dames* and Chaucer's *Legend of Good Women*.[54] The general assumption of *écriture féminine*—that there is a relationship between a woman's body and her life and her writing—underlies the depictions of women in the work of both Rudolph M. Bell and Caroline Walker Bynum.[55]

The new attention to economic matters promoted by the Marxist critics also provides insights into the nature of women in other historical periods. In *Writing Woman: Women Writers and Women in Literature, Medieval and Modern*, Delany states explicitly that "this is not a feminist book"[56] because her ideological perspective is Marxist. But by focusing on economic and social factors that oppress women, Delany nonetheless provides an analysis of interest to feminists: she demonstrates that in *Flore and Jehane*—a work which reflects the high economic status of middle-class Franco-Flemish women who could own businesses and belong to guilds without their husbands' permission—one can find a "literary heroine who is neither victim nor cheat [and] who does not rely on sexuality to make her mark in the world."[57] Delany shows that issues of concern to feminists are often broader than sexual oppression, and, in one sense, her work is non-Marxist, because it does not focus narrowly on economic oppression.

Christine E. Fell's *Women in Anglo-Saxon England* also offers a counter-response to the strict form of Marxism by arguing against the inevitability of class oppression. "Scholarship [she argues] does not require us to read only, always and inevitably, a history of oppression and exploitation of the female sex. The real evidence from Anglo-Saxon England presents a more attractive and indeed assertive picture."[58] Just as French women were in a stronger position before the French Renaissance than in the modern world,[59] the evidence of the sources of Anglo-Saxon England suggests that English women were in a stronger position before the Norman Conquest than they were in subsequent centuries. It is likely, therefore, that feminist studies of Anglo-Saxon literature and history will follow along the lines of Delany and Fell, who make use of the economic insights of the Marxist critics but do not do so in a doctrinaire, ahistorical way.

Fell's book follows most of the books on medieval women in being a *feminist reading* or a *feminist critique* in its broadest sense. As noted above, a feminist reading is an interpretative method used to examine the works of both men and women, which is comparative, historical in orientation, and revisionist in intent.

Since it "probes the ideological assumptions of literary phenomena," a feminist reading is one which considers and, if necessary, corrects and revises "the images and stereotypes of women in literature, the omissions and misconceptions about women in criticism, and woman-as-sign in semiotic systems."[60] Because it is revisionist and corrective, it mirrors the purpose of feminist activism in the United States. Showalter's criticism of the *feminist critique* as a critical approach is that it is responsive and derivative because it is based largely on texts written by men and on literary critical approaches that are male-instituted. Too often, Showalter argues, the effect of such readings is only to "fit women between the lines of the male tradition."[61] Although she may be right about bad critics, she underestimates good ones. Her sweeping indictment is open to qualification, because it is difficult to see how a feminist critic, following either gynocriticism or the feminist reading as a critical approach, could avoid examining male-authored texts and male-generated theories, since feminist criticism is new and since the essence of its method is interdisciplinary and comparative. Critical activity, as a cultural phenomenon, is by its very nature responsive and derivative because its task is to examine and correct something already in existence. Even the theories of the *écriture féminine* "derive" from Lacan, Freud, de Saussure, Derrida, and Barthes.[62]

At its best, a feminist interpretation of early English literature is more than merely a negative study of women in relationship to the Anglo-Saxon men who define their existence: it is a positive attempt to recover the nature of the feminine in earlier societies and thereby understand the heritage of both male and female in today's society. Women have not been on the periphery of human civilization throughout the ages, even though contemporary readings of historical and literary documents have been colored by male-centered preconceptions and preoccupations. A feminist reading aims (in Nina Auerbach's words) to fill "a vacuum in our knowledge" and to "build, restore, reconstruct a peopled female past."[63]

To say that the endeavor to reconstruct women's past and to make visible and whole women's inheritance will have great cultural and historical benefit is to say the obvious. But since the obvious is often overlooked, the effort becomes especially meaningful for the literature written before the beginning of the modern women's movement, literature that is particularly distant and difficult to recover, either because of language barriers or because of scarcity of documents. If one is to come any closer to understanding and evaluating women's experience in the English-speaking world and, by extrapolation, to reassessing men's, one is obligated to turn to the literature and art of Anglo-Saxon England from a feminist reader's point of view. Any conclusions regarding the nature of women's inheritance and the tenet that gender shapes society would be incomplete without the testimony of the historical and fictional women from the Anglo-Saxon period.

OLD ENGLISH LITERARY CRITICISM ON WOMEN

Feminist readings of Old English literature re-open an area of Old English studies that remains dominated by the scholarly consensus established in the nineteenth century. Nineteenth-century studies of the Anglo-Saxon period (as of other literary eras) were androcentric, written by males for a male audience from a male perspective and experience. In the nineteenth and early twentieth centuries, Anglo-Saxon literature also served as a mine for philologists. In 1936, Tolkien's "The Monsters and the Critics" departed from the purely philological approach, treating *Beowulf* as a work of literary interest, and the work of Arthur G. Brodeur, Adrien Bonjour, and Francis P. Magoun, Jr., among others,[64] continued to develop new literary readings of the poetry. In scholarship on representations of women, however, critical discourse often viewed the work with ideas about the "heroic" nature of the society in which it was composed and about female "passivity" and male "activity" within that culture. These assumptions have become our ideological heritage.

Historically, studies of women in Anglo-Saxon literature have presented a stereotypical picture. The first surveys began to appear in the last quarter of the nineteenth century, and they followed contemporary expectations concerning women, finding the familiar "Angel in the House" and "Woman on a Pedestal."[65] Richard Burton saw the Anglo-Saxon woman as "housekeeper, weaver, and childbearer," the queen (particularly in *Beowulf*) as "the tactful hostess" seen "in the heartfelt relations of kin and family," and the women in the Christian poems as showing the "humanizing influence of this more gentle religion."[66] The German studies of Fritz Roeder in 1899 and Ada Broch in 1902 placed the women in stereotypical roles and stressed their passivity and dependency (Roeder, in particular, does this).[67] Roeder's work amassed material from legal and historical sources, placing literary characters in a Germanic and Christian context, and his discussion is naturally influenced by his own understanding of Germanic women. The same could be said for G. F. Browne's discussion of Tacitus's depiction of Germanic women and for Bede's of women among the Picts as a preface to analyzing "the evidence of the actual position of women" in Anglo-Saxon England.[68]

Twentieth-century literature surveys that examine women in Old English literature are more restrained and empirical in their use of evidence, even though their conclusions reinforce the conventional view: women were passive, victimized, and peripheral.[69] Even Chance, in a book that requires readers to look at the women in Old English literature in new ways, speaks of the "ideal of the aristocratic woman as primarily a passive, peaceful, and colorless addition to society,"[70] despite Sklute's effective argument that the *freoþuwebbe* 'peace-weaver' (which Chance views as passive) is an active role akin to that of a diplomat.[71] Most interpretations of women in Old English literature make them resemble the passive women of the novel, which (as Myra Jehlen has demonstrated) describes men of action and women of emotion. Such a general characterization does not reflect the actual representation of women in Old English literature. Rather, it reduces them to comfortably familiar entities. It rehabilitates stereotypes rather than "deconstructs" them.

Several of the critical approaches traditionally used by Anglo-Saxonists impact on this book.[72] They have tended often to obfuscate rather than to illuminate the female characters. All Anglo-Saxonists, for example, must be trained philologists. But some of the philologists of the nineteenth and early twentieth centuries tended to be pedantic (as suggested in Graves's anecdote quoted earlier) and refrained from using philological inquiry to illuminate the characterization not only of women, but also of men. More recent philological approaches by critics—some of them represented in this volume—do place emphasis on the literary and aesthetic considerations of characters and themes. Source study—another critical approach—has demonstrated "the fund of common narrative material associated with the Teutonic Migration period"[73] and the importance of classical and patristic works that underlie Old English, but the effect of this approach, too, has been to reject the women as active narrative agents. W. W. Lawrence dismisses the poem now called *Wulf and Eadwacer* as "the first riddle of Cynewulf."[74] Edith Rickert discusses the story of Modthrytho in *Beowulf* (1931b–62b) in the light of historical sources but ignores what the homicidal Modthrytho and her "digression" contribute to the poem's aesthetic force.[75] As effectively, Kemp Malone disengages women from their literary environments by discussing only the possible sources for the stories of Geat and Maethild in *Deor* and for *Wulf and Eadwacer* instead of addressing the problems of characterization and meaning.[76] Likewise, Otto Glöde has studied the sources of *Elene* and *Juliana* and James M. Garnett those of *Juliana,*[77] but both concern themselves with details of narrative and dictional parallels. These are important matters, to be sure, but should not be allowed to overshadow character analysis as they almost exclusively have done in the past. The study of analogues and sources is important, but such study must lead back to the poetry and prose before it can elucidate the reality of women in Anglo-Saxon narrative. Several of the essays in this collection address the difficulties inherent in adaptation of source material and the significance of the changes made by the Anglo-Saxon writer in delineating the women characters.

Allegory has been another canonical approach to Old English poetry.[78] Although allegorical readings broaden the scope of a poem by allowing the reader to see it in a different context, in their abstraction they tend at the same time to destroy character—male and female—and immediate situation. Allegory reduces the person to a less-than-human figure who stands for something more than human. Elene is a "figure or type of the Church"; Juliana is "the initiator, embodiment, and new exemplar" of "central and potent Christian events."[79] The result of such interpretations is to diminish the reader's engagement with what is essentially feminine in the flesh-and-blood heroine. They represent an interpretative style feminist critics like Patricia Meyer Spacks see as exclusively androcentric.[80] Typological critics claim to provide an objective description of how a medieval audience would have received a poem, and, in some cases, claim it to be the only valid description. Feminist critics of the same poems (as this collection offers) suggest that a medieval audience would have had other perceptions, some still of interest today.

Not all early criticism backed away from analyzing the female characters as representations of real women. In two poems, it would be difficult to disregard the female character, since the main speaker appears to be a woman: W. H. Schofield, for example, entitles *Wulf and Eadwacer* "Signy's Lament,"[81] a change that not only takes into account correspondences with Old Norse materials but also accepts the female voice as the primary means of expressing emotion. Critics from Lawrence to Greenfield have interpreted both *Wulf and Eadwacer* and *The Wife's Lament* (the other lyric with a female speaker) as poems about "the emotions of women" and "the love between man and woman and the tribulations such love has had to endure."[82]

The eroticism in the poems even sparked a controversy as to whether such poetry was possible in Europe before the introduction of courtly love. The opposing views are exemplified, on the one hand, by Clifford Davidson's strong argument that there was "a continuity of tradition in love poetry" during the Middle Ages and that "erotic songs"[83] existed in Old English and, on the other, by R. C. Bambas's denial that "the idea of undying passion between a man and a woman existed among the early Teutons."[84] Bambas carries his argument to an unsupportable conclusion when he proposes that the feminine endings of *geomorre* 'mournful' and *minre sylfre* 'my own self' (which identify the speaker undeniably as a woman) are scribal errors,[85] and that the speaker is a man. One might see in Bambas's criticism the culmination of androcentricism progressing from nineteenth-century paternalism to twentieth-century misogyny.

The *frauenlieder* speak of the human condition, and the voices which give shape and authority to the subject are female. They are not the only female voices that testify to the rigors, challenges, deprivations, and glory in human experience: Wealhtheow, Judith, Juliana, Elene, and Eve speak a language as vibrant as their experience. Yet the women of the *frauenlieder* and the women in *Beowulf,* except for Grendel's Mother, have been customarily looked upon as passive figures, shadows in an otherwise brilliantly illuminated heroic world. The woman is the "victim" of the husband-lover; Wealhtheow is a "tragic queen," caught in the net of male political intrigue; Hildeburh in *Beowulf* and the speaker in *Wulf and Eadwacer* are "lonely and innocent victims of fate."[86] Some critics assert that the poets were aware of the passive and victimized nature of the female characters and used it rhetorically to express "human pain and weakness" because they believed that women had a "greater share in human suffering and anguish"[87] than men during the Anglo-Saxon period. This type of assessment not only denigrates men's emotional capacity, but also identifies the activity of suffering and experiencing pain as passive and marginal. Therefore, it comes to exemplify a kind of male-centered literary criticism in which women in literature are viewed as "passive victims of male authorial desire."[88] Such male-centered criticism looks upon the women as passive victims of critical desire as well. If one continually describes women *in* literature as passive, victimized, over-whelmed by, rather than expressing, emotion and desire, one can eventually persuade women *outside* literature to believe it, a belief that would effectively either immobilize them or pervert their action.

The beginning of the systematic study of the position of women in Anglo-Saxon England came with the work of the Stentons and Whitelock.[89] They suggested for the first time that the social position of the aristocratic woman in Anglo-Saxon England was much stronger than previously believed. By using the laws, charters, and wills from the Anglo-Saxon period, they demonstrated that Anglo-Saxon women exercised considerable economic independence and enjoyed a relationship of "rough equality" to men.[90] Women could own property and inherit and dispose of it at their will; they could free slaves; and they had the power of naming land they owned. One deleterious effect of the Norman Conquest was the weakening of their "independent status,"[91] a status, as Lady Stenton argues, women were never fully to regain "within the changing pattern of English society."[92] The subsequent work of social historians Betty Bandell, Mark Meyer, Sheila Dietrich, and Anne L. Klinck has clarified the life of women in Anglo-Saxon England.[93] But it has been only recently that comprehensive studies like Pauline Stafford's *Queens, Concubines and Dowagers: The King's Wife in the Early Middle Ages* and Christine E. Fell's *Women in Anglo-Saxon England* have provided enough information about all aspects of Anglo-Saxon society to demolish the nineteenth-century portrait of the dependent and passive Anglo-Saxon lady of gentility.[94]

Recent work thus suggests that women were not in conflict with their society in Anglo-Saxon England, and that the period has something to teach us today which requires that we temper the narrowly martial image. There were, for example, women writers in the Anglo-Saxon period such as Eadburg, Bucge, Leoba, Ælflæd, and Berhtgyd. But because they wrote in Latin, they have not been part of the college curricula[95] and remain unknown to the majority of students. Regrettably, if naturally, since the familiar authors in Old English—Caedmon, Cynewulf, Ælfric, Alfred, Wulfstan, et al.—are male, people have tended to assume that the authors of anonymous works must be men as well. The fact that a great number of Old English texts are anonymous[96] makes this assumption crucial. Students interested in the history of women's writing and in the differences between male and female language might well pay close attention to these anonymous works, which may be identified and explained by these very differences. A new literary history could result. Old English was in origin a dual-gender language, and an author may use gender inflections to differentiate character. The feminine inflections of *minre sylfre* and *geomorre* of *The Wife's Lament* establish the speaker as female.[97] Such gender inflections may have been important because the poetry was orally performed, as most popular literature in the Middle Ages was,[98] suggesting a female speaker. But the feminine endings may also have been used because the poet—like the *trobairitz* of Provence[99]—was a woman who, like Kristeva's poet, is pressed by an inner drive to express the meaning of her experience.

THE NATURE AND DIRECTION OF NEW READINGS

The essays in this volume are part of the recent informal movement by scholars like Chance, Damico, Dietrich, Fell, Olsen, and Stafford to restore historical and cultural balance by recovering "women's inheritance" from Anglo-Saxon England. Hence, these essays complement the primary task of the larger feminist critique by correcting "false visions"[100] of women and their status and by articulating reality anew. The essays are revisionist. Renoir, for example, challenges the notion of woman's lesser intellectual capabilities, and Frese argues that the agony accompanying the loss of a child may be as great or greater than that which might accompany the loss of a lover. Each essay proposes alternative conceptions of women and thus asserts an ideology which challenges that held by many nineteenth-century and contemporary scholars. The essays, however, do not attempt to present anything like a manifesto about either women or the representation of women in Anglo-Saxon culture and literature. Rather, they represent a "plurality" of approaches and positions with a common objective. They seek to reassess women as women actually appear in the laws, in works written by women, and in canonical literature. In dealing specifically with Anglo-Saxon literature, these essays widen the scope of feminist studies in general.

In particular, they question the uncritical image of Anglo-Saxon women as passive victims. The result of this questioning supports the studies of other feminist literary critics, who have shown that in other literary periods "women emerge . . . as powerful figures" even when specific texts are "crafted to appropriate or to mute their difference."[101] The women who emerge from the essays in this collection are individuals, not sexist clones but what Abel has characterized as "artful renditions of sexual difference,"[102] not exactly like the men in character or action but neither more nor less. All told, these investigations suggest that the Anglo-Saxon man did not view a woman only as a "silent bearer of ideology (virgin, wife, mother)" and, therefore, as a "necessary sacrifice to male secularity, worldliness, and tampering with forbidden knowledge."[103] Since modern women have not always fared as well, a fresh picture of women active in word and deed may contribute to a just and encouraging understanding of women as they have been and are now—*dydon swa hie cuðon* 'they have done as they know how to do'.[104]

THE PLAN OF THIS VOLUME

Part I of this collection deals with sources that depict women's early medieval experience, mostly in Anglo-Saxon England. Christine E. Fell initiates this section with "Some Implications of the Boniface Correspondence," a study of letters written from women to men and men to women, which expands our knowledge of female literacy and women writers at a particular historical time. The thrust of the essays in this part is to "reconstruct a peopled female past,"[105] what Nina Auerbach (and other feminist literary critics as well) sees as indispensable to the understanding of a literature of a particular historical period. In her consideration of the interrelationship between art and life, Virginia Woolf noted that "fiction, imaginative work that it is, is not dropped like a pebble upon the ground," but rather "is attached to life."[106] All Anglo-Saxon writing is of necessity bound up with the life of the times. Several of the following essays—F. T. Wainwright's "Æthelflæd, Lady of the Mercians," Pauline Stafford's "The King's Wife in Wessex, 800–1066," and Frank M. Stenton's "The Historical Bearing of Place-Name Studies"—are classic works that elucidate particular features of the social conditions of early English society. Mary P. Richards's and B. Jane Stanfield's "Women and Anglo-Saxon Laws" considers especially how the concepts of women in the laws accord with evidence of their power in the charters and in other documentary writings. Concluding the first part of the collection is Carol J. Clover's "The Politics of Scarcity: Notes on the Sex Ratio in Early Scandinavia," which argues that the Old Icelandic laws present us with a world in which women were restrained but that the sagas depict the actual situation, in which women by their scarcity had assumed considerable informal power. Together these essays re-evaluate the historical record.

Part II extends the investigation of the historical record by turning to folklore and myth concerned with women and sexuality. In her evaluation of the contributions made by contemporary French feminists to the study of women's sexuality and its literary representation, Mary Jacobus has contrasted former appraisals of women's desire with more contemporary judgments. She concludes that "contemporary feminist criticism is more likely to stress pleasure than suffering—the freeing of repressed female desire; *jouissance* and *'la mère qui jouit'* (no longer barred from sexual pleasure) as against the burden of womanhood."[107] Edith Whitehurst Williams's "What's So New about the Sexual Revolution?" opens part II by directly addressing misapprehensions of female sexuality. She argues that the Anglo-Saxons possessed "wholesome and spontaneous" values about women's sexuality but that over the years these attitudes have become almost unrecognizable in the process of transmission. Paul Szarmach's "Ælfric's Women Saints: Eugenia" also deals with the sexuality of Anglo-Saxon women. He shows that Ælfric preserves the erotic details found in traditional female saints' lives, so that his works reflect how women's sexuality was perceived. An issue related to female sexuality, witchcraft, has received the attention of French feminists in particular because of the danger the figure of the witch has "pose[d] . . . to phallocentric society."[108] In "The *Ides* of the Cotton Gnomic Poem," Audrey L. Meaney discusses the term *ides* as it was applied to women in their "sacral and mysterious aspect," which is to say, witches, who acted in a way potentially antisocial. It seems that the *idisi* were as much of a problem for the West Germanic peoples as were the witches in more recent times. Meaney's investigations balance a too idealistic view of a liberated Anglo-Saxon society by suggesting that there were limitations set on women by phallocentric concerns. The Germanic cognates of the term *ides* referred to the valkyries, women who were part of a female warrior enclave. Helen Damico's "The Valkyrie Reflex in Old English Literature" surveys the dual representation of the valkyrie in Germanic culture and argues for its appearance in Old English literature, thus providing reasons for reassessing the representations of women in heroic poetry.

Part III deals with differences in the nature and use of language by and about women. In an essay growing out of the work of Julia Kristeva, Patricia A. Belanoff's "Women's Songs, Women's Language: *Wulf and Eadwacer* and *The Wife's Lament*" continues the discussion of the two elegies in the context of the Indo-European *frauenlieder*. She concludes that the anomalies of voice and environment in these poems represent levels of female discourse foreign to men. L. John Sklute's "*Freoðuwebbe* in Old English Poetry" and Paul Beekman Taylor's "The Old English Poetic Vocabulary of Beauty" examine words that distinguish the character and appearance of women, especially in the context of dual-gender language. Taylor's re-examination of linguistic evidence further calls into dispute the consensus (derived from the work of Julius Pokorny) that all that needs to be known about the etymologies of words has already been discovered. The concluding essay of Part III engages the supposition of women's articulateness. Alexandra Hennessey Olsen's "Cynewulf's Autonomous Women: A Reconsideration of Elene and Juliana" argues that women in Old English poetry use language assertively and luxuriantly: they are not paralyzed or constrained by want of elegant and effective words.

Part IV reinterprets women whom critics in the past have either neglected or stereotyped. Joyce Hill's " 'Þæt wæs geomuru ides!' A Female Stereotype Examined" investigates the victimized woman in her legendary guise and shows that many facets of the female role are concerned with power complexes and tribal politics. Jane

Chance's "The Structural Unity of *Beowulf:* The Problem of Grendel's Mother" argues that we can understand the accepted pattern of the queen as *freoþuwebbe* 'peace-weaver' by comparing her to the antitype Grendel's Mother. Alain Renoir's "Eve's I.Q. Rating: Two Sexist Views of *Genesis B*" overturns the common view that Eve is intellectually inferior to Adam. He also reminds us that the Middle Ages held no single view of women. Dolores Warwick Frese's "*Wulf and Eadwacer:* The Adulterous Woman Reconsidered" argues that the poem is not a woman's lament for a husband or a lover but "the eloquent lament of a grieving mother reciting a formal *giedd* for her son." Anita R. Riedinger's "The Englishing of Arcestrate: Woman in *Apollonius of Tyre*" concludes Part IV by discussing the often-neglected character Arcestrate. Riedinger demonstrates how the translator adapted the tale for his English audience by making Arcestrate representationally English: literate and creative and involved in a romantic pursuit of Apollonius.

THE OBJECTIVE

In a 1976 article in *Signs* concerned with characterizing feminist literary criticism in its "purest" sense, Showalter describes feminist literary criticism as "a radical alteration of . . . vision, a demand . . . [to] see meaning in what had previously been empty space."[109] This, of course, may be said of all *new* literary criticism that addresses its subject from a particular and specialized point of view and which challenges established ideas. The authors of the essays in this book are not "feminist literary critics" in the usual sense of the term. They are Anglo-Saxonists, trained in the Anglo-Saxon tradition. But they are feminists in the sense that they have been concerned with and have confronted the "empty space" that was peopled by the women of the Anglo-Saxon period. Their essays round out the nineteenth-century critical tradition in that they—like feminist literary critics—address, correct, and begin fresh exploration of a neglected area of study in Old English literature. The essays are meant to form the basis for more extensive and controversial examinations of the women in Anglo-Saxon literature and culture. It is spirited dialogue on a controversial area of study that may effectively remove the study of Old English language and literature from a critical pedantry that provokes scholars and teachers of more modern literary periods to regard this highly sophisticated and beautiful literature as stultifying and oppressive and of interest only to "linguists and antiquarians."[110] Anglo-Saxon studies—and its contemporary students—deserve the fullest and richest approach. To take any other would be to deny students access to a rich and full world view that is inclusive of able-bodied women with power and complexity as well as men of power and complexity. As Cynewulf's Elene says, living people must be aware of the *fyrngewritu* 'ancient writings' and remember them *þurh snyttro cræft* 'through skilful wisdom'[111]—and this truth fits both sexes and the traditions passed down by and about them.

NOTES

1. Robert Graves, *Goodbye to All That* (Garden City, N.Y.: Anchor Books, 1957), pp. 292–93.

2. Carolyn G. Heilbrun, "Bringing the Spirit Back to English Studies," in *The New Feminist Criticism: Essays on Women, Literature, and Theory,* ed. Elaine Showalter (New York: Pantheon Books, 1984), pp. 21–28, especially p. 22. The collection is hereafter cited as *NFC*.

3. J. R. R. Tolkien, "The Monsters and the Critics," *Proceedings of the British Academy* 22 (1936): 245–95. Rpt. in *An Anthology of* Beowulf *Criticism,* ed. Lewis E. Nicholson (Notre Dame, Ind.: Notre Dame University Press, 1963), pp. 34–35.

4. In the past, the term Old English was used when referring to the language, and the term Anglo-Saxon when referring to the language and literature. We use the term alternately for both the language and literature, as has become customary. The chronological boundaries of the Anglo-Saxon period are from A.D. 600 to A.D. 1200.

5. H. L. Rogers, "Beowulf's Three Great Fights," *Review of English Studies* 6 (1955): 339–55; Kathryn Hume, "The Theme and Structure of *Beowulf,*" *Studies in Philology* 72 (1975): 1–27; Jane Chance (Nitzsche), "The Structural Unity of *Beowulf*: The Problem of Grendel's Mother," *Texas Studies in Language and Literature* 22 (1970): 287–303, rpt. herein, chap. 16.

6. Sheila C. Dietrich, "An Introduction to Women in Anglo-Saxon Society (ca. 600–1066)," in *The Women of England from Anglo-Saxon Times to the Present: Interpretive Bibliographic Essays,* ed. Barbara Kanner (Hamden, Conn.: Archon, 1979), pp. 32–56. See also Christine E. Fell with Cecily Clark and Elizabeth Williams, *Women in Anglo-Saxon England and The Impact of 1066* (Bloomington: Indiana University Press, 1984); Pauline Stafford, *Queens, Concubines and Dowagers: The King's Wife in Wessex in the Early Middle Ages* (Athens, Ga.: University of Georgia Press, 1983); Jane Chance, *Woman as Hero in Old English Literature* (Syracuse: Syracuse University Press, 1986); Helen Damico, *Beowulf's Wealhtheow and the Valkyrie Tradition* (Madison: University of Wisconsin Press, 1984); and Alexandra Hennessey Olsen, *Speech, Song, and Poetic Craft: The Artistry of the Cynewulf Canon* (New York: Peter Lang, 1984). Other works of interest are Mary Anne Gould's "Women's Roles in Anglo-Saxon and Old Norse Poetry," Diss., University of Oregon, 1974, which examines women's function in heroic poetry along stereotypical lines; Anne Lingard Klinck's "Female Characterization in Old English Poetry," Diss., University of British Columbia, 1976, which discusses methods of characterizing females and argues that it is the *passivity* of women which allowed the poets at times to attempt more individual characterization; Patricia A. Belanoff's "The Changing Image of Women in Old English Poetry," Diss., New York University, 1982, which is a comprehensive lexical examination; and Bernice W. Kliman's "Women in Early English Literature, 'Beowulf' to the 'Ancrene Wisse'," *Nottingham Medieval Studies* 12:1 (1977): 32–49, which posits a disintegrating development in women's roles. These are but a few of the works on the women in Old English literature; we have gathered some 190 items for a bibliography in preparation about publications concerning women in Old English literature.

7. Dietrich, "Introduction," p. 33.

8. In *Woman as Image in Medieval Literature from the Twelfth Century to Dante* (New York: Columbia University Press, 1975), Joan Ferrante observes, "I was alerted to the importance of the blending of male and female characteristics in literature by Heilbrun's *Toward a Recognition of Androgyny* (New York: Knopf, 1973), a book which played no small part in arousing my interest in this subject and to whose thesis I hope this study offers added support" (p. 4).

9. For feminist studies of Old French literature, see *Romance Notes* 25 (1985), a special edition, ed. E. Jane Burns and Roberta L. Krueger; on Christine de Pisan, see especially *Ideals for Women in the Works of Christine de Pizan,* ed. Diane Bornstein (Medieval and Renaissance Monograph Series; Michigan Consortium for Medieval and Early Modern Studies, 1981). For Margery Kempe, see Mary Mason, "The Other Voice: Autobiography of Women Writers," in *Autobiography: Essays Theoretical and Critical* (Princeton: Princeton University Press, 1980), pp. 207–35, and Hope Phyllis Weissman, "Margery Kempe in Jerusalem, *Hysterica Compassio* in the Middle Ages," in *Acts of Interpretation: The Text in Its Contexts, 700 to 1600: Essays on Medieval Literature in Honor of E. Talbot Donaldson,* ed. Mary J. Carruthers

and Elizabeth D. Kirk (Norman, Okla.: Pilgrim Books, 1982), pp. 201–17. For Julian, see especially Jennifer P. Hummel, *"God Is Our Mother"*: *Julian of Norwich and the Medieval Image of Christian Female Divinity* (Salzburg: University of Salzburg, 1982). Middle English specialists have also examined feminist concerns in the works of male authors like Chaucer— see, for example, Maureen Fries, " 'Slydynge of Corage': Chaucer's Criseyde as Feminist and Victim," in *The Authority of Experience: Essays in Feminist Criticism*, ed. Arlyn Diamond and Lee R. Edwards (Amherst: University of Massachusetts Press, 1977), pp. 45–59—and Gower—see, for example, Linda Barney Burke, "Women in John Gower's *Confessio Amantis*," *Mediaevalia* 3 (1977): 238–59.

10. Susan Schibanoff, "The Crooked Rib: Women in Medieval Literature," in *Approaches to Teaching Chaucer's "Canterbury Tales,"* ed. Joseph Gibaldi (New York: Modern Language Association, 1980), pp. 121–28.

11. For definitions of terms in feminist social and literary criticism, see *Feminist Dictionary*, ed. Cheris Kramarae and Paula A. Treichler (London: Methuen, 1986). John Stuart Mill, "The Subjection of Women," in *Essays on Sexual Equality*, ed. Alice S. Rossi (Chicago: University of Chicago Press, 1970), pp. 184–85. Mary Wollstonecraft, *A Vindication of the Rights of Woman, with Strictures on Political and Moral Subjects* (repr. of 1792 edition; New York: Source Book Press, 1971). Mary Astell, *A Serious Proposal to the Ladies* (repr. of the 1701 edition of Parts I and II; New York: Source Book Press, 1970), and *Some Reflections Upon Marriage* (repr. of the 1730 edition; New York: Source Book Press, 1970), both excerpted in *First Feminists: British Women Writers 1578–1799*, ed. Moira Ferguson (Bloomington: Indiana University Press and Westbury, N.Y.: Feminist Press, 1985); Margaret Fuller, "The Great Lawsuit. Man versus Men. Woman versus Women," *The Dial* 4:1 (1848): 1–47, excerpted in *The Feminist Papers from Adams to de Beauvoir*, ed. Alice S. Rossi (New York: Columbia University Press, 1973), pp. 158–82.

12. Simone de Beauvoir, *Le deuxième sexe* (Paris: Gallimard, 1949), trans. H. M. Parshley, *The Second Sex* (Harmondsworth: Penguin, 1972), pp. 49–50; and de Beauvoir, Interview with Alice Schwarzer, *MS* (July 1972), rpt. in *New French Feminisms*, ed. Elaine Marks and Isabelle de Courtivron (New York: Schocken Books, 1981), p. 143 [this collection is hereafter cited as *NFF*]; and Alice Schwarzer, *Simone de Beauvoir Today. Conversations with Alice Schwarzer, 1972–1982* (London: Chatto and Windus, 1984), p. 32.

13. Betty Friedan, *The Feminine Mystique* (New York: Dell, 1963). For a comprehensive introduction to the relationship between the feminist political movement and feminist literary theory, see Toril Moi's *Sexual/Textual Politics: Feminist Literary Theory* (London: Methuen, 1985). It is essential reading (although one may hold differing positions), because Moi discusses clearly and in detail the major figures of Anglo-American and French feminism and feminist literary theory and criticism. See also K[enneth]. K. Ruthven, *Feminist Literary Studies: An Introduction* (Cambridge: Cambridge University Press, 1984), the first survey in this field written by a man, and Moi's assessment of it in *Sexual/Textual Politics*, pp. 174–75.

14. Julia Kristeva makes this observation in "Women's Time," trans. Alice Jardine and Harry Blake, in *Feminist Theory: A Critique of Ideology*, ed. Nannerl O. Keohane, Michelle Z. Rosaldo, and Barbara C. Gelpi (Chicago: University of Chicago Press, 1982), pp. 31–53; quotation from p. 45; see Moi, *Sexual/Textual Politics*, pp. 150–72, for an examination of Kristeva's theories. For individual views by separatists and integrationists, see *Sisterhood Is Powerful: An Anthology of Writings from The Women's Liberation Movement*, ed. Robin Morgan (New York: Random House, 1970) and *Woman in Sexist Society: Studies in Power and Powerlessness*, ed. Vivian Gornick and Barbara K. Moran (New York: Basic Books, 1971).

15. Catherine A. MacKinnon, "Feminism, Marxism, Method, and the State: An Agenda for Theory," in Keohane, Rosaldo, and Gelpi, *Feminist Theory*, pp. 1–30, especially pp. 2, 5, 14–15, 21–25, 29. MacKinnon's article clarifies, incorporates, and makes distinctions between the thought of major feminist theoreticians in the formation of her theoretical system. See also Moi, *Sexual/Textual Politics*, pp. 91–95; and Mary O'Brien, "Feminist Theory and Dialectical Logic," in Keohane, Rosaldo, and Gelpi, *Feminist Theory*, pp. 99–112, esp. p. 100.

16. MacKinnon, in Keohane, Rosaldo, and Gelpi, *Feminist Theory,* pp. 8–10; Moi, *Sexual/Textual Politics,* pp. 94–95, 141–42. See also Jean Bethke Elshtain, "Feminist Discourse and Its Discontents: Language, Power, and Meaning," in Keohane, Rosaldo, and Gelpi, *Feminist Theory,* pp. 127–45, esp. pp. 135–38.

17. For a discussion of de Beauvoir's influence on subsequent feminists and their works, see Moi, *Sexual/Textual Politics,* esp. pp. 92, 98.

18. Mary Ellmann, *Thinking About Women* (New York: Harcourt, 1968); Kate Millett, *Sexual Politics* (London: Virago, 1977); Katharine M. Rogers, *The Troublesome Helpmate: A History of Misogyny in Literature* (Seattle: University of Washington Press, 1966); Virginia Woolf, *A Room of One's Own* (1929; rpt. London: Granada, 1977).

19. Sandra M. Gilbert and Susan Gubar, *The Madwoman in the Attic: The Woman Writer and the Nineteenth-Century Literary Imagination* (New Haven: Yale University Press, 1979); Ellen Moers, *Literary Women: The Great Writers* (New York: Doubleday, 1976); Elaine Showalter, *A Literature of Their Own: British Novelists from Brontë to Lessing* (Princeton, N.J.: Princeton University Press, 1976).

Showalter's "Feminist Critical Revolution," in *NFC,* pp. 3–17, offers a summary of the development of feminist literary criticism (with a particular emphasis on the American branch) and the issues with which it is concerned. For working definitions of *androcentric* (male-centered), *phallocentric* (holding the additional psychological associations with male identity, alienation, and desire), and *phallocratic* (patriarchal), see Ruthven, *Feminist Literary Studies,* pp. 1–3, 51–55.

20. The characteristics have been outlined by both feminists and non-feminists, the latter group using them as charges against the reliability of feminist critical perspectives. See, for example, the articles by Lydia Blanchard ("Feminist Literary Criticism: The Feminist Criticism of Literary Criticism," pp. 31–56), Catherine Stimpson ("Feminist Criticism and Feminist Critics," pp. 57–63), and E. Jane Burns ("For Those Who Were Not Persuaded," pp. 107–109) in *Feminist Literary Criticism: A Working Paper,* no. 3 (Research Triangle Park, N.C.: National Humanities Center, August, 1981). See also the articles by Gilbert ("What Do Feminist Critics Want? A Postcard from the Volcano," pp. 29–45) and Annette Kolodny ("A Map for Rereading: Gender and the Interpretation of Literary Texts," pp. 46–62) as well as the three Showalter articles ("The Feminist Critical Revolution," pp. 3–17; "Toward a Feminist Poetics," pp. 125–43; and "Feminist Criticism in the Wilderness," pp. 243–70) in *NFC* (see note 2 above). As an example of the antitheoretical censure of the American feminist literary critics, see Alfred Hornung's response to the feminist papers collected in *Feminist Literary Criticism: A Working Paper,* "Defusing the Minefield: The Context of Feminist Criticism," pp. 113–22; and Toril Moi's introductory chapter "Who's Afraid of Virginia Woolf?: Feminist Readings of Woolf," in *Sexual/Textual Politics,* pp. 1–18, 46–48, et passim. See also Ruthven (*Feminist Literary Studies,* p. 21), who rightly points to the difference between French and what he calls "anglophone" critical stances, the former being characterized by its "passion for abstraction, particularly the theorizing of theory" and the latter by its resistance to any theory that has no practical application.

21. For a generalized definition of *politics,* see Ruthven, *Feminist Literary Studies,* pp. 30–31: " 'Politics' in this wider sense means 'power' or rather 'power relations': who does what to whom and in whose interests" (p. 31). For the relationship between politics and aesthetics and on the issue of making evaluative judgments on literary works by women, see Moi, *Sexual/Textual Politics,* pp. 73–74.

22. Feminists make the distinction between sex (biology) and gender (the cultural inculcation of sexual identity) which had its origins in de Beauvoir's statement that "one is not born, but rather becomes, a woman" (*Second Sex,* p. 273). See Ruthven's argument for male critics participating in feminism and in feminist literary studies, *Feminist Literary Studies,* pp. 11–15, especially p. 13. Ruthven sees feminism as a "new knowledge" comparable in importance to our understanding of Marxism and psychoanalysis as forces that shape society (pp. 24–25).

23. See especially the writings of Gilbert and Showalter, in particular Gilbert, "What Do

Feminist Critics Want?" in *NFC*, p. 36, and Showalter, "Feminist Criticism in the Wilderness," in *NFC*, pp. 246–47.

24. For discussions on the speciousness of this critical stance, see Myra Jehlen, "Archimedes and the Paradox of Feminist Criticism," in *Feminist Theory*, ed. Keohane, Rosaldo, and Gelpi, pp. 194–97; and Moi, *Sexual/Textual Politics*, pp. 51–52. Moi defines feminist literary criticism as "political criticism, sustained by a commitment to combat all forms of patriarchy and sexism" (p. 52). See also Showalter in *NFC*, "Towards a Feminist Poetics " pp. 126–29, and "Feminist Criticism in the Wilderness," p. 244.

25. Quoted by Showalter, "Feminist Criticism in the Wilderness," in *NFC*, p. 244, from the title of Arlyn Diamond's and Lee R. Edward's anthology, *The Authority of Experience;* see note 9 above.

26. See, for example, Kolodny's "A Map for Rereading: Gender and the Interpretation of Literary Texts," in *NFC*, pp. 46–62, where she takes issue with Harold Bloom's *Anxiety of Influence* (New York: Oxford University Press, 1973) which presents as universal a "shared and coherent literary tradition" that excludes women writers (see especially pp. 59–60). In this same article, Kolodny effectively illustrates the lack of sensitivity of male critics in their interpretation and evaluation of two short stories by the early twentieth-century American writers Charlotte Perkins Gilman and Susan Glaspell.

27. Heilbrun, "Bringing the Spirit Back to English Studies," in *NFC*, pp. 21–28, quotation from pp. 22–23.

28. The "resisting reader" is Judith Fetterley's descriptive attribute which she deems essential for the feminist literary critic, in *The Resisting Reader: A Feminist Approach to American Fiction* (Bloomington: Indiana University Press, 1978); the "suspicious reader" is Annette Kolodny's, based on Paul Ricoeur's "hermeneutics of suspicion," in *Freud and Philosophy: An Essay on Interpretation*, trans. Denis Savage (New Haven: Yale University Press, 1970), pp. 32–36.

29. Ruthven, *Feminist Literary Studies*, pp. 15–23.

30. In "What Do Feminist Critics Want?" (*NFC*, pp. 29–45), Gilbert assesses the change that has taken place thus far: "We live the way we live now, and think the way we think now, because what was once a wholly masculinist, patriarchal culture has begun fragmentarily, haltingly, sometimes even convulsively, but, I suspect, irreversibly to evolve into a masculinist-feminist culture . . . whose styles and structures will no longer be patriarchal in the old way" (p. 43).

31. Showalter, "Feminist Criticism in the Wilderness," in *NFC*, p. 247.

32. Showalter, "Towards a Feminist Poetics" and "Feminist Criticism in the Wilderness," in *NFC*, pp. 125–43, 243–70, respectively.

33. Showalter, "Feminist Criticism in the Wilderness," in *NFC*, pp. 128–29.

34. Joan Ferrante, *Woman as Image;* Katharina M. Wilson, ed., *Medieval Women Writers* (Athens: University of Georgia Press, 1984); Peter Dronke, *Women Writers of the Middle Ages: A Critical Study of Texts from Perpetua (†203) to Marguerite Porete (†1310)* (Cambridge: Cambridge University Press, 1984); Eleanor Shipley Duckett, *Women and their Letters in the Early Middle Ages* (Northampton, Mass.: Smith College, 1965); Frances and Joseph Gies, *Women in the Middle Ages* (New York: Barnes and Noble, 1980); Rosmarie Thee Morewedge, ed., *The Role of Women in the Middle Ages* (Albany: State University of New York Press, 1975); Susan Mosher Stuard, ed., *Women in Medieval Society* (Philadelphia: University of Pennsylvania Press, 1976). For other studies, see note 8.

35. Elaine Showalter, "Feminist Criticism in the Wilderness," in *NFC*, p. 128. For discussions on gynocritics, see Moi, *Sexual/Textual Politics*, pp. 76–78, 104–107, and Ruthven, *Feminist Literary Studies*, pp. 93–128.

36. Hélène Cixous and Catherine Clément, *The Newly Born Woman*, trans. Betsy Wing (Minneapolis: University of Minnesota Press, 1986); Luce Irigaray, "Ce sexe qui n'est pas un," trans. Claudia Reeder, in *NFF*, pp. 99–106; for a discussion on French feminist criticism, see Moi, *Sexual/Textual Politics*, pp. 89–126.

37. Cixous and Clément, *The Newly Born Woman*, p. 7.

38. Cixous, "The Laugh of the Medusa," trans. Keith and Paul Cohen, *Signs* 1 (1976); rpt. in *NFF*, p. 245.

39. Moi, *Sexual/Textual Politics*, pp. 102–104, 125–26.

40. Annie Leclerc, "Woman's Word," trans. Gillian C. Gill, in *NFC*, p. 79.

41. Julia Kristeva, *La Révolution du langue poétique: l'avant-garde à la fin du XIXe siècle, Lautreamont et Mallarmé* (Paris: Edition du Seuil, 1974); *Desire in Language: A Semiotic Approach to Literature and Art*, ed. Leon S. Roudiez; trans. Thomas Gora, Alice Jardine, and Leon S. Roudiez (New York: Columbia University Press, 1980). Kristeva argues that even feminists participate in the phallocentric nature of language by speaking of "Woman," a term which denies "the singularity of each woman" ("Woman's Time," trans. Alice Jardine and Harry Blake, in Keohane, Rosaldo, and Gelpi, *Feminist Theory*, p. 51). See also Moi, *Sexual/Textual Politics*, pp. 163–54.

42. Kristeva, *Desire in Language*, pp. 17–18, 19, 24–28, 133–87.

43. Ibid., pp. 135–37, 144–45. See Moi's statement about the importance of the idea of the "disrupted subject" (i.e., "the subject-in-process") to Kristeva's ideology, *Sexual/Textual Politics*, pp. 172–73.

44. See note 41.

45. David Aers, "Introduction," in *Medieval Literature: Criticism, Ideology and History*, ed. David Aers (New York: St. Martin's Press, 1986), p. 2.

46. Marxist-Feminist Literature Collective, "Women's Writing: *Jane Eyre, Shirley, Vilette, Aurora Leigh*," *Ideology and Consciousness* 1:3 (1978): 27–48.

47. See Moi's discussion of the British feminist literary critics in *Sexual/Textual Politics*, pp. 93–96.

48. This is Shoshana Felman's term; see her "Woman and Madness: the Critical Phallacy," *Diacritics* 5 (Winter 1975).

49. Showalter, "Feminist Criticism in the Wilderness," in *NFC*, p. 255.

50. Showalter, "Toward a Feminist Poetics," in *NFC*, p. 129.

51. Annis Pratt, *Archetypal Patterns in Women's Fiction* (Bloomington: Indiana University Press, 1981).

52. See Myra Jehlen, "Archimedes and the Paradox of Feminist Criticism," in Keohane, Rosaldo, and Gelpi, *Feminist Theory*, pp. 210–13.

53. See Nancy Reinhardt, "New Directions for Feminist Criticism in Theatre and the Related Arts," *Soundings* 14 (1981): 361–87. For her discussion of women in classical tragedy, see especially pp. 366–71.

54. Sheila Delany, "Rewriting Woman Good: Gender and the Anxiety of Influence in Two Late-Medieval Texts," in *Chaucer in the Eighties*, ed. Julian N. Wasserman and Robert J. Blanch (Syracuse: Syracuse University Press, 1986), p. 75.

55. Rudolph M. Bell, *Holy Anorexia* (Chicago: University of Chicago Press, 1985); Caroline Walker Bynum, *Jesus as Mother: Studies in the Spirituality of the Late Middle Ages*, Center for Medieval and Renaissance Studies, UCLA Publications, vol. 16 (Berkeley: University of California Press, 1982); *Holy Feast and Holy Fast: The Religious Significance of Food to Medieval Women* (Berkeley: University of California Press, 1987); Caroline Bynum et al., eds., *Gender and Religion: On the Complexity of Symbols* (Boston: Beacon Press, 1986).

56. Sheila Delany, *Writing Woman: Women Writers and Women in Literature, Medieval to Modern* (New York: Schocken Books, 1983), p. 1.

57. Delany, *Writing Woman*, p. 22.

58. Fell, *Women in Anglo-Saxon England*, p. 21.

59. Marks and de Courtivron, "Introduction I: Discourses of Anti-Feminism and Feminism," in *NFC*, p. 8.

60. Showalter, "Toward a Feminist Poetics," in *NFC*, p. 128; "Feminist Criticism in the Wilderness," in *NFC*, p. 245.

61. Showalter, "Toward a Feminist Poetics," *NFC*, p. 129.

62. For a more precise classification, which sees feminist literary criticism organized in five basic categories, see Ellen Messer-Davidow, "The Philosophical Bases of Feminist Literary Criticism," *New Literary History* 19 (1987): 65–103.

63. Nina Auerbach, "Feminist Criticism Reviewed," in *Gender and Literary Voice*, ed. Janet Todd, *Women and Literature*, n.s., vol. 1 (New York: Holmes and Meier Publishers, Inc., 1980), p. 259.

64. See Arthur G. Brodeur, *The Art of Beowulf* (Berkeley: University of California Press, 1959); Adrien Bonjour, *The Digressions in Beowulf* (Oxford: Blackwell, 1950) and *Twelve* Beowulf *Papers: 1940–1960, with Additional Comments* (Neuchâtel: Faculté des lettres, 1962); and Francis P. Magoun, Jr., "Oral-Formulaic Character of Anglo-Saxon Narrative Poetry," *Speculum* 28 (1953): 446–67, and "The Theme of the Beasts of Battle in Anglo-Saxon Poetry," *Neuphilologische Mitteilungen* 56 (1955): 81–90.

65. For a discussion of these and other stereotypes in English literature, see Mary Anne Ferguson, *Images of Women in Literature* (Boston: Houghton Mifflin Co., 1973).

66. Richard Burton, "Woman in Old English Poetry," *Sewanee Review* 4 (1895): 2, 8, 11.

67. Fritz Roeder, *Die Familie bei den Ags. Eine Kultur- und Literaturhistorische Studien auf Grund gleichzeitiger Quellen*, vol. 1: *Mann und Frau, Studien zur englischen Philologie*, 4(1899); Ada Broch, *Die Stellung der Frau in der ags Poesie* (Zurich, diss., 1902).

68. G. F. Browne, "The Importance of Women in Anglo-Saxon Times," *Studies in Church History* (London: Society for Promoting Christian Knowledge, 1919), p. 15.

69. See, for example, the comment in Stanley B. Greenfield's and Daniel G. Calder's *A New Critical History of Old English Literature* (New York: New York University Press, 1986) that *Wulf and Eadwacer* and *The Wife's Lament* "deal . . . with patterns of concord and discord in the relations between men and women" (p. 291). They find *Wulf and Eadwacer* interesting because of its "obscurity" and "thematic patterning" (p. 292) rather than because of its female speaker and find *The Wife's Lament* interesting because of "the speaker's miserable state of mind" (p. 293) and "stoic fortitude, frozen in time present" (p. 294). Ironically, the effect of such views on feminists can be seen in the introduction to the section on the "Middle Ages and the Renaissance" in *A Norton Anthology of Women Writers* edited by Sandra M. Gilbert and Susan Gubar (New York: W. W. Norton, 1985). Gilbert and Gubar state: "The Anglo-Saxon culture which predated Christianity in England was oblivious or hostile to women. . . . In *Beowulf*, . . . women are objects of exchange, servants to men, monsters, or mothers of monsters" (p. 5).

70. Chance, *Woman as Hero*, pp. xiii–xiv.

71. Larry M. Sklute, " 'Freoðuwebbe' in Old English Poetry," *Neuphilologische Mitteilungen* 71 (1970): 534–41; reprinted in this anthology (chap. 12) under "L. John Sklute."

72. Literary studies in Old English have been characterized by lively debate on the language, the methods of composition, and the genres and sources of the works. For a survey both of the genres and of the most common critical approaches thereto, see Greenfield, *A Critical History of Old English Literature* (New York: New York University Press, 1968), and Greenfield and Calder, *A New Critical History*, pp. 297–98.

73. Greenfield and Calder, *A New Critical History*, p. 134.

74. William Witherlee Lawrence, "The First Riddle of Cynewulf," *Publications of the Modern Language Association* 10 (1902): 247, 250.

75. Edith Rickert, "The Old English Offa Saga," *Modern Philology* 2 (1905): 55.

76. Kemp Malone, "Mæðhild," *English Literary History* 3 (1936): 253–56; "The Tale of Geat and Mæðhild," *English Studies* 19 (1937): 193–99; "On *Deor* 14–17," *Modern Philology* 40 (1942): 1–18; "Two English *Frauenlieder*," *Comparative Literature* 14 (1962): 108; rpt. in *Studies in Old English Literature in Honor of Arthur G. Brodeur*, ed. Stanley B. Greenfield (Eugene: University of Oregon Press, 1963), pp. 106–17.

77. Otto Glöde, "Üntersuchung über die Quelle von Cynewulf's *Elene*," *Anglia* 9 (1886): 271–318; Glöde, "Cynewulf's *Juliana* und ihre Quelle," *Anglia* 11 (1889): 146–58;

James M. Garnett, "The Latin and Anglo-Saxon *Juliana*," *Publications of the Modern Language Association* 14 (1889): 279–98.

78. The scholar whose cogent discussions are most responsible for popularizing the allegorical method as an authoritative approach to Old English poetry is Thomas D. Hill; see especially "Figural Narrative in *Andreas:* The Conversion of the Mermedonians," *Neuphilologische Mitteilungen* 70 (1969): 261–73, and "Sapiential Structure and Figural Narrative in the Old English *Elene*," *Traditio* 27 (1971): 159–77.

79. Catharine A. Regan, "Evangelicalism as the Informing Principle of Cynewulf's 'Elene'," *Traditio* 29 (1973): 27–52; Joseph Wittig, "Figural Narrative in Cynewulf's *Juliana*," *Anglo-Saxon England* 4 (1975): 37–55.

80. Patricia Meyer Spacks, *The Female Imagination* (New York: Alfred A. Knopf, 1975; rpt. Avon Books, 1975).

81. William Henry Schofield, "Signy's Lament," *Publications of the Modern Language Association* 17 (1902): 262, 267.

82. W. W. Lawrence, "The Banished Wife's Lament," *Modern Philology* 5 (1908): 387 and 405, respectively. See Greenfield's comparable remark that the lyrics are "devoted to the love between man and woman and the tribulations such love has had to endure" (*A Critical History*, p. 163).

83. Clifford Davidson, "Erotic 'Women's Songs' in Anglo-Saxon England," *Neophilologus* 59 (1975): 460 and 451 respectively.

84. Rudolph C. Bambas, "Another View of the Old English *Wife's Lament*," *Journal of English and Germanic Philology* 62 (1963): 303–309; rpt. in *Old English Literature: Twenty-Two Analytical Essays,* ed. Martin Stevens and Jerome Mandel (Lincoln: University of Nebraska Press, 1968), p. 229.

85. Bambas, "Another View," p. 230.

86. Elaine Tuttle Hansen, "From *freolicu folccwen* to *geomuru ides:* Women in Old English Poetry Reconsidered," *Michigan Academician* 9 (1976): 113.

87. Ibid.: 117 and 114.

88. Elizabeth Abel, "Introduction," in Abel, ed., *Writing and Sexual Difference* (Chicago: University of Chicago Press, 1982), p. 16.

89. See Doris Mary Stenton, *The English Woman in History* (London: George Allen and Unwin, 1957); Frank M. Stenton, *Anglo-Saxon England* (Oxford: Clarendon Press, 1943) and "The Historical Bearing of Place-Name Studies: The Place of Women in Anglo-Saxon Society," *Transactions of the Royal Historical Society,* 4th. ser., 25 (1943): 1–13, rpt. herein, chap. 4; Dorothy Whitelock, *The Beginnings of English Society* (Harmondsworth: Penguin Books, 1954); Dorothy Whitelock, ed., *Anglo-Saxon Wills* (Cambridge: Cambridge University Press, 1930), and ed. and trans., *The Will of Æthelgifu* (Oxford: Oxford University Press, 1968).

90. Doris Stenton, *English Woman,* p. 28.

91. Ibid., p. 28.

92. Ibid., p. v.

93. See Betty Bandell, "The English Chroniclers' Attitude toward Women," *Journal of the History of Ideas* 16 (1955): 113–18; Marc A. Meyer, "Land Charter and Legal Position of Women," in Kanner, *Women of England,* pp. 57–82; Dietrich, "Introduction"; and Klinck, "Female Characterization," and "Anglo-Saxon Women and the Law," *Journal of Medieval History* 8 (1982): 108–21.

94. For Fell and Stafford, see note 6.

95. Fell, *Women in Anglo-Saxon England,* pp. 110–14, discusses the fact that the original audience of Aldhelm's *De Virginitate* was composed of nuns and that "eighth-century-letter-writers, such as the nun Leoba, show themselves much influenced by his style and vocabulary" (p. 110). Indeed, many historians acknowledge that female literacy was important in Anglo-Saxon England; Patrick Wormald argues that "women were actually better

educated than men" ("The Uses of Literacy in Anglo-Saxon England and Its Neighbors," *Transactions of the Royal Historical Society,* 5th. ser., 27 [1977]: 98).

96. Feminist critics have been concerned with works authored by named women, allowing themselves to be governed by masculinist assumptions about literature, authority, and history. In the *Norton Anthology of Women Writers,* for example, Gilbert and Gubar omit all anonymous poetry, thereby decontextualizing medieval authors they include like Margery Kempe.

97. Raymond P. Tripp, Jr., has pointed out to us that the feminine inflections could possibly refer to a feminine speaker but not necessarily to a flesh-and-blood woman; since a noun like *sawol* 'soul' is grammatically feminine, the speaker could be a soul; see his "The Narrator as Revenant: A Reconsideration of Three Old English Elegies," *Papers on Language and Literature* 8 (1972): 339–61.

98. Although the means whereby Old English poems were composed is still a matter of debate, it is clear that they were *performed* orally. Ruth M. Crosby has pointed out that "oral delivery of popular literature was the rule rather than the exception in the Middle Ages" ("Oral Delivery in the Middle Ages," *Speculum* 11 [1936]: 110).

99. In *The Woman Troubadours* (New York: W. W. Norton, 1976), Meg Bogin discusses the *trobairitz* 'the female troubadours', twenty of whom are known from their *vidas* 'biographies' and nineteen of whom are known from extant poetry. Bogin points out that they are "the first female witnesses we have . . . from a culture that has profoundly influenced our own and which has hitherto been represented only by its men" (p. 4) and argues that we cannot understand the literature of romantic love unless we read the *trobairitz.* The women write about love but do not idealize it or present the lady and lover allegorically, and their language uses less word-play than that of men because they "prefer the more straightforward speech of conversation" (p. 13). It is noteworthy that one of the *trobairitz* was Garsenda de Forcalquier, wife of Alphonse II, who ruled Provence after Alphonse's death—a situation reminiscent of that of Æthelflæd of Mercia.

100. Diamond and Edwards, *Authority of Experience,* p. xii.

101. Abel, "Introduction," in Abel, *Writing and Sexual Difference,* p. 2.

102. Ibid., p. 2.

103. Mary Jacobus, "The Difference of View," in Jacobus, ed., *Women Writing and Writing about Women* (New York: Barnes and Noble Books, 1979), p. 25.

104. *Daniel,* 1. 257b, in *The Junius Manuscript,* ed. George Philip Krapp, vol. 1 of *The Anglo-Saxon Poetic Records* (New York: Columbia University Press, 1969), p. 118.

105. Auerbach, "Feminist Criticism Reviewed," in Todd, *Gender and Literary Voice,* p. 259.

106. Woolf, *A Room of One's Own,* p. 43.

107. Jacobus, "The Difference of View," in Jacobus, *Women Writing,* pp. 11–12.

108. Xavière Gauthier, "Pourquoi Sorcières?" trans. Erica M. Eisinger, in *NFC,* p. 203.

109. Showalter, "Literary Criticism," *Signs* 2 (1976): 435.

110. Brigid Brophy, Michael Levey, and Charles Osborne, *Fifty Works of English and American Literature We Could Do Without* (London: Rapp and Carroll, 1967), p. 1.

111. *Elene,* 373b and 374a, in *The Vercelli Book,* ed. George Philip Krapp, vol. 2 of *The Anglo-Saxon Poetic Records* (New York: Columbia University Press, 1969), p. 76.

The Historical Record

CHRISTINE E. FELL

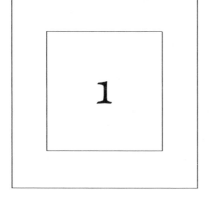

Some Implications of the Boniface Correspondence

> Suscepi desiderii mei epistolam, charissima, ues-tram, et amplexus animotenus scripta non tantum legi sed etiam condidi in thesauro cordis mei.[1]

> (Most beloved, I have received the letter I desired from you, and having clasped what you wrote to my soul, I have not merely read it, but have laid it away in the treasury of my heart.)

Æðelweard may have cherished the letters of his *consobrina* 'kinswoman' Matilda but since the letters themselves do not survive it is impossible for us to know in what formal or informal terms the two of them corresponded. Of the letters written by women that do survive from the Anglo-Saxon period, by far the most illuminating and informative are the much earlier ones that form part of the corpus known as the Boniface correspondence. The reason these are still extant may be that they were known and copied on the Continent, whereas most equivalent material in England either failed to survive the Viking raids, the Norman Conquest, or the Dissolution of the Monasteries and related hazards, or was not thought worthy of preservation in the first instance. Bede in gathering together information for his *Historia Ecclesiastica* was doubtless as assiduous in collecting it direct from the scriptoria of abbesses as from any other reputable and reliable source. It is likely that, given what we know of the response of women to the intellectual challenge of Christian learning and literacy in the eighth century, letters between members of different religious communities were commonplace, perhaps letters to friends and kin as well. Yet though Bede quotes letters in his *Historia Ecclesiastica,* we do not have a "Bede correspondence" in the same way that we have a "Boniface correspondence." And though Aldhelm and Alcuin were assiduous letter-writers, again we have nothing like the range of reciprocal material that is the delight of the Boniface mission. It must, I think, be assumed that though our immediate reaction to the Boniface correspondence is inevitably charmed surprise at its volume, its range, its quality, and its intimacy, it nevertheless represents only a tiny fragment of a vast Anglo-Saxon corpus of letters.

Firm evidence, however, is as usual hard to come by, and speculation involves us in many uncertain areas. We do not as yet know enough about possible distinctions between lay and learned literacy, nor, in spite of King Alfred's wise analysis of a changing pattern in education, do we know enough about the difference between centuries in the overall period we call Anglo-Saxon. Æðelweard's correspondence with his *consobrina* may have been much less typical of the late tenth century than any of the surviving eighth-century letters are of theirs. A further problem is the question of what we mean by a "personal" letter. The great fascination of much of the Boniface correspondence is the concentration on friendly detail. We appear to see a good deal of the emotional life of these Anglo-Saxon men and women, especially those on foreign soil isolated from their kin and homeland. Yet the mere fact of these letters having been formally copied and preserved indicates that the copier or compiler of the first codex saw a formal dimension to them. The laments of loneliness, the feelings of exile or solitude, are perhaps neither more nor less personal than the laments of the shadowy personae of *The Seafarer* and *The Wanderer*.

THE ''BONIFACE CORRESPONDENCE''

The Boniface correspondence survives in a variety of manuscripts of which the most significant is probably the ninth-century Vienna codex MS Nationalbibliothek Lat. 751.[2] When we are discussing the contents of this manuscript, the shorthand term "Boniface correspondence" turns out to be misleading in a number of ways. Granted that the majority of the letters are linked with the German mission that originated with Boniface himself, the letters nevertheless span a full century, the first probably from the 670s, the latest from the last quarter of the eighth century, and those which center on the successor of Boniface, Lull, and his contacts are no less illuminating than the earlier group. Also the manuscript contains letters which have no apparent connection with the Boniface mission itself and are merely representative of late seventh- or early eighth-century religious correspondence. In this group one must place some of the Aldhelm letters and that of the Whitby abbess Ælflæd.

Ways in which the Boniface correspondence has been presented to the general reader can also be misleading. M. Tangl has edited *Die Briefe des heiligen Bonifatius und Lullus*[3] with meticulous care and scholarly precision; yet his careful ordering of the letters necessarily obscures the order of presentation in individual manuscripts, and letters which the compiler of the Vienna codex put consecutively are in this edition widely separated. Furthermore, the well-known behavior of historians in singling out politically relevant items has led to far more translations of Boniface's own letters than of those from more obscure members of his mission.[4] E. Emerton's comment is not untypical:

> The present translation has been made from the text as published by Tangl. Some few letters there published have, however, been omitted from the translation, *since they have no reference to the great bishop*.[5] (my italics)

In the various collected translations I have looked at, I have not yet found any rendering of Berhtgyð's unhappy letters to her brother.[6] They admittedly have little importance in the political scenario if that has to be the criterion for inclusion.

Tangl's collection using all major manuscript sources contains 150 letters. In this number he includes, but does not reprint, half a dozen from the Aldhelm correspondence, considering them to have been adequately edited elsewhere. In the total of 150 there are sixteen letters from men to women as well as two from Boniface written generally to all brothers and sisters in religious communities (Tangl 41 and 46). The first of these (41) is addressed to named brothers in the first instance but adds *et omnibus fratribus ac sororibus nostrum* 'and to all our brothers and sisters'. The second (46) specifies status and includes abbesses, virgins *consecratis et Deo devotis* 'consecrated and devoted to God', and *cunctis consecratis ancillis Christi* 'all consecrated women in Christ's service', which I suppose to comprise all women vowed to God who were neither abbess nor virgin. There must certainly have been widows enough who found refuge in the religious life.

As well as letters to women, named or anonymous, there is one important letter (Tangl 105) in which a woman of distinction is used as introduction and referee. Æðelbert of Kent makes it clear that it is only on the recommendation of the abbess Bucge that he has the temerity to address himself to Boniface—though his urgent need for good falcons may have motivated him also.

The letters to named women include one from Aldhelm to an otherwise unknown Sigegyð (Tangl 2), nine from Boniface himself, and probably six from Lull,[7] of which one is by joint authors Lull, Denehard, and Burghard. The five Aldhelm letters in the Vienna codex have most recently been discussed and edited by Michael Herren,[8] including the one to Sigegyð. Here, as usual, a single surviving letter implies the loss of others. It is clear that Aldhelm is replying to a request, but it is the reply only, not the letter of asking, that is preserved. The number of lost letters cannot of course be estimated, but some indication is given by the sparsity of reciprocal letters in the entire collection. When we look at the letters written to and from Boniface this is particularly clear.

Four letters written by Boniface to Eadburg, abbess of Thanet, are preserved. So is one from Lull. Letters from Boniface regularly mention gifts and greetings he has received from Eadburg. It is conceivable but unlikely that these were accompanied only by verbal messages. Lull, in writing to Eadburg (Tangl 70), specifically asks for a return letter: *Interea rogo, ut mihi litteras tuae dulcidinis distinare non deneges* 'Meanwhile, I ask that in your kindness you will not refuse to write to me'. But no letter from Eadburg is extant. This pattern we see quite clearly repeated a number of times. Leoba asks Boniface for a kindly reply to her first letter. It is unlikely that he failed to send one, but in this instance we have Leoba's request and not Boniface's answer. This implies haphazard survival. It is not that Boniface's words were considered more worthy of preservation, in spite of the immense veneration in which he was held.[9]

Letters from women that are preserved are nine in number, and to these we should add one (Tangl 55) that purports to be from the heads of three religious communities, one abbot and two abbesses, but is in fact clearly the composition of Cneoburg, one of the abbesses named. We may also note that at the end of Ecgburg's letter (Tangl 13) to Boniface a postscript is added by a man, saying in effect, "Please remember me, too." I mention this, because such indications of friendly cooperation between men and women in religious communities would have seemed so unlikely in the post-Conquest period. Only one letter is from woman to woman, the one from Ælflæd, abbess of Whitby (Tangl 8), to Adola, abbess of Pfalzel (near Trier). It is in itself sufficiently interesting as one of the few bits of firm evidence of Whitby's contacts with Europe in the post-Hild era, but the content of the letter, recommending yet another of those committed women on pilgrimage to Rome to the care of the Pfalzel community on her journey south, must have been duplicated in dozens of others from all English houses.

Of the remaining eight letters written by women, five are to Boniface himself, and three (probably) are from the nun Berhtgyð to her brother *in Domino et in carne Balthardo* 'in the Lord and in the flesh Baldhard'. Because the survivals are so haphazard, generalizations about the nature of the correspondence are dangerous. In one sense we may see the letters as representative of two or even three generations, one generation being the earliest friends of Boniface and another that of his successor, Lull. Even here the links between the generations make glib distinctions impossible. Yet because Boniface's own letters have received more attention than those of his successor, I propose to concentrate on the letters of the second and third generation, though some cross-reference to the earlier period will be inevitable. In this group I include six letters from Lull to women, including the one for which he is only one-third responsible (Tangl 49), and the ones from Berhtgyð to her brother.

THE LETTERS OF LULL

Tangl 49 is in Tangl's dating circa 740. It is from Lull, Denehard, and Burghard to an otherwise unidentified abbess in England, Cyniburg. The relationship between these young men and their abbess was probably not unlike that of Hild's brilliant scholars (who went on to become bishops) with their distinguished superior. The tone of the letter certainly suggests that Cyniburg continued to be regarded by these earnest young men as their spiritual mentor and secular lord.

She is their *domina dilectissima,* their 'most loved lady', and they are her 'sons and fellow-countrymen', *filii tui ac vernaculi*. The whole letter is written with love and deference:

> Some little gifts accompany this letter, frankincense, pepper and cinnamon—a very small present but given with deep love. Please do not look at the size of the gift, but remember the loving spirit. We ask you also to correct the *rusticitas* of this letter, and send us a few of your own sweet words, which we eagerly await.

I quote this only to establish the tone. The real importance of the letter is the degree of administrative control it implies. We all know of the plight of the "lordless" man in this period—one of the first Old English poems any student reads is *The Wanderer*, the lament of the lordless man. The first necessity for people visiting any part of England was to attach themselves firmly to a *hlaford*, a 'lord', even if only on a temporary basis. The laws of Ine of Wessex spell out the situation with clarity and precision.[10] If anyone kills a man from abroad who has no kin, the fine for his death, the *wergild*, is divided between the king and the one who took this person under his or her protection. If the protector *abbod sie oððe abbodesse* 'is either an abbot or an abbess', he or she has full rights to half the *wergild*.

This law makes it quite clear that a traveller from abroad might choose to put himself in the protection or overlordship of an abbess, that a "lordless" man might choose an abbess as his *hlaford,* and that she would then have the full responsibility for him as a member of her community, and legal obligation to press for redress on his behalf, if he were killed or injured. This might seem an unlikely hypothesis (though Anglo-Saxon laws are usually too laconic to make provision for unlikely occurrences), but in fact this is clearly the situation outlined by Lull, Denehard, and Burghard in their letter to Cyniburg. 'We also wish it known to your care and wisdom that if any of the three of us should visit Britain we should not seek to put ourselves in obedience to the government of anyone else, but only in subjection to your benevolence': *nullius hominis oboedientiam et institutionem antea querimus, quam tuae bonevolentiae subiectionem.* They add 'for in you we have the most complete confidence': *quia in te firmissimam spem mentis nostrae positam habemus.*

Another paragraph in the same letter is equally important and revealing. Lull, Denehard, and Burghard assume that the abbess Cyniburg is entirely capable of protecting the legal interests of two boys who have recently been manumitted. They want her to make arrangements for these boys to come out and join the German mission, 'if it is their wish and if they are under your control': *illorum voluntas sit et in tua potestate sint.* Since they have been freed, *tua potestate* self-evidently does not mean they might be 'in her power' in the sense of slavery, but must clearly mean that she functions as their *hlaford,* their 'lord'. If anyone should try to prevent these boys from going out to join the missionaries *sine iustitia* (i.e., anyone without legal right to do so) then would Cyniburg please undertake their defense, *eos defendere digneris.* The whole letter implies no small degree of power and legal responsibility resting in the position of the abbess.

Lull writes also to Eadburg of Thanet, and here, though the tone of deference is no less than when he writes to Cyniburg, the letter is much less personal. The implications are, I suggest, that Lull knew Eadburg rather as Boniface's friend than his own. Doubtless she was a lady with a formidable reputation, as Boniface's letters make clear, but generous also in the sending of gifts to her fellow countrymen as Lull's gratitude shows. His courteous thank-you letter goes by the messenger Ceola, who also carried Boniface's letters and gifts to Æðelbald of Mercia (Tangl 69). It was written only a few years later than his letter to Cyniburg, when he was still young and *diaconus* 'a deacon', but is a very much more formal composition.

Also from this period are two letters attributed to Lull written to unidentified recipients. One (Tangl 98) is to an abbess and one of her nuns jointly; the other (Tangl 140) is to an anonymous and unknown nun whom he addresses as *soror* 'sister'. The other four letters, where the ascription to Lull is certain, are found in more than one manuscript, but these two are in the Vienna codex only. Tangl gives the reasons for ascribing these letters to Lull, and there seems little reason to challenge the attribution. If they are not Lull's letters, they would be the only two in the complete collection sent from men to women which were not from the three major names Aldhelm, Boniface, and Lull. In the following pages I accept the attribution to Lull.

Stylistically they are somewhat different from Lull's other letters to women, being a good deal more "Aldhelmian." Both contain Latin verse, and it is clear that Lull (like many of his contemporaries) enjoyed experimenting with form and meter.

In the letter he and others sent to Cyniburg, he apologized with some diffidence for the *rusticitas* of their joint Latinity. No such scholastic humility is found in his letters to Eadburg, Leoba, and Swiða. In the one to the unnamed abbess and nun, however, he is clearly striving after literary effect. It is a most open and revealing letter, and the author's desire to impress is part of the candor. We learn that he had been afflicted with severe illness during which time he was nursed back to health in the house of this unknown abbess, *benigna caritatis humanitate memini susceptum* 'I remember with what loving-kindness I was cared for'.[11] His letter continues with shy delight: *eandem quoque actenus parum pigrae fraternitatis affectus dilectionem divini amoris obtentu conplentes observare dinoscimini* 'and to this day you have displayed towards me as towards a brother this same unwearying affection in consideration of the divine love'.

It is clear, however, that during this period of ill health and convalescence, the author was impressed not only by the loving-kindness of his nurses, but also by their erudition. The unnamed nun, who perhaps more than the abbess had charge of the patient, was *non solum exteriore litterarum studio, verum etiam interiore divinae scientiae luce inlustrate* 'illuminated not only by the outer brilliance of learning, but by the inner light of divine wisdom'. Thus, in what can only strike the reader as an immense effort to impress by his own literary skills, he indulges more than is his wont in picturesque vocabulary, romantic and sentimental description—*relictaque fecundissima natalis patriae insula, quam glauca spumantis maris cerula infligentia scopolosis marginibus undique vallant* 'leaving the fruitful soil of my native land whose craggy coasts the dark green waves of the foaming sea hem in on every side'—and ultimately in learned and enigmatic verse, which he begs in desperately authentic accents shall not be shown to anyone else. He is confident that the two women to whom he writes will be gentle literary critics: *ubi pro certo scio nullam dirae fraudis suspicione mentem distinantis mordere nec dictantem hostili vituperatione lacerare, licet vitiosa pagina scabraque scedula repperiatur* 'for with you I am certain that the tooth of suspicion will not bite, nor the claws of harsh judgment rend the writer, though the contents be faulty and the composition rough'. There are few letters in the collection more evocative than this one.

This letter, which survives only in the Vienna codex, contained in its original form the full text of poems where the manuscript has only a couple of lines. These poems from Lull's description evidently included play on words and names. The delight of the Boniface circle in cryptography and other forms of learned game-playing is well known, and it is therefore quite likely that the cryptogram, runic names, and other word-games which immediately follow this letter in the manuscript were a part of Lull's original composition, intended as a pleasurable intellectual pastime for his learned correspondents. The general tenor of the letter encourages this interpretation, though René Derolez is inclined to the view that the scribe of the manuscript may have been responsible for an addition here simply in order to fill up the end of a quire.[12]

The letter which Lull writes to an unknown *soror* (Tangl 140) is basically a simple request that she should give him the help of her prayers, but here too the prose is determinedly "literary," and Lull ventures again with suitable deprecation into

Latin verse. This and the preceding letter are so similar both in the degree of affection they display and in their delight in shared aesthetic and learned pursuits, that it is not impossible that the *soror* of Tangl 140 and the young nun of Tangl 98 were the same. But such speculations are not to open to proof, and it may be that one should not appear to underestimate the numbers of men and women involved in the exploration and challenge of learning and literature.

Lull offers his poems *non arroganter mea commendans, sed humiliter tua deposcens* 'not arrogantly commending my own but asking humbly for yours'. He includes two verses in different meters: first, standard hexameters:

in caelo flagrans iam iustis vita perennis
(shining in heaven now, life with the righteous and everlasting)

but this is followed by the less common rhyming octosyllabic formula:

Vale Christo virguncula   Christi nempe tiruncula.
(Farewell in Christ, young virgin, truly Christ's novice.)

Lull is of course imitating Aldhelm's *Carmen Rhythmicum* here, and it is interesting to note the background. Aldhelm's *Carmen* is preserved only in the same Vienna codex (751) that is a major source for the Boniface correspondence, and Lull is thought to have been the mastermind behind the assembling of materials which the compiler of this codex used. Lull, in a letter to an English brother (Tangl 71), specifically asked to be sent the works of Aldhelm *seu prosarum seu metrorum aut rithmicorum* 'whether in prose or meter or rhyme'. Michael Lapidge suggests that the *Carmen Rhythmicum* is a verse form "on which [Aldhelm] left the imprint of his originality and of which he was possibly the inventor."[13] It is worth noting that Lull in his letter to an unknown nun and Berhtgyð writing to her brother indulge themselves in interesting if not profound experiments with this innovation.

It is clear that in considering Lull's letters to women, even given the small number that survive, we are able to distinguish up to a point between the formal and the personal. His letter to Leoba (Tangl 100)—headed in Tangl, *Bitte um Fortdauer der Freundschaft* and in E. Kylie's translation "Lull asks Leoba not to doubt his affection for her"—seems to me a magnificent piece of thinly disguised irritation. The rhetoric he employs is heavily characterized by the device of *occupatio*. He begins *Non inmemorem tuae sagacitatis industriam estimo* . . . 'I do not believe that you forget, in your wisdom and energy . . .'. He continues with emphatic negatives, *Nec enim* . . . *arbitreris* and *neque* . . . *autumes:* Leoba is not to judge Lull "forgetful" nor to think him "negligent." Here certainly we have the reply to one, or probably more than one, *cri de coeur* from Leoba which has not been preserved. There is evidence enough in Berhtgyð's letters of how lonely and isolated these women could feel, and in Leoba's biography we get some indication of this. Boniface's exhortations to her a little before his death not to grow weary of her work and not to abandon her adopted land imply at least that she had had hopes and thoughts of returning home. It is also true that not all of Boniface's followers regarded Lull with the same degree of devotion and affection with which they had looked up to Boniface.

Abbot Eigil's biography of Sturm, for example, reveals a good deal of friction and rivalry.[14] In spite of the ostensible friendliness of Lull's letter to Leoba, the underlying feeling is one of some tension between them.

In writing to Leoba, Lull was writing to a colleague more or less of his own generation, the generation of younger people who had been inspired to go out and join Boniface's team. In writing to the abbesses named above, Lull was writing rather to women of Boniface's own generation and this presumably accounts for the much greater degree of deference. However, there is one other letter to note here, and that is from Lull to the abbess Swiða (Tangl 128), a letter in a totally different register from any of the others we have considered. Swiða, too, must have been one of approximately his own generation since in his letter Lull refers to her having been a disciple of their common master Boniface.

In considering the achievements of the seventh and eighth centuries, it is frequently pointed out that of all the great double houses scattered over England the only one of which scandal is reported is Coldingham. This was neglect of religious observance within the monastery itself, the cells which should have been devoted to prayer being filled instead with feasting, gossip, and so on. Other kinds of scandal are sometimes mentioned in the Boniface correspondence. Boniface himself rebukes King Æðelbald of Mercia for fornication with nuns and consecrated virgins (Tangl 73) and, in a letter to Archbishop Cuthbert of Canterbury (Tangl 78), asks that the practice of women undertaking pilgrimage to Rome should be restricted since so many of them end up as prostitutes in foreign towns. He mentions almost in parenthesis that many of them die, but he is clearly rather more concerned about those that fail to preserve their chastity *magna ex parte pereunt paucis remanentibus integris* 'a great part of them perish, and few of the rest remain virtuous'. When he tells us that there are few towns in *Longobardia vel in Francia aut in Gallia* 'Lombardy or in Frankland or in Gaul' where there is not *adultera vel meretrix generis Anglorum* 'an adulteress or a prostitute of the English race', one is inclined to be sceptical of a statement so clearly based on hearsay.

If King Æðelbald indulged himself in sexual relationships with nuns and consecrated virgins in convents, Boniface commented with severity on the man but not on those in charge of the said convent. It must be implicit that an abbess was unable to protect her nuns from a licentious king. If women on pilgrimage ended up as prostitutes, Boniface suggests that perhaps their religious superiors were at fault in allowing them to travel, or, at any rate, that if they had not already taken responsibility in this area they should now do so. But we do not have an example from Boniface's pen of an abbess rebuked for not taking better care of her nuns.

I have digressed here in order to provide some kind of context for Lull's letter to Swiða. It was, I think, necessary to do so because though the letter is extraordinarily harsh in tone, the offense in question is not set out with maximum clarity. Also we know nothing of the abbess Swiða except what Lull's letter tells us, not even where she was in charge. That she was an abbess is to be inferred from the fact that the letter is addressed to *Suithan eiusque subiectis* 'Swiða and her subordinates', but she is given no greater courtesy of address than this. The letter is one of stern rebuke and indeed threatens excommunication. The fault of Swiða is that she has allowed two women to go *in longinquam regionem* 'into a distant region' wherever that may be *propter arrogantiam ac voluptatem laicorum explendam*. If one translates *voluptatem* as 'lust', then the suggestion would be that laypeople had in their pride and lust taken off two of Swiða's nuns. But Lull is certainly putting the blame firmly on the women (unlike Boniface in his rebuke to the Mercian king). Moreover, the women are subsequently castigated not for their sex lives but for being *vagas et inoboedientes* 'wandering and disobedient'. And an earlier remark of Lull's indicates that a major part of the fault was that Swiða allowed this to happen without his permission and advice, *sine licentia et consilio meo*. The implication must be not that they have been unchaste, but that they have run the risk of falling into the devil's noose—*in laqueum diaboli*. It sounds as if Lull were trying to impose a sterner discipline on and greater control over the convents in his diocese than we have evidence for in Anglo-Saxon England at this period. The women were not precisely "disobedient" to their abbess, if their abbess allowed their absence, and it seems to be assumed that this absence was temporary since Lull tells Swiða what penance they are to undergo on their return. A visit to kin or even a pilgrimage undertaken in the company of lay kinsmen seems a possible explanation of all these not easily reconcilable factors in Lull's denunciation. Swiða herself is instructed to abstain from flesh food and from any honey-sweetened drink—*abstinendo ab omni carne et ab omni potu qui melle indulcoratur*—which does not sound in itself a penance of sufficient severity to fit in with the general harshness of Lull's tone. In another letter (Tangl 113), he asks his dearest sons to abstain from meat and honey-drinks for one week as part of a plea to the Almighty to release them from the continuous rains. I would suggest that Lull's letter to Swiða is more an indication of petulant authority than of serious corruption within the community, but the evidence is slight and judgments based on tone are necessarily subjective.

THE LETTERS OF LEOBA AND BERHTGYÐ

There are three women of the second and third generations of the Boniface mission whose letters are extant. The letter from Leoba (Tangl 29) to Boniface features enough in general discussion to be better known than the others. The letter from Cena to Boniface (Tangl 97) is too timidly deferential and conventional to have warranted much attention. The letters from Berhtgyð have (pre-Peter Dronke) received virtually none. There is another and more important factor which differentiates these letters from those of the other women friends of Boniface. The first group—Ecgburg, Eangyð, Eadburg, and Bucge—are all settled in England. Leoba, Cena, and Berhtgyð are apparently in Germany. Leoba's first letter, it is true, was probably written from England, but she chose exile to become part of the Boniface team. Cena's letter suggests that she is similarly a disciple of Boniface settled in a remote province, while Berhtgyð may never even have had the choice. She was evidently either not yet born or, more probably, an infant when her mother first came to Germany.

I am not perfectly sure which women John Lingard had in mind when he wrote:

> Even the women caught the general enthusiasm: seminaries of learning were established in their convents; they conversed with their absent friends in the language of ancient Rome; and frequently exchanged the labours of the distaff and the needle, for the more pleasing and elegant beauties of the latin poets.[15]

For the skills of Leoba and Berhtgyð with either needle or distaff we have no evidence. But they are the only two women in the range of the Boniface correspondence who venture into Latin verse. Leoba's only surviving composition is the four-line one included in her early letter to Boniface when she was still very young and introducing herself to his notice. She calls her lines *versiculi* 'unpretentious verses' and is suitably diffident about their merit, but they scarcely deserve the severity with which they have been treated:

> It is sad to say that, although Leoba declares she has not done this audaciously, it is an audacious piece of copying, from the treatise on the construction of Latin verse by Aldhelm of Malmesbury.[16]

It is perfectly true that the four lines are heavily Aldhelm-dependent, but as the sketchiest glance at Tangl's footnotes makes clear, so is a very considerable amount of the Boniface correspondence, both prose and verse. Given what we know about the composition of vernacular verse in Old English with its reiterated use of stock phrases, it is a little absurd to rebuke Leoba in accordance with twentieth-century concepts of the rights of individual authorship. Leoba says herself she was taught the art by her *magistra* 'female teacher', and the text book from which she would have learned is Aldhelm's *De Metris*. As obviously did Lull and Berhtgyð.

There are almost certainly three letters from Berhtgyð to her brother Baldhard. These letters occur only in the Vienna codex, and they are on adjacent folios (33-35). The first (Tangl 143) is, in the manuscript, without names. The second (Tangl 147) names both the sender *Berthgyth* and recipient *Balthardus*. The third (Tangl 148) names the recipient again, *fratri unico Baldhardo* 'her only brother Baldhard', but not the sender. Nevertheless, stylistic detail, similarity of content, and positioning in the manuscript suggest single authorship.

We know of Berhtgyð from Otloh's *Vita Bonifatii*. The women who came out to join Boniface's mission were:

> feminae vero religiosae, matertera scilicet sancti Lulli nomine Chunihilt et filia eius Berhtgit, Chunitrud et Tecla, Lioba et Waltpurgis, soror Willibaldi et Wunnebaldi. Sed Chunihilt et filia eius Berhtgit, valde eruditae in liberali scientia, in Turingorum regione constituebantur magistrae.[17]

> (truly religious women, namely the maternal aunt of Saint Lull named Cynehild, and her daughter Berhtgyð, Cyneðryð and Tecla, Leoba and Waldburg, the sister of Willibald and Wynnebald. But Cynehild and her daughter Berhtgyð, very learned in the liberal arts, were appointed as teachers in the region of Thuringia.)

If Cynehild was Lull's aunt and Berhtgyð's mother, it is perhaps a little difficult to know where to place Berhtgyð in age. When Boniface writes a loving letter to Leoba, Cynehild, and Tecla, he addresses them as "daughters." It is the only time he uses this term, for whenever he writes to abbesses in England he always calls them "sister." This suggests perhaps that though Cynehild was probably a mother when she came over to join the mission, she was young enough to be envisaged along with Tecla and Leoba as "the younger generation." Otloh's *Vita* however makes no mention of Cynehild's son. Attempts have been made to identify him. Tangl suggests he was the first abbot of Hersfeld, and, since Hersfeld was founded by Baldhard's cousin Lull, this is not improbable. That he or his sister is to be identified in the Durham *Liber Vitae* lists of those who are to be remembered in prayers at the altar seems to me not very probable given the fact that these names are not uncommon.[18] It is certainly to be inferred from Berhtgyð's letters that her brother was somewhere in the monastic or missionary world since she addresses him as *crucicola* 'servant of the cross'. It is mildly curious that, in one letter to him, she implies that where he is there also are the graves of both their parents. It is not impossible that Cynehild, when she came to join the Boniface mission, came with husband as well as young children and that they went their separate ways into evangelical work. Lull himself claims that almost all his kin came with him. But it certainly represents a sidelight on family involvement which we do not get elsewhere in the Boniface letters.

The comments on the learning of Cynehild and her daughter are so reminiscent of Lull's letters to an unnamed abbess and nun (Tangl 98) that one could be tempted to identify the recipients of Lull's letter with his kinswomen. What militates against this is the fact that he addresses the abbess as *splendida virginitatis castimonia* 'splendid purity of virginity'. Also, the extent to which he provides information in that letter about his own background would scarcely have been news to an aunt and cousin. Nevertheless, we might note that what Lull says of the learning of the young nun to whom he writes and the fact that he sends examples of his poetry does indicate that the circle of learning and literature was a fairly impressive one. It is not within the scope of this essay to discuss the works of the nun Hygeburg, but their existence is a reminder of the range of this highly intellectual community, and Berhtgyð is unlikely to have been the only woman poet among them. Tangl assumes the recipients of this letter to be in England. I do not see any firm evidence for this assumption; on the contrary, one or two phrases suggest Lull is writing to fellow exiles.

Berhtgyð's letters have at last received attention in Dronke's recent publication.[19] His translations convey well the sentimental rhetoric of the originals, but his discussion of them implies that he thinks of them as the work of a woman in her thirties. At any rate he suggests she was a child in the 740s, and her letters might be attributed to the 770s. I am inclined to disagree. Kinship was taken very seriously among the Anglo-Saxons, and I find it difficult to believe that Berhtgyð would have written so poignantly of her solitary state—*ego sola in hac terra et nullius alius frater visitet me neque propinquorum aliquis ad me veniet* 'I am alone in this country and have no other brother to visit me nor any other relative to come to me' and, again, *ego enim sola derelicta et destituta auxilio propinquorum* 'for I am alone, forsaken, and deprived of the support of kin'—while her first cousin Lull was still living and archbishop of Mainz. He died in 786. We also note that Lull, in his letter to an unknown abbess and nun, tells us that he crossed the seas to Germany with a great band of almost all his kindred *cum totius propinquitatis meae propemodum caterva.* This great band, one presumes, included some of Cynehild's kin as well. The word used of the relationship between Lull and Cynehild is *matertera* 'maternal aunt'. We know much of the relationship between uncles and their sisters' sons, less of the relationships between aunts and their sisters' sons in the Germanic world. Yet, considering what sources tell us of the far-flung nature of kinship obligations, considering even that it was remembered by the time Otloh wrote that Cynehild was Lull's *matertera,* it would, I think, be absurd to assume that Lull was so negligent of his young cousin that she would have written quite such desolate letters in his lifetime.

One should also note that Berhtgyð quite probably learned her rhyming and alliterative octosyllabic meters through Lull's agency. It is Lull who begs to be sent copies of Aldhelm's rhythmical work, doubtless Lull who is responsible for the preservation of the various octosyllabic compositions in the Vienna codex. It is not likely that there was such a plethora of this material available in Germany that Berhtgyð had independent access to a wide range of Aldhelmian verse. The heavy stylistic indebtedness to Aldhelm that she and Lull share was quite likely a matter of copied or exchanged manuscripts between the cousins. We know of course that Boniface also was a writer both of octosyllabic verse and of a treatise on metrics, but the particular style of Lull and of Berhtgyð appears to owe more to Aldhelm than to Boniface. I suggest that Berhtgyð's letters to her brother were probably not written in Lull's lifetime and that she was beginning to think of herself as an old woman when she sent them. Her stress on her imminent death is not necessarily fantasy or illness. She begs to come where the graves of their parents are *et temporalem vitam ibi finire* 'and there end this transitory life'. Dronke sees parallels to the tone of Berhtgyð's letters in "the two extant Anglo-Saxon women's love laments, known as 'The Wife's Complaint' and 'Wulf and Eadwacer'."[20] I myself see her letters as more evocative of the isolation, age, and exile tones in *The Wanderer.* Berhtgyð, I would suggest, can see no reason *for hwan modsefa   min ne gesweorce* 'why my mind should not grow dark' (59) and expects no final refuge except *frof[or] to Fæder on heofenum / þær us eal seo fæstnung is* 'consolation from the Father in Heaven, where all our security is' (115)—or as she puts it *ubi perfecta mansio esse cernitur et regio vivorum et gaudia angelorum sine fine laetantium* 'where will be seen a perfect mansion, the land of the living, and the joy of the angels rejoicing without end'.[21] (I take it *mansio* is an echo of "in my father's house are many mansions" John, 14/2 Vulgate *In domo Patris mei mansiones multae sunt.*)

However, all this is to assume a fairly intensive personal kinship background including the extended kinship range. The other factor that needs to be remembered when looking at Berhtgyð's letters is the nature of the record. Who preserved these letters and why? It is perhaps a little unlikely that Berhtgyð herself preserved copies of her own letters for posterity but not the one that her brother had obviously sent her between her letters two and three. Did her brother preserve her letters and hand them over to a compiler of "Bonifacian correspondence?" I am inclined to think this unlikely too. My own suggestion would be that Berhtgyð's letters, passionate as they are, are nevertheless by no means informal. As Dronke has shown, even the prose can in modern English be rendered in something approximating to verse form. In other words it is highly formalized rhetoric. And her verse is, as said above, one of the few surviving examples from this part of the world of the influence of Aldhelm's *Carmen Rhythmicum*. I think these letters survive, not because of the apparent and urgent personal note, but because of the embedded literary skills, and that they were intended so to survive. In other words, I suppose them to be formal literary compositions of which copies were carefully made before the originals were despatched. I do not wish to depersonalize Berhtgyð's grief and loneliness any more than I would depersonalize the desperation of Gerard Manley Hopkins's "No worst, there is none." But the compiler who put these letters together for posterity is hardly likely to have preserved them solely for the note of personal anguish. Their value must have been in their formalization of that emotion.

We are also doing a disservice to the women of the Bonifacian correspondence if we depict them as more emotional or more self-pitying than their male counterparts. The letters from men, the letters from Boniface and Lull, over and over again reveal mental, emotional, and physical suffering and stress. The effect of Christianity was, it seems, partly to encourage a greater emotional openness than had been traditional in a more stoical Germanic ethos. Boniface and Lull are ready enough to invite sympathy for their extensive and various problems. Berhtgyð, in using every Aldhelmian device known to her, is well within both the literary and the emotional etiquette of her background.[22]

The Boniface correspondence is probably still one of the more neglected areas of Anglo-Saxon studies. All I have been able to do in this essay is to signal a few aspects that seem to me of interest. The work I should like to see done would be a close analysis of the Anglo-Saxon vocabulary and concepts underlying the acquired Latinity. But that would require a scholar of infinitely greater linguistic expertise than myself.

NOTES

1. *The Chronicle of Æthelweard*, ed. A. Campbell, Nelson's Medieval Texts (London: Nelson and Co., 1962), p. 1.

2. F. Unterkircher, *Sancti Bonifacii Epistolae. Codex Vindobonensis 751 der öster-reichischen Nationalbibliothek, Codices selecti phototypice impressi XXIV* (Graz: Akademische Druck-und-Verlagsanstalt, 1971). It is difficult to be consistent in the spelling of Old English names. The manuscript forms (Berthgyth, etc.) are unacceptable to scholars accustomed to Old English. Old English forms however look odd where we have such standard modernizations as Cuthbert. I have settled for Berhtgyð, Baldhard, Cyniburg, etc. rather than Beorhtgyð, Bealdheard, Cyneburg, but kept Leoba rather than Leofa simply because she seems too well known under that form for me to change it. The abbess Swiða (Tangl, "Suitha") presents a particular and interesting problem. The Vienna codex has the name twice, once in the heading and once in the first sentence. In the main text the MS reads *osuuitha*, and it is possible that we have here, accurately, a Latinized form of the name Oswið which scribe and editor have reinterpreted as apostrophe plus personal name.

3. M. Tangl, ed., *Die Briefe des heiligen Bonifatius und Lullus,* Monumenta Germaniae Historica: Epistolae Selectae, vol. 1, 2nd ed. (Berlin: Weidmann, 1955).

4. Note, for example, the selection in D. Whitelock, *English Historical Documents I,* 2nd ed. (London: Eyre Methuen, 1979), pp. 168ff.

5. E. Emerton, trans., *The Letters of Saint Boniface* (New York: Columbia University Press, 1940), p. 19.

6. Emerton, see note 5 above; Whitelock, see note 4 above; see also E. Kylie, *The English Correspondence of Saint Boniface* (New York: Cooper Square Publishers, 1966), and C. H. Talbot, *The Anglo-Saxon Missionaries in Germany* (London and New York: Sheed and Ward, 1954). Berhtgyð's letters are, however, discussed by Peter Dronke in his *Women Writers of the Middle Ages* (Cambridge: Cambridge University Press, 1984), pp. 30–35.

7. Tangl discusses Lull's authorship of letters for which the manuscript has no ascription, see his footnotes, pp. 218 and 279. A fuller discussion is in his *Studien um den heiligen Bonifatius* published in *Das Mittelalter in Quellenkunde und Diplomatik I* (Berlin: Akademie-Verlag, 1966), pp. 25ff.

8. Michael Lapidge and Michael Herren, trans., *Aldhelm: The Prose Works* (Cambridge: D. S. Brewer, 1979), pp. 136ff.

9. The only surviving translation into Old English of any of Boniface's letters was probably of interest because of its account of a vision, not because of its authorship; see Kenneth Sisam, *Studies in the History of Old English Literature* (Oxford: Clarendon Press, 1953), pp. 199ff.

10. F. Liebermann, ed., *Die Gesetze der Angelsachsen* (Halle: M. Niemeyer, 1903–16), vol. 1, pp. 98 and 99.

11. Finding myself floundering in the translation of this ornate prose I have relied on Kylie's translations, see note 6 above.

12. R. Derolez, *Runica manuscripta: The English Tradition* (Brugge: De Tempel, 1954), pp. 197ff.

13. Michael Lapidge and James L. Rosier, trans., *Aldhelm: The Poetic Works* (Cambridge: D. S. Brewer, 1985), p. 171.

14. Eigil's *Life of Sturm,* trans. Talbot, see note 6 above. Lull's *Vita* composed by Lambert of Hersfeld in the eleventh century has also material on this controversy; see Ioannes Bollandus, et al., *Acta Sanctorum* (Brussels: Société des Bollandistes, 1845), October 7, pp. 1050ff.

15. John Lingard, *The Antiquities of the Anglo-Saxon Church,* 2nd ed. (Newcastle: Edward Walker, 1810), pp. 317–18.

16. G. F. Browne, *Boniface of Crediton and his Companions* (London: Society for Promoting Christian Knowledge, 1910), p. 81. That Leoba is, with entire propriety, following Aldhelm in putting formulaic patterns together is pointed out by Lapidge in "Aldhelm's Latin Poetry and Old English Verse," *Comparative Literature* 31 (1979): 209–231, esp. 230.

17. W. Levison, ed., *Vitae Sancti Bonifatii,* Scriptores Rerum Germanicarum, vol. 57 (Hanover: Hannsche Buchhandlung, 1905), p. 138.

18. H. Sweet, ed., *The Oldest English Texts,* Early English Text Society, o.s., vol. 83 (London: Oxford University Press, 1885; rpt. 1966), pp. 154ff. The *Liber Vitae* certainly has two characters named *berhtgid* among the *nomina reginarum et abbatissarum,* but this is not evidence for an identification with the letter-writer of the same name. H. Hahn first propounded the identification in "Die Namen der Bonifazischen Briefe im liber vitae ecclesiae Dunelmensis," *Neues Archiv der Gesellschaft für ältere deutsche Geschichtskunde* 12 (1887): 111–27. He also discusses these names briefly in his *Bonifaz und Lul: Ihre angelsächsischen Korrespondenten* (Leipzig: Veit and Co., 1883), pp. 138–39. Levison in *England and the Continent in the Eighth Century* (Oxford: Clarendon Press, 1946) appears to accept Hahn's and Tangl's identification of Baldhard with the Hersfeld abbot (p. 168). We may note that if this abbot was Berhtgyð's brother he outlived Lull by twelve years, dying in A.D. 798.

19. Dronke, *Women Writers of the Middle Ages;* see note 6.

20. Ibid., p. 31.

21. The names at the end of Berhtgyð's octosyllabics run as follows: *elonqueel. et michael. accadai. adonai. alleuatia alleluia.* Some of these are clearly Hebrew divine and angelic names; others, though the spelling is confused, are probably of the same order. My colleague in Classics at Nottingham, Professor Alan Sommerstein, has kindly looked at this for me and writes: "The first word may be corrupt but probably includes some form of *El* and *Elo(h)im* (both 'God'). Michael is the archangel; the following two words may well, as Traube thought, conceal *ac Saddai Adonai* 'and the Almighty (Hebrew *Shaddai*), the Lord'. The penultimate word may be either a modified or a corrupt form of *alleluia.*" Dronke (see note 6) suggests that this is a "magic spell": "It would seem that Berhtgyth tried every method known to her in order to obtain the loved brother's assent" (Dronke, *Women Writers,* p. 32). This is to trivialize Berhtgyð's knowledge and skills. As Mr. Windos has pointed out to me in a personal communication, the line represents a perfect alleluia trope, such as might reasonably be expected in the context. That the names are not all correctly spelt reflects on the learning and understanding of the ninth-century scribe but not on the competence of Berhtgyð herself. She should perhaps be given credit for more Christian integrity and less credulity than Dronke has allowed. One might also note here that the layout in Tangl's edition makes the run of names look more separated from the preceding hymn than does the manuscript itself. This is, moreover, one of the very few occasions in the Vienna codex where octosyllabics are not formally set out as poetry. In addition to the more obvious stylistic features that these lines share with Old English vernacular poetry, they share the presentation pattern of being written out as if prose rather than verse.

22. Texts and translations of some of these letters, especially Berhtgyð's, will be published with commentary in my forthcoming *Letters and Letter-writers in Anglo-Saxon England.*

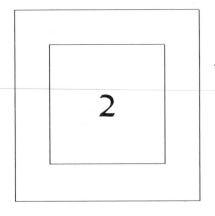

2

Æthelflæd, Lady of the Mercians

Æthelflæd was the daughter of Alfred the Great, the sister of Edward the Elder, the wife of Ealdorman Æthelred of the Mercians, and herself ruler of the Mercians for seven years after her husband's death. She played a vital role in England during the first quarter of the tenth century. The success of Edward's campaigns against the Danes depended to a great extent upon her cooperation. In the midlands and the north she came to dominate the political scene. And the way in which she used her influence helped to make possible the unification of England under kings of the West Saxon royal house. But her reputation has suffered from bad publicity, or rather from a conspiracy of silence among her West Saxon contemporaries.

In a later age William of Malmesbury saw her as a forceful, even a formidable woman, and he recognized the importance of her contribution to Edward's military successes against the Danes.[1] Her achievements, however, are pointedly ignored in the West Saxon version of *The Anglo-Saxon Chronicle*,[2] represented during these years by a remarkably full record of events in MS A. Here her death is recorded, and with it the statement that Edward thereupon occupied Tamworth and secured the submission of all her Mercian subjects. There is no word of her victories, no word of her share in the national program of fortress-building, no word of her high reputation in the north, and no word of her loyal and successful cooperation with Edward. It is clear that the blanket of official policy has kept her achievements out of the national record.

Fortunately, a fragment of a lost Mercian chronicle has survived. It was later incorporated into other versions of the *Chronicle,* and it is usually known as *The Mercian Register.* From it we get the basic facts of Æthelflæd's military operations within Mercia. Reliable though it is, however, *The Mercian Register* gives no more than the basic facts, a selection only, and that limited by the horizon of immediate Mercian interests. No attempt is made to relate them either to Edward's campaigns against the Danes or to events in the troubled areas of the north. To assess her contribution to Edward's campaigns and to obtain anything like a true picture of her power and reputation in the north we must piece together the details of her cooperation with Edward, examine her operations against their wider political background, and consult non-English sources for a less prejudiced appraisal of her achievements.

The Mercian Register gives us the following facts about Æthelflæd. She built fortresses at *Bremesburh* (910), *Scergeat* and Bridgnorth (912), Tamworth and Stafford (913), Eddisbury and Warwick (914), and Chirbury, *Weardburh*, and Runcorn (915). In 916 she sent a Mercian army to punish the king of Brycheiniog for the murder of Abbot Egbert and his companions. In 917 she captured the town of Derby from the Danes and the area of which it was the military center (*mid eallum þam ðe þærto hyrde* 'and all of those who were subject thereto'). Early in 918 she gained control of Leicester without a struggle, and most of the Danish army of Leicester submitted to her. The men of York (*Eoforwicingas*) also approached her with offers of submission and allegiance. Then, very soon after that, she died at Tamworth on 12 June 918, in the eighth year of her dominion over the Mercians, and her body was buried at Gloucester.

She was the firstborn child of Alfred.[3] Her mother was Ealhswith, daughter of Æthelred, Ealdorman of the Gaini, and of Eadburh, a member of the royal house of Mercia.[4] Æthelflæd, therefore, was half-Mercian by birth. She was already the wife of Ealdorman Æthelred of Mercia when Asser was writing his Life of King Alfred. He says that she was given to Æthelred *adveniente matrimonii tempore* 'as the time for matrimony approached',[5] which probably means that she was under twenty at the date of her marriage. Three or four years earlier, in 886, Alfred had recovered the Mercian city of London from the Danes and had given it into the keeping of Ealdorman Æthelred. Æthelred was older, perhaps a great deal older, than Æthelflæd. He had emerged as the effective ruler of Mercia some years before 886. The marriage was intended to cement the friendship between Æthelred and Alfred and to strengthen the bonds between Mercia and Wessex. Æthelflæd was about forty, perhaps a little over forty, when Æthelred died in the first half of 911. She was still under fifty when she herself died in June 918.

The Mercia to which Æthelflæd went as a young bride was a revived and rejuvenated Mercia. By the date of her marriage the lamentable failures under Burgred and the national degradation under Ceolwulf II were memories which, if not forgotten, were being neutralized under the leadership of Æthelred. Ceolwulf is not heard of after 877, and within the next four or five years Æthelred became the effective ruler of Mercia. He accepted Alfred as his lord, and there followed a period of close and successful collaboration between Wessex and Mercia. In the 890s the Danes turned their attacks against northwest Mercia, but joint action by Mercians and West Saxons repelled the threat. When Alfred died in 899 the Danes were still securely in possession of the eastern half of Mercia, but a new era had already dawned. So far as we can see, Æthelred never aspired to the vacant throne of the Mercian kingdom. He was subordinate to King Alfred, but his position as Ealdorman of the Mercians apparently satisfied him. He seems always to have been the loyal ally and supporter of his father-in-law. And he seems to have been content to stand in the same relationship to his brother-in-law Edward.

Æthelflæd was personally acceptable to the Mercians. She was, as noted above, half-Mercian by birth, and she seems to have won their approval as a ruler long before Æthelred died. Medieval chroniclers were aware that Æthelred was a sick man for some time before his death in 911,[6] and modern historians have more than once suggested that in the last years of his life he was incapable of shouldering the full responsibility of government.[7] Neither the main version of *The Anglo-Saxon Chronicle* nor *The Mercian Register* mentions his illness or his incapacity, but the former records that in 909 and 910 Edward sent the Mercian fyrd against the Danes, and the latter records that in 910 Æthelflæd built the fortress at *Bremesburh*. It is significant that neither refers to Æthelred, and the assumption is that, though still alive, he was not in any condition to command or direct Mercian forces. The *Three Fragments*,[8] an Irish source which preserves much interesting information in an unconvincing setting, specifically mentions Æthelred's illness, and indeed lays great emphasis on it. He is repeatedly described as "in a disease" or "on the point of death." It was Æthelflæd who granted lands to Ingimund and his followers in Wirral, and it was Æthelflæd who installed the garrison in Chester in 907. Her husband could do no more than offer advice from a sickbed. If we are to believe the *Three Fragments*, he was precluded from active participation in government from at least 902 onwards.[9]

There is good reason, then, to believe that Æthelflæd was responsible for the government of Mercia before 911. When her husband died in that year, she was accepted at once by the Mercians, and thereafter in *The Mercian Register* she is described as *Myrcna hlæfdige* 'Lady of the Mercians'. Whatever the precise significance of this title may be, it is the exact equivalent of *Myrcna hlaford*, the title by which Æthelred was known in Mercia. The implication is that she succeeded without qualification to the position which he had held.

No such title is accorded to her in the West Saxon version of *The Anglo-Saxon Chronicle*, where official policy no doubt dictated that on her death she be described only as King Edward's "sister." It is clear that Edward was pressing for the closer integration of Mercia and Wessex under his own undivided authority. It has already been noted that he was giving orders to the Mercian fyrd before 911. As soon as Æthelred died he took London and Oxford into his own hands, a direct reversal of the policy followed by Alfred in 886. And the fact that his son Athelstan was brought up in the household of Æthelred and Æthelflæd is a clear indication of the ultimate intention behind his policy.

There is no evidence that Æthelflæd took offense at Edward's policy or offered any resistance to it. On the contrary, she seems to have acquiesced willingly in the subordinate role allotted to her and to have supported her brother's schemes loyally and energetically. His assumption of authority over London, Oxford, and the southern territories of Mercia, an act which was scarcely less than formal annexation, should perhaps be regarded not only as an example of his policy of integration but also as an example of the understanding that existed between brother and sister. Edward was probably the more compelling personality, and he was certainly the dominant partner, but it would be difficult to exaggerate the importance of Æthelflæd's contribution to their joint achievement. Together they planned and worked for the destruction of the independent Danish armies in England, and their collaboration was highly successful.

The central feature of their collaboration between 910 and 916 was the building of additional fortresses to provide bases for operations against the Danes and, at the same time, to protect their territories from sporadic Danish raids. While Æthelflæd was building the ten fortresses listed above, Edward was building a parallel series farther south: one at Hertford in 911, one at Witham and a second at Hertford in 912, two at Buckingham in 914, one at Bedford in 915, and one at Maldon in 916. By the end of 916 Edward had already made considerable advances into Danish territory, and he was ready to launch the great offensive of 917.

The Danes were not Æthelflæd's only problem, and her fortresses served more than one purpose, but for the moment we may concentrate on what has the best claim to be called the main theme of the national policy, i.e., Edward's determination to reconquer the Danish half of England. The military value of strongly fortified positions had been recognized by Alfred, and under Edward the fortress became the essential unit of Anglo-Danish strategy. Each stronghold dominated the surrounding district and proved a surer defense than a mobile army, which was always difficult to maintain in the field except for limited periods in times of immediate crisis. The fortress-system was the most effective answer to sudden Danish raids. Fortresses could block important routes, and the Danes became increasingly reluctant to undertake expeditions that would involve either the preliminary destruction of strong positions or the risk of leaving unreduced garrisons in their rear to harass their retreat and to rob them of their loot. Edward had changed the character of the Anglo-Danish struggle. It was no longer an interchange of lightning raids but a war of attrition, and the Danes, unrivaled in raiding, were ill equipped for war. The fortress-system had equally an offensive value, for territorial gains could be consolidated only by the erection of permanent fortresses. The fortresses built by Edward and Æthelflæd in the years 910–16 at once drew a firm offensive line against the Danes, secured the English frontier, and protected vulnerable areas (see map).

This is not the place to examine the fortress-system in detail or to explain the military significance of each unit in it. It is enough to emphasize that Æthelflæd's fortresses were conceived as part of the national system. *Bremesburh*, built immediately after the Battle of Tettenhall (910), probably shared with Hereford, Worcester, and Gloucester the defense of southwest Mercia, and no doubt proved its worth in 914 when a large Scandinavian force sailed from Brittany to attack Wales and the areas adjacent to the Severn estuary. Bridgnorth (912) commanded an important Severn crossing much favored by the Danes, and higher up the river was perhaps *Scergeat* (912). Chirbury (915), within two miles of Offa's Dyke, controlled the main route through Montgomery into central Wales. Stafford (913), Tamworth (913), and Warwick (914) formed, with Buckingham (914), the main line of defense against the strong concentrations of Danish forces in the midlands. They directly fronted the Danish armies in Derby, Leicester, and Northampton respectively, and each fortress was within thirty miles of its opposite number. Stafford controlled the Trent Gap leading from Derby, Nottingham, Lincoln, and, indeed, from the heart of Danish England. Tamworth, within two miles of Watling Street, and Warwick, within five miles of Fosse Way, guarded direct routes from Leicester, Lincoln, and the further north. Warwick and Buckingham together menaced the Danish army of Northampton and brought increased security to Oxford and the district southwest of Banbury,

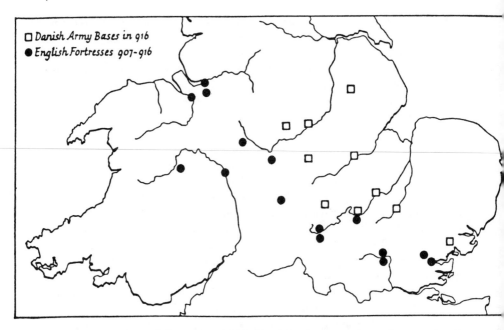

□ *Danish Army Bases in 916*
● *English Fortresses 907-916*

The preparations of Edward and Æthelflæd for the campaigns of 917 and 918.

which had been ravaged in the previous year (913) by raids from Northampton and Leicester. The two fortresses at Buckingham secured the submission of the leading men of the army of Bedford and many of the army of Northampton (914), enabling Edward to advance to Bedford and build a fortress there (915). This submission belongs to Edward's sphere of activity rather than to Æthelflæd's, but the two are closely linked, and Æthelflæd's fortress at Warwick no doubt brought it home forcibly to the Danes, especially to the Danes in Northampton, that they were being pinned down; and it probably helped to persuade some of them that the time had come to offer submission. In 907 the primary function of the fortress at Chester was to overawe the Irish-Norwegian settlers in Wirral, and the erection of fortresses at Eddisbury (914) and Runcorn (915) was probably intended to strengthen the northern frontier of Mercia against the hordes of their kinsmen in Lancashire and in Ireland. But they also became part of the long line of fortresses which by (916) stretched from the Mersey to Essex and menaced the Danes in their midland strongholds (see map).

It is, however, only from a closer study of the events of these years that the full extent of Æthelflæd's cooperation becomes apparent. It was probably no accident that Æthelflæd was building fortresses at *Scergeat* and Bridgnorth in 912 while Edward was building a fortress at Witham and a second fortress at Hertford. They probably remembered that in 893–95 an earlier attempt to pin down the Danes in Essex had produced three spectacular break-out raids into northwest Mercia and that a Danish force had spent the winter of 895–96 in Bridgnorth. Both Edward and Æthelflæd's husband had been involved at close quarters in the earlier series of events, and it is clear that Edward was guarding against a repetition of the Danish break-out to the northwest. The following year provides another example of coordinated action: after Easter (28 March) 913 Danish raiders from Northampton and Leicester penetrated areas under Edward's control, and within a month or two Æthelflæd had fortified Tamworth 'in the early summer' (*on foreweardne sumor*) and Stafford in July (*foran to hlafmæssan* 'before Lammas', or August 1). In 914 the only serious gap in the line of fortresses which faced and confined the Danish armies of the midlands, the gap between Tamworth and Hertford, was closed by the fortification, within a few weeks of each other, of Warwick and Buckingham—the former by Æthelflæd *on ufeweardne hærfest* 'late in the harvest' and the latter by Edward *foran to Martines mæssan* 'before Martinmas'. Such examples emphasize the close and constant cooperation between Edward and Æthelflæd in matters of detail no less than in the broader issues of national policy.

The same cooperation is seen in the campaigns of 917. These are described in remarkably full detail in the West Saxon version of the *Chronicle*. Before Easter (13 April) Edward ordered the occupation and fortification of Towcester, and in July a Danish force from Northampton, Leicester, and "the north" was provoked to take offensive action. Another Danish force built a fortress at Tempsford and launched an attack on Bedford. A third Danish force, from East Anglia and Mercia, attacked a position which Edward had fortified at *Wigingamere,* apparently a few miles southeast of Cambridge. The struggle reached the peak of its intensity (and of its complexity) in the height of the summer, in the six weeks between the third week of June and the second week of August. Before the year ended the army of Northampton had surrendered, Huntingdon had been occupied, and the whole army of East Anglia, including the army of Cambridge, had offered submission and allegiance to Edward.

The details of these moves and countermoves do not concern us here. What does concern us is that in July (*foran to hlammæssan*) Æthelflæd attacked and captured Derby. This is recorded in *The Mercian Register.* The West Saxon version of the *Chronicle,* for all its wealth of detail, altogether ignores this important event, the fall of the first of the five great strongholds in the Danish midlands. Æthelflæd's move to Derby took place while Edward was heavily engaged in the confused fighting around Towcester, Bedford, *Wigingamere,* and Tempsford, an excellent example of well-timed and successful coordination. It has been suggested that her object was to relieve the pressure on Edward's front,[10] but there is reason to believe that her chief concern was to take advantage of the temporary absence of the army of Derby from its base.[11] The two explanations are to some extent complementary. A brilliant move seldom has a single result, and this coordinated strategy deserves to be called brilliant.

By the end of 917 the Danish armies of East Anglia, Cambridge, Bedford, Huntingdon, and Northampton had ceased to exist as independent military units; and Derby, one of the five great midland strongholds, had fallen. There remained only the four centers of Stamford, Leicester, Nottingham, and Lincoln, but they lay in the most Danish areas of England, and it might be thought that their reduction would call for the closest of coordination between Edward and Æthelflæd. The final campaign was planned for 918. In the four weeks between the middle of May and the middle of

June Edward advanced to Stamford, built a fortress on the south bank of the Welland, and secured the submission of all the people previously under the authority of the Danish fortification on the north bank. Meanwhile Æthelflæd had entered Leicester without opposition, and most of the army there had submitted to her. The road to Nottingham and Lincoln lay open, but Æthelflæd died on 12 June and so by six months missed seeing the collapse of the last independent Danish armies in the midlands.

The careful preparations of 910–16 and the dramatic campaigns of 917 and 918 were all part of a single coherent policy, the policy of a man with vision, patience, tenacity of purpose, and an aptitude for war. Organized Danish armies had controlled a large part of England for forty years, but at last all non-English elements south of the Humber had been reduced to subjection and compelled to recognize the authority of the king of the West Saxons. To Edward belongs the credit for this sustained and successful operation, but it is doubtful if he could have subdued the Danes, especially those of the north midlands, if the support and cooperation of the Mercians had been withheld. Perhaps Æthelflæd did no more than carry out her brother's instructions loyally, but her assistance was all-important. Without it Edward's ambitious schemes might well have failed. That is the measure of her contribution to the destruction of the Danish armies in England.

But Æthelflæd had other problems and other interests, and in these she seems to have followed a more independent line of action. In the early years of the tenth century large numbers of Norwegian and Irish-Norwegian settlers arrived in north-west England and southwest Scotland. The movement amounted to a mass migration in scale and intensity. It is unnoticed by English annalists, but it is reflected unam-biguously in the place-names of these areas.[12] Most of the immigrants settled north of the Mersey, in what remained of the ancient kingdom of Northumbria, but more than a few settled in Wirral. Their arrival under Ingimund and their subsequent activities in Wirral, including their attack on the city of Chester, are recorded with much legendary detail in the *Three Fragments*. The settlement of potentially hostile Scan-dinavians within Mercian territory must have alarmed Æthelred and Æthelflæd, fully occupied as they were with problems arising from the Danish settlements in the east midlands. As the event showed, the Scandinavians in Wirral were a dangerous and disruptive element in the population, and there was always the possibility that they might combine with or give assistance to the still unsubdued Danish armies of eastern England. Æthelflæd's fortification of Chester in 907 was intended to control disaffec-tion in Wirral, and the subsequent attack on the city proves that she had not misjudged the situation.[13]

She was also concerned with the political implications of the far heavier immigration of Irish-Norwegian Scandinavians into Northumbria. They were outside her own territory, it is true, but they constituted a serious threat to the security of Mercia, and that was her responsibility. The kingdom of Northumbria had never recovered from the defeat of 867. The central government had then collapsed. The preservation of law and order was apparently in the hands of local magnates, but there was no authority strong enough to cope with problems posed by a large-scale immigration of alien settlers. Confusion in Northumbria was increased in or about

914 when Ragnald grandson of Ivar arrived, fought a battle at Corbridge on the Tyne, and seized control of lands between the Tees and the Wear. The impact of this meteoric figure on the already troubled north made all the northern peoples aware— if they were not aware of it before—that a new scourge had come to afflict them. Æthelflæd's reaction was prompt. To the fortress already at Chester she added fortresses at Eddisbury (914) and Runcorn (915). These three fortresses, and possibly that at *Weardburh* (also built in 915),[14] were directed against the Irish-Norwegians. Their function was to protect the northern frontier of Mercia against the new Scandinavian menace and to control the lines of communication which, through the Dee and the Mersey, linked Ireland with the alien settlers in Lancashire and with the areas occupied by Ragnald's followers in northeast England. There is no reason to believe that Æthelflæd sent Mercian forces to oppose Ragnald during or after the first Battle of Corbridge in 914, but the additions to her fortress-system prove that she was interested in and alarmed at conditions and events north of the Mersey and the Humber.

According to the *Three Fragments* she was more than interested and alarmed.[15] We are told that she played a leading part in a battle against the Norwegians, a battle which took place in 918 and which may perhaps be equated with the second battle against Ragnald at Corbridge. Indeed, we are told that Æthelflæd's direction of the battle brought victory to the opponents of Ragnald and that "her fame spread abroad in every direction." The details of this story, like the details of Ingimund's attack on Chester, are obviously legendary accretions, but there would be no reason to doubt the truth of a plain statement that Æthelflæd sent a force of Mercians to join the many opponents of Ragnald in the battle of 918. She had already reacted sharply to his arrival and to the events which led up to the first Battle of Corbridge, and in 918 all the northern peoples—the Picts, the Scots, the Britons of Strathclyde, the Angles, and the Danish settlers in Northumbria—were ready to combine against the common enemy.

It comes less as a surprise, therefore, to find that the *Three Fragments* go on to state that Æthelflæd made an alliance with the Britons and the "men of Alba" (the Picts and the Scots), she to assist them and they to assist her against the Norwegians, and that her new allies proceeded forthwith to attack positions held by the enemy. The claim is that Æthelflæd was recognized and accepted as the leader of an anti-Norse coalition in the north.

This claim is not so wild and unconvincing as it might at first appear. It is true that no other chronicle accords such a role to Æthelflæd, but her death is recorded in Irish and Welsh sources,[16] and that alone is a fair indication of her reputation outside Mercia. The *Annals of Ulster,* for example, pass over in silence the deaths of both Alfred and Edward, but they enter Æthelflæd's and they describe her as *famosissima regina Saxonum.* The title "queen" has no great significance in Irish and Welsh sources, perhaps, but it is clear that in Ireland and Wales Æthelflæd was regarded as holding a position of power and dignity.

And what little is known of northern politics in this period squares well enough with the suggestion that Æthelflæd was the active leader of a coalition against the Norwegians. It is reasonable to believe that she would be interested in the formation of an anti-Norse coalition and in the stabilization of the north. Such a policy would be no more than the natural extension of her defensive arrangements on the Mercian frontier, the security of which was her main concern. There is also the unimpeachable but otherwise enigmatic statement in *The Mercian Register* that in 918 the men of York (*Eoforwicingas*) offered to her their submission and their allegiance. They were one of the peoples threatened by Ragnald, and their approach to Æthelflæd may be explained convincingly as an attempt to secure protection for themselves. It is impossible to dissociate their action from the issues at stake in the battle of 918, and it is reasonable to see their submission as part of an Anglo-Celtic alliance under Æthelflæd's leadership. Ragnald's seizure of York in the following year confirms this explanation of their approach to Æthelflæd and, incidentally, proves that their fears had not been groundless.

Further confirmation comes from Edward's own actions after Æthelflæd's death. He continued her policy of strengthening the Mercian frontier by building a fortress at Thelwall in 919, by occupying and installing a garrison in Manchester at the same time, and two years later by building a fortress at the mouth of the Clwyd in north Wales.[17] And it was as the leader of an anti-Norse coalition that he was able to secure the submission of Ragnald and the general pacification of the north in 920.

It is possible, therefore, to see Æthelflæd as the architect of victory in the north. She may have been the subordinate partner of Edward in the campaigns against the midland Danes, but in the north it was she who laid down the policy and took the lead in shaping the course of events. Edward inherited her policy when he inherited her position in Mercia. As in the midlands, the final triumph came only after her death, but she had made it possible. She was an important figure in her own right and she exerted a controlling influence on northern politics. Her achievements impressed themselves on her contemporaries and, as the Irish annalist says, "her fame spread abroad in every direction." He was not to know that West Saxon policy could not countenance the development of an Æthelflæd legend in Mercia.

Very little is known of Æthelflæd's relations with Wales. The one recorded event, the punitive expedition to Brycheiniog in 916, suggests that the traditional hostility between the Mercians and the Welsh was still strong enough to produce incidents and reprisals in the Marches. In 914 the Scandinavian raiders from Brittany captured a Welsh bishop, and Edward paid a ransom of forty pounds to secure his release. It was as easy for the West Saxons to appear as the protectors of the Welsh as it was inevitable that the Mercians should be their traditional enemies. That relationship had been determined by proximity since the time when the Mercians and the Welsh first came into contact with each other. Æthelflæd's fortresses along the Welsh border would not improve relations. It is probable that they were directed chiefly against Scandinavian raiders, raiders who might reach England from the west through Wales,[18] and raiders from the Danish midlands who, as in 893–96, might escape into Wales after attacking west Mercia. But the Welsh cannot have regarded with equanimity the erection of fortresses along their march with Mercia, especially as they might be used to discomfit the Welsh as well as the Scandinavians. Chirbury, as noted above, controlled an important route into Wales (and from Wales); *Bremesburh* and perhaps *Weardburh*, to say nothing of Chester, Bridgnorth, and perhaps

Scergeat, could all be used against the Welsh. Even though they gained some protection against the Scandinavians from these fortresses, they cannot have been unconcerned at such proofs of the increasing strength of Mercia, for a strong Mercia was always a threat to Wales.

It may be, however, that the Scandinavian menace had reconciled the Welsh princes to submission; and it may be that they were willing, if unenthusiastic, members of Æthelflæd's Anglo-Celtic coalition. Enmities as fierce and as traditional had been temporarily stilled in the north by the arrival of Ragnald. *The Anglo-Saxon Chronicle* records that on Æthelflæd's death in 918 all the Welsh peoples sought Edward as their lord. This can hardly have been a voluntary act arising from love or respect for the king of the West Saxons. It is probable that it was the formal transfer of allegiance from one ruler of Mercia to the next. It would seem that Æthelflæd had already brought the Welsh princes at least nominally under her authority, and that Edward stepped into her shoes in Wales as he did in the north. He used his new position to build a fortress at the mouth of the Clwyd in 921. By the end of his reign, however, the Scandinavian menace had been removed, and the traditional hostility of the Welsh towards the ruler of the English midlands had broken into open rebellion. Friendship between Wales and Wessex counted for nothing when the king of Wessex was also ruler of the English midlands. William of Malmesbury has preserved an ancient account of trouble at Chester, where Mercians and Welshmen had combined in an attempt to throw off the yoke of the West Saxons.[19]

There can be no question that Edward stepped into Æthelflæd's shoes in Mercia. As soon as he heard of her death on 12 June 918 he at once occupied Tamworth, and all Æthelflæd's subjects submitted to him. For about six months he allowed her daughter Ælfwyn to hold some nominal position, but early in December she was "deprived of all authority among the Mercians" and carried off to Wessex. Another submission to Edward followed, a submission of all people, Danes and English, who lived in Mercia.[20] Thereafter Mercia was no more than a province of Edward's enlarged kingdom.

Æthelflæd probably knew what Edward had in mind. Yet she seems neither to have resented nor to have opposed his schemes. She must have been aware that he had placed Athelstan in her charge so that he might come to know the Mercian noblemen and be more acceptable to them when he became king. She seems never to have thrust her own daughter forward, or even to have found a husband for her, though she was approaching thirty years of age in 918. It would be pointless to speculate on the reasons for Ælfwyn's single state, for it may be that they have no political significance at all. But we can be sure that Edward would frown on all separatist tendencies in Mercia. There is no doubt that many Mercians resented the subordination of their ancient kingdom to Wessex. The words of the annalist who wrote of the deposition of Ælfwyn in *The Mercian Register* are heavy with resentment, and even the West Saxon annalist implies that at least a display of force was required to secure the submission of the Mercians to Edward on Æthelflæd's death. The trouble at Chester in 924 probably shows that even after six years many Mercians still deplored the loss of their national identity and their absorption into the West Saxon state. Æthelflæd could have formed a strong nationalist party in Mercia before

918, had she wished to do so, but so far as we can see her influence was always thrown on the side of Edward and his plans for the integration of Wessex and Mercia.

Edward dared not do anything to encourage the separatist forces in Mercia. And so a blanket of official silence had to be thrown over all Æthelflæd's achievements. She was, after all, Lady of the Mercians, and her reputation could be used with effect by nationalists who hoped to revive the independent kingdom of Mercia. She had made possible Edward's reconquest of the Danish midlands; she had extended English authority over the princes of Wales; she had helped to bring about the immediate integration of Mercia and Wessex; and by her intervention in northern politics she had paved the way for the unification of all England under the kings of Wessex. It is ironic that the policy of integration, to which she had contributed so much, should also demand her own virtual elimination from the national record.

NOTES

1. William of Malmesbury, *De gestis regum Anglorum*, ed. W. Stubbs, Rolls Series (London: Eyre and Spottiswoode, 1887–89), vol. 1, p. 136.

2. B. Thorpe, ed. *The Anglo-Saxon Chronicle*, 2 vols., Rolls Series (London: Longman, Green, Longman, and Roberts, 1861); R. Flower and A. Smith, ed., *The Parker Chronicle and Laws*, Early English Text Society, o.s., vol. 208 (London: Early English Text Society, 1937).

3. Asser, *De rebus gestis Ælfredi*, ed. W. H. Stevenson (Oxford: Clarendon Press, 1904), ch. 75.

4. Ibid., ch. 29. On the territory occupied by the Gaini see F. M. Stenton, *The Early History of the Abbey of Abingdon* (Reading: University College Studies in Local History, 1913), p. 26, n.

5. Asser, *De rebus*, ch. 75.

6. See Henry of Huntingdon, *Historia Anglorum*, ed. T. Arnold, Rolls Series (London: Longman and Co., 1879), p. 157.

7. See F. M. Stenton, *Anglo-Saxon England*, 2nd ed. (Oxford: Clarendon Press, 1947), p. 320; J. M. Lappenberg, *Geschichte von England*, 2 vols. (Hamburg: F. Perthes, 1834–37), vol. 1, p. 355; compare J. M. Lappenberg, *A History of England under the Anglo-Saxon Kings*, trans. B. Thorpe, 2 vols. (London: J. Murray, 1845), vol. 2, p. 90.

8. J. O'Donovan, *Annals of Ireland, Three Fragments* (Dublin: Irish Archaeological Society, 1860).

9. For these and other details of the story of Ingimund's activities in the Wirral, see F. T. Wainwright, "Ingimund's Invasion," *English Historical Review* 63 (1948): 145–69.

10. Stenton, *Anglo-Saxon England*, p. 324.

11. It will have been noticed that the Danish force which attacked Towcester came from Northampton, Leicester and "the north," and that the force which attacked *Wigingamere* came from "the East Angles and the land of the Mercians." Either of these forces could have contained contingents from Derby (and also from Nottingham, Stamford, and Lincoln). At first glance it might seem reasonable to regard the army from "the north" as Northumbrian, but, if this were the correct interpretation, it would be the only recorded occasion on which the Northumbrian Danes intervened in the struggle against Edward after their disastrous defeat at Tettenhall in 910, and by 917 they had troubles of their own to cope with (see below). It would be surprising, on the other hand, if armies from all the midland Danish boroughs were not represented among the forces which opposed Edward in 917, for his advance carried an unmistakable threat to the security of every part of the Danish midlands.

The suggestion that the army of Derby was operating in the south in July 917 is further supported by the fact that Æthelflæd was able to capture Derby. It is doubtful if she could have done so if the army had been at home. It was not easy to storm a fortress, and successful attempts are comparatively rare. Edward took Tempsford and Colchester by force, it is true, but against these two examples must be set the peaceful or unopposed occupation of Northampton, Huntingdon, Cambridge, Stamford, Leicester, Nottingham, Lincoln, and, apparently, Bedford. It is interesting also to note that Danish attacks on English fortresses (Towcester, Bedford, *Wigingamere,* and Maldon) all failed. It seems highly probable, therefore, that Derby had only a skeleton defense in July 917 and that its main forces were engaged in the south midlands.

12. For references to the place-name evidence, see Wainwright, "The Submission to Edward the Elder," *History* 37 (1952): 117.

13. For details of conditions and events in Wirral and for a discussion of the reliability of the *Three Fragments,* see Wainwright, "Ingimund's Invasion."

14. The site of *Weardburh* is not yet satisfactorily identified. The name *Weardburh* cannot be equated with the name Warburton, Cheshire, as used to be thought possible, but there is a general presumption that it belongs to this area. Recently, however, numismatic evidence has suggested that we ought to look farther south for *Weardburh,* perhaps somewhere between Shrewsbury and Hereford. For this evidence see F. Elmore Jones and C. E. Blunt, "The Tenth-Century Mint 'Æt Weardbyrig'," *British Numismatic Journal* 28 (1958): 494–98.

15. For discussion of the evidence underlying the conclusions and the interpretations put forward in the next five paragraphs, see Wainwright, "The Battles at Corbridge," *Saga-Book of the Viking Society* 13 (1946–53): 156–73, and Wainwright, "Submission."

16. See W. M. Hennessy, ed., *Annals of Ulster,* vol. 1 (Dublin: A. Thom and Co., 1887); E. Phillimore, ed., "*Annales Cambriae,*" *Y Cymmrodor* 9 (1888): 141–83; T. Jones, ed., *Brut y Tywysogyon, Peniarth MS 20* (Cardiff: University of Wales Press, 1941); T. Jones, ed., *Brut y Tywysogyon, Red Book of Hergest Version* (Cardiff: University of Wales Press, 1955).

17. See Wainwright, "Cledemutha," *English Historical Review* 65 (1950): 203–12.

18. Ibid.: 207–208, for examples which prove that this danger was a real one.

19. William of Malmesbury, *De gestis,* vol. 1, pp. 144–45. See also Stenton, *Anglo-Saxon England,* p. 335.

20. For this dating of the deposition of Ælfwyn and for the distinction between the two submissions of Æthelflæd's subjects to Edward see Wainwright, "The Chronology of the Mercian Register," *English Historical Review* 60 (1945): 388–89, and Wainwright, "The Anglian Settlement of Lancashire," *Transactions of the Historic Society of Lancashire and Cheshire* 94 (1942): 53–55.

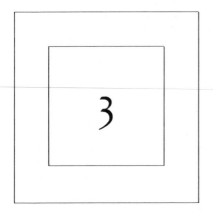

The King's Wife in

Wessex, 800–1066

For the people of the West Saxons do not suffer a queen to sit next to the king, nor do they even permit her to be called a queen but only wife of the king.[1]

Writing from the vantage point of Alfred's Court, Asser sums up the obscurity of most ninth-century West Saxon royal women. The limited political role of royal wives in Wessex had been noted by a West Frankish chronicler in the *Annales de Saint-Bertin* in 856. When King Æthelwulf, Alfred's father, married Judith, he formally conferred the title of queen, "something hitherto unusual for him or his people."[2] The absence of royal women from the history of ninth-century Wessex bears out these statements: Asser omits even the name of Alfred's wife Ealhswith;[3] earlier wives are almost anonymous;[4] charter witness lists ignore them, and no oral or written memory survived into the historical legends of the twelfth century.[5] Only two royal wives in Wessex made any impression on historical record. Judith, wife successively of Æthelwulf and his son Æthelbald, was the daughter of the West Frankish king Charles the Bald. Hearing of the low status accorded to West Saxon wives, Charles took the precaution of having her consecrated as queen before she left West Frankia.[6] As the first certainly anointed queen she has a place in the history of queen-making, but her brief career in Wessex from 856 to ca. 861 has left little trace. At the beginning of the century Eadburh, daughter of Offa of Mercia, was the wife and queen of King Beorhtric. Her dominance at his court culminated in her alleged poisoning of her husband[7] and consequent flight to the safety of the Carolingian court. Her actions have undoubtedly been exaggerated in the interests of later West Saxon propaganda: against Mercia, against Beorhtric, and in justification of the limited role allowed to royal wives. The details of Eadburh's career were given to Asser by Alfred himself to explain why the West Saxons did not have queens. To the extent that her power was real, it belongs to earlier West Saxon traditions and reflects the dominant position of her father Offa in the politics of late eighth-century England.

The only native West Saxon women to make an impact on ninth-century history did so as wives of Mercian rulers (see pp. 68–70 for genealogies). Alfred's sister Æthelswith who married Burgred of Mercia was his *queen* in every sense.[8] Alfred's eldest daughter Æthelflæd was wife and then regnant widow of Æthelred of Mercia. At first jointly with her husband and then alone after his death, Æthelflæd played a vital role in the military conquest of Danish England, masterminding the building of fortifications, receiving the submission of armies, leading an alliance of the rulers of northern Britain against the Viking menace.[9] Æthelflæd was not so much daughter of Alfred as wife of Æthelred, ruler of Mercia.[10] She was the beneficiary of a tradition of queenly importance in Mercia. That tradition, so ably utilized by Æthelflæd herself, culminated in the unprecedented events which occurred at her death. Her only child, a daughter, Ælfwynn, was chosen by a section of the Mercian nobility as her mother's successor in preference to her West Saxon uncle Edward the Elder. Edward had to remove this queen of Mercia by force.[11] To marry into the West Saxon ruling family in the ninth century was to sink into obscurity, yet outside Wessex its women could achieve the height of fame and power.

By the later tenth and the eleventh centuries a radical change had occurred. Four women in succession were of first importance in the history of the enlarged West Saxon kingdom. Eadgifu, the third wife of Edward the Elder, was a key figure during the reigns of her sons, Kings Edmund and Eadred; she was deeply involved in the succession dispute on Eadred's death, and was rewarded by Edgar, the grandson whose accession she helped to secure. Ælfthryth was the third wife of that same Edgar. Her political role began during her husband's reign but came to its peak during the succession dispute after his death and in the early years of the reign of her son Æthelred II. Emma, second wife of Æthelred II, was important during the later stages of his reign, but was increasingly significant under her second husband Cnut and her son Harthacnut. Edith, wife of Edward the Confessor, replaced Emma at Edward's court, and her influence waxed strong in the last years of Edward's reign.[12] Disputes over the throne provided an arena for the activities of the first three queens in 956, 975, and 1035.[13] All four were ecclesiastical patronesses, manipulators of church appointments.[14] Emma and Edith both commissioned written works, the *Encomium Emmae* and the *Vita Edwardi regis*.[15] Their authors combined praise and apologia for their respective queens into highly charged political works, especially relevant to arguments over the succession to the throne.[16] The history of England from the 940s until 1066 bears the imprint of the activity of these four women.

The century immediately preceding the Norman Conquest and spanning the monastic revival is documented by a sudden wealth of evidence. Many traditions survived from it into the chronicles of the twelfth century. By contrast the ninth and early tenth centuries are exiguously documented; the history of the ninth century was largely written in retrospect from the perspective of Alfred's court. Limelight and obscurity, dominance and ineffectiveness, the contrasts in our picture of queens may reflect only the state of the source material. Yet charters cover the whole period, and tell the same tale. Ninth-century Mercian queens like the later Eadgifu and her successors are regular witnesses, their appearance in charters reflecting their position at court: West Saxon royal wives before Eadgifu are conspicuously absent.[17] Even in the most obscure periods of English history, powerful queens can be tantalizingly glimpsed: Seaxburg, who briefly ruled Wessex;[18] Ine's queen, Æthelburh, who attacked Taunton.[19] Ninth-century West Saxon women are cloaked in silence, and Asser is explicit about their low status.

Whatever changes occurred in the status of West Saxon royal wives in the mid-tenth century were neither all-embracing nor irrevocable. Many later wives remain no more than names, and some are denied even the dignity of explicit contemporary historical record.[20] Eadgifu, Ælfthryth, Emma, and Edith themselves had chequered careers. Eadgifu played little part during the reign of her husband Edward or of her stepson Athelstan; her prominence is greatest under her sons. Ælfthryth enjoyed the height of her power in the early years of her young son's reign and suffered a period of obscurity in the late 980s and early 990s. Emma was powerful under her second husband Cnut, was the standard bearer of her son Harthacnut in the disputed succession on Cnut's death, but endured exile when her attempts on behalf of Harthacnut failed and was totally eclipsed when her older son Edward the Confessor came to the throne and took a new wife. Any changes in the status of West Saxon royal wives between the ninth and eleventh centuries were not independent of political circumstances.

Asser attempted to explain and justify the low status of West Saxon kings' wives by reference to the story of the wicked Eadburh. Contemporary justifications should not be accepted at face value. Personalities do make an impact on political change, but explanations couched solely in such terms are inadequate. Asser's own story also suggests that the low profile of royal wives was a deliberate decision imposed by the rulers and thus probably linked to the politics of ninth-century Wessex. The fluctuating status of West Saxon wives in political life is common to much early medieval history. In Anglo-Saxon England the age of conversion was one in which women in general and royal women in particular found a political role; in the eighth century they appear to have been less important. The greatest obscurity of West Saxon women, from the mid-eighth until the mid-tenth century, coincides with the greatest prominence of Mercian queens. The circumstances of conversion and of female monasticism opened opportunities for royal women whether in England, Frankia, or later in Ottonian Saxony.[21] The unique position of Æthelflæd of Mercia was a product of personality acting upon traditions which had their origins in dynastic insecurity and succession strategies. Fundamental factors may determine the status and define the role of a royal wife, but short-term political changes affect her ability to secure, continue, and enhance that role.[22]

Certain factors affected the standing of all kings' wives in the early middle ages. Royal marriage practices were conducive neither to individual security nor importance for the king's wife. Unilateral repudiation of wives by their husbands remained common in the ninth and tenth centuries in spite of ecclesiastical opposition.[23] Royal marriage remained a political affair. The paramount desire for an adequate number of sons to ensure dynastic survival, coupled with shifting alliances, fostered serial monogamy with wives taken and divorced as need required. As long as women could be discarded with relative ease they lacked that assurance of a long-term future necessary to a queen who hoped to build up a faction at court. A succession of wives cast doubt over whether the sons of any particular woman were destined for the throne; again the certainty which attracted supporters to queen and potential heir might be denied her. However, with royal wives wedded for the alliance of their families, those families could in certain circumstances ensure security. A wife who was also daughter of a powerful noble clan might not readily be discarded. Where kindred could not or did not provide backing, formal designation as queen, even the ceremony of anointing, could help. Anointing in particular confirmed the queen with the strength of divine approbation. It was no guarantee of survival, but it set a wife apart, enhanced her position, and provided another argument to deploy in favour of the throne-worthiness of her sons.

Concern for the future and a natural desire to advance her own sons drew a king's wife into the area of succession. The question of inheritance to the throne engrossed politics. When it was disputed between rival dynasties, royal women were often the most loyal supporters of husbands and sons. To enhance the position of the queen was at such times a method of emphasizing the uniqueness of her sons and their claims against rivals. It is no coincidence that the struggles between the Carolingians and the Capetians in tenth-century Frankia produced the strong tradition of queenly anointing.[24] When the struggle was confined within the royal family, queens emerged as supporters of their own sons and grandsons. They were actively engaged in the maneuvering before a king's death and in the disputes which followed his passing. Success could bring the coveted position of queen mother. Where male relatives were feared as potential rivals, mothers were the safest choice as formal regents for minors; where such regency was unknown, they qualified as closest counselors.

Succession practices helped determine the part a queen might play. Fraternal succession aims to ensure the claims of younger brothers. It may require discouragement of the ambitions of a reigning king's wife for her sons; the role of the king's wife at court may be deliberately reduced. Fraternal succession aims to produce a line of adult kings; the possibility of minorities and the opportunity for the queen mother gaining power is less. But the best regulated systems of fraternal succession are troubled by uncertainty and conflict, especially on the death of the youngest brother. Prior agreement rarely obviates the ensuing struggle among the sons of several brothers all of whom have ruled. "Dynastic shedding," that is, restricting the claims to sons of a king who has ruled, may reduce the number of claimants, but it encourages rebellion by princes who fear that failure to secure the throne will extinguish all claims for their sons. By stressing the throne-worthiness of *all* sons, fraternal succession encourages rebellion at all times.

Vertical succession often brings minors to the throne, needing the secure support of a queen mother. Kings may attempt to control their succession either by designating an heir or by leaving the question open among all their sons. A king who wishes to keep all sons and rivals guessing, who desires to retain exclusive control of the succession in order to use it and subsequent marriages as political tools, will be loath to see his options pre-empted by raising one wife to the status of heir-producing consort. Such a strategy again requires equal throne-worthiness for all sons and fosters discord. Designation may lessen but rarely removes conflict. Wives seek designation for their sons: it guarantees their long-term security. Yet the eventual consequences of designation, as of any other determinate system such as primogeniture, reduce the queen's role. The designated or firstborn son requires less support from his mother, and the succession is in the long term removed from the center of politics. Ironically, wives who sought designation for short-term personal advantage hastened on this development.

Succession practices change with circumstances. To describe them is to give an impression of prescriptive arrangements which in reality were open to challenge. It is difficult to eradicate the throne-worthiness of all sons, especially in a society like Anglo-Saxon England which was slow to recognize primogeniture at any level. Succession struggles become the focus of other discontents and grievances and assume greater proportions at periods of general change and tension. In practice the succession is usually determined within the ranks of potential claimants by the strength of rival alignments on the king's death. The queen's ability to take part in the struggle is inseparable from her ability to produce sons, to control them, and to attract a faction and following of her own.

A queen's capacity to hold and inherit land was crucial to her status, as it is to that of all women in all societies.[25] Her power was greater if she could add to this capacity the control of the household in its economic aspects[26] and exert influence over royal patronage. Intimate access to the king gave her informal powers in the royal household even if her formal role there was minimal. The wealth, influence, and connections which formed the basis of the queen's role at court could be utilized in favor of her son. Ironically, the very same marital practices which worked against wives could foster struggles which opened roles for them. Divorce and remarriage created bitter family conflict between stepmothers and stepsons, contests for the throne between half-brothers, and exacerbated the question of succession. Family backing could help a royal wife as mother, as could a formal position at court with its opportunities for winning allies. Throughout the early middle ages queens looked to the royal court and especially to its ecclesiastical members for their friends: a succession of accusations of adultery by the king's wife with high-ranking household officials is testimony to their frequent and close alliance. Church politics were ever an ideal arena for female activity; like the succession they brought queens to the center of the stage. As patronesses in their own right and as manipulators of husbands and sons,[27] kings' wives forged friendships with churchmen who gave them practical and ideological support. Moral arguments concerning marriage and legitimacy acquired the utmost significance in the context of the conflicts over the succession to the throne.

The effects of these factors on the status of royal women can be seen in the history of Wessex between 800 and 1066. West Saxon kings were convinced serial monogamists, not always troubling to await the death of a previous wife before remarriage. Edward the Elder married three times, to Ecgwyna, Ælfflæd, and Eadgifu. Ecgwyna is called a concubine, perhaps a noble concubine of youth taken by Edward before his father's death.[28] Edward married Ælfflæd ca. 901. Since she appears to have survived Edward as a nun at Wilton in the company of her daughters,[29] Edward may have repudiated her to take a third wife, that same Eadgifu who outlived him to play such a large part under her sons. Edward's grandson Edgar followed his example, taking three wives at least one of whom was repudiated[30] while the conquering Danish Cnut kept two wives simultaneously.[31] Summary disposal of wives was not confined to the royal family. Æthelwine, ealdorman of East Anglia, had at least three wives and we cannot be certain that death preceded remarriage.[32] Uhtred, Earl of Bamburgh, was as adept as any king at changing his wives to suit his political advantage: a daughter of the bishop of Durham was repudiated in favor of a prominent York noblewoman, but she was in turn set aside when Uhtred had the chance of marrying a royal princess, daughter of Æthelred II.[33] The exploits of Harold Godwinson show that such practices were not confined to the backward north.[34]

Kings chose their wives with an eye to political advantage. Æthelred II, for example, first married the daughter of Thored of York because he needed to cement the loyalty of a man whose rule in a difficult area was itself part of a rebellion.[35] Æthelred's later marriage to Emma was the result of long negotiations with the duke of Normandy against the Vikings. Cnut's first alliance with Ælfgifu of Northampton linked him to a noble family with extensive power and property in the north midlands, a clan disaffected with King Æthelred II and of obvious utility to Cnut's plans of conquest.[36] His second marriage was to Emma, Æthelred's own widow. The marriage may have carried legitimation for a foreign conqueror; more important, it neutralized both Emma's and Norman support for her sons by Æthelred II, the obvious rivals for Cnut's throne. In the ninth century Asser recorded the genealogy of Alfred's mother, Osburh. Her noble family and putative descent from Stuf and Wihtgar presumably determined her original choice by King Æthelwulf.[37]

But kings could not always keep the control of their marital affairs in their own hands. In 958 Archbishop Oda forcibly separated King Eadwig and his wife Ælfgifu on the grounds of consanguinity;[38] they probably both shared the same great-great-grandfather in King Æthelwulf. A later king like the Capetian Robert the Pious was able to contract such a marriage with impunity; Eadwig's problem was less his relationship to Ælfgifu than the weakness of his political position. Ælfgifu belonged to an important royally-descended family in southern England. Eadwig's marriage to her strengthened his hand in the palace revolution and succession dispute which accompanied his accession in 956. Among Eadwig's opponents were Bishop Dunstan and his ally Archbishop Oda; Dunstan appears from the first to have opposed the marriage.[39] By 958 Eadwig's position had been weakened by the successful revolt of his brother Edgar, who had been set up as king of England north of the Thames. His enemies now felt strong enough to act against him and separate the young king from his wife.

If circumstances forced divorce on Eadwig, they were later to prevent Edward the Confessor from disposing of Edith, to the final undoing of the dynasty of Cerdic. Edward's marriage to Edith was barren. It had been contracted in 1045 as part of Edward's attempts to woo the loyalty of her powerful family: Edith was the eldest daughter of Earl Godwin. By 1050 Edward was at odds with this noble family; the desire to divorce the barren Edith may have been an important factor in the souring of relations. Godwin's enemy, Archbishop Robert, himself urged divorce on the king.[40] In 1051 Godwin and his family were banished and Edith sent into the custody of the king's half-sister in the nunnery of Wherwell. Her repudiation was short-lived. In 1052 Godwin and his sons swept back to power by force, and Edith was restored to the royal bed in their wake.

The marriage practices of the West Saxon dynasty cannot have helped queens and go some way to account for their initially low status during the ninth century. However, the period between the ninth and eleventh centuries saw a consolidation of noble as much as royal power in England. Royal wives were drawn from the same families which provided local rulers for the king and endowment for the monastic revival,[41] families which dominate the history of the tenth and eleventh centuries. All royal wives between 800 and 1066 were of high birth and married for political considerations. But the extent to which this provided security for a woman depended on an intricate balance of circumstance. In the case of Edith, survival was assured by the weight of a family whose authority the king could not successfully challenge, a tribute both to their importance and to his difficulties. Edith's career might be seen as the culmination of a trend in which kings through marriage found themselves not capturing great noble clans but captured by them. Eadwig chose a wife similarly well-connected, but the overall weakening of his position by 958 left him unable to withstand his enemies, even with her family's support. In each case the king's immediate political position as much as the power of individual families determined the fate of husband and wife. The growth of powerful noble clans was a significant factor in the status of royal women, partly because it provided individual wives with backing, but largely because it threatened royal security and contributed to a series of disputed successions in the tenth and eleventh centuries. Æthelflæd of Damerham, second wife of King Edmund, was the daughter of one ealdorman of Essex and sister-in-law of the next. But with her husband dead and no son, and thus with no lever on the succession, she was unable to put her kindred and their wealth to any practical use. Her history after Edmund's death is one of virtual obscurity. The link between the power of nobles and queens is neither simple nor straightforward.

In 856 the twelve-year-old Carolingian princess Judith married the West Saxon King Æthelwulf, probably already turned fifty. Judith was going far from the protection of her own kin into a kingdom known for the low status it accorded to a king's wife. She was acquiring an elderly husband whose procreative powers might possibly be in doubt and a brace of stepsons, two of them already adult. It is no surprise that her father Charles the Bald took every precaution to ensure her security, most notably the unprecedented step of having her anointed as queen. Judith's anointing was to work the church's magic in her favor. Her position was to be enhanced by the deep changes brought about by the pouring of holy oil; her fertility was to be assured and the claims of the son she would therefore produce would be enhanced by the special status of his mother. Judith's stepsons appraised the implications and the eldest of them, Æthelbald, rose in revolt. Judith was made queen by anointing, but the event had no immediate repercussions on West Saxon women, unless it added to Alfred's conviction that a formal role for a queen which precipitated such troubles was undesirable. The first recorded anointing of a native West Saxon queen was that of Ælfthryth in 973, and the queenly titles *regina* and *seo hlæfdige* 'the Lady' came into common use after this date to describe her and other consecrated queens. In this sparsely documented age, however, first record need not mean first occurrence, and it is possible that anointing was used earlier when Edward the Elder underlined the status of his wife and cousin Ælfflæd.[42] Anointing was not the only way a woman could be designated as queen, though it was the most effective. From the time of Cynethryth at the end of the eighth century, the wives of kings of Mercia had been raised to queenly dignity, though anointing of queens at this date is unlikely.[43] Asser clearly felt that a queen could and should sit beside the king on the throne of the kingdom, suggesting that he too recognized the possibility of formally designated queens with a special position at court. That formal position was denied to West Saxon royal women in the ninth century, and possibly to others later. It was enjoyed by Ælfthryth and those of her successors known to have been anointed. But the title of queen was applied to Ælfthryth before 973, and there are instances of its use to describe Eadgifu and some other mid–tenth-century wives, although the evidence here is mostly late.[44] Consecration of queens may have been used in the early tenth century in Wessex, but its history after this was at best spasmodic. By mid-century West Saxon kings had begun formally to designate certain of their wives and mothers as queen, but the confirmation of that status through anointing can be proved only from 973.

Designation as queen, and especially anointing, brought the benefits of additional security and more formal powers at court. There could not be two queens in the royal household. As long as his mother, Ælfthryth, was alive, Æthelred II did not have a consecrated wife; his marriage to Emma and her anointing followed Ælfthryth's retirement and death. Emma outlived Edith's marriage and consecration in 1045, but retired into a nunnery; Edith, not Emma, was in control of the lands and treasures of the queen in 1051. Eadgifu, like Dunstan, may have disliked the marriage of her grandson Eadwig in 956 with its threat of raising a new queen in the royal court. Loath to relinquish power, she became involved in the attempts to replace Eadwig by his brother Edgar. If formal designation of a queen could lead to such problems, there might be good reasons why the ninth-century dynasty eschewed the practice.

The power she acquired at court could only help the efforts of a queen to gain the succession for her son. Especially where anointing and its status-change was involved, a son's claims might be enhanced. In the succession dispute of 975, Ælfthryth's party backed Æthelred with the argument of his mother's anointing.[45] Raising a wife as queen had implications for the succession. Offa of Mercia had been concerned to secure the throne for his son Ecgfrith; one element in his strategy was the designation of Ecgfrith's mother, Cynethryth, as queen. Mercian royal wives continued to enjoy this dignity throughout the ninth century. The Mercian throne was bitterly disputed between rival families; no king could be certain that a son would succeed him. Every additional security and argument counted; a claimant needed the advantage of birth from a true queen.

The practices, let alone the rules, of succession in Wessex are elusive. Fraternal succession long remained a possibility. From the death of Æthelwulf in 858 until the accession of Edward in 1042, brother succeeded brother on every possible occasion.[46] This fact gives a misleading impression of a fixed rule. The accidental death of Ælfweard led to the accession of his brother Athelstan in 924;[47] the premature death of Edmund secured that of Eadred in 946, overruling the claims of Edmund's minor sons in order to ensure the rule of adult kings. Neither Athelstan nor Eadred appears to have married and produced legitimate heirs, again allowing the succession of brothers' sons.[48] The fraternal successions from 956 onwards were all the result of succession disputes in which two brothers claimed the throne and one was ousted from his capture of it by the other.[49]

The terminology of kingship throughout the period is consistent with fraternal or indeterminate succession. The term *ætheling* and its Latin equivalent *clito* indicate throne-worthiness. They are applied to all royal sons as late as the reign of Æthelred II.[50] But there is not complete indeterminacy: sons invariably succeed in order of age; the throne does not go simply to the strongest, fittest candidate.[51] In the late ninth century fraternal succession was a policy, witness Alfred's succession to a brother who had sons.[52] King Æthelwulf had made arrangements for his inheritance with a joint settlement on the brothers Æthelbald, Æthelred, and Alfred, perhaps suggesting that each should succeed.[53] To the claims of all sons was added the complication of designation, perhaps even of associating an heir to the throne in the kingship.[54] Although the term *ætheling* was applied to *all* sons of a king, it could also be used as a title and seems to have a particular significance when attached in this way to a prince's name.[55] The fact that claims of designation were made suggests that they were considered possible by the eleventh century if not before. Emma, for instance, claimed that her sons Edward and Harthacnut had been designated heirs of their respective fathers, Edward while he was still in the womb. In both cases the nobility are alleged to have sworn oaths to the princes.[56]

The succession strategies of the West Saxon dynasty are not entirely clear. In response to Viking attack and possibly also to dynastic insecurity, fraternal succession may have been attempted in the ninth century.[57] The fact of the succession of brothers from 858 to 956, whether deliberate or not, provided strong arguments for those who wished to push the claims of rival brothers after this date. The pressures necessitating adult kings were less compelling by the mid-tenth century, but a brother could still find supporters to back his challenge. Disputes were fostered by the apparent fluctuations between fraternal and vertical succession, by the recognized throne-worthiness of any son of a king and by the possibility of success. The fact that in 975 and 1035 the rivals were in fact half-brothers, sons of different mothers, fanned dispute and drew women further into the conflict. In her propaganda for her own son Harthacnut, Emma could cast aspersions on the character of her stepson's mother. The low status of royal wives in Wessex in the ninth and early tenth centuries may have been deliberately engineered to facilitate fraternal succession or indeterminacy. Struggle over the throne did occur at this date, but women were in no position to influence it. The disputes of the tenth and eleventh centuries allowed women a wider role. This was not simply because the succession of young children was now possible; only Ælfthryth secured the accession of a son who was a minor with consequent hope of quasi-regency. It was more important that wives were able to deploy substantial support in the struggles, influence their outcome, and use their support to continue their power.

Influence over the succession and power in the new reign require, first, that a wife have a son to support and, second, that she retain effective control over his rearing. Many West Saxon princes were reared away from court by foster mothers,[58] removing them from the arena of palace intrigue and establishing links with the noble families who nurtured them. As the tenth century advanced, there are instances of heirs to the throne raised in the queen's household, though it is impossible to say whether this became a rule. Alfred's mother played a role in his education though he was raised by *nutritores*.[59] At the end of the tenth century Ælfthryth had the upbringing of her son and later of her grandsons.[60] When Emma took over the position of queen, she took over this role; she reared not only her own sons but the younger sons of Æthelred II's first marriage.[61] Under Cnut, Emma was to be separated from her son Harthacnut. He was sent to rule Denmark, though this may have been late in Cnut's reign.[62] The events of 1035–37 demonstrate how the physical presence of a son was crucial. Emma gained the initial advantage in the succession dispute, securing the support of Godwin and capturing the royal treasure. But the ground she had won was lost when Harthacnut lingered in Denmark. Emma had long been estranged from her older son, Edward the Confessor. No bonds of affection bound her to this son of her first marriage whom she had abandoned in 1017, and his accession in 1042 brought her scant comfort or influence. The development of the formal position of queen may have been accompanied by the growth of a queen's court and the control there of heirs to the throne. Edith, for example, produced no sons of her own, but in 1066 she was the guardian of Ralf of Mantes's son Harold, great-grandson of King Æthelred II.[63]

As noble women, royal wives, and queens, women like Ælfthryth and Edith disposed of land, fortune, and influence, the raw material of political power. Their wills indicate that tenth-century Anglo-Saxon noble women had rights of possession and free disposal of land. The wills of two dowagers, Æthelflæd, widow of Edmund, and Ælfgifu, probably widow of Eadwig, reveal extensive properties derived from family and royal bequest.[64] Ælfgifu paid a heriot to the king, which suggests that her status was virtually that of an ealdorman. Their link with the royal house contributed substantially to the fortunes of both women, as it brought Eadgifu all King Eadred's booklands in Kent and a stream of less spectacular grants to other royal wives.[65] Inalienable endowments for wives were also made from the royal demesne.[66] These endowments often passed from queen to queen, ensuring personal fortune, and could not apparently be used more flexibly. Both Æthelflæd and Ælfgifu in their wills returned such property to the king or used it to endow royal monasteries such as Winchester and Glastonbury, effectively returning it to the spiritual use of the royal family. The derivation of much of our knowledge of these estates from wills makes it difficult to know whether we are dealing with the dower lands of the West Saxon house or with all the property at the disposal of a king's wife. That property appears to have been more extensive than the inalienable endowment: Edith's lands in Domesday Book were valued at some £900;[67] Judith held property in Wessex which she was able to sell before returning to Frankia in 862;[68] Eadgifu received bookland (that is, alienable land) from Eadred in addition to the probably dower estates of Wantage, Amesbury, and Basing. Members of the royal family had opportunities to acquire many lands,[69] and even inalienable land was a source of important income. The apparent growth in movable cash wealth in tenth- and eleventh-century England may have been important in consolidating the queen's position, as it was for those of kings and nobles.[70]

Their access to royal wealth and patronage was equally important to queens. Eadburh fled from Beorhtric's court with treasure, either his or her own. By the eleventh century both Emma and Edith held royal treasure. Unfortunately we only hear of this when the queen is disgraced, either absconding with it or deprived of it: Emma was twice deprived of treasure in 1035 and 1043, Edith of land and treasure in 1051.[71] It is thus impossible to tell whether all wives held treasure, or only formally designated queens, as all the above happen to have been. Control of royal treasure had been a key to the part played by Merovingian queens;[72] if late Saxon queens had secured similar control it can only have contributed to their enhanced position.

Ælfthryth's power at court led men to woo her with gifts and seek her favor in disputes.[73] Intimate access to royal favor, sexual desirability, and formal position at court were factors which enabled individual wives and mothers to influence royal patronage; Ælfthryth was reputedly a great beauty, and slanderous accusations were later to suggest that Edgar had murdered her first husband to secure possession of her charms. She used her position at court to exercise ecclesiastical patronage with clear political repercussions. As Edgar's queen she had general responsibility for nunneries and was foundress of the nunneries of Wherwell and Amesbury as well as taking over Barking.[74] Her special alliance was with Winchester and Bishop Æthelwold. She championed Winchester causes,[75] and in exchange Winchester became the center of a new ideology and of propaganda for Ælfthryth's cause. It was there that the iconography of Mary Queen of Heaven was developed;[76] Winchester and Æthelwold may have provided the impetus for Ælfthryth's consecration. At New Minster, Winchester, the peculiarly legitimate nature of Ælfthryth and her son Edmund were stressed at the expense of her stepson and rival Edward.[77] It was Abbot Ælfric, a product of the Winchester school, who defined an *ætheling* in such a way as to suggest that his claims to the throne were affected by the status and consecration of his mother.[78] In the succession crisis of 975–79 Æthelwold probably supported Ælfthryth and Æthelred her son; certainly in the early years of the new reign Winchester was the most prominent recipient of royal favor.

Churchmen who had made alliances with queens at court could provide support and arguments in their patronesses' struggles over the succession. Eadgifu had persuaded her sons Edmund and Eadred to advance the careers of Æthelwold but especially of Dunstan. Dunstan and Eadgifu were involved together in the dispute of 956; Dunstan suffered exile and Eadgifu confiscation of her property as a result of their opposition to Eadwig.[79] In 975 Ælfthryth was able to use arguments about throne-worthiness based on the question of consecration against her stepson Edward. In 1035 Emma and her party questioned the paternity of Harold Harefoot. Among her supporters was the archbishop of Canterbury, Æthelnoth, who refused to consecrate Harold as long as any son of Emma's lived.[80] Such arguments do not alone win political battles, but they attract allies, legitimate resistance, and discredit opponents. Queens by the later tenth century could rely on ecclesiastical allies for ideological and practical support. The progress of the monastic revival in tenth-century England dominated the politics of the court and provided a new context in which royal women, with their powers of patronage and influence, were well equipped to operate. They used their new friends to help secure the throne for their sons and grandsons.

Succession struggles are one aspect of a royal insecurity which saw kings searching for allies and support. A queen or queen mother could hope to survive only as long as she remained useful. Emma dominated Harthacnut's brief and insecure reign, but had less to offer Edward; she soon found herself in a nunnery. Ælfthryth may have been relegated from a dominant position at Æthelred's court by his coming-of-age ca. 985, but the strength of her position and the changing tides of his reign returned some influence to her by the 990s. Eadgifu occupied an unrivaled place at the courts of her two sons Edmund and Eadred. Yet both sons were adults at their accession; both apparently succeeded without question.[81] Nothing is known of Eadgifu's role in securing the accession of either, thus the background to her power remains obscure. The key to Eadgifu's initial influence may lie in her connections in Kent, which determined Edward the Elder's choice of her as wife, and also in the obscure politics of Athelstan's reign. Athelstan's claim to the throne was clouded by the less than legitimate circumstances of his birth.[82] He may have been destined to rule in Mercia, while his legitimate half-brother Ælfweard held Wessex; only Ælfweard's death days after his father's allowed Athelstan's accession to the whole kingdom. Ælfweard was son of Ælfflæd, Edward the Elder's second and repudiated wife, and his full brother Edwin staged a rebellion against Athelstan in 933.[83] Ælfflæd and Eadgifu presented Athelstan with two dowager stepmothers, each with sons of her own, a situation which augured ill for the tranquility of his reign. Eadgifu played some role, albeit limited, at her stepson's court.[84] Athelstan may have played her and her young sons off against his older and more dangerous half-brothers, the sons of Ælfflæd, perhaps even designating Eadgifu's eldest son Edmund as his successor.[85] Eadgifu's role in Athelstan's reign, if any, is now lost; she may have helped determine Edmund's designation. If Edmund was the obvious successor in the late 930s, she had all the influence of a future queen mother. During Edmund's reign his mother, Eadgifu, and his brother Eadred *together* dominated at court. No other adult male of the West Saxon house was ever given such prominence before his accession. Such a demonstration of unity in the royal family may suggest fear of challenge, even an agreement between the brothers guaranteeing the succession to Eadred, with Eadgifu presiding over their harmony. Eadgifu's long political career must have provided opportunities to build up alliances indispensable to her sons.

Emma's expertise in the English court was later to prove useful to Cnut, the Danish conqueror who became her second husband. Especially during the early years of his reign, Cnut felt unsure of the loyalty of many English noble families; throughout his reign, his long absences in Scandinavia necessitated regents in England. Emma's career, like that of her ally Earl Godwin, owed much to these circumstances of Cnut's kingship. The prominence of both at Cnut's court suggests that he relied heavily on them.

Edith's fortunes mirrored those of her family—eclipsed during their fall from

West Saxon Genealogy†

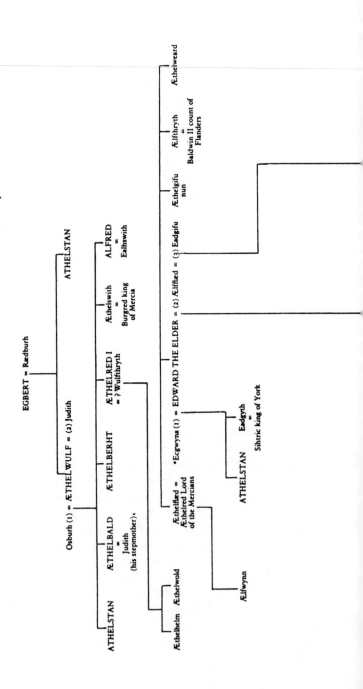

EGBERT = Rædburh

Osburh (1) = ÆTHELWULF = (2) Judith

ATHELSTAN

ATHELSTAN   ÆTHELBALD   ÆTHELBERHT   ÆTHELRED I   Æthelswith   ALFRED
              =   = ? Wulfthryth   =   =
              Judith   Burgred king Ealhswith
              (his stepmother),   of Mercia

Æthelhelm   Æthelwold   Æthelflæd =   *Ecgwynn (1) = EDWARD THE ELDER = (2) Ælfflæd = (3) Eadgifu   Æthelgifu   Ælfthryth   Æthelweard
                          Æthelred Lord   nun   =
                          of the Mercians   Baldwin II count of
                                                                                                                             Flanders

Ælfwynn   ATHELSTAN   Eadgyth
                                        =
                                        Sihtric king of York

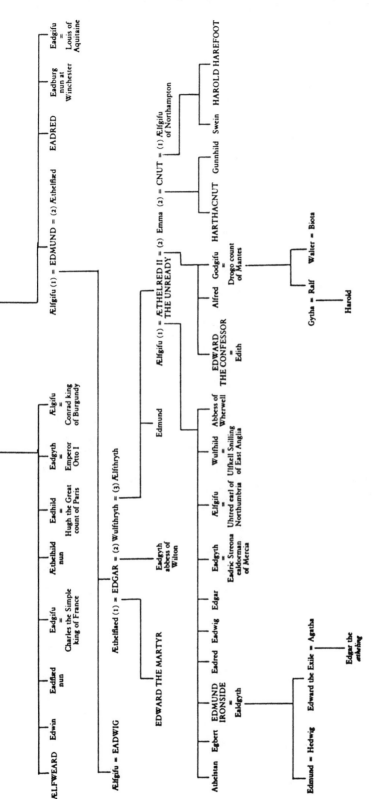

† Order of marriage and children not always certain. Names of West Saxon kings are in capitals.
* Asterisk signifies concubine.

SOME FAMILY CONNECTIONS OF CERTAIN WEST SAXON ROYAL WIVES†

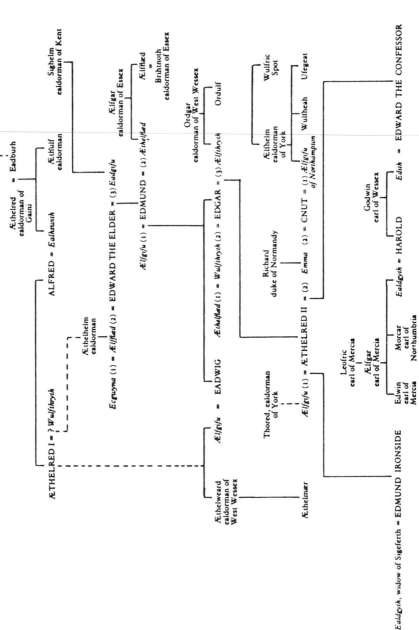

† Names of West Saxon kings are in capitals. Names of wives of West Saxon kings are in italics.

power in 1051–52, at their zenith at the end of Edward's reign when her brothers between them controlled the bulk of England, successfully fought the Welsh, and began to entertain hopes of determining the English succession. Edward's long continental exile had made Edith and her family essential to his establishment on the throne; the events of his reign demonstrate his continued need for their support. Accidents which produced one foreign king and the protracted exile of another resulted in each case in a lack of expertise in English politics and enhanced the importance at court of two consecutive women. Edith was living proof of that noble power which made for the insecurity of kings.

From the mid-tenth to the mid-eleventh century, kings of Wessex needed queens and queen mothers to help them secure accession and retain power. Ninth-century wives had been the victims of succession practices and strategies which deliberately reduced their position. At that time military pressure had inhibited dispute to a certain extent, but, more important, royal wives lacked the political advantages which would have enabled them to capitalize on disputes. Succession struggles were intensified in the tenth century by the additional ambitions of a powerful aristocracy, an outgrowth of the enlargement of the kingdom, and by the increased availability of movable wealth and changes in the church. The rapidity with which the families of Godwin and Leofric rose to fill the vacuum left by such clans as those of Athelstan Half-King, Ælfhere of Mercia, and Wulfric Spot shows such an aristocracy to be a structural part of West Saxon politics by this date. Royal wives drawn from it partook in the growing importance of their own families. With the backing of aristocratic clans and the support of churchmen themselves waxing in power, queens had an essential role in the manipulation of royal family intrigues, which had assumed the importance of national politics, and in the royal household. The monastic revival brought allies and the buttresses of ideology, even queenly consecration. Ecclesiastical politics, position at court, and control of patronage raised queens to a prominence from which they could maximize the opportunities offered by royal insecurity and succession politics. The coincidence of four consecutive women of great ability ensured that these opportunities were fully exploited, and they themselves helped create the circumstances of their own advance. The process was cumulative; a tradition of the acceptability of a queen's power was created. Yet this role was transient. When succession questions ceased to focus noble rivalries and when the alliance of court and church was ruptured, women saw their arenas of political activity at court reduced. The ultimate irony is that some of these developments were hastened on by queens themselves.

NOTES

I am very grateful to Jane Hyam, Professor Henry Loyn and especially Dr. Janet Nelson for their generous criticisms of an earlier draft of this paper. However, the opinions expressed are not necessarily theirs, and the faults are entirely my own.

1. Asser, *Life of King Alfred*, ed. W. H. Stevenson (Oxford: Clarendon Press, 1904; rpt. 1959), *cap.* 13.

2. F. Grat, J. Vielliard, and S. Clémencet, eds., *Annales de Saint-Bertin* (Paris: C. Klincksieck, 1964), p. 73.

3. Ealhswith is known only from Alfred's will and from brief references during the reign of her son Edward the Elder; see F. Harmer, ed., *Select English Historical Documents of the Ninth and Tenth Centuries* (Cambridge: Cambridge University Press, 1914), no. 11; J. Earle and C. Plummer, eds., *Two of the Saxon Chronicles Parallel*, 2 vols. (Oxford: Clarendon Press, 1892–99; hereafter *Anglo-Saxon Chronicle*), MS. A, 903, 905; MS. D, 903, 905; MS. C, 902. She witnesses two charters: S.349, a forgery, and the suspicious S.363 (Anglo-Saxon charters are cited by their numbers in P. H. Sawyer, *Anglo-Saxon Charters: An Annotated List and Bibliography* [London: Royal Historical Society, 1968]).

4. Wulfthryth *regina* in S.340 may be Æthelred I's wife; cf. Asser, *Life of Alfred*, p. 201, n. 4. Egbert's consorts are unknown.

5. This is in sharp contrast with earlier women and their ninth-century Mercian contemporaries. Legends concerning Anglo-Saxon England current after the conquest are discussed by C. E. Wright, *The Cultivation of Saga in Anglo-Saxon England* (London: Oliver and Boyd, 1939).

6. Grat, Vielliard, and Clémencet, eds., *Annales de Saint-Bertin*, p. 73. I have discussed Judith's marriage and anointing in my "Charles the Bald, Judith and England," in M. Gibson and J. Nelson, eds., *Charles the Bald: Court and Kingdom*, British Archaeological Reports, International Series, vol. 101 (Oxford: British Archaeological Reports, 1980).

7. Asser, *Life of Alfred, caps.* 13, 14, 15, 17.

8. Æthelswith was a prominent witness of Burgred's charters with the title *regina*, and made grants jointly with the king and in her own name: S.210, 214, 1201. She is called *cwen* in the *Anglo-Saxon Chronicle*, MS. A, 888, a title also applied to Judith in the same source *sub anno* 855.

9. F. T. Wainwright, "Æthelflæd, Lady of the Mercians," in his *Scandinavian England*, ed. H. P. R. Finberg (Chichester: Phillimore, 1975), pp. 305–24, reprinted in the present volume. Æthelflæd grants land jointly with her husband in S.221, 223; alone in S.224, 225.

10. Æthelred was an independent ruler of Mercia. Æthelweard the Chronicler calls him king (*rex*): A. Campbell, ed., *The Chronicle of Æthelweard* (London: Nelson and Co., 1962), pp. 49–50. It is also stated that he "then ruled the parts of Northumbria and Mercia," A. Campbell, ed., *Chronicle*, p. 52; cf. pp. xxviii–xxix. Asser, *Life of Alfred, cap.* 80, describes how the independent Welsh princes submitted to Alfred "in the same way as Æthelred did with the Mercians." The *Anglo-Saxon Chronicle* MSS. B and C refer to Æthelflæd throughout as *seo hlæfdige*, a title which always translates *regina*.

11. Florence of Worcester, *Chronicon ex chronicis*, ed. B. Thorpe, 2 vols., English Historical Society (London: Sumptibus Societatis, 1848–49), vol. 1, pp. 128–29.

12. The witnesses of these women are described and discussed in A. Campbell, ed., *Encomium Emmae reginae*, Camden Society, 3rd ser., vol. 72 (London: Royal Historical Society, 1949), appendix 2; F. Barlow, *Edward the Confessor* (London: Eyre and Spottiswoode, 1970), pp. 77, 93, 163.

13. On the role of Ælfthryth and Emma in Æthelred's reign, see my "The Reign of Æthelred II: A Study in the Limitations on Royal Policy and Action," in D. Hill, ed., *Ethelred the Unready*, British Archaeological Reports, British series, vol. 59 (Oxford: British Archaeological Reports, 1978), pp. 15–46. On Ælfthryth, Emma and Edith, see my "Sons and Mothers: Family Politics in the Early Middle Ages," in D. Baker, ed., *Medieval Women* (Oxford: B. Blackwell, 1978), pp. 79–100. On Eadgifu and Ælfthryth, see C. Hart, "Two Queens of England," *Ampleforth Journal* 82 (1977): 10–15, 54. On Emma, see M. W. Campbell, "Queen Emma and Ælfgifu of Northampton: Canute the Great's Women," *Mediaeval Scandinavia* 4 (1971): 66–79; M. W. Campbell, "Emma, reine d'Angleterre: mère denaturée ou femme vindicative?" *Annales de Normandie* 23 (1973): 97–114.

14. On Eadgifu and Ælfthryth, see M. A. Meyer, "Women and the Tenth-Century English Monastic Reform," *Revue bénédictine* 87 (1977): 34–61, esp. 38–45, 51–61. On Emma, see F. Barlow, *The English Church, 1000–1066* (Hamden, Conn.: Archon Books, 1963), pp. 14, 40–41, 103, 223. On Edith, see Barlow, *The English Church*, pp. 82, 104, 109, 114. Cf. A. Robertson, ed., *Anglo-Saxon Charters* (Cambridge: Cambridge University Press,

1956), nos. 14, 81, 96, pp. 462, 472; F. Harmer, ed., *Anglo-Saxon Writs* (Manchester: Manchester University Press, 1952), nos. 57, 70; A. Campbell, ed., *Encomium Emmae*, pp. xlvii–xlviii.

15. F. Barlow, ed., *The Life of Edward the Confessor Who Lies at Westminster* (London: Nelson and Sons, 1962). As Barlow remarks elsewhere, this work brings immediately to mind the *Encomium Emmae*, and its overt purpose is to praise Edith: Barlow, *Edward the Confessor*, pp. 291–92. He feels (p. xxiv) it might aptly be renamed as *Encomium Edithae reginae*.

16. On the purposes of the *Encomium Emmae*, see S. Körner, *The Battle of Hastings: England and Europe, 1035–66* (Bibliotheca Historica Lundensis, vol. 14; Lund: C. W. K. Gleerup, 1964), pp. 47–74. On the purpose of the *Life of Edward*, see Barlow, *Edward the Confessor*, appendix A, though his conclusion that it was designed to suggest that Edith was Edward's heir is not entirely convincing.

17. S.349 and S.363 are both suspicious charters and contain the only West Saxon witnesses of women in the late ninth and early tenth century.

18. *Anglo-Saxon Chronicle*, MS. A, begins with a regnal list recording the one-year reign of Seaxburg, Cenwalh's queen.

19. *Anglo-Saxon Chronicle*, MS. A, 722; William of Malmesbury, *De gestis regum Anglorum*, ed. W. Stubbs, 2 vols., Rolls Series (London: Eyre and Spottiswoode, 1887–89), vol. 1, pp. 35–36, 39, on Æthelburg, "a woman of royal birth and spirit," and on her alleged role in persuading Ine to resign his crown.

20. Charter evidence suggests a negligible role for St. Ælfgifu and Æthelflæd, wives of King Edmund, and for Æthelflæd the White and Wulfthryth, wives of King Edgar, and Ælfgifu, first wife of Æthelred II. The last three are recorded only in post-conquest sources: Æthelflæd, "the white surnamed *Eneda*," in Florence of Worcester, *Chronicon ex chronicis*, vol. 1, p. 140; Wulfthryth in, for example, "La vie de S. Wulfhilde par Goscelin de Canterbury," ed. M. Esposito, *Analecta Bollandiana* 32 (1913): 17; Ælfgifu, in Ælred of Rievaulx, *Vita S. Edwardi regis*, in *Patrologiae cursus completus*, ed. J.-P. Migne, Series latina, vol. 195 (Paris: Garnier Fratres, 1855), col. 741.

21. See J. T. Schulenberg, "Sexism and the Celestial Gynaceum from 500 to 1200," *Journal of Medieval History* 4 (1978): 117–33; K. Leyser, "The Women of the Saxon Aristocracy," in his *Rule and Conflict in an Early Medieval Society: Ottonian Saxony* (Bloomington: Indiana University Press, 1979), pp. 49–73.

22. See the study of two Merovingian queens by J. L. Nelson, "Queens as Jezebels: The Careers of Brunhild and Balthild in Merovingian History," in Baker, ed., *Medieval Women*, pp. 31–77.

23. See P. Daudet, *Études sur l'histoire de la jurisdiction matrimoniale* (Paris: Librairie du Recueil Sirey, 1933); G. H. Joyce, *Christian Marriage* (London: Sheed and Ward, 1933). Archbishop Hincmar counted divorce and remarriage as grave sins, but acknowledged their prevalence: Hincmar, *De divortio Lotharii regis*, in *Patrologiae cursus completus*, ed. J.-P. Migne, Series latina, vol. 125 (Paris: Garnier Fratres, 1852), cols. 734–35, para. 672.

24. See M. F. Facinger, "A Study of Medieval Queenship: Capetian France, 987–1237," *Studies in Medieval and Renaissance History* 5 (1968): 3–48; J. Verdon, "Les femmes et la politique en France au Xe siècle," in *Économies et sociétés au moyen âge: mélanges offerts à Edouard Perroy* (Paris: Publications de la Sorbonne, 1973), pp. 108–19.

25. J. Goody, "Inheritance, Property and Women: Some Comparative Considerations," in J. Goody, J. Thirsk and E. P. Thompson, eds., *Family and Inheritance: Rural Society in Western Europe, 1200–1800*, Past and Present Publications (Cambridge: Cambridge University Press, 1976), pp. 10–36.

26. D. Herlihy, "Land, Family and Women in Continental Europe, 701–1200," *Traditio* 17 (1962): 89–120; J. A. McNamara and S. Wemple, "The Power of Women through the Family in Medieval Europe, 500–1100," in M. S. Hartmann and L. Banner, *Clio's Consciousness Raised: New Perspectives on the History of Women* (New York: Harper and Row, 1974), pp. 103–18. Not all women enjoyed these economic powers.

27. For the patronage of queens, see n. 14 above.

28. William of Malmesbury, *De gestis regum Anglorum,* vol. 1, para. 126, calls her "illustrious woman"; para. 131 states that Athelstan was born "of a concubine," while in para. 139 she is "daughter of a shepherd." Florence of Worcester, *Chronicon ex chronicis,* vol. 1, p. 117, calls her "most noble woman." The alliance between Edward and Ecgwyna was contracted before Alfred's death.

29. S.1719, quoting William of Malmesbury, "De antiquitate Glastoniensis ecclesiae," in Adam of Domerham, *Historia de rebus gestis Glastoniensibus,* ed. T. Hearne (Oxford: E. Theatro Sheldoniano, 1727), p. 72, has a queen Ælfflæd alive during the reigns of Athelstan and Edmund. The accuracy of this source is questionable: it has an otherwise unknown tenth-century queen Ælfswith in S.1761, 1762. For Ælfflæd and Wilton, see William of Malmesbury, *De gestis regum Anglorum,* vol. 1, para. 126.

30. Edgar's first wife Æthelflæd was daughter of the otherwise unknown *dux,* Ordmær: Florence of Worcester, *Chronicon ex chronicis,* vol. 1, p. 140. His second wife Wulfthryth, who came from an important noble family, was repudiated and sent to Wilton: Esposito, ed., "Vie de S. Wulfhilde": 13–14, 17. His third wife Ælfthryth was daughter of Ordgar, ealdorman of West Wessex: *Anglo-Saxon Chronicle,* MS. D, 965.

31. Emma, Æthelred's widow, was married in 1017 and was Cnut's queen throughout his reign. Ælfgifu of Northampton was married to Cnut before 1017, was sent to Norway as regent for their son Swein, and outlived Cnut; See F. M. Stenton, *Anglo-Saxon England,* 3rd ed. (Oxford: Clarendon Press, 1971), pp. 397–98, 405–406.

32. C. Hart, "Athelstan Half-King and his Family," *Anglo-Saxon England* 2 (1973): 136.

33. Simeon of Durham, "De obsessione Dunelmi," in *Symeonis Monachi opera omnia,* ed. T. Arnold, 2 vols., Rolls Series (London: Longman and Co., 1882–85), vol. 1, pp. 215–17.

34. On his mistresses and his contemplated marriage to a daughter of William of Normandy, see E. A. Freeman, *The History of the Norman Conquest of England, its Causes and its Results,* 6 vols. (Oxford: Clarendon Press, 1867–79), vol. 3, pp. 638–39, 690–93. On his marriage to Ealdgyth, sister of Edwin and Morcar, see *The Ecclesiastical History of Orderic Vitalis,* ed. M. Chibnall, Oxford Medieval Texts (Oxford: Clarendon Press, 1969), vol. 2, p. 138.

35. See my "Reign of Æthelred II," p. 24 (see note 13); cf. D. Whitelock, "The Dealings of the Kings of England with Northumbria in the Tenth and Eleventh Centuries," in P. Clemoes, ed., *The Anglo-Saxons: Studies in Some Aspects of Their History and Culture Presented to Bruce Dickins* (London: Bowes and Bowes, 1959), pp. 79–80.

36. *Anglo-Saxon Chronicle,* MS. E, 1036. On her family, see P. H. Sawyer, ed., *Charters of Burton Abbey* (London: Oxford University Press, 1979), pp. xxxviii ff.

37. Asser, *Life of Alfred, cap.* 2.

38. *Anglo-Saxon Chronicle,* MS. D, 958.

39. "Life of Dunstan" [Auctore B], in W. Stubbs, ed., *Memorials of St. Dunstan, Archbishop of Canterbury,* Rolls series (London: Longman and Co., 1874), *cap.* 21, pp. 32–33.

40. According to the *Anglo-Saxon Chronicle,* MSS. D, 1052, and E, 1048, she was sent to Wherwell. Barlow, ed., *The Life of Edward the Confessor,* p. 23, has her sent to Wilton and cites Robert as urging divorce.

41. Ælfgifu, wife of Eadwig, had a brother who became ealdorman of West Wessex and a nephew who founded Cerne and Eynsham: S.911, 1217. The family of Æthelflæd, Edmund's second wife, were the major patrons of Ely and other eastern houses, and provided two consecutive ealdormen of Essex: D. Whitelock, ed., *Anglo-Saxon Wills* (Cambridge: Cambridge University Press, 1930), nos. 8, 14, and 15; E. O. Blake, ed., *Liber Eliensis,* Camden Society, 3rd ser., vol. 92 (London: Offices of the Royal Historical Society, 1962), pp. 133–36, 422–23. Ælfthryth was a daughter of an ealdorman of the southwest, and her brother founded Tavistock: S.838; William of Malmesbury, *De gestis pontificum Anglorum libri quinque,* ed. N. E. S. A. Hamilton, Rolls series (London: Longman and Co., 1870), pp. 202–203. Ælfgifu

of Northampton's father was ealdorman at York, and her uncle Wulfric Spot lavishly endowed Burton: Sawyer, ed., *Charters of Burton Abbey,* pp. xxxviii ff. Eadgifu was daughter of ealdorman Sighelm of Kent; see S.350, 1211.

42. Ælfthryth's consecration is described in "The Anonymous Life of Oswald," in *The Historians of the Church of York and its Archbishops,* ed. J. Raine, 3 vols., Rolls Series (London: Longman and Co., 1879–94), vol. I, p. 438. The *Anglo-Saxon Chronicle,* MS. E, 1048, states that Edith was "hallowed . . . as queen (*gehalgod . . . to cwen*)"; she has these titles. The titles are applied to Emma, though there is no precise reference to her consecration. She is shown crowned in the manuscript of the *Encomium Emmae:* British Library, Additonal MS. 33241, fo. iv. The case for the anointing of Ælfflæd has been put by J. Nelson, "The second English Ordo," in her collected essays, *Politics and Ritual in Early Medieval Europe* (London: Ronceverte, 1986), p. 367.

43. On Mercian queens and the history of queenly anointing, see my "Charles the Bald, Judith and England," pp. 142–43, 140–42.

44. Ælfthryth is *regina* in S.731, 767, 771, 779, 785, all dated before the year 973. In Asser, p. 202, n. 4, Stevenson noted that these charters were dubious, but did not dispose of the evidence in Robertson, ed., *Anglo-Saxon Charters,* no. 45, pre-971, where she is *regina,* and no. 49, pre-970, where she is *seo hlæfdige.* Whitelock, ed., *Anglo-Saxon Wills,* no. 11, calls Eadgifu *seo hlæfdige* in the mid-century, and she is *regina* in a German gospel book entry from Athelstan's reign: D. Bullough, "The Continental Background to the Reform," in D. Parsons, ed., *Tenth-Century Studies* (London: Phillimore, 1975), p. 34. Ælfgifu, Edmund's wife, is *regina* in A. Campbell, ed., *Chronicle of Æthelweard,* p. 54, but this is a late tenth-century source. Æthelflæd, Edmund's second wife, is *cwen* in *Anglo-Saxon Chronicle,* MS. D, 946, but this is an eleventh-century manuscript and untrustworthy for tenth-century terminology; for example, it calls Edgar *ætheling* in 973, although he was already crowned. See J. L. Nelson, "Inauguration Rituals," in P. H. Sawyer and I. N. Wood, eds., *Early Medieval Kingship* (Leeds: School of History, University of Leeds, 1977), pp. 65–67.

45. Certain nobles objected to Edward because although his mother was legally married, neither she nor his father had been consecrated at the time of his conception: Eadmer, "Life of Dunstan," in Stubbs, ed., *Memorials of St. Dunstan,* p. 214.

46. Æthelwulf was succeeded in turn by his four sons; Alfred by his son Edward. Edward's only known brother Æthelweard predeceased him, and Edward was succeeded in turn by four sons: Ælfweard, Athelstan, Edmund, and Eadred. Eadred was succeeded by his brother's sons, Eadwig and then Edgar; Edgar by his sons, Edward the Martyr and then Æthelred. Cnut was followed first by Harold Harefoot and then by Harthacnut.

47. For the brief reign of Ælfweard, see the regnal list in Ernulphus, *Textus Roffensis,* fo. 8ᵛ (P. H. Sawyer, ed., *Early English Manuscripts in Facsimile* [Copenhagen: Rosenkilde and Bagger, 1957]); cf. *Anglo-Saxon Chronicle,* MS. D, 924. His reign disposes of the theory of a brief interregnum between Edward and Athelstan as suggested in M. L. R. Beaven, "The Regnal Dates of Alfred, Edward the Elder and Athelstan," *English Historical Review* 32 (1917): 525.

48. Did they fail to marry in order to assure the succession to brother or brother's sons? The evidence that they did not marry is too negative to be certain.

49. There is a possibility that Harold Harefoot had a son, passed over in favor of his uncle Harthacnut; see W. H. Stevenson, "An Alleged Son of Harold Harefoot," *English Historical Review* 28 (1913): 112–17.

50. *Clito* describes all the king's sons; see, for example S.909, 910, 911. William of Malmesbury, *De gestis regum Anglorum,* p. 70, defined *æthelingas* as "sons of the Kings of England." The *Institutes of Cnut,* iii, 56 (ed. F. Liebermann, *Die Gesetze der Angelsachsen,* 3 vols. in 4 [Halle: M. Niemeyer, 1903–16], vol. I, p. 615) defines *ætheling* as "a king's son by a legal wife." When Edward the Confessor wanted to make Edgar his heir, "he named him ætheling": *Leges Edwardi Confessoris,* para. 35 (Liebermann, ed., vol. I, p. 665), where it is shown that *ætheling* denoted not simply royal blood, but a king's son (Edgar was grandson of a king and thus not by right an *ætheling*); cf. Beornoth, in *Anglo-Saxon Chronicle,* MS. A, 905,

termed as "son of an *ætheling.*" See D. Dumville, "The Ætheling: A Study in Anglo-Saxon Constitutional History," *Anglo-Saxon England* 8 (1979): 1–33.

51. Ælfweard, the younger but more legitimate brother of Athelstan, succeeded before him. But Athelstan's strong claims of age-precedence were expressed in his kingship of Mercia and in the fact that he made good his claim to Wessex on Ælfweard's death, over the head of Ælfweard's younger brother.

52. See the will of Alfred, in Harmer, ed. *Select English Historical Documents,* no. 11. Asser, *cap.* 29, refers to Alfred as *secundarius* during his brother's lifetime. Interestingly, this formal position is mentioned in connection with his marriage.

53. However, Eric John's suggestion, in his *Orbis Britanniae and Other Studies* (Leicester: Leicester University Press, 1966), pp. 38–44, that Æthelwulf had Alfred consecrated by the pope to ensure his succession to his brothers, has been persuasively rebutted by J. L. Nelson, "King Alfred's Royal Anointing," *Journal of Ecclesiastical History* 18 (1967): 145–63.

54. Egbert made his eldest son Æthelwulf under-king in Kent, and Æthelwulf gave Kent to his eldest son Athelstan; see my "Charles the Bald, Judith and England," pp. 143–44.

55. I am grateful to Professor Loyn for drawing my attention to this fact. *Anglo-Saxon Chronicle,* MS. E, 933, applies the title *ætheling* to Edwin, the eldest surviving brother of Athelstan; *Anglo-Saxon Chronicle,* MS. A, 937, 941, applies it to Athelstan's brother and successor, Edmund; *Anglo-Saxon Chronicle,* MS. C, 1015, to Edmund, the eldest surviving son of Æthelred II, though his younger brother is not so designated when the same source refers to him in 1014. The term *edlyg* was borrowed into Welsh in the tenth century to denote the designated heir to the throne, though this need not be taken to imply that it had the same meaning in England; see D. A. Binchy, "Some Celtic Legal Terms," *Celtica* 3 (1956): 221–31. If the term does denote a prince to whom additional expectation has been given, it underlines the possible designation of Ælfthryth's son by Edgar, over his elder brother; *Anglo-Saxon Chronicle,* MS. A, 971, gave the title to her eldest son Edmund, though the entry was subsequently expunged.

56. A. Campbell, ed., *Encomium Emmae,* p. 33; Barlow, ed., *Life of Edward the Confessor,* pp. 7–9.

57. Cf. M. Southwold, "The Succession to the Throne in Buganda," in J. Goody, ed., *Succession to High Office* (Cambridge: The University Press, 1966), pp. 82–126, for a comparable adoption of this practice.

58. Athelstan was brought up by his aunt Æthelflæd: William of Malmesbury, *De gestis regum Anglorum,* vol. 1, para 133; Edgar by the wife of Athelstan Half-King: *Chronicon abbatiae Rameseiensis,* ed. W. D. Macray, Rolls series (London: Longman and Co., 1886), pp. 11, 53; Æthelred II's eldest son by a certain Ælfswith: Whitelock, ed., *Anglo-Saxon Wills,* no. 20; Edward the Confessor perhaps by Leofrun (but since the same lady is said to be the wife of Earl Tostig there are chronological difficulties): S.1137.

59. Asser, *Life of Alfred, caps.* 22, 23.

60. Æthelred was physically part of her household when she visited Ely after 972: Blake, ed., *Liber Eliensis,* p. 86. The sons of Æthelred's own first marriage normally appear at court with their grandmother; see, for example, S.876, 877, 878, 888, 891, 896; Whitelock, ed., *Anglo-Saxon Wills,* no. 20.

61. They attended court with her and accompanied her to Normandy in 1013: *Anglo-Saxon Chronicle,* MS. E, 1013.

62. *Anglo-Saxon Chronicle,* MS. C, 1023, has Cnut entrust his son to Thorkell the Tall in Denmark. It does not specify which son, and although Harthacnut was in Denmark before his father's death, there is difficulty in accepting that he was sent there in 1023; see Campbell, ed., *Encomium Emmae,* pp. 35, 75; *Anglo-Saxon Chronicle,* MS. D, 1023.

63. Barlow, *Life of Edward the Confessor,* pp. 197, 219.

64. Whitelock, ed., *Anglo-Saxon Wills,* nos. 14, 8. Some twenty-seven estates are the objects of Æthelflæd's bequests, among which Damerham, Lambourn, and Cholsey are royal land, but most are from her family; cf. the wills of her father and sister in Whitelock, ed., *Anglo-Saxon Wills,* nos. 2, 15. Ælfgifu bequeathed fourteen estates, some very substantial,

plus a great fortune in cash, about 720 mancuses of gold. She left seven estates to the king and ætheling, at least one of which had originally come to her through royal gift.

65. There are grants, for example, to Ælfthryth: S.725, 742, 877; to Emma: S.925; to Æthelflæd, Edmund's wife: S.513; to an Ælfflæd, who may be the wife of Edward the Elder: S.1719, 474, 399; to Eadgifu: S.489, 562, 811; to Ælfgifu, wife of Eadwig: S.737, 738.

66. Wantage, for example, was left to Ealhswith in Alfred's will and to Eadgifu by Eadred. It is royal demesne in 1066. Amesbury was granted to Eadgifu by Eadred, and Ælfthryth later founded a nunnery there; again it is royal demesne in 1066. Lambourne was left to Ealhswith by Alfred, was one of the estates returned to the king by Æthelflæd, and was in royal hands in 1066. A large area of Rutland was in the queen's possession in 1066. Geoffrey Gaimar, Lestoire des engles, ed. T. D. Hardy and C. T. Martin, 2 vols., Rolls Series (London: Eyre and Spottiswoode, 1888–89), vol. 1, ll. 4135–40, states that Ælfthryth and Emma had held it. On the possibility that it may go back as a royal estate, perhaps in the hands of the queen, to the Mercian kingdom, see C. Phythian-Adams, "Rutland Reconsidered," in A. Dornier, ed., Mercian Studies (Leicester: Leicester University Press, 1977), pp. 63–84. Exeter and Winchester also have queenly connections: see Gaimar, Lestoire des engles; Anglo-Saxon Chronicle, MS. C, 1003; Freeman, History of the Norman Conquest, vol. 3, p. 640. On the evidence of Domesday and Robertson, ed., Anglo-Saxon Charters, nos. 114, 118, it is clear that Hayling Island and Wargrave were consecutively held by Emma and Edith. Cf. the lands allocated to the upkeep of princes and allegedly inalienable, referred to in S.937.

67. Barlow, Life of Edward the Confessor, p. 74.

68. Grat, Vielliard, and Clémencet, eds., Annales de Saint-Bertin, sub anno 862.

69. See the will of the ætheling Athelstan, in Whitelock, ed., Anglo-Saxon Wills, no. 20.

70. I am grateful to Dr. Janet Nelson for drawing my attention to this point.

71. Asser, Life of Alfred, cap. 15; Anglo-Saxon Chronicle, MSS. C and D, 1035, 1043; MS. E, 1048 (recte 1051).

72. Nelson, "Queens as Jezebels," esp. pp. 74–75.

73. Whitelock, ed., Anglo-Saxon Wills, nos. 8, 9, 15; Robertson, ed., Anglo-Saxon Charters, no. 66.

74. Ælfthryth's foundations are discussed in Meyer, "Women and the Tenth-Century English Monastic Reform," pp. 55–61.

75. Robertson, ed., Anglo-Saxon Charters, nos. 45, 49.

76. R. Deshmann, "Christus rex et magi reges: Kingship and Christology in Ottonian and Anglo-Saxon Art," Frühmittelalterliche Studien 10 (1976): esp. 397–98.

77. In S.745 Ælfthryth is legitima prefati regis conjunx 'legitimate wife of the above king'; Edmund is clito legitimus prefati regis filius 'ætheling, legitimate son of the above king'; while the older Edward is placed after Edmund and referred to as eodem rege clito procreatus 'ætheling born to the above king'.

78. See Ælfric's statement that "the queen (cwen) gives birth and the ætheling by his birth thrives to the throne": The Homilies of the Anglo-Saxon Church, ed. B. Thorpe, 2 vols. (London: The Ælfric Society, 1844–46), vol. 1, p. 110, where cwen should probably be understood with a specific meaning of queen, even anointed queen. The post-conquest definition in the Institutes of Cnut, iii, 56 (Liebermann, ed., Gesetze der Angelsachsen, vol. 1, p. 615) also referred to the nature of the marriage in determining throne-worthiness.

79. On Eadgifu's fortunes, see Harmer, ed., Select English Historical Documents, no. 23. On Dunstan and Eadgifu, "Life of Dunstan" [Auctore B], in Stubbs, ed., Memorials of Dunstan, caps. 21, 24.

80. A. Campbell, ed., Encomium Emmae, p. 41.

81. Edmund succeeded an unmarried brother, and all the other children of his prolific father were dead or disposed of by 939. Only his full brother Eadred survived.

82. For his birth by a concubine, see William of Malmesbury, De gestis regum Anglorum, vol. 1, para. 131. Such arguments were evidently advanced against him.

83. Anglo-Saxon Chronicle, MS. E, 933. William of Malmesbury, De gestis regum Anglorum, vol. 1, para. 126, makes Edwin to be the son of Ælfflæd, and his account of the family of Edward the Elder is altogether more accurate than that in Florence of Worcester,

Chronicon ex chronicis, vol. 1, p. 119, where Edwin is made a son of Eadgifu. Further details of Edwin's rebellion are in William of Malmesbury, *De gestis regum Anglorum,* vol. 1, para. 139.

84. She never appears in witness lists but was associated with Athelstan in the grant of a gospel book to a German community; see D. Bullough, "The Continental Background to the Reform," p. 34. The possibility that the Eadgifu in question is the sister of Athelstan and wife of the Frankish king, Charles the Simple, has been raised by S. Keynes, "King Athelstan's Books," in *Learning and Literature in Anglo-Saxon England,* eds. M. Lapidge and H. Gneuss (Cambridge: Cambridge University Press, 1985), pp. 190–93.

85. See n. 55 above on the possibility that *ætheling* used as a title implies such designation. Edwin, son of Edward the Elder's earlier marriage, was referred to by this title in 933, but Eadgifu's son Edmund enjoyed it by 939. Was Edwin's rebellion in 933 the result of a scheme to pass him over in favor of Edmund?

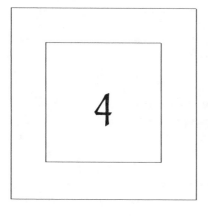

The Historical Bearing of Place-Name Studies

The Place of Women in Anglo-Saxon Society

One of the interesting features of Anglo-Saxon history is the number of women who impressed themselves on the consciousness of their time. They appear in all periods from the legendary foreworld to the eve of the Norman Conquest, and they occur in the religious as well as the temporal sphere. The illustrious Hild of Whitby, who made her house a nursery of bishops, stands for many of her sex and order, whose right to rule communities of men and women was never challenged by the native leaders of the English church. Among women of the world, if *The Anglo-Saxon Chronicle* can be trusted—and its authority in this section is good—Seaxburg, the widow of Coenwalh king of Wessex, reigned after him for a year, late in the seventh century. Cynethryth the wife of Offa, who passed into history as the great example of a tyrannous queen, was of such consequence in her own day that coins were struck in her name. In the tenth century, Æthelflæd the Lady of the Mercians, at the head of a military household, planned and carried out a series of momentous campaigns. Ælfgifu of Northampton, the first wife of Cnut, after ruling Norway with a severity which made "Ælfgifu's time" an evil memory in the North, brought the leading men of England to accept her son Harold as their king. A generation later, the lady who was known in at least seven counties as Eddeve "the fair," Eddeve "the rich," or Eddeve "the rich and fair," commanded a following of free landowners which would have done credit to an earl. There is no doubt that Old English society allowed to women, not only private influence, but also the widest liberty of intervention in public affairs.

The prominence of these and other women in the life of the state is in curious contrast with the vagueness which overhangs the position of women in Old English law. On many important points the Anglo-Saxon codes give no information of any kind. On others, the information which they give is confused, touched with homiletic, or overconcise. The obscurity is perhaps at its densest around the fundamental question of the conditions under which women could acquire and enjoy the possession of land. There is no doubt as to the bare fact that women could inherit land before the Norman Conquest. But on the circumstances under which an inheritance would fall to them, there is little to be gathered from the primary authorities for Old English legal history. They give no clear direction even in regard to the basic problems which center round the daughter's right to a share in her father's land. It is significant that on the most urgent of these problems, Felix Liebermann, after editing the *Gesetze,* attempted no more than the statement that "on the evidence of the Old English laws, the exclusion of the sister by the brother in the inheritance of landed property can neither be proved nor disproved."[1]

For further light on questions like these, it is necessary to pass beyond the enactments of Old English kings to materials of narrower range—to the wills, the private charters, and the royal diplomas of the Anglo-Saxon period. They have little to tell about the inheritance of unprivileged land—the land of the free peasant and the lesser thegn. But they give valuable information about the descent of estates held as "bookland" under the terms of a royal charter. One of the liberties normally attached to land thus held was the power of bequeathing or otherwise regulating the descent of the property. The power was often used to keep the estate in the male line of its recipient. There was a strong preference for the male line in the West Saxon royal house itself. In his own will, King Alfred remarks that his grandfather, King Egbert, had bequeathed his land "to the spear-side, not to the spindle-side."[2] But with regard to certain lands which had been acquired by the royal family since Egbert's death, Alfred observes that he is free to bequeath them to men or women as he wishes, and the history of many estates in the next two centuries shows that there was no general custom adverse to the inheritance of bookland by women. Even before King Alfred's time, cases of such inheritance are on record. The most interesting of King Egbert's few surviving charters was made in favor of three sisters, who had inherited an estate of this kind from their father, but had lost their *anteriora scripsiuncula.*[3]

Documents from the century before the Conquest, and especially the wills and narrative charters which are characteristic of this age, show large numbers of women possessed of land by virtue of grant, bequest, or inheritance. They also show that these women were able to dispose of their landed property with a freedom which was not permitted to their successors of the feudal age. A woman could alienate her "morning-gift," or dower, though it would be well for such a transaction to be confirmed by the king. In Alfred's time, a woman says explicitly that she is free to sell a particular estate "because it had been her morning-gift."[4] In the eleventh century, it was possible for a woman to disinherit her son, ostentatiously, in favor of a female relative. Few characters outside the mainstream of Old English history stand out more clearly than the lady who received a deputation from the local shire-court with the outburst "Here sits Leofflæd, my kinswoman, to whom after my death I grant my land and my gold, my robes and my raiment, and all that I have. Behave like thegns, and give my message to the good men in the court, and tell them to whom I have given my land and my property—and to my son, nothing."[5] That women had the power of bequeathing land is proved by many wills of this age, which show that their freedom of bequest was not restricted to their kin but extended to their servants, to ecclesiastical persons, and to churches.[6] The fact that the king is often asked to confirm these bequests merely proves that he was interested in any important change in the distribution of land among his subjects. The number of men who make the same request shows that it was not the sign of any special limitation imposed on the woman testator.

The royal charters of the pre-Conquest age, formal as they are, contain many passages which illustrate the position of the woman landowner. A considerable number of them are grants to women. Some of these women seem to have been under vows of religion, but many of them, to all appearances, were living in the world. Other charters show incidentally that the properties with which they are concerned had been owned by women at some time in the past. Among the earliest of them is a charter of Edward the Elder relating to Water Eaton near Oxford, which sketches the history of the estate during the previous thirty years.[7] It states that Burgred and Æthelswith, the king and queen of Mercia, had granted the village to Alhhun bishop of Worcester; that Alhhun's successor, bishop Werferth, had exchanged it for other land with Ceolwulf II king of Mercia; that King Ceolwulf had granted it to a woman named Hungyth; and that Hungyth had sold it to a certain Wigferth in the presence of the Mercian *witan*. The whole tenor of the passage is against the idea that there was any religious purpose behind Ceolwulf's grant to Hungyth, and the way in which the story is told suggests that those who recorded it saw nothing remarkable in her acquisition of the estate or, for that matter, in her alienation of it by sale.

It is clear from *Domesday Book* that there were many women among the English landowners of the Confessor's reign. Several of them have left their names to the estates which they possessed. The hamlets of Goodcott and Lovacott in Devon obviously derive their names from the women called Godgifu and Lufu who were their pre-Conquest owners.[8] Afflington in Dorset seems to be named after Ælfrun, the holder of one of the manors into which the place was divided in 1066.[9] The case of Tolpuddle in the same county is more interesting.[10] In *Domesday Book,* the village is described among the possessions of Abbotsbury Abbey under the name *Pidele*— the name of the stream by which the place is situated. The first syllable of the modern name, which was added in order to distinguish the manor from other places near the same stream, represents the name of Tola, the wife of Urk, a housecarle of King Cnut, who with her husband, or more probably after his death, gave Tolpuddle to the abbey. The addition had the curious result that a Scandinavian woman's name, which is extremely rare even in Danish England, became permanently associated with a manor in the heart of southern Wessex.[11]

The place-names which contain the names of women form a useful supplement to the documentary evidence for the pre-Conquest woman landowner.[12] Few of them can be closely dated; but, as a group, it is probable that they belong to the later rather than the earlier centuries of Anglo-Saxon history. Wulfrun, for example, the great Staffordshire lady whose *hēah tūn*, or chief manor, has become Wolverhampton, lived in the second half of the tenth century.[13] It is suggestive that no names of this type occur in the writings of Bede, or in the oldest sections of *The Anglo-Saxon Chronicle*. The first for which there is ancient authority seems to be Bamburgh in Northumberland, which appears in King Alfred's translation of the *Historia Ecclesiastica* in the form *Bebbanburg* and, according to the dubious testimony of Nennius, was derived from Bebbe, wife of Æthelfrith king of the Bernicians.[14] Names of this kind are rare in the earliest charters. Bognor in Sussex, "Bucge's bank or shore," occurs in a charter which is dated 680, but was probably written in the tenth century.[15] Fladbury in Worcestershire, "Flæde's *burh,*" was the subject of a grant by Æthelred king of Mercia, shortly after 690.[16] The next undoubted case of a village-name thus formed seems to be the unidentified *Cyneburgingctun* which is mentioned in a west-midland charter of 840.[17] It is not until the tenth century is well advanced that such formations begin to appear in appreciable numbers.

More than seventy of these names appear in *Domesday Book.* The number would have been much larger if the *Domesday* enumeration of hamlets and villages had been more nearly complete. Elson in Gosport, for example, is not mentioned in *Domesday Book,* but its name, which means "Ethelswith's *tūn,*" occurs in a tenth-century charter.[18] There are many names of this type which are not recorded before the twelfth or thirteenth century but are clearly of Old English origin. Under the social conditions which prevailed in the Norman age, few Englishwomen were in a position to leave their names to manors or villages. Names such as Aylton in Herefordshire—"Æthelgifu's *tūn,*" Edburton in Sussex—"Ēadburg's *tūn,*" Chellington in Bedfordshire—"Cēolwynn's *tūn,*" or Harvington in Chaddesley Corbet, Worcestershire—"Herewynn's *tūn,*" though ignored by *Domesday Book,* can safely be referred to the Old English time. It is easier to imagine conditions in which the names of Englishwomen could appear at a later date in place-names of a topographical kind, such as Goodwood in Sussex—"Godgifu's wood," Whaberley in Worcestershire—"Hwætburg's clearing," Adney in Shropshire—"Ēadwynn's island," or Wilberfoss in Yorkshire—"Wilburg's ditch" [*sic*]. But the number of cases in which such names are known to have arisen after the Conquest is so small that these names also are best taken as Old English survivals.

In any case, for historical purposes, they are much less interesting than the names which combine a woman's name with a word denoting a place of settlement—*hām, burh, tūn, wīc,* or *worth,* and in Danish England, *by* or *thorp.* There are cases in which it is hard to decide the nature of the settlement described by such a name. It is only a comparison with other names of the same kind and a review of local circumstances which make it probable that *wīc* in the Hertfordshire *Æthelflæde wīc* meant a dairy-farm,[19] and that the original *Cynehilde worth,* which has become Kenilworth, was a farmstead in Arden.[20] But in regard to the more important of these terms of settlement, the meaning is plainer. There is direct evidence that *tūn,* the commonest of all, which at first meant no more than "enclosure," had acquired the sense of "village" before the end of the seventh century.[21] In innumerable place-names, this word is preceded by the name of a man or woman in the genitive case.[22] Few examples occur in the earliest authorities, but by the eleventh century the type had arisen everywhere. In Derbyshire alone, more than thirty of these names are mentioned in *Domesday Book.* Historically, they are important because they show that in the Old English period it was not unusual for an individual to hold a position of such prominence within a village that his or her name became attached to it. The nature of this position is a difficult question. It may well have varied in different cases between the ownership of the village with all its lands and informal precedence among a group of peasant proprietors. Whatever its character, it must have been permanent, and recognized, not only within the village itself, but also by the men of the surrounding country.

Among the names of this type recorded in *Domesday Book*, more than thirty contain the names of women. There are isolated examples in most parts of England. In Nottinghamshire, Darlton, Kinoulton, and Kneeton contain the feminine names Dēorlufu, Cynehild, and Cēngifu, of which the last appears again in Kniveton, Derbyshire, and Knayton, Yorkshire. In Suffolk, Dennington, Alpheaton, and Wiston contain Denegifu, Ælfhild, and Wīgswīth. In Sussex, Binderton, Warbleton, and Walberton contain Beornthryth, Wǣrburg, and Wealdburg. Wǣrburg appears again in Warburton, Cheshire. In Berkshire, Elton in Welford is derived from Æthelflǣd; Eddington near Hungerford, from Ēadgifu. Wollaton in Devon is derived from Wulfgifu; Offerton in Worcestershire, from Ealhflǣd; Wollerton in Shropshire, from Wulfwynn; Willington in Cheshire, from Wynnflǣd; Wilburton in Cambridgeshire, from Wilburg; Abberton in Essex, from Ēadburg. The only county in which there is anything resembling a concentration of these names is Kent, where the feminine names Ælfgyth, Bilswīth, Hringwynn, Sǣgifu, Sigeflǣd, Cēolwaru, Æthelwaru, and Gārwynn have given rise to the place-names Elvington, Bilsington, Ringleton, Sevington, Siffleton, Chilverton, Elverton, and Garrington.[23] But even without the Kentish examples there are enough names of this kind to suggest that in Old English times it was not uncommon for a woman to be the lady of a *tūn*.

Although *tūn* is among the most widely distributed of place-name elements, it is not prominent in the local nomenclature of the earliest times. So far as can be seen, in the age of the settlement, and for many generations thereafter, the word generally used for an important place of habitation was not *tūn* but *hām*. On the other hand, it is doubtful whether *hām* was much employed in the formation of new place-names after, at latest, the end of the eighth century, and it is therefore of some interest that the word occasionally appears in combination with a woman's name. Among the cases as to which there is no serious doubt, Babraham and Wilbraham in Cambridgeshire contain the feminine names Beaduburg and Wilburg; Asheldham in Essex contains Æschild; Hardham in Sussex, Heregyth; Worldham in Hampshire, Wǣrhild; Alpraham in Cheshire, Ealhburg; Abram in Lancashire, Ēadburg; Hubberholme in Yorkshire, Hūnburg. In view of the rarity of late place-names formed from *hām*, these examples can reasonably be accepted as an addition to the evidence for the ownership of land by women in the pre-Alfredian age.

It is more remarkable that in at least ten place-names, apart from the archaic Bamburgh, a woman's name is compounded with the element *burh*. Harbury in Warwickshire means the *burh* of a woman named Hereburg. Bibury and Tetbury in Gloucestershire contain the feminine names Bēage and Tette. Heytesbury and Alderbury in Wiltshire are derived from Heahthrȳth and Æthelwaru. Adderbury in Oxfordshire, Fladbury in Worcestershire, Bucklebury in Berkshire, Queniborough in Leicestershire, and Alberbury in Shropshire, were named from women called Ēadburg, Flǣde, Burghild, Cwēne, and Alhburg. The original meaning of *burh* was fortress, or place of defense. Apart from the specialized usage which survives in the modern "borough," the word was applied to ancient forts of stone or earthwork and to houses surrounded by defenses which could be held against an enemy. It is often difficult to determine the sense which it bears in a particular place-name, and it is unlikely that it had the same meaning in all the names which have been quoted. The most interesting feature of this group of names is that in one of them, and probably in others, *burh* meant neither a fort nor a defensible house but a monastery. In a charter of the late seventh century which comes from Malmesbury but is probably genuine, the estate afterwards known as *Tettan byrig* and now as Tetbury is described as 15 *cassati,* or hides, *prope Tettan monasterium.*[24]

There is other evidence that *burh* and *monasterium* could be used interchangeably. Westbury on Trym in Gloucestershire appears as *Uuestburg* in an original charter of Offa and as *Westmynster* in a document of 804 preserved in Heming's Worcester cartulary.[25] The usage presumably refers to the enclosure which surrounded the monastic buildings, and it provides the most natural explanation of several other names, such as Malmesbury, in which the word *burh* was used to denote the site of a religious house.[26] It probably accounts for the appearance of the word in the name of Fladbury, which is described as a *monasterium* in a charter of the early eighth century.[27] In composition with a woman's name, *burh* is more likely to have meant "monastery" than "fortress," and it may well be a mere accident that Fladbury and Tetbury are the only names in this series which can definitely be connected with an early religious foundation.[28]

In every county, *Domesday Book* records many place-names which originally denoted topographical features such as trees, springs, woods, or clearings. Some of these names contain the names of women. Buckden in Huntingdonshire, "Bucge's valley," and the lost *Hatheburgfelda* in Suffolk, "Heathuburg's open ground," are examples. Eythorne in Kent, "Hēahgyth's thorn-tree," though not mentioned in *Domesday Book,* had become a village-name as early as the ninth century.[29] The Old English *lēah* 'clearing' is perhaps the commonest of all the elements which occur in these names, and it is frequently compounded with the name of a woman. Among the names of this kind which are certainly of pre-Conquest origin, Alveley in Shropshire and Aveley in Essex contain the feminine name Ælfgyth; Avely in Suffolk contains Ælfwynn; Balterley in Staffordshire, Bealdthrȳth; Audley in Staffordshire, Ealdgyth; Kimberley in Norfolk, Cyneburg; Wilderley in Shropshire, Wilthrȳth; Anslow in Staffordshire, Ēanswith. Without overstressing these names, it can at least be said that they illustrate the part which women had played in the reclamation of woodland for tillage during the later centuries of the Old English period.[30]

The best recorded names of this type come from the boundary clauses of Old English charters. They have not yet been studied exhaustively from this point of view, but a casual search is enough to show the number and variety of the elements which were compounded with the names of women. It is doubtful whether there was any common feature of the countryside which somewhere or other was not associated with a woman's name. Feminine names occur in connexion with *mere* 'pool', *wiella* 'spring', *flēot, burna,* and *gelād* 'stream' or 'watercourse', *mutha* 'creek', *dīc* 'ditch', *trēow* 'tree', *stocc* 'stump', *stān* 'stone', *bricg* 'bridge', *weg* 'way', *stīg* 'path', *bece* and *denu* 'valley', *beorg* 'hill' or 'mound', *hyrst* 'wooded hill', *grāf* 'brushwood', *worthig,* generally 'homestead', *hamm,* generally 'water-meadow', and *ford.*[31] Most names of this kind come from regions of long established cultivation, but *Wynburge spær*[32] was the name of a Sussex swine-pasture, *Edswythe torr*[33] was a hill near Meavy beneath Dartmoor, and *Eanburge mere*[34] was near Wootton Underwood in the original Bernwood Forest. Names formed in this way had arisen by the tenth century in all the parts of England from which charters have survived.[35] Examples of an earlier date are rare, because charters themselves are comparatively rare, and charters containing detailed boundaries are very rare indeed. But the names which have been preserved suggest that the part which women had taken in the occupation of new lands for settlement had been by no means inconsiderable.

In many charters, the boundary of an estate is drawn for part of its course along the border of an adjacent property, which is identified by its owner's name. The line is said to pass *andlang Wynsies mearce* 'along the border of Wynsie' and *andlang Wistanes gemere* 'along the lake of Wistan'. Among the landowners whose names are thus recorded, at least ten were women. They are scattered over Berkshire, Hampshire, Wiltshire, Kent, Essex, Oxfordshire, and Warwickshire.[36] The only one of them of whom anything is otherwise known is Eadgifu, the boundary of whose land is mentioned in a charter relating to Leverton in Berkshire.[37] The neighboring village of Edington near Hungerford takes its name from a woman called Eadgifu, and there is no reason to doubt that she was identical with the woman of this name who appears in the Leverton charter. There is nothing to suggest that she was a more important person than the other women of this group, and there seems no particular significance in the fact that she alone has given name to a village.

The names which have so far been quoted are all of English origin. Most of them belong to Wessex or English Mercia. For the position of women in Danish England there is less evidence. Few collections of early charters have survived from the Danelaw, and for the northern part of this region there is little documentary material earlier than *Domesday Book*.[38] Nevertheless, the clearest description of an independent woman landowner which has come down from early England relates to this part of the country. In the statement of disputed claims to land at the end of the Yorkshire *Domesday*,[39] it is asserted that the whole land of a woman named Asa ought to belong to Robert Malet,

> because she had her land separate and free from the lordship and power of Bernulf her husband, even when they lived together, so that he could make neither gift nor sale of it, nor could he forfeit it. Moreover after their separation, she withdrew with all her land, and possessed it as lady.

The passage agrees remarkably with the general tenor of Norse literature about the position of women in the North, and it carries the authority of a public court—of a wapentake, if not of a riding. It is perhaps more important to note that the statement is not introduced into *Domesday Book* as the record of a legal anomaly. There would have been no reference to the rights of Asa over her land if it had not been for the practical complications raised by her departure from her husband.

In view of this passage, it is natural to expect that here and there among the early place-names of the North, there should be traces of the ownership of land by women who, like Asa, bore names of Scandinavian origin. The place-names which are in point are few, but their evidence, so far as it goes, is conclusive. South of the Humber, the only clear examples are Gunthorpe in Nottinghamshire and Raventhorpe in Lincolnshire, which contain the feminine names Gunnhildr and Ragnhildr. But in Yorkshire, at least eight of these names are well recorded. The feminine names Ingirithr and Gunnhildr occur in Ingerthorpe in the West Riding and Gunby in the East Riding. Raventhorpe in the East Riding is a doublet of Raventhorpe in Lincolnshire. Helperthorpe in the East Riding and Helperby in the North Riding each contains the rare feminine name Hjalpr, and in each case this name appears in the correct genitive form *Hjalpar*. The same Scandinavian genitive occurs in early spellings of Burythorpe in the East Riding and Thorlby in the West Riding, which are derived from the feminine names Bjǫrg and Thorhildr. Hinderskelfe in the North Riding means the ledge or shelf of land belonging to a woman called Hildr, and in this name also the true genitive in -*ar* has been preserved. Apart from Ingerthorpe, which is not mentioned before the late twelfth century, each of these names is recorded in *Domesday Book,* and one of them is known to have arisen within a hundred years of the Danish settlement in Yorkshire. Helperby is mentioned in a list of properties acquired for the see of York by archbishop Osketel, who died in 971.[40]

When all is told, the place-names into which the names of women enter form a minute proportion of the place-names of all England. It would be easy to exaggerate their significance. Nevertheless, there are enough of them to carry a few modest generalizations. They show that before the Norman Conquest it was not unusual for women, like men, to leave their names to villages, hamlets, and parcels of land brought into cultivation from brushwood or forest. They imply that a considerable number of women possessed estates which can properly, if untechnically, be described as manors. Regarded as a whole, they give the impression that women were associated with men on terms of rough equality in the common life of the countryside. They suggest, in fact, that the independence which women had enjoyed in the Migration Age was never completely lost during the centuries of Old English history.

NOTES

1. Felix Liebermann, ed., *Die Gesetze der Angelsachsen* (Halle: M. Niemeyer, 1903–16), vol. 2, no. 2, p. 390.

2. Florence E. Harmer, *Select English Historical Documents of the Ninth and Tenth Centuries* (Cambridge: Cambridge University Press, 1914), p. 19.

3. Walter de Gray Birch, *Cartularium Saxonicum* (London: Whiting and Co., 1885–93), p. 410.

4. Harmer, *Select English Historical Documents,* p. 31.

5. A. J. Robertson, ed., *Anglo-Saxon Charters* (Cambridge: Cambridge University Press, 1939), p. 152.

6. Ten out of the 39 documents printed in Miss D. Whitelock's *Anglo-Saxon Wills* (Cambridge: Cambridge University Press, 1930) were made by women.

7. Birch, *Cartularium Saxonicum,* p. 607.

8. J. E. B. Gover, A. Mawer, and F. M. Stenton, *The Place-Names of Devon* (Cambridge: Cambridge University Press, 1931–32), pp. 305 and 108.

9. A. Fägersten, *The Place-Names of Dorset* (Uppsala: Uppsala University Årsskrift, 1933), p. 117.

10. Ibid., p. 179.

11. The name does not seem to be recorded in Swedish or in the West Scandinavian dialects, but was common in Old Danish (see O. Nielsen, *Olddanske Personnavne* [Copenhagen: Trykthos J. Jørgensen, 1883], p. 100). Two examples have been noticed in the English Danelaw.

12. It should be emphasized at this point that any list of these names which can be compiled at the present time is bound to be seriously incomplete. In dealing with the short forms of personal names which occur in countless place-names, it is always difficult, and generally impossible, to distinguish between the names of men and women. It is reasonable to assume that Bibury in Gloucestershire takes its name from a woman called Beage because in the eighth century the place, which until then had had no fixed name, was granted to a local nobleman *et filiæ suæ quæ vocatur Beage* (Birch, *Cartularium Saxonicum*, p. 166). Without this information, few scholars would have hesitated to derive the name from the masculine form *Bæga*. The evidence which place-names supply for the existence of the woman land-owner comes almost entirely from compound names which are proved to be feminine by the nature or arrangement of their elements.

13. Her name does not seem to have become permanently attached to the site until a century after her time. The first example of the compound Wolverhampton occurs in a late writ of William I. In *Domesday Book,* the place appears as "Hantone" and "Handone."

14. Nennius, *Historia Brittonum,* ed. Theodor Mommsen, Monumenta Germaniae Historica, Auctores Antiquissimi, vol. 13 (Berlin: Weidmannos, 1894), part 1, p. 206. According to a northern tradition preserved in the late manuscript "E" of the *Chronicle* the fortress was walled by the Bernician king Ida at about the middle of the sixth century.

15. Birch, *Cartularium Saxonicum*, p. 50. Bucge is a short form of a feminine name beginning or ending in the element *Burg.*

16. Ibid., p. 76. On this name see below.

17. Ibid., p. 430; Historical Manuscripts Commission, *Report on the Manuscripts of Lord Middleton* (London: H. M. Stationery Office, 1911), p. 208.

18. Birch, *Cartularium Saxonicum,* p. 865, where the name appears in the compound *Æthelswithetuninga lea.*

19. W. W. Skeat, *The Place-Names of Hertfordshire* (Hertford: East Herts Archaeological Society, 1904), p. 181. The site is now represented by Beauchamps in Layston.

20. There seems to have been a doublet of Kenilworth in the *Cynilde worth* which occurs as a boundary-point near Whittington in Worcestershire.

21. A law of Hlothhere prescribes that a man who wishes to clear himself from the charge of stealing a slave must produce a number of free witnesses, of whom one must come from the *tun* to which he himself belongs (see Liebermann, *Die Gesetz,* vol. I, pp. 9–10).

22. See, for example, *Eadnothes tun, Deorlafestun,* and *Beadurices tun,* now represented by Ednaston in Derbyshire, Darlaston in Staffordshire, and Barcheston in Warwickshire.

23. The history of these Kentish names was first worked out by J. K. Wallenberg in *The Place-Names of Kent* (Uppsala: Uppsala University Årrskrift, 1934). Chilverton and Elverton are not, apparently, recorded before the thirteenth century, but there does not seem to be any reason for separating them from the other names of this group.

24. Birch, *Cartularium Saxonicum,* p. 58.

25. Ibid., pp. 274 and 313.

26. Congresbury in Somerset, in which the first element is a saint's name, is probably another example.

27. In an endorsement by bishop Ecgwine of Worcester to a charter of Æthelred of Mercia granting Fladbury to the seventh-century bishop Oftfor (Birch, *Cartularium Saxonicum,* p. 76).

28. There are several place-names in which the word *mynster* is compounded with a personal name, but the only case in which the name is that of a woman seems to be the *Bebingmynster* of Birch, *Cartularium Saxonicum,* p. 535. The first element in this name is

clearly the Old English Bebbe. The site has been identified with Beaminster in Dorset, but the medieval forms of the latter name do not agree very well with this suggestion. In Alvechurch, Worcestershire (*Ælfgythe cyrcan*, Ibid., p. 1320), and Peakirk, Northamptonshire (*æt Pegecyrcan*, Kemble, *Codex Diplomaticus* (see note 31 below), p. 726), a woman's name is associated with the Old English *cyrice* 'church'. Nothing is known about the Ælfgyth of Alvechurch, but there is no reason to doubt the Pege of Peakirk was the well-recorded sister of St. Guthlac of Crowland.

29. Birch, *Cartularium Saxonicum*, p. 318

30. The name Anslow, which does not occur in *Domesday Book*, appears in the form *Eansythelege* in the boundaries of Wetmoor, Staffordshire, in a fourteenth-century copy of a charter of Æthelred II (see C. G. O. Bridgeman, "Staffordshire Pre-Conquest Charters," *William Salt Archaeological Society*, 1916, p. 124).

31. As no systematic collection of these names seems to have been made, it may be useful to give a selection of them here. (In the references, CD stands for J. M. Kemble, *Codex Diplomaticus Aevi Saxonici* [London: Sumptibus Societatis, 1839–48] and CS, for Birch, *Cartularium Saxonicum*.) *Eanburge mere* near Wootton Underwood, Bucks., CS 452; *Cynewynne wylla* near Ardley, Oxon., CD 1289; *Hunburge fleot* in South Hams, Devon, CS 451; *Beadgithe burna* near Bilston, Staffordshire, Monasticon Anglicanum VIII 1444; *Eanflæde gelad* near Hinksey, Berks, CS 1002; *Eanflæde mutha* near Reculver, Kent, CS 880; *Sigwynne dic* near Fovant, Wilts., CD 687; *Beornwunne treow* near Creedy, Devon, CS 1331; *Winburge stoc* near Eynsham, Oxon., CD 714; *Byrngythe stan* near Wolverhampton, Staffordshire, CD 650; *Wulfgythe bricg*, near Mickleton, Gloucestershire, CD 714; *Æthelburge weg* near Bath, CS 1257; *Æthelflæde stig* near Phepson, Worc., CS 937; *Ceoldrythe bece* near Oldbarrow, Worc., CS 124; *Beornwynne denu* near Pershore, Worc., CS 1282; *Mægnhilde beorh* near Taynton, Oxon.; Bouquet, *Recueil des historiens de la Gaule . . . XI*, p. 655; *Cyneburgæ hyrst* near Droxford, Hants., CS 742; *Denegithe graf* near 'Newton', Northants., CS 712; *Heatheburhe weorthyg* near Pershore, Worc., CS 1282; *Wihtlufe hamm* near Lyford, Berks., CD 746; *Sithrithe ford* near Weston on Trent, Derbyshire, Charter in William Salt Library, Stafford.

32. Birch, *Cartularium Saxonicum*, p. 834.

33. Kemble, *Codex Diplomaticus*, p. 744.

34. Birch, *Cartularium Saxonicum*, p. 452.

35. To the examples recorded in charters, there may be added a number of ancient hundred-names which are formed from the names of women. A complete list is given by O. S. Anderson, *The English hundred-names* (Lund: C. W. K. Gleerup, 1939), vol. 3, p. 206. Among the most interesting are *Auronhelle* in Sussex—"Ælfrun's hill," *Celfledetorn* in Gloucestershire—"Ceolflæd's thorn," *Winburge treow* in Worcestershire—"Wynnburg's tree," *Redbornstoke* in Bedfordshire—"Rædburg's place," and *Underditch* in Wiltshire—"Wynnthryth's dyke."

36. Phrases referring to the boundary of a woman's land occur in 753, *Ælfgythe mearc on eastan . . . oþ Eadgife mearce* ("Oswalding tun," Kent); Birch, *Cartularium Saxonicum*, p. 984, *on Ælflæde mearce* (Padworth, Berkshire); Ibid., p. 1077, *be Byrhtswyþe mearce* (Kilmiston, Hampshire); Ibid., p. 1101, *andlang Ælfwenne mearce* (Vange, Essex); Kemble, *Codex Diplomaticus*, p. 636, *to Ælfflæde gemære* (Clyffe Pypard, Wiltshire); Ibid., p. 641, *on Wilburge imare* (Tisbury, Wiltshire); Ibid., p. 724, *on Ælflæde gemæro* (Bishopton, Warwickshire); Ibid., p. 792, *andlang stremes oð Eadgife gemære* (Leverton, Berkshire); Ibid., p. 1307, *on Leofrune gemære* (Whitchurch, Oxfordshire); *Ordnance Survey facsimiles, ii, Winchester College 4, to Leofwinne mearce* (Drayton, North Hampshire).

37. Kemble, *Codex Diplomaticus*, p. 792.

38. It may be noted that in regard to Scandinavian, as to English names, it is often hard to distinguish between masculine and feminine forms. There is nothing, for example, in *Touetun*, the Domesday spelling of Towton in Yorkshire, to show whether the first element is the masculine *Tófi* or the feminine *Tófa*. Ambiguities like this are frequent.

39. *Domesday Book*, vol. 1, fo. 373.

40. Robertson, *Anglo-Saxon Charters*, p. 112.

MARY P. RICHARDS AND B. JANE STANFIELD

Concepts of Anglo-Saxon Women in the Laws

5

What can the Old English laws tell us about the lives and legal status of women in Anglo-Saxon England? The answer depends upon the way in which these curious, quasi-historical materials are analyzed. The temptation is to view them as historical documents providing an accurate representation of the status, relationships, punishments, and privileges afforded women in the Anglo-Saxon period.[1] They have even been used comparatively to trace changes in women's legal position over time.[2] In fact, the laws reflect at best a partial view of actual practice. Unless their tenets can be verified from contemporary documents such as wills and writs, they must be used with caution as proof for assertions concerning women's position in Anglo-Saxon England at any particular point in time. The problem is this: the dominant legal tradition was comprised of folk-law, a Germanic heritage of custom known to the people and governing the everyday lives of each class. On occasion a king might be motivated to issue a formal code addressing particular points of concern; a few kings attempted more comprehensive codes that embodied a significant portion of folk-law. But everyone understood that any one expression of the law, whether oral or written, informal or formal, was incomplete. This principle is clear, for example, in the legal compendia that survive from Anglo-Saxon England, where codes are collected and arranged often by topic, and where no code appears to supercede its predecessors. These matters will be explored in more detail in the course of this chapter. For the moment it suffices to say that the picture of women in the laws reflects the nature of the texts, and therefore is neither complete nor easily datable.

Nevertheless, a comparison of statements in the Old English laws with those regarding women in other types of contemporary documentary evidence and in literature reveals a fundamental consistency in the legal position of women lacking, for example, in the records of medieval Iceland. In Old English law, we can compare the strictures regarding the inheritance and remarriage of widows in Anglo-Saxon England with extant wills to see how those provisions worked in practice. One such will reflects statements in the laws regarding the extent of a widow's control over inherited property and her husband's power over her even beyond the grave.[3] Women from the aristocracy held positions of leadership and authority in the nunneries and used religious houses as places of retreat. These roles and privileges were recognized in the Old English laws. In literature the dominant roles for women usually were as saints, but their appearance in secular literature is consistent with the conditions prescribed for them in the laws. In short, there is no significant disparity between the laws and other evidence regarding the legal status of women in Anglo-Saxon England. On the other hand, we must be cautious not to expect a complete picture of women's status from the laws; these are not comprehensive documents, and they reflect changes from era to era. Yet, if we look for clusters of related ideas supported by patterns of language, there is much to be learned from a close examination of the Old English laws affecting women. Our purpose in this essay is to examine the laws as texts, rather than as historical materials, for whatever they can add to our understanding of the lives of women before the Conquest.

This approach requires explanation. The Old English laws are unique vernacular texts composed over the course of five centuries beginning with the reigns of the first Christian kings of Kent (ca. 604). Many of the legal codes have royal authority, but a smaller number are not associated with a specific ruler and seem to address particular circumstances, for example, relationships between the English and Welsh peoples living in the mountainous border regions between the two countries. Both types of written laws survive primarily in compilations made at major ecclesiastical centers in England from the ninth through the twelfth centuries. The collections are not arranged historically and give evidence of having been compiled for specific purposes[4]—that is, the manuscript contexts of the laws imply that they were regarded as texts to be used as sources for newer legislation and related instructional purposes, rather than as static records of the past. Although individual codes remain unchanged through successive recopyings, the order and arrangement of the materials varies substantially in the surviving collections. Thus the laws differ significantly from other prose records such as the *Anglo-Saxon Chronicle,* which maintained a standard chronological format no matter where it appeared.

In one major respect the laws resemble the *Chronicle,* however, and that is in their use of formulaic language. The statements in the laws follow certain syntactical patterns, as do entries in the *Chronicle,* and show vocabulary preferences consistently from the earliest to the latest codes.[5] Thus the laws must be viewed as written texts, conforming to a tradition probably established and maintained by the ecclesiastical foundations at which they were copied and often composed (as is the case with the *Chronicle*), but separate from the oral folk-law that actually operated in the courts. As Patrick Wormald and others have shown, there is no evidence that the written laws as we know them were consulted during judicial proceedings.[6] In only one instance that survives are instructions provided for circulation of the code, a situation that could suggest these directions were the exception rather than the rule, and therefore that the written law had relatively little impact on judicial procedure.[7] Judges were encouraged to be fair, to judge correctly and impartially by learning as much as they could about the "good old law," but this was the law as it existed in the collective memory of the people rather than in a written compilation. For, as M. T.

Clanchy has shown, law courts in illiterate communities draw on the living legal sense of the people, and the law is learned by hearing cases and recalling precedent.[8]

Why, then, did certain kings issue codes of law which came to be collected and recorded? They seem to have begun to do so following the example of their contemporaries on the Continent, particularly the Frankish kings whose laws foreshadow the early royal codes from England. Frankish influence betrays itself in the organization, and even the language, of the Kentish and Ælfredian codes.[9] It seems that successive English rulers wanted to reaffirm the "good old law" and to restore certain provisions that had been lost or neglected, hence they issued proclamations that were collected, and often rewritten, by the Church. The example of Ælfred is instructive here. The preface to his code states clearly that he does not intend to issue his own laws, which have yet to stand the test of time, but to compile previous legislation that reflected the custom of the people.[10]

With the help of Bede, the English laws became closely tied to the history of Christianity in England. The Christian kings of Kent were the first law-givers, and by the time of Ælfred the link to Mosaic law emerged as justification for that king's issuance of the first comprehensive royal code.[11] Secular and ecclesiastical laws operated jointly, to the point that the Church administered ordeals to determine guilt or innocence and played a role in the courts. Under these circumstances, it clearly was in the Church's interest to maintain a record of written legislation, especially since it had the resources to do so. If there was a royal secretariat engaged in recording legislation, no evidence of this function has survived.[12] To the contrary, the fact that the major collections of the laws were copied at ecclesiastical centers in the seat of government or very near it (Winchester, Worcester, York, London, Canterbury, Rochester) suggests that the Church may have assumed this function from the beginning.

From this sketchy overview of the genesis of the Old English laws, some observations emerge that hold particular significance for those who hope to learn more about the status of women in Anglo-Saxon England. We must begin by understanding that the Church is the intermediary for our materials. Its view of women controlled the statements in the laws, and in the later period Archbishop Wulfstan performed the actual drafting and recording.[13] Second, the written laws represent only a fraction of the laws affecting women, and in some cases they may have applied to women in a restricted geographical area at a specific point in time.[14] The extent to which a given code was operative thus will always be in doubt, as will the unwritten customary laws affecting women. Third, it is often difficult to tell whether men and women—or only men—were affected by the majority of the laws that survive. The pronoun references can be ambiguous, sometimes meaning all persons collectively and other times referring to men only.[15] Since the unique features of women's lives are potentially the most interesting, the present study will consider only those laws which explicitly refer to women.

These are the caveats. On the other hand, the laws are a rich source of information about women—their occupations, comparative status, rights in marriage, and criminal activities—to be placed alongside literary as well as documentary accounts of the activities of women. They help to fill out the picture of the Anglo-

Saxon female as long as we remember to use them as texts instead of historical facts. Just as we can learn about the "peace-weaving" functions of noble women in marriage alliances from reading *Beowulf* and about the power widows could exercise over their property from reading narrative accounts in the Old English charters, so we can accumulate certain clusters of information from examining the laws as a group of related texts within the larger body of Old English literature.

To begin, women appear in many of the royal codes but very few of the anonymous codes. The laws of Æthelberht, Ælfred-Ine, and Cnut contain the greatest number of references to women, which is not surprising since each of these codes attempts comprehensiveness—that is, each covers a large number of crimes, secular and ecclesiastic, and contains lists of punishments. From the time of Æthelberht, the first Christian king of Kent and the earliest law-giver on record in England, laws mentioning women reflect certain concerns. These statements address mainly sexual crimes and women's marital or religious state, and they are often subclassified according to the woman's social status or that of her partner. It appears that a truly comprehensive code traditionally would cover matters specifically affecting females, but that shorter legal codes, often written for a particular purpose, might not mention women. Thus, women normally received notice in the laws when the range of society was being addressed, but their presence in proportion to the whole is roughly the same as it is elsewhere in Old English literature—relatively slight.

Nowhere else in the records of Anglo-Saxon society, however, does there appear a broader cross-section of classes and occupations of women than in the laws. Although we would like to know more about the work performed by women, they seem to have had major responsibilities for dairying (including cheesemaking), grinding, and general work as serving maids.[16] They also served as nursemaids to children.[17] Wives, on the other hand, kept the keys of the household and therefore were culpable if goods disappeared or if contraband were found in one of the areas under their control.[18] Other female occupations addressed in the laws include nuns, abbesses, and, perhaps, prostitutes, depending upon how one translates *horcwene*. The latter are often connected to witches and wizards in codes forbidding their activities, which could imply that all three were remunerative. The gender of witches is never stated in the laws, but elsewhere in Old English literature they are female.[19]

Perhaps the most telling characteristic of these occupations is that they imply male counterparts—that is, the laws affecting women as they function in these groups usually include male referents or occur in the context of a list of male occupations. Phrases such as *abbod oððe abbodesse* 'abbot and abbess' occur, along with statements such as the following:

> *Ine* 63: Gif gesiðcund mon fare, þonne mot he habban his gerefan mid him 7 his smið 7 his cildfestran.
>
> (If a nobleman moves his residence he may take with him his reeve, his smith, and his children's nurse.)
>
> *VI Æthelred* 2: . . . 7 huruþinga Godes þeowas—biscpas 7 abbodas, munecas 7 mynecena, canonicas 7 nunnan—to rihte gecyrran 7 regollice libban 7 for eall Cristen folc þingian georne.

(and most all of the servants of God—bishops and abbots, monks and nuns, canons and women under religious vows—shall revert to a proper discharge of their duties and live according to their rule, and earnestly intercede for all Christian people.)

VI *Æthelred* 7: 7 gif wiccan oððe wigeleras, scincræftcan oððe horcwenan, morð-wyrhtan oððe mansworan ahwar on earde wurðan agytene. . . .

(And if [witches] or sorcerers, magicians or prostitutes, those who secretly compass death or perjurers be met with anywhere in the land. . . .)

The latter two examples, written by Wulfstan, are repeated in later codes he drafted, I *Cnut* 6a and II *Cnut* 4a. Certain of his pairings are formulaic in Old English literature, especially *munecas* 7 *mynecena,* but he expands on this tendency to link male and female counterparts by grouping them in lists. Except when a woman's occupation forms part of her legal status, for instance, the serving maid of a reeve as opposed to the serving maid of a lord, she is usually defined by males in related occupations.

But a woman's legal status and worth also were dependent in many cases on those of a male. In Æthelberht's code (14 and 16) a man's fine for lying with a serving maid changes according to the status of her owner, be he a nobleman or a commoner. This principle appears again in *Ælfred-Ine* 10, where the fine depends on the *wergeld,* or worth in monetary terms, of her wronged husband. If the woman is single, however, compensation is to be proportionate to her own *wergeld* (11.5), and compensation is doubled if she is a nun (18). These points are not addressed in such detail in the later codes, though the underlying philosophy seems to be the same. *II Cnut* 50.1 indicates that it is wrong for a pious man to have sexual intercourse with an unmarried woman but much worse if the woman is the wife of another man or has taken religious vows. Although the actual *wergeld* of a woman depended upon the class into which she was born, compensation for crimes committed against or with her usually was determined by another man's interest in the matter, if another were involved.

Women appear in the laws predominantly as wives, widows, and nuns, though maidens, too, receive some notice. Their virginity, or lack of it, determines the type of protection they receive under the law. All but the last of these were legally recognized states that separated women from the control of their own families and enabled them to act independently to a degree—that is, the written laws suggest that women were able to make certain decisions concerning their lives and were not fully ruled by men, their own families, or the religious establishment. Although there is an element of buying (and selling) implied in the laws concerning marriage, women seem to have had some voice in the process. *II Cnut* 74 states this point directly, but it is implied even in the earliest Kentish codes. In *Æthelberht* 31 we find the following statement:

Gif friman wið fries mannes wif geligeþ, his wergelde abicge, 7 oðer wif his agenum scætte begete 7 ðæm oðrum æt ham gebrenge.

(If one freeman lies with the wife of another freeman, he shall pay his [or her] wergeld, and procure a second wife with his own money, and bring her [at his expense] to the other man's home.)

Although to a twentieth-century reader this may sound like an arrangement in which the women had no choice, the language used suggests otherwise. The verb *begete<begitan* occurs elsewhere in Old English literature in the sense of obtaining a wife, and it implies the process of doing so rather than a simple financial transaction.[20] Although money and property certainly were involved, there is nothing in the phrase to indicate that the process could take place without the woman's acquiescence. Rather, the emphasis in *Æthelberht* 31 is on the wrongdoer's responsibility to cover all expenses involved in a new marriage if the parties are willing. Another, anonymous law concerning the betrothal of women contained in two twelfth-century manuscript collections of laws states forcefully that women must agree to their marriage arrangements.[21] Its contents have been used to argue for a late date of composition, which may be correct given the statement on the topic in *II Cnut*. But, with what we now know about the genesis and preservation of the laws, it is safer to say that the issue of the female's assent to marriage negotiations was of greater interest later in the Anglo-Saxon period than it had been at an earlier time.

Marriage certainly was a business contract. Two additional statements in the early laws command our attention:

Æthelberht 77: Gif mon mægþ gebigeð, ceapi geceapod sy, gif hit unfacne is.
   1. Gif hit þonne facne is, eft þær æt ham gebrenge, 7 him man his scæt agefe.

(If a man buys a maiden, the bargain shall stand, if there is no dishonesty. If, however, there is dishonesty, she shall be taken back to her home, and the money shall be returned to him.)

Ine 31: Gif mon wif gebyccge, 7 sio gyft forð ne cume, agife þæt feoh 7 forgielde 7 gebete þam byrgean, swa his borgbryce sie.

(If anyone buys a wife and the marriage does not take place, he shall return the bridal price and pay as much again, and he shall compensate the trustee of the marriage according to the amount he is entitled to for infraction of his surety.)

In the *Maxims,* the verb *gebycgan* is used to advise a king about obtaining a queen and, more generally, the word implies the acquisition of a much-desired object, such as spiritual salvation. These meanings distinguish *gebycgan* in its varying forms from *bycgan,* which consistently means "purchase."[22] *Gebycgan* differs, too, from *begitan* quoted above, where the marriage transaction alone was implied. Despite the fact that marriage constituted a business agreement, the language suggests a matter of high importance in the lives of the individuals involved. Other laws amplify and clarify these early statements, but their point of view is remarkably consistent.

Further statements in the laws concerning marriage support the premise that women had a voice in the transaction, to the extent that they could leave if they wished. According to Æthelberht's code, the wife's share of the property under these circumstances depended upon whether she took the children with her or left them with her husband. In *VI Æthelred* 26, widows are instructed to remain single for a year, after which they may marry if they wish: *ceose syþþan þæt heo sylf wille.* Throughout the laws, wives who act independently and refuse to participate in their husbands' illegal activities avoid punishment and indeed are rewarded with their share of the property in the marriage (*Wihtred* 12; *Ine* 7, 57; *VI Æthelstan* 1). An interesting corollary to this principle occurs in *II Cnut* 76.1, where the wife is required to allow her husband to bring whatever he wants into their cottage, but if he brings stolen goods, she will not be charged with complicity unless they are discovered in a place under her lock and key.

Concubinage seems to have been practiced from pre-Christian times in England, and is condemned legally first by Wihtred, one of the Kentish kings.[23] The women in question are never mentioned, however; the laws address only those men who participate in illicit unions under threat of excommunication. Certain laws concerning abduction, to be discussed below, may relate to women who willingly participate in such a union, and hence have no survivor's benefits for themselves or their children, unless the latter are claimed by the father.

Widows and women under religious vows (nuns, anchoresses, canonesses, and so forth) receive the greatest protection afforded to women under the laws. As stated in *VI Æthelred* 39,

> 7 gif hwa nunnan gewemme oþþe wydewan nydnæme, gebete þæt deope for Gode 7 for worolde.

> (And if anyone injures a nun or does violence to a widow, he shall make amends to the utmost of his ability both towards church and state.)

In the much earlier Kentish laws, the special status of widows is made clear by the large compensation to be paid for violating their *mund*, or right of protection (*Æthelberht* 75, 76). Ælfred's code (8, 18) assigns significantly higher penalties to those who seize nuns against their wishes and notes that the compensation for nuns should be at least double that for laywomen. Widows have inheritance rights as well as maintenance for minor children until they reach maturity (*Ine* 38, *II Cnut* 70.1, 72). In the later codes written by Archbishop Wulfstan, they are enjoined against remarrying for a year after the deaths of their husbands, nor are they to enter a convent too hastily. With their inherited property, widows were attractive marriage prospects, and one suspects that the purpose of the paternalistic legal statements, authored by Wulfstan for Æthelred and Cnut in the eleventh century, was to strengthen the traditional protection afforded these women in accordance with the Church's teaching. He may, too, have aimed to lay the groundwork for instituting the Church in the role of guardian for these women.[24] In the same codes, he exhorts nuns and other members of religious orders to embrace chastity.

The problem for these and other groups of women comes when they are abducted, at which point they seem to lose all rights and be treated as if they are guilty:

> *Æthelberht* 82: Gif man mægþmon nede genimeþ: ðam agende L scillinga 7 eft æt þam agende sinne willan ætgebicge.

> (If a man forcibly carries off a maiden, [he shall pay] 50 shillings to her owner, and afterwards buy from the owner his consent.)

There is an additional fine if she is already betrothed, and part of the compensation must be paid to the king if she is returned.

Ælfred 8: Gif hwa nunnan of mynstere ut alæde butan kyninges lefnesse oððe biscepes, geselle hundtwelftig scill', healf cyninge, healf biscepe 7 þære cirican hlaforde, ðe ðone munuc age.

(If anyone takes a nun from a nunnery without the permission of the king or bishop, he shall pay 120 shillings, half to the king, and half to the bishop and the lord of the church, under whose charge the nun is.)

The statement goes on to say that if the nun lives longer than her abductor, neither she nor any child she may have will inherit property, the presumption being that she has chosen to remain in an illegal relationship, possibly concubinage. And if her child is slain, the portion of the *wergeld* due her family will be paid to the king, though the father's family will receive its share. In *Ælfred* 11, compensation is indicated for a young woman "of the commons" when she is assaulted by a man. If she is raped, and then accused of having previously engaged in sex with a man, she must clear herself with an oath of sixty hides of land, or lose half the compensation due to her. *II Cnut* 73 states that even if a widow is compelled by force to marry before a year has elapsed since her husband's death, she will lose her possessions unless she returns home and forsakes the new husband forever. Thus the laws convey the message that a woman is somehow responsible for her abduction unless she can escape and prove her innocence. Compensation for such an offense is paid to the king and her male guardian, but rarely to the female herself. Although the specific case addressed changes from code to code, the underlying philosophy remains constant.

Aside from potential complicity in unlawful acts committed by their husbands, women are mentioned as participants in relatively few crimes: thievery, incest, adultery, prostitution, and sorcery. Harsh penalties fall on women or men who steal from their masters. The fullest statement of these is in the Latin code, *IV Æthelstan* 6. Illicit or incestuous unions are forbidden throughout the laws, with equal punishments meted out to men and women for these crimes. In the matter of fornication and adultery, however, it appears that women paid more dearly, with mutilation rather than money, perhaps because they often held few possessions in their own right (*II Cnut* 53). Again and again, men are instructed to pay for raping a woman or lying with another man's wife and are told not to marry nuns on pain of losing the right to a Christian burial or otherwise incurring spiritual harm. According to *Ælfred* 32, only if a slave rapes a slave is mutilation the punishment, presumably because all the slave has to lose are his body parts. Betrothed women who commit fornication must pay the surety of the marriage to their intended spouses, but nowhere in the laws does a table of compensation appear for the wife who commits adultery. This implies that the statement in *II Cnut* may have been the traditional punishment, which came to be written down in a late, comprehensive code authored by Archbishop Wulfstan, a man ready to condemn all aspects of unchristian behavior.[25]

The ecclesiastical flavor of the royal codes culminates in Wulfstan's work, which stresses the importance of knowing one's role and status and living within it. Women are not major figures anywhere in the laws, and where they appear their roles are often the traditional ones for a Christianized, male-dominated society. Wulfstan writes in stronger language than his predecessors, but his legal compendia build on their earlier codes. His most original contribution lies in his vocabulary. The term *horcwene* for prostitute is unique to Wulfstan, and he, more than other writers, uses *æwbrycan* in its narrow sense of "rape" rather than general law-breaking.[26]

The surprise is that women seem to have had some freedom in marrying and in determining the course of their lives after marriage. Women always remained under the protection of male guardians, however, so their independence was limited, at best. As was the case for men, fines for offenses against women were based on their social status, but certain principles underlying the determination of a crime seem to remain constant regardless of the victim's social class. A rape was to be punished, for instance, no matter the class of the two parties involved. New statements do appear in the later law codes, an example being the declaration that a widow must wait one year to remarry. It is unwise, however, to read these as necessarily reflecting new developments, especially since many of them involve restating long-held positions of the Church.

Thus when we use the Old English laws to learn more about the condition of Anglo-Saxon women, we should interpret them as a group of related texts conveying in their entirety a portrait, at times inconsistent, of a distant but compelling group of women. From the laws we receive hints about the kinds of situations involving women conveyed elsewhere in Old English literature. In *The Wife's Lament*, for instance, relatives seem to have interfered in the marriage and to be holding the wife away from her spouse while she sings her song of sorrow. The husband has committed a crime, however, and she stands to be implicated if she had prior knowledge of the planned murder.[27] In *Beowulf* we find marriage used, not always successfully, as a vehicle to mend alliances and effect political stability. The women in the poem seem not to have married against their will, but they are aware that their union serves a larger purpose than their own happiness or security. The point here is that any one source of information about the lives of women in Anglo-Saxon England is incomplete and should not be interpreted as fact, whether it be quasi-historical material or imaginative literature. This is especially true of the Old English laws, which give the appearance of authoritative documents but in fact are as much the product of the Church as they are of the State. Although the laws do not contradict what we know about the legal status of Anglo-Saxon women from other written sources, and indeed they are the most substantial body of information we have on the subject of women's lives, they are most useful when examined in depth for the underlying concepts they convey about the legal status of women from the period.

NOTES

1. The most responsible use of the laws to understand the status of women in the Anglo-Saxon period is found in Christine Fell with Cecily Clark and Elizabeth Williams, *Women in Anglo-Saxon England and the Impact of 1066* (Bloomington: Indiana University Press, 1984). The standard edition of the Old English laws is by Felix Liebermann, *Die Gesetze der Angelsachsen*, 3 vols. (Halle: Max Niemeyer, 1903–16; rpt. 1960). For convenience of reference, all quotations from the laws (including translations) in this essay are drawn from F. L. Attenborough, *The Laws of the Earliest English Kings* (Cambridge: Cambridge University Press, 1922) and A. J. Robertson, *The Laws of the Kings of England from Edmund .*

Henry I (Cambridge: Cambridge University Press, 1925). Both of these editors take their Old English texts from Liebermann.

2. One recent example is the study by Anne L. Klinck, "Anglo-Saxon Women and the Law," *Journal of Medieval History* 8 (1982): 107–21.

3. Old English will of Ealdorman Ælfred (871–888) trans. in Dorothy Whitelock, ed., *English Historical Documents c. 500–1042*, 2nd ed. (London: Eyre Methuen, 1979), pp. 537–39.

4. Mary P. Richards, "The Manuscript Contexts of the Old English Laws: Tradition and Innovation," in *Studies in Earlier Old English Prose*, ed. Paul E. Szarmach (Albany, N.Y.: State University of New York Press, 1986), pp. 171–92.

5. For specific examples of these features, see Mary P. Richards, "Elements of a Written Standard in the Old English Laws," in *Standardizing English: Essays in the History of Language Change in Honor of John Hurt Fisher*, ed. Joseph B. Trahern, Jr., Tennessee Studies in English, vol. 31 (1989), pp. 1–22.

6. Patrick Wormald, "Æthelred the Lawmaker," in *Ethelred the Unready: Papers from the Millenary Conference*, ed. David Hill, B A R British Series 59 (1978): 47–80.

7. See the discussion of *IV Edgar* by Hanna Vollrath in "Gesetzgebung und Schriftlichkeit—Das Beispiel der Angelsachsischen Gesetze," *Historisches Jahrbuch* 99 (1979): 46–47.

8. M. T. Clanchy, "Remembering the Past and the Good Old Law," *History* 55 (1970): 165–76.

9. J. M. Wallace-Hadrill, *Early Germanic Kingship in England and on the Continent* (Oxford: Oxford University Press, 1971), pp. 33–39; Patrick Wormald, "*Lex Scripta* and *Verbum Regis:* Legislation and Germanic Kingship, from Euric to Cnut," in *Early Medieval Kingship*, ed. P. H. Sawyer and I. N. Wood (Leeds: University of Leeds, 1977), pp. 105–38; Rosamund McKitterick, "Some Carolingian Law-Books and their Function," in *Authority and Power*, ed. Brian Tierney and Peter Lineham (Cambridge: Cambridge University Press, 1980), pp. 13–27.

10. Liebermann, *Die Gesetze* 1:46.

11. Ibid., 1:26–42.

12. Simon Keynes, however, has argued for the existence of a royal secretariat during the reign of King Æthelred in *The Diplomas of King Æthelred 'The Unready' 978–1016* (Cambridge: Cambridge University Press, 1980).

13. Doris Mary Stenton, *The English Woman in History* (London: Allen and Unwin, 1957), pp. 11–12. On Wulfstan's authorship of the laws, see three articles by Dorothy Whitelock: "Wulfstan and the so-called Laws of Edward and Guthrum," *English Historical Review* 56 (1941): 1–21; "Wulfstan and the Laws of Cnut," *English Historical Review* 63 (1948): 433–52; and "Wulfstan's Authorship of Cnut's Laws," *English Historical Review* 70 (1955): 72–85.

14. Fell, *Women in Anglo-Saxon England*, p. 56.

15. Ibid., p. 17.

16. See for example *IV Æthelred* 12 and *Æthelberht* 11, 14, 16.

17. *Ine* 63.

18. Christine E. Fell, "A *friwif locbore* revisited," *Anglo-Saxon England* 13 (1984): 157–65, and *II Cnut* 76.

19. For this and subsequent discussions of vocabulary items, I am indebted to the information found in *A Microfiche Concordance to Old English*, ed. Richard Venezky and Antonette diPaolo Healey (Newark: University of Delaware, 1980). In support of my interpretation of *wiccan*, see Marc A. Meyer, "Land Charters and the Legal Position of Anglo-Saxon Women," *The Women of England from Anglo-Saxon Times to the Present*, ed. Barbara Kanner (Hamden, Conn.: Archon Books, 1979), p. 69. For an opposing view, see Fell, *Women in Anglo-Saxon England*, p. 66.

20. See *Genesis A*, 1130 *and wif begeat* and *Orosius* 3–7.112.8 *he begeat Arues dohtor him to wife.* Commentary on *wif begietan* is found in Andreas Fischer, *Engagement, Wedding and Marriage in Old English* (Heidelberg: Carl Winter, 1986), p. 138.

21. Liebermann, *Die Gesetze* 1:442–44.

22. Fell, *Women in Anglo-Saxon England,* p. 16, discusses *bycgan* but does not distinguish it from *gebycgan.*

23. Margaret Clunies Ross, "Concubinage in Anglo-Saxon England," *Past and Present* 108 (1985): 3–34.

24. Margrit Haussner, "Entgegnung auf Th. J. Rivers: 'Widows' Rights in Anglo-Saxon Law'," *Zeitschrift für Anglistik und Amerikanistik* 33 (1985): 161–63.

25. See further Dorothy Bethurum, *The Homilies of Wulfstan* (Oxford: Oxford University Press, 1957).

26. Wulfstan uses *horcwene* formulaically in *Edward-Guthrum* 11, *VI Æthelred* 7, and *II Cnut* 4; the formula is quoted in Sermon 60 of Arthur Napier's *Wulfstan. Sammlung der ihm zugeschriebenen Homilien nebst Untersuchungen über ihre Echtheit I Text und Varianten,* Sammlung englischer Denkmälern in Britischen Ausgaben, 4 (1883; rpt. with a bibliographical supplement by Klaus Ostheeren, Dublin and Zurich: Weidmann, 1967). As Fell points out in *Women in Anglo-Saxon England,* p. 66, it is impossible to specify the meaning of *horcwene* from these contexts.

27. *Three Old English Elegies,* ed. R. F. Leslie (Manchester: Manchester University Press, 1961), p. 6.

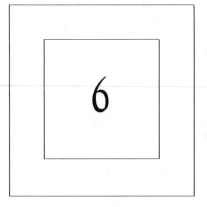

The Politics of Scarcity

Notes on the Sex Ratio in Early Scandinavia

On the subject of women, the Old Norse sources speak—notoriously—in two voices. One voice tells of "proud" and "independent" women who arrange their own betrothals, dominate their husbands, initiate divorce (and new marriages), spend extravagantly, play an aggressive role in the politics of feud, and so on. The other voice tells a different story: of women given in marriage without their consent, excluded from the judicial and legislative arenas, severely constrained in their use of what small property they are allowed, and so on. Generally speaking, the "powerful" women populate Eddic poetry and the sagas (chiefly the sagas of Icelandic families, but also those of Norwegian kings), and the "powerless" women the laws and *Sturlunga saga*.[1] With Sigurður Nordal's evaluation of the sagas as fiction,[2] and the concomitant privileging of the laws and contemporary sagas as history, the "powerful" woman was consigned to the realm of fantasy. If an earlier generation, more trustful of the Icelandic sagas as sources, construed her as the pagan original and the "powerless" woman as the degraded voice of Christianity, the generation of scholars after Sigurður Nordal has exactly reversed the priority. For them, the "powerless" woman is the real one, and the "powerful" woman a medieval fiction. Rolf Heller reads the "powerful" woman as a romantic throwback to the grand figures of heroic legend,[3] while Jenny Jochens suspects her of having been cultivated by the Church as part of a campaign to stabilize consensual, monogamous marriage in the North.[4]

Jochens's statement of the problem is worth quoting at length:

> In the literary sagas, then, women clearly exercised considerable rights and priv-
> ileges over their own lives, and their advice—for good or bad—carried weight in the
> men's world. This does not mean, to be sure, that women were equal to men. They
> enjoyed no legal or judicial responsibilities; they could not witness, nor prosecute
> directly in law. Their influence was only felt indirectly in this area by the affinal resources
> and responsibilities a man received through his wife. Women could not speak at the
> Thing assemblies, although they often accompanied their fathers and husbands for social

purposes. Once in Iceland they did not travel abroad unless they intended to settle permanently in new countries as in the case of the colonial expeditions to Greenland and Vinland. Women did not fight and were ineligible for the office of *goði,* although they may have participated in the religious cult in a minor capacity. Even without complete equality, however, the power of the Icelandic heroine of the literary sagas is so impressive and her range of activity and influence so at variance with her Continental sisters that the question of her authenticity has to be raised. Did the Icelandic heroine have a counterpart among historical women, and if so, when?[5]

Her answer is a firm no. Neither *Grágás* (the earliest legal codex) nor *Sturlunga saga* supports the saga picture of female marital consent, easy divorce, or involvement in bloodfeud, and "given the relative proximity [of *Grágás* and *Sturlunga*] to the events and society described, we can conclude that these sources, while containing some distortion, present a picture that is at least more coherent and most likely more reliable than the literary sagas."[6] The "domineering Icelandic heroine of the family sagas," she concludes, "bears little resemblance to female existence and, *hélas,* should be consigned to the realm of male fiction—a fiction stemming from the pagan period but conveniently perpetuated as a form of social control by the medieval Church."[7]

But as readers of the sagas know, the evidence does not distribute itself so neatly over the documentary categories. Both voices speak loudly within the genre of the *Íslendingasögur,* within the individual saga, and even, of course, within the scene. So Hallgerðr names her own child and grandchild against the understanding that naming is the father's prerogative (*Njáls saga*); Jófríðr (in *Gunnlaugs saga*) countermands her husband's orders to get rid of a baby daughter (a decision that is properly his); Finnbogi's wife gives away her daughter in marriage without her husband's consent (*Finnboga saga*); and Asgerðr tells her husband, when he objects to her adultery, either that he can live with it, or that she'll kick him out of bed for all time and divorce him (*Gísla saga*); and so on and on. Are these really tales that can be "unlayered"? To designate Jófríðr's act as fiction and her husband's command as historical truth (or conversely to designate her act as fact and his command as fiction) is to undo the sense of the scene. In fact, these anecdotes and hundreds like them, long and short, precisely turn on the discrepancy between what women *ought* to do and what they *really* do. Remove the discrepancy and you have no story.

R. George Thomas put his finger on the systematic nature of the split when he noted, in passing and without further purpose, that the sagas' two "voices" address and reflect two spheres. "The sagas," he wrote, "give two versions of the status of women in the Saga Age Society—theoretically and legally, a low and unimportant place, but, in practice, an honoured and effective one."[8] Such was Thomas's loyalty to Sigurður Nordal's project that he did not pursue the implications of his own distinction: namely, that what he called the sagas' "*consistent* inconsistency" (emphasis mine) on the subject of women—that is, the discrepancy between legal theory and quotidian practice—is at least as likely to stem from real historical ambiguity as from authorial ambivalence. He did not, in other words, ask the question his distinction between low-status theory and high-status practice begs: whether it might not have been the case, during the settlement period itself, that women were in fact short in official power but long in unofficial power and that this bimodality was sensed and highlighted by those who transmitted and eventually wrote the stories down.

This essay begins, then, where Thomas broke off. Its premise is that there was indeed a breach, during the settlement period, between women's de facto status and their de jure rights; that the former could and on occasion did override the latter; and that such excesses quickly became the stuff of oral tradition. The question then is what historical circumstance might reasonably give rise to such a state of affairs. The answer I shall propose has to do with the sex ratio. There is reason to suppose that the sexes were not in numerical balance in settlement Iceland, and that the imbalance might well have "split" women's status in just the way the sagas suggest.

Generally speaking, the sex ratio at birth is 105:100 (that is, 105 males to 100 females).[9] Owing to the greater mortality of males throughout the lifespan, the sex ratio in a stable and stationary society will in general be roughly even. The younger brackets will have more males, the older brackets will have more females, and the middle brackets, like the population as a whole, will show a balance. Only two factors can affect this ratio: a differential death rate and a differential migration rate. Migration from country to city can involve females disproportionately, but migration to frontiers is by definition a completely or largely male phenomenon. On the mortality side we may list prolonged and large-scale warfare, which has reduced the number of adult men at certain historical moments. Epidemic illness can also strike the sexes differentially (if only for the man-made reason that women are more likely to be evacuated from infected areas). On the other hand, death in childbirth is not as common as it is often assumed to be: "There is little, if any, evidence for the systematic, stable, and widespread elimination [statistically speaking] of females at or near the time of birth."[10] Far more decisive categories of sex-based mortality are preferential female infanticide or preferential female neglect. Preferential female infanticide refers to the outright killing or abandonment of larger numbers of girl than boy babies. Preferential female neglect (or excess female mortality) refers to a pattern whereby, despite their greater natural fitness, females die in unreasonable numbers at various stages in the life cycle owing to their being stinted "nutritionally, emotionally, and with respect to medical care."[11]

Our first intuition, on bringing these considerations to bear on settlement Iceland, is likely to be that men, not women, were in short supply there. It is after all of male death—in feud, duels, outlawry, fishing accidents, foreign travel, and soldiery abroad—that the sagas lavishly speak. But there are two other social processes of which the sagas (and other sources) also speak, albeit less loudly, that are surely more significant in the Icelandic case and that point in the other direction: infanticide and migration. This is not to say that many men did not die in the course of risky activities; it is to suggest that such a male death rate would have to be unbelievably high to offset the female shortage potential in the processes of infanticide and frontier migration. In short, infanticide and frontier migration can create a male-heavy population, regardless of high male death rates in feud and fishing; and a male-heavy population can in turn result in precisely the set of social peculiarities that the Icelandic sagas chart so eloquently.

FEMALE INFANTICIDE

There is no doubt that the Scandinavians practiced infanticide. This is clear among other things from the laws that forbid it. According to Ari's *Íslendingabók,* when the parliament decided around the year 1000 that the official religion and law of Iceland would henceforth be Christian, two heathen practices were specifically exempted: the eating of horseflesh and the exposure of children.[12]

> Þá var þat mælt í lǫgum, at allir menn skyldi kristnir vesa ok skírn taka, þeir es áðr váru óskirðir á landi hér en of barnaútburð skyldu standa en fornu lǫg ok of hrossaskjǫtsát. Skyldu menn blóta á laun, ef vildu, en varða fjǫrbaugsgarðr, ef váttum of kvæmi við. En síðarr fám vetrum vas sú heiðni af numin sem ǫnnur. (*Íslendingabók,* ch. 7)[13]

> (It was established in law, that all people should be Christian and undergo baptism, those still unbaptized in the country; but on the matter of child exposure, the old laws should stand, as on the matter of the eating of horseflesh. People might sacrifice [to the heathen gods] in secret, if they wished, but under penalty of lesser outlawry if witnesses were to observe them. But a few years later, this heathenism was abolished like the others.)

Óláfs saga Tryggvasonar in mesta expands on the matter of the exemptions. The reason, as Þorgeirr lǫgsǫgumaðr tells it, is strictly economic:

> En því at þeir menn er mest hafa í móti gengit kristniboðinu koma varla skilning á, at þat megi saman fara at fœða upp bǫrn ǫll þau er alin eru, svá fatækra manna sem auðigra, en afneita ok banna til mannfœðu þá hluti sem áðr er alþýðunni mestr styrkr í. Því skulu þeir hafa sitt mál um þat hin fornu lǫg skulu standa um barnaútburð ok hrossakjǫtsát. (vol. 2, 197)

> (But because those who have most vigorously opposed the Christian mission can scarcely imagine rearing all the children born, to poor and rich alike, given the banning and abolition as human food of those things which the public at large have as their mainstay, they shall have their way in this: that the old laws shall stand with respect to the exposure of children and the eating of horseflesh.)

Following the lead of the sagas themselves, scholars have relegated the practice of infanticide to the poor *because* they are poor; exposure was the way the poor limited the number of mouths to be fed, and horseflesh was what they ate. The exemptions were thus less an act of charity than a means of trying to contain the numbers and the poverty of the slave population at manageable levels.[14] We shall return to this assumption later; for the present, let us simply say that the passage above does not implicate the poor exclusively (the word *alþýða* in its early usage refers to people in general, not common people only) and, further, that there is reason to imagine that rich as well as poor people had an economic interest in limiting the number of daughters they raised. For the moment we need only note that whatever they were, the reasons must have been compelling, for these decidedly unchristian behaviors were allowed to continue not for just another "few" years, as Ari says, but another seventeen or so.

From references to infanticide elsewhere in Scandinavia it is clear that the Icelanders were hardly alone in the practice. "Every child born in our country shall be raised and not gotten rid of," the Swedish *Gutalagen* states, and other of the Swedish provincial laws, under the clear influence of the Church, define and set penalties for child-murder, particularly "overlying," or *oppressio infantium*. [15] Likewise the Norwegian laws, which speak repeatedly and sometimes luridly not only of exposure but also of strangling babies in bed. Even Christian law permitted the elimination of defectives, and the statutes pay close attention to just what qualifies as defective. The Swedish *Guta saga* states that babies were sacrificed to the gods: "Before that time and for a long while thereafter, people believed in groves and mounds, in temples and stave-sanctuaries, and in heathen gods. They sacrificed their sons and daughters and livestock, as well as food and drink." And the Arab traveller Al Tartushi claimed that the Danes of Hedeby threw their extra babies "into the sea." [16]

Reykdæla saga too speaks of ritual sacrifice:

> Þá gerði vetr mikinn þar eptir inn næsta, ok eigu þeir fund, Reykdœlir, at Þverá, at Ljóts hofgoða. Ok þat syndisk mǫnnum ráð á samkomunni, at heita til veðrabata. En um þat urðu menn varla ásáttir, hverju heita skyldi. Vill Ljótr því láta heita, at gefa til hofs, en bera út bǫrn ok drepa gamalmenni. En Áskatli þótti þat ómæliligt ok kvað engan hlut batna mundu við þat heit, sagðisk sjá þá hluti, at honum þótti líkara at batna myndi, ef heitit væri. Ok nú spyrja men, hvat þat væri. En hann sagði, at ráðligra var at gera skaparanum tígn í því at duga gǫmlum mǫnnum ok leggja þar fé til ok fœða upp bǫrnin. Ok svá lauk nú þessu máli, at Áskell réð, þó at margir menn mælti í móti í fyrstu. Ok ǫllum þeim, er réttsýnir váru, þótti þetta vera vel mælt. (*Reykdæla saga*, ch. 7)

> (After the second severe winter in a row, the men of Reykjadalr held a meeting at Þverá at the farm of Ljótr, the temple-chieftain. And it seemed advisable to the assembled company to offer propitiation (*heita*) for an improvement in the weather. But there was disagreement about how to go about it. Ljótr wished to propitiate by a temple offering— by exposing children and killing old people. But Áskell thought that unspeakable, declaring that no good could come of such a propitiation, and saying that he could see a better way, more likely to be an effective propitiation. And now men ask what that might be. And he said that more honor would be done to the Creator by caring for the old people and contributing money to raise the children. And the discussion ended with Áskell prevailing, even though many men spoke against it at first. And all right-thinking people thought the case had been well put.)

In reality, during periods of famine in an economy as marginal as the Scandinavian one, infants presumably stood a chance of being eliminated in some numbers. Whether such decisions were made programmatically on the part of community elders, however, remains an open question (one suspects Old Testament interference here). Nor is it entirely plausible that the gods would want in sacrifice most the people the community needed least: unproductive dependents. In the end, the *Reykdæla saga* passage tells us less about pagan religious practices than it does about the need of a Christian apologist to identify infanticide and murder of the aged as systemic evils of heathendom. Still, to the extent that it concedes the existence of infanticide and relates it to economic pressures, the passage is of some interest.

The other eight Icelandic sources are remarkably consistent and may be outlined as follows:

A. A woman gives birth and her husband announces the child is to be exposed. If he expects to be absent at the time of delivery, he gives his instructions in advance. Thus Þorsteinn says to Jófríðr (in *Gunnlaugs saga*), "Svá er háttat . . . at þú ert með barni, ok skal þat barn út bera, ef þú fœðir meybarn, en upp fœða, ef sveinn er" ("It appears . . . that you are pregnant; and that child shall be exposed if it is a girl, but brought up if it is a boy."), and so Ásbjǫrn says to Þorgerðr (in *Finnboga saga*), "Nú ætla ek til þings ríða eptir vanda, en ek veit, at þú ert með barni ok mjǫk framat. Nú hvárt sem þat er, þá skal eigi upp ala, heldr skal bera út þetta barn" ("Now I'm planning to ride to the Thing, as before, and I realize that you are pregnant and rather far along. Now, whichever it is, the child shall not be brought up, but shall be abandoned"). If the woman is unmarried, the decision to keep or kill the baby falls to her male guardian (*Harðar saga, Þorsteins þáttr uxafóts*). In only one case is the decision made by a woman—not the mother, but the lawful wife of a man who impregnated a concubine (*Vatnsdœla saga*). Wives sometimes argue with their husbands' decisions, and the husbands' decisions sometimes override their wives' wishes.

B. Someone, often the saga narrator, expresses disapproval of this practice, which is repeatedly attributed to former times and poor people. "Ok þat var þá siðvanði nǫkkur, er land var allt alheiðit, at þeir menn, er félitlir váru, en stóð ómegð mjǫk til handa, létu út bera bǫrn sín, ok þótti þó illa gǫrt ávallt" ("And at that time, when the land was still fully heathen, there was a certain custom whereby those people who were poor and had many dependents had their children exposed—though this was always disapproved of"; *Gunnlaugs Saga*). In two cases (*Gunnlaugs saga* and *Finnboga saga*), wives object that their husbands are too rich to have their children exposed.

C. The baby is not water-sprinkled or named. In *Harðar saga*, Torfi keeps the infant from being sprinkled on the expectation that it will be exposed. It is found by a man who has her sprinkled and named Þorbjörg. The baby is then brought back to Torfi, who takes her in but now dares not kill her "því at þat var morð kallat at drepa börn, frá því er þau váru vatni ausin" ("because it was called murder to kill children after they were water-sprinkled"). Life, it seems, was defined as beginning not at the moment of physical birth, but at some later moment, with the administration of an incorporating act—water sprinkling, first feeding, naming.[17] Until the infant was officially incorporated into the family, it was in spiritual limbo and could be killed with impunity.[18] Vilhelm Grønbech remarkably argued that "The act of the father is clearly just as much an act of birth as is the mother's delivery. . . . So effective a part is that of the father in making a human being of the newly born, that one might be tempted to regard the consecration as itself the real birth. What can be the value of simply being born, when the child, until adopted by the father or male kin, is after all but a thing one does not even need to kill, but can merely thrust out as not belonging to humanity at all?"[19] That we are in any case dealing with not just a Scandinavian but a Germanic practice is suggested by the eighth-century Frisian story of Liafburga, who was ordered killed at birth on account of her sex. But because Frisian custom allowed a child to be killed before but not after it had tasted "earthly food," a servant intervened and saved the baby by feeding her something, thereby forcing the parents to keep the girl and bring her up.[20] Naming/water sprinkling was supplanted by baptism in the Christian era, and the detailed prescriptions in the early Christian laws (e.g, the opening section of *Grágás*) concerning immediate and proper baptism must reflect a concern with infanticide.[21]

D. The task of getting rid of the baby is entrusted to a third party, who takes the baby to a remote spot and leaves it there, perhaps swaddled in clothes with a piece of pork in its mouth. On her husband's orders, and explicitly fearful of his temper, Þorgerðr "fekk menn til at bera út barnit ór garði út ok lögðu niðr milli steina tveggja ok ráku yfir hellu mikla ok létu flesk í munninn barninu ok gengu síðan brott" ("got men to expose the child away from the farm, and they laid it down between two stones and set a flat stone across the top and put some pork in the mouth of the child and then went away"). The widespread use of the term *bera út* (*barnaútburðr*, etc.) suggests that abandonment was the standard form of infanticide in the North (as it is among many preindustrial peoples, including the Eskimo).[22] The concern in the Christian laws of Norway with strangling and smothering probably reflects the progressive effects of Christianity on public ethics. The banning of exposure seems to have turned what was once a passive act to an active one, and by the same token what was once a father's right to a mother's crime.[23]

E. The baby is saved. In most cases it is simply discovered and rescued by good-hearted people (a childless couple in *Finnboga saga*). In *Vatnsdœla saga*, two Christian men learn of an exposure and, eager to incur God's mercy, find and save the child. "Ok sá þeir, at breitt hafði verit yfir andlitit ok kraflaði fyrir nǫsunum, ok var þá komit til bana. Þeir tóku barnit ok fluttu heim til Þóris, ok hann fœddi upp sveininn" ("And they saw that [the baby] had a cloth spread over its face and that it was clawing about the nose and was nearly dead. They took the child and brought it to Þórir's, and he raised it"). In *Harðar saga,* a man is instructed to throw a baby in the river, but his nerve fails and he leaves it at a farmyard gate instead, where it is found and saved. In *Gunnlaugs saga,* the exposure never happens, for Jófríðr defies her husband's orders and has a shepherd spirit the infant to safety. "Ok þeim ástaraugum renni ek til barns þessa, at víst eigi nenni ek, at þat sé út borit" ("And so dear to my sight is this child that I will not stand to have it exposed"). The rescued babies are then water-sprinkled and named, thus guaranteeing their safety.

As far as the procedural details are concerned, the texts are in rough agreement and we have no reason to disbelieve them.[24] Indeed, Icelandic/Scandinavian practice is in close accord with practices in exposure societies worldwide. Only John Boswell has taken exception. Boswell argues that scholars have wrongly conflated infanticide and child exposure or abandonment (*expositio*). The former may be murder, he claims, but the latter is not; it refers rather to the practice of leaving children out so they can be found—a kind of primitive adoption system. The ON *barnaútburðr,* he argues, answers the Latin *expositio* and implies nothing more than an act of removal. "*Expositio* was an *alternative* to infanticide," he writes. To leave a child out was "not without risk, but exposing a child to danger or injury was certainly not the point."[25] How Boswell could arrive at this conclusion from his reading of the saga passages mentioned in his essay is a mystery; even in them, and certainly in other passages, not to speak of the Norwegian laws, it is unambiguously clear that the term "bearing out" a child means intending to kill it. The child ordered *borne out* in

Þorsteins þáttr tjaldstæðings and *Landnámabók* asks to be spared "turf or blade" in order that he can "live among people" (remain among the living); the child *borne out* in *Þorsteins þáttr uxafóts* is found by a man who wonders why such a healthy male child should be put out to *die;* the babies of *Reykdœla saga* are to be *borne out* to propitiate the gods; the child ordered *borne out* in *Harðar saga* is to be *destroyed* (*tortíma*) by being thrown into the river; and the Norwegian laws use "bear out" as a generic term to refer to all manner of child murder, including exposure. (It is no coincidence that the term *bera út* also refers to the removal of the dead.)[26] Infanticide seems everywhere to be attended by shame, even where it is not illegal and is in fact widely practiced;[27] if babies in the North were sometimes left swaddled in discoverable places, even with food in their mouths, that surely attests to nothing so much as the need of the community, and of parents in particular, to participate in a collective fiction of salvation, possibly articulated as a religious belief. Against Boswell's remarkable claim that "few abandoned children actually died," we cite not only our documentary evidence but also archaeological evidence (see below) and the so-called dead child folk traditions, the immense spread and popularity of which give a chilling intimation of the scale of child killing, commonly through exposure, in the North.[28] Finally there is the matter of the Nordic winter; we must wonder how an open-air adoption service might have worked in temperatures that can freeze a healthy adult to death in a matter of hours.

But if the sagas can be believed on the fact and details of the practice, the *cases* themselves must be exceptional, preserved by tradition because they *are* special cases. For example, every description we have ends with the infant's being found and saved and growing up to be an important person—like Moses or Oedipus, both stories of failed infanticide. In reality, of course, the number of exposed babies who ended up as happy foundlings must have been very small, and—given the relative frequency of exposure among the poorest classes—the number of foundlings who grew up to be important persons about whom sagas were told must have been even smaller. Moreover, all but two of the saga passages would also have us believe that infanticide involved healthy male infants. In reality it was probably the sickly, the malformed (presumably few in number),[29] and above all the female who were selected for elimination.[30] Hints to this effect are found even in the stories of the healthy males. Þorsteinn uxafótr is unusually large at birth: "Þat var sveinbarn svá mikit, at menn þóttust ekki barn meira nyfætt sét hafa" ("It was a boy, so large that people thought they had never seen a larger newborn"). His grandfather opposes the idea of exposure for exactly this reason: "Hann talaði um, at sveininn skyldi eigi út bera, sagði sér svá hug um segja, at sá sveinn mundi ekki lítill fyrir sér verða, ef hann hæði lífa at halda" ("He argued that the boy should not be exposed, saying that he had the feeling that the boy would surely amount to something if he were allowed to live"). The father persists, however, and the baby is set out in the forest. The man who finds it marvels that someone should want to get rid of such a large and well-formed *male* child:

En með því at . . . hann sá, at þat var bæði glæpska ok skaði, at þar dæi svá *mannligt* barn ok líkligt til stórra afdrifa, þá tók hann þat upp ok hafði heim með sér. (*Þorsteins þáttr uxafóts;* my emphasis)

(And because . . . he realized that it was both foolish and wasteful to get rid of a child so *manly* and capable of great deeds, he picked it up and took it home with him.)

In *Finnboga saga,* the father orders the pregnant mother to have the baby exposed when it is born. This baby too is a model specimen:

Litlu síðar fæðir Þorgerðr sveinbarn. Þat var mikit ok þrifligt ok fagrt mjök. Allir lofuðu þat, þeir er sá, bæði konur ok karlar.

(A little later Þorgerðr gave birth to a baby boy. It was large and healthy and very good looking. Everyone who saw it, both women and men, praised it.)

The discovery of this fine infant so excites the finder that he rushes home with the news: "ok hefi ek ekki sét jafnfagrt barn" ("and I have never seen an equally 'fair' [well-formed] child"). The implication in both cases is that healthy, well-formed males are not the usual candidates for exposure.

In fact, healthy boys are exposed in the stories only under special circumstances and for special reasons: Þorkell krafla and Þorsteinn uxafótr because they are illegitimate; Knútr (in *Jómsvíkinga saga*) because he is the product of incest; Finnbogi because his father wishes to punish his mother for an earlier act of insubordination (she had given an older daughter in marriage without his consent); and Þorsteinn Ásgrímsson because his father wants to leave home on a Viking voyage. The ostensible motive for exposing Helga the Fair (in *Gunnlaugs saga*) is a premonitory dream on the part of her father which he takes to mean that a future daughter of his will cause the death of two men. In fact, however, when the time comes for him to pronounce on the subject of his wife's forthcoming childbirth, he offers no explanation, but says simply:

"Svá er háttat," segir hann, "at þú ert með barni, ok skal þat barn út bera, ef þú fœðir meybarn, en upp fœða, ef sveinn er."

("It appears," he says, "that you are with child. If the baby is a girl it is to be exposed, but reared if it is a boy.")

Femaleness itself is justification; no other explanation is necessary. Femaleness itself seems also to be the justification for the decision to expose Hervör (in *Hervarar saga*):

Nú er þar til at taka, at dóttir Bjartmars jarls fœddi meybarn, ok þótti flestum ráð, at út væri borit.

(Now it will be told that Earl Bjartmarr's daughter bore a baby girl, and it seemed advisable to most that it be exposed.)

The same sentiment, though not explicitly connected with infanticide, is expressed by the hero of *Áns saga bogsveigis* when he tells the father of the woman he has impregnated: "Ef þat er sveinn, þá sendið til mín . . . en sjá þú sjálfr fyrir, ef mær er" ("If the baby is a boy, send it to me . . . but if it is a girl, keep it yourself").

Especially revealing is the phrase used by Ásbjörn (in *Finnboga saga*) when he orders his pregnant wife to get rid of the child:

"Nú ætla ek til Þings ríða eptir vanda, en ek veit, at þú ert með barni ok mjök framat. Nú *hvárt sem þat er,* þá skal eigi upp ala, heldr skal bera út þetta barn" (my emphasis).

("Now I plan to ride to the Thing, as usual, and I know that you are pregnant and rather far along. Now *whichever it is,* the child shall not be brought up, but shall be exposed.")

Hvárt sem þat er "whichever it is" can in this context mean only one thing: *regardless of sex.* In other words, Ásbjörn is so angry at his wife that he wants the child killed *even if it is a boy.*[31]

Bjarnar saga Hítdœlakappa (chap. 20) contains what appears to be a joke hinging on the practice of female infanticide. In the lampoon known as *Grámagaflím,* Bjǫrn ridicules Þórðr's conception and birth. The third stanza reads:

Sveinn kom í ljós,
sagt hafði drós
auðar gildi,
at hon ala vildi;
henni þótti sá
hundbítr, þars lá,
jafnsnjallr sem geit
es í augu leit.

(The boy came to light. The mother said to her collector-of-wealth [her husband] that she wished to raise it up. As he lay there he seemed to her a dog-biter, just as bold as a she-goat, when she looked in his eyes.)

"The doting mother's decision to rear the boy," Joseph Harris writes, "must be understood as a decision *not* to expose the infant; but such a decision was properly that of the father. And by specifying the decision at all Bjorn manages to imply that Þórðr's was one of those poor families for which the possibility of exposing its infants, a practice frowned on even during the pagan period, was a real alternative; the phrasing further suggests that Þórðr was actually a marginal case—the decision could have gone either way!"[32] Harris must be right that the point here is that Þórðr was a candidate for exposure. But the aim of the insult was surely more than fiscal. It must also imply physical weakness or malformation, and it must also imply femaleness—or better yet, sexual ambiguity. Like the great majority of insult jokes in Old Norse tradition, this one too, in this reading, is ultimately sexual. Scanty though our passages are, they all point in the same direction. Healthy male babies are regarded as unusual candidates for exposure; and when sex (that is, femaleness) is used as the sole criterion for exposure, no further explanation is necessary. Sons, it is fair to conclude, were likelier to survive the first days of infancy than daughters.

The infanticidal practices of the early Scandinavians are by no means exceptional.[33] Infanticide has been practiced "on every continent and by people on every level of cultural complexity, from hunters and gatherers to high civilizations. . . . Rather than being the exception, it is the rule."[34] One ethnographic survey found evidence for infanticide in 302 of the 393 societies examined (and the remaining ones were merely those in which there was no overt evidence).[35] Where birth control methods and abortion are ineffective, as they necessarily are to a greater or lesser

degree in preindustrial economies, infanticide is a straightforward means of controlling family size.[36] A likely explanation of slow population growth during the
Pleistocene are rates of infanticide at 15 to 50 percent of livebirths, figures based on
evidence from Paleolithic burial sites and supported by analogy with modern hunter-
gatherers.[37]

Strictly speaking, infanticide has two advantages over abortion, at least in
preindustrial societies. One is that it does not endanger the life of the mother, who is
after all a more valuable member of society than a newborn. (It has been claimed that
to the extent primitive abortion affects population growth at all, it does so only by
eliminating an adult female from the childbearing pool.)[38] The other is that one can
see the child first and then decide. Some infanticides may be scheduled beforehand,
sight unseen as it were: for example, when the child is known to be illegitimate, when
spacing is important (the Japanese word for infanticide means literally "weeding" or
"thinning rice seedlings,"[39] or where it is clear in advance that the family cannot
afford another mouth to feed, no matter what sort of child it is.

Commonly, however, the decision to keep or kill is made only after birth, when
the child's salient characteristics are visible. Thus sickly or malformed children are
commonly eliminated—or one of twins, or overly dark-skinned or otherwise unac-
ceptably marked children. But postpartum selection is made above all on the basis of
sex, and in that case, females are overwhelmingly selected for elimination. "When
infanticide is practiced, female infanticide is usually the rule."[40] Very few cases of
preferential male infanticide are known,[41] whereas preferential female infanticide is
richly attested, from a great range of geographical areas and historical periods, and at
rates ranging from substantial to phenomenal. The classic formulation is Mildred
Dickeman's: "The data confirm that preferential female infanticide operates in a
variety of human socioeconomic systems as a significant contributor to the maintenance of social structures at rates ranging from 10–100% of female livebirths per
social unit."[42] The Yanamamö show a childhood sex ratio (ages 1–14) of 129:100
(140:100 in the first two years of life, and in some villages much higher), the Xavante
124, the Peruvian Cashinahua 148; Eskimo groups have shown childhood sex ratios
of up to 200; Tikopia shows a ratio of 153 in cohorts under the age of 27; the
enormously high sex ratios in nineteenth-century northern India have fallen, but even
in the 1950s and 1960s, some areas showed ratios of 115 to 166 males per 100
females; and turn-of-the-century China shows childhood sex ratios of up to 460:100
and 200:100 in the adult population.[43]

Because population growth is directly linked to the size of the childbearing
pool, female infanticide works on a general level to control a society's raw numbers.
"Whatever the reason given, the effect of female infanticide is to check population
growth, since removing female infants, potential child bearers, is more effective than
male deaths in limiting births."[44] Thus it is likely that the slow rate of population
growth during the Pleistocene rests not only on infanticide but on preferential female
infanticide. In practice, however, the parent who decides to expose a baby girl
because of her femaleness is probably not thinking on such a grand or long-term
level; he is more likely to have his own family's immediate configuration and
resources in mind.[45]

Although the stated reasons may vary, they are usually economic or apparently economic in nature. A typical explanation is the "life insurance" one offered by the Netsilik Eskimos to Knud Rasmussen (they had, in the previous generation, eliminated about a third of their newborns, nearly all of them female): sons take care of their parents in their old age, whereas daughters are of benefit only to their future husbands' families.[46] Nursing a daughter, moreover, may delay the arrival of a hoped-for son by reducing the probability of conception during the nursing period. The nature of male labor is also named as a factor; thus sons may be kept and daughters eliminated where, for example, hunting or heavy plowing is thought central. In reality, however, there are few if any societies, not even those based on hunting, in which women are not more productively valuable per capita than men;[47] the fact that female infanticide exists even in those economies in which women's labor is overtly crucial reminds us that factors other than immediately practical ones are at work.[48]

Dowry is a common consideration. In dowry systems, daughters may be eliminated as potentially too costly. Not only is a son "free," he may actually bring *in* a dowry, which will prove beneficial to his parents as well. The *locus classicus* in this connection is the wealthy and high-status caste of the Jharaja Rajput caste of northern India, which until relatively recent times killed nearly all of its female infants, thereby forcing its sons to marry into the caste below and in so doing guaranteeing the upward flow of dowry wealth.[49] Here, as in other Indian caste groups, we have a case not of poor families trying to survive, but of rich people trying to get even richer. Female infanticide, in other words, can be practiced for "oysters and champagne" as well as "bread and butter" reasons.[50] Mary Douglas, for one, has argued that the "focus of demographic inquiry," with particular respect to infanticide, "should therefore be shifted from subsistence to prestige, and to the relation between the prestige structure and the economic basis of prosperity."[51]

Female infanticide has long existed in China (it is estimated that in Imperial China, even in the modern era, a quarter to a third of the men in the peasant class could never hope to find wives); and, although Mao Tse Tung outlawed the practice, the recent policy of one child per family has given it new impetus. What is at stake now is not simply the family economy but the vaguer matter of the "family name"— a fact acknowledged by the government's recent ruling that daughters may now, for the first time, carry it on.[52] (Government billboards show happy families consisting of parents and daughter.) These cases, and others like them, remind us that economic motivations cannot be separated from, and are often synonymous with, structural misogyny.[53]

Of particular interest for our purposes is the claim of Divale and Harris that warfare and female infanticide are reciprocals and interact to produce stationary or near-stationary populations—in other words, the optimal level of growth in preindustrial societies, particularly those that stand in a delicate relation to the environment. Again, rates of population growth are determined by rates of female, not male, survivorship. A moderately healthy population (one with a life expectancy at birth of 47 years) will "become stationary if about one third of all females born never survive to reproductive age, and if each female who survives to reproductive age has on the average three live births. If the average woman in a population has four live births, about half of all the females born cannot live to reproductive age if the population is to remain stationary."[54] Male warfare, then, is not only a balancing mechanism but a balancing mechanism that is self-perpetuating. The more a society commits itself to warfare as a way of life, economically and otherwise, the more sons will be valued as future warriors and the more daughters will be regarded as worthless—and indeed, the more the society may find itself making war for purposes of capturing women to make up the shortage.[55] In the history of such societies, warfare "perpetuated and propagated itself because it was an effective method for sustaining the material and ideological restrictions on the rearing of female infants."[56] Whether or not Divale and Harris are right that male warfare and female infanticide interact to create the most primitive and effective form of population control, the fact remains that "female infanticide is common in societies where a high death rate among men would otherwise create an imbalance in adult sex ratios."[57] (This is not to say that female infanticide and warfare are coextensive; as Miller notes, the "distribution of female infanticide even within primitive societies, is far more widespread than warfare.")[58] For Mildred Dickeman,[59] the issue is reproductive politics. Where women are scarce, men are forced to compete for them; and males at the top of the social ladder, thanks to health, wealth, and control of their immediate environment, will therefore enjoy a maximum number of (known) offspring under optimal conditions. In so doing, of course, they consolidate their social rank. In either case—population control or reproductive advantage—the principle remains the same: the high sex ratio to which so many early or primitive societies seem to aspire may be costly in the short run but serves a long-run purpose.

In Europe, the documentary evidence for female infanticide begins in the classical world. A Milesian statistic from 225 B.C. indicates that the 79 families who appealed for citizenship had a total of 118 sons and 28 daughters. The named relatives of Epicteta (ca. 200 B.C.) include 25 males and 7 females. Of the 600 families documented on the second-century B.C. Delphic inscriptions, only one percent raised two daughters.[60] A fourth-century Athenian statistic indicates that 61 families had 87 sons and 44 daughters. A study of the "propertied and influential families" listed in Johannes Kirchner's *Prosopographica Attica* shows that, of "346 families, 271 had more sons than daughters and that the ratio of boys to girls is roughly five to one."[61] Tarn concludes that "throughout the whole mass of [ancient Mediterranean] inscriptions, cases of sisters [two girls in a family] can almost be numbered on one's fingers."[62] Burial and skeletal evidence, although spotty, gives much the same picture. To the extent that these proportions reflect reality, they can be accounted for by "no natural cause," as Tarn puts it.[63] Or J. C. Russell: "If there are marked divergences from the normal, some tampering with human life is to be suspected."[64] Some scholars doubt the more extreme figures and wonder whether women were not underenumerated in life and undercommemorated in death. An ingenious recent analysis of Athenian court records that attempts to correct for this bias concludes that rates of 143 to 174 (men to 100 women) obtained during the fourth century—still a high ratio, but one within the range of probability.[65] That preferential female infanticide is the chief cause of such imbalances is assumed from references to the practice. Poseidippos remarked that "even a rich man always exposes his daughter,"[66] and in classical comedy the exposure of girl babies is the subject of jokes.[67] In a papyrus letter dating from first-century B.C. Alexandria, a certain Hilario wrote in a letter to his sister: "If—good luck to you!—you bear offspring, and it is a male, let it live; if it is a female, expose it."[68] The so-called Law of Romulus obliged the Roman father to raise all his male children but only the firstborn girl, and though it is "not to be accepted at face value that every father regularly raised only one daughter," it is "nevertheless indicative of official policy and foreshadows later legislation favoring the rearing of boys over girls."[69]

Although Tacitus claimed that the Germans, unlike the Romans, did not practice infanticide,[70] the comparison is so blatantly invidious that, like others of its kind in the *Germania,* it must be doubted: "Numerum liberorum finire aut quemquam ex adgnatis necare flagitium habetur, plusque ibi boni mores valent quam alibi bonae leges" ("To limit the number of their children, to make away with any of the later children is held abominable, and good habits have more force with them than good laws elsewhere"). In fact, as David Herlihy points out, Merovingian and other sources attest to the elimination of infants, and one of Bathaldis's marks of saintliness was her opposition to the practice. "That most evil and impious institution ought to be ended, according to which many men seek to kill their offspring and not to rear them," she exhorted her husband.[71] The Frisian account of Liafburga, mentioned earlier, attests at once to the particular mechanisms of Germanic custom and to femaleness as a category of discrimination. When an old pagan woman, so vicious as to be unmentionable by name, learns that her newly born grandchild is a girl, she orders it killed. "She sent *lictores* who were to seize the then delivererd girl from the breast of the mother, and kill her, before she took milk. For this was the custom of the pagans: if they wished to kill a son or daughter, they did so before they took material food" ("qui sic erat mos Paganorum, ut si filium aut filiam necare voluissent, absque cibo terreno necarentur").[72] The child was saved by a serving woman who fed her honey, thereby forcing her parents to bring her up.

In the centuries that followed the criminalization of infanticide in A.D. 374, Christian writers inveighed against the practice of throwing babies to rivers, latrines, famine, cold, and dogs. But to judge from a rich variety of evidence—statutes, cases, statistics on foundlings and wet-nursing, tax and census records, cemetery evidence, dead-child and other infanticide folklore, and witchcraft accusations (witchcraft being "far away the most common social crime imputed to the aged women of Europe by demonologists")[73]—Church views were one thing and popular practice quite another. "A prima facie case does . . . exist for continuity," as Richard Trexler puts it.[74] That continuity extended to the preferential elimination of girl children: "In law, in the family, and in the family home, European society preferred boys. This meant more deaths for infant girls."[75]

Just how many deaths is suggested by the statistics preserved in the polyptych of Saint Germain des Prés, an immense tax census of the peasantry dating from early ninth-century France. It shows ratios as high as 4:1 on smaller, poorer farms and among larger families—patterns that point, in the eyes of the analyst, toward systematic female infanticide.[76] According to David Herlihy, Europe in general suffered a shortage of women up through the early Middle Ages. At some point during the coming centuries, before the high Middle Ages, the situation reversed itself; a body of "scattered but consistent comment . . . indicates that between the early and the later Middle Ages, women had gained a superiority over men in life expectancy which they have since retained."[77] As reasons for the change, he cites the improved economic conditions of the later Middle Ages, which affected women disproportionately; the rise of cities, in which women worked at less exhausting tasks; and under Christianity the diminution of violence toward society's weaker members, including children.[78] Although female infanticide is still attested, it is no longer so pervasive as to produce the generally high ratios of the earlier period. To an extent, the rise of women's houses both inside and outside the Church served to absorb daughters who would earlier have fallen victim to "turf or blade."[79]

In the absence of equivalent tax or census records from early Scandinavia, we are obliged, in our efforts to arrive at sex ratios, to rely on lesser forms of evidence. One of these is cemetery evidence, problematic because the sexes may have been buried differentially (so that, for example, males will be overrepresented and females underrepresented in the usual burial areas); because the sex of a burial is not always obvious (the skeletal remains and/or grave goods being insufficient and/or ambiguous); and because, more generally, it is always a question whether the found remains constitute a representative sample of the contemporary population.

The second question—how burials are sexed—is a particularly knotty one. If an older generation of archaeologists tended to sex graves on the basis of the presence of a single "gendered" object, thus presumably misidentifying sex in an unknown percentage of cases (for as osteological analysis has revealed, gendered objects do not always follow sex), more recent analysts have preferred either to rely wholely on osteological analysis or, where that is impossible, to "tighten" the analysis of grave goods. Thus Liv Helga Dommasnes, in her study of the Later Iron Age burials in Sogn, Norway (not analyzed osteologically),[80] counts twice: once on the basis of *two* gendered objects (the "certain" category), and once on the basis of just one gendered object (the "uncertain" category). Of a total of 264 graves, only 68 can be sexed certainly; of these 49 are male and 19 female. If to the certain category is added the uncertain one, the figure becomes more extreme: 162 male graves and 51 female graves ("Et gravmateriale," 99 and passim). A later study provides comparative data. In the seventh century, Sogn shows a male-to-female ratio of 8:1 and Nordland one of 2:1. In the eighth century, Sogn shows 6:1, Gloppen 20:1, and Nordland 3:1. In the ninth century, Sogn, Gloppen, and Nordland all show around 2:1, while Upper Telemark shows 8:1. In the tenth century, Sogn shows 4:1, Gloppen 6:1, Nordland 3:1, and Upper Telemark 30:1. (I have rounded all figures.) Dommasnes concludes from the greater relative frequency of women's graves in the coastal areas during the ninth century ("only two men buried for each woman" [!]) that "women's status has been high" at that time and place.[81] One is perhaps more impressed by the fact that the ratios everywhere and unremittingly favor the male and, more to the point, that even the lowest of them, 2:1, taken at face value, indicates a female mortality rate twice that of males. A ratio of 2:1, moreover, is demographically speaking not a slightly but a radically skewed sex ratio, one disruptive to traditional social and economic structures if it emerges suddenly, and one accompanied by a variety of social and economic accommodations if it has obtained for some time.

The Danish material has been conveniently summarized by Berit Jansen Sellevold, Ulla Lund Hansen, and Jørgen Balslev Jørgensen. They report (on the sole basis of osteological analysis) 62.6 percent males in the Early Roman Period, 55 percent males in the Late Roman Period, and 53.8 percent males in the Viking Period.[82] Klavs Randsborg notes with some surprise that male skeletons outnumber female ones by about 2:1 even in towns; in fortress areas the difference is even larger than that, although in agricultural areas the ratios are close to even.[83]

Sellevold et al. puzzle at some length over the "very low numbers of children observed in the Danish and other material from the Iron Age," noting that even if all the possible biasing factors (excavation practices, soil conditions, disturbances by nature or modern man, and such possible "cultural practices" as burying children separately) are corrected for, the percentages would still remain seriously low.[84] The early Danes, they conclude, must have engaged in the practice of "setting out most of the *dead* children, and only burying in proper graves those who had either a certain social status of their own or belonged to a family of a certain social status"[85] (emphasis mine).

The authors puzzle similarly over the shortage of women:

> The predominance of males over females in the present material must be attributed either to: 1) the fact that there *really* was a surplus of males (in the Early Roman period especially), or 2) that many females were buried elsewhere than in the usual cemetery (but such graves have not been found), or 3) that female bones, being more fragile, have disappeared. However, since we have a surplus of males in all three major groups [= chronological phases], the last hypothesis does not seem very tenable. Perhaps the same holds true with regard to females as seems to have been the case with children: only those of a certain social position were deemed worthy of being buried in a grave.[86]

It is odd, given the attention paid it in historical and anthropological circles during the last decade, that infanticide, more particularly preferential female infanticide, is not raised as a possible explanation for these two shortages. Indeed, insofar as it presents a single answer to two questions, it is a peculiarly economic suggestion: the exposure or drowning of infants would account for the paucity of children's skeletons, and the preferential selection of girls for that fate would account for the shortage of adult women. It seems in any case hasty to conclude that high sex ratios necessarily indicate an unrepresentative burial ground. Dommasnes similarly writes that the 4:1 sex ratio in the Iron Age graves at Sogn "supports our hypothesis that the sample is not representative of the population, since it must be assumed that the male/female ratio is constant at about 1:1."[87] The Sogn burials may well be unrepresentative, but the high sex ratios indicated in pre- and early medieval European materials, together with the frequency of high sex ratios in preindustrial societies in general, emphatically suggest that the adult male/female ratio in historical reality was *not* 1:1 but something higher than that.

As the closest thing to a census from early/medieval Scandinavia, the list of Icelandic settlers and their descendants known as *Landnámabók,* for all its shortcomings as a source, deserves some attention. Offspring, we note, are listed in two ways. One is by sexual category:

> [Ísólfr's] son var Hrani á Hranastǫðum, en dóttir Bjǫrg (328).

> ([Ísólfr's] son was Hrani á Hranastǫðum, and his daughter Bjǫrg.)

Where both sons and daughters are mentioned, sons usually outnumber daughters, sometimes by four or five—or as many as nine—to one. The majority of such "son/daughter" entries, however, mention no daughters at all, only sons:

> Lǫðmundr enn gamli á Sólheimum átti sex sonu eða fleiri. Váli hét son hans . . . Sumarliði hét annarr . . . Vémundr hét enn þriði (334).

> (Lǫðmundr enn gamli á Sólheimum had six sons or more. Váli was the name of his son . . . Sumarliði was the name of the second . . . Vémundr was the name of the third.)

And so on, through all six sons. It is not clear, in such a case, whether Lǫðmundr also had daughters who for whatever reason were not mentioned, or whether he had in fact only sons. Cases of daughters only are few and far between.

The other sort of entry simply enumerates *children (bǫrn)*:

> Hans [Arngeirr's] bǫrn váru þau Þorgils ok Oddr ok Þuríðr (285–86).

> (His [Arngeirr's] children were Þorgils and Oddr and Þuríðr.)

In such "children" entries, too, sons repeatedly outnumber daughters; the number of daughters mentioned is commonly none or one, whereas sons often run to six or more. There are some spectacular exceptions—Hrólfr rauðskeggr's three daughters and one son, Óláfr feilan Þorsteinsson's four daughters and one son, Þorsteinn rauðr's six daughters and one son, and so on—but they are very definitely departures from the rule.

Landnámabók has long been suspected of underenumerating women, and that is clearly so in the case of the "implied wives" we encounter on virtually every page in such entries as this one:

> Vémundr hét maðr, er nam Fáskrúðsfjǫrð allan ok bjó þar alla ævi; hans son var Qlmóðr (307).

> (Vémundr was the name of a man who took all of Fáskrúðsfjǫrðr and lived there his whole life; his son was Qlmóðr.)

It may be, however, that there were better reasons for remembering daughters than wives. Especially wives of foreign or lesser birth (as a number of the implied wives must have been) were less important, genealogically speaking, to their descendants than were those wives' daughters, who after all provided the link to the founding father and so to the ancestral property. As *Landnámabók* itself makes clear, women can and do figure prominently in lineages, and it seems unlikely on the face of it that a descendant would "forget" the link, even if it were female, that took him/her back to

Ketill flatnefr. If this is so, and if infanticide was practiced preferentially on females at even the minimal rate of ten percent of livebirths, the shortage of women in the offspring lists of *Landnámabók* may be as much a function of the actual survival of females as it is of their underenumeration. So suggests Icelandic archaeology, in any event. According to Kristján Eldjárn, of the 126 sexable prechristian burials (of a total of 246), 78 are male and 48 female—a ratio of about 170:100.[88]

The argument so far can be summed up as follows.

1. The early Scandinavians are known to have practiced infanticide, and the wording of the saga passages indicates firmly that girls were likelier candidates than boys. Again, this accords with the summary claim that "when infanticide is practiced, female infanticide is the rule." 2. The shortage of female skeletons from early Scandinavia accords with the further claim that where preferential female infanticide is practiced, it is practiced at rates ranging from 10 to 100 percent of female livebirths. 3. The possibility of a shortage of women in Scandinavia accords with the presumed shortage of women in early medieval Europe in general. The European ratios are attributed variously to preferential female infanticide and excess female mortality in all age brackets (again, owing to the stinting of quality food, medical care, and the like). We can assume that whatever pressures produced the high ratios on the Continent would have operated even more harshly on the northern periphery. Viking Scandinavia, we conclude, was very probably male heavy—if not in every district, then overall.

The next question is one of extent: was the shortage of women during the Viking Age within the normal (that is, traditional) range of variation, or was it unusually large? This far, needless to say, the cemetery evidence does not reliably take us, and we are obliged, as all speculators on the causes of the Viking Age are obliged, to turn to the dreamier witness of historical circumstances. The chief of these circumstances, of course, is the apparent fact that the spillage of people out of the North from the eighth to the tenth centuries was by and large a spillage of males—a bachelor movement, it has been called. Just how large that spillage was, and what its aims were, remain matters of debate. Against the case of Peter Sawyer that the numbers were few and the activities chiefly peaceful (settling, trading), Patrick Wormald has recently tried to revive the specter of large, violent, and rootless warbands that ravaged Europe in much the way the annals and chronicles claim.[89] This is not the place to rehearse the arguments; our point is rather to ask the obvious, but seldom asked, question: what about the women? Are we really to believe—as the assumption of a roughly even sex ratio requires us to believe—that for every Scandinavian male off raiding, trading, or soldiering there was a lone woman back in Scandinavia? If that is so, and if the "rootless warbands" of which Wormald speaks numbered in fact in the thousands or even tens of thousands, we are led to the remarkable conclusion—since at any given moment more than one warband might be active— that the quotidian economy of at least certain parts of Scandinavia was for all practical purposes in the hands of women. This is unlikely on the face of it, nor does it square with the oversupply of male skeletons in Scandinavian burial finds—an oversupply all the more impressive in light of the fact that a fair percentage of the travelling males presumably did not come home to die.

Nor does the oversupply of male skeletons square with the apparent fact that one of the things the Vikings took for themselves in their foreign travels was women.[90] This we glimpse both in the Norse documents and in such foreign notices as the entry for the year 821 in the *Annals of Ulster,* stating that the Vikings plundered north of Dublin, taking a "great prey of women therefrom,"[91] or various entries in other Irish annals referring to the seizure of women, or the entry in *The Anglo-Saxon Chronicle*[92] mentioning that in expectation of a Scandinavian attack, the English locked away their ships, property, and women. Did the Scandinavians sell their female captives abroad, or did they take them home as slaves, concubines, or wives? If they took them home, did the imported women displace or coexist with Scandinavian women? Again, neither displacement nor coexistence seems likely on the face of it; if every travelling male had a female opposite number back in Scandinavia, the influx of yet more women would surely have placed a grave strain on any but the wealthiest households. As for those men who went abroad not as pirates but as settlers in new areas, they seem in some cases to have brought women with them,[93] but in other cases, to judge from the sagas of Orkney and the Faroes and even *Landnámabók,* they took foreign wives.[94] Again, are we to suppose, contrary to the cemetery evidence, that the taking of an English wife created a Norwegian spinster?

It is not impossible that widows, spinsters, and abandoned wives made up the bulk of the adult population in the coastal areas of Scandinavia; that local economies and social structures adjusted, in a relatively short period of time, to accommodate that imbalance; and that the bones of all these "extra" women have for whatever reason simply not come to light. But common sense and the witness of comparative evidence suggest otherwise. A far more efficient and realistic explanation for the oversupply of Scandinavian males both dead in cemeteries and on the loose in Viking Age Europe is simply that there were, relatively speaking, too many—perhaps far too many—of them. This is emphatically not to suggest that the Viking Age came about because men went out looking for women (although they appear on occasion to have found them); it is to suggest that a shortage of women at home may have contributed, in much the same way that primogeniture has been claimed to contribute, to the alienation of younger or "extra" sons from the social structure and native economy.

The presuppositions of this claim are (1) that the sex ratio rose, perhaps sharply, at roughly the time the Viking Age began, and (2) that it remained unusually high for the better part of the era. As it turns out, the first presupposition accords well with the standard, if sometimes maligned, overpopulation hypothesis of Johannes Steenstrup.[95] Thanks to polygyny, Steenstrup argued, Scandinavia experienced a population boom just before the Viking Age. It is when the burgeoning numbers began to strain the available resources that the exodus began. This moment would also, of course, be an optimum one for high rates of female infanticide. Particularly if the weather turned bad while the resources were bearing a maximum population load, families would surely have responded by rearing fewer girls.[96]

But surely, it may be objected, the practice of polygyny (on which Steenstrup's overpopulation hypothesis is based) is inconsistent with the claim of a high sex ratio? On the contrary, polygyny (and/or concubinage) routinely flourishes in such a context: the scarcer women are, the more potent a status symbol is the ownership of more than one. The apparently paradoxical fact that the practice of polygyny where women are scarce to begin with worsens the mating situation for men further down the social ladder, thereby intensifying the sex ratio difference, is much discussed.[97] Divale and Harris's assumption is that the longer-range interests of population control in a primitive society must override the interests of immediate social harmony.[98] Dickeman takes a different tack. She too notices the frequency of the combination female infanticide/polygyny (concubinage) and concludes that exacerbation must be the whole point; the more that males are forced to compete to reproduce, the more the males at the top will deserve (reproductively speaking) their success. This is not to say that the overpopulation thesis is wrong; it is to suggest that polygyny (the extent of which in early Scandinavia is less than clear) was in either case not a contributing factor. We repeat that, generally speaking, all that is required to bring about a rise in population is that the group in question rear more than two-thirds of the females born into it. If Scandinavia enjoyed a period of prosperity in the era preceding the Viking Age, thanks to good weather or to economic development, families might well have achieved those levels.

But if polygyny is not required to explain overpopulation, neither is overpopulation required (though it may have pushed the process along) to explain the detachment of males from the native economy. Indeed, no climactic event at all is required to explain that detachment if we extend to Scandinavia the generality that "female infanticide is common in societies where a high death rate among men would otherwise create an imbalance in sex ratios" (long-term absenteeism would presumably have the same effect) and the further generality that female infanticide, male warfare/absenteeism, and polygyny/concubinage fuel each other in an escalating syndrome—whether in the service of reproductive stratification or population control or both. We need only posit that for whatever straightforward material reasons— "sheer and ugly greed," as Kendrick put it[99]—some Scandinavian males went abroad as raiders and traders and were successful in their ventures and that their success encouraged parents to prefer sons to daughters. Then: the more sons were preferred to daughters, the greater the shortage of females in the adult population; the greater the shortage of females in the adult population, the greater the destabilization of traditional socioeconomic structures; the greater that destabilization, the more men were thrown onto the new economy of foreign ventures of one sort or another; the more men were thrown onto that new economy, the more they disappeared from the old one; the more they disappeared, the more likely daughters were to be regarded as supernumerary and not raised; and so on. (Dickeman would in addition stress the institutionalization of male competition for women.) It is not so much the precise steps in this chain that are at issue—they may be subtracted, supplemented, or modified—as it is the principle of a vicious circle: when male attrition rates are high, female infanticide is used *not just to correct but to overcorrect* for that attrition, with the result that males are driven in even greater numbers into the activities that bring about their attrition to begin with.

We can sum up our proposition in the form of a question. Is it possible that a generative context for the male movements of the Viking Age was a serious shortage of women—a shortage brought about by unusually high rates of female infanticide (and possibly preferential female neglect) triggered in the first instance by a population squeeze or later by a rise in male mortality and absenteeism, but once begun, perpetuated to compensate or overcompensate for attrition? This line of reasoning is the early medieval equivalent of the argument Dickeman makes about the high sex ratios in pre-war Japan: "Once preexisting governmental ideology found support in industrialization and overseas expansion, the largely masculine excess [that is, the high sex ratio resulting from high rates of female infanticide] that was preserved in response provided the labor and military force for an episode in modern imperialism." [100]

I have by now strayed deep into what are for me the alien territories of historical demography and Viking Age history and archaeology. My conviction, admittedly impressionistic, is that the hypothesis of a sex-ratio imbalance makes good sense of what we know of the Viking Age. It may well be that there is Scandinavian evidence of which I am not aware that speaks against the claim. But if the preceding discussion does nothing more than remind us that theorizing about large-scale demographic events like the Viking Age cannot base itself on male activities alone, no matter how eye-catching those activities may be, but must also take into account the role of women in the economy, no matter how mundane that role may seem, its purpose will have been served.

FRONTIER MIGRATION

We turn now to Iceland and the second of the two demographic phenomena with which this essay concerns itself: frontier migration.

The commonplace that frontiers attract men disproportionately is nowhere more amply illustrated than in North America, like Iceland a *terra nova* in the first instance and after that, for a period of some 250 years, a series of further frontiers opening to the west. We tend to think of migration to the United States as a family matter, but it has in fact been a largely male matter from the beginning right up to the present. "In the initial period of colonization, both the New England colonies and Virginia had a considerable excess of males," Guttentag writes. "In New England, this amounted to about three adult males for every two women, a sex ratio of 150 [to 100]; and in Virginia, up to about 1640, there were seven males over 20 years of age for each woman, a sex ratio of 700!" [101] Likewise the frontier migration from east to west. States like Ohio, Illinois, Iowa, and Kansas show sex ratios ranging from 114 to 126 in their early censuses—this in spite of the fact these were largely agricultural settlements in which women's productive and reproductive labor was particularly valuable. Some of the "single" men had wives back east or in Europe whom they expected to bring out at a later date; others were simply bachelors. The ratios in these states remained imbalanced in favor of males even in the year 1900 (ranging from 102 to 110). The astronomical ratios of the next frontier, the far west, are well known. California in 1850 had a ratio of 1228:100 and Colorado in 1860 had one of 1659:100. These high figures reflect, of course, the selective recruitment of males in mining, but again, the western states showed an overall ratio of 150:100 even in the year 1900. It is a measure of just how male the U.S. immigration has been that the national sex ratio did not even out until the Second World War.[102]

We have, of course, no reliable information on the relative numbers of men and women involved in the migration to Iceland. References to accompanying family (e.g., "Hrollaugr went to Iceland, and had with him his wife and sons" [*Landnámabók* 317]) are few and far between; for the most part we hear only of the man and his "people" (*menn*). Nor does *Landnámabók* shed much light on the marital status of the founding fathers. Some are unambiguously married to named wives:

> Eilífr ǫrn nam land inn frá Mánaþúfu til Gǫnguskarðsár ok Laxárdal ok bjó þar; Eilífr átti Þorlaugu dóttur Sæmundar ór Hlíð (227–28).

> (Eilífr ǫrn took land in from Mánaþúfa to Gǫnguskarðsá and Laxárdalr and settled there; Eilífr was married to Þorlaug, the daughter of Sæmundr from Hlíð.)

Whether such wives were acquired before or after the migration is not clear.

The great majority of "wives," however, are the implied or invisible ones of such entries as this one:

> Geiri hét maðr norrœnn, er fyrstr bjó fyrir sunnan Mývatn á Geirastǫðum; hans son var Glúmr ok Þorkell (284).

> (Geiri was the name of a Norwegian, who first settled south of Myvatn at Geirastaðir; his sons were Glúmr and Þorkell.)

The question is why, in a culture preoccupied with lineage on both sides, so many wives should be nameless. Perhaps these passages provide the clue:

> Vilbaldr hét maðr, bróðir Áskels hnokkans [*H*: þeir váru synir Dofnaks]; hann fór af Írlandi til Íslands ok hafði skip þat, er hann kallaði Kúða, ok kom í Kúðafljótsós; hann nam Tunguland á milli Skaptár ok Holmsár ok bjó á Búlandi. Hans bǫrn váru þau Bjólan, faðir Þorsteins, ok Ǫlvir muðr ok Bjollok, er átti Áslákr aurgoði (326).

> (Vilbaldr was the name of a man, the brother of Áskell hnokkan; he went from Ireland to Iceland, with the ship he called Kúða, and arrived at Kúðafljótsóss; he took Tunguland between Skaptá and Holmsá and settled at Búland. His children were Bjólan, the father of Þorstein, and Ǫlvir muðr and Bjollok, whom Áslákr aurgoði married.)

> Hildir and Hallgeirr ok Ljót, systir þeira, váru kynjuð af Vestrlǫndum; þau fóru til Íslands ok nam land milli Fljóts ok Rangár, Eyjasveit alla upp til Þverár. Hildir bjó í Hildisey; hann var faðir Móeiðar. Hallgeirr bjó í Hallgeirsey; hans dóttir var Mábil (355).

> (Hildir and Hallgeirr and Ljót, their sister, were natives of the British Isles; they went to Iceland and took land between Fljót and Rangá, Eyjasveit all the way up to Þverár. Hildir settled in Hildisey; he was the father of Móeiðar. Hallgeirr settled in Hallgeirsey; his daughter was Mábil.)

We suggested earlier that the name of the founding father's wife is especially subject to syncope in Icelandic oral tradition. The founding father will be remembered by virtue of his status as founding father (a status often fixed in place-names), regardless of his family background, and his children will be remembered as links to the founding father, but his wife will be remembered only if her own family background is such that her descendants will want to count back *through* her. Thus Þórunn hyrna (wife of Helgi magri) is mentioned by name because she is the daughter of Ketill flatnefr; and so Rafarta Kjarvalsdóttir (wife of Eyvindr austmaðr Bjarnarson) is mentioned by name because she is the daughter of a king. The implied wives of Vilbaldr, Hildir, and Hallgeirr in the above passages are presumably Irish. But because they are not (it seems) daughters of kings, they are in Icelandic terms genealogically irrelevant and hence not worth remembering or mentioning by name. Again, the majority of founding fathers' wives in *Landnámabók* are implied and nameless; if even a quarter of them are nameless by virtue of lower social class and/or foreign birth, that would in itself suggest a shortage, perhaps a severe shortage, of "like" women in the adult population. It is in any case clear from references to children "slave born" (*prælborin*) on the mother's side that some men married down, just as it is clear from references to *named* women of foreign birth that some men married "out": the mother of Helgi magri (Rafarta) and the grandmother of Bjǫrn Hǫfða-Þórðarson (Fríðgerðr) are Irish, both daughters of kings; Melkorka (another Irish princess) is brought to Iceland as a concubine, but once there is married off to a landowner; Grélǫð was acquired by Ánn rauðfeldr in the course of harrying in Ireland (*hann herjaði á Írland ok fekk þar Gréladar dóttur Bjartmars jarls* [176]), and Auðun stoti, settler of Hraunsfjǫrðr, is married to Mýrún Maddaðardóttir Írako- nungs. Scandinavian wives of good birth, it appears, were at a premium.

Yet another immigration scenario is suggested in this passage:

> Ásbjǫrn hét maðr, son Heyjangrs-Bjarnar hersis ór Sogni; hann var son Helga Hel- gasonar, Bjarnarsonar búnu. Ásbjǫrn fór til Íslands ok dó í hafi, en Þorgerðr, kona hans, ok synir þeir kómu út ok námu allt Ingólfshǫfðahverfi á milli Kvíár ok Jǫkulsár (320).

> (Ásbjǫrn was the name of a man, the son of Heyjangr-Bjǫrn chieftain from Sogn; he was the son of Helgi Helgason, the son of Bjǫrn búna. Ásbjǫrn was on his way to Iceland but died at sea, and Þorgerðr, his wife, and their sons came on out and took all of Ingólfs- hǫfðahverfi between Kvíá and Jǫkulsá.)

The pattern of migration in two stages—first the man, then the woman (and chil- dren)—is well known from American settlement history. In the above passage it is the man who dies. But it was surely more commonly the case that, for any number of reasons, the wife failed to show—an eventuality that *Landnámabók* would have no interest in recording. In such cases, men who thought themselves married would find themselves single after all. Even in the cases of wives who did make the journey, there would be a lag time of at least a year (two or three? more?), and these lag times, staggered throughout the period of settlement, would have placed an additional strain on whatever sex ratio imbalance already existed. *Laxdœla saga* also tells of a woman (Þorgerðr) who after the death of her husband in Iceland returns to her kinspeople in Norway; if this too reflects a pattern, it is one more way that the pool of women would have been reduced.

Finally there are the men who seem to have no wives at all, neither absent nor invisible:

Sveinungr ok Kolli námu víkr þær, er við þá eru kenndar, Sveinungsvík ok Kollavík (287).

(Sveinungr and Kolli took those inlets which are known after them, Sveinungsvík and Kollavík.)

Such entries are less frequent than the "invisible wives" entries, but given the aim of *Landnámabók*—to establish the forward lineages of the original land claimants— and further given the fact that the land claim of a childless and brotherless man is likely to pass into other hands at his death, it is surprising that there are as many such notices as there are; perhaps they owe their survival to the place names they purport to explain.

The demographic picture that *Landnámabók* paints of Iceland during the settlement years is consistent, if impressionistic. Sons outnumber daughters in the genealogies; a fair number of men appear to be childless, which must in many cases mean they were wifeless; and an unknowable but potentially large number of men appear to have imported wives or married beneath them. *Grænlendinga saga* (chap. 7) states that when Þorfinnr Karlsefni mounted an expedition to Vinland with permanent settlement in mind, he gathered a company of sixty men and five women, and we must wonder whether that shipload represents the standard proportion (12 to 1). Even if we treble the number of women and reduce the number of men accordingly, the ratio is still 3 to 1. Archaeology provides the lowest ratio, but that is still 1.7 to 1. There is, in short, every reason to believe, and none to disbelieve, that Iceland suffered the demographic consequences shared by frontier societies everywhere. To correct a sex ratio imbalance takes about a century of equal treatment under stable conditions. If the Icelanders continued to eliminate more girls than boys (as infanticide cultures notoriously persist in doing even to their social peril) and if the continuing immigration continued to be disproportionately male, the imbalance would have obtained for longer than that. But it would in any case have existed in its most acute form during the Saga Age.

But what happens in a community that has, in effect, too many men in it? One of the usual concomitants of a high sex ratio we have already mentioned: institutionalized male violence, commonly in bloodfeud or warfare. Another concomitant, also mentioned earlier, is polygyny, the chief effect of which is to exacerbate the shortage of women for men further down the social scale. Other consequences of a high sex ratio are more predictable.[103] One is male competition for women, that competition often taking the form of official duels or wife theft, real or threatened. Another is male depression and suicide. Another is the emigration of males to new lands. Another is the importation of women, frequently women procured through war. Another is male homosexuality. Another is the early betrothal of girls. Another is a high incidence of adultery, despite a claimed intolerance of it. Another is a high rate of divorce, obtainable by women as well as men. Another is easy remarriage for women, leading to a pattern of multiple marriages for women—serial polyandry, in effect. (These last two—the relative ease for women in obtaining divorce in the first instance and remarrying in the second—are part and parcel of the unofficial or informal power that accrues to women by simple dint of their scarcity. Rasmussen tells of Eskimo women who went through seven or eight trial marriages before finally settling down, remarried freely when their husbands died, and enjoyed a certain sexual freedom in practice despite its official proscription.)[104] To the question of why a group continues with a practice that is so socially dysfunctional, we answer again that infanticide is almost always a decision made within the family and on the basis of custom and immediate tensions; it is *not* a decision made by the community, and it is not made on the basis of projected community needs twenty years hence (as the present patterns in China confirm). As Dickeman puts it: "In a discordant sociopolitical system, decisions regarding population limitation or growth must fall to the most constricted, local unit of cognition and the lowest level of social organization, namely the family, which must operate without benefit of any wider information flow"—even when, again, personal short-term advantage is at odds with group long-term advantage.[105]

Readers of the Icelandic sagas will of course recognize this list of social ills proceeding from high sex ratios as a veritable roster of Icelandic saga themes and situations. Consider the popularity of the triangle story in which two men want the same woman, seldom the other way around; we think first and foremost of the skald sagas here, though the theme is well represented elsewhere as well. Wife theft, real or threatened (as in *Gísla saga* and *Grettla*) is a staple of saga literature. Likewise male dueling, including dueling over women. (By the third winter in Vínland, according to *Eiríks saga rauða* [chap. 12], "quarrels broke out over the women, the unmarried men attacking the married men, with great trouble as a result.") We note too that although the sagas, as dynastic literature, concern themselves chiefly with married men of property, they also present us with numbers of wifeless men: not only *einhleypir* 'single men without fixed household, unmarried' alone or in bands of berserks or Vikings (who steal women, among other things), but also men of some importance (Hœnsa-Þórir, Þorgeirr, Þórmóðr, etc.). Consider too the number of betrothal negotiations in which (as in *Njála* and *Laxdœla*) the focus is on whether the man will succeed or fail in getting the woman and not the other way around. Then there is adultery, presented as a fact of life for both sexes; when Ásgerðr (in *Gísla saga*) is confronted by her husband on the matter of her extramarital relations with Vésteinn, she tells him to drop the subject or she'll divorce him on the spot—a threat grave enough to silence him and bring him back to bed. Divorce is, moreover, notoriously easy to obtain—for women as well as for men. ("The statistics on saga divorce suggest that women were thought to have the upper hand in this procedure: of the twelve divorces performed in the family sagas, nine are demanded by women; of the five threatened divorces, all are initiated by women."[106]) The two grandest female figures in saga literature, Guðrún and Hallgerðr, are multiple widows—a condition that seems to affect their appeal not a whit. Nor, to judge from the sagas, is female chastity the issue in early Iceland that it was on the Continent. Further: the sagas hint at the practice, particularly useful in a high sex ratio society, of leviratic marriage, whereby a man marries his brother's widow "to keep a good woman in the family" (*Gísla saga*, chap. 1; also *Egils saga*). Finally there is the institutionalized male violence that the sagas are *about*—in the form of vendetta, dueling, and piratic or mercenary ventures. These are hardly minor themes; they account, in sum, for the better part of the literature.

Although various commentators have remarked in passing on the link between scarcity and privilege, it is to my knowledge Marcia Guttentag who first formulated the principle. Her analysis rests on a distinction between structural power and dyadic power. Structural power refers to the power granted by law and custom (the right to vote, for example, or to inherit property or make laws); bound up with the traditions of society, structural power is slow to respond to changes in real conditions. Dyadic power has to do with the purchase one has in a one-on-one relationship; it is the more volatile sort of power, responding directly to social or economic changes. Structural power everywhere favors the male, whereas dyadic power favors the "individuals whose gender is in short supply; they are able to negotiate more favorable terms [for themselves] within the dyad, or two-person relationship" because they are more easily able to leave it.[107] That is, the higher the sex ratio, the greater the dyadic power of women—to the point, indeed, where it may undermine, override, or even alter structural expectations. Supply and demand, in a phrase; blackmail, in a word.

Guttentag draws much of her support for the relation between scarcity and dyadic power from the American example.[108] So oversupplied with men were the colonies that women were frequently imported. "As for women," wrote a Maryland observer in 1658, "they no sooner arrive than they are besieged with offers of matrimony." Many of these women were European servants, or other undowered poor, for whom the United States offered a chance for upward mobility. "Maid servants of good honest stock may choose their husbands out of the better sort of people," a seventeenth-century plantation owner wrote. As with social class, so with age and race; the higher the sex ratio, the more younger men married older women and the more white men married, or otherwise availed themselves of, black or Native American women. Widows too found themselves in demand: "A young widow with four or five children, who, among the middling or inferior ranks of Europe, would have so little chance for a second husband, is [in America] frequently courted as a sort of fortune," wrote Adam Smith. Indeed, widows were often social belles, and numerous cases are known of women who married three, four, or five times. Women were evidently quick to grasp the advantages scarcity conferred on them. An early governor of Virginia complained that too many women committed themselves to more than one man ("Women are yet scarce and in much request, and this offence has become very common, whereby great disquiet arose between parties, and no small trouble to the government"); New England daughters quickly learned that they could choose their own suitors against their parents' wishes; and women throughout frontier America divorced their husbands—often eloping with other men—at considerably higher rates than those of their European counterparts. If it is so, as David Herlihy surmises, that the relatively high status of women in the early Middle Ages (as indicated in the laws of the Alamanni and the Salian Franks) is a function of their scarcity and that the decline in that status during the coming centuries is a function of their growing numbers, we have a historical instance of women's dyadic power actually influencing men's structural power.[109] Another such instance may be the enfranchisement of American women first in those states with the highest sex ratios.[110] More typically, however, an expansion in women's informal power results in a contraction in their structural power as (male) lawmakers seek to enforce traditional expectations. According to Guttentag, an improvement in women's *structural* rights correlates with a low, not a high, sex ratio.

Guttentag's distinction between structural and dyadic power brings us full circle back to the distinction saga scholars have drawn between women's low theoretical status and high informal status. But where saga scholars see an inconsistency in need of reconciling, Guttentag sees reciprocals: in a high sex ratio situation, women will be empowered in the private sphere for precisely the same reason—their scarcity— that they will be *dis*empowered in the public one; and the higher the ratio, the greater the split. That scheme, I suggest, makes perfect sense of the Icelandic case. When *Grágás* speaks of annulment or separation but makes no provision for divorce or remarriage and the sagas tell us that divorce and remarriage were frequently and easily arranged, we need not choose one account over the other; we can rather assume that the laws represent what lawmakers *wished* were true all of the time, whereas the sagas reflect, at least roughly, what *was* true at least some of the time. Likewise the individual saga: when it shows us women excluded from the judicial consideration of wergild on one page but playing a directorial role in bloodfeud on the next, we need not assume the latter to be a fictional intrusion; as the American example shows, a high sex ratio can propel women's behavior in practice well beyond their rights in theory, even in the same time and place. And it is precisely, as R. G. Thomas perceived, in personal relations, not the public sphere, that saga women exert their authority. Predictably enough, the great majority of examples of women's "proud and independent behavior" (including those listed by Thomas himself) constitute acts of insubordination against *husbands*. Husbands are the thwarted parties in Hallgerðr's naming of her own child, Finnbogi's wife's betrothal of her daughter, Jófríðr's rescue of a baby daughter, Ásgerðr's threat of divorce, and so on and on. It is true that women also commit acts of insubordination against fathers and uncles, which would seem to speak against the "available partners" explanation; but it is also the case that such acts against fathers and uncles typically involve the woman's wish to marry or not marry, or to divorce, against her male guardian's wishes, and so constitute a kind of secondary or spillover effect in the supply-and-demand situation. Hildigunnr and Hallgerðr in *Njáls saga* and Gúðrún in *Laxdæla saga* can demand more prestigious husbands because they know, to put it crudely, their own market value. They may also know that they can make separate arrangements of a sort that might bring discredit on the family. Blackmail, one step removed.

Perhaps some version of blackmail underlies the statistic that early medieval farms bearing women's names compounded with -*staðir* are about seventeen times more numerous in Iceland than in Norway.[111] "This important difference," Barði Guðmundsson wrote, "shows that Icelandic women of old enjoyed by far more liberty of action and respect than their kindred sisters in Norway."[112] It more probably attests to the purchase (the downside of respect) women enjoyed in family politics during the frontier period, thanks to the demographic effects of selective migration. Finally there is Jón Steffensen's well-known claim that the change in women's nicknames, from laudatory in the earliest period to uncomplimentary in later centuries, reflects the erosive effects of Christianity on women's status. Again, whatever decline such slim evidence may attest is surely more likely to have been dictated by demography than religion; women's commodity value, boosted artificially in the frontier period, fell as their numbers slowly rose.

(A few words on the thirteenth century, when the sagas took their full and final form. Our premise is that there was a shortage of women in Iceland during the settlement period and that the themes of oral tradition stem from this demographic context. But what of the next two hundred years? Given the fact that the American West took over a hundred years to even out under relatively modern conditions; and also given the evidence that Europe in general did not even out until the eleventh or twelfth century, long after the advent of Christianity; and further given the witness of anthropology that infanticidal habits are very hard to break, even when they are no longer required; and finally given the political and economic climate of Iceland in the thirteenth century, which would presumably not have been fully discouraging of infanticidal tendencies; I would suggest that it is possible, even likely, that there was still a shortage of women, though perhaps not as acute, even during the thirteenth century. I am suggesting, in short, that an imbalance in the sex ratio may be the demographic context both for the original events and stories of the tenth century, whatever they might really have been, and also, though to a lesser extent, for the saga authors and audiences of the Sturlung Age. The chronicle of that age ought, then, to give us a mixed picture; and so it does. That is, it shows nearly all the themes mentioned earlier, some of them in quite spectacular form; but it also shows some other tendencies—for example, fewer accounts of multiple marriages for women, and in general fewer displays of feminine self-will or defiance. Perhaps the mixed picture of *Sturlunga saga* can be explained this way: first, that in the economic and political elite whose lives are chronicled there, there were individuals who could and did transcend demographic realities, and second, that it was exactly people of this social class who would, during the Christian period, have the lowest rates of infanticide and hence the least skewed sex ratios. That is, we conjecture, by analogy with historical and anthropological examples, that in prechristian Iceland infanticide was practiced in all social classes—among the poor for "bread and butter" reasons, but also among the not-poor for "oysters and champagne" reasons—and that it was only in later times that the practice declined among the wealthy, who could afford to be good Christians. I suspect that when we read in the sagas that infanticide was only practiced by poor people, we are listening to the ashamed voice of the thirteenth-century elite.)

I have argued on textual, comparative, and archaeological grounds that settlement Iceland, thanks to its frontier status and its tradition of preferential female infanticide, was short of women. At the risk of circularity, I argue further that the sagas themselves offer circumstantial evidence for such a shortage. From men fighting over women to woman-initiated marriage and divorce, the themes and circumstances of the sagas seem to reflect a world in which women were in short supply. The distinction between de jure and de facto status, coupled with the understanding that the latter is flexible and in certain conditions—in this case a high sex ratio—may override or contradict the former, is crucial to any historical study of women. In the case of Iceland, the distinction is all-important, for by obviating the need to make a choice between right and wrong sources, it recuperates the sagas not as strictly historical sources but as realistic social documents that stand in a complementary, not contradictory, relation to the laws and *Sturlunga saga*. Women in the Icelandic sources seem to have two statuses not because the sources got it wrong, in other words, but because they got it right; women in settlement Iceland had two statuses in fact and simultaneously. By the same token, when the sagas themselves speak with two voices, they are both telling the truth. Perhaps not surprisingly, that truth is often reflexive: that is, the stories the sagas choose to tell of women repeatedly both illustrate and turn on the tension between theory and practice. They are informed by the discrepancy, as we said earlier, between what women ought to do and what they really do; take away that discrepancy and you have no story. It is not just that the sagas happen to relate the social side effects of a high sex ratio; it is that they worry over women's capacity for excessive words and deeds, defiance of male authority, and control in family affairs—their uncontainability, in a word. To the extent that their uncontainability is the point of the stories told about them, it may be that women's very presence in the sagas, or at least their peculiar visibility, is itself a function of demographic realities during the settlement period. Indeed, to the extent that the sagas' "womanless" passages (tales of male violence and male travels) may likewise ultimately derive from real-life "womanlessness" (in the ways I have suggested above), the sagas as a literature may be said to owe, ironically enough, the circumstances of their making on the one side to a practice they decry and on the other to the social fallout of the very historical event they seek to glorify.

NOTES

1. The standard edition of Icelandic texts is found in the series Íslenzk Fornrit (Reykjavík: Hið Íslenzka Fornritafélag, 1933 to date). Other editions used are as follows: *Ála-Flekks saga*, in *Drei Lygisǫgur: Egils saga einhenda ok Ásmundar berserkjabana. Ála flekks saga. Flores saga konungs ok sona hans*, ed. Åke Lagerholm (Altnordische Saga-Bibliothek, vol. 17; Halle: Niemeyer, 1927); *Flateyjarbók*, ed. Sigurður Nordal (4 vols.; Akranes: Prentverk Akranes, 1944–45); *Harðar saga ok Holmverja*, ed. Sture Hast, Editiones Arnamagnaeanae A:6 (Copenhagen: Munksgaard, 1960), also ed. Guðni Jónsson, in *Íslendingasögur*, vol. 12 (Reykjavík: Íslendingasagnaútgáfan, 1953; rpt. 1968); *Hervarar saga*, in *Heiðreks saga (Hervarar saga ok Heiðreks konungs)*, ed. Jón Helgason, Samfund til Udgivelse af Gammel Nordisk Litteratur, vol. 48; Copenhagen: Jørgensen, 1924); *Óláfs saga Tryggvasonar en mesta*, ed. Ólafur Halldórsson (Editiones Arnamagnaeanae A:1–2; Copenhagen: Munksgaard, 1958–61).

2. See especially Sigurður Nordal, *The Historical Element in the Icelandic Family Sagas* (Glasgow: Jackson and Sons, 1957).

3. Rolf Heller, *Die literarische Darstellung der Frau in den Isländersagas*, Saga: Untersuchungen zur nordischen Literatur und Sprachgeschichte, vol. 2 (Halle: Niemeyer, 1958).

4. Jenny Jochens, "Consent in Marriage: Old Norse Law, Life, and Literature," *Scandinavian Studies* 58 (1986): 142–76, and "The Medieval Icelandic Heroine: Fact or Fiction?" *Viator* 17 (1986): 35–50.

5. Jochens, "Heroine": 41.

6. Ibid.: 47.

7. Ibid.: 50; see also Jochens, "Consent."

8. R. George Thomas, "Some Exceptional Women in the Sagas," *Saga-Book of the Viking Society* 13 (1946): 323–24.

9. On variations, see Marcia Guttentag and Paul F. Secord, *Too Many Women? The Sex Ratio Question* (Beverly Hills: Sage, 1983); see also Barbara D. Miller, *The Endangered Sex: Neglect of Female Children in Rural North India* (Ithaca: Cornell, 1981), pp. 38–41.

10. Sheila Ryan Johansson, "Deferred Infanticide: Excess Female Mortality during Childhood," in Glenn Hausfater and Sarah Blaffer Hrdy, eds., *Infanticide: Comparative and Evolutionary Perspectives* (New York: Aldine, 1984), p. 471.

11. Johansson, "Deferred Infanticide," p. 468; David Herlihy, "Life Expectancies for Women in Medieval Society," in *The Role of Woman in the Middle Ages*, ed. Rosmarie Thee Morewedge (Albany: State University of New York Press, 1975), 1–20. Some scholars (e.g., Sheila Johansson) consider deferred mortality or excess female mortality (EFM) to be of greater demographic significance than outright infanticide. Rural economies seem especially prone to the syndrome. When women eat after men, for example, they frequently suffer vitamin/mineral deficiencies; iron is particularly problematic, since women need larger quantities than men and since deficiencies affect immunological fitness (Johansson, "Deferred Infanticide," p. 471). Unfortunately, however, our sources give us practically no information on practices that might lead to excess female mortality, and for that reason I have let the issue lie in favor of outright infanticide—which is, against all odds, clearly documented.

12. As Bo Almqvist points out ("Folk Beliefs and Philology: Some Thoughts Evoked by Juha Pentikäinen's Thesis *The Nordic Dead-Child Tradition*," *Arv* 27 [1971]: 69–95), the use of the word "law" in this formulation is curious ("but on the matter of exposure, the old law should stand"). The word *lǫg* normally means law, not custom or habit, and "Ari is wont to pick his words with care." "But, on the other hand, if child exposure was a generally accepted practice, allowed without qualifications, there would hardly be any need for laws about it. Is it not likely, then, that Ari's phrasing betrays a knowledge that child exposure was not practiced indiscriminately but regulated by rules of a legal nature, stating in what cases it was allowed and perhaps how it should be done? Such an hypothesis gets some support from the fact that in the sagas, too, we hear of *lǫg* in connexion with child exposure, even though too much importance should perhaps not be attached to this, since the possibility of an influence from *Íslengingabók* cannot be ruled out. If we take it, however, that there were legal rules about child exposure in heathen times, what may these have contained specifically?" His suggestions accord perfectly with the saga material (and with practices in other non-Christian cultures): "Some such regulations as to how child exposure should be carried out and at what stage in a child's life it became impermissible may have formed part of the pagan law which Ari refers to." He also suggests that the early law may have distinguished between justified and unjustified infanticide (pp. 74–76).

13. Christianity is by no means the only religion or authority to ban infanticide. "All unifying political systems, whether of expanding conquerors or nationalizing elites, apparently encourage fertility and discourage traditional means of limitation. Muhammed attempted to suppress female infanticide in Arabia, as did the Mogul emperor Jahangir in India two hundred years before the British, and Tokugawa and Meiji rulers in Japan, employing Buddhist sanctions" (Mildred Dickeman, "Demographic Consequences of Infanticide in Man," *Annual Review of Ecology and Systematics* 6 [1975]: 133).

14. Árni Pálsson, "Um lok þrældóms á Íslandi," *Skírnir* 97 (1932): 191–203; Jón Jóhannesson, *A History of the Old Icelandic Commonwealth: Íslendinga Saga,* University of Manitoba Icelandic Studies, vol. 2 (Winnipeg: University of Manitoba Press, 1974), pp. 136–38.

15. Carl Johan Schlyter and H. S. Collin, *Corpus iuris Sueo-Gotorum antiqui. . . . Samling af Sweriges gamla lagar, på Kong. Maj:ts. nådigste befallning,* 12 vols. (Stockholm: Haeggström, 1827–69), p. 88; Arthur Thomsen, *Barnkvävningen: En rättshistorisk studie,* Skrifter utgivna af Kung Humanistiska Vetenskapssamfundet i Lund, vol. 58 (Lund: Gleerup, 1960), pp. 1–24; Julia Pentikäinen, *The Nordic Dead-Child Tradition: Nordic Dead-Child*

Beings: A Study in Comparative Religion, Folklore Fellows Communications, vol. 202 (Helsinki: Suomalainen Tiedeakatemia, 1968), pp. 99–100.

16. The main saga passages referring to infanticide are *Gunnlaugs saga* (ÍF 3, ch. 3); *Vatnsdæla saga* (IF 13, ch. 37); *Finnboga saga* (IF 14, ch. 2); *Reykdæla saga* (IF 10, ch. 7); *Harðar saga ok Holmverja* (ch. 8); *Jómsvíkinga saga* (ch. 1); *Áns saga bogsveigis* (ch. 5); *Þorsteins þáttr uxafóts* and *Þorsteins þáttr Ásgrímssonar* (*Flateyjarbók*). I have excluded *Ála-Flekks saga* (ch. 2) from consideration here on grounds that it is a patently fantastic romance, set in England and obviously dependent on international folktale motifs; see Laugerholm (esp. lvi–lvii and lxvii). Al Tartushi's observations are documented in Harris Birkeland, *Nordens historie i middelalderen etter arabiske kilder* (Oslo: Dybwad, 1954), p. 84.

17. Incorporating ceremonies are widespread. Compare Netsilik Eskimo practice: "Naming had a restrictive influence on infanticide. . . . It was essential that infanticide take place prior to naming, since killing a named child might offend the spirit of the reincarnated person" (Asen Balikci, *The Netsilik Eskimo* [Garden City, N.Y.: Natural History Press, 1970], p. 149). See also Vilhelm Grønbech, *The Culture of the Teutons*, 3 vols. (London: Oxford University Press, 1932), vol. 1, pp. 292–93, and Konrad Maurer, *Über die Wasserweihe des germanischen Heidenthumes*, Abhandlungen der Philos.-philol. Classe der kgl. Bayer. Akademie der Wiss., vol. 15 (Munich: Verlag der k. Akad., 1880), esp. pp. 179–83.

18. Jón Steffensen, "Aspects of Life in Iceland in the Heathen Period," *Saga-Book of the Viking Society* 17 (1968): 199–205; Pentikäinen, *Nordic Dead-Child Tradition*, pp. 59–62; Grønbech, *Culture*, vol. 2, pp. 291–92.

19. Grønbech, *Culture*, vol. 2, pp. 291–92.

20. Herlihy, *Medieval Households* (Cambridge, Mass.: Harvard University Press, 1985), pp. 53–54.

21. Maurer, *Die Wasswerweihe;* Pentikäinen, *Nordic Dead-Child Tradition*, pp. 75–86.

22. Again compare Netsilik practice. "Several different techniques were used to put the newly born female child to death. In winter the infant was placed in the igloo entrance, where she lay screaming until she froze to death—usually not very long. Suffocation was practiced in all seasons by bringing a furry skin over the infant's face. In summer a small stone grave was dug near the family's dwelling and the infant placed inside, where it cried for several hours until it died. Apparently no active killing methods were used" (Balikci, *Netsilik Eskimo*, pp. 148–49).

23. R. Keyser and P. A. Munch, eds., *Norges Gamle Love indtil 1387*, 5 vols. (Oslo: Gröndahl, 1846–49), esp. vol. 1, pp. 340, 375–76; Pentikäinen, *Nordic Dead-Child Tradition*, pp. 76–86.

24. Almqvist, "Folk Beliefs": 75–76.

25. John Boswell, "*Expositio* and *Oblatio:* The Abandonment of Children and the Ancient and Mediaeval Family," *American Historical Review* 89 (1984): 13.

26. See Richard Cleasby and Gudbrand Vigfusson, eds., *An Icelandic-English Dictionary* (Oxford: Clarendon Press, 1975).

27. Dickeman, "Demographic Consequences": 115.

28. The best-known branch of the dead child complex is the "utburd" tale, which in Pentikäinen's view is "tradition-historically . . . a Christian innovation which spread widely during the Viking Period" (*Nordic Dead-Child Tradition*, p. 360). Almqvist sees no reason to assume Christian innovation: "While it is true that the conditions for the spread and expansion of the belief in dead-child beings are much more favorable after the introduction of Christianity than before, the factual background for such belief is not lacking in pagan times" ("Folk Beliefs": 76).

29. The provincial laws of medieval Norway allow the abandonment of malformed children. Numerous statutes attempt to distinguish acceptable from unacceptable malformation. As Pentikäinen points out, however, these descriptions appear to derive from Continental laws (*Nordic Dead-Child Tradition*, pp. 77–81). Nor is the incidence of malformations identifiable at birth in preindustrial or disadvantaged groups more than around 1 percent (see Dickeman, "Demographic Consequences": 117–20).

30. See Jóhannesson, *History*, p. 136.

31. To the extent that ordering a *daughter* killed as an act of anger toward a *wife* constitutes a form of gender punishment, it may also provide a context for the motif, widespread in the North, of a wife's having her *sons* killed and serving them up to her *husband* (as Guðrún does to Atli in Eddic tradition, for example). Daly and Wilson point out that "mothers' interests may be violated by female-selective infanticide, a practice imposed by a larger social group demanding the production of warriors" (Martin Daly and Margo Wilson, "A Sociobiological Analysis of Human Infanticide," in Hausfater and Hrdy, *Infanticide*, p. 495).

32. Joseph Harris, "Satire and the Heroic Life: Two Studies (*Helgakviða Hundingsbana I*, 18 and Bjǫrn Hítdœlakappi's *Grámágflím*)," in *Oral Traditional Literature: A Festschrift for Albert Bates Lord*, ed. John Miles Foley (Columbus, Ohio: Slavica, 1980), pp. 330–31; Ursula Dronke, "*Sem jarlar forðum:* The Influence of *Rígsþula* on Two Saga Episodes," *Speculum Norroenum: Norse Studies in Memory of Gabriel Turville-Petre*, ed. Ursula Dronke, Guðrun P. Helgadóttir, Gerd Wolfgang Weber, and Hans Bekker-Nielsen (Odense: Odense University Press, 1981), pp. 71–72.

33. The data and examples that follow—from societies worldwide and from historical Europe—constitute only a selected fraction of available information. Readers wishing more details should first consult Susan Scrimshaw, "Infanticide in Human Populations: Societal and Individual Concerns," and Daly and Wilson, "Sociobiological Analysis," in Hausfater and Hrdy, eds., *Infanticide*, pp. 439–63 and 487–502, respectively; Laila Williamson, "Infanticide: An Anthropological Analysis," in *Infanticide and the Value of Life*, ed. Marvin Kohl (Buffalo, N.Y.: Prometheus, 1978), pp. 61–75; Dickeman, "Demographic Consequences" and her "Female Infanticide, Reproductive Strategies, and Social Stratification: A Preliminary Model," in *Evolutionary Biology and Human Social Behavior: An Anthropological Perspective*, ed. Napolean A. Chagnon and William Irons (North Scituate, Mass.: Duxbury Press, 1979), pp. 321–67; Miller, *The Endangered Sex;* Guttentag, *Too Many Women?;* and Sarah Pomeroy, *Goddesses, Whores, Wives, and Slaves: Women in Classical Antiquity* (New York: Schocken, 1975).

34. Williamson, "Infanticide," p. 61; Hermann Heinrich Ploss and B. Renz, *Das Kind in Brauch und Sitte der Völker: Völkerkundliche Studien* (3rd ed.; Leipzig: Grieben, 1911–12), vol. 1, pp. 160–96.

35. See William Tulio Divale and Marvin Harris, "Population, Warfare, and the Male Supremacist Complex," *American Anthropologist* 78 (1976): 521–38.

36. John T. Noonan, Jr., *Contraception: A History of Its Treatment by the Catholic Theologians and Canonists* (Cambridge, Mass.: Belknap-Harvard, 1966); Dickeman, "Demographic Consequences": 131.

37. Williamson, "Infanticide," p. 66; J. B. Birdsell, "Some Predictions for the Pleistocene Based on Equilibrium Systems Among Recent Hunter-Gatherers," in *Man the Hunter*, ed. R. B. Lee and I. DeVore (Chicago: Aldine, 1968), p. 239; W. Penn Handwerker, "The First Demographic Transition: An Analysis of Subsistence Choices and Reproductive Consequences," *American Anthropologist* 85 (1983): 5–25.

38. Divale and Harris, "Population": 530.

39. Dickeman, "Demographic Consequences": 126.

40. Guttentag, *Too Many Women?*, p. 51; Harris, "Satire," p. 204; Dickeman, "Demographic Consequences": 126.

41. Mary Douglas gives the example of the Rendille of Kenya, who—in an effort to maintain a delicate balance between camels and the boys who herd them—kill all male children born on Wednesdays or after the circumcision of the eldest brother ("Population Control in Primitive Groups," *British Journal of Sociology* 27 (1966): 263–73.

42. Dickeman, "Demographic Consequences": 130.

43. Dickeman, "Reproductive Strategies."

44. Williamson, "Infanticide," p. 67; Dickeman, "Demographic Consequences."

45. On the centrality of the family as a caretaking unit and the father as decision-maker in early Iceland, see Steffensen, "Aspects of Life": 197–98.

46. Knud Rasmussen, *The Netsilik Eskimos: Social Life and Spiritual Culture* (Report of the Fifth Thule Expedition 1921–24; Copenhagen: Gyldendal, 1931), passim.

47. Divale and Harris, "Population": 526.

48. See, for example, Miller, *The Endangered Sex*, pp. 107–32.

49. Kanti Pakrasi, *Female Infanticide in India* (Calcutta: Edition Indian, 1970); Miller, *The Endangered Sex;* Dickeman, "Demographic Consequences" and "Reproductive Strategies."

50. See Douglas, "Population Control."

51. Douglas, "Population Control": 272; also Dickeman, "Reproductive Strategies."

52. See *Time* and *Newsweek,* 30 April 1974.

53. Scrimshaw, "Infanticide," p. 447; Divale and Harris, "Population."

54. Divale and Harris, "Population": 53; Bjorn Ambrosiani, *Fornlämningar och bebyggelse: Studier i Attundalands och Södertörns förhistoria* (Uppsala: Almqvist and Wiksell, 1964), pp. 204–205.

55. Divale and Harris, "Population"; Peggy Reeves Sanday, *Female Power and Male Dominance: On the Origins of Sexual Inequality* (Cambridge: Cambridge University Press, 1981), pp. 45–51.

56. Divale and Harris, "Population": 531.

57. Williamson, "Infanticide," p. 67.

58. Miller, *The Endangered Sex,* pp. 42–43.

59. See Dickeman, "Reproductive Strategies."

60. W. W. Tarn and G. T. Griffith, *Hellenistic Civilization* (3rd ed.; London: Arnold, 1952), p. 101.

61. Pomeroy, *Goddesses,* p. 70.

62. Tarn and Griffith, *Hellenistic Civilization,* p. 101.

63. Ibid.

64. Josiah Cox Russell, *Late Ancient and Medieval Population* (Philadelphia: American Philosophical Society, 1958), p. 14.

65. Guttentag, *Too Many Women?,* pp. 41–42; Donald Engels, "The Problem of Female Infanticide in the Greco-Roman World," *Classical Philology* 75 (1980): 112–20; cf. Pomeroy, *Goddesses,* pp. 227–28 and passim.

66. Jack Lindsay, *The Ancient World: Manners and Morals* (London: Weidenfeld and Nicolson, 1968), p. 168.

67. Peter Astbury Brunt, *Italian Manpower. 225 B.C.–A.D. 14* (London: Oxford University Press, 1971), p. 149.

68. Mary R. Lefkowitz and Maureen B. Fant, *Women's Life in Greece and Rome: A Source Book in Translation* (Baltimore, Md.: Johns Hopkins University Press, 1982), p. 111.

69. Pomeroy, *Goddesses,* p. 164; Lefkowitz and Fant, *Women's Life,* p. 173; Brunt, *Italian Manpower,* pp. 148–55.

70. Tacitus, *Germania,* ed. J. G. C. Anderson (Oxford: Clarendon, 1938), chap. 19.

71. Herlihy, *Medieval Households,* p. 53.

72. Ibid., pp. 55, 195.

73. Richard C. Trexler, "Infanticide in Florence: New Sources and First Results," *History of Childhood Quarterly: The Journal of Psychohistory* 1 (1974): 103.

74. Ibid.: 99.

75. Ibid.: 110.

76. Emily K. Coleman, "Infanticide in the Early Middle Ages," in *Women in Medieval Society,* ed. Susan Mosher Stuard (N.p.: University of Pennsylvania Press, 1976); Dickeman, "Reproductive Strategies," pp. 360–62.

77. Herlihy, "Life Expectancies," p. 11; Russell, *Late Ancient and Medieval Population.* The change, Herlihy notes, is accompanied by a shift in medical doctrine, which earlier claimed men to be naturally longer-lived by virtue of their greater warmth, but later claimed

women to be naturally longer-lived by virtue of their cleaning menses ("Life Expectancies," pp. 10–11).

78. Herlihy attributes the shortage of women to infanticide on the one hand and on the other to excess female mortality resulting from overwork, inferior care, and maltreatment. See also Johansson, "Deferred Infanticide."

79. Boswell, "*Expositio*"; Dickeman, "Reproductive Strategies," pp. 354–58.

80. Liv Helga Dommasnes, "Et gravmateriale fra yngre jernalder brukt til å belyse kvinners stillings," *Viking* 62 (1979): 95–105.

81. Liv Helga Dommasnes, "Late Iron Age in Western Norway: Female Roles and Ranks as Deduced from an Analysis of Burial Customs," *Norwegian Archaeological Review* 15 (1982): 70–84.

82. Berit Jansen Sellevold, Ulla Lund Hansen, and Jørgen Balslev Jørgensen, *Iron Age Man in Denmark,* Nordiske fortidsminder B:8 (Copenhagen: Det Kongelige Nordiske Old-skriftselskab, 1984), p. 235.

83. Klavs Randsborg, *The Viking Age in Denmark: The Formation of a State* (New York: St. Martin's, 1980), p. 81; Randsborg, "Burial, Succession and Early State Formation in Denmark," in *The Archaeology of Death,* ed. Robert Chapman, Ian Kinnes, and Klavs Randsborg (London: Cambridge University Press, 1981), p. 113.

84. Cf. Anne-Sofie Gräslund, "Barn i Birka," in *Tor: Meddelanden från Institutionen för Nordisk Fornkunskap vid Uppsala Universitet* 13 (1969): 161–79.

85. Sellevold et al., *Iron Age Man,* p. 214.

86. Ibid.

87. Dommasnes, "Late Iron Age," p. 73.

88. Kristján Eldjárn, *Kuml og haugfé úr heiðnum sið á Íslandi* (Reykjavík: Bókaútgáfan Norðri, 1956), pp. 194, 248–49.

89. See Peter Sawyer, *The Age of the Vikings,* 2nd ed. (London: Arnold, 1971) and Patrick Wormald, "The Vikings: Whence and Whither?" in *The Vikings,* ed. R. T. Farrell (London: Phillimore, 1982), pp. 128–53.

90. Ingeborg Schröbler, *Wikingische und spielmännische Elemente im zweiten Teile des Gudrunliedes* (Halle: Niemeyer, 1934), pp. 9–10.

91. *Annals of Ulster,* ed. William E. Hennessey (Dublin: Her Majesty's Stationery Office, 1887), p. 279.

92. *The Parker Chronicle* for A.D. 894, in *The Parker Chronicle, 832–900,* ed. Albert Hugh Smith (Methuen's OE Library; London: Methuen and Co., 1935).

93. Christine E. Fell with Cecily Clark and Elizabeth Williams, *Women in Anglo-Saxon England and the Impact of 1066* (Bloomington: Indiana University Press, 1984), pp. 130–37.

94. Fell points to the relatively high incidence of Scandinavian women's names in English materials and wonders whether it reflects a high incidence of actual Scandinavian women or the tendency of mixed marriages—Scandinavian male, English female—to give their children Scandinavian names. She leans toward the former explanation, but a cursory glance at naming patterns in *Orkneyinga saga, Færeyinga saga,* and *Landnámabók* suggests that children of Scandinavian fathers commonly bear Scandinavian names.

95. Johannes C. H. R. Steenstrup, *Normannerne,* 4 vols. (Copenhagen: Klein, 1876–82). See also Andreas Holmsen, *Norges historie fra de eldste tider til 1660* (Oslo, Bergen: Universitetsforlaget, 1961), pp. 101–10.

96. Weather fluctuations meant, of course, more to early Scandinavians than they did to early Frenchmen. As E. R. Wrigley put it, "Slight variations in summer temperature in, say, Beauce might make only a minor difference to the date of the harvest and its size. Similar variations in parts of Scandinavia might make the difference between a crop to be harvested and the failure of the grain to ripen at all. And the whole economy hinged on the harvest" (*Population and History* [New York: World University and McGraw-Hill, 1969], p. 76). To other evidence adduced for worsened economic conditions around the time of the Viking Age may be added the observation that, in Denmark, after a steady increase from the Early to the Late Roman period, the skeletal stature of both males and females, but especially females,

decreases significantly. The Viking Age decrease "might be indicative of poorer living conditions during this or the preceding period" (Sellevold, Jansen, Hansen, and Jørgensen, *Iron Age Man*, p. 227).

97. Dickeman, "Reproductive Strategies," esp. pp. 363–67; Guttentag, *Too Many Women?*, p. 49; Divale and Harris, "Population."

98. Divale and Harris, "Population": 526–27.

99. T. D. Kendrick, *A History of the Vikings* (New York: Scribner's, 1930), p. 22.

100. Dickeman, "Demographic Consequences," p. 129.

101. Guttentag, *Too Many Women?*, p. 115.

102. Ibid., pp. 113–52.

103. Balikci, *Netsilik Eskimo*, pp. 147–93; Guttentag, *Too Many Women?* p. 51; Dickeman, "Reproductive Strategies."

104. Rasmussen, *The Netsilik Eskimos*, p. 193.

105. Dickeman, "Demographic Consequences," p. 133.

106. Roberta Frank, "Marriage in Twelfth- and Thirteenth-Century Iceland," *Viator* 4 (1973): 473–84.

107. Guttentag, *Too Many Women?*, p. 23.

108. Ibid., esp. pp. 115–24.

109. Herlihy, "Life Expectancies"; Brunt, *Italian Manpower*, pp. 151–53.

110. See Eleanor Flexner, *Century of Struggle* (Rev. ed.; Cambridge, Mass.: Belknap-Harvard University Press, 1975).

111. See Magnus Olsen, *Farms and Fanes of Ancient Norway* (Oslo: Instituttet for Sammenligende Kulturforskning, 1928); Barði Guðmundsson, *On the Origin of the Icelanders* (Lincoln: University of Nebraska Press, 1967).

112. Guðmundsson, *Origin*, p. 40.

Sexuality and Folklore

EDITH WHITEHURST WILLIAMS

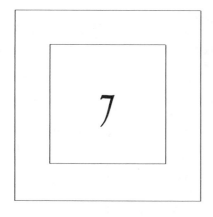

What's So New about the Sexual Revolution?

Some Comments on Anglo-Saxon Attitudes toward Sexuality in Women Based on Four Exeter Book Riddles

Although the Anglo-Saxon strain is only one in the cultural heritage of present-day America, it is a significant one. If we look far enough back into this culture we discover that a number of wholesome and spontaneous attitudes once prevailed that are strikingly similar to those which energetic young people of this century are struggling so earnestly to reestablish. A regard for certain values, such as those pertaining to property rights and individual liberties, has been transmitted in an almost unbroken line through the channel of the common law. But others, particularly those having to do with the position of women and with their role in the area of sexuality, have been shunted off and distorted with the infusion of other streams of culture from the continent. To examine these attitudes we must look backward far behind the time of Thomas Bowdler, John Calvin, St. Augustine, and St. Jerome.[1] We must examine mores which had their inception long before the latter patriarch established the doctrine of antifeminism which defined woman as nothing short of bestial—lecherous, shrewish, evil in every way. Above all, we must bear in mind that we are looking backward to the time before the English woman had been corseted into a fragile doll apparently not endowed with the full complement of anatomical features.

The centuries we are concerned with are the eighth to tenth centuries in England. Although the island had been Christianized very rapidly—within approximately a century and a half following the arrival of St. Augustine of Canterbury in 597—the outlook of a race of people is not overturned so easily. Mass conversions usually took place at the behest of a king, and the behaviors of the people at large continued firmly in the Germanic tradition. Actually it was not until the advent of the Normans several centuries later that real alterations occurred, such as the introduction of the "chattel" concept of women. Sir Frank M. Stenton, a meticulously reliable historian, remarks, "one of the interesting features of Anglo-Saxon history is the number of women who impressed themselves on the consciousness of their time. They appear in all periods from the legendary foreworld to the eve of the Norman

Conquest, and they occur in the religious as well as the temporal sphere. . . . There is no doubt that Old English society allowed to women, not only private influence, but also the widest liberty in public affairs."[2] These socio-political aspects of the life of the Anglo-Saxon woman can be pieced together from the few remaining laws, deeds, wills, and records of religious houses. A glimpse of a much more intimate and subjective phase of her existence is revealed in a handful of astonishing poems which survive in the collection from the ninth or tenth century known as the Exeter Book.

The ninety-five riddles in the collection represent the nearest approach to the short lyric to be found in Old English poetry.[3] They are heterogeneous in subject matter and range in length from four lines to more than a hundred. Although undoubtedly transcribed in an atmosphere of (nominal) celibacy in the scriptorium of some monastery and preserved for almost a thousand years in the library of Exeter Cathedral, eight or ten of these secular riddles deal with sexuality in a frankly enthusiastic and descriptive manner. The riddles were first solved in the latter half of the nineteenth century and the first decade of the twentieth and as a consequence of the time were unfortunately labeled "obscene." Victorian scholars seem to have stumbled upon them in dismay and were confronted with the task of dealing with them as delicately as possible. One turn-of-the-century editor, Frederick Tupper, speaks with nervous embarrassment of the fact that "a few descend into the depths of greasy *double entente* [*sic*]."[4] Another, A. J. Wyatt, falls back upon the cautious term "lubricity."[5] All sooner or later employ the word "obscene." But it is one of the significant purposes of my remarks to point out that our classification of what is obscene changes from period to period. When we clear away all preconceived notions of lewdness and examine them carefully, particularly with a view toward discovering what we can about women's functions and women's feelings in the sexual area, two points emerge distinctly: (1) sexual pleasure clearly lay within the province of women; (2) there was no sanction against this pleasure since women are not portrayed as degraded nor exploited in this context.

Guiseppe Pitrè, as quoted by Tupper, states as a fundamental definition, "a riddle is an arrangement of words by which is understood or suggested something that is not expressed; or else it is an ingenious and witty description of this unexpressed thing by means of qualities and general traits that can be attributed quite as well to other things having no likeness or analogy to the subject."[6] These characteristics are essentially the characteristics of poetic diction as they apply to metaphor and allegory. We first read a poem for the nominal or surface meaning; it is when we re-read for the expanded meanings of the double entendre that we begin to perceive the rich depth of the poem. A carefully selected diction reveals the clues to the second level, and it is in this realm of poetic art that we discover the subjective overtones which are carried in associative connotations. This is especially true of Old English alliterative verse. The metrical requirements demand a very compact expression. Ideas are expanded through repetition and parallel variation, but within the metrical unit of the half-line, notional expressions are highly compressed into the descriptive compound and the kenning. These two components of poetic language—the *sine qua non* of Old English poetry—are always heavily loaded with connotative values, but this is also possible for individual word choices. It is legitimate, then, to give free rein to the associative process in the effort to experience an Old English metaphor to its widest limits. It is essential, of course, to consider the word first in its immediate context; then we may bring to bear all the semantic possibilities current during the period. This can be accomplished by making comparisons to its use in other settings in the corpus of Old English literature.[7]

The first point, that sexual pleasure was a prerogative of Anglo-Saxon women, is displayed clearly in two short poems, No. 23 (K-D 25), which is nominally solved as "Onion" and No. 43 (K-D 45), "Dough."[8] The first reads:

> Ic eom wunderlicu wiht,   wifum on hyhte,
> neahbuendum nyt.   Nængum sceþþe
> burgsittendra   nymþe bonan anum.
> Staþol min is steapheah;   stonde ic on bedde,
> neoþan ruh nathwær.   Neþeð hwilum
> ful cyrtenu   ceorles dohtor,
> modwlonc meowle,   þæt heo on mec gripeð,
> ræseð mec on reodne,   reafað min heafod,
> fegeð mec on fæsten.   Feleþ sona
> mines gemotes   seo þe mec nearwað,
> wif wundenlocc—   wæt bið þæt eage.

(I am a remarkable creature, a joy to women, useful to neighbors; I harm no citizen except my slayer alone. Lofty is my position, I stand in a bed, am shaggy somewhere beneath. Sometimes a very beautiful daughter of a freeman, a proud-minded woman, ventures to get hold of me, rushes upon me who am red, ravages my head, binds me in a fastness. She soon feels that encounter with me, she who confines me, the woman with braided locks. Her eye becomes wet.)

Here the woman is indeed portrayed as a lively participant. The phrase *wifum on hyhte* 'joy to women' is self-explanatory; the nature of the joy is expanded when we recognize that *hyht* is also used to mean "expectation," "desire," and "comfort." But the tone of the poem is conveyed in the alliterating verbs *ræsan* and *reafian* (8), both of which imply not only willingness but aggressiveness. Extended meanings of *ræsan* include "to move violently or impetuously," while *reafian* can also mean "to take by force." Both follow logically upon *neþeð* (5), meaning "to dare or venture." *Riddle* No. 43, "Dough," follows very much the same vein:

> Ic on wincle gefrægn   weaxan nathwæt,
> þindan ond þunian,   þecene hebban.
> On þæt banlease   bryd grapode,
> hygewlonc hondum;   hrægle þeahte
> þrindende þing   þeodnes dohtor.

(I heard of something growing in a corner, swelling and standing up, raising its cover; a bride, elated in mind, the daughter of a prince, felt that boneless object with her hands, covered the swelling thing with her garment.)

Again there is evidence of the bride's eagerness, implied by the verb *grapian* 'to feel', 'touch', or 'grope for', and reinforced by the adjective *hygewlonc*. *Wlonc* is often glossed as "proud" or "haughty" but in combination with *hyge* 'mind' or 'disposition' it seems particularly appropriate to read it to mean "elated" or "exultant," both of which are acceptable interpretations. The narrative content of these two poems demonstrates a completely unselfconscious approach to a sexual situation on the part of women. Nothing indicates that the poet equates his joyous account with the lechery so dear to the hearts of the patriarchs and to the later Calvinists. Insight on this point can be gained from a careful examination of the terms chosen to delineate the women; this leads to the second point, that women are not portrayed as degraded in the sexual situation.

The word *ceorl* (No. 23, 6), ancestor of modern *churl,* meant at that period a free man; he was, indeed, a free man at the lowest level of the social order, but the term is not in itself pejorative. The girl can be envisioned as rustic, but not necessarily as wanton. *Cyrten,* in the same line, is, on the other hand, a notably elevated term for "beautiful." It is used in association with the Biblical Esther in the Homilies and as an element in complimentary epithets, often in association with priests. *Meowle* (7) is a respectable term for "girl," "damsel," "woman"; it is applied in repeated instances to the Hebrew heroine Judith and to the Virgin Mary. *Wundenlocc* (11) is a highly connotative word. It means in a literal sense either "braided" or "curled" locks which were considered an accessory of great beauty. Certain laws of the period verify that free-flowing locks were also the sign of freedom.[9] This descriptive detail strengthens the notion of the girl as daughter of a freeman, and it is for this reason that I read *modwlonc* (7) as "proud-spirited" or "courageous," especially fitting since she ventures or dares. The poem in its entirety conveys a clear impression of impulsive, independent action in an atmosphere of beauty and freedom.

We do not have to argue the position of the *bryd* 'bride' in No. 43. She is a prince's daughter and *hygewlonc,* discussed earlier, bears a favorable connotation. Some comment might be added with regard to the *hrægl* 'garment' (4) with which she covers the swelling thing. *Hrægl* is a very common word meaning "garment" or "raiment." It is regularly used in connection with ecclesiastical vestments and royal raiment, very often in association with jewels and ornamentation. We cannot argue that it occurs only in these contexts, for we also have instances of a beggar pleading for *hrægles and alemessan* 'a garment and an alms'; but its common usage is consistent with the high position of the lady and maintains a tone of dignity and charm.

Two additional *Riddles,* No. 59 (K-D 61) and No. 87 (K-D 91), illustrate the points we are considering. The surface meaning of No. 59 is of slight importance. It has never been solved conclusively and is usually taken to mean either a helmet or a shirt—in short, something of value or beauty which a lord thrusts himself into from beneath.

> Oft mec fæste bileac freolicu meowle,
> ides on earce; hwilum up ateah
> folmum sinum ond frean sealde,
> holdum þeodne, swa hio haten wæs.
> Siðþan me on hreþre heafod sticade,

nioþan upweardne   on nearo fegde.
Gif þæs ondfengan   ellen dohte,
mec frætwedne   fyllan sceolde
ruwes nathwæt.   Ræd hwæt ic mæne.

(Often a comely woman, a lady, locked me fast in a chest. Sometimes she took me out with her hands and gave me to her lord, a gracious prince, as she was commanded. Afterwards he stuck his head into my interior, pointing upwards from beneath, joined tightly in a narrow place. If the strength of him who was received, was capable, something shaggy must fill me, adorned as I am. Tell what I speak of.)

Again the description of the activity is explicit. The phrase *mec bileac . . . on earce fæste* 'locked me fast in a chest' cannot be applied in a literal way to the secondary meaning, but it is undoubtedly a metaphoric statement for the lady's great modesty which is set aside only in the proper circumstance—when her lord commands. This latter point may offend the liberationist, but we must recognize that the situation is not based on the principle of male-female status but on the high position of a lord or prince in relation to all his retainers—a relationship by no means resented in the heroic culture, but one adhered to with great loyalty to the mutual benefit of all parties. That the pattern extended into the marriage relationship is reflected throughout Old English poetry and prose. The concept is supported by the heroic terminology which pervades this poem, as for example *ellen dohte* (5). The phrase is a familiar formula "if his valor avails" and fits admirably into the context.[10]

The subject of this riddle is distinctly feminine and once more the diction is elevated. *Freolic,* the adjective used in conjunction with *meowle* (1) sometimes means "free" but more often "noble," "comely," "goodly." Its most frequent contexts relate to noble rulers, comely children (heirs, first-born), and fair and comely wives. *Ides* is a word limited almost exclusively to poetic usage. According to Grimm, it applied in earliest times to superhuman beings, occupying a position between goddesses and mere women.[11] If someone is recalling that this term is applied to Grendel's dam, remember that it is used for purposes of comparison only: *Þæra oðer wæs . . . idese onlicnes* 'one of these was the likeness of a lady' (*Beowulf,* 1349b–51a). Used with reference to the outcast marsh-wanderer, the contrast is both ironic and tragic. In the same poem, the term *ides* is regularly applied to Wealhþeow, when she makes her gracious appearance to honor the victorious Beowulf.

The question might be raised whether any *un*favorable epithets are ever applied to women in the *Riddles.* They are, indeed. *Riddle* No. 10 (K-D 12, "Leather") speaks of the dark-haired Welsh girl as *dol droncmennen* 'stupid, drunken slave girl' and refers to her *hygegalan hond* 'wanton hand'. Here, again, the degradation does not rest on a male-female distinction but on one of class, a slave-free difference. The fact that the word *gal* is used in the compound *hygegalan* to mean "lustful, wanton" underscores the point that such denigrating words are not used in sex-oriented riddles where the participants are of the upper class.

No. 87 is a complex poem and has in the past been treated, mistakenly I believe, as a difficult one:

Min heafod is   homere geþuren,
searopila wund,   sworfen feole.
Oft ic begine   þæt me ongean sticað,
þonne ic hnitan sceal   hringum gyrded,
hearde wið heardum,   hindan þyrel—
forð ascufan   þæt mines frean
mod·p· freoþað   middelnihtum.
Hwilum ic under bæc   bregde nebbe
hyrde þæs hordes,   þonne min hlaford wile
lafe þicgan   þara þe he of life het
wælcræfte awrecan   willum sinum.

(My head is beaten by a hammer, wounded by a pointed instrument, rubbed by a file. Often I open wide to that which pricks against me. Then, girded with rings, I must thrust hard against the hard, pierced from the rear, press forth that joy which my lord cherishes at midnight. Sometimes, by means of my countenance, I move to and fro, backwards, the entrance of the treasure when my lord wishes to receive what is left of that which he commanded from life (i.e., to death), which he thrust with deadly power according to his desire.)

This riddle has been almost universally read to mean "Key" but I depart from that reading to offer the solution "Keyhole." That is, instead of forcing certain distorted meanings to apply rather doubtfully to a male instrument, I suggest accepting the very obvious allusion to a female receptacle, active though it appears to be. Apparently it lay beyond the limits of decency for the nineteenth-century readers to admit to certain clear implications; they skillfully sidestepped primary meanings of words, choosing innocuous synonyms, and major elements in the poem were sacrificed in the process. For example, when they came to a term such as *begine* 'to open the mouth wide' whose possibilities they could not bring themselves to cope with, they dismissed it as "meaningless" and emended indiscriminately.[12] If the solution "Key" were accepted, the poem would become scarcely more than a literal statement with occasional heavy sexual overtones; it would not meet the requirements of riddling where the subject possesses "traits that can be attributed quite as well to other things." When, on the other hand, the meaning "Keyhole" is admitted, the elements fall into place revealing an intricate metaphor which operates on not two but three levels of meaning. The initial interpretation of the keyhole being penetrated by the key in order to yield the treasure poses no difficulty; the theme of conjugal pleasure follows the same pattern identically; the two are united in meaning by a broader metaphor of conquest couched in battle imagery which is in no way inappropriate to the sexual encounter. The diction which conveys this ever widening circle of meaning merits attention.

If the first two lines referred to a male instrument, the image would be too excruciating to contemplate—hammered, wounded, filed! Applied to the female counterpart, the terms contain fairly standard symbols and at the same time establish the conquest motif. The atmosphere of power and force, introduced by *geþuren* 'hammered' (1) is sustained by *wund* 'wounded' (2), which refers specifically to a wound inflicted by a blow. The common meaning of *begine*, mentioned earlier, is "to open wide the mouth" and extends to include "gape" or "yawn." There is no ambiguity here and certainly no justification for altering the word to escape its meaning. *Hnitan* (4) is used extensively with reference to battle encounters and can indicate "to come together with a shock." The word *hring* has a multiplicity of meanings and its figurative possibilities lead in many directions. Primarily it means "ring" as in "ring-mail" or "armor"; only rarely does it refer to a ring as a piece of jewelry. Metrically *hringum gyrded* 'girded with rings' comprises a perfect half-line and could simply mean "armored as I am," i.e., psychologically "prepared for battle as I am." Other meanings are "an object having a circular form"; a "circular fold or coil"; "the surroundings or border of a circular object." Fortunately, the reading of metaphor does not force us to an either-or position; we can settle upon a central meaning without forfeiting an awareness of all the attendant connotations. My choice for this passage is "girded with rings," implying preparedness for battle, while keeping in mind all the possibilities for physical description.

Lines 5–7 are fairly explicit with regard to statement and contain none of the puzzling subtleties found in the last four lines. The word *nebb* (7) can mean "bill" or "beak-shaped object" but just as frequently means "face" or "countenance," that is, the exterior of the subject speaking. I take *hyrd* (8) not as a form of *hierd* 'keeper' or 'guardian' but as the noun *hyrd* meaning "door," therefore "entrance." This makes it possible to deal honestly with the verb *bregdan* (8), another word which gave earlier editors pause. It simply means to "move to and fro" or "vibrate." Rearranged, this portion of the sentence reads "Sometimes by means of my countenance I move the entrance of the treasure to and fro, backwards . . . ." The sentence concludes with the very complex statement ". . . when my lord wishes to take the remainder of that which he commanded from life (i.e., to death) with deadly power according to his desire." This very compact ending unifies the metaphoric statement at all three levels. The key to the passage lies in the word *laf*, a poetic word which appears repeatedly in periphrastic expressions. It means "what is left," "remainder," "inheritance," or "survivor," and the Anglo-Saxon mind would have been attuned to searching its meanings for what amounts to a narrative in miniature. The first meaning of the above passage summarizes the fact that the tumblers of a lock, within a keyhole, vibrate and fall back when the owner wishes to take the treasure thus contained—that is, the plunder left behind from those whom he has caused to be slain. Pursuing the conquest theme, it is the woman who is the survivor who has been captured when her tribe was defeated; she is the "leavings" of her kinsmen whom the lord has killed. In the light of the erotic theme, the image is a vivid presentation of a familiar notion, that the culmination of the sex act is a symbolic death. The subject vibrates and draws back as the lord takes what is left—the final moment of the experience—of that which he himself according to his savage power and his own desire caused to die. This theme has been explored in the psychological literature, but it is not necessary to go to esoteric sources to find analogues for this interpretation. We need go no further than *Antony and Cleopatra* (I, ii) to find a classic example of this concept developed as a literary symbol, when Enobarbus observes "I do think there is a mettle in death which commits some loving act upon her, she hath such a celerity in dying."

This poem moves rapidly with a sense of power that amounts to violence. At the same time, it offers the strongest argument of all for the mutuality of the sex experience. A female persona relates the incident; four of the significant verbs in the poem describe her own actions which seem to be both voluntary and vigorous. Her allusions to joy and pleasure place the same high value on the circumstance that we have seen in the other *Riddles*. As for the conquest, she seems to take an Amazonian delight in it—except for the figurative "wounded" there is no other word which suggests either discomfort or distaste.

This unexpected point of view gives rise to all manner of questions as to the authorship of a poem which found its way to us by way of monasteries and a cathedral. It is quite possible that the author was, indeed, a woman. There were many double religious houses in the Anglo-Saxon period and the behavior of their inmates often lapsed into a secularity which caused consternation among the Church fathers. Bede quotes Adamnan's description of the ill-fated monastery at Coldringham which was struck down by fire: "All of them, men and women alike, are either sunk in unprofitable sleep, or else awake only to sin. Even the cells which were built for prayer and study, are now converted into places for eating, drinking, gossip, or other amusements."[13]

Thomas Wright, an antiquarian of the last century, offers evidence that the pre-Christian priesthood of the Anglo-Saxons was a family office, passed down by heredity; the Roman Church had great difficulty in establishing the concept of a celibate clergy.[14] The depraved behavior which distressed Bede, among others, may have been nothing more reprehensible than marriage. The above *Riddles* might well have been the product of the "gossip and other amusements."

There are five other *Riddles* in the Exeter collection which can be termed sex-oriented. They have been solved as "Key," "Churn," "Poker," and two as "Bellows." They deal predominantly, as their titles suggest, with male prowess and do not add any notable insights into feminine psychology. Only in one area do they, without exception, support my conclusions. Even when describing mildly ludicrous circumstances, the language continues to be elevated; all the customary epithets for noblemen and warriors are employed—*þegn, frean, hæleð, secg, rinc,* and *gumrinc.* Nothing in the diction brands them as "lewd" or "coarse."

These comments make no argument for or against irregular sex practices; the information is too scanty to warrant conclusions. The lord-lady terminology of many of the poems points very strongly toward a regularized marital situation. However, our concern is not so much with institutions as with the more intimate problem of the definition of the Anglo-Saxon woman as a psychological entity. Even on such slight evidence we get a picture of her as a spirited individual, fully capable of physical and emotional gratification in this most important area of human life. We could do worse than try to recapture this image in our own time.

NOTES

1. For the discussion of this viewpoint, see St. Jerome's letter replying to Jovinian's defense of marriage which bears the brunt of the Wife of Bath's ridicule in lines 7–157 of her

prologue; John Hurt Fisher cites this and other antifeminist references in *The Complete Poetry and Prose of Geoffrey Chaucer* (New York: Holt, Rinehart and Winston, 1977), p. 107.

2. Sir Frank M. Stenton, "Place-Names as Evidence of Female Ownership of Land in Anglo-Saxon Times," *Academy* 7 (July 1906); rpt. in *Preparatory to Anglo-Saxon England,* ed. D. M. Stenton (Oxford: Clarendon Press, 1970), p. 6.

3. John F. Adams, "The Anglo-Saxon Riddle as Lyric Mode," *Criticism* 7 (Fall 1965): 335.

4. Frederick Tupper, Jr., ed., *The Riddles of the Exeter Book* (Boston: Ginn, 1910; rpt. Ann Arbor: University Microfilms, 1971), p. xci.

5. A. J. Wyatt, ed., *Old English Riddles* (Boston: D. C. Heath, 1912; rpt. Ann Arbor: University Microfilms, 1971), p. xxx.

6. Tupper, *Riddles of the Exeter Book,* p. xiii.

7. Usages cited are for the most part those given in Joseph Bosworth, ed., *An Anglo-Saxon Dictionary,* enlarged by T. Northcote Toller (Oxford: Clarendon Press, 1898; rpt. 1972; *Supplement,* 1898).

8. Craig Williamson, ed., *The Old English Riddles of the Exeter Book* (Chapel Hill: University of North Carolina Press, 1977); quotations and citations by line number of the riddles are taken from this collection; numbers in parentheses refer to *The Exeter Book,* ed. George Philip Krapp and Elliott Van Kirk Dobbie (New York: Columbia University Press, 1936).

9. Laws of Aethelbert, No. 73: "If a freeborn woman, with long hair misconducts herself, she shall pay 30 shillings as compensation." The usual interpretation is that the long hair denotes the freeborn woman as opposed to the slave. F. L. Attenborough, ed. and trans., *The Laws of the Earliest English Kings* (New York: Russell and Russell, 1963), pp. 15; n. 1, 178.

10. Tupper, p. 202.

11. Jacob Grimm, cited in Bosworth-Toller.

12. Moritz Trautman, cited by Krapp-Dobbie, n., p. 379.

13. Bede, *A History of the English Church and People,* trans. and ed. Leo Sherley-Price, rev. R. E. Latham (London: Penguin, 1968), p. 256.

14. Thomas Wright, *A History of Domestic Manners and Sentiments* (London: Chapman and Hall, 1862), p. 55.

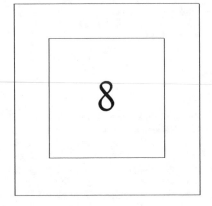

Ælfric's
Women Saints
Eugenia

In the last few years three major books in Old English studies have looked at women and the literary image of women in Anglo-Saxon England, while at the same time several articles and conference papers have also sought to bring new perspectives to bear on similar themes.[1] Yet this new movement continues this century's characteristic disregard of Old English prose—not to mention its major figure, Ælfric—and at best downplays the vast corpus of prose and its potential contribution to the field. With this paper I begin a study of women saints in Ælfric's *Lives of the Saints,* offering a reading of Ælfric's views on women. The focus here will be on sexuality in the *Life of Eugenia,* and the depiction of transvestism will also be a major theme. How Ælfric treats sexual or erotic details found in his sources is a necessary issue. Known for the "sobriety" of his doctrinal views and for a style that is "less strained" than that of his contemporaries, does Ælfric react with comparable "sanity" to the excesses of Latin hagiography?[2] Thus, by treating Ælfric in the context of the issues of women's studies this circumscribed study can lead to a revised estimate of Ælfric *and* contribute to the valid incorporation of new views into approaches to the whole of Old English literature. While perhaps any of Ælfric's major lives of women could provide an appropriate beginning for this study, the *Life of Eugenia* has, as will be seen, some special claim because of its treatment of sexuality.[3]

Ælfric's *Life of Eugenia* is a complex narrative that like so many saints' lives relates an exemplary life from birth through triumphant martyrdom, which should in turn inspire the reader (or the audience) to a moral conversion and ultimately salvation—or at least the hope of it. Conversion of self, family, and miscellaneous antagonists, particularly secular authorities, becomes not only a kind of moral triumph in the genre, but, in its fundamental form, a metamorphosis. Eugenia is virgin and martyr and, as is to be expected, the preservation of her virginity is a major narrative motif. What sets Eugenia apart from other female saints is that she is a transvestite; i.e., she disguises herself as a man, living the life of a monk so successfully that she becomes the abbot of her community after three years of exemplary monastic rigor.[4] Only when her inverted sexuality inspires the lust of another woman does disguise lead to recognition at a trial presided over by Eugenia's father. Deuteronomy may condemn transvestism and St. Paul rail against it,[5] but Eugenia nevertheless triumphs unto salvation as do those converted by her moral ways. It is inverted sexuality that creates the narrative and moral complexities of this story, making comparatively unusual demands on Ælfric's skills as storyteller and moral teacher. To see how Ælfric treats these erotic and sexual details, it will be necessary to offer a close analysis of the *Life*.

Eugenia is born into an excellent pagan family: her father Philip has an imperial commission to rule Alexandria, and he sends his only daughter to study Greek philosophy and Latin eloquence. The deep and irreconcilable conflict with *saeculum* 'the world' is telegraphed in these sketchy, understated background details, but Ælfric suspends the political theme here to focus on Eugenia and her education. In the course of Eugenia's studies, St. Paul's teaching comes into her hand—*becom hyre on hand* (24)[6] is the casual expression—and her mind *mycclum onbryrd* (26). Skeat translates her reaction as "greatly aroused," but the contemporary reader can be misled by the Modern English: Eugenia is not emotionally or sexually stimulated; rather, hers is a religious feeling related to, if not actually, compunction, which includes weeping as part of a change of heart.[7] What is not clear from her hopeful reaction to St. Paul's teaching is her father's reaction. Ælfric suppresses any elaboration of the father-daughter relationship here: after all, Eugenia asks her father for permission to search for Christian teachers that he himself had driven away (28–34). After this narrative fact, Ælfric gives only another: *Hwæt þa Eugenia ardlice færde* 'So then Eugenia quickly journeyed' (35). The simple sequential *þa* glosses over defiance or (unlikely) acquiescence or any potential dramatic conflict between pagan father and near-Christian daughter, which narrative option in the genre remains only latent.

When Eugenia encounters the Christians and their hymn-singing, she has a second attack of compunction, this time with weeping, and she decides to join the Christians. But Eugenia is not traveling alone. She has two companions, Protus and Jacintus, who had been schoolmates learning Latin and Greek with her. As Ælfric introduces Protus and Jacintus, he emphasizes that Eugenia's *twægen cnihtas* 'two young men'

> . . . wæron *eunuchi*, þæt synt belisnode
> and wæron heora hlæfdige holde and getrywe.
> (46–47)
>
> (. . . were *eunuchi*, that is to say, castrated, and were to their mistress true and faithful.)

Whatever Philip's prudent or practical intentions might have been in giving his daughter two such companions, Ælfric now makes sexuality a major theme in this *Life* by his straightforward, glosslike explanation of the Latin word. For this *Life*, *cnihtas* now carries a major contextual definition, "eunuch," which is hardly its customary signification.[8] This quiet, but important, semantic shift is in the background of Eugenia's more daring action:

> Ða nam eugenia hi [Protus and Jacintus] on sundor spræce.
> het hi gebroðra . and bæd þæt hi
> hyre fæx forcurfon wæpmonna wysan .
> and mid wædum gehiwodon . swylce heo cniht wære .
> wolde ðam cristenan genealecan
> on wærlican hiwe . þæt heo ne wurde ameldod .

$$(48-53)$$

> (Then Eugenia took them apart in conversation, called them brethren, and besought that they would shear her hair after the fashion of men, and disguise her with garments as if she were a boy. She desired to approach the Christians in the garb of a man, that she might not be betrayed.)

Eugenia's conversion of heart to Christianity requires a transformation of sex, or at least the appearance of sex. And her transformation is dual: she wishes to appear as a man and she wishes to be brother to her eunuchs. Note the collocation *heo cniht* 'she boy' (51), which is good syntax, technically bad grammar (because of the pronominal reference), but correct sexuality in this *Life*. Eugenia is repudiating her own sexuality, which is *de rigueur* for those who join "sex-negative" Christianity, and she is presumably changing her social status. As Vern L. Bullough has explained, female cross-dressing—here Eugenia's desire to be a man—has generally proven acceptable in Christianity, biblical proscriptions to the contrary, for such a change is a healthy desire, as Bullough puts it, "a normal longing not unlike the desire of a peasant to become a noble."[9] In fact at several times in this *Life*, Ælfric repeats this theme and the phrase *in wærlican hiwe* 'in the garb of a man' or similar phrases.[10] The further complication of this *Life* is Eugenia's desire to become a brother to her companions, who are presumably below her in social class, and who are themselves deprived of their male organs. Eugenia's sexual inversion to male and to (brother-) eunuch and her accompanying social change can only obliterate her sexual identity. These changes symbolize the totality of her conversion to Christianity. The announced motivation in the narrative for her disguise, that she would not be betrayed (or disclosed), *ameldod* (53), has a touch of the tautological about it. Females often disguise themselves as males to protect their chastity, but it is hard to see how that concern should be present when joining a group of presumably chaste Christians. Pagans would also presumably be welcome among Christians, for after all they are ripe for conversion. One can thus only infer Eugenia's need to change status to enter the group as the motivation more implied than expressed.

These thematic inversions and the narrative complication of transvestism create problems for plot and story. However devout the disguised Eugenia and her companions might be, they are still unbaptized. True baptism would require Eugenia's real identity and discovery. Fortunately, the bishop Helenus has a vision that informs him of the entire situation. It is a masterstroke to have the narrative device of vision overcome the narrative problem posed by disguise.[11] With full knowledge of who

Eugenia and her companions are, Helenus baptizes the three in secret. He praises Eugenia's virginity and prophesies persecutions because of it; he encourages her companions, elevating their status by citing Christ's words, "I do not call you servants, but on the contrary you are my friends."[12] Eugenia and her companions thus receive episcopal endorsement for their actions, and indeed Helenus bids them continue their secret lives in the service of the minster. On the whole, however, Helenus is a plot figure, the recipient of a timely vision and a prophesier of further incidents in the *Life*. As far as thematics are concerned, the need for disguise now could be considered nonfunctional: Eugenia and her companions have become Christians. The continuation of disguise, however, allows Eugenia and her companions to achieve further moral perfection. Eugenia lives in the minster *mid wærlican mode* 'with virile intent' (93), such that she is further transformed; Ælfric says she is *awend of wulfe to sceape* 'changed . . . from a wolf to a sheep' (100). The image is startling because Eugenia has hardly been wolvish in any of her actions or thoughts, but it does emphasize the fundamental redirection of her moral life.

The narrative tension of disguise increases with Eugenia's success as a servant of God. When her abbot dies, the brothers, implicitly considering her to be the best of their own and not knowing that she is in a basic way not one of their own, choose her as abbot. Eugenia's reaction to the burdens of office is human and real:

Ða wearð þæt mæden mycclum hohful .
hu heo æfre wæras wissian sceolde.

(121–22)

(Then became the maiden extremely anxious how she was ever to direct men . . .)

Virtue triumphs as Eugenia excels as moral exemplar and administrator, further given divine aid to act as healer and exorcist. Yet to this point Eugenia, earlier praised for her virginity, has never had her virginity tested. As Milton would have it, hers has been a "fugitive and cloistered virtue," and one protected by disguise to boot. The logic of the plot would seem to require that Eugenia-the-man be the object of lustful attention by a woman. And so it is that Melantia, a wealthy and wanton woman who has been cured of fever by Eugenia, attempts to seduce her transvestite physician. The inverted situation is the stuff of Roman comedy or Restoration farce, but the context of hagiography and Ælfric's treatment control the comic potential.[13] The persistent and lust-struck Melantia offers gifts, whispers sweet nothings, and feigns illness to see her physician again. Melantia, evidently saying that she and her deceased husband had had no intercourse, offers her virginal self along with her inherited wealth. Eugenia responds with pieties, and Melantia tries the direct approach with an embrace. Blessing herself, Eugenia responds as Jankyn might have to the Wife of Bath, saying that

. . . heo soðlice wære
galnysse ontendnyss . and gramena mæge .
þeostra gefæra . and mid sweartnysse afylled .
Ðeaðes dohtor and deofles fætel.

(172–75)

(. . . she verily was
a kindler of lust, a child of wrath,
a companion of darkness, and filled with blackness,
a daughter of death, and the devil's vessel.)[14]

Yet the sharp rebuke helps rob the scene of any comic potential, while Melantia's reaction further underlines the seriousness of the situation. Melantia, though ashamed,
opts not for conversion but for falsehood to cover her lustful advances lest Eugenia
~~hyre word ameldian~~ 'her words disclose' (179). The word *ameldian* echoes Eugenia's
earlier, more moral choice (53) to seek moral perfection, not mere deception,
through disguise. The falsehood consists of lying accusations to Philip that the
transvestite abbot was the initiator of the lust. The ironies deriving from Eugenia's
disguise are here multiple. Unbeknownst to all, the pagan Philip is called upon to
defend the apparent virtue of the wanton widow against his transvestite Christian
daughter who is in fact virtuous beyond reproach. The scribes of the Otho and Julius
versions, in fact, cannot agree on how to present Eugenia's switching, the former
considering her a "he" and an "abbot" while the latter considers her a "she" and
"Eugenia."[15] At the trial Melantia marshals false witnesses, her servants, who offer
damaging testimony that enrages Philip. But Eugenia's defense is irrefutable. She
tears off her clothes, baring her breast to her father-judge, and declares:

> . . . þu eart min fæder
> and þin gebædda claudia . gebær me to mannum
> and ðas ðine gesætlan synd mine gebroðra .
> auitus . and særgius . and ic soðlice eom
> eugenia gehaten . þin agen dohtor .
> and ic for cristes lufe . forlæt eow ealle .
> and middaneardlices lustas swa swa meox forseah.
> Her synd eac þa cnihtas . þe ic cydde mine digolnysse
> protus . et iacintus . þine fostercyld .
> mid ðam ic becom to cristes scole .
> and þær on drohtnode oð þisne andwærdan dæg .
> and ðam ic wylle æfre oð ende þeowian.
>
> (235–46)

> (. . . "Thou art my father!
> and thy spouse Claudia bore me as a child,
> and these that sit beside thee are my brethren,
> Avitus and Sergius, and verily I am
> named Eugenia, thine own daughter.
> And I, for Christ's love, abandoned you all,
> and despised as dung the lusts of the world.
> Here are also the servants to whom I told my secret,
> Protus and Jacinctus, thy foster-children,
> with whom I went to the school of Christ.
> and therein have ministered unto this present day,
> and Him will I serve ever, even unto the end.")

This somewhat lengthy speech, effectively a plot summary, closes the disguise motif and serves as a multiple recognition scene just as in "classic" romance: daughter to father (and family), accused to accuser, individual to all of society. There are narrative complexities within each kind of recognition. Philip and his family thought Eugenia dead, having erected a golden statue of her in memory, and she is now resurrected, so to speak. Melantia, her cold and calculating viciousness exposed, is undisguised woman at her moral worst, contrasting with de-sexed Eugenia. Melantia's punishment comes not from Philip, Eugenia interceding, but rather directly from Christ who sends a fire that totally destroys her mansion. So much for woman's lust. The harsh, almost personally vindictive punishment, is in harmony with "black farce."

The public recognition opens what is effectively the second half of the *Life*, which affects *saeculum* in direct ways. After a public celebration where Eugenia is decked with gold (somewhat unwillingly), Philip follows his daughter into Christianity; the people choose him as bishop; and a new governor has Philip murdered on imperial command. Eugenia moves to Rome, where she is well received by her father's friends. The Roman scene has several counterpoints to the Alexandrian scene. Eugenia's Christian activities attract Basilla, a heathen maiden, who cannot approach Eugenia because of opposition. Eugenia sends her eunuchs, now described as *twægen halgan* 'the two saints' (348), to teach Basilla, with the result that Bishop Cornelius secretly baptizes her. The two virgins now work together to advance Christianity, along with the pure widow Claudia (Eugenia's mother), and Protus and Jacintus. In narrative structure it is clear that Eugenia and Basilla are heroine and surrogate, or perhaps more succinctly, doubles. Eugenia is the foreground character, Basilla the background character.[16] Genre demands that both (indeed all Christians) face martyrdom. The presence of Basilla in the narrative allows Ælfric a form of narrative economy. Eugenia's virginity has already been tested and proven, if somewhat unconventionally. There is no narrative or thematic need to test Eugenia again. Basilla, however, can face the conventional test of virginity when the pagan Pompeius seeks to marry her. Of course, Basilla *hæfde gecoren crist hyre to brydguman* 'had chosen Christ as her Bridegroom' (352), and she refuses. Pompeius appeals to the Emperor, who orders Basilla to marry Pompeius or face death *mid heardum sweorde* 'with hard sword' (360), and all Christians to return to heathendom or face death. The emperor's edict links virginity and Christian belief in such a way as to suggest that to be a Christian is to be a virgin. Basilla accordingly suffers martyrdom, Ælfric repeating that

> . . . nolde basilla . brydguman geceosan .
> nænne butan crist þe heo gecoren hæfde.
>
> (364–65)

(. . . would not Basilla choose as her bridegroom
any other but Christ, whom she had chosen. . . .)

The eunuchs Protus and Jacintus face death too. While theirs is a simple test to worship false gods, Ælfric emphasizes after their execution that

> . . . næron næfre on life
> þurh wif besmytene . ac hi wundeon on clænnysse .
> oð heora lifes ænde . mid mycclum geleafan.
>
> (380–82)

([These martyrs] were never, throughout their lives,
defiled with women, but continued in purity
unto their lives' end, with much faith. . . .)

Faith and chastity are moral equivalents even when within the bounds of "conventional" Christian morality; the moral agents are not capable of sexual activity.

The martyrdom of Eugenia, however, brings the several sexual and moral themes together in Christian triumph. With a quiet and unmentioned irony, Eugenia is asked to sacrifice to Diana, the goddess of chastity in classical mythology.[17] She refuses, bringing down Diana's temple through prayer, and hence faces successively and successfully drowning and fiery baths. Thrown into a dark prison for twenty days without food, Eugenia finds relief when a radiant and visionary Christ offers her a snow-white loaf, promising martyrdom on the day that he *com to mannum* 'came to humanity' (410). The phrase denotes Christ's physical appearance on earth, but further it connotes his Incarnation, the transformation of transformations when the divine became human, if you will, that makes salvation possible for all. Christ's birthday is Eugenia's birthday into eternity. Claudia sees her daughter in a celestial vision, adorned with gold, which confirms her final transformation. The mention of gold echoes previous golden moments of transformation for Eugenia, one will recall: when she was thought dead but only converted to Christianity, her family made a golden statue of her, and when she was discovered at the trial, she too was adorned with gold. This recurrent image helps unify the main parts of the narrative.

Ælfric's *Life of Eugenia* derives of course from the Latin tradition. It is not at all established which version of the *Vita Sanctae Eugeniae* Ælfric might be following, and indeed the scholarship on the Latin tradition itself has not developed in any full or complete way.[18] The apparent mainline version, popular and early, is a considerably more extensive treatment, offering many more details about Eugenia, her life, and its background than Ælfric gives. Ælfric's characteristic method of abbreviation is obviously at work here, if the mainline Latin version is a reliable guide. An exhaustive point-for-point comparison with a Latin version of uncertain status is likely to raise more problems than it solves—and this treatment is clearly provisional pending Patrick Zettel's promised study—but a selective treatment can highlight Ælfric's apparent intention to hold first to a narrative line that creates a coherent story. Thus, in the Latin, Helenus and the first Christians Eugenia meets play a considerably more important role. For instance, a full chapter (cap. v) of the thirty in the Latin *vita* recounts the struggle between Helenus and the sorcerer Zareas. This struggle with dark but ineffectual powers has no direct narrative bearing on Eugenia's progress toward salvation. The incident highlights the theme of sorcery, a charge Christians face whenever they are successful against pagan persecution. This theme is present at the end of both Latin and Ælfrician treatments when Eugenia foils the pagans, but in the latter it is merely incidental. Likewise the Latin text gives much exposition or background material on the Christians, their observances, and their fervor. The history of early Christianity could have proven an interesting byway for Ælfric to follow, but he gives only the amount of information necessary to establish a credible basis for Eugenia's conversion.

It is Ælfric's avoidance of source material supporting his treatment of the sexual theme that presents more interesting problems. In cap. ii the unknown author of the Latin gives personal information about Eugenia:

> Erat enim acris ingenii, et tam memoriae capax, ut quidquid audiendo semel vel legendo potuisset arripere, perpetuo retineret. Erat autem Eugenia pulchra facie et eleganti corpore. . . . (PL 73, 607)

> (She had a sharp mind, and so retentive a memory that whatever she learned quickly by hearing or reading she retained forever. She was, moreover, good-looking and had a good figure. . . .)[19]

This intellectual and physical beauty leads to marriage proposals, including a potential match with the son of the consul, all of which Eugenia *animo castitatis obsisteret,* 'resisted with the soul of chastity' (PL 73, 607). Ælfric gives nothing of this material. As the discussion above indicated, Eugenia's first real moral test in Ælfric is the attempted seduction by Melantia. This suppression of biographical information is the first of several places where Ælfric eschews details or incidents or speeches that advance the theme of sexuality in the Latin. For example, when Eugenia introduces herself to Helenus as "Eugenius," Helenus says: *Recte tu Eugenium vocas; viriliter enim agis* 'You rightly call yourself Eugenius; you act in a manly way' (PL 73, 610). Possibly the most important passage in the Latin and not in Ælfric is part of the recognition scene speech that Ælfric otherwise quotes directly. Before she bares herself Eugenia says:

> Tanta est enim virtus nominis ejus ⟨Christi⟩, ut etiam feminae in timore ejus positae virilem obtineant dignitatem; et neque ei sexus diversitas fide potest inveniri superior, cum beatus Paulus apostolus, magister omnium Christianorum, dicat quod apud Dominum non sit discretio masculi et feminae, omnes enim in Christo unum sumus [Galatians 3:28]. Hujus ergo normam animo fervente suscepi, et ex confidentia quam in Christo habui, nolui esse femina, sed virginitatem immaculatam tota animi intentione conservans, virum gessi constanter in Christo. Non enim infrunitam honestatis simulationem assumpsi, ut vir feminam simularem; sed femina viriliter agendo, virum gessi, virginitatem quae in Christo est fortiter amplectendo. (PL 73, 614)

> (So great indeed is the power of His Name that even women standing in fear of it may obtain a manly dignity; nor can a difference in sex be considered superiority in faith, when blessed Paul the Apostle, the master of all Christians, says that before God there will be no distinction between masculine and feminine, we are "all indeed one in Christ." Therefore, his precept I have followed with a burning heart, and from the firm trust which I have had in Christ, I have not wanted to be a woman, but preserving a spotless virginity with a total effort of the soul, I have acted consistently as a man. I have not put on a senseless pretense of respectability so that as a man I might imitate a woman, but I, a woman, have acted as a man by doing as a man, by embracing boldly a virginity, which is in Christ.)[20]

This passage gives the moral explanation for Eugenia's transvestism, deriving its ultimate justification from Galatians: masculine and feminine will be one in Christ.[21] Whether in Paradise this state is true androgyny or true sexlessness one might leave to mystical theology. Eugenia also makes public her motivation and explains further her search for (moral) status or how a woman can be like a man. In the Latin *vita* this speech provides the thematic foundations for much of the narration. In Ælfric, by contrast, six lines present only one of the ideas in the Latin, Eugenia's preservation of virginity:

> Hwæt ða eugenia seo æþele fæmne .
> cwæð þæt heo wolde hi sylfe bediglian .
> and criste anum hyre clænnysse healdan .
> on mægðhade wuniende . mannum uncuð .
> and forðy underfænge æt fruman þa gyrlan .
> wærlices hades . and wurde geefsod.
>
> (227–32)

> (Well then, Eugenia, the noble woman,
> said that she had desired to keep herself secret,
> and to preserve her purity to Christ alone,
> living in virginity, unknown to man,
> and therefore at the first had assumed the robes
> of a man's garb, and had had her hair shorn.)

Why did Ælfric render this speech in so limited a way? John Anson suggests that some early baptismal rites, particularly those with Gnostic associations, have sexual themes, including transvestism, in actions seeking to be *enim in Christo* 'one in Christ Jesus'.[22] It is not likely that Ælfric would have particular knowledge of these early rites. More likely is Ælfric's perception that the doctrine expressed and implied in Galatians 3:28 requires a great deal of complicated analysis to present, including notions of the resurrection of the body and the beatified state, while the idea of preservation of virginity is a simple enough concept to relate. Incomplete or incorrect explication of Galatians 3:28 could inspire irregular Christian conduct or observance. There is something blatant and heavy-handed about this part of the speech too, but a purely literary explanation may be not as compelling in this case.

What then do a close reading of the *Life of Eugenia* and a comparative analysis with the Latin *vita* reveal about Ælfric's treatment of sexuality? Ælfric's literary architectonics has fashioned from the looser Latin a two-part *Life*, which can be characterized by systematic contraries as Alexandria and Rome, Eugenia and her surrogate(s), disguise and (public) recognition, "unconventional" and "conventional" sexuality, among other contraries. Ælfric's power of abstraction has sharpened and focussed incidents from the Latin in such a way that transvestism (or the Melantia incident) takes on a central importance in narrative and theme that it did not have in the Latin. The romance motifs of disguise and recognition have a comparatively greater narrative impact in Ælfric, thus bringing forward the theme of sexuality in high relief, while the "doubling" of Eugenia and Basilla balances and contrasts, and verbal echoes contribute a unifying effect among narrative elements rather more disparate in the Latin. But the high relief is unelaborated in its verbal style. Ælfric's treatment of scenes and situations tends toward understatement and, on the surface, unselfconsciousness. Melantia's attempts at seduction are unelaborated, and Eugenia's recognition speech is shortened by eliminating most of its sexual content. In a sense, Ælfric's shaping of incident and his telling of incident work in a harmonious contrariety: he offers an erotic story with no erotic content.

Does the *Life of Eugenia* repudiate women and woman's sexuality? It would be mere simplistic surface-reading to say "yes." Rather, it is Galatians 3:28 and its complex view of sexuality that is operating in the deep structure of Ælfric's *Life*. Eugenia has un-womaned herself, Protus and Jacintus are un-manned, and these three sexless saints anticipate on earth the state in heaven. Melantia and Pompeius are too much of this world in seeking sexual satisfaction, while Claudia as chaste widow and Basilla as virgin are ready for the beatific life. However many sexes there may finally be, the Pauline vision of none is metaphysical indeed.

The *Life of Eugenia,* therefore, is a complex narrative about sexuality that within the boundaries of hagiography demonstrates Ælfric's special talents as teacher and storyteller. Yet Ælfric's *Life of Eugenia* is not at all known in the field of hagiography, where it should be a part of the saint's narrative history, and it is not a work that occupies any particular place in Old English literary studies. The developing field of women's studies, bringing with it a new interest in the corpus of literature and in new themes therein, can on the other hand become the occasion for a reinvestigation of various areas in Old English literature that hitherto have received little literary attention. Old texts can come out as new. These new critical interests thus fulfill their promise when they stimulate a positive reconsideration of Ælfric's *Lives of the Saints* and provide a framework for approaching this collection. Only one of the *Lives* was the subject of this paper. Further consideration of other women in the *Lives of the Saints* should enhance and develop the study of the major prose writer of the Old English period and extend the impact of the critical interests of women's studies.

NOTES

1. Helen Damico, *Beowulf's Wealhtheow and the Valkyrie Tradition* (Madison: University of Wisconsin Press, 1984); Jane Chance, *Woman as Hero in Old English Literature* (Syracuse, N.Y.: Syracuse University Press, 1986); Christine Fell with Cecily Clark and Elizabeth Williams, *Women in Anglo-Saxon England and The Impact of 1066* (Bloomington: Indiana University Press, 1984). These books have useful bibliographies directing the reader to other secondary sources. For a sense of the latest developments in this fast-moving field see the Appendix "Abstracts of Papers in Anglo-Saxon Studies," published in each Spring issue of the *Old English Newsletter.*

2. The best overview of Ælfric is still Peter Clemoes, "Ælfric," in *Continuations and Beginnings,* ed. E. G. Stanley (London: Thomas Nelson and Sons Ltd, 1966), pp. 176–209, esp. 184–85; in the same collection, see also Rosemary Woolf, "Saints' Lives," pp. 37–66, esp. 60–62. See also James Hurt, *Ælfric,* Twayne English Author Series, vol. 131 (New York: Twayne Publishers Inc., 1972), esp. 60–83 on the Lives of the Saints. Stanley B. Greenfield and Daniel Calder, with Michael Lapidge, offer the latest treatment of Ælfric in the context of prose writers contemporary to him: *A New Critical History of Old English Literature* (New York: New York University Press, 1986), pp. 68–106.

3. The standard collection is Walter W. Skeat, ed., *Ælfric's Lives of the Saints,* Early English Text Society, o.s., vols. 76, 82, 94, 114 (London: Oxford University Press, 1881–1900; repr. in two vols., 1966); I cite here the reprint, vol. I, pp. 24–51, with trans. *en face,* by line number. Not all the *Lives* printed are Ælfric's: nos. 23, 23b, 30, and 33 are not his. No. 33, the *Life of Eufrasia,* who is another transvestite saint, is relevant to the present study. I give Skeat's translation for Old English passages. Skeat did translate the *Life of Eugenia* and others, but the "greater part" of the translation appearing in the edition is owed to the Misses Gunning and Wilkinson, who are generally uncredited in the scholarship and on whose work, Skeat says, he made "inconsiderable" alterations; see Skeat's Preface to Volume II, liv–lv. Robert Alexander criticizes aspects of Skeats' edition and calls for a new edition in "W. W. Skeat and Ælfric," *Annuale Mediaevale* 22 (1982): 36–54. For a discussion of Ælfric's canon, see Peter Clemoes, "The Chronology of Ælfric's Works," in *The Anglo-Saxons: Studies in Some Aspects of Their History and Culture Presented to Bruce Dickins,* ed. Peter Clemoes (London: Bowes and Bowes, 1959), pp. 212–47 (repr. with additions as *Old English Newsletter Subsidia* 5 [1980]), and John Collins Pope, ed., *Homilies of Ælfric: A Supplementary Collection,* Early English Text Society, o.s., vol. 259 (London: Oxford University Press, 1967), vol. 1, pp. 136–45. Students of Ælfric owe Luke Reinsma a considerable debt for his *Ælfric: An Annotated Bibliography* (New York and London: Garland Publishing, Inc., 1987); Reinsma annotates some twelve items relevant to the *Life,* published through 1982 (see *Index of Works* under *LS* 2 Eugenia).

4. For transvestism and transvestite sainthood, see the following: John Anson, "The Female Transvestite in Early Monasticism: the Origin and Development of a Motif," *Viator* 5 (1974): 1–32; Vern L. Bullough, "Transvestites in the Middle Ages," *American Journal of Sociology* 79 (1974): 1381–94; Hippolyte Delehaye, *The Legends of the Saints,* trans. Donald Attwater (New York: Fordham University Press, 1962), pp. 150–56. Delehaye studies St. Eugenia in *Études sur le legendier Romain,* Subsidia Hagiographica 23 (Brussels: Société des Bollandistes, 1936), pp. 171–86. The Bollandist Delehaye is interested in disentangling the reality of the saint from fiction, a recurrent theme in early scholarship but not of interest here. For transvestitism in early modern France and particularly "Women on Top," see Natalie Zemon Davis, *Society and Culture in Early Modern France* (Stanford: Stanford University Press, 1975), pp. 124–51. Perhaps the most famous transvestite in the Middle Ages was Joan of Arc; see Marina Warner, *Joan of Arc: The Image of Female Heroism* (Harmondsworth: Penguin Books, 1983), pp. 146–63, for Joan as the ideal androgyne.

5. Deuteronomy 22:5, *Non induetur mulier veste virili, nec vir utetur veste feminea; abominabilis enim apud Deum est qui facit haec* 'The woman shall not put on men's clothing, and the man shall not put on women's clothing; for the one who does so is abominable before God'; 1 Corinthians 11:14–15, *Nec ipsa natura docet vos, quod vir quidem si comam nutriat, ignominia est illi; mulier vero si comam nutriat, gloria est illi; quoniam capilli pro velamine ei data sunt* 'For does not nature itself teach you, that if a man has long hair, it is a shame to him; but truly if a woman has long hair, it is a glory to her; because her hair is given to her as a covering'. But see the discussion of Galatians 3:28 below.

6. What is lost in the transmission here is a possible link to early Christian belief and observance, some of which comes forward trailing Gnostic associations. See Anson, "Female Transvestite": 21 and 1–11 for the background.

7. See *onbryrdan* and *onbryrdness* s.v. in Joseph Bosworth and T. Northcote Toller, *An Anglo-Saxon Dictionary* (Oxford: Oxford University Press, 1898; repr. 1964) and Toller's *Supplement* (Oxford: Oxford University Press, 1921; repr. 1955); hereafter cited as Bosworth-Toller. Alcuin describes compunction in cap. xi of his *Liber de Virtutibus et Vitiis,* in *Patrologia Latina,* ed. J. P. Migne (Paris: 1844–91), 101, 620–21; hereafter cited as PL by volume and column.

8. See *belisnian* s.v. in Bosworth-Toller.

9. Bullough, "Transvestites": 1392.

10. To summarize: see lines 53, 84, 93, 232. Perhaps one might also count *on læces hiwe* 'in a physician's garb' (186, 203).

11. The *Vita Eugeniae* [presented by Heribert Rosweyde, *Vitae Patrum* (Antwerp: 1628)] can be found twice in the PL: among the works of Rufinus in PL 21, 1105–22, where there are helpful chapter headings, and as part of the *Vitae Patrum* in PL 73, 605–20. There is also a version in Boninus Mombritius, ed., *Sanctuarium Seu Vitae Sanctorum*, 2 vols. (Paris: Apud Albertum Fontemoing, Editorem, 1910), considered earlier and not of as wide currency, which Delehaye compares in part to the Rosweyde version in *Étude sur le legendier Romain*, pp. 176–77. The details presented by Delehaye suggest that Ælfric did not follow the Mombritius version. For the Helenus chapters, see PL 73, 607–10. In Ælfric's treatment, where there are fewer details, the narrative function of vision is correspondingly sharper.

12. John 15:15, *Iam non dicam vos servos . . .; vos autem dici amicos* 'For I do not call you servants: but I call you friends'.

13. Humor and comedy exist in saints' lives, but it is not always easy to tell when there is a jest, particularly when Ælfric's style is so measured and cool. For humor in hagiography, see Ernst Robert Curtius, *European Literature and the Latin Middle Ages,* trans. Willard R. Trask (New York and Evanston: Harper and Row Publishers, 1963), pp. 425–28; Charles W. Jones, *Saints' Lives and Chronicles in Early England* (Ithaca: Cornell University Press, 1947), pp. 67–69. Marina Warner has pointed out to me that St. Dympna, fleeing her incestuous father, left with her confessor and the court jester.

14. Compare PL 73, 612–13.

15. See Skeat's notes at the bottom of pp. 34, 36, 38. Line 204 is exemplary in its gender confusion.

16. See generally Robert Rogers, *The Double in Literature* (Detroit: Wayne State University Press, 1970), esp. pp. 1–17 on varieties of doubling; and also Otto Rank, *The Double: A Psychoanalytic Study,* ed. and trans. Harry Tucker, Jr. (Chapel Hill: University of North Carolina Press, 1971), esp. pp. 8–33 on doubles in literature.

17. Ælfric discusses the gods of both classical and Scandinavian mythology in "De Falsis Diis," in *Homilies of Ælfric: A Supplementary Collection,* vol. 2, ed. John C. Pope, Early English Text Society, o.s., vol. 260 (London: Oxford University Press, 1968), pp. 677–712, esp. pp. 681–86, but he does not mention Diana.

18. Patrick H. Zettel's "Saints' Lives in Old English: Latin Manuscripts and Vernacular Accounts: Ælfric," *Peritia* 1 (1982): 17–37, offers a key from his study of the "Cotton-Corpus Legendary," a collection later than Ælfric but closer to the source which Ælfric probably used for his *Lives* than many printed editions cited in prior studies. Zettel has promised a more detailed study beyond this introduction in *Peritia.* For the *Life of Eugenia,* Zettel cites Hereford, Cathedral Library, MS P 7 vi, one of the four extant manuscripts of this Legendary (written at Hereford, c. 1150), as offering "a strikingly close textual correspondence" (37), but he does not offer specific parallels to the *Life of Eugenia* as such, focusing rather on other examples. For a sense of the complexities of the Latin tradition in the tradition of the Old English Martyrology, see J. E. Cross, "Passio S. Eugeniae et Comitum and the Old English Martyrology," *Notes and Queries* n.s. 29 (1982): 392–97.

19. The free translations here and following are mine.

20. See also Anson's translation ("Female Transvestite": 23).

21. Galatians 3:28: *Non est Iudaeus, neque Graecus; non est servus, neque liber; non est masculus, neque femina. Omnes enim vos unum estis in Christo Iesu* 'There is not Jew, nor Greek; there is not slave, nor free; there is not male, nor female. For you are all one in Christ Jesus'.

22. Anson, "Female Transvestite": 23.

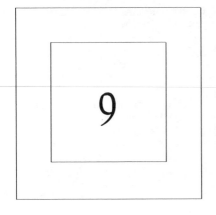

The Ides of the Cotton Gnomic Poem

Ides sceal dyrne cræfte
fæmne hire freond gesecean   gif heo nelle on folce geþeon
þæt hi man beagum gebicge.[1] (43b–45a)

Elliott Van Kirk Dobbie translates this passage, "A woman must visit her friend with hidden craft (i.e., secretly), if she does not wish to bring it about among the people that she is bought with rings," and comments, "The passage is somewhat complicated in phraseology and the meaning is not entirely clear."[2] R. Macgregor Dawson says of it:

> It does not fit in with the content of the surrounding gnomes, nor does it follow clearly in thought; yet it is bound in by alliteration and cannot be dismissed as interpolation. There is, however, the possibility that the word *dyrne* is the key. It may have been suggested by the weather and demon gnomes just before. *Dyrne* is a term used of Grendel and his kin (*Beowulf* 1357) and it may be that the *þyrs* prompted the standard form *dyrne cræfte*.[3]

However, Professor Dawson may be unduly pessimistic; and a close study of the vocabulary and total meaning of the passage may suggest other links in the chain of ideas.

First, the word *ides* itself appears to be common to Old English and West Germanic, and maybe even to general Germanic. Old Saxon *idis* and Old High German *itis* are applied to Mary; and, most important, *idisi* is the word used for the women who sit working spells of binding and loosing in the Old High German *First Merseburg Charm*. It would seem that an *ides* was no ordinary woman; and indeed Jakob Grimm believed that, like the Greek νυμφη, the word was applied in earliest times to superhuman beings, midway between goddesses and ordinary women.[4] More recent writers have tended to discount this view; but perhaps *ides* may have been originally a word for woman in her sacral and mysterious aspect, as described by Tacitus:

Inesse quin etiam sanctum aliquid et providum putant, nec aut consilia earum aspernantur, aut responsa neglegunt. Vidimus sub divo Vespasiano Veledam diu apud plerosque numinis loco habitam; sed et olim Auriniam et complures alias venerati sunt, non adulatione nec tanquam facerent deas.[5]

(Moreover, they [the Germani] think there is something sacred and prophetic [about women], and they do not despise their counsel, nor neglect their replies. We ourselves saw in the time of the deified Vespasian, that Veleda was regarded by many for a long time as divine. But some time ago Aurinia and many others were venerated, not out of servility, nor as if they were making goddesses.)

Moreover, although Tacitus declares that among the Germani lots were cast by the priest in a public inquiry, and by the father of the family if in private,[6] Caesar says that it was reported to him that "it was a custom among the Germans that their matrons should declare by lots and divinations whether it was expedient or not to engage in warfare."[7]

Can we assume that, if the word *ides* was used with such connotations among the Germani, it would have retained any of them in Old English? It appears as a gloss for *virgo invencula(m)* 'prescient maiden', but otherwise only in poetry[8] where it is applied to all sorts and conditions of women—for example, in the Old English *Genesis* it is used for Eve, for the wives of Cain and Lamech, for Sarah and her Egyptian handmaid Hagar, and for the women of Sodom and Gomorrah.[9] It is always, however, used in a complimentary sense; and three times the woman (Eve, Cain's wife, Hagar) is described in the immediate context as *freolicu mæg* 'noble woman'. As applied to Hagar, the words are put into Sarah's mouth when she is commending her handmaid to Abraham so that he might beget an heir upon her; as for the women of Sodom and Gomorrah, they appear to have been described as *monig blachleor ides* 'many a pale-faced lady' in order to emphasize their pathetic qualities (1969b–72b).

In *Beowulf, ides* is used not only for the exemplary queens Wealhtheow (620, 1168, 1649) and Hildeburh (1075, 1117), but also for Offa's bloodthirsty wife, with the comment:

> Ne bið swylc cwenlic þeaw
> idese to efnanne, þeah ðe hio ænlic sy,
> þætte freoðuwebbe[10] feores onsæce
> æfter ligetorne leofne mannan.[11]
>
> (1940b–43b)

(That is no womanly custom for an *ides* to perform, though she be peerless, that she, weaver of peace, should seek the life of a dear man because of false anger.)

There may be a suggestion here that an *ænlic ides* is not necessarily to be judged by the standards of ordinary women—but this kind of behavior is going too far! More significantly, and more strangely, *ides* is a term employed for the monstrous mother of Grendel the *þyrs* (1259, 1351); in this usage it resembles the words *æglæca* and *mære,* applied both to Beowulf and Grendel.[12]

The word *ides,* then, appears to have no moral connotations; but clearly to mean "noble woman, lady" rather than simply "woman." The next question is: would such a woman have retained, in Anglo-Saxon times, any of the feminine mystique attributed to the women of the Germani by Tacitus? Poetry can help us no further with this; but a hint that it might have been so is given by the occurrence of crystal balls—often in suspension slings of silver—and of perforated and ornamental circular-bowled spoons in the graves of rich (and almost certainly also important and even royal)[13] women, mostly in Kent, and mostly from the heathen period. The function of these objects has never been established, but most archaeologists agree that it must have been symbolic rather than utilitarian or purely ornamental. It seems very probable that the crystal balls represent woman as the guardian of the hearth and perhaps also of the family's health and that the spoons symbolize her function as the dispenser of wine.[14] The graves of early Anglo-Saxon women show also that they were more addicted to the use of amulets than were men;[15] but, in this, there is no distinction between the rich and the poor. Nor is any such distinction made in the laws and penitentials, where many provisions show that the suspicion of working magic, especially love-magic, frequently fell upon women.[16]

The *Penitential* attributed to Theodore of Tarsus, archbishop of Canterbury (669–690), prescribes penance for seven years for a woman *quae semen viri sui in cibo miscens ut inde plus amoris accipiat*[17] 'who [mixes] the semen of her husband in food in order to receive more love thereby', and for anyone who kills a man *per poculum vel artem aliquam*[18] 'by means of a philtre or some device'. This latter appears to be a version of a provision that occurs frequently in the various penitentials, concerned with an accidental killing by means of a magic potion intended as an aphrodisiac or as a drug to confuse the mind of a suspicious husband or unwanted lover. It appears to derive ultimately from Canon 6 of the early fourth-century Council of Elvira, where it is made clear that the practice of magic was idolatry.[19] The same idea was expressed in fuller form in one of the Canonical Epistles attributed to Basil of Caesarea, which were known to and cited by Theodore of Canterbury. There (Canon 188) the fact that women often used incantations and amulets to attract love to themselves is commented upon. There is also, in the Theodore *Penitential* (xv 4), a general prohibition against women performing "incantations or diabolical divinations" for which a year's penance is prescribed; and to this prohibition were added the words of a canon (closely resembling "Isidore Mercator's" Latin version of Ancyra 23) forbidding anyone to receive magicians into their home. Theodore also prescribed penance for a woman who attempted to cure a daughter's fever by placing her on a roof or in an oven (perhaps with attendant incantations or magic practices?).[20]

Since at least some of Theodore's provisions derive from earlier, non-English sources, can they be considered relevant to conditions in early Anglo-Saxon society? Very probably so, since the Theodore compilation, however much of it may have been due to the archbishop himself and however much to later redactors, gives clear signs of a concern to make its provisions and penalties appropriate to the current situation. No sources are known for the prohibitions against magically curing a daughter's fever or mixing semen with food. This latter may have been a general Germanic superstition, since it is repeated in later Frankish penitentials, including the ninth-century Pseudo-Theodore,[21] which was known in late Anglo-Saxon England.[22] Theodore's provisions, then, clearly reflect a belief current in late seventh- and early eighth-century England that women were capable of working magic, and especially love-magic.

The other penitentials that have been considered to emanate from eighth-century England add little to Theodore;[23] and after this, there is a long interval before any more penitentials are known that have any clear connection with England. In the late ninth century, however, in the preface—and therefore not to be regarded as a part of current legislation—to King Alfred's laws, in place of the Exodus verse (xxii 18), *Maleficos non patieris vivere* 'You shall not permit magicians to live', there is the expansive

> Đa fæmnan þe gewuniað onfon gealdorcræftigan 7 scinlæcan 7 wiccan ne læt þu ða libban.[24]

> (Do not allow the women who are accustomed to receive enchanters and magicians and witches to live.)

This would seem to be related to the Ancyran canon quoted in Theodore concerning those who entertain soothsayers in their homes, but unfortunately it is not possible without further evidence to argue from this that Alfred knew the Theodore compilation. Æthelstan's and Edmund's laws have only general prohibitions against sorcery, without specific reference to women or to love-magic.[25]

Penitential literature becomes important again with the ninth-century Frankish "Pseudo-Theodore," and appears to have been well known to the late Anglo-Saxon ecclesiastical legislators; it contains a general prohibition against love-magic derived from earlier Continental sources.[26] In Old English, there is the *Scrift-boc* (or so-called *Pseudo-Egbert Confessional*) of uncertain, perhaps tenth-century, date, which contains successive provisions against the woman who succeeds in her purpose *mid drycræft and galdorcræft and unlibban*[27] 'with sorcery and incantation and philtres', and the one who accidentally kills someone with her philtres. The prohibitions against a woman's putting her daughter on a roof or in an oven to cure fever and against mixing semen with food to increase love are also translated; the latter runs:

> Wif seo ðe mencð weres sæd in hire mete and þone þigeð, þæt heo þam wæpnedmen sy ðe leofre, fæste III winter (Spindler XVII 19x).

> (Let the woman who mixes a man's seed in her food and eats it so that she may be the dearer to the male fast for three winters.)

The Old English translation of the Latin (see above) is clearly very literal; and it is difficult to tell whether the compiler of the *Confessional* is here automatically repeating the Theodore or the Egbert *Penitentials* or whether he has deliberately chosen these provisions because they were still relevant to contemporary conditions.

Certainly the probability that love-magic was still believed to be practiced in late Anglo-Saxon England is given support by a lengthy provision in the *Penitential of Pseudo-Egbert*, another Old English compilation which appears to have connections with Ælfric and Wulfstan. It runs:

Gif hwa wiccige ymbe æniges mannes lufe and him on æte sylle oððe on drence oððe on æniges cunnes galdorcræfte, þæt heora lufe for þam þe mare beon sceole: Gif hit læwede man do, fæste [he] healf ger. . . . Gif hit bið cleric, fæste an ger. . . . Gif he beo diacon, fæste III ger. . . . Gif hit bið mæsse-preost, fæste V ger.[28]

(If anyone practices witchcraft concerning any man's love and gives him [something] in food or in drink, or with any kind of incantation, so that their love shall thereby be the greater: If a layman do it, let him fast half a year. . . . If it be a cleric, let him fast a year. . . . If he be a deacon, let him fast three years. . . . If it be a priest, let him fast five years.)

The care taken to produce a conflation in this provision and the elaborate scheme of penalties indicate that it was not an antiquarian curiosity, though the increasing scale of penance for the various grades of ecclesiastics proves that it was certainly not specifically aimed at women. However, in Ælfric's homily *De Auguriis* there is a passage concerning superstitions of women clearly influenced by the penitentials, and it appears, in part, directly dependent on the *Pseudo-Egbert Penitential,* since it shows at times the same order of ideas and even uses the same vocabulary. One part of it runs:

Sume hi wyrcað heora wogerum drencas oððe sumne wawan þæt hi hi to wife habban (157–58).[29]

(Some [women] make philtres for their wooers or some wickedness, that they may have them as wives.)

Some foolish women, he says, are also accustomed to draw their children through the earth at crossroads (148–49), presumably for the sake of their health.[30]

All the evidence seems to show that women—especially, perhaps, if they were outstanding in any respect—were regarded as dangerous by the good men of Anglo-Saxon England, because they were suspected of possessing dark powers not so readily tapped by the masculine genius.

Is the interpretation of these lines in the *Cotton Gnomic Verse* helped by the assumption that the use of magic was somehow involved? Long ago, in C. W. M. Grein's *Sprachsatz der angelsächsische Dichter,*[31] the phrase *dyrne cræfte,* which is instrumental in case, was glossed "*durch Zaubermittel?*" in this passage; and, perhaps independently, A. Mawer also suggested that *dyrne cræfte* should be translated "by magic."[32] This interpretation has, however, received little acceptance; and it remains to examine the phrase to see if it will indeed bear it.

The basic meaning of *dyrne* is "secret," and this is clearly its meaning in *dyrne-geliger* 'adultery' and *dyrn-licgan* 'fornicate'—it is later used as a regular term for "courtly love." At times, however, it bears a stronger meaning than this, more akin to the modern English "dark." As applied in *Beowulf* to Grendel and his kin (*dyrnra gasta* 1357), and perhaps also to the dragon's home within the barrow (*dryhtsele dyrnne* 2320), its connotation is decidedly sinister. More telling, however, is the constant association in other poetry of the adjective *dyrne* with the devil. In the *Later Genesis,* it is applied to a devil's messenger (*dyrne deofles boda* 490) and his intentions (*dyrne geþanc* 532);[33] in *Juliana* it is used to describe devilish blandishments, secret errors (*dyrnra gedwilda* 368);[34] and in *The Whale* it is by means of the devil's *dyrne meaht* 'secret might' (33),[35] that he deceives men. In all these contexts *dyrne* bears a moral connotation and could be translated "deceitful, evil."

Similarly, the phrase *dyrne cræfte* may mean, as Sweet suggested, simply "secretly, clandestinely"; but it is also possible to see something more sinister in this "secret skill." In *Salomon and Saturn* (453) it is said of the devil that he made for himself a standard and a broad coat of mail *ðurh dierne cræftas*.[36] In *Beowulf, dyrnum cræfte* appears twice, once in the description of the man who first entered the dragon's lair: *he to forð gestop / dyrnan cræfte   dracan heafde neah* 'he stepped forward . . . near the head of the dragon' (2289b–90b). Bosworth-Toller translates "with evil craft"; Grein-Kohler suggests "*sich durch Zauberei unsichtbar machend?*" The poet adds, however,

> Swa mæg unfæge   eaðe gedigan
> wean and wræcsið   se ðe Waldendes
> hyldo gehealdeþ!
>
> (2291a–93a)

(So may a man not fated to die, he who possesses the favor of the Lord, easily survive misery and exile!)

If this comment is intended to refer directly to the man who violated the dragon's hoard, it would be difficult to reconcile the fact that he had God's favor with an interpretation of *dyrne cræfte* as "sorcery"; but if this passage is merely supplying a hypothetical parallel case—and *dyrne cræft* for the one is, as it were, equivalent to God's favor for the other—then a sinister connotation for *dyrnan cræfte* is still possible. On the whole, the second interpretation appears the more probable, since it is difficult indeed to take *dyrne cræft* in any morally good sense; and since *swa* appears often to introduce a gnomic simile, bearing the meaning "likewise" rather than "thus."[37]

The other occurrence of the phrase in *Beowulf* is not only gnomic in form, but also recalls the passage on Offa's wife already quoted. Beowulf has just presented to Hygelac, his lord and kinsman, the war-gear which had belonged to Hiorogar, erstwhile king of the Danes, who, Beowulf says, had not wished to give it to his son Heoroweard. Beowulf adds to this gift four horses; and then the poet comments, in another gnomic simile:

> Swa sceal mæg don
> nealles inwitnet   oðrum bregdon
> dyrnum cræfte   deað ren(ian)
> hondgesteallan.
>
> (2166b–69a)

(So ought a kinsman to do, not at all weave a net of malice for another . . . prepare death for a companion.)

This passage is certainly metaphorical; but, since weaving is frequently associated with magic,[38] it is tempting to interpret *dyrnum cræfte* here as "by magic."

In short, it seems quite possible that *dyrne cræft* here is equivalent to *maleficium* or *maleficius ars* 'sorcery' or to *veneficium* 'magic' from *venenum* 'a magic love-potion > a magic potion > poison'. It need not always bear such a definite meaning; what is clear is that *dyrne cræft* appears to be morally and socially evil and that implications of the use of magic underlie it. We can be quite sure that the *ides* of the *Cotton Gnomes* was "up to no good."

Few of the other words in the *ides* passage are immediately clear in meaning, however. The other epithet used for the lady in this passage is *fæmne*, which appears to bear the technical meaning of "virgin," although it is also used for a young married woman, e.g., in *Beowulf* 2034; perhaps "young woman" would be an acceptable translation. The verb *gesecan* has several meanings that would be appropriate in the context: (1) to seek, go to, visit; (2) to try to find; (3) to try to get; (4) to go to [a person] (a) for residence or communication (b) for help or protection. Perhaps "seek out" would most nearly represent a general meaning encompassing most of the specific alternatives. The word *freond* here clearly must mean "lover," even if there were no parallels; but in *The Wife's Lament* one of the protagonist's causes for complaint is that, while she is alone in the early morning in her wretched hut:

> Frynd sind on eorþan,
> leofe lifgende,   leger weardiað.[39]
> (33b–34a)

(There are lovers on the earth, living beloved, occupying their beds.)

Hire in the *ides* passage is probably a reflexive dative; and so we arrive at "A lady, a young woman, must seek out for herself a lover by means of magic" for 43b–44a.

In the next half-line, *gif heo nelle on folce gepeon*, the meaning of the verbs is doubtful. The basic meaning of *gepeon* is "to flourish, prosper"; but the verb appears capable of bearing the meaning "to be of good reputation," especially when it is combined with phrases meaning something like "among the people." Parallels are in *Beowulf*, in a gnomic utterance: *Lofdædum sceal / in mægþa gehwære   man gepeon* 'In every people a man shall prosper with praiseworthy deeds' (24b–25b), and in the *Exeter Gnomic Poem* I: *Eadig biþ se ðe in his eðle gepihþ,   earm se him his frynd geswicaþ* 'Blessed is he who prospers in his country, wretched is he whom his friends betray' and *Ne sceal hine mon cildgeongne forcweþan,   ær he hine acyþan mote; / þy sceal on þeode gepeon,   þæt he wese þristhycgende* 'One shall not rebuke him when he is a young child, before he can speak for himself; by that means he will prosper among the people, that he may be strong-willed'.[40] In this last passage it is possible to take the meaning of *gepeon* as intransitive, and the last clause '[in] that he be strong-willed' as explanatory; or it could be that here, as in *Christ* 375–77,[41] *gepeon* is transitive and means "accomplishes, brings it about" with the clause "that he be strong-willed" as object. "Bring it about" is another possible meaning for *gepeon* in the *ides* passage.[42]

The obvious meaning of *nelle* would be "does not wish"; but it can also have reference to habitual conduct. In the *Riddles,* which have many similarities to the

Gnomic Poems, willan is quite frequently used for an often-repeated, characteristic action;[43] and a parallel use of the negative is found in the *Bow Riddle* No. 23:

Nelle ic unbunden   ænigum hyran
nymþe searosæled.

(15a–16a)

(I will not obey anyone unbound, only if skillfully bound.)

This passage, then, like some of those from the other *Riddles* using the positive *willan,* appears to show a blending of the idea of habitude with that of willing or wishing—an idea that may also be present in the *ides* passage under discussion. Therefore, the meaning of 44b could be variously, at either extreme, "if she is not of good reputation among the people" or "if she does not wish to bring it about."

The meaning of 45a is certainly "contract a public marriage," as S. J. Crawford pointed out, citing a passage from the *Heliand* where Mary is said to have been "bought" by Joseph. There is a similar usage in Æthelberht's laws (77), *Gif mon mæg gebigeþ* 'If a man buys a woman'. The position of the woman "bought with rings" was clearly respected and honorable; by no means was she equated with slaves or cattle.

Perhaps the aim of the *ides* was to attract a man into marriage, as it is in the passage from Ælfric's *De Auguriis,* in which case a possible translation of the whole passage would be

A lady, a young woman, must seek out for herself a lover by means of magic, so that she may be married, if she is not of good reputation among the people.

An alternative, however, is to take *nelle* in the sense of 'does not wish, is unwilling' followed by the infinitive *gepeon* in the sense of 'bring about' and a noun clause beginning with *þæt.* The translation might then run

A lady, a young woman, must seek out for herself a lover by secret means, if she does not wish to bring it about among the people that she should be married.

Both interpretations appear to have validity, and we have no reason to suppose that Old English poetic language is only ever capable of bearing one meaning.

In order to appreciate the literary value of these two lines of Old English verse, we need to reach an understanding not only of their possible primary meaning, or denotation, but also of their connotations,[44] and, therefore, must first look at the context of the passage.

The three gnomes preceding that of the *ides* run:

Scur sceal on heofenum
winde gebanden,   in þas woruld cuman.
Þeof sceal gangan þystrum wederum.   Þyrs sceal on fenne gewunian
ana innan lande.

(40b–43a)

(A shower, mingled with wind, in [or from] heaven must come into this world. A thief must go about in dark weather. A water-demon [*þyrs*] must dwell in a fen, alone within the land.)

The progression so far appears fairly straightforward. The stormy shower makes the poet think of the evil-living man, the only one who by choice goes about in such weather, and then in turn of the *þyrs* who has not only to go about, but to live in unpleasant wet conditions, far from the normal habitations of men. The next step, to the *ides*, could have come about in two ways. The first, a verbal connection, has been partially suggested by Dawson:[45] *dyrne* is a word applied in *Beowulf* to Grendel the *þyrs;* the similar sound as well as the meanings of the words could have caused the idea of the *ides* to come forth. One could push the verbal connection even further: as we have seen, *ides* itself is a word applied to Grendel's Mother; and, if it often carried the connotation of a woman of power and even of magic-working, it may itself have provided a link with the preceding gnome of the *þyrs*.[46]

The second possible link is a thematic one—the *þyrs* and the *ides* may be much closer than appears on the surface if we accept the idea that Old English literature has been influenced by "Old Testament apocrypha." Robert E. Kaske has argued that the *Beowulf* poet knew the story of the uniting of the angelic Watchers with the daughters of men, based on Genesis vi 2, and described most fully in the *Book of Enoch*.[47] Kaske has pointed out that Grendel, the *þyrs*, appears to be just such a cannibalistic giant[48] as was said to have been born of the union between a corrupt spirit and a human woman, whose subsequent fate was to be degraded into a "siren," that is, a water-dwelling monster. For the sequence of gnomes under discussion the description of the seduction of the women is particularly interesting:

> VII. And all [the Watchers] . . . took unto themselves wives, and each chose for himself one, and they began to go in unto them and defile themselves with them, and they taught them charms and enchantments, and the cutting of roots, and made them acquainted with plants.[49]

The imparting of forbidden knowledge to mankind is stated as one of the chief reasons for the condemnation of the leaders of the fallen Watchers: when the flood is foretold, it is said that those on earth are ruined because "they have learnt all the secrets of the angels, and all the violence of the Satans, and all their powers—the most secret ones—and all the power of those who practice witchcraft, and the power of those who make molten images for the whole earth: and how silver is produced . . ." (lxv 6–7, p. 130).

Obviously the gnomic poet was not describing the union of a Watcher with a human woman; nor is it necessary to imagine the *þyrs* to be a possible mate for a woman who does not seek ordinary human marriage. However, a chain of association, in which these passages from the *Book of Enoch* played a part, can easily be envisaged. If a *þyrs* was a creature that could be the child of a spirit and a human woman, what more natural than that the idea of a woman working magic for sexual purposes should come into the poet's mind directly after he had described the *þyrs?*

The mention of the normal married state of womanhood, however, makes the poet turn back to the theme of the normal order of nature, which appears to be his prime concern in this poem. It may or may not be relevant, in view of the trans-mogrification of the wives of the Watchers into water-monsters, that he takes up this thread again with a description of the sea, before going on to mention briefly the earth and the heavens. Yet the thematic sequence is equally understandable as a natural progression from the two evil-doing and outcast male creatures, excluded from normal human intercourse, to the female who does not tread the straight and narrow path, and who, therefore, has to gain for herself a lover by socially unacceptable means.

There is a similar succession of ideas in the first set of the *Exeter Gnomic Verses*, beginning with the brave warrior, then turning to the woman in her proper place—at home—to whom is contrasted the despised gadabout. The next line contrasts the righteous with the unrighteous man:

> Eorl sceal on eos boge,   eorod sceal getrume ridan,
> fæste feþa stondan.   Fæmne æt hyre bordan geriseð;
> widgongel wif word gespringeð,   oft hy man wommum belihð
> hæleð hy hospe mænað,   oft hyre hleor abreoþeð.
> Sceomiande man sceal in sceade hweorfan,   scir in leohte geriseð.
>
> (62a–66b)

Unfortunately, although the general sense of this is clear enough, many of the words are ambiguous; and a translation can only offer one of several possible alternatives:

> A noble must be on a horse's back; the horse-troops must ride in company; the foot-troops stand fast. A young woman belongs at her embroidery; a roving woman causes gossip; often she is accused of vices; men speak of her with contempt; often her face deteriorates. A man shamed must move in the shade; the pure man belongs in the light.

The same train of thought is developed in much more detail in the second *Exeter* set, where we have a picture of two virtuous women, at different levels of society. The first is a queen:

> Cyning sceal mid ceape   cwene gebicgan
> bunum ond beagum;   bu sceolon ærest
> geofum god wesan.   Guð sceal in eorle
> wig weaxan,   and wif geþeon
> leof mid hire leodum,   leohtmod wesan,
> rune healdan,   rumheort beon
> mearum and maþmum,   meodorædenne,
> for gesiðmægen   symle æghwær
> eodor æþelinga   ærest gegretan
> forman fulle   to frean hond
> ricene geræcan   and him ræd witan
> boldagendum bæm ætsomne.
>
> (81a–92a)

Again a translation can only be put forward tentatively:

A king shall buy a queen for a price, with goblets and rings: both must first be generous with gifts. Warfare, martial qualities, must grow in a brave man, and a woman must be of good reputation (prosper), dear among her people, be glad at heart, keep counsel, be generous with horses and treasures; with mead always and everywhere first greet the protector of princes above the companion, quickly present the first cup to the hand of her lord, and know counsel for both of the householders together.

The responsible and honored position of a high-born married woman may be judged from this. But the gnomic poet is also interested in the situation of a woman further down the scale, and he turns to the meeting of and the relationship between a returning sailor and his wife:

> leof wilcuma
> Frysan wife,   þonne flota stondeð;
> bið his ceol cumen   and hyre ceorl to ham,
> agen ætgeofa,   and heo hine in laðaþ
> wæscað his warig hrægl   and him syleþ wæde niwe
> liþ him on londe   þæs his lufu bædeð.
> Wif sceal wiþ wer wære gehealdan,   oft hi mon wommum belihð;
> fela bið fæsthydigra,   fela bið fyrwetgeornra,
> freoð hy fremde monnan,   þonne se oþer feor gewiteþ.
> Lida biþ longe on siþe;   a mon sceal seþeah leofes wenan,
> gebidan   þæs he gebædan ne mæg.
>
> (94b–104a)

(Dear is the welcome man to the Frisian woman, when the ship stops moving; his vessel has come, and her husband is at home, her own provider; and she invites him in, washes his clothing stained with seaweed and gives him a new garment; grants him on land what his love commands. A woman must hold faith towards a man—often she is accused of vices; many a one is steadfast in mind, many a one is eager in her curiosity; she cares for a stranger when the other departs far away. A ship is long on its voyage; always, however, a man must look forward to his beloved; wait for what he cannot command.)

A recurring theme in Old English gnomic verse, then, is the idea of the proper place of woman; and how she may lose the respect due to her by unchastity or merely by immodesty—her behavior should be such that she is above suspicion; for there are many ready to condemn her. It is remarkable how closely the picture of the honored noble woman, and of the shame of the dishonored one, echoes that given by Tacitus in his description of the women of the Germani:

Dotem non uxor marito, sed uxori maritus offert. intersunt parentes et propinqui ac munera probant, munera non ad delicias muliebres quaesita nec quibus nova nupta comatur, sed boves et frenatum equum et scutum cum framea gladioque. in haec munera uxor accipitur, atque in vicem ipsa armorum aliquid viro adfert: hoc maximum vinculum, haec arcana sacra, hos coniungales deos arbitrantur. ne se mulier extra virtutum cogitationes extraque bellorum casus putet ipsis incipientis matrimonii auspiciis admonetur venire se laborum periculorumque sociam, idem in pace, idem in proelio passuram ausaramque. . . . Ergo saepta pudicitia agunt . . . paucissima in tam numerosa gente adulteria, quorum poena praesens et maritis permissa: abscisis crinibus nudatam coram propinquis expellit domo maritus ac per omnem vicum verbere agit; publicatae enim pudicitiae nulla venia: non forma, non aetate, non opibus maritum invenerit (chs. xviii and xix).[50]

(The wife does not bring a dowry to the husband, but the husband to the wife. The parents and kinsmen are present and approve the gifts: gifts not selected with regard to feminine pleasures nor with which the bride may be adorned, but oxen, and bridled horses, and shield with spear and sword. The wife is received in respect to these gifts, and in turn she herself brings something in the way of arms to the husband: this they believe the greatest bond; these the sacred mysteries; these the matrimonial deities. That the woman may not think herself excluded from considerations of martial courage, excluded from the chances of war, she is warned by the very omens attending the beginning of the marriage that she is coming as a companion in hard work and dangers and that she is destined to suffer and dare in peace and war alike. . . . Therefore they live hedged about by chastity; very few among such a numerous people are adulteries, for which the penalty is immediate and the prerogative of the husbands. The husband expels her from the house naked, with hair cut off, in the presence of kinsmen, and drives her with blows through the whole village. There is no forgiveness for violated chastity; neither beauty nor age nor possessions will find her a husband.)

No wonder she might at times be reduced to using magic!

It is clear that within Old English poetry the respected *ides* is represented most clearly by the exemplary queens in *Beowulf*, Wealhtheow and Hygd. It is not quite so clear that we also have a picture of the *ides* rejected by society, in the two lyrics in the *Exeter Book* in which the speaker is a woman bewailing her fate. Certainly many of the same elements as are present in the gnomic verses are found also in these poems—but with the difference that in *Wulf and Eadwacer* and *The Wife's Lament*, the poet does not reject the woman, whatever society might do, and her unhappy situation is used to give added poignancy to her personal grief.[51] A brief examination of these poems will illustrate the point and also give force to the argument that the *ides* passage fits normally and naturally into its place in the chain of ideas of the *Cotton Gnomes*. It will inevitably be necessary, at times, to choose which of various conflicting interpretations of these poems seems the most probable.

In the brief *Wulf and Eadwacer*,[52] a woman, the speaker, is on an island; Wulf is on another surrounded by marsh, where there are cruel men. It appears that he is in danger both from them and from her own people. She longs for him. When it was rainy weather and she sat weeping *se beaducofa* 'the warrior'—who, it appears to me, can be no other than Wulf[53]—embraced her; this was both pleasant and hateful to her. At the end of the poem she breaks out into an apostrophe:

Gehyrest þu, Eadwacer?   Uncerne earne hwelp
bireð Wulf to wuda.

(16a–17a)

(Do you hear Eadwacer? Wulf (or a wolf) (will) bear(s) our wretched pup to the wood.)

It is usually, but not universally, agreed that Eadwacer is her unloved husband and the father of her child.[54] If so, she would be the kind of wife the gnomic poets disapprove of so strongly, involved with a man who seems to have been banished to the fringes of society. The fenny island and the rainy weather at the time of their meeting, which presumably provide cover for it, all emphasize that Wulf is unacceptable to society and that she herself offends society by loving him. Surely it is the Anglo-Saxon poet's recognition of the fact that powerful passion will not be constrained by the normal bonds of society that gives this poem its universal appeal.

The woman of *The Wife's Lament*[55] bewails her lot at greater length and with less force. Her lord, like the sailor of the *Exeter Gnomes,* went away; but instead of waiting quietly for his return, she set out on a journey, evidently feeling herself friendless. Thereupon, it seems, her husband's kinsmen plotted to keep them furthest apart from and most hateful to each other. Her distress was caused because she found the man well-matched to her "unhappy, sad at heart, concealing his mind, intending great wickedness" (19–20). Whether his evil intent was directed at herself or at another has often been disputed; but the succeeding lines which speak of their earlier vows never to part, and which recognize with despair that their relationship is now over, seem to me to indicate that it was directed toward her:

> eft is þæt onhworfen
> is nu . . . swa hit no wære
> freondscipe uncer.   Sceal ic feor ge neah
> mines felaleofan   fæhðu dreogan
>
> (23b–26a)

(that is now changed; our relationship as if it had never been. I must far and near suffer hostility because of my beloved.)

Her husband[56] commands her to take up her dwelling in that same land where before she had found herself so friendless (cf. *heonan of leodum* 'hence from my people', 6; *on þissum londstede* 'into this land', 16), in an old "miserable earth-hut" beneath an oak tree. The high hills, dark valleys, and encroaching brambles of this dry landscape are as harsh as the fens. Here the departure of her lord often afflicted her—she remembers that other *frynd* 'lovers' are in bed, while she wanders at dawn through her earthen dwellings. There she must sit the summer-long day, bewailing her many hardships.

The reference of the next part of the poem is the most difficult of all. What is important in this context, however, is not whether the woman is wishing exile upon her husband, or imagining him suffering it, but the dreary wet surroundings which she allots to him in her mind:

> þæt min freond siteð
> under stanhliþe   storme behrimed
> wine werigmod,   wætre beflowen
> on dreorsele.
>
> (47b–50a)

(that my lover, [my] lord weary in mind, sits under a rocky slope, in a sad hall surrounded by water.)

She ends with a gnomic reflection which is strangely reminiscent of the ending of the passage concerning the Frisian woman, and which refers back to her own painful longing for her husband:

> Wa bið þam þe sceal
> of langoþe   leofes abidan.
> (52b–53b)

(There is grief from longing for the beloved for the one who must wait.)

Looking back at the earlier part of the gnomic passage concerning the sailor's wife, it seems legitimate to wonder whether what the wife describes as an innocent journey to seek help for herself is supposed to have been interpreted as infidelity by her husband's kin, who therefore accused her to her husband.[57] He drove her, or had her driven, out of the house, as a man of the Germani would have done: she, lacking kindred and friends to support her, must drag out a miserable existence remembering her own past joys and the present happiness of others. Her husband will not return joyously from a sea-voyage, as the Frisian woman's did.

It seems to me that the Old English gnomic poems have been too long dismissed as belonging "to an early stage in poetic development" and as having "no great beauty."[58] Their own appeal is not immediate, but to those who teach them year after year they have always new delights to reveal and new insights to offer. Moreover, they can help us to understand contemporary poetic themes and to appreciate the way in which other poets have interpreted and transformed these themes. They epitomize Anglo-Saxon social attitudes: attitudes already in existence in Tacitus's time, but modified by Christianity. Ancient modes of thought are preserved within them—it is for a dragon to live in a burial mound, guarding treasure, just as it is for a king to distribute rings in a hall. Conflict between opposites is also inevitable—good must strive against evil, youth against age, life against death, as the poet of the *Cotton Gnomes* writes in his concluding lines, paraphrasing Ecclesiasticus xxxiii 15.[59] The *ides,* embodying by her immodest and anti-social behavior man's inherent distrust of woman, epitomizes "natural disorder"—a disorder that is still "part of God's providential order."[60]

NOTES

My gratitude is due to Dr. Hilda Davidson and Miss Doreen Gillam, who read earlier versions of this article, and to Prof. Elizabeth Liggins for constant help and encouragement.

1. Elliott Van Kirk Dobbie, ed., *The Anglo-Saxon Minor Poems,* vol. 6 of *The Anglo-Saxon Poetic Records* (New York: Columbia University Press, 1968), pp. 56–57. For convenience, other Old English poems will be cited in editions in this series.

2. Ibid., p. 176.

3. R. MacGregor Dawson, "The Structure of the Old English Gnomic Poems," *Journal of English and German Philology* 61 (1962): 22.

4. Jakob Grimm, *Deutsche Mythologie,* 4th ed. (Gütersloh: 1875), vol. 1, p. 332; see also J. de Vries, *Altgermanische Religionsgeschichte,* 2nd ed. (Berlin: Walter de Gruyter and Co., 1956), §230, for a possible etymological connection between *ides* and the ON *dís* 'sister; female guardian angel, goddess; maid'.

5. Tacitus, *Cornelii Taciti De Origine et Situ Germanorum,* ed. J. G. C. Anderson (Oxford: The Clarendon Press, 1938), ch. 8. My thanks are due to Dr. H. Jocelyn and Dr. A. Emmett for advice concerning the translations from Tacitus.

Jane Crawford, in "Evidences for Witchcraft in Anglo-Saxon England," *Medium Ævum* 32 (1963): 99–116, argues that the relevance of the first quoted sentence to the conditions of Anglo-Saxon England is questionable, without corroborative evidence. However, if one starts from the Anglo-Saxon side, it is surely permissible to quote Tacitus in corroboration.

6. Tacitus, ch. 10.

7. Caesar, *The Gallic War,* ed. H. J. Edwards, Loeb Classical Library (London: William Heinemann, 1917), vol. 1, p. 50.

8. Joseph Bosworth and T. Northcote Toller, *An Anglo-Saxon Dictionary* (Oxford: Oxford University Press, 1954; *Supplement,* 1966 reprint) *sub ides;* hereafter cited as Bosworth-Toller.

9. Lines 896, 1054, 1076, 1728, 1970, 2229 respectively; George Philip Krapp, ed., *The Junius Manuscript,* vol. 1 in *The Anglo-Saxon Poetic Records* (New York: Columbia University Press, 1964), pp. 30–67.

10. The feminine noun *freoðuwebbe* is listed in Bosworth-Toller as occurring in Old English only here and in *Widsith* (6), and it has usually been interpreted metaphorically. However, one is reminded of the twelve women weaving war in *Njál's Saga* (ch. 157) and of the passage in Burchard's *Corrector, Decretum,* ch. 19 (J. P. Migne, ed., *Patrologiae Cursus Completus, Series Latina,* vol. 140 [Paris: 1890], col. 961) where, whatever the exact meaning may be, magic practices are clearly connected with weaving. The idea of woman as weaver is also symbolized by the iron weaving-swords found in some rich women's burials of the sixth to seventh centuries, sometimes in the same burials as the crystal balls and silver spoons mentioned below. See Sonia Chadwick (Hawkes), "The Anglo-Saxon Cemetery at Fingelsham, Kent: a Reconsideration," *Medieval Archaeology* 2 (1958): 30–35.

11. Elliot Van Kirk Dobbie, ed., *Beowulf and Judith,* vol. 4 of *The Anglo-Saxon Poetic Records* (New York: Columbia University Press, 1953), p. 60.

12. See D. M. Gillam, "The Use of the Word 'Æglæca' in *Beowulf* at lines 893 and 2592," *Studia Germanica Gandensia* 3 (1961): 145–69.

There is a general discussion of the Anglo-Saxon *ides* (partly based on this paper) in chap. 1 of Jane Chance, *Woman as Hero in Old English Literature* (Syracuse, N.Y.: Syracuse University Press, 1986).

13. In some of the same graves have also been found gold braids, which appear to be a sign of royal rank; see Elisabeth Crowfoot and Sonia Chadwick Hawkes, "Early Anglo-Saxon Gold Braids," *Medieval Archaeology* 11 (1967): 42–86.

14. See discussion in A. L. Meaney, *Anglo-Saxon Amulets and Curing Stones,* British Archaeological Report, vol. 96 (Oxford: British Archaeological Reports, 1981), pp. 82–88 and 90–96.

15. Meaney, *Anglo-Saxon Amulets and Curing Stones,* pp. 245–62.

16. J. Helterman has pointed this out in *"Beowulf:* The Archetype Enters History," *Journal of English Literary History* 35 (1968): 15–16.

The Anglo-Saxon penitential material has recently been assessed by A. J. Frantzen in "The Tradition of Penitentials in Anglo-Saxon England," *Anglo-Saxon England* 11 (1983): 23–56; *The Literature of Penance in Anglo-Saxon England* (New Brunswick, N.J.: Rutgers University Press, 1983). I have examined the earlier penitential provisions and ecclesiastical pronouncements against "idolatry" in "Anglo-Saxon Idolators and Ecclesiasts: From Theodore to Alcuin," forthcoming in *Anglo-Saxon Studies in Archaeology and History;* "Women, Witchcraft and Magic in Anglo-Saxon England" was read at a conference on Anglo-Saxon Magic and Popular Medicine held by the Manchester University Centre for Anglo-Saxon Studies on June 25, 1988, and appears in the Conference Proceedings (ed. D. G. Scragg).

17. A. H. Haddan and W. Stubbs, *Councils and Ecclesiastical Documents,* vol. 3 (Oxford: 1871), p. 188, and P. W. Finsterwalder, *Die Canones Theodori Cantuariensis und*

ihre Überlieferungsformen (Weimar: H. Böhlaus Nachfolger, 1929), p. 308. B. Thorpe's *Ancient Laws and Institutions of England* (London: 1840) is unreliable.

18. Haddan and Stubbs, p. 180.

19. José Vives, *Concilios visigóticòs e hispano-romanos,* España Cristiana, textos, vol. I (Barcelona: Consejo Superior de Investigaciones Científicas, Instituto Enrique Flórez, 1963), section I, p. 3.

20. Haddan and Stubbs, p. 190.

21. I [16] §30; F. W. H. Wasserchleben, ed., *Die Bussordnungen der abendländischen Kirche* (Halle: 1851), p. 576. Note the significant addition of a related practice to prevent childbearing.

22. D. Bethurum, "Archbishop Wulfstan's Commonplace Book," *Publications of The Modern Language Association* 57 (1942): 916–29; and T. P. Oakley, *English Penitential Discipline and Anglo-Saxon Law in Their Joint Influence* (New York: Columbia University Press, 1923), pp. 31–32.

23. The shorter Penitentials attributed to Bede do not concern themselves with superstitious practices at all. The *Egbert Penitential* copies Theodore's provisions concerning women working magic, but places two of them in juxtaposition, altering the wording slightly to imply that death may be caused inadvertently (Haddan and Stubbs, p. 424); however, in the form we have it, this seems to me to be a later Frankish compilation. The *Liber de remediis peccatorum* which Albers attributed to Bede (but which appears merely to combine parts of the other 'Bede' and the 'Egbert') simply repeats the 'Egbert' provisions against idolatry. See the discussion of these compilations in J. T. McNeill and H. Gamer, *Medieval Handbooks of Penance,* Records of Civilization: Source and Studies, vol. 29 (New York: Columbia University Press, 1938), pp. 217–43; M. W. Laistner, *The Intellectual Heritage of the Early Middle Ages,* ed. C. G. Starr (Ithaca, N.Y.: Cornell University Press, 1957), pp. 165–77; Frantzen, "Tradition": 30–35, and Meaney, "Ecclesiasts."

24. F. Liebermann, *Die Gesetze der Angelsachsen,* vol. I (Halle: M. Niemeyer, 1903), pp. 38–39.

Crawford, "Witchcraft": 107–108, prefers an alternative version from the mid-eleventh-century manuscript British Library Cotton Nero A.i (N. R. Ker, *Catalogue of Manuscripts Containing Anglo-Saxon* [Oxford: The Clarendon Press, 1957], no. 163) which begins *Pa fæmnan ðe gewuniað anfon galdorcræft 7 scinlæcan 7 wiccan . . .* 'The women who are accustomed to practice enchantments, and magicians and witches'. However, the mid-tenth-century version in the Parker manuscript (Cambridge Corpus Christi College 173) quoted here is supported by the reading *galdercræftigan* in the Textus Roffensis.

25. F. L. Attenborough, *The Laws of the Earliest English Kings* (Cambridge: Cambridge University Press, 1922), pp. 130–31; A. J. Robertson, *The Laws of the Kings of England from Edmund to Henry I* (Cambridge: Cambridge University Press, 1925), pp. 6–7.

26. Wasserschleben, pp. 596–97; cf. *Burgundian Penitential* (8th c.) and *Halitgar's Roman Penitential* (ca. 830); see McNeill and Gamer, pp. 274 and 305. See also n. 22 above.

27. Canon 29 in Thorpe, *Ancient Laws;* XVI, 19e and f in R. Spindler, *Das altenglische Bussbuch* (Leipzig: B. Tauchnitz, 1934), p. 184. This arrangement repeats that in the *Egbert Penitential.* See also the discussion of the later penitentials by Frantzen, "Tradition": 35–49.

28. J. Raith, *Die altenglische Version des Halitgarschen Bussbuches* (Hamburg: Henri Grand, 1933), IV 14, pp. 53–54. This provision is also found in an abbreviated form in the derivative "Late Old English Handbook for the Use of a Confessor," ed. Roger Fowler, *Anglia* 83 (1965): 25, lines 267–68, almost certainly to be attributed to Wulfstan and his circle.

29. Ælfric, *Lives of the Saints,* ed. W. W. Skeat, Early English Text Society, o.s, vols. 76 and 82 (London: The Early English Text Society, 1881), pp. 374–75.

30. For full discussions of Ælfric's strictures against magic and heathen practices, see my two articles "Ælfric and Idolatry," *Journal of Religious History* 13 (1984): 119–35; and "Ælfric's Use of his Sources in his *Homily on Auguries,*" *English Studies* 66 (1985): 477–95.

31. C. W. M. Grein, *Sprachsatz der angelsächsiche Dichter,* rev. J. J. Kohler (Heidelberg: C. Winter, 1912) *sub dyrne.*

32. Reported by S. J. Crawford, *"The Ways of Creation,* 43–45," *Modern Language Review* 19 (1924): 107. This suggestion has been repeated by N. K. Bollard, "The Cotton Maxims," *Neophilologus* 59 (1975): 139–40, in a note that appeared after the completion of this paper.

33. Krapp, *The Junius Manuscript,* pp. 18–19.

34. George Philip Krapp and Elliot Van Kirk Dobbie, *The Exeter Book,* vol. 3 of *The Anglo-Saxon Poetic Records* (New York: Columbia University Press, 1966), p. 123.

35. Krapp and Dobbie, *The Exeter Book,* p. 172.

36. Dobbie, *The Anglo-Saxon Minor Poems,* p. 47.

37. *Beowulf,* lines 20, 1534, 2166, and 2444, in Fr. Klaeber, ed., *Beowulf and the Fight at Finnsburg,* 3rd ed. (Boston: D. C. Heath and Co., 1950).

38. See n. 10.

39. Krapp and Dobbie, *The Exeter Book,* p. 211.

Moreover, in *Juliana,* line 102 (Krapp and Dobbie, *The Exeter Book,* p. 116) there is the sentence *He is to freonde god;* and since the reference is to a bridegroom the interpretation could well be 'He is good as a lover'.

40. Krapp and Dobbie, *The Exeter Book,* p. 158, lines 37 and 49.

41. Krapp and Dobbie, *The Exeter Book,* p. 13.

42. J. M. Kirk, in a recent, privately printed posthumous edition of the Gnomic Poems, takes *geþeon* "as an ironic reference, 'make her living among the people', i.e. be a prostitute." This is merely an extension of the basic intransitive meaning.

43. For example, in 16, line 7; 39, line 5; 44, line 5; Krapp and Dobbie, *The Exeter Book,* pp. 189, 199, and 205 respectively.

44. See D. M. E. Gillam, "A Method for Determining the Connotations of O.E. Poetic Words," *Studia Germanica Gandensia* 6 (1964): 85–101.

45. See n. 3.

46. It may also be relevant that the basic meaning of *helrunan* used in *Beowulf,* line 163, for Grendel and his kin, appears to be "witches, sorceresses, necromancers." See Klaeber, *Beowulf,* p. 134; de Vries, *Altgermanische Religionsgeschichte,* vol. 1, p. 323; §231.

47. Robert E. Kaske, *"Beowulf* and the Book of Enoch," *Speculum* 46 (1971): 421–31.

48. Or an evil spirit that went forth from the giant: see Kaske's discussion of the corporeal and incorporeal concepts of Grendel; ibid., 424–25.

49. R. H. Charles, trans., *The Book of Enoch* (Oxford: The Clarendon Press, 1912), p. 18.

50. Anderson (Tacitus, *Germania,* p. 110) claims that Tacitus misunderstood the marriage ceremony and that the father of the bride gave the bridegroom a sword as a symbol of the transference of power over her; but this does not affect the present argument.

51. See the discussion of these poems in C. Davidson, "Erotic 'Women's Songs' in Anglo-Saxon England," *Neophilologus* 59 (1975): 451–62.

52. Krapp and Dobbie, *The Exeter Book,* pp. 179–80. There is a valuable study of the poem by A. Renoir, *"Wulf and Eadwacer:* A Noninterpretation," in *Franciplegius: Medieval and Linguistic Studies in Honour of Francis Peabody Magoun, Jr.,* ed. Jess B. Bessinger, Jr., and Robert P. Creed (New York: New York University Press, 1965), pp. 147–63.

53. Cf. the parallels between lines 9, 11, and 13–14.

54. The pronoun *us* and the possessive adjective *uncer* appear always to refer to her relationship with Eadwacer.

55. Krapp and Dobbie, *The Exeter Book,* pp. 210–11.

M. J. Swanton, *"The Wife's Lament* and *The Husband's Message:* A Reconsideration," *Anglia* 82 (1964): 269–90, argues that the *Wife's Lament* is an exploration of "the relationship between Christ and the Church, which yearns for the re-establishment of a previous union. . . . Such an interpretation seems to present the only rational and comprehensive resolution for the apparent inconsistencies." However, such an allegory could have no force unless it were related to ordinary experience, and I therefore discuss it here as if it were a human marriage relationship.

56. R. F. Leslie, ed., *Three Old English Elegies* (Manchester: Manchester University Press, 1961), p. 7, argues that the *mon* of line 27 is impersonal; and that therefore there is a difference between *Het mec hlaford min herheard niman* of line 15 and *Heht mec mon wunian* of line 27. In view of the fact that the wife twice refers clearly to her husband as the "man" (11 and 18), it seems to me that he is to be understood as giving the command here too.

57. See S. B. Greenfield, *"The Wife's Lament* Reconsidered," *Publications of The Modern Language Association* 68 (1953): 907–12.

58. The earlier critical view of the Cotton Gnomic verse, that it lacks integrity (Blanche C. Williams, *Gnomic Poetry in Anglo-Saxon* [New York: Columbia University Press, 1914], p. 110) and is "abrupt and disconnected" (introduction to the edition Cotton Gnomic Verses in Henry Sweet, *Anglo-Saxon Reader* [Oxford: Clarendon Press, 1882] and still repeated in D. Whitelock's 1967 revision), is giving way to an appreciation of the literary skill of the poet; see Greenfield and R. Evert, *"Maxims II:* Gnome and Poem" in *Anglo-Saxon Poetry: Essays in Appreciation,* ed. L. E. Nicholson and D. W. Frese (Notre Dame: Notre Dame University Press, 1975), pp. 337–54. However, it must be conceded that every critic of the poem appears to read it differently!

59. T. D. Hill, "Notes on the Old English 'Maxims' I and II," *Notes & Queries* 215 (1970): 445–47.

60. Ibid.: 447.

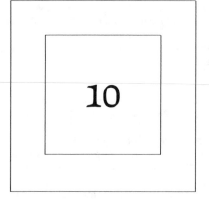

The Valkyrie Reflex in Old English Literature

Figures corresponding to the valkyries may be found in various Indo-European cultures, where they have been associated with the Irish war-goddesses, the Vedic *Divo duhita*, the Teutonic *idisi*, and certain twin sky-goddesses of ancient Greek lore.[1] In Old Norse literature, two distinct, antagonistic perceptions of valkyries essentially exist: they are seen as fierce, elemental beings and as benevolent guardians. This bifurcated vision may reflect a deeper understanding of the war-maids as representing differing concepts of the worship of Óðinn and the nature of the afterlife.[2] A complete inquiry into this motif understandably would exceed the bounds of this study; the ensuing discussion, therefore, will consider the valkyries as literary rather than religious figures, and will examine only those elements that bear directly on elucidating the construction of the heroines in Old English epic in light of the valkyrie tradition.

In both their benevolent and malevolent aspects, the valkyries are related to a generic group of half-mortal, half-supernatural beings called *idisi* in Old High German, *ides* in Old English, and *dís* in Old Norse, plural, *dísir*.[3] Both groups are closely allied in aspect and function: they are armed, powerful, priestly. They function as arrangers of destinies and intermediaries between men and the deity. The major difference between the categories is that some *dísir* are worshipped through sacrificial rites, at a kind of shrine, or altar, or sanctuary called a *hǫrgr*. Freyja, in her role as *Vanadís* 'the goddess of the Vanir', for example, is assured of Óttarr's devotion to her because of his many burnt offerings that have worn the rough stone of her *hǫrgr* to a glassy smoothness (Hyndl 10). Some of the *dísir* were believed to be ghosts who roamed and ruled the night and who were appeased by sacrifice at the *hǫrgr*.[4] A resonance of this kind of sacrificial rite is found in *Beowulf*, where, after the attack of the *helrūnan* 'demons, sorceresses' (referring to Grendel and, by extension, to his mother), the Danes offer *wīgweorþunga* 'honors of war, sacrifice' at the *hærgtrafum* 'heathen temples' as appeasement (163, 175–178a).[5] Of course, not all *dísir* require sacrificial appeasement. There are those who function as brides and guardians of the hero and whose environment is the court as well as the battlefield. The valkyries Sigrún, Sváva, and Brynhildr exemplify these.

The concept of the valkyrie as a fierce battle-demon was apparently of southern Germanic origin.[6] Part of this sinister, southern group are the Teutonic *idisi* 'the divine ladies' of the *First Merseburg Charm,* the title—in this case, as in Old English and Old Norse—referring to the status of the creatures. The charm presents these "divine ladies" as baleful war-spirits, who bind and fetter the host and, in essence, inflict a kind of paralysis upon the warriors.[7] Several female characters in Old Norse literature are related to these malevolent figures: the darker dream woman who comes to the hero "covered in men's blood" in *Gísla saga* (Ch. 24) is of this class, as is the cult-figure, Þorgerðr Hölgabrúðr, the troll-like (yet beautiful) *dís* who delights in human sacrifice (Jóms 32–33), and the three valkyries who weave a bloody death for the hero-king in *Darraðarljóð.* Binding and fettering, as well as engendering battle-paralysis, are considered to be functions of Óðinn's valkyries. One of the war-maids, in fact, is called *Herfjǫturr* 'war-fetter', or 'warrior-fetter'. As a group, the valkyries are called *valmeyjar* 'battle-maidens', *hjálmvitr* 'helmet-creatures', *skjaldmeyjar* 'shield-maidens', among many other epithets that refer to their function and physical appearance.

Occasionally, the Old Norse documents juxtapose the sinister battle-demon with the radiant, courtly figure. Thus, in *Helgakviða Hjǫrvarðssonar,* Hrímgerðr, the corrupt, lustful warring-giantess, vies with the gold-adorned Sváva for possession of the hero-king; in *Helreið Brynhildar,* Brynhildr overcomes the giantess who bars her path to Sigurðr; and in *Hyndluljóð,* Freyja opposes Hyndla. It is this adversarial relationship that Ellis Davidson sees as possibly being reflective of two distinctive religious conceptions of the afterlife, the destructive battle-figure representing the earlier tradition.[8]

In Old English literature, resonances of both the grim and benevolent aspects of the valkyrie-figure occur as well, although, for the most part, only the earlier concept of the valkyrie as a baleful war-spirit has been previously remarked upon. *Wælcyrge* 'chooser of the slain', the Old English equivalent of ON *valkyrja,* consistently refers to creatures who are malevolent, destructive, corrupt, and associated with slaughter. In the glosses and vocabularies of the eighth through the eleventh centuries,[9] in Wulfstan's *Sermo Lupi ad Anglos,* and in Cnut's letter to his subjects, the *wælcyrgean* are seen as sinister war-spirits and baleful influences in society, in concert with murderers, slayers of kinsmen, and fornicators.[10]

The barbarous nature of the valkyrie is also documented in the *Beowulf* codex. In the prose catalogue of marvels, *The Wonders of the East,* the battle-figures are associated with the Gorgons. The valkyries, the narrator informs the reader, were begotten in *Gorgoneus,* and apparently had the horrific eyes of the Gorgons, for, earlier in the travelogue (in recounting the marvels of Lentibelsinea, a location near the Red Sea), the narrator describes indigenous beasts that had *eahta fēt* 'eight feet' and *wælcyrigean ēagan* 'the eyes of the valkyrie'.[11] The description not only evokes the image of Óðinn's eight-legged steed, Sleipnir, but also brings to mind the picture of the sinister female-rider advancing into battle, the sight of whom strikes the warrior with terror.

Squadrons of galloping female riders appear in two Old English pagan charms. As a metaphor for a sudden, unexpected attack of physical pain, "For a Sudden Stitch" employs a horde of malevolent spear-throwing female riders advancing for attack over a barrow and screaming out their battle cry:

> Hlude wæran hy, la, hlude   ða hy ofer þone hlæw ridan,
> wæran anmode,   ða hy ofer land ridan.
> Scyld ðu ðe nu, þu ðysne nið   genesan mote.
> Ut, lytel spere,   gif her inne sie!
> Stod under linde,   under leohtum scylde,
> þær ða mihtigan wif   hyra mægen beræddon
> and hy gyllende   garas sændan;
> ic him oðerne   eft wille sændan,
> fleogende flane   forane togeanes.
>
> (3–11)

(Loud were they, lo, loud, when they rode over the barrow. Bold were they, when they rode over the land. Shield thyself now, thou might escape this violent attack. Out little spear, if here inside you be! I stood under the linden, under the light shield, when the mighty women made ready their strength, and they sent forth screaming spears. I will send back another, a flying arrow against them.)

And in another Old English charm, the female squadron is a metaphor for swarming bees:

> Sitte ge, sigewif,   sigað to eorþan!
> Næfre ge wilde   to wuda fleogan.
> Beo ge swa gemindige   mines godes,
> swa bið manna gehwilc   metes and eþeles.
>
> (9–12)

(Descend, victorious women, settle to earth! Never fly wild to the woodlands. Be you as mindful of my goods, as each man is of food and homeland.)

Nora K. Chadwick and Ellis Davidson identify both the *mihtigan wīf* mustering their troops and (as do others) the *sigewīf* as valkyries.[12] This latter reference, however, suggests a more benevolent aspect of the warrior-maids, one that evokes the dignified women of the Helgi lays who ride above land and sea and alight to protect the hero; it thus provides the one possible exception in Old English literature to the prevailing view of the valkyries as baneful.

The *Beowulf* poet follows the tradition of depicting the valkyrie-figure as a deadly battle-demon in his characterization of Grendel's Mother. As Chadwick has argued, Grendel's Mother, that *wælgǣst wǣfre* 'roaming slaughter-spirit' epitomizes the earlier concept of the valkyrie.[13] Certainly, an examination of her epithets lends support to Chadwick's statement. Grendel's Mother has a formidable strength. She is a *merewīf mihtig* 'mighty sea-woman', a *mihtig mānscaða* 'mighty evil ravager', a *micle mearcstapa* 'great boundary stalker', and she delights in carnage—she is a 'horror, glorying in the carrion', *atol ǣse wlanc*. Her protective covering is analogous to helm and byrnie, since Beowulf's sword "sang out its greedy war-song" as it clanged against her head (1520–1522a). Moreover, she is ambisexual as are the *skjaldmeyjar* whom Saxo describes as possessing the "bodies of women . . . [but] the souls of men."[14] Grendel's Mother has the 'likeness of a woman' (*idese onlīcnes*, 1351a) but is characterized as a *sinnigne secg* 'sinful man' (1379a), and several of her pronominal references are in the masculine (1260, 1392, 1394). Finally, the force of her surprise attack on the hall—which the poet compares to an onslaught by a number of battling women against a single armed man (1279–1299)—creates in the warriors a terrifying panic, a paralysis, that reasonably identifies the *ides āglǣcwīf* 'divine lady, monstrous warrior woman' with the *idisi* of the *Merseburg Charm* and the *dísir* of Old Norse literature.

As a complement to Grendel's Mother, the *Beowulf* poet presents the earlier view of the valkyrie as a grim battle-demon in another, more provocative guise. Yet even when he metamorphizes the figure into a splendid creature—as he does in the rendering of the *goldhroden* Modthrytho—he retains the malevolent traits of the early battle-demon:

nǣnig þæt dorste   dēor genēþan
swǣsra gesīða,   nefne sinfrēa,
þæt hire an dæges   ēagum starede;
ac him wælbende   weotode tealde
handgewriþene;   hraþe seoþðan wæs
æfter mundgripe   mēce geþinged,
þæt hit sceādenmǣl   scȳran mōste,
cwealmbealu cȳðan.   No bið swylc cwēnlīc þēaw
idese tō efnanne,   þēah ðe hīo ǣnlicu sȳ,
þætte freoðuwebbe   fēores onsǣce
æfter ligetorne   lēofne mannan.

(1933–1943)

(No brave one among her own champions, save the great lord, dared to venture that—to gaze on her openly with his eyes; but he could reckon fetters of the slain would be ordained for him, woven by hand; quickly thereupon, after his seizure, the sword was appointed, so that the damascened blade was obliged to settle it, to make known the baleful death. Such is no queenly custom for a lady to perform, although she be peerless, that a peace-weaver should exact the life of a beloved man because of a pretended injury.)

Although the environment is courtly and the queen a *freoðuwebbe* 'peace-weaver', Modthrytho's weaving of slaughter-bonds is reminiscent of the weaving of chains and twisting of shackles in which the *idisi* of the *Merseburg Charm* engage, and the paralytic state that grips her victim is analogous to the terror that the *idisi* generate in theirs.

Modthrytho is assuredly a court figure. In contrast to Grendel's Mother, who is an abstract rendering of the battle-demon, Modthrytho is a specific personage. She is *ides ǣnlīcu* 'lady of peerless beauty', and she is 'gold-adorned' *goldhroden*. Although, as will be discussed presently, these characteristics would associate her with the later aspect of the valkyrie-figure—the benevolent battle-maid in a courtly environment—in the poem's formal arrangement, Modthrytho must nevertheless be considered primarily a baleful valkyrie-figure in the tradition of the *idisi*. A distinct parallel drawn between the regal manslayer and the "evil ravager," Grendel's Mother, emphasizes this bond. In accord with the structural pattern in the poem, Modthrytho's sequence (quoted above) is a repetition of an earlier moment of terror, one that, as always with the grim war-spirits, was swift, sudden, and deadly for the warrior, in this instance, for Beowulf's surrogate, Aeschere:

> Cōm þā tō Heorote,   ðǣr Hring-Dene
> geond þæt sæld swǣfun.   Þā ðǣr sōna wearð
> edhwyrft eorlum,   siþðan inne fealh
> Grendles mōdor.   Wæs se gryre lǣssa
> efne swā micle,   swā bið mægþa cræft,
> wīggyre wīfes   be wǣpnedmen,
> þonne heoru bunden,   hamere geþrūen,
> sweord swāte fāh   swīn ofer helme
> ecgum dyhtig   andweard scireð.
> Ðā wæs on healle   heardecg togen
> sweord ofer setlum,   sīdrand manig
> hafen handa fæst;   helm ne gemunde,
> byrnan sīde,   þā hine se brōga angeat.
> Hēo wæs on ofste,   wolde ūt þanon,
> fēore beorgan,   þā hēo onfunden wæs;
> hraðe hēo æþelinga   ānne hæfde
> fæste befangen,   þā hēo tō fenne gang.
> Sē wæs Hrōþgāre   hæleþa lēofost
> on gesīðes hād   be sǣm twēonum,
> rīce randwiga,   þone ðe hēo on ræste ābrēat,
> blǣdfæstne beorn.   Næs Bēowulf ðǣr. . . .
>   (1279–1299)

(Then she came to Heorot, where the Ring-Danes slept throughout the hall. Then immediately, there was reversal for the noblemen, when Grendel's Mother penetrated into [the hall]. The terror, the war-terror of the woman, was lesser [than Grendel's]—just as great as is the strength of maidens compared with a weaponed man when the bound blade, the sword, hammer-forged and shining with gore, strong in its edges, shears through the opposite boar-image cresting the helm. Then within the hall, the hardened-edge, the sword was seized from the seat, many a broad shield lifted steady in hand; no one heeded helm nor broad byrnie, when the terror seized him. She was in haste, she wanted out from thence, wanted to save her life, when she was discovered; quickly she had seized firmly one of the nobles; then she went out to the fen. He was of heroes in the rank of champion, the dearest to Hrothgar; between the two seas, a mighty shield-warrior, a man established in his glory, whom she had cut down in his bed. Beowulf was not there. . . .)

The details of both sequences—the doomed beloved champion, the hand-seizure, the victim's enthrallment, the shearing sword, the personal injury, and the baleful death—all point to similarity in action between the *ides āglǣcwīf* 'lady, monstrous-warrior woman' and the peerless peace-weaver.

Modthrytho, of course, is not entirely vicious. The poet records her conversion from evil to virtuous queen after her marriage to Offa. And although the movement of the character's change of temper exemplifies that found in the reluctant-bride or tamed-virago motif,[15] it also parallels the evolution of the archetypal figure that Modthrytho is modelled upon, the progression of fierce war-demon to gold-adorned warrior-queen.

For the most part, it is the later perception of the valkyrie—the warrior-maid in her benevolent aspect—that is the prominent one in Old Norse heroic poetry. Both the pictorial and early poetic tradition conceive of the valkyries as dignified gentlewomen, generally pictured either astride their horses in full armor, riding through the air over land and sea, or welcoming the *einherjar* to Valhalla with cup or horn outstretched. In the skaldic poems—*Hákonarmál, Hrafnsmál,* and *Eiríksmál*—and in the mythological poems of the *Edda,* they are entirely supernatural with few individualizing attributes. With the exception of Freyja, whose qualities and functions are complex, the characters are stereotypes. In *Hákonarmál,* the figure appears in shining armor on the battlefield with the "thoughtful features" that distinguish those who arrange destinies. In *Hrafnsmál,* the valkyrie has shining eyes, is wise, fair-skinned, and golden-haired: these traits romanticize the physical and mental brilliance of the martial maidens. And in *Eiríksmál,* she is no more than a dream-figure, a symbol of a portentous event in Óðinn's mind.[16] In essence, the war-maids have been neutralized from characters of volition to elements of heroic machinery.[17]

The valkyries of the Eddic heroic lays are distinctly different in kind. They are legendary personages and, as such, have idiosyncratic personalities. The heroines of these poems—Sigrún, Sváva, Brynhildr, and Guðrún (referentially)—are figures of the royal court, with ties and obligations to a worldly environment. Sigrún, for example, is caught between her loyalty to her brother and her loyalty to her husband (HH II 30–38), and Brynhildr either must obey Atli's command to marry Gunnarr or battle her brother in defiance of that wish (Sigsk 35–40). At the same time, the valkyrie-brides (so called because of their erotic attachment to the hero) have supernatural powers (they are not limited by spatial and temporal considerations). As Óðinn's maids, they determine the outcome of central issues that concern the Germanic warrior society—battle and the warrior's afterlife. In all respects, their roles are consonant with the subject matter of the poems—heroic deeds in battle.

Terms like *skjaldmeyjar* and *hjálmvitr* describe their appearance as armed warriors bearing shield and helmet. Their physical beauty is emphasized by epithets dealing with gold ornamentation of helmet and bright byrnie. The battle-maids are *bjǫrt í brynio* 'bright in byrnie' (Gríp 15), *gullvarið* 'gold-adorned' (HH II 45), *marggullin* 'richly decked with gold' (HHv 26), *baugvarið* 'ring-adorned' (HH II 35). They are *sólbjǫrt* 'sun-bright one(s)' (HH II 45) and *brúðr biartlituð* 'bride(s) of clear brilliant hue of countenance' (HHv 7). In addition, they are wise, keen-witted, and articulate. Brynhildr and Sváva impart hidden knowledge to their respective hero-kings (Gríp 17–18, Sd 5–13, HHv 8–9),[18] and Sigrún is first characterized as *snót svinnhuguð* 'wise, quick-minded woman' (HH II 11), a quality recalled later in the poem when she is addressed on the battlefield as *alvitr* 'all-wise' (HH II 26). The latter epithet is used as an identifying term for the valkyries in *Vǫlundarkviða* (1, 3) where it appears as a refrain.

Acuity and wisdom are buttressed by sagacity of speech, and a decidedly supernatural coloration informs the utterances. Sváva and the Sigrúns declaim speeches characteristic of *hvatir*—exhortations to action—and benisons. On their initial encounters with Helgi, they chastise the hero for his behavior, incite him to his duty, and heap blessings upon him as a reward. They place a command upon him that, once accepted, will set him apart from other men, transform his personality, and invest him with a glory that is akin to the divine. This otherworldly dimension likewise characterizes Brynhildr's speeches to Sigurðr and Gunnarr. If the battle-maid's rune lesson to Sigurðr provides the hero at the onset of his journey with the tools that will help him carve out his heroic destiny, her prophecy to Gunnarr outlines, in words latently sacerdotal, the final bitter unraveling of the Gjúking's life. These qualities of wisdom, acumen, and eloquence, and the attributes of brightness and radiance of physical appearance are traits that are an essential part of each valkyrie-bride's basic characterization, so much so that it becomes apparent that, despite their idiosyncratic personalities, Sigrún, Sváva, and Brynhildr, as well as the other heroines, were each constructed according to a distinct character type.

Conventions for the characterization of females in heroic poetry were part of the Old Norse literary tradition. In *Skáldskaparmál* (31), Snorri counsels the skalds to identify their female characters through epithets that give them a supernatural and martial dimension: (*Kona er ok kend við allar ásynjur eða valkyrjur eða nornir eða dísir*) 'Woman', says Snorri, 'is also kenned by the names of goddesses, or valkyries, or norns, or *dísir* [or as Brodeur translates the last term, 'women of supernatural kind']'.[19] Earlier in the chapter, he advises the poets to characterize the female by referring to *gull ok gimsteina* 'gold and jewels' and *gimsteina eða glersteina* 'jewels or agates', and in terms alluding to their "conduct, or properties, or family." Old Norse heroic poetry follows these stylistic prescriptions, for the generic norm is the appearance of a brightly adorned noblewoman, metamorphized into a valkyrie and/or a *dís*.

No comparable *ars poetica* exists for Old English heroic poetry, and any assumptions regarding the poets' stylistic conventions for the characterization of females must derive from empirical investigations of the extant literature, assumptions that, by nature, must be provisional, because the Old English poetic corpus is so limited. In general, however, the treatment of the female warriors of Old English heroic poetry—Elene, Judith, and Juliana—corresponds closely to the treatment given the Old English heroic male warrior. In an examination of the rhetorical figures used to describe these three female characters, Patricia A. Belanoff demonstrates that the epithets used to define Beowulf, Hrothgar, and Andreas are likewise employed to distinguish the Cynewulfian and Old Testament heroines.[20] Although the female characters undergo slight alterations—their femininity is diffused, while their heroic attributes (soberness of mind, nobility of birth, courage in action) are emphasized—the heroic temperament is rendered as equally appropriate to male and female.

Admittedly, one hesitates to assign the warrior-woman role to Juliana. The Christian saint neither sets out on a military campaign leading her comitatus as does Elene, nor does she brandish a sword to slay the enemy as does Judith. The tortures and humiliations she undergoes are not heroic features, but are details found in the trials of other saints.[21] Furthermore, although she does engage in single combat (a heroic commonplace), it does not entail the physical agony that, for example, Beowulf undergoes in contesting with Grendel and Grendel's Mother. In the Demon, Juliana battles not a foe of the flesh, but one of the spirit and the mind. And her weapons are words. If, however, one conceives of battle for spiritual salvation as viable subject matter for a heroic poem and the rhetorical mode as a means of battle, Juliana can be perceived as a triumphant warrior-maid. She confronts her antagonist in *þām engan hofe* 'in the narrow place' (532a), a suitable place for heroic encounter. On God's command, the heroine grasps her antagonist, binds him in fetters—bonds that he is powerless to break (433–434a, 534b–536a)—and does not release him until he has capitulated to her (547b–556a).

In the main, there is a close correspondence in the treatment of Elene, Judith, and Juliana. Similarities in their mental qualities and their emotional and physical traits point to the possibility that each heroine is a particularized rendering of a character type, the warrior-woman. Their attributes, moreover, closely resemble those of the valkyries of the heroic lays. The Nordic and Anglo-Saxon characters are parallel in their physical appearance, in qualities, status, and, in part, activity. These likenesses suggest that both the pagan and Christian warrior-maids may be related to the same conventional stock character—the Germanic warrior-woman.

Conceptual equivalents to *gullvarið* and *baugvarið*, for example, are terms like *goldhroden, golde gehyrsted, golde gefrætwod*, and *bēahhroden*, epithets describing the physical appearance of Modthrytho, Elene, and Judith. Like the valkyrie-brides, a striking attribute of Elene and Judith is that each is splendidly adorned, and the keynote of the ornamentation is its metallic and martial properties. When Elene speaks out to the assembly, she is *geatolīc gūðcwēn golde gehyrsted* 'splendid battle-queen adorned with gold' (329–331). The terms *geatolīc* and *gehyrsted* have strong military associations throughout Old English poetry. Elsewhere in *Elene*, *geatolīc* is used to describe the splendid byrnies (*geatolīc gūðscrūd*) of the warrior-queen's comitatus on the march towards Jerusalem (258–259a). These martial overtones are also evident in *Beowulf* where, in addition to its employment as a descriptive term for Hrothgar and Heorot (215a, 1401a), *geatolīc* denotes the splendor of the sword that kills Grendel's Mother (1562a).[22]

Closely allied with motifs of warfare is *gehyrsted*, the past participial form of *hyrstan* 'to adorn, to decorate'. The noun *hyrste* means "armor, decoration," and is used in the former sense in *Elene—hilderincas hyrstum gewerede* 'the warriors were outfitted in armor' (263)—as it is in *Beowulf* where it refers to Ongentheow's battle dress (2988a). Moreover, *-hyrsted* and the second element of *goldhroden* are etymologically related to OHG *hrust*, which carries the signification of armor.[23]

Dress of metallic brightness is also attributed to Judith. Both she and the war-trappings of the soldiers are *golde gefrætwod* (171b–328b). *Golde gefrætwod*, as well as *golde gehyrsted*, appear to be part of a formulaic system that expresses the idea of adornment with gold of military equipment.[24] This is not to suggest that only military objects are adorned with gold,[25] but rather that the expression "adorned with gold" is most commonly invoked to praise splendid military dress.

Judith is also *bēahhroden*, the term that is conceptually equivalent to *baugvarið*, an epithet for Sigrún. Exactly what the meaning of *bēahhroden* might be in the

Judith context is difficult to determine. In the *Poetic Edda,* Helgi's valkyrie-bride is described as *brúðr baugvarið* 'ring-bedecked woman' (HH II 35). In addition to a general sense of evoking jeweled adornment, *baugvarið* could also refer to Sigrún's wearing of bent rings, either spiral or round in form, interlocked or single, that in Old English and Old Icelandic literature are used primarily as treasure or currency (ON *baugr;* OE *bēag,* pl. *bēagas*).[26] But since Sigrún is neither dispensing treasure when she is termed *baugvarið,* nor being praised for her physical beauty, but is instead pronouncing doom on her brother, Dag, it is conceivable that the term is meant to denote another aspect of the character.

In Old Norse poetic diction, *baugr* had an additional specialized sense that heightened its heroic coloration. A *baugr* often signified a circle painted on a shield within which scenes of mythological subjects were depicted.[27] As Snorri relates, through what apparently was a process of synecdoche, *baugr* eventually came to stand for the shield itself (Skáldsk 48). An instance of *baugr* as a metaphor for shield appears in *Hákonarmál* (8.2).[28] A term like *baugvarið,* then, might refer to a woman who is either decorated with shields or who carries a shield, the ring of battle, as an ornament. Although this understanding of the term is at first difficult to visualize, there is a description of the *skjaldmeyjar* 'shield-maidens' in Saxo which is helpful in this regard. Describing the she-captains who fought at Bravalla (Wisna, in particular), Saxo writes (Bk. VIII):[29]

> Wisna, a woman, filled with sternness, and a skilled warrior, was guarded by a band of Sclavs: her chief followers were Barri and Gnizli. But the rest of the same company had their bodies covered by little shields, and used very long swords and targets of skiey hue, which, in time of war, they either cast behind their backs or gave over to the baggage-bearers: while they cast away all protection to their breasts, and exposed their bodies in every peril, offering battle with drawn swords.

Such a garment worn by the historical warrior-women—a byrnie covered with metal shields—would have had a metallic, ornamental radiance, particularly in battle and under the glare of the sun.

Bēahhroden in *Judith* likewise might possess connotative value closely related to battle or activity on the battlefield. The term appears in a highly martial environment and refers to both Judith and her maid, an anomalous description, since to be *bēahhroden* (in the conventional sense) would conform neither with the maid's social status nor with her function in the poem. She neither appears as a treasure-giver, nor is she *bēahhroden* as an allurement for a man, a reason Huppé suggests for Judith's "adornments."[30] Some other, more immediate explication of the word is called for, one that would encompass both maid and mistress, as well as the environment:

Eodon ða gegnum þanonne

þa idesa ba   ellenþriste,
oðþæt hie becomon,   collenferhðe,
eadhreðige mægð,   ut of ðam herige,
þæt hie sweotollice   geseon mihten
þære wlitegan byrig   weallas blican,
Bethuliam.   Hie ða beahhrodene

feðelaste   forð onettan,
oð hie glædmode   gegan hæfdon
to ðam wealgate.

(132b–141a)

(Then they went forward thence, both the women, bold in courage, until they, bold-spirited, passed through, out from the host, maidens blessed in triumph, so that they clearly might see Bethulia, the walls of the fair city shining. Then, the ring-adorned ones, they hastened forth with footsteps, until they, gracious in spirit, had gone to the wall-gate.)

The cluster of epithets—*ellenþriste, collenferhðe, eadhrēðige mægð*—not only distinguishes the characters as heroic figures (earlier the maid is referred to as a *foregenga* 'one who goes before', evoking the image of a standard-bearer [127b]), but defines the women as a character pairing, a characterization device whereby a minor figure is endowed with similar (or contrasting) traits belonging to the hero in an effort to enhance his person. The heroic qualities possessed by the warrior-woman, Judith, are properties of her maid: she is thoughtful and prudent (*higeðoncolre*, 131a and *þancolmōde*, 172b). She is also decorous, possessing 'excellence of custom' *ðēawum geðungen* (129a). The *þīnenne* 'servant', in fact, is a mirror-image of her mistress, enjoying all the qualities appropriate to the warrior-woman—superiority of mind, conduct, courage, and obedience. *Bēahhroden* further unites the women in a heroic sense, suggesting a concept of them, not as servant and mistress, but as victors in a campaign against the enemy. It is as *bēahhrodene* 'ring-adorned ones' that they march through the horde of an invading army with dauntless courage, carrying their battle-prize—the head of Holofernes—in triumph. A meaning of "shield-adorned" for *bēahhroden* would make appropriate its use for both Judith and her maid, since it would describe warrior-dress. As were the *skjaldmeyjar* and Sigrún, the Old English female warriors might conceivably have been adorned with shields, the jewels of the battlefield, as they moved through the enemy troops.

Judith possesses one further physical characteristic that is a feature of the valkyrie-brides. The lucency that is a common trait of the Nordic figures is a vital feature of Judith, who is *beorht mæg* 'bright maiden' (Jud 58, 254) and has the shining brilliance of the sun about her. She is *ælfscīenu* 'shining like an elf', or 'elfin-bright', a term that possibly refers to a class of elf—the light elves, the *ljósálfar* of Old Norse mythology—reportedly fairer than the sun itself (Gylf 17).

Paradoxically, the brightness and radiance of physical appearance that distinguishes the valkyrie-brides is the prime attribute of the most Christian of the Old English female warriors, Juliana. The warrior-saint is defined by epithets expressing the ideas of sunshine and the brightness of the sun. In a passage original with Cynewulf, Juliana becomes luminosity itself. She is called *sunna scīma* 'shining of the sun', the only instance in Old English poetry where the term has a human referent (166b).[31] Elsewhere, again in a passage that is Cynewulf's alone, Juliana is identified as *sunscīene* 'the sun-bright one', a unique appearance of the term in Old English poetry (229a). *Sunscīene* is allied conceptually with *sólbiǫrt* 'the sun-bright one', an epithet for Sigrún (HH II 45).

There is, moreover, a resemblance in action between Juliana and Óðinn's maids. Not far removed from the fettering and the shackling of warriors which the *idisi* engage in, nor for that matter from Modthrytho's hand-seizure of the hall-champion, is Juliana's grasp of the Demon. It will be remembered that when first encountering the formidable maid, the Demon (the sinning *þegn*) is seized by the warrior-saint and becomes physically paralyzed—"powerless to resist"—as if chained in shackles:

> þu me ærest saga,
> hu þu gedyrstig   þurh deop gehygd
> wurde þus wigþrist   ofer eall wifa cyn,
> þæt þu mec þus fæste   fetrum gebunde,
> æghwæs orwigne.
>
> (430b–434a)

("Tell me first how you, you daring through deep thought, became thus bold in battle beyond all races of women, so that you might bind me thus, fast in fetters, powerless to resist in every way.")

There is, of course, difference in point of view: the Christian heroine is virtuous; the *idisi* and Modthrytho are villainous. Yet the nature and effect of Juliana's action upon the Demon is, in essence, that of the fell valkyries.

Boldness in battle and resoluteness of mind are major constituents of Juliana's character. Elsewhere in the poem, the Demon testifies that neither patriarch nor prophet had ever engaged him in combat as *þriste* 'boldly' as had the maid, none had laid bonds upon him as "boldly" as she (*bealdlice bennum bilegde*, 519), none were more relentless or "bolder" in thought (*þristran geþohtes ne þweorhtimbran*, 549). These qualities of severity of mind, tenacity of purpose, and courage are components of Elene's and Juliana's personalities.[32] They are, moreover, reminiscent of those belonging to another battle-maid, the *harðugðictman* 'hard-minded woman' Bryn-hildr (Gríp 27), who enters the battlefield *bǫll, í brynio* 'bold, in her byrnie' (Sigsk 37, Helr 3).

Vestiges of other qualities common to the Old Norse valkyrie-brides arise in the characterizations of the Old English female warriors. Like their Nordic parallels, they have profundity and agility of mind. Judith is twice referred to as *snoter* 'wise, intelligent', once when she is escorted by Holofernes's men into his bedchamber (55a) and, again, later (as *snotere mægð*) when, no longer the victim but the victor, she carries out his bloody head to her servant (125a). This combination of wisdom and acumen implied by *snoter* is likewise found in Elene who is granted *snyttro cræft* 'power of wisdom and discernment' after the recovery of the cross (Ele 1171).

Searoðoncol 'clever-minded' (145a), *gearoðoncolre* 'quick-witted' (341a), and *gleaw* 'wise' also point to Judith's keenness of wit and wisdom. The Jewish widow is first described as *gleaw on geðonce* 'wise in mind' (13b); subsequently is referred to as being *ferhðgleawe* 'wise in spirit, prudent' (41a), a *gleawhydig wíf* 'wise-minded woman' (148a); and, finally, as *séo gleawe* 'the wise one' when she commands her handmaid to uncover the battle-treasure, the head of Holofernes (171a). That trait that enabled Judith to defeat the Assyrian invader is identical to that which allowed Juliana to best the Demon. Juliana is *gleaw* 'wise' and dear to God (131a). And all three Christian female-warriors are *gemyndig* 'mindful' of their duty to a higher authority (Ele 266b, 267b; Jud 74b–77a; Jln 601b–602a), obligations they fulfill with rhetorical brilliance. Elene repeatedly commands and goads the Jewish elders and warriors to reveal the whereabouts of the true cross; Judith exhorts her soldiers into battle; and Juliana's speeches progress from forensic argument to evangelical utterance.

Lastly, the status of the Old English heroines in their respective narratives resembles that of the valkyrie-brides. Juliana's position in the narrative as spokesman and instrument of God is an appropriate one for the conventional saint-type; she stands on a plane midway between the human and the divine, used by men for help and intercession (696, 716) and by God as "chosen" to effect his will (605, 613). This office is analogous to the authority held by the valkyries who were also "high-born" and "chosen" of the gods. Their function was likewise to serve as intermediaries between men and the deity. That they comprised an elite group selected by Óðinn and set apart from the other aristocratic females is stressed in appelations used to identify them: they are known as *nǫnnur Herjans* 'nuns of Herjan' (a name for Óðinn) and *ǫskmeyjar* 'adopted or chosen maids'.

In essence, this intermediate status is applicable not only to Juliana, but to Judith and Elene as well. The female warriors are functionaries, chosen servants of God. Judith, in fact, is called *Nergendes þēowen* 'servant or handmaiden of the Savior', at the moment she is about to strike off Holofernes's head. And even though Elene is the emissary of her son, the emperor, in actuality she is on God's business, for it is his truth she struggles to have revealed. Juliana's action during her night-struggle with the Demon is analogous to that of the battle-maids in combat. At the command of God, she binds and fetters the foe and pronounces his fate. This is not to imply that either Cynewulf or the anonymous poet of Judith was consciously creating a combination saint and valkyrie type. Rather, that the parallels suggest that both the Nordic and Anglo-Saxon poets availed themselves of a stock female character that was so embedded in Germanic heroic literary tradition that, in its depiction, religious or national boundaries were ignored.

In light of these remarks, the valkyrie-figure seems to be as much a part of the Anglo-Saxon literary consciousness as it is of the Old Norse. The glosses, charms, and prose documents clearly depict a figure essentially derived from the early war-spirits of Germanic origin. Resonances of the later concept of the valkyrie, exemplified in the *Poetic Edda* by Brynhildr and the Sváva-Sigrún character of the Helgi lays, can be detected in the female warriors of the Old English Christian epics, and, although not touched upon in this article, in Wealhtheow as well. Correspondences in epithets, traits, and action are understandably subtle. That they exist at all is remarkable. A Christian poet working within the Germanic heroic tradition that had the valkyrie-figure as one of its conventional character types would undoubtedly have been constrained to use some delicacy in selecting characterizing details for delineations of his warrior-saints and sympathetic queens.

NOTES

1. For a general discussion of the valkyries, see Jan de Vries, *Altgermanische Religionsgeschichte*, 3rd ed., 2 vols. (Berlin: Walter de Gruyter & Co., 1970), I, 273–74 (193), II, 59 (380); Jakob Grimm, *Teutonic Mythology*, trans. James Steven Stallybrass, I (London: George Bell & Sons, 1883), 401–402, 417–26; John Arnott MacCulloch, *The Mythology of All Races: Eddic*, II (New York: Cooper Square Publications, Inc., 1964), 248–57. The association of the valkyries with the Irish war-goddesses is made by Charles Donahue, "The Valkyries and the Irish War-Goddesses," *Publications of the Modern Language Association* 56 (March 1941): 1–12. Alexander Haggerty Krappe, "The Valkyries," *Modern Language Review* 21 (1926): 55–76, argues for an identification of the valkyrie with the *alaisiagis* and with the female dioscuri, the "daughters of the sky" that appear throughout Indo-European literature.

2. Hilda Roderick Ellis [Davidson], *Road to Hel: A Study of the Conception of the Dead in Old Norse Literature* (1942; rept. New York: Greenwood Press, 1968), pp. 65–73, 77–78, 135–38, and her concluding remarks on pp. 198–201.

3. For an examination of Old English *ides* in gnomic poetry, see Audrey L. Meaney's "The *Ides* of the Cotton Gnomic Poem," *Medium Ævum* 48, no. 1 (1979): 23–39; reprinted herein. Old Norse *dís* is also used to refer to the "luck" guardian figures, the *fylgjukona* 'female follower or guardian', and the *hamingja* 'guardian spirit'. There is a confusion of identity among the four classes: a *fylgja* 'follower or preceder', for example, sometimes appears in helmet and byrnie as do the *dísir* and the valkyries (*Hallfreðarsaga*, chap. 2), sometimes as an animal or troll figure (HHv, Prose before 31). For discussions on the distinctions in function and aspect of these guardian figures, see de Vries, *Alt. Rel.*, I, 222–28 (161, 162–64), 273–74 (193); II, 297–99 (528–29); Grimm, I, 400, 419; II, 874–77; see also Ellis [Davidson], *Hel*, pp. 130–38; MacCulloch, II, 235–37; E. O. G. Turville-Petre, *Myth and Religion of the North: The Religion of Ancient Scandinavia* (New York: Holt, Rinehart and Winston, 1964), pp. 221–30; Folke Ström, *Diser, nornor, valkyrjor*, in *Kungliga vitterhets historie och antikvitets akademiens handlingar*, Filologisk-filosofiska serien 1 (Stockholm: Almqvist och Wiksell, 1954); and Else Mundal's discussion on the *dísir* and the *fylgjur* in chap. 4 of *Fylgjemotiva i norrøn litteratur* (Oslo: Universitetsforlaget, 1974). Textual references to and quotations from the poems of the *Poetic Edda* are from Gustav Neckel, ed., *Edda: Die Lieder des Codex Regius nebst verwandten Denkmälern*, 4th ed. revised by Hans Kuhn (Heidelberg: Carl Winter, 1962). The translations of the poems are mine although references are also made to the translations of Henry Adams Bellows, *The Poetic Edda* (New York: The American Scandinavian Foundation, 1923), and Lee M. Hollander, *The Poetic Edda* (Austin: University of Texas Press, 1962). The abbreviations used for Old Norse Texts are as follows: HHv, *Helgakviða Hjǫrvarðssonar;* HH I, *Helgakviða Hundingsbana I;* HH II, *Helgakviða Hundingsbana II:* Helr, *Helreið Brynhildar;* Hyndl, *Hyndluljóð;* Jóms, *Jómsvíkinga saga;* Sigsk, *Sigurðarkviða en skamma;* Gríp, *Grípisspá;* Gylf, *Gylfaginning.*

4. Ellis [Davidson], *Hel*, pp. 134–37; Grimm, I, 402.

5. Through an association of words in the Old English glosses, *helrūne* is connected with the earlier concept of the valkyrie as a grim battle-spirit. As a gloss for *pythonissa*, *helrūne* appears as an alternative for *hægtesse* = *erenis*, *eumenides*, *furia*, *parcae*, all terms that gloss *walcrigge*, *wælcyrre*, *wælcyrge;* see Thomas Wright, *Anglo-Saxon and Old English Vocabularies*, ed. Richard Paul Wülcker, 2nd ed. (London: Trübner and Co., 1884), I, 188.33, 189.12, 392.18, 392.19, 404.33, 344.4, 470.27, 471.31, 472.1, among other entries. For an examination of OE *hearg* (ON *hǫrgr*), see Thomas L. Markey, "Germanic Terms for Temple and Cult," in *Studies for Einar Haugen*, eds. E. S. Firchow, et al. (The Hague: Mouton, 1972), pp. 365–78, esp. pp. 367–70. Textual references to and quotations from *Beowulf* are to Fr. Klaeber's edition, *Beowulf and the Fight at Finnsburg*, 3rd ed. (Lexington, Mass.: D. C. Heath and Co., 1950). Unless otherwise noted, all textual references to and quotations from other works in the Anglo-Saxon poetic corpus will rely on the collective edition, *The Anglo-*

Saxon Poetic Records, eds. George Philip Krapp and Elliott Van Kirk Dobbie, 6 vols. (New York: Columbia University Press, 1931–1953).

6. Bellows, pp. 14, no. 31; 296, n. 17; Donahue, "Valkyries & Irish War-Goddesses": 4; Grimm, I, 401; MacCulloch, II, 255–56. Based on the writings of Latin and Greek historians, MacCulloch and Ellis Davidson, as well as others, suggest that the concept of the valkyries originated in actual Germanic female warriors; MacCulloch, II, 256, 375, n. 37; H. R. Ellis [Davidson], *Gods and Myths of Northern Europe* (Penguin Books, 1973), p. 61.

7. *Eiris sazun idisi, sazun hera duoder. / suma hapt heptidun, suma heri lezidun, / suma clubodun umbi cuoniouuidi; / insprinc haptbandun, unuar uigandun* ('In days gone by, the *idisi* sat and they sat here and yonder. Some made firm the fetters, some hindered the host, and some picked apart the chains; escape from fetters, escape from foes.') Quoted from Charles C. Barber, *An Old High German Reader* (Oxford: Basil Blackwell, 1964), p. 65.

8. *Hel*, pp. 73, 77.

9. Latin equivalents for the term *wælcyrge (walcyrge, walcrigge)* refer to the *Erinyes (Herines, Erinys, Eurynes, Herinis), Allecto, Tisiphone, Parcae*, and the Roman goddess of war, *Bellona*; Wright, *Vocabularies*, I, 19.44, 25.27, 417.12, 347.32, 533.26, 50.40, 189.11, 360.3, 527.17, 94.15, 12.12.

10. Although *wælcyrgean* is usually translated as 'sorceresses' in Wulfstan and Cnut, there is no indication in either text that the creatures being referred to are not the war-spirits. See Dorothy Bethurum, ed., *The Homilies of Wulfstan* (Oxford: Clarendon Press, 1957), pp. 273, 363, n. 160–66; Dorothy Whitelock, ed., *Sermo Lupi ad Anglos*, 3rd ed. (London: Methuen & Co., Ltd., 1963), pp. 64–65, n. 171; Dorothy Whitelock, David Douglas, and C. W. Greensway, eds., *English Historical Documents: c. 500–1042*, I (London: Eyre & Spottiswoode, 1955), 414 f., 858–59, n. 1.

11. *Three Old English Prose Texts in MS. Cotton Vitellius A. xv*, ed. Stanley Rypins, Early English Text Society, o.s., 161 (London: Oxford University Press, 1924), pp. 52, 55.

12. Nora K. Chadwick, "The Monsters and *Beowulf*," in *The Anglo-Saxons: Studies in Some Aspects of Their History and Culture Presented to Bruce Dickins*, ed. Peter Clemoes (London: Bowes & Bowes, 1959), pp. 171–203, esp. p. 176; Ellis Davidson, *Gods & Myths*, p. 63; Krappe, "Valkyries": 55; MacCulloch, II, 248, 253.

13. Chadwick, "Monsters & *Beowulf*," pp. 176–77.

14. *The Nine Books of Saxo Grammaticus*, trans. Oliver Elton (Norroena Society; rpt. Nendeln/Liechenstein: Kraus Reprint Limited, 1967), Bk. VIII, p. 310.

15. Klaeber, p. 195, note to 1931b–1962.

16. Textual references to these poems rely on Nora Kershaw's dual-language edition, *Anglo-Saxon and Norse Poems* (Cambridge: The University Press, 1922), pp. 82–87, 96–99, 104–109.

17. C. M. Bowra parallels the evolution of the valkyrie with that of the *vile*, the fierce female battle-spirits of Yugoslavian heroic song, and sees the neutralizing of divinities as part of the development of heroic poetry into an anthropocentric genre; *Heroic Poetry* (New York: St. Martin's Press, 1966), pp. 84–86.

18. This is, of course, accepting the assumption that *Sigdrífa* is an epithet for Brynhildr. The rune-lesson sequence likewise appears in *Vǫlsunga saga*.

19. In *Edda Snorra Sturlusonar*, ed. Finnur Jónsson (Reykjavík: Sigurður Kristjánsson, 1907); Arthur Gilchrist Brodeur, *The Prose Edda by Snorri Sturluson* (New York: The American Scandinavian Foundation, 1923), p. 143. Because the nature and function of the *dísir* is so complex and ambiguous, I have chosen not to translate the term.

20. See her unpublished article, "Elene, Juliana, and Judith: Women of Old English Heroic Poetry"; see also "The Changing Image of Woman in Old English Heroic Poetry" (Diss.: New York University, 1982). I am grateful and indebted to Professor Belanoff for her generosity in permitting me to quote from her work.

21. For discussions of Juliana as a conventional saint-type, see Gordon Hall Gerould, *Saints' Legends [The Types of English Literature]* (Boston and New York: Houghton Mifflin and Company, 1916), pp. 1–62.

22. The comprehensive contextual study of these terms in the poetic corpus has been made possible through the use of *A Concordance to The Anglo-Saxon Poetic Records*, ed. J. B. Bessinger, Jr., prog. by Philip H. Smith, Jr. (Ithaca: Cornell University Press, 1978).

23. Jan de Vries, *Altnordisches etymologisches Wörterbuch*, 2nd ed. (Leiden: E. J. Brill, 1962), pp. 257–58, *hrjóða*, 2; Alois Walde, *Vergleichendes Wörterbuch der indogermanischen Sprachen*, herausgegeben und bearbeitet von Julius Pokorny (Berlin und Leipzig, 1930), I, 477. The Old Norse equivalent of *goldhroden—gull-roðinn, gull-hroðinn*—in fact carries the signification of "the gilt of warriors' helmets and shields"; *An Icelandic-English Dictionary*, ed. Richard Cleasby, enlarged and completed by Gudbrand Vigfusson (Oxford: The Clarendon Press, 1874), p. 220, cmpd., *gull-hroðinn*.

24. *Golde gegirwan*, for example, employed in *Waldhere* to praise the sword made by Weland (II.7a), and *golde gegyrwed* used in *Beowulf* to extol the hero's woven mail shirt (553a), are variations of the formula as is *golde geweorðod*, which describes the gold-studded armor that is Waldhere's inheritance from Aelfhere (II.9b).

25. In *Andreas* and *Elene*, for example, *gefrætwod* refers to miraculous statues (*And* 715b, 1518a) and angels (*Ele* 742a).

26. Cleasby-Vigfusson, *baugr*, p. 53; Klaeber, *bēag*, glossary; Knut Stjerna, *Essays on Questions Connected with the Old English Poem of Beowulf*, trans. and ed. by John R. Clark Hall, The Viking Club Society of Northern Research, E. S., vol. 3 ([Coventry], 1912), pp. 251–54, glossary.

27. Cleasby-Vigfusson, *baugr*, II.2.

28. *Blendusk við roðnum und randar himni / Sköglar veðr, léku við skýum bauga* 'Skogul's storms mingled, reaching towards, under the reddened canopy of the shield; they contested with the clouds around the shields'; Kershaw, *Anglo-Saxon & Norse Poems*, notes to *Hákonarmál*, p. 190, 8; the translation is mine.

29. Saxo, pp. 310–11.

30. Bernard F. Huppé, *The Web of Words* (Albany: State University of New York Press, 1970), p. 164.

31. The only other appearance of the term has the literal meaning 'shining of the sun' (Dan 263).

32. Elene, for example, is described as *þriste on geþance* 'bold in thought' as she marches towards Jerusalem and (along with Judas and her warriors) as *stiðhycgende* on the approach to Calvary (267, 716).

PART

III

Language and Difference
in Characterization

PATRICIA A. BELANOFF

11 Women's Songs, Women's Language
Wulf and Eadwacer *and* The Wife's Lament

The speakers of *Wulf and Eadwacer* and *The Wife's Lament*[1] make us uncomfortably aware of how rarely we hear female voices in Old English poetry expressing those emotions which poets tell us they have. The *Beowulf* poet does say of Hildeburh: *ides gnornode* 'the lady mourned' (1117b); but we do not hear *her* voice, nor that of the lamenting woman at Beowulf's funeral pyre, nor those of the sorrowing women of *Deor*. There are, of course, a number of poems in which non-sorrowing female voices are presented to us directly, but except for *Wulf and Eadwacer* and *The Wife's Lament,* all female words expressing grief are filtered through the undeniably male voice of a narrator. The uniqueness of these poems suggests that our reading and understanding of them will be enriched if we view them as expressions of the feminine in a literary milieu seemingly dominated by heroic male action.

Some twenty-five years ago, building on the work of Theodor Frings and Leo Spitzer, Kemp Malone argued that our two Old English poems were the Germanic representatives of an international genre of women's songs designated by their German name, *frauenlieder.*[2] *Frauenlieder* are popular rather than courtly songs, apt to appear in unlikely contexts. Except for the *muwassahas*—mozarabic poetry of the tenth and eleventh centuries which Spitzer considers urban poems—other national *frauenlieder* are marked by references to nature. In addition, they are enigmatically allusive, usually focused on pain and sorrow brought about by separation from a male, and explicit in their references to sexual activity. Our two Old English *frauenlieder* manifest all these traits. As we seek the image of the feminine embedded in *Wulf and Eadwacer* and *The Wife's Lament,* we should expect them to exhibit cross-cultural, as well as culture-dependent, traits. To appreciate them fully, we must read them as both Old English poems *and as frauenlieder.*

Of course, it is not mainly the content of *The Wife's Lament* and *Wulf and Eadwacer* that differentiates them from the bulk of Old English poetry and associates them with the *frauenlieder;* but, more strikingly, it is their form and the nature of their language, the peculiarities of which have been fodder for many articles. Most critics agree with Malone that *Wulf and Eadwacer* diverges more from classical Old English poetic style than *The Wife's Lament* does; it is not "done in the classical literary formulaic style usual in what has come down to us of Old English poetry"; he, in fact, thinks it more akin to certain forms of Old Icelandic poetry. Of *The Wife's Lament*, he says:

> The proportion of the whole composed in short sentences is much greater than one usually finds in classic OE poetry. . . . The run-on lines and the long, involved sentence (lines 43b–50a) . . . link the poem to the classical tradition, but these features are not nearly so prominent as one would expect in a strictly classical composition. We have here a popular poem, composed indeed under the influence of the prevailing literary mode of its day but not bound by the conventions of that mode.[3]

This acknowledgement of the differentness of the language, coupled with the acknowledged differentness of approach and content and the identification of *The Wife's Lament* and *Wulf and Eadwacer* as *frauenlieder*, suggests that we need to read them with different expectations than we read the bulk of Old English poetry. By so doing, we will respond to their "differentness" as something other than divergence.

The crucial point about "differentness" in the genre as well as "differentness" in the language of *The Wife's Lament* and *Wulf and Eadwacer* is that they are interrelated: the language is different because the poems are women's songs, a genre which inevitably entails a differentness of language. Such an observation accords with the theories of women's language put forth by modern French feminists Hélène Cixous and Luce Irigaray, and, in particular, by Julia Kristeva. The fragmented, disjointed syntax of the Old English *frauenlieder* finds clarification in Irigaray's theories. She advises readers to hear "an 'other meaning' always in the process of weaving itself, of embracing itself with words, but also of getting rid of words in order not to become fixed, congealed in them."[4] Cixous celebrates what she calls women's writing of their bodies; they must "make up the unimpeded tongue that bursts partitions, classes, and rhetorics, orders and codes, must inundate, run through, go beyond the discourse. . . ."[5] Kristeva's theories of language permit us to articulate and to discuss the differentness we experience in the language of *Wulf and Eadwacer* and *The Wife's Lament*. It is on Kristeva's theory of language acquisition that we will focus.

Kristeva associates female language with the semiotic and male language with the symbolic. She hypothesizes a pre-Oedipal unorganized flow of bodily pulsations and rhythms—the semiotic—which possesses languagelike qualities. This is the primary stage of language acquisition. When the child emerges from this stage, it enters a world of symbolic language in which there is a one-to-one correspondence between signifier and signified, a correspondence which implies that language is a window through which one has access to truth provided one can compose in "transparent" words. The symbolic is thus a fixed system of signifiers and signifieds, which make meaning-in-language possible. It manifests itself in linear strings of words which are analyzable through use of traditional and fixed systems of grammar, syntax, and semantics. When one enters the world of symbolic language, however, the semiotic does not disappear; it remains, repressed by the symbolic, although not entirely repressible. It erupts into the symbolic flow of language, pushing it beyond the limits of its own meaning. The semiotic—unfixed in reference, nonlinear, fluid, and related to prelinguistic meaning-making—disrupts and infuses the symbolic with meaning not entirely containable in the symbolic. Revealed through rhythm, stress, intonation, repetition, echolalias, glossalalia, the semiotic is "a distinctive mark, trace, index, the premonitory sign, the proof, engraved mark, imprint—in short a *distinctiveness* admitting of an uncertain and indeterminate articulation because it does not yet refer . . . or no longer refers . . . to a signified object."[6] Although Kristeva links the symbolic to a male, patriarchal system and the semiotic to the maternal, she does not so limit the gender of those who produce language. In fact, Kristeva speaks of the heterogeneity of language, stating that it is characterized by both the symbolic and the semiotic: "Language as social practice necessarily presupposes these two dispositions, though combined in different ways to constitute *types of discourse,* types of signifying practices."[7]

Thus, all languages have both a symbolic and a semiotic character as a result of *being* language, but various genres and languages also have genre-specific and language-specific ways of manifesting their character. Within the context of Old English poetry, we can think of the symbolic order as the structure which underlies the poetry: the four-stress line with its limited number of metrical and alliterative patterns, the formulaic basis of the word patterns, the use of envelope structuring, and the collocative, recurrent themes of the heroic code: male bonding, heroism, battles, exile, the search for *lof* 'praise' and *dom* 'glory'. Both of the Old English *frauenlieder* adhere to some part of this symbolic underpinning of the period's poetry. The rhythmic template on which both depend is the four-stress alliterative line; both poems draw upon the connotative force of formulas and formulaic expressions: *wineleas wræcca* 'friendless exile' (WL10b), *ofer yþa gelac* 'over the rolling of the waves' (WL7a), *a scyle* . . . 'always shall' (WL42a), *fæst is þæt eglond* 'fast is that island' (WE5a), *murnende mod* 'mourning spirit' (WE15a). The typical themes of the heroic code are muted in both poems—more so in *Wulf and Eadwacer,* as we shall see, than in *The Wife's Lament.* We can hear echoes of typical heroic themes in phrases such as *folgað secan* 'to seek service' (WL9b), *fæhðu dreogan* 'to endure/suffer feud' (WL26b), *beaducafa* 'battle-bold one' (WE11a), *giedd* 'poem/song' (WL1a; WE19), *on þreat* 'in a company' (WE2b, 7b), *wælreas weras* 'slaughter-rough men' (WE6), and in the maintenance of *bliþe gebæro* 'cheerful bearing' (WL20a, 44a), despite being *hygegeomorne* 'sad at heart' (WL19b) and in anguish *breostceare* 'grief of heart' (WL44b). But erupting through these masculine, symbolic traits which connect these poems to the mainstream of Old English poetry is another thread of meaning which I associate with the semiotic, a thread of meaning which ties them to the *frauenlieder* genre more than to Old English poetry.[8]

Of the most immediately obvious characteristics of the vocabulary of the poems is the heavy use of first-person pronouns[9] which emphasizes the physical presence of the speaker vis-à-vis an other. The *I* in both *frauenlieder,* though physically isolated, is grammatically surrounded by possessive pronouns. In *The Wife's Lament,* twelve of these are forms of *min* 'mine'; these connect the narrator to the man or men in her life—*min hlaford* 'my lord' (5a), *min leodfruma* 'my lord' (8a), *mines felaleofan* 'my dearly beloved one' (26a)—and to her own sorrowful thoughts—*minre weaþearfe* 'my woeful need' (10b), *min hyge geomor* 'my sad mind' (17b), *minra wræcsiþa* 'my journey of exile' (6b), *modceare minre* 'my heartache' (40a). The first-person possessive functions similarly in *Wulf and Eadwacer: leodum is minum* 'it is to my people' (1a), *Wulfes . . . mines* 'my Wulf' (9a), *Wulf, min Wulf* 'Wulf, my Wulf' (13a). Fortifying the narrators' connections are forms of dual pronouns which generate highly charged emotional moments. In *The Wife's Lament*, we read: *ful oft wit beotedan / þæt unc ne gedælde nemne deað ana* 'very often we-two promised that nothing except death alone would divide us-two' (21b–22b), and *is nu . . . swa hit no wære / freondscipe uncer* 'is now as though it never were, the friendship of us-two' (24a–25b). Dual pronouns are notably lacking in the final gnomic section of *The Wife's Lament;* their disappearance emphasizes the finality of the narrator's separation from the man she describes. Much of the ambiguity of reference in *Wulf and Eadwacer* derives from the pronouns in *ungelic(e) is us* 'it is unlike/different for us' (3, 8) and *uncerne . . . hwelp* 'the whelp of us-two' (16b); and the dual pronoun in the final line, *uncer giedd geador* 'the song/poem of us-two together' (19), infuses both power and mystery into its paradoxical conclusion. The French feminists emphasize the significance and, indeed, the presence of the body in female language; in keeping with such assertions, each of our narrators feels her own self strongly as a bodily presence situated in a particular situation with a particular connection (or lack of connection) to others. Neither narrator is able to escape the I-ness of her situation.

The *I*'s in these poems come to us embedded in presentness. Both narrators project themselves out of the present and into the past and out of their confining locations into others, but those other times and places are incorporated into a present forcefully expressed. Phyllis G. Whittier points to the high number of finite forms of *beon* 'to be' and *wesan* 'to be, occur' in *The Wife's Lament*.[10] These create a powerful sense of enduring immediacy. We must remember that contemporary audiences experienced these poems aurally. Standing before them would be a poet speaking of present sorrow, and the illusion created would be that of a person expressing feelings while actually experiencing them. We know from our own personal interactions, when we attempt either to express feeling or to understand another's experience, that we always sense in the immediacy of the communicative act the presence of the uncommunicable, and that this sense becomes part of the communicated feeling. In Kristeva's terms, the presence of the uncommunicable is a part of the semiotic. *The Wife's Lament* and *Wulf and Eadwacer* exploit this mode of communication. If we think of this in relation to modern popular singing, we come to realize that what is significant is the emotional situation of the singer as she reflects, mourns, rejoices in events and people. Knowing the specifics of the events or the identity of the people might well detract from our response. What resonates throughout the two Old English poems is that men not currently present are responsible for emotions which *are* current.

The free-floating nature of semiotic language is quintessentially apparent in its polysemous nature, a pronounced feature of the two Old English *frauenlieder*. Most critics of these poems have sought to clarify the meaning of individual words and phrases in order to interpret the poems in a way that gives consistency both to the narrators' emotions and to the embryonic hints of linear narrative. The very disparity of such interpretations indicates the polysemous quality of disputed words, phrases, and punctuation. Arnold E. Davidson concretizes this quality of *Wulf and Eadwacer*'s language by presenting a translation which incorporates the most argued for meanings of disputed words. A glance at just the first two lines of his translation suggests the rich polysemous nature of the poem's vocabulary:

Is to my people as if one might give them (a battle/
          sacrifice/gift/message/game),
Will they (receive/consume/oppress/relieve) him if he
          comes (with a host/in violence/in need)?[11]

This piling up of possibilities taps a semiotic response in listeners and allows us to ingest multiple meanings simultaneously which mandate a constant deferral of meaning and definition: "nothing is ever to be posited that is not also reversed and caught up again in the supplementarity of this reversal."[12]

In *The Wife's Lament*, it is not only the polysemy of the diction that creates tension in the communicative process, but the seeming discordance between speaker and utterance. Those who argue that the speaker is not a woman[13] single out phrases such as *folgað secan* 'to seek service' (9b), *beotedan* 'vowed' (20b), and *fæhðu dreogan* 'to endure/suffer feud' (26b), as language not applicable to a male-female relationship. We need to recognize that the very fact of these words' *not* being in their expected contexts lends a particularly effective resonance to them. Perhaps it *is* inappropriate for a woman to *folgað secan*, but perhaps the very inappropriateness creates meaning in the poem and for the speaker. A number of critics assert that *leodfruma* (8a), *hlaford* (6a, 15a), *frean* (33a), and *wine* (49a, 50b), all translatable as "lord," are inappropriate epithets for a woman to use of her husband.[14] But it is the effectiveness of contrast between these words and other designators such as *freond* 'friend' (47a), and *felaleofan* 'much loved one' (26a), which enables the narrator's full expression of her condition. Kristeva's emphasis on the polysemous nature of semiotic language makes us appreciate the richness of the simultaneous manifestation of all these possibilities. Alternative segmentation of the language of the manuscript (that has been the basis for critical debate for decades) generates an added dimension to the poems' communicated meaning. Should *bliþe gebæro* (21a) be read as the end or the beginning of a sentence? We need to recognize the potential for it to be read as both, for, to a listening audience, the phrase is more effectively polysemous. Print requires a decision; orality keeps the polysemy alive.

Furthermore, both the structure and the sequencing of ideas in the two *frauenlieder* suggest a lack of interest on the part of their narrators in traditional forms, logic, and chronology, thus pointing to meanings which lie outside customary, or symbolic, language. Whittier notes the smaller number of dependent clauses in *The Wife's Lament* in comparison to *The Wanderer* and *The Seafarer*, which results in a syntactically looser structure: "Such syntactical looseness may correlate with or contribute to the disjointed effect of the poem and our impression that it is, more than the other three elegies (*The Wanderer, The Seafarer, The Husband's Message*), an emotional rather than an intellectual or a philosophical statement."[15] The rhythm imparted to the poem by the higher number of independent clauses mirrors the pulsations of the semiotic. Lines 29a–32a demonstrate this rhythm most overtly:

> Eald is þes eorðsele,   eal ic eom oflongad,
> sindon dena dimme,   duna uphea,
> bitre burgtunes,   brerum beweaxne,
> wic wynna leas.

> (Old is this earth-hall, I am all in-longing
> the dales are dim, the dunes up high,
> the bitter strong enclosures, by briars grown about,
> the dwelling place joyless.)

Here each half-line is a complete unit of sense, and each—beginning with 30b—manifests the topic-comment structure which Kristeva sees as an early stage in language development.

The heavy end-stopping in *Wulf and Eadwacer,* particularly in the first eight lines, accentuates (or pushes to the very limits) the natural rhythm of the four-stress line. This rhythm is abruptly overturned twice at the beginning by the two short lines of the refrain and twice at the end by two more shortened lines. Such abbreviated lines emphasize the gaps and silences in which meaning grows out of the unsaid rather than the said. Irigaray advises writers to "insist upon those *blanks* in discourse which recall the places of her [woman's] exclusion and which, by their *silent plasticity,* ensure the cohesion, the articulation, the coherent expansion of established forms. . . ."[16] This alternation of short and long lines plus the lack of temporal, causal, or consecutive elements disrupts the symbolic order, the traditional rhythm of Old English poetry. Disruption occurs within half lines also, particularly in line 13a *Wulf, min Wulf,* the focal emotional outburst of the poem which as George P. Krapp and Elliott Van Kirk Dobbie comment, "cannot be emended without loss of effectiveness."[17] The last four lines are also metrically anomalous, suggesting an erratic functioning of normal bodily rhythms which would be far more evident to a listening audience than to a reading audience. And, finally, the paradox built into the language of the final two lines aptly concludes our developing awareness of the alogical language and structure.

Attempts to impose chronological order on the events alluded to by the narrators of these poems, the goal of most early commentators[18] and even of Malone in his article, are doomed to failure. The difficulties encountered in these readings have caused such divergent interpretations that none has gained wide acceptance. Narrative is irrelevant to poems which express such potent present feeling; emotional memory is rarely chronological. In both poems seemingly narrative or objective sections are concluded with emotional or subjective reactions: e.g., *mec longade* 'it made me long' (WL14b), and *eal ic eom oflongad* 'I am all in-longing' (WL29b).[19] This alternation of subjective and objective passages contributes to the attitude, mood, and tone of the poem. In *Wulf and Eadwacer* the emotion breaks out in the repeated lines *ungelic(e) is us* and *Wulf, min Wulf,* each of which follows allusions to apparently actual events. The subjective contains the objective as the present contains the past; and, obviously, this alternation of subjective and objective crisscrosses the patterning and unpatterning of the metrical flow. In Kristevan terms, the symbolic language cannot quite contain the pulsations of the semiotic which, never far below the surface, erupt in outbursts of heightened emotion and disrupted patterns.[20]

Echoic rhythm found in both *frauenlieder* points toward semiotic meaning also. In *The Wife's Lament,* we hear it in the repetition of similar roots in *longade, oflongad, langaþes/langoþe.* The emotions responsible for these rhythms break through at times with such power that the narrator perceives herself as being controlled by them. Her language reveals this control-by-emotion in the impersonal construction *mec longade* and the passive *eal ic eom oflongad* and in her sense of being possessed by longing *þe . . . in þissum life begeat* 'that seized [her] in this life' (41b), and events which *Ful oft . . . her wraþe begeat* 'which very often seized [her] here harshly' (32b). The accumulated echoic weight increases the tension in the last lines between the proverbial tone of stasis centered on the verb of condition (*bið*) and the emotion of longing (*langoþe*). The alliterating *h*'s in lines 15–19, to a listening audience, impart a sighing, almost breathless, quality to these lines of the poem, growing out of and reinforcing the initial articulation of *longade* in line 14. In *Wulf and Eadwacer,* repetition of whole lines and half lines, of words and ideas—*on iege* 'on an island' (4a), *þæt eglond* 'that island' (5b), and *on ige* 'on an island' (6b)—and of the name Wulf create aural linkages which weave their own pattern through the narrator's words. The speaker's almost obsessive preoccupation with Wulf is reënforced by and generates the high number of lines (five out of nineteen) alliterating on *w,* another sound with heavy breath quality. A number of these repetitions blend together to create an embryonic suggestion of strophic structure. R. F. Leslie points to "the regularity with which each passage is rounded off with outbursts of feeling which become in places almost refrains" as a "remarkable feature" of *The Wife's Lament.*[21] This tendency is far more obvious in *Wulf and Eadwacer.*

The tension in our two poems between the set patterns and customary linguistic contexts of words in Old English poetry and the intermittent disruption of them fuels the emotional impact. Throughout both poems we are exposed to alternations which demonstrate that both control and release are always present even though only one may be manifest at a given point. I sense a similarly charged confrontation of forces in the narrators' situations: both are physically confined (whether by circumstances or force, we cannot tell), but their emotions are free and volatile, far-ranging geographically and temporally. Thus the tensions of form and content interpenetrate; in both, the semiotic and the symbolic interact, "allowing what is said and what is not said to float haphazardly."[22] Kristeva has given us a means of talking about the "differentness" in the language of the Old English *frauenlieder.* That Kristeva's theories are a twentieth-century phenomenon should not deter us from seeing their applicability to works of the tenth. The poetic impulse to express emotion transcends time and place. In essence, Kristeva has provided names for the differentness of poems' communicative process which former scholars have been aware of but could not fully articulate. In his analysis of *Wulf and Eadwacer,* A. C. Bouman comes closest to responding to its language in ways which foreshadow Kristeva's theories:

> The poem is spoken as if in a state of trance, or in a dream. To make out the trend of semi-conscious thought or feeling one has to collect loose fragments, to listen more carefully and with a deeper sympathy than to an epic narrator. No one may feel sure that the first or

any other line will contain a clue to a better understanding of what follows. Every word is like a sudden, unexpected flash from a burdened mind.[23]

The differentness of genre, content, form, and language in these poems raises questions about the ideology of the feminine embedded in them. The general consensus seems to be that the composers were male, even though literary historians acknowledge that women may have both composed and recited poems and songs during the period under consideration.[24] Even if our two *frauenlieder* were composed by men, their artfulness is an outgrowth of ancient and popular female-voiced songs, deeply rooted in the bodily rhythms of dance. Men may have built upon the tradition, but the tradition itself was and is constituted by a language homogeneity which allows a thread of uncapturable significance to intertwine into the necessarily significant patterning of the language. In sum, our two poems, whether female- or male-composed, are powerful representations of an age-old poetic tradition which found a way to signify that which ordinary language could not.

Ultimately the feminine image underlying these poems has political implications. If suffering caused by male activity (or even by female activity when women function in stereotypically male roles as they do in *Juliana, Elene,* and *Judith*) can be so vividly portrayed, the activity itself cannot be viewed as ideal and unflawed. The very power of the emotion in these poems demonstrates that suffering and separation are not subordinate to the heroic ethos and cannot be judged solely from that point of view; they, *with* the heroic ethos, comprise the world view of the composers of Old English poetry. Frings collects in his appendix examples of *frauenlieder* in many languages of the world. The similarity of women's suffering evident in this collection blurs divisions among peoples. These voices of women remind us all that life cannot be single-mindedly focused on competitive confrontations and defense.

But because physical confrontation in battle has seemed to determine the course of history, it has been privileged. As a consequence, critics may accept the powerfulness of women's suffering, such as that in the two Old English *frauenlieder,* yet see the women speakers as passive and ineffective. Before coming to such a conclusion, I believe we need to consider more closely the function of poems such as these. We need to guard against judging female-voiced language on the basis of schooled and acculturated norms which mandate our seeing it in limited ways. Heroic poems, whether having male or female protagonists, portray their heroines/heroes confronting overwhelming odds. Such poetry appeals to its audience by depicting the resulting action. But *frauenlieder* make a different appeal; they ask their audiences to share emotions with them, to be present at the creation of meaning which can never be fully articulated. Far from being weak, these women triumph because they have created emotional and psychological bonds with their audiences. These poems represent triumphs in the management of the audience's feelings. We resist being like the narrators (particularly if we are women) but through the impact of their emotional life and its presentness, through the illusion of its creation and eruption *as* we listen or read, we gradually, but eventually fully, identify ourselves with the narrators. In the process we define ourselves while the narrators are defining themselves; we hear their words in relation to the events and people in our own lives. The multiplicity of possible meanings, readings, and interpretations strengthens rather than weakens the narrators. Such realizations bring into question our customary ways of reading Old English poems and encourage us to develop receptivity to so-called irregularities in them, to enrich our reading and listening by incorporating these into our responses rather than explaining or emending them out of existence.[25]

If *The Wife's Lament* and *Wulf and Eadwacer* were once parts of larger epic cycles, it is instructive that only they survived. What has endured through them is a message about the value, strength, and universality of our connections to others in a world characterized by strife and alienation, both physical and emotional, from other human beings—no matter what might be the causes. The French feminists speak of "differentness," but here in these 1000-(at least)-year-old *Frauenlieder*, the very differentness of the language serves (ironically) to give force to the still relevant need we all have to be linked to others and to the still overwhelming emotion and sense of loss we experience when we are not.

NOTES

1. All quotations from the Old English are from George P. Krapp and Elliott Van Kirk Dobbie, eds., *The Anglo-Saxon Poetic Records,* 6 vols. (New York: Columbia University Press, 1969). Translations are mine.

2. Kemp Malone, "Two English *Frauenlieder,*" in *Studies in Old English Literature,* ed. Stanley B. Greenfield (Eugene: University of Oregon Press, 1963), 106–17; Theodor Frings, *Minnesinger und Troubadours* (Berlin: Deutsche Akademie der Wissenschaften zu Berlin, 1949); Leo Spitzer, "The Mozarabic Lyric and Theodor Frings' Theories," *Comparative Literature* 4 (1952): 1–22. See also Peter Dronke, *The Medieval Lyric* (New York: Harper and Row, 1969), p. 91, who likewise sees *The Wife's Lament* and *Wulf and Eadwacer* as Germanic examples of women's songs connected to the entire continental secular vernacular tradition. Such songs existed in societies widely separated by geography and culture and antedated male lyrics. In "Poesia griega de amigo y poesia arabigo-espanola," *Emerita* 40 (1972): 329–96, Elvira Gogutia Elicegui traces the lineage of women's songs back to ancient cult songs, then forward through the Greeks and Phoenicians to pre-Islamic Spain. In *Medieval Lyric* (233), Dronke considers the evidence presented inadequate; but Elicegui does quote a number of representative examples of the genre which have much in common with later examples.

3. Malone, "*Frauenlieder,*" pp. 110, 116.

4. Luce Irigaray, *This Sex Which is Not One,* trans. Catherine Porter and Carolyn Blake (Ithaca: Cornell University Press, 1985), p. 29.

5. Hélène Cixous, *The Newly Born Woman,* trans. Betsy Wing (Minneapolis: University of Minnesota Press, 1986), pp. 94–95.

6. Julia Kristeva, *Desire in Language,* ed. Leon S. Roudiez; trans. Thomas Gora, Alice Jardine, and Leon S. Roudiez (New York: Columbia University Press, 1980), esp. pp. 133–34.

7. Ibid.

8. I do not doubt that the semiotic makes some appearance in male voices in Old English poetry also. What comes to mind immediately is the dreamlike quality of *The Wanderer* (37a–55b), which concludes *swimmað on weg* 'they swim away'. With Kristeva, I do not limit semiotic discourse to women's voices.

9. Alain Renoir, "A Reading of *The Wife's Lament,*" *English Studies* 58 (1977): 7, comments on this feature in *The Wife's Lament* and connects it to the use of *ic* in the riddles, suggesting one basis for the poem's enigmatic flavor.

10. Phyllis G. Whittier, "Syntax and Poetry in Four OE Elegies," Diss. University of Oregon, 1968, p. 80.

11. Arnold E. Davidson, "Interpreting *Wulf and Eadwacer,*" *Annuale Mediaevale* 16 (1975): 25.

12. Luce Irigaray, *Speculum of the Other Woman,* trans. Gillian C. Gill (Ithaca: Cornell University Press, 1985), pp. 79–80.

13. A. N. Doane, "Heathen Form and Christian Function in 'The Wife's Lament'," *Mediaeval Studies* 28 (1966): 77–91, considers the speaker to be "a cast-off heathen minor deity"; M. J. Swanton, " 'The Wife's Lament' and 'The Husband's Message': A Reconsideration," *Anglia* 82 (1964): 269–90, and W. F. Bolton, " 'The Wife's Lament' and 'The Husband's Message': A Reconsideration Revisited," *Archiv* 205 (1960): 337–51, read the poem as an "exploration of the relationship between Christ and the Church, which yearns for the re-establishment of a previous union" (Swanton, " 'The Wife's Lament' ": 289). For example, Doane, "Heathen Form" (85), Swanton, " 'The Wife's Lament' " (285), and Rudolph C. Bambas, "Another View of the OE 'Wife's Lament'," *Journal of English and Germanic Philology* 62 (1963): 306–307, object to *folgað secan;* Doane, "Heathen Form" (84), and Bambas, "Another View" (305), object to *beotedan;* Swanton (284–85), and Martin Stevens, "The Narrator in 'The Wife's Lament'," *Neuphilologische Mitteilungen* 69 (1968): 84, object to *fæhðu dreogan.*

14. Doane, "Heathen Form": 83; Stevens, "The Narrator": 83–84; Swanton, " 'The Wife's Lament' ": 271; Bambas, "Another View": 305.

15. Whittier, "Syntax and Poetry": 67.

16. Irigaray, *Speculum,* p. 142.

17. George P. Krapp and Elliott Van Kirk Dobbie, eds., *The Exeter Book, The Anglo-Saxon Poetic Records,* vol. 3 (New York: Columbia University Press, 1969), p. 320.

18. See Edith Rickert, "The OE Offa Saga," *Modern Philology* 2 (1905): 29–76, 321–76; William W. Lawrence, "The First Riddle of Cynewulf," *Publications of the Modern Language Association* 17 (1902): 247–61; Sir Israel Gollancz, "(Review of) *The Sigurd Cycle and Britain,*" *Athenaeum* 25 (25 October 1902): 551c–552a.

19. The Old English captures in these phrases (*mec longade* and *eal ic eom oflongad*) meaning which is not quite translatable into modern English. Literally these phrases mean something like "it longed me" and "I am all longed." Modern English renderings perforce blunt the passivity and impersonality of these phrases.

20. In the larger context of *The Exeter Book,* the poems also demonstrate an eruptive quality. Although they have affinities both to the other elegies and to the riddles, they are unique within the collection, and, in fact, unique in the corpus. For that reason alone, some critics have asserted that they cannot be women's songs. (See Bambas, "Another View": 303–4; Doane, "Heathen Form": 82; Swanton, " 'The Wife's Lament' ": 271; and Stevens, "The Narrator": 82.)

21. R. F. Leslie, ed., *Three Old English Elegies* (Manchester: Manchester University Press, 1969), p. 11.

22. Kristeva, *Desire in Language,* p. 120.

23. A. C. Bouman, "*Leodum is Minum:* Beadohild's Complaint," *Neophilologus* 33 (1949): 100.

24. Jeff Opland, *Anglo-Saxon Oral Poetry* (New Haven: Yale University Press, 1980), pp. 64, 150; Dronke, *Women Writers,* pp. 98–99.

25. One of the earliest examples of emending away difficulties was the conclusion by Levin L. Schücking, "Das angelsächsische Gedicht von der *Klage der Frau,*" *Zeitschrift für deutsches Altertum* 48 (1906): 436–49, that the first two lines of *The Wife's Lament* were not part of the poem, thus eliminating the female endings altogether. In his *Kleines angelsächsisches Dichterbuch* (Cöthen: Schulze, 1919), Schücking returned to a less radical position. *Wulf and Eadwacer* has been the victim of more elaborate attempts to dispense with its female narrator. Donald K. Fry, "*Wulf and Eadwacer:* A Wen Charm," *The Chaucer Review* 5 (1971): 247–63, reads it as a charm against wens; Norman E. Eliason, "On *Wulf and*

Eadwacer," in *Old English Studies in Honour of John C. Pope,* ed. Robert B. Burlin and Edward B. Irving, Jr. (Toronto: University of Toronto Press, 1974), p. 228, considers it a "private communication" which "playfully" protests "the mishandling of their poetry, which instead of being kept intact—as it should if it is to be appreciated properly—has been separated"; W. J. Sedgefield, "OE Notes I: 'Wulf and Eadwacer'," *Modern Language Notes* 26 (1931): 74–75, reads it as the dream of a female dog!

L . J O H N S K L U T E

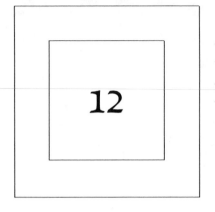

Freoðuwebbe in Old English Poetry

12

The compound, *freoðuwebbe,* is an easily understood compound presenting no interesting problems to the philologist. It means, clearly, "peace-weaver," commonly thought of as a metaphor or epithet for "woman."[1] But the overtones that radiate both from the term itself and from its context are of poetic interest because they affect our understanding of related compounds in similar and different contexts, and they interpenetrate with our understanding of other metaphorical weavers, the poets themselves who *wordum wrixlan* 'vary words'.

Because *freoðuwebbe* appears only three times in Old English poetry, once in *Widsith,* once in *Beowulf,* and once in Cynewulf's *Elene,* we must conclude that if it was a metaphor intended to indicate a woman, it was by no means commonly used. Yet, since each of its appearances is in a different book of the preserved records of Old English poetry—*The Exeter Book, MS Cotton Vitellius A XV,* and *The Vercelli Book*—we may assume that it was common enough to have been understood readily by the audiences of these poems. Moreover, in *Widsith* and *Elene,* the compound is part of an alliterative formula. In *Widsith, fælre freoðuwebban* 'faithful peace-weaver', a dative, appears in the first halfline modifying the dative form of the name Ealhild in the second half of the line before;[2] in *Elene* it is in the same formula, *fæle friðowebba,* an accusative, also in the first half-line.[3] In *Beowulf,* however, the compound is not a part of an alliterative formula, but alliterates with the /f/ phoneme— *feores onsæce* 'exact life'—of the second half of the same line in which it appears.[4] Since it is likely that the alliterative formula was available to the *Beowulf* poet but that he chose instead to connect it by alliteration to the formula in the second half-line, we may assume a precise intention behind its use and a special literary effect intended by it.

It has generally been assumed that epithets like *beag-gyfa* 'ring-giver' reflect an actual practice exercised by the person to whom they are attached, that the metaphorical quality of the term or terms is rooted in an historical reality of Old English society. A similar assumption pertains to *freoðuwebbe*. In his translation of *Beowulf*, for example, E. Talbot Donaldson suggests as an explanation for *freoðuwebbe:* "Daughters of kings were frequently given in marriage to the king of a hostile nation in order to bring about peace."[5] The practice about which Donaldson is speaking did exist, so far as we know, and continued among royal families at least through the Renaissance. But whether the term *freoðuwebbe* functions only or primarily to describe this phenomenon is a moot question. Since the historical realities reflected in the poetry are generally obscure and since our well-intentioned reconstructions of those realities are, at best, tentative, it seems to me more important and even valid to try to understand the function and meaning of the term in its literary context than to speculate about the possible historical practice it might represent.

In *Beowulf*, *freoðuwebbe* is used to characterize Offa's queen. Although she is commonly known as Thryth, Modthryth, or Cynethryth,[6] the same as queen Drida according to the *Vitae Duorum Offarum*, her historical identity is actually a mystery.[7] The *Beowulf* poet says only that she had a rather violent period of adolescence, because of which she put to death all the suitors who dared to look upon her (1931–1934); she is, thus, reminiscent of Brünhild and the other great ladies of the Valkyrie tradition. He also says that she became an excellent queen after marrying Offa (1945–1962). If the poet, by calling her *freoðuwebbe*, means merely that she is a woman, there is no cause to pursue the issue further. But it is clear that the literary motivation behind the poet's use of the term for this complex woman requires us to seek a fuller range of possibilities and a more particularized definition.

The specific meaning of *freoðuwebbe* is clearest in the context of *Elene*. The *fæle friðowebbe*, also called *halga* 'holy'—*þæs halgan* 'of the holy one' (86a)—appears to the emperor Constantine in a vision:

> Þuhte him wlitescyne   on weres hade
> hwit ond hiwbeorht   hæleða nathwylc
> geywed ænlicra   þonne he ær oððe sið
> gesege under swegle.
>
> (72a–75a)
>
> (It seemed to him that a certain beautiful warrior appeared in the form of a man, white and radiant, more beautiful than he earlier or later saw under the sky.)

He is an angel functioning as a messenger from God, *wlitig wuldres boda* 'beautiful messenger of glory' (77a), sent to proclaim the coming victory of Constantine over the Huns by directing the king's eye to the *sigores tacen* 'sign of victory' (85a), appearing in the sky in the form of *wliti wuldres treo* 'the beautiful tree of glory' (89a) or, again, *se blaca beam* 'the shining tree' (91a). As a peace-weaver, therefore, his function is clear. By the sign, he indicates that he is weaving together a peace between God and man, for the message he brings causes Constantine to accept Christianity (153–202). This action in turn provides the impetus for St. Helen's subsequent journey to the Holy Land in search of the rood. On the basis of its use in *Elene*, *friðowebbe* has nothing at all to do with a woman—angels by definition are masculine. Unless we can prove that Cynewulf is here refurbishing a secular metaphor, by no means impossible, any attempt to connect the compound with an historical practice is purely speculative. A more secure identification of the term would take into account the angel's quality as messenger and bearer of good tidings.

In *Widsith, fælre freoþuwebban* is an epithet for Ealhild. As suggested by Richard Heinzel[8] and elaborated by R. W. Chambers in his early study of the poem,[9] Ealhild is the historical wife of Eormanric, king of the Ostrogoths. It is usually argued about the opening of the poem that Widsith the scop is accompanying the maiden Ealhild on her wedding journey from her home in Angle to the court of Eormanric where she will be wed. Hence, as Chambers himself suggested,[10] "peaceweaver" in line eight would seem a specific appellation for a woman given in marriage to establish amity between two tribes. But this argument is by no means decisive since it too assumes what cannot be proven by the historical record.

If we are looking in the poetry for an example of a woman given as a peace exchange, we find it openly presented in *Beowulf*. In his recapitulation of his experiences in Denmark, Beowulf tells Hygelac about Hroðgar's daughter Freawaru:

> Sio gehaten (is)
> geong goldhroden,   gladum suna Frodan;
> (ha)fa ð þæs geworden   wine Scyldinga,
> rices hyrde,   ond þæt ræd talað,
> þæt he mid ðy wife   wælfæhða dæl,
> sæcca gesette.
>
> (2024b–29a)

(She is promised, young and gold-adorned, to the gracious son of Froda; the lord of the Scyldings, the guardian of the kingdom, has brought that about, and he considers it good counsel that he should settle part of his deadly feuds and battles with the woman.)

But Beowulf is himself openly wary of the value of such a practice:

> Oft seldan hwær
> æfter leodhryre   lytle hwile
> bongar bugeð,   þeah seo bryd duge!
>
> (2029b–31b)

(Seldom anywhere does the deadly spear sink to rest for a little while after the fall of men, although the bride is of worth!)

To demonstrate that such an exchange cannot actually settle the enmity between warring tribes, the hero narrates the so-called Ingeld digression (2032–69).

Although both the passages quoted above and the Ingeld episode concern the exchange of a woman to secure peace, not once is the compound *freoðuwebbe* used. Of course, there was no semantic necessity compelling the poet to select the term for use here; yet, the fact that it appears elsewhere in Old English as an alliterative formula, and elsewhere in *Beowulf*, suggests its availability as a half-line to a poet whose context requires a phrase dealing with the very practice that *freoðuwebbe* has been supposed to represent. However, the poet's failure to use a term in a context that seems relevant does not prove that the term means something different from what we thought; it merely tells us that the poet chose not to use it at this particular time. For a more solid method of establishing the meaning of *freoðuwebbe* we must return to the context where it is used, to *Widsith* where the alliterative formula in the dative refers undeniably to the dative form of Ealhild. She is a *freoðuwebbe*.[11]

Kemp Malone glosses *freoðuwebbe* as "peace-weaver, queen."[12] Although a more generalized term than "peace-weaver," "queen" is not nearly as broad in meaning as "woman." A queen is not only a member of the female sex; she is a particular member in an important political position and has certain duties to perform. In a later passage of *Widsith,* for instance, we are told that after Eormanric gave Widsith a precious ring as a gift exemplifying his magnanimity (89–92), his wife did the same (97–98). Because of this action the scop is grateful and sings her praises (99–101) whenever he wants to tell of a *goldhrodene cwen giefe bryttian* 'gold-adorned woman dispensing treasure' (102). In other words, by giving a ring to the poet, Ealhild has her reputation and the reputation of her husband's largess spread throughout the world so that men acclaim not only her nobility, but the graciousness and splendor of Eormanric's court. Like the angel in *Elene* whose magnificence boded well for Constantine's future, Ealhild's munificence and gracious behavior incline the scop to sing the praises of the Ostrogothic court. In both cases, the peace-weavers have functioned to cement relationships, but the acts they perform are not concerned with marriage.

A more fully developed example of queenly munificence occurs in *Beowulf.* Wealhþeow's chief function in the meadhall is to walk among the retainers, to pass out drink, and to give rings. She does this on three occasions in the poem. Especially in her second appearance, however, we are shown how Wealhþeow functions on duty. She gives to Beowulf

>   wunden gold
> estum geeawed,   earm(h)reade twa,
> hrægl ond hringas,   healsbeaga mæst
> þara þe ic on foldan   gefrægen hæbbe.
>   (1193b–96b)

(twisted gold graciously presented, two bracelets, a corselet and rings, and the greatest of necklaces that I have heard of on earth.)

When he returns to Geatland, Beowulf gives the necklace to queen Hygd and extols the virtues of Wealhþeow and of Hroðgar's court (2016–19), in much the same way as Widsith did. But Wealhþeow does more. She offers *freondlaþu / wordum* 'words of friendly invitation' (1192b–93a).[13]

Wealhþeow recognizes that there might be trouble in the line of inheritance to the Danish throne after Hroðgar's death. Very early in the poem the audience is made aware of the future family feud between the sons and the nephew of Hroðgar that will ultimately cause the destruction of Heorot and of the Danish royal line (83–85). The poet abruptly and strikingly reintroduces this tragic subject in a series of hypermetric lines that bring forth Wealhþeow to utter her second speech of the poem (1162–65). And indeed throughout her speech the noble queen is preoccupied with what will become of her children, her nephew, and, one might add, herself after Hroðgar is gone. Her discussion of what she hopes will be the behavior of Hroðulf toward

Hreðric and Hroþmund (1181–87) has the tone of tragic irony that makes her appeal to Beowulf as future protector of the Danes (1225–31) all the more intense and meaningful.[14]

Wealhþeow's function at the court of Hroðgar is, then, precisely the same as the combined actions of Ealhild in *Widsith* and the angel in *Elene*. Like Ealhild, she gives jewels to honor her guests and to enhance the reputation for magnanimity at her particular court. Like the angel, she speaks words of friendship and words of prophecy although she herself may not realize fully the implications of her admonitions. If, as I have been suggesting, *freoðuwebbe* is related to the idea of weaving bonds of peace by means of personal behavior or action, the poet of *Beowulf* would find in Wealhþeow's function at court an excellent embodiment. Although this term is never attached to Wealhþeow, a similar one is.

Beowulf refers to Wealhþeow as *friðusibb folca* (2017a) 'peace-bond of the people'. Friederich Klaeber calls attention to the semantic similarity between *friðusibb* and *freoðuwebbe*.[15] Defined by John Earle as "a bond of peace to the nations,"[16] *friðusibb*, it is assumed, refers to the kind of exchange in which Freawaru was given to Ingeld as a peace offering. But again, lack of historical evidence prohibits such an automatic assumption. For instance, we know nothing whatever of Wealhþeow's historical existence before she became the wife of Hroðgar. Chambers's otherwise exhaustive study of the genealogies of the characters in *Beowulf* makes no mention of historical references to her early life or to the conditions that brought her to Hroðgar's court.[17] Thus we can conclude only that whatever the precise semantic meaning of *friðusibb*, it seems to function in the same way as *freoðuwebbe*.

As far as we can discern from an examination of the texts and contexts in which the compound appears, *freoðuwebbe*/*friðuwebbe*—and, relatedly, *friðusibb*—does not necessarily reflect a Germanic custom of giving a woman in marriage to a hostile tribe in order to secure peace. Rather it is a poetic metaphor referring to the person whose function it seems to be to perform openly the action of making peace by weaving to the best of her art a tapestry of friendship and amnesty. The warp of her weaving is treasure and the woof is composed of words of good will. The compound *freoðuwebbe* expresses the duty of the king's wife (or of the king's messenger in *Elene*) to construct bonds of allegiance between the outsider and the king and his court. If it reflects anything of the social system of the Anglo-Saxons, it is that of the diplomat. Although a peace-weaver is not the sole securer of good will, her presence and her actions help the lord at his task.

We can, therefore, recognize the special irony present in *Beowulf* when we are told about the early behavior of Offa's queen:

> Ne bið swylc cwenlic þeaw
> idese to efnanne,   þeah ðe hio ænlicu sy,
> þætte freoðuwebbe   feores onsæce
> æfter ligetorne   leofne mannan.
>
> (1940b–43b)

(That is not a womanly custom for a lady to follow, although she be beautiful, that a peace-weaver should deprive a beloved man of life after a fancied insult.)

For, just before the poet moralizes by telling us that peace-weavers ought not to behave so violently, he has shown us that this particular woman, skilled artisan that she was, was anything but a weaver of peace. Any man who dared to look upon her by day, he tells us, *ac him wælbende weotode tealde / handgewriþene* 'but he might consider slaughter-bonds woven by hand to be prescribed for him' (1936a–37a). Thus Offa's queen was, if anything, a war-weaver before Offa deprived her of her fatal shuttle and put the powerful hands with which she bound up her victims (1938) to the far more peaceful, and womanly, occupation of being diplomatic.

NOTES

1. Joseph Bosworth and T. Northcote Toller, ed., *An Anglo-Saxon Dictionary* (Oxford: Oxford University Press, 1973), pp. 336 and 339.

2. George Philip Krapp and Elliott Van Kirk Dobbie, ed., *Widsith* (*The Anglo-Saxon Poetic Records*, vol. 3 [New York: Columbia University Press, 1939]), p. 149, ll. 5–6. Further references to *Widsith* will be from this edition.

3. George Philip Krapp, ed., *Elene* (*The Anglo-Saxon Poetic Records*, vol. 2 [New York: Columbia University Press, 1932]), p. 68, l. 88. Further references to *Elene* will be from this edition.

4. Fr. Klaeber, ed., *Beowulf and the Fight at Finnsburg* (3rd ed.; Lexington, Mass.: D. C. Heath and Co., 1950), p. 73, l. 1942. Further references to *Beowulf* will be from this edition.

5. E. Talbot Donaldson, trans., *Beowulf* (New York: W. W. Norton and Co., Inc., 1966), p. 34, note 3. In answer to a letter I sent him asking about his motivations for writing this note, Professor Donaldson replied: "The most likely explanation is that I made it up, relying on the context (where it's ironical) and Klaeber. It is quite likely wrong—indeed, I take it that your researches make it certainly wrong." Actually, my researches show that only the explanation, not his reading of the poetry, is wrong.

6. Frank M. Stenton calls her this in "The Historical Bearing of Place-Name Studies: The Place of Women in Anglo-Saxon Society," *Transactions of the Royal Historical Society*, 4th ser., 25 (1943), 1–13; rpt. herein, chap. 4.

7. She is commonly known as Thryth. For a full account of the name and its problems, see R. W. Chambers, *Beowulf: An Introduction to the Study of the Poem*, 3rd ed., with Supplement by C. L. Wrenn (Cambridge: Cambridge University Press, 1963), pp. 36–40, 238–43, and 541–42. Klaeber, *Beowulf*, pp. 195–99, prefers Modþryðo. Although suspect, the suggestion that Offa's queen was queen Hygd herself in a first marriage is put forth by Norman E. Eliason, "The 'Thryth-Offa Digression' in *Beowulf*," in *Franciplegius: Medieval and Linguistic Studies in Honor of Francis Peabody Magoun, Jr.*, ed. Jess B. Bessinger, Jr., and Robert P. Creed (New York: New York University Press, 1965), pp. 124–39.

8. Richard Heinzel, "Über die Hervarasaga," *Sitzungsberichte des kaiserliche Akademie der Wissenschaften zu Wien*, Philologisch-historische Klasse 114 (1887), p. 102.

9. R. W. Chambers, *Widsith: A Study in Old English Heroic Legend* (Cambridge: Cambridge University Press, 1912), pp. 21–28.

10. Chambers, *Widsith*, p. 28.

11. Besides, in his edition of *Widsith*, Kemp Malone has argued that the traditional reading of the opening lines raises some perplexing questions. First we would have to assume that Ealhild, the daughter of King Eadwine, is an Angle. The royal genealogies, at least, do not testify to the existence of an Eadwine. Even if we disregard the historical document and assume Eadwine, nevertheless, to have been an Anglian king somehow overlooked by the records, we still are left to wonder what Widsith, a Myrging, is doing conducting an Anglian princess to the court of the Ostrogoths. He himself testifies later in the poem (43–44) to the enmity between the Myrgings and the Angles who have conquered them. Because of these

problems, Malone suggests that when the poem opens, Ealhild is already the wife of Eormanric and is at the Ostrogothic court. Widsith is speaking about her but is travelling alone. Malone's suggestion is, of course, also a speculation exhibiting the tendency to reconcile all the conflicts of the Germanic Dark Ages in much the same way as the Schoolmen tried to do with Biblical history. See *Widsith,* ed. Kemp Malone, 2nd ed. (Copenhagen: Rosenkilde and Bagger, 1962).

12. Malone, *Widsith,* p. 121, col. 1.

13. For a study of Wealhþeow, which was published much after this article first appeared in print, see Helen Damico, *Beowulf's Wealhtheow and the Valkyrie Tradition* (Madison, WI: University of Wisconsin Press, 1984).

14. That Wealhþeow's admonition makes a deep impression upon Beowulf is clear from the amount of space he devotes to the queen in his recapitulation to Hygelac. Of the 151 lines comprising the speech, the first 69 are concerned with Wealhþeow, Freawaru, and the situation at the Danish court (including the Ingeld digression). Only 74 lines, few in comparison to the proportion of lines the action originally took, are concerned with Beowulf's fight against Grendel and his mother.

15. Klaeber, *Beowulf,* p. 335, col. 1.

16. Quoted in Klaeber, p. 335, col. 2.

17. Ibid., pp. xvi, 25, 27–37, 126, 426, 428, and 447; see also Chambers, *Beowulf.*

13

The Old English Poetic Vocabulary of Beauty

THE LEXICON

"What is beautiful is good," says Sappho in a surviving fragment, and the equation is a universal etymological as well as ontological truism. In Plato's *Timaeus* (87), Socrates reverses the order of terms in an argument that the good is necessarily beautiful. In *Cratylus* (416), Socrates, with tongue in cheek, suggests that Beauty and Mind are one, since χαλόν 'beauty' shares the same etymological root as χαλεῖν 'to name'. Our word *beauty* derives from the Latin *bellus*, through French *beau*, a doublet form of *bon* 'good' which derives from an earlier Latin *benlus* (IE **duonos* or **dwenos*).[1] The semantic bind between beauty and goodness flourishes in expressions such as "a handsome gesture" and "a fair exchange," associations exploited mercilessly by purveyors of advertising copy who hawk specious goods with the bait of specious beauty.[2] Latin *pulcher,* most likely akin to the Greek πεϱχυός 'spotted, dark', designates 'prosperous', and the adverb *pulchre* matches English *well* (*pulchre! bene! recte!* 'beautifully! well! correctly!' exclaims Horace in *Ars Poetica,* and *sat pulchra si sat bona* 'fair enough is good enough' is a tried and true proverb).[3] Though the stoics of the late Empire may have frowned upon beauty as a dubious virtue, Augustine reiterated the Platonic view that Beauty is the visible sign of an invisible good (*Confessions,* VII, 16–21).[4] The popular discourse of the Medieval Church regularly associated wisdom with men and beauty with women, and these associations have prevailed into modern times. Such alignments are alien to early Germanic conceptions. The contexts of Old English and Old Norse terms for beauty are not fixed sexually, and fair-seeming is not equated universally with fair-doing. With rare exceptions, terms for beauty in the Germanic traditions are free of pejorative implications. In Old English poetry particularly, beauty is a positive force imbuing all aspects of creation.

I recognize four distinct classes of terms which reflect beauty in Old English poetry (see the appendices for an expanded classification). My criteria of selection are arbitrary and incomplete but representative. My intent in classifying these words in specific categories is not to offer new definitions but to indicate meanings which the words convey in specific poetic contexts. I search for concrete senses which glossaries eschew in favor of abstract translations such as "appealing," "choice," "elegant," "glorious," "magnificent," "noble," "splendid," and "stately," to note but a few examples. (One is inevitably struck by the number of romance words used to gloss Old English diction.) Boundaries for the semantic field of fair-seeming are indeterminate, partly because of the polysemous character of Old English vocabulary and partly because of subjective reader response to their textual environment. I exclude from my lists terms such as *gōd* 'good', *swǣs* 'dear', *swēte* 'sweet', *dēor* 'dear', and others whose links with physical forms are rarely effected in the verse. *Swēte* 'sweet' does qualify physical forms when it modifies affections, taste, and smell (Whl 65b). *Æþele* 'noble', *blǣd* 'glory', *dōm* 'glory', *ēad* 'prosperity', *sēl* 'better', and *til* 'good' are included because they refer, although rarely, to physical posture.[5]

Few of these terms signify "beauty" *per se,* but each of them designates a form which appeals to the eye or to a value judgment made from sight in the cited context. Some commentary on the words in context is, therefore, in order. The words classified under category A in the appendices—Beauty as Brightness—require little explanation. The association of radiance with beauty and goodness is of long Indo-European tradition. Augustine elaborates on the scriptural aptness of light images for God in *Confessions* (X, 8). The Old English homily *De Sancto Johannes* (also known as "The Phoenix Homily") describes the saint with *his ēagene twā ǣðele . . . swā clǣne swā cristal,*[7] *swā scīre swā sune lēoma* 'his two noble eyes as clean as crystal, and as bright as the sun'.[6] Nothing quite matches the poetic collocation of terms for radiance in the description of Christ arriving on Mount Sion:

Þonne semninga   on Syne beorg
sūþanēastan   *sunnan lēoma*
cymeð of scyppend   *scȳnan lēohtor*
þonne hit men mǣgen   mōdum ahycgan,
beorhte blīcan . . .
Cymeð wundorlīc   Cristes onsȳn,
æþelcyninges *wlite*   ēastan fram roderum
of sefan swēte   sīnum folce.

. . . .
Hē bið þām gōdum   glædmōd on gesihþe,
wlitig, wynsumlīc . . .
                    frēond ond lēoftǣl
lufsum ond līþe   lēofum monnum
tō scēawianne   þone *scȳnan wlite.*
                    (Chr 899a–914b, my italics)

(Then quickly to Mount Sion from the southeast the light of the sun comes from the Creator shining brighter than men might imagine in their minds, brightly gleaming. . . . The sight of Christ comes to them in splendor, the beauty of the noble king out of the skies in the east, pleasing in heart to his folk. He is joyous in sight to good men, beauteous and appealing . . . a friend and a pleasure, lovely and gracious for beloved men to look upon that shining radiance.)

The beauty of Christ is ineffable.

Descriptions of beauty as light are common currency among many cultures, so there is little cause to assume that Old English terms for beauty are local adaptations of a Mediterranean vocabulary. *Wuldor* 'splendor', for one, echoes the name of an early Germanic god known for his bright countenance.[7] But however the pagan Goths used the term, Ulfilas renders Latin *gloria* with it, though its etymology seems to be connected with "knowing" rather than with "shining." The term appears often in Old English in epithets for God and angels. In *Menologium* (149a), *wīfa wuldor* 'splendor of women' designates the Virgin Mary. Although a sense "glory" is apt here, her glory is not so much of fame as it is of splendor.

Words such as *hīw* 'hue', *blēoh* 'color', and *blāc* 'pale' would appear to be color referents, but the *blēo* of the Cross (DrR 22a) is its glistening ornaments. The Jewish women of Sodom and Gomorrah, about to be carried into captivity (Gen 1970a) as well as Judith's handmaiden carrying the head of Holofernes (Jud 128a) are *blāchlēor* 'bright-cheeked'. *Ælfscīenu* 'elf-bright' (?) always designates the fair form of a woman who is the object of sexual attention. Judith is so described as she is led to the tent of Holofernes (Jud 14a),[8] and Sarah when Abraham surrenders her to other men (Gen 1827a, 2731a). Perhaps, though the evidence is scant and circumstantial, *ælfscīenu* can be understood as an incitement to sin rather than as an inspiration to noble deeds. *Deall* is commonly glossed "proud" or "excellent" but its etymological sense is "bright, brilliant" (Old Norse *döll* and *mardöll* are terms for Freyja). The phoenix is a *fugel feðrum deal* 'feather-bright bird' (Phx 266a) and the troops in *Beowulf* (494a) who are *þrýþum dealle* 'proud in their strength', display their pride in the strength of their carriage. The common word *fæger* 'fair' qualifies things as often as people. Angels are God's *fægre frēoþeowas* 'fair free servants' (Gen 79a), Eve is *frēo fægrost* 'free, most fair' (Gen 457a), and so forth. Juliana's *glæm* 'radiance' incites lust. Eliseus's apostrophe to her denigrates her radiance:

Mīn se swētesta,   sunnan scīma,
Iuliana!   Hwæt, þū glæm hafast,
ginfæste giefe,   gēoguðhādes blæd!
                                 (Jln 166a–68b)

(My sweetest light of the sun, Juliana! Lo, you have radiance, an enduring gift, the blossom of youth!)

Hwīt, lēoht, scīr, scīne, scīma, and *torht* all signify 'light' while designating radiance of form, particularly of the face. It is worth noting that *scīn* is homophonous with the neuter noun *scin(n)* 'spectre, evil spirit' (see SnS, 101a). Both senses seem to be at play in the description of the fallen angels: *blāce hworfon / scīnnan forscepene* 'the bright ones (the dark ones) departed / the radiant ones (the fallen angels) with beauty transformed' (XSt 71b–72a). Indeed, Bosworth-Toller cannot choose between them, translating "beauty transformed" under the headword *forsceppan* and "fallen angels" under the headword *scinnan*. *Wlitig* is "fair aspect" or "brightness of form,"

but suggests an attraction to one or more of the senses. *Wlitig* describes the earth in
Phoenix (7a), the giant sword in Grendel's cave (Bwf 1662b), the enticing aroma of
the panther (Pnt 65a), and the sound of God's voice (Jln 283a). Eve is *wīfa wlitegost*
'fairest of women' (Gen 627a).[9]

The words classified under B—Beauty in Appealing Physical Form—refer to
general attractiveness. *Ǣnlīc* denotes "singular," though in poetic context it regularly designates "excellence" or "superiority" of physical form. It qualifies Modthrytho's fair exterior belied by her malefic character (Bwf 1941b), the heavenly sign
which converts Constantine (Ele 74a), and the appearance of Beowulf to the Danish
coastguard as he measures the hero's *wlite* 'beauty' (Bwf 250b) and *ansȳn* 'countenance' (Bwf 251a). *Cȳmlic* 'fair' describes the iceberg of *Riddle* 33 and Scyld
Scefing's funeral ship (Bwf 38b).[10] *Cyrten* (Vulg. L *cortinus*, ON *kurteiss*) appears
only in *Riddle* 25.6—*ful cyrtenu ceorles dohtor* 'the very beautiful daughter of a
churl'—where the context implies sexual attraction. *Dōm* 'glory' is admittedly
questionable under this category. *Dōm unscynde* 'honorable [shining, brilliant]
glory' (Ele 365b) is Saint Helen's expression for man's original sinless state. Beowulf's *dōm* as he enters Hrothgar's hall after the fight against Grendel's Mother does
project a stateliness and resplendence of form in contrast to the loathsome head of
Grendel.[11]

Geatolīc 'adorned' is an exclusively poetic term for excellence of appearance.
Hrothgar is *geatolīc* (1401a) on the way to Grendel's pond, and Saint Helen is
geatolīc gūðcwēn golde gehyrsted 'a splendid war-queen adorned with gold' (Ele
331). Christ is *wilsum in worlde* 'resplendent in the world' (Vgl 81a), 'resplendent'
rather than 'desirable'. Beowulf is met at Heorot by the *wlonc* 'brave' warrior
Wulfgar (Bwf 331b), and the hero is called *wlanc* by the poet a few lines later (Bwf
341a). His boldness is of posture before it is of speech. The hair of the Hebrew
warriors in *Judith* (325a) is resplendent rather than bold. *Wrǣst,* from *wrīðan* 'to
twist' or *wrīdan* (?) 'to flourish', is clearly a quality of physical excellence in *Riddle*
40.26b, where Creation boasts *ic ēom wrǣstre þonne hēo* 'I am more splendid than
she'. *Wrǣtlic* alludes to excellence of craftsmanship. The waters of the Phoenix's
paradise are *wundrum wrǣtlice* 'wonderfully splendid' (Phx 63a; Lactantius' verse
has *lenis, dulcibus* 'calm, sweet').[12] *Wynn* usually designates 'joy' or 'delight', but
in the contexts cited, it refers to the best of a class. The Virgin Mary is *wīfa wynn* 'joy
of women' (Chr 71a), not so much a joy to women as the 'fairest' of them. God's
heavenly fruit is *wynlīc* 'beautiful' (Gen 255a), appealing because of its beauty.[13]
Wynsum 'pleasant', occasionally glossing Latin *pulcher* 'beautiful', qualifies the
appeal to eye and thirst of the world's water (Phx 65a) and to the nose of the whale's
odor (Whl 54b).

The words under category C—Quality Recognizable in Form or Stance—
designate qualities associated occasionally with fair appearance to the eye. *Ǣþele*
'noble' and *ēadige* 'blessed' refer to moral virtue, though the former is associated
etymologically with good birth and the latter with riches. As nouns they mark a
physical posture which displays virtue. *Blǣd* is etymologically associated with
"growth." The *līfes blǣd* of the *Seafarer* (Sfr 79b) is perhaps "worldly prosperity,"
but *blǣd is gehnǣged* 'prosperity is brought low' in line 88b of the same poem
implicates physical forms. The reading "glory" here is too vague.[14]

Frēolīc carries into poetic contexts physical, social, and moral values. The term may well qualify the free-born and noble status of Hrothgar's queen Wealhtheow (Bwf 615a, 641a)—in pointed contrast with a latent implication of servitude in her name—but Sarah is *frēolīc* in a context which insists on her apparent femininity and womanly attributes (Gen 1722a).[15] ON *fríðleik,* 'personal beauty', as well as *fríðust* 'beauty' and *fríðleikskona* 'personal beauty of a woman', implies woman's beauty, though the noun *fríðr* in personal names signals a womanly affection (*friðr* with a short *i* is 'peace'). In Old English, however, the adjective is not restricted to women. King Edward, for example, is *frēolīce* 'comely' (D Ew 22b), and the masculine voice of the *Riming Poem* (38b) calls himself *frēolīc.*

Lēoftæl is, literally, "a portion of love." Both Christ (Chr 912b–13a) and the Panther (Pnt 32a) are *lēoftæl* 'loving' and *lufsum* 'lovable'. The terms seem to be almost synonymous. *Lustgryre* (SBI 23b) is the "fierce grip of desire." *Myne* 'desire' is open to question as a term signaling beauty. OHG *munilîca* and ON *munaðr* are glossed "voluptuous," and ON *munr* means "delight." These senses are not entirely inappropriate to *myne* in some of its Old English poetic contexts. Juliana's *mōdes myne* (Jln 379a, 657a) as well as Christ's (Chr 1358a) is "desire of mind" or "excellence of courage." *Myne* is both "desire" and "that which is desired." Sarah before the Pharaoh (Gen 1861a) is *wífmyne* 'womanly desirable' (simply *pulchra* 'beautiful' in the Vulgate text).[16] Perhaps in *Beowulf* (169b) it is possible to understand that what is denied either Grendel or Hrothgar is that which is desirable, the good or the beautiful gifts of God (or Hrothgar).[17]

Sēl 'better' is a moral or social qualification. Beowulf is praised tautologically as *sēlra* 'a more better' shield bearer (Bwf 860b). The Danish troops at the celebration feast are called *sēl* (Bwf 1012b), certainly not because of their past exploits, but most likely for their posture. *Til* is uncertain as a term for beauty. Etymologically related to *tilian* 'to till', it carries a sense of good-doing rather than fair-seeming. When *Elene* speaks of words *swā tiles swā trages* 'either good or evil' (Ele 325a), however, it contrasts fair words with foul, truth with lies. Those who hold their faith in God are *til* (Wan 112a) of spirit, but why Hrothgar's brother Halga is called *til* (Bwf 61b) is a mystery to me.

Category D—Beauty by Array—needs no explication. It is a brief selection of the many terms for adornments which render or enhance beauty. The two words I include here for women's hair—*wundenlocc* 'with plaited locks' and *bundenheord* 'with hair bound up'—designate female status rather than appearance.[18] Helen Damico has reviewed the role of female adornment and concludes that the radiance of martial women is "ornamental radiance, particularly in battle and under the glare of the sun."[19] A woman's array also signals as well as emphasizes her sexual force, distinct from, and in many cases superior to, masculine battle strength. Indeed, the ornaments worn in battle by males emulate female forces in a fetish appropriation of life-giving and life-sustaining power.[20]

READING THE EVIDENCE

First of all, the words which commonly designate fairness of physical form cluster in poetic contexts. So the habitat of the phoenix is described:

Wlitig is se wong ēall,   *wynnum* geblissad
mid þǣm *fǣgrestum*   foldan stencum.
Ǣnlīc is þæt īglond,   *æþele* se wyhrta. . . .
(Phx 7a–9b, italics mine)

(Lovely is the entire plain, blessed with delights, with the fairest perfumes of the earth. Singularly beautiful is that waterland, excellent its maker. . . .)

The heavenly sign which incites Constantine's conversion is similarly described, with greater emphasis on radiance:

. . . frætwum *beorht*
wliti wuldres trēo   ofer wolcna hrōf,
golde gelenged,   (gimmas *līxtan*);
wæs se *blāca* bēam   bōcstafum awrīten,
beorhte ond *lēohte.* . . .
(Ele 88b–92a, italics mine)

(. . . bright with treasures, beautiful tree of glory over the roof of the clouds, gold-decked, gems glistening; the bright beam was carved with letters, bright and shining. . . .)

Second, the beauty of women is not a fragile virtue. Grendel's Mother, who is not beautiful, is said to be less frightening than an armed warrior, and she shows fear scurrying from the hall. On the other hand, the devil cowers before an *unforhte* 'unafraid' Juliana (Jln 147a, 209b, 601a). Judith is *ides ellenrōf* 'a remarkably brave woman' (Jud 109a, 146a) and *collenferhðe* 'bold-spirited' (Jud 134b), unlike Ælfric's homily version of her as *lytel ond unstrang* 'little and weak'.[21] Woman's beauty is, generally, a sign of strength and not a seductive lure. The allegorical body of man may be *lustgryre* 'gripped by desire', but there seems to be no handy poetic term in Old English for a woman's sexual attraction, unless it is the term *ælfscīenu*, usually glossed as "elf-bright." *Cyrten* glosses Latin *venustus* 'beauty, elegance', but occurs only once in the poetry to qualify a churl's daughter, though her appeal may not be purely sexual.[22] Old Norse poetry contains many examples of a woman's physical attractiveness as an incitement. Helgi Hundingsbani battles rival suitors for the maiden he pursues; Freyja seduces gods and giants alike with her sexual appeal; and the most famous rivalry is that between two women—Gudrun and Brynhild—for the attention of Sigurd.[23]

Third, beauty is rarely an isolated or single quality, or even a dominant one.[24] Judith has *ellen* 'courage' (95a), *rǣd* 'wisdom' (97a), *riht* 'justice' (97a), and *list* 'imagination' (101a), besides being *hālig* 'holy' (56b). She is also *glēaw on geðonce, / ides ælfscīnu* 'wise in thought, elf-bright woman' (13b–14a). Juliana is *ēadge* 'blessed' (105a, 130a) and *glēaw* 'wise' (131a). She is also *wuldres mæg / ānrǣd ond unforht* 'maiden of radiance, single-minded and unafraid' (600b–601a), as well as *hālge . . . / ungewemde wlite* 'holy one with unblemished beauty' (589b–90a). I can distinguish at least five virtues combined in the persons of Judith and Juliana: strength of character (*ellenrōf*), wisdom (*glēaw*), moral and social superiority (*æþele*), beauty (*wlite*), and piety (*hālig*). The piety of saints is perhaps comparable to the assiduity or resoluteness of secular heroines, though one might include piety under strength of character. Elene and Wealhtheow have similar virtues that include quickness of mind, sagacity of speech, thoughtful intent toward duty, and shining physical appearance.[25] Beauty is not simply a visible or outward sign of an interior virtue. It is a particular force in itself whose frequent manifestation in words for brightness suggests a *natural* power. Women of beauty and boldness of character have preternatural strength.[26] Their powers border on the monstrous. As Anacreon observed long ago: who has beauty is more formidable than fire and iron.

APPENDICES

A. Beauty as Brightness

beorht 'bright'	(XSt 520a, Jud 58b)
blāchlēor 'bright-cheeked'	(Gen 1970a, Jud 128a)
blēo(h) 'color'	(DrR 22a, Jln 363a)
deall 'bright'	(Bwf 494a, Phx 266a, R31.22b)
fæger 'fair'	(DrR 73a, Gen 457a, Mnl 148b, Phx 291a)
glǣm 'radiance'	(Ele 1266a, Glc 1278b, 1289b, Jln 167b)
hīwbeorht 'hue-bright'	(Ele 73a)
hwīt 'white'	(Ele 73a)
lēoht 'light'	(XSt 165a, Gen 265b, 676b, R29.3a)
lēoma 'light'	(Chr 234a, as metaphor)
scīr 'light'	(Bwf 496a, 979a, Exo 125a, Phx 308a)
scīene/scēone 'light'	(Gen 549a, 656b, Phx 308a)
ælfscīenu 'elf-bright'	(Gen 1827a, 2731a, Jud 14a)
sunscīene 'sun-bright'	(Jln 229a)
wlitescīene 'bright-faced'	(Ele 72a, Gen 527a, Jln 454a)
scīma 'light'	(Chr 697b, Gen 137a, Jln 166b)
torht 'light'	(Jud 43a, Phx 200b)
wlite/wlitig 'fair aspect'	(Bwf 93a, GfM 35a, Jln 163a, 590a)
wuldor 'splendor'	(Mnl 149a)

A word remarkable for its absence from a list of terms for "radiance, brightness," hence "beautiful" is *bealdor* 'lord' (ON *baldr*, Gothic *balþs* 'bright one' and *bala* 'white-faced horse', Greek φαλιός 'clear, white, shining', IE **bhel* 'to gleam brightly'). The etymologies are unclear, but it appears that whatever the links with radiance might be, the noun *bealdor* had, in both Old English and Old Icelandic linguistic developments, ties with titles of eminence and with a name for a god. It is entirely possible that the OE *bald/beald* 'bold' became associated with *bealdor* and that the sense "lord" carried with it an appropriate sense of radiance. *Beald* glosses Latin *virtuosus*.

B. Beauty in an Appealing Physical Form

ǣnlīc 'singular'	(Bwf 251a, 1941b, Ele 74a, Phx 312a, R74.2a)
cȳmlīc 'fair'	(Bwf 38a, R33.2a)
dōm 'glory'	(Bwf 1645b, Ele 365b)
geatolīc 'adorned'	(Bwf 215a, 308a, 1401a, Ele 258a, 331a)
ungewemde 'unblemished'	(Jln 590a)
unwemme 'uninjured'	(Phx 46a)
wilsum 'resplendent'	(Vgl 81a)
wlanc 'brave'	(Bwf 341a, Jud 325a)
wrǣst 'splendid'	(P146.11.3b, R40.26b)
wrǣtlīc 'excellent'	(Phx 63a, R26.14a)
wyn 'joy'	(Chr 71a, Phx 7b, 290a)
wynlīc 'beautiful'	(Gen 255a)
wynsum 'pleasant'	(Gen 1855a, Phx 65a)

C. Quality Recognizable in Form or Stance

æþele 'noble'	(Jud 256a, Phx 2b)
blǣd 'prosperity'	(Chr 1635b, Phx 662b)
ēadge 'blessed'	(Jln 130a)
frēolīc 'comely'	(Bwf 615a, 641a, GfM 34b)
lēoftǣl 'loving'	(Chr 912b, Pnt 32a)
lufsum 'lovable'	(Chr 913a, Pnt 32a)
lustgryre 'gripped by desire'	(SB1 23b)
myne 'desirable'	(Bwf 169b, Chr 1358a, Jln 379a, 657a, Wan 27b, Wds 4a)
sēl 'better'	(Bwf 860b, 1012b, Mnl 168b)
til 'good'	(Ele 325a, Gen 1810b, Wan 112a)

D. Beauty by Array

bēaghroden 'ring-adorned'	(Bwf 623b, R14.9)
bēahhrodene 'adorned, ring-adorned'	(Jud 138b)
bundenheord 'with hair bound up'	(Bwf 3151b)
gefrætweod 'adorned'	(Jud 171b)
gehlæste 'adorned'	(Jud 36b)
gehyrsted 'ornamented'	(Ele 331b)
goldhroden 'gold-adorned'	(Bwf 614a, 640b, 1948a, 2025a, Wds 102a)
sinchroden 'treasure-adorned'	(HbM 14a)
wundenlocc 'with plaited locks'	(Jud 77b, 103b, R40.98–99, 104)

NOTES

1. See the *Oxford Dictionary of English Etymology*, ed. C. T. Onions (Oxford: Clarendon Press, 1957) and Joseph T. Shipley, *The Origins of English Words* (Baltimore: Johns Hopkins University Press, 1984).

2. English *pretty*, on the other hand, derives from OE *prættig* (ON *prettugr*) 'cunning, conniving': *wille ge beon prættige (versipelles) oþþe þusenthiwe on leasungum, lytige on spræcum, onglæwlice?* 'do you want to be cunning (crafty) or of a thousand hues in falsehood, do you want to be crafty in speech?' asks Ælfric in his *Colloquy*, opposing prettiness to wisdom. See *Ælfric's Colloquy*, ed. G. N. Garmonsway (New York: Appleton-Century-Crofts, 1966), p. 43.

3. Horace, *Ars Poetica*, line 428, in *The Works of Horace*, vol. 2 (Oxford: Clarendon Press, 1891), p. 427; Hugh Percy Jones, ed., *Dictionary of Foreign Phrases and Classical Quotations* (Edinburgh: John Grant, 1913), p. 107.

4. Augustine, *Confessions*, trans. R. S. Pine-Coffin (Baltimore: Penguin Books, 1971), pp. 150–56. In *City of God* (XII, 6), Augustine absolves beauty of the charge of inciting lust. If two men differ in their reactions to beauty, he argues, their difference is attributable to will and not to nature. See *The City of God*, trans. Gerald G. Walsh et al. (Garden City, N.Y.: Doubleday and Co., 1958), pp. 250–53.

5. Abbreviations and citations follow the Bessinger-Smith *A Concordance to the Anglo-Saxon Poetic Records* (Ithaca: Cornell University Press, 1978). Old English quotations are from *The Anglo-Saxon Poetic Records* (New York: Columbia University Press, 1931–1953). In order to regularize spelling, I have added macrons over the vowels and diphthongs to indicate length. For additional meanings of the terms, see Joseph Bosworth, *An Anglo-Saxon Dictionary*, ed. and enlarged by T. Northcote Toller (London: Oxford University Press, 1898; rpt. 1976); hereafter cited as Bosworth-Toller.

6. "The Phoenix Homily," in *Early English Homilies*, ed. Rubie D-N. Warner, Early English Text Society, o.s., vol. 152 (London: Oxford University Press, 1917), p. 147.

7. The Gothic form of the word *wulþus* is cognate with Latin *vultus*. The names of gods normally reflect common nouns and adjectives, so that it is likely that *wuldor* was first a quality and then a god; but poets are prone to play on the associations of the two. So, Snorri Sturluson, in *Gylfaginning* (31): *Ullr* [the son of the gold-haired Sif] . . . *er ok fagr álitum* 'Ullr is also fair of face' (*Edda Snorra Sturlusonar*, ed. Finnur Jónsson [Reykjavík: Sigurður Kristjánsson, 1907]). Scriptural links between godhead and light are common as well. *Ego sum lux mundi* 'I am the light of the world', says Christ in John 8:12 (*Biblia Sacra, Vulgatae Editionis* [Rome: Editiones Paulinae, 1957], p. 1117). Various terms for God in the Psalms include *lux, splendor,* and *lumen,* 'light'.

8. At this point in the story, the Vulgate has *femina* 'woman' and *bona puella* 'good girl' (Judith 12:11 and 12, *Biblia Sacra*, p. 410).

9. In comparison with Old English, Old Icelandic poetry is poor in terms for beauty, though it shares part of the vocabulary linking radiance to fair-seeming. Gudrun is *liósa brúði, biart í buri, scírleita, gaglbiart* 'bright bride, bright one in the bower, bright-faced, bright as a goose'. Svanhild is *hvítari . . . sólar geisla* 'whiter than the sunbeam' and *sæmleitr sólar geisli* 'a sunbeam fine to look at'. Billing's daughter is *sólhvíta* 'white as the sun'. Thor's daughter is *fagrglóa* 'fair-glowing' and *miallhvíta* 'snow-white'. Sigrlin in the Helgi poems is *meyna fegrsto* 'fairest of maids' and Sigrun is *sólbiart* 'sun-bright'. Brynhild, curiously, is not described as beautiful; see *Edda: Die Lieder des Codex Regius nebst verwandten Denkmälern*, ed. Gustav Neckel, 4th ed. rev. Hans Kuhn (Heidelberg: Carl Winter, 1962). On saga terms for beauty, see Wolfgang Krause, *Die Frau in der Sprache des altisländischen Familienge-schichten* (Göttingen: Van der Breck und Ruptecht, 1926), p. 73ff. In Old Icelandic, *hvítr* 'white' applied to men is often an insult, alluding to a face pale with fear. The most common Modern Icelandic term for beautiful is *fallegur*, deriving from *falla* 'to be useful or worthy'. See *An Icelandic-English Dictionary*, ed. Richard Cleasby, enlarged and completed by Gudbrand Vigfusson (Oxford: Clarendon Press, 1874; rpt. 1969).

10. Scyld's funeral ship, like the Rood which carries Christ, is associated with female generative forces whose making and destroying powers reflect God's.

11. According to Jan de Vries, *Altnordisches Etymologisches Wörterbuch* (Leiden: Brill, 1962), OE *dōm* and *dǣd* 'deed', like *deall*, are cognate with ON *dǣll* 'gentle, familiar, forbearing', whose modern Norwegian form *deilig* is a common word for "attractive."

12. Lactantius, "De Ave Phoenice," line 26, in *Minor Latin Poets*, ed. J. Wight Duff and Arnold M. Duff (Cambridge, Mass.: Harvard University Press, 1961), p. 652.

13. *Wynlice* is glossed "beautiful" here by F. J. Cassidy and Richard Ringler, *Bright's Old English Grammar and Reader* (New York: Holt, Rinehart and Winston, 1971), p. 492.

14. For the polysemy of *blǣd* in this line, see Stanley B. Greenfield, *The Interpretation of Old English Poems* (London: Routledge and Kegan Paul, 1972), p. 89.

15. Richard J. Schrader, *God's Handiwork: Images of Women in Early Germanic Literature* (Westport, Conn.: Greenwood Press, 1983), p. 36, notes that *frēolīc* reflects aristocratic values. Helen Damico, *Beowulf's Wealhtheow and the Valkyrie Tradition* (Madison: University of Wisconsin Press, 1984), p. 22, translates "free-born." There is ironic aptness for *frēolīc* describing Sarah as such, since her husband is offering her up as a slave. Damico discusses terms for womanly beauty, pp. 68–69, et passim.

16. Genesis 12:11, *Biblia Sacra*, p. 9.

17. C. L. Wrenn's note to the line offers "mind, purpose" or "love" for *myne* (*Beowulf, with the Finnesburg Fragment*, 1973 ed. rev. W. F. Bolton [London: Harrap, 1973]). Fr. Klaeber rejects "desire" in favor of "gratitude" or "thought" (*Beowulf and the Fight at Finnsburg*, 3d ed. [Lexington, Mass.: D. C. Heath, 1950]). Stephen A. Barney, *Word-Hoard* (New Haven, Conn.: Yale University Press, 1977), notes the romance cognates for the word but ignores the Germanic cognates which might be brought to bear upon this context.

18. Schrader, *God's Handiwork*, p. 45, states that *bundenheord* signals a married state, but he offers no supporting evidence. The word is a crux, for -*heord* is unknown in Old English for "hair." If, as most editors assume, the word is cognate with ON *haddr* 'braided hair', then hair bound-up would betoken a state of suspended or latent fertility.

19. Damico, *Beowulf's Wealhtheow*, pp. 29–34, points out that Judith is *golde gefrǣtewod* 'adorned with gold' (171b) by her military equipment, so that *bēaghroden* can be understood as "shield-adorned" (138b). In the ON *Völundarkviða*, Nidud's troops in armor reflect the bright moonshine: *scildir blico beira við inn scarða mána* 'their shields shone under the waning moon' (stanza 6).

20. See P. B. Taylor, "The Traditional Language of Treasure in *Beowulf*," *Journal of English and Germanic Philology* 85 (1985): 191–205.

21. Ælfric, "Judith," in Bruno Assmann, *Angelsächsische Homilien und Heiligenleben* (Kassel: G. H. Wigland, 1889), p. 410.

22. Sharon Farmer, "Persuasive Voices: Clerical Images of Medieval Wives," *Speculum* 61 (1986): 517–43, provides an informative survey of late Medieval Church attitudes towards the relationship between a woman's beauty and her ability to use it in moving her husband to virtue.

23. See *Helgaqviða Hundingsbana II* and *Prymsqviða* in *Edda;* for translations, see *Corpus Poeticum Boreale. The Poetry of the Old Northern Tongue*, ed. and trans. Gudbrand Vigfusson and F. York Powell, 2 vols. (Oxford: Clarendon Press, 1883); *Vǫlsunga saga, The Saga of the Volsungs*, ed. and trans. R. G. Finch (London: Thomas Nelson and Sons, 1965).

24. The description of Christ's bright aspect in *Christ*, 899–914, however, emphasizes no other aspect besides his radiance.

25. Damico, *Beowulf's Wealhtheow*, p. 31. Schrader, *God's Handiwork*, p. 71, notes that holy women in early Germanic literature balance physical beauty with mental acuity. The heroic women of the Old Norse traditional poetry are more often wise—*horskr, kenndr, frōðr*—than beautiful.

26. Standards of beauty in the Old English period and the beauty-morality bind were heavily influenced by Christian iconography which equated beauty with the good and ugliness

with evil. Native Germanic thought tends to disregard such an association. Neither Thor nor Odin are handsome gods. The evil Loki is. In the sagas, romance types such as Gunnar of Hlidarend and Olaf Peacock are handsome, but the great heroes such as Egil Skallagrimsson and Skarphedin Njálsson are notably ugly (*ljótr*). Hallgerd Höskuldsdóttir, Gunnar's wife, is most beautiful but murderous, while the most heroic of women, Njál's wife Bergthora, is a prophetess, loyal wife, and mother of heroes and marked by her ugly features.

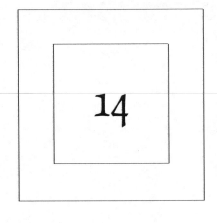

Cynewulf's Autonomous Women

A Reconsideration of Elene and Juliana

Critics have tended to view the female char-
acters in Old English secular literature from the perspective of patriarchal culture, in
which relationships to men define reality for both men and women. They describe
women in Anglo-Saxon England as passive figures within a world of active, heroic
men. This attitude is heightened in respect to women of the religious literature.
Modern readers often assume that women who adopted religious life were even more
passive than secular women because they voluntarily put themselves under the
governance of the male hierarchy of the Catholic church, which many modern
readers believe to have been more rigidly patriarchal than secular society. Such an
attitude ignores the fact that Christianity gave women the chance to operate as full
human beings. Peter Brown observes that women had been a "blank on the map of
the classical city" but that Christian women "achieved a new prominence through
participation in Christian charity and church building associated with the cult of the
saints,"[1] and Christine E. Fell has demonstrated that the advent of Christianity
permitted Anglo-Saxon women to exercise both personal and public autonomy.[2]
When studying religious literature, many readers assume that the female saint merely
re-enacts patterns developed in respect to male saints because hagiographic narratives simply reduplicate predictable patterns; as James Whitby Earl summed up this
attitude, "When you've read one saint's Life, you've read them all."[3] This attitude
seems to be confirmed from medieval texts themselves, which often demonstrate
what Charles W. Jones calls the "principle of duplication" by which one author
borrows passages from others because "all things are common in the communion of
saints."[4] Anne L. Klinck has, however, argued persuasively that "female characterization in Old English poetry" is often associated with "the growth of psychological
realism" rather than with suffering and that *Christ I* and *Genesis B* in particular show
"an interest in persons as individuals apart from their functions as members of a
group."[5] Although Klinck's study is one of those that free us to view women in both
secular and religious literature in a new light, the habit of treating female saints and

saintly figures like Judith as mere allegorical counters in typological narratives is strong enough that even Klinck concludes that the portrayal of these women in Old English poetry is "quite stilted."[6] I should like to suggest that such an attitude derives from the fact that critics fail to understand not only the nature of Old English poetry, which represents a literature more personal and more human in our terms than the Roman literature from which the stories are drawn, but also the nature of female sanctity.

One question that critics never address is why, considering the many women saints treated in Old English and Anglo-Latin literature, the stories of Judith, Juliana, and Elene survive in the poetic form that blends elements of common-Germanic culture with Romanized Judeo-Christian tradition. I would argue that they were considered appropriate for poetic treatment because all three women are active and heroic. Judith is clearly active, because she goes to the enemy camp, decapitates the Assyrian leader, and returns home as "the heroine on the beach";[7] so is Elene, responsible for the finding of the True Cross, journeying to Jerusalem, convening councils, and imprisoning Judas when he refuses to speak. Cynewulf even eliminates Elene's death, which is found in the Latin versions, and ends the narrative of the Invention with her activity: *Hio wæs siðes fus / eft to eðle*[8] 'She was eager for the journey back to her native land' (1218b–19a). Her activity, however, has caused many to view her with disfavor, presumably because she is not the passive and inactive female many scholars want women in Old English literature to be. James Doubleday, for example, calls her "one of the most unpleasant saints in the calendar,"[9] and Jackson J. Campbell recounts an anecdote about a fellow Anglo-Saxonist who once referred to Elene as a "cruel, hardbitten old harridan."[10] I believe that both Cynewulf and his original audience would have been surprised by these descriptions. Elene is certainly no more unpleasant than male heroes like Odysseus, but like Judith and Juliana, she makes men submit to her will. I believe that Cynewulf and his audience would have been even more surprised at the lack of criticism of Affricanus and Heliseus, the men who torture Juliana to try to force her to submit to their wills. In contrast to such criticism of Elene's activity, readers have tended to view Juliana as a passive person, primarily because she refuses marriage, and those who have perceived her choice of virginity as active have tended to view that action as negative. As I have shown elsewhere, Cynewulf adapts his source to eliminate at least one action,[11] that in which Juliana throws the devil *in locum stercoris*[12] 'on the dung-heap'. I believe that he does so not to make Juliana more passive than her source, but to focus on her "mental rather than physical strength"[13] and on the verbal actions that Juliana chooses in preference to the actions prescribed by her pagan father and suitor. Juliana in fact chooses the chain of circumstances that leads to her martyrdom; martyrdom is not forced upon her, so that it is impossible to treat her as the passive victim of circumstances beyond her control.

The response of literary critics to the problems raised by Elene and Juliana has been to retreat from discussing them as women at all, depicting them instead as allegorical counters in typological narratives.[14] Such readings are often of great interest because of what Thomas D. Hill has called "the importance of a figural interpretation of history in the intellectual life of the [Old English] period."[15] The problem, however, is that the scholars who make such statements refuse to see the female characters as human beings but reduce them to counters manipulated by the poet. Robert E. Bjork, for example, focuses exclusively on the speeches made by characters in the poems and the typological importance thereof, speaking of "Elene's discourse" as "the iconographic norm to which Judas will eventually totally conform" and of Juliana's speech as revelatory of "Juliana's achieved sainthood and the process through which she must move to reach it."[16] Although I do not deny that such readings have been of value because they have shown readers in the twentieth century that Cynewulf's poems are of intrinsic literary merit, I believe that they have gone too far; they dehumanize the heroines, and, more important, they limit—even negate— the literary effect of the poems. Elene may well represent the Church and Juliana events in Christian history, but they are first women whom we must interpret in terms of what we know about women in Old English society. I would argue that a reading of the two poems that is feminist in the broad sense of the term shows that Cynewulf has created two heroines who are models of personal autonomy, albeit on different patterns. Furthermore, both are heroines in a tradition that merges the Christian and the heroic, and to understand Elene and Juliana, we must understand both.

The Latin Helena is an assertive figure, but one cannot truly call her autonomous because she is always acting as her son's representative, and, once Judas converts and becomes Bishop Cyriacus, she submits to his authority. When Helena wishes to find the Nails, she *dixit* 'said' to Cyriacus that she wishes him to find them and begs him, *accede adhuc*[17] 'agree to this'. In contrast, the Old English Elene *bald reordode* 'spoke boldly' (1072b) to Cyriacus and, in a twenty-line speech that translates the brief (eighteen-word) sentence in the Latin, she orders him to find the Nails *hrædlice* 'quickly or at once' (1086b). After he has done so, Cynewulf observes that *hæfde Ciriacus / eall gefylled swa him seo æðele bebead, / wifes willan* 'Cyriacus had completely done as the noble woman bade him do, the will of the woman' (1129b–31a). By adding this passage to his source, Cynewulf emphasizes that his Elene is the person who controls the situation.

It is not surprising that, in comparison to Elene, Helena seems to lack autonomy. In the Latin tradition, good women are usually depicted as passive.[18] In the *Waltharius,* for example, Hildegund is a *timidam . . . puellam*[19] 'timid girl' who hides in the woods during the battle, in contrast to Hildegyth of the Old English *Waldere* fragments, who *hyrde*[20] 'encouraged' (1b) Walter during the battle. In his essay on *Genesis B* included in this volume, Alain Renoir warns us to avoid assuming that the entire Middle Ages viewed and depicted women in only one way. He points out that the attitude toward women which was held by "the Gothic warriors who followed Odoacer to Rome in the fifth century was [not] necessarily the same as that of a major theologian in fifteenth-century Paris" and that the Germanic tradition differs from "the Latin monastic tradition" which is the one that scholars view as quintessentially medieval.[21] It seems probable that when Cynewulf decided to translate the Latin monastic legend of the Invention of the Cross, he would have noted that Helena resembled women of the heroic tradition, assertive in speech and capable of acting authoritatively when necessary, especially when her son, her protector, is absent. I should like to suggest that Cynewulf heightened the portrait in his Latin source to make Elene the strong, autonomous figure that she is and that we need to understand women of Germanic tradition to interpret her and her role in the poem properly.

Those who assume that the woman's role in Anglo-Saxon society was passive disapprove of the fact that Elene resorts to torture to persuade Judas to divulge the hiding place of the Cross, because they assume that she has more in common with Grendel's Mother than with Hildeburh. In order to understand the nature of the heroic women in the common-Germanic culture that underlies our extant Old English texts, we must consult texts from other Germanic cultures. We must, of course, use texts from Germanic societies other than that of Anglo-Saxon England with care, bearing in mind Jeff Opland's warning that scholars have assumed "too readily that there was absolute uniformity within the various Germanic . . . traditions."[22] Nevertheless, the analogy is useful, especially in the case of a woman like Elene, who acts more like the women of Old Norse literature than like Graeco-Roman women saints. Daniel G. Calder has pointed out that Cynewulf "combines the Christian saint, the figure of Mary, and the church striving against . . . evil"[23] with the figure of the Germanic *guðcwen* 'war-queen' (254a) who journeys over the sea *gumena þreate* 'with a troop of men' (254b).

One point that critics like Calder have not noted in respect to Elene is that in Germanic tradition, women normally use speech rather than action to achieve their purposes, but they resort to action when speech fails. The Latin Helena knows Old Testament and classical history and can discuss both the prophets and the Fall of Troy, but Cynewulf places a special emphasis on Elene's ability to remember past events and remind her audience of them. She uses the interjection *Hwæt* 'Lo' five times (293a, 334b, 364a, 397a, and 670a), and the use recalls the openings of poems like *Beowulf* and *The Dream of the Rood*. Helen Damico has argued that Elene's qualities—"severity of mind, tenacity of purpose, and courage"—link her to those "half-mortal, half-supernatural beings called *idis* in Old High German, *ides* in Old English, and *dís* in Old Norse."[24] She points out that the *ides* in heroic poetry is characterized by "acuity and wisdom . . . buttressed by sagacity of speech," and she suggests that Elene manifests this aspect when she "repeatedly commands and goads the Jewish elders and warriors to reveal the whereabouts of the true cross."[25] I should like to suggest that Cynewulf deliberately recast the depiction of Helena to evoke memories of the *ides* and of human women who have similar sagacity of speech.

In particular, Cynewulf makes Elene resemble the women of Germanic tradition who admonish their male kinsmen to act in accordance with the heroic code, especially what Michael Murphy defines as the "strong-willed and forceful women of the sagas," who, as Carol J. Clover emphasizes, use both speech and actions in scenes of "*hvǫt* or incitement" to action.[26] In *Laxdœla Saga,* for example, Thorgerthr Egilsdóttir incites her sons to avenge their murdered brother and finally accompanies them on their journey because they need *brýningina* 'someone to egg them on'; her son Halldorr observes, *ekki munu vér þér þat kenna, móðir, þótt oss lifði ór hug þetta*[27] 'we would not be able to blame you for it, mother, if this should slip out of our memories'.

Women in Old Norse texts are not passive, but they are usually "taunters" who do not themselves participate personally in the feuds, and Clover observes that "in the feud situation, women's (and old men's) words are the equivalent of men's deeds" and that the "whetting women . . . [are] repeatedly described in admiring terms."[28] Women do not usually seek vengeance personally, although, like Thorgerthr, they may accompany the men on what is not considered a *kvennaferðir*[29] 'journey appropriate for a woman' in order to continue to incite them. Exceptional are the women like Authr of *Laxdæla Saga*, who uses a sword to avenge herself on the man who divorced her. In Old Norse poetry, women are strong and assertive, and they act physically rather than verbally when they must. In *The Waking of Angantyr*, Hervor goes alone at night to her father's grave to ask his ghost for the sword Tyrfingr in order to avenge his death and takes the sword even though it will *ætt . . . allri spilla*[30] 'destroy all her family'. In *Atlakvitha*, Guthrun personally avenges her brothers' murders by killing her husband Atli and burning the hall with his drunken retainers inside, and by so doing she gains the approval of the Eddic poet:

> Fullrœtt er um þetta:
> ferr engi svá siðan
> brúðr í brynio
> brœðr at hefna.[31]

(This whole tale is told: no woman since her has gone in a byrnie to avenge her brothers.)

Elene uses the various tactics found among Old Norse heroic women at various times in her quest for the True Cross. As I have shown elsewhere, "*Elene* is characterized by speech acts and by the poet's concern with the ethical use of speech,"[32] and Cynewulf uses formulaic language like *maðelode* 'spoke formally', *wið þingode* 'addressed', and *wordum (ge)negan* 'approach with words' to emphasize the importance of speech in his poem. At this point, I would like to observe that his use of such verbs—in contrast to the use of *dixit* 'said' throughout the *Inventio*—suggests that Cynewulf expected his audience to compare Elene to Germanic secular heroic women (assuming that we can use women from the later saga tradition to explain women from the Old English period). Elene sometimes resembles women like Thorgerthr, using speech to incite men to action as she does when she orders Cyriacus to find the Nails. Sometimes, however, she acts when other courses fail, especially in the case which has caused critics to heap opprobrium upon her, ordering Judas incarcerated without food or water. Although the latter is a verbal action rather than a physical one like those of Authr, Hervor, or Guthrun, it differs from her verbal actions as a taunter in respect to the Jewish elders.

Juliana differs from Elene because she is not the dowager empress of the Roman Empire but a young girl living under her father's rule, and in both Roman and Anglo-Saxon societies, an elderly widow had more legal autonomy than an unmarried woman. In addition, she is a virgin martyr rather than an active quester for the holiest relic of Christendom. Most important, the subtlety with which Cynewulf adapts heroic tradition in his depiction of Juliana is elusive,[33] because, in contrast to *Elene*, heroic concepts often play "a basically negative" role as the "secular concepts and inadequate values against which Christian concepts and values work."[34] Even those who allegorize the heroic tradition in Old English hagiographic narratives have observed that although "Juliana conforms to the warrior-martyr type within the *miles Christi* tradition . . . , there is no noun or nominal phrase in the poem that defines Juliana as a warrior figure."[35] Cynewulf uses some heroic values positively. Like Elene, Juliana is depicted as a Germanic *ides,* and her main attribute is the "brightness and radiance of physical appearance"[36] characteristic of the *ides.* Furthermore, "boldness in battle and resoluteness of mind are major constituents of Juliana's character,"[37] recalling the heroic women of Old Norse literature like Brynhildr rather than the meek virgins of Roman literature.

Although Cynewulf expresses suspicions about traditional heroism in *Juliana,* they concern the world of men and male action. He presents the verbal action of heroic women positively. Like Elene, Juliana is characterized by "sagacity of speech,"[38] and like the Invention legend, that of St. Juliana focuses on speeches and dialogues rather than on physical actions. In *Juliana,* Cynewulf frequently uses formulaic language both to introduce speeches and within speeches; his use of the formulaic word-hoard derived from heroic oral tradition shows the importance of that tradition for our understanding of the character of Juliana. *Juliana* uses a high density of formulaic language, and the speeches of the positive characters are more formulaic than those of the negative ones: "Juliana has 24% formulas, compared with 13% for Heliseus, 18% for Affricanus, and 21% for the devil."[39] The formularity of Juliana's speeches both shows that she is the hero of the poem and suggests that Cynewulf omits the action in the *Passio* in which Juliana throws the devil on the dung-heap in order to heighten the likeness of Juliana to heroic Old Norse women who act verbally. The direction of this emphasis is confirmed by Marie Nelson, who applies the speech-act theory of John L. Austin and John Searle to show that *Juliana* has a "confrontational" verbal structure. Nelson observes that "in the ordinary course of events, the person who threatens makes the conditions (the form is often 'If you don't —————, then I will —————'). Here Juliana's freedom of choice has been threatened, but . . . she makes the conditions under which she will marry Heliseus."[40] This fact shows her desire for autonomy and the heroic nature of her speech, reminiscent of the "confrontational" mode used by women like Gudrun Osvifsdóttir.

Once we grant that Cynewulf's intention is to emphasize speech in *Juliana* and that this emphasis resembles that in heroic Old Norse narratives about women whose speech is action, there are still interpretative problems for a modern audience. Women like Thorgerthr incite men to kill others, sometimes, as Michael Murphy notes, even "goading their men into courses of action, . . . very much against those men's good judgment and mutual friendship . . . , on behalf of the *family,* of blood relations, the closest and most basic of all ties."[41] Even though on the face of it Juliana goads nobody to do anything, she actually goes so far as to goad her father into permitting her to be tortured and Heliseus into killing her. This emphasis is unpleasant to a twentieth-century sensibility. It is more comfortable for critics to deal with an allegorical Juliana. I believe that in order to interpret *Juliana* properly, we must understand its use of the dual traditions of heroic Germanic literature and of Patristic hagiography. In particular, we need to examine the reasons why women became virgin martyrs during the Patristic period and ascetic nuns during the Middle Ages: they sought to assert their personal autonomy.

When one reads the Latin *Passio* side by side with *Juliana*, one is immediately struck by the nature and implications of Juliana's demands. When the Latin Eleusius first asks to marry Juliana, she refuses because he has not achieved *dignitatem præfecturæ*[42] 'the rank of prefect'. When he obtains the rank from the Emperor, she requires even more for her hand, saying, *credideris deo meo: et adoraueris patrem et filium et spiritum sanctum*[43] 'believe in my God: and adore the Father, the Son, and the Holy Spirit'. Cynewulf eliminates the first condition; his Juliana promises to marry Heliseus if he meets the second and worships *soðne God* 'the true God' (47b). Although it is probable that Cynewulf made the change so that his Juliana's refusal is based solely on religious considerations rather than on worldly ones involving the bridegroom's wealth and power, many critics find it puzzling. R. Barton Palmer, for example, believes that the *Passio* "presents a plot sequence in which a strong emphasis is placed on the dynamic, developmental relationship between character and action" and that "for the all-too-human figures of the *vita*, with their failings and virtues, Cynewulf substitutes allegorical representations of the contending forces in the never-ending battle of God against his enemies."[44] In contradistinction, I would like to suggest that the changes Cynewulf makes serve two functions. First, they make Juliana's actions more psychologically appropriate to a woman who lives an autonomous and active religious life. Second, the changes eliminate the promise that Juliana obviously has no intention of keeping, a promise which shows her to be duplicitous and therefore lacking in sanctity and which would undoubtedly be unacceptable to an audience familiar with heroic Germanic tradition, even when that audience was composed of Christians attuned to Christian stories. A woman may make an ambiguous promise as does Gudrun Osvifsdóttir to Thorgils Holluson in *Laxdœla Saga*, but she always keeps the letter if not the spirit thereof. To a modern audience, Juliana's promise to marry Eleusius if he attains a certain rank recalls the fact that Gyda Ericsdóttir refused to marry Haraldr Hárfagr unless he became king of all Norway, and she had no intention of reneging on the promise. To an audience raised on stories of such a nature, the promise of the Latin Juliana, which she breaks as soon as its terms are fulfilled, would be unacceptable.

Another interpretative problem with Cynewulf's *Juliana* involves the fact that Cynewulf tells us that Juliana *hogde georne / þæt hire mægðhad   mana gehwylces / fore Cristes lufan   clæne geheolde* 'thought eagerly how she should keep her virginity pure of any sin/man/marriage for the love of Christ' (29b–31b), a statement which seems at odds with Juliana's promise to marry Heliseus if he converts. Some of the difficulties of interpretation have a linguistic basis. Cynewulf uses a pivotal pun in lines 29b–31b to show his heroine's character. Juliana longs to keep herself clean of *man*. If the *a* is long, the statement means that she wishes to keep herself free from sin; if the *a* is short, it means that she wishes to keep herself clean of any *mann* 'man'. The word with the long vowel also suggests a play on *gemāna* 'marriage', implying that Juliana wishes to reject the secular world that prescribes marriage as the proper role for women. Above all, however, Juliana wishes to avoid a *sinful* marriage, and if she must marry, she will only marry a Christian. Her longing recalls the plight of Emily in Chaucer's *Knight's Tale*, who wishes "noght to ben a wyf and be with childe" but knows that she will probably have to forsake virginity for marriage and therefore asks Diana, "sende me hym that moost desireth me."[45] Unlike Emily, Juliana preserves her virginity and therefore her autonomy.

Scholars have shown that virginity is not passive in Christian literature but rather represents "an active choice" made by both men and women, "a vocation and an emblem of spiritual leadership."[46] In his study of this active form of virginity, John Bugge analyzes *Juliana* as a work which suggests "that virginity is the source of their [the female virgins'] ability to resist tempters and tormentors alike."[47] Bugge argues that the "real threat to her [Juliana's] virginity is the devil" rather than Heliseus and that the diction in the *flyting* between Juliana and the devil "establishes the implication that the devil's penetration is symbolic of sexual sin."[48] If we accept the validity of Bugge's observations, then it is clear that the most important aspect of Juliana's virginity is spiritual. In defending her virginity, she defends her soul, and she does so in a manner reminiscent of the female heroes of Germanic story, by speech. In contrast to Bugge, most critics[49] have treated Juliana's desire to protect her virginity only as a physical matter, in spite of its clear significance for her personal autonomy. As I have pointed out elsewhere, Juliana rejects the *mægrædenne* 'maid-ruling' (109a) which is Heliseus's view of marriage, "not only because she is interested in 'mægðhad' (l. 30a) [maidenhood], but also because she refuses to accept his heroic values"[50]—and his patriarchal view that the nature of secular society dictates that a woman must be ruled by a man.

Even critics favorably inclined to the Old English *Juliana* often argue that "Cynewulf portrays Juliana's physical acts typically as passive"[51] and her character "as a nearly hysterical . . . and unswerving Christian."[52] The ideals, however, that would have been familiar to Cynewulf's audience show that Juliana is neither passive nor hysterical. In contrast to Chaucer's Emily, she views virginity, not as a desirable but unattainable ideal, but as an ideal she can attain by goading her father and suitor into killing her. In this respect, Cynewulf follows his Latin source—which is motivated by the same ideals that underlie Old English monasticism—in which, as Palmer judiciously observes, "Juliana, quite literally, molds him [Eleusius] single-handedly into the instrument of her torture and death."[53] In other words, Juliana is active in both word and deed. A historical approach to Cynewulf's *Juliana* proves more useful than that taken by literary critics, because it obliges us to see the motivations of holy women in a fuller context. Although there are many studies of asceticism that could help in this endeavor, most pertinent to the study of *Juliana* is Rudolph M. Bell's *Holy Anorexia*. Even though Juliana is a martyr of the early Church whereas Bell deals with women of the late Middle Ages, his study is of great value in understanding Juliana.

According to Bell, the holy anorexic seeks "the suppression of physical urges and basic feelings—fatigue, sexual desire, hunger, pain—[which] frees the body to achieve heroic feats and the soul to commune with God."[54] He supports his analysis of this traditional goal with recent medical literature which shows that modern young women become anorexic in search of "identity, *autonomy,* and perfection."[55] Bell concludes that the holy anorexic seeks "to obliterate every human feeling of pain, fatigue, sexual desire, and hunger" in order "to be master of [herself]."[56] His study of Catherine of Siena shows that "it was Catherine's *will* that shaped the course of her infirmity and gave it meaning," especially since "she convinced people that behaviour commonly thought to be insane or demonic was holy."[57] Her family's response to her austerities resembles that of Affricanus and Heliseus to Juliana's self-assertion: "Mother, father, and brothers all determined to teach the girl a lesson, to break her will and make her agree to do as they wanted. Their concern was discipline."[58] Discipline is also the concern of Affricanus and Heliseus, who believe that Juliana exhibits *geaþe* 'foolishness, lightmindedness, or mockery' (96b), *unræd* 'lack of counsel' (120a), and *orlegu* 'strife' (97a) and torture her to force her to *onwend[an]* 'change direction' (144a) in her thought and speech and do as they want. Because the struggle between Juliana and her father and suitor occurs during the persecution of the early Church, Juliana does not need to practice the austerities of anorexic behavior and self-flagellation practiced by Catherine of Siena. The reaction to her decisiveness is swift and violent, but it is analogous to that in the biography of Catherine. Bell argues that it is only when Catherine was "exhausted by her austerities and broken emotionally by her failure to reform the Church" that her "will to live gave way to an active readiness for death."[59] The Old English *Juliana* shows the greater strength of Juliana's will in respect to the wills of others and her active readiness for death. She forces Affricanus and Heliseus to martyr her, a theologically acceptable course of action, of which Cynewulf—and presumably his audience—approves because *hyre sawl wearð / alæded of lice   to þam langan gefean* 'her soul was led from the body to lasting joy' (669b–70b).

Cynewulf depicts both Elene and Juliana as autonomous women, complex and strong, although on different models. *Elene* develops the dowager empress found in the Latin *Inventio* into an assertive Germanic woman whose speech is action but who acts when she must. *Juliana* presents a woman who is heroic in two ways. In terms of heroic Germanic culture, Juliana resembles the "taunters"[60] of the sagas who initiate the men's violent actions. In terms of heroic monastic culture, in which the saint rejects the secular world, she exhibits the same behavior on a spiritual plane. Each is, in her own way, an active woman whose indomitable will and assertive speech make her an exemplar of female autonomy. When we read *Elene* and *Juliana* from a feminist point of view, we do not have to reduce the characters to allegorical commonplaces or the narratives to typological paradigms but can admit that Cynewulf depicts his female characters as human beings only a little less vivid than Catherine of Siena. I submit that Old English literature and scholarship will be of greater interest to a wider audience if we do so.

NOTES

1. Peter Brown, *The Cult of the Saints: Its Rise and Function in Latin Christianity*, Haskell Lectures on History of Religions, n.s., vol. 2 (Chicago: University of Chicago Press, 1981), pp. 46 and 47.

2. See Christine E. Fell, "The Religious Life," in Fell with Cecily Clark and Elizabeth Williams, *Women in Anglo-Saxon England and The Impact of 1066* (Bloomington: Indiana University Press, 1984), pp. 109–28.

3. James Whitby Earl, "Literary Problems in Early Medieval Hagiography," Diss., Cornell University, 1971, p. 7.

4. Charles W. Jones, *Saints' Lives and Chronicles in Early England*, Romanesque Literature, vol. 1 (Ithaca, N.Y.: Cornell University Press, 1947), p. 61; italics deleted.

5. Anne L. Klinck, "Female Characterization in Old English Poetry and the Growth of Psychological Realism: *Genesis B* and *Christ I*," *Neophilologus* 63 (1979): 597, 607.

6. Klinck, "Female Characterization": 597.

7. Donald K. Fry, "The Heroine on the Beach in *Judith*," *Neuphilologische Mitteilungen* 68 (1967): 168.

8. All quotations from *Elene* are from *Cynewulf's "Elene*," ed. P. O. E. Gradon (Exeter: University of Exeter, 1977), and all quotations from *Juliana* are from *Cynewulf's "Juliana*," ed. Rosemary Woolf (Exeter: University of Exeter, 1977). Line references to both poems appear in the text. *ȝ* has been normalized to *g* and *þ* to *w*.

9. James Doubleday, "The Speech of Stephen and the Tone of *Elene*," in *Anglo-Saxon Poetry: Essays in Appreciation, for John C. McGalliard*, ed. Lewis E. Nicholson and Dolores Warwick Frese (Notre Dame: University of Notre Dame Press, 1975), p. 116.

10. Jackson J. Campbell, "Cynewulf's Multiple Revelations," *Medievalia et Humanistica*, n.s., 3 (1972): 257.

11. See Alexandra Hennessey Olsen, *Speech, Song, and Poetic Craft: The Artistry of the Cynewulf Canon*, American University Studies, series IV, vol. 15 (New York and Bern: Peter Lang, 1984), p. 88.

12. Boninus Mombritius, ed., *Passio Sancte Ivlianae Martyris*, in *Sanctuarium Seu Vitae Sanctorum*, vol. 2 (Paris: Apud Albertum Fontemoing Editorem, 1910), p. 79.

13. Olsen, *Speech*, p. 88.

14. See discussion of the allegorical approach to Old English literature in the Introduction to the present volume.

15. Thomas D. Hill, "Sapiential Structure and Figural Narrative in the Old English 'Elene'," *Traditio* 27 (1971): 161.

16. Robert E. Bjork, *The Old English Verse Saints' Lives: A Study in Direct Discourse and the Iconography of Style* (Toronto: University of Toronto Press, 1985), pp. 65 and 45.

17. Boninus Mombritius, ed., *Sanctae Crvcis Inventio*, in *Sanctuarium Seu Vitae Sanctorum*, vol. 1 (Paris: Apud Albertum Fontemoing Editorem, 1910), p. 379.

18. The following six paragraphs are adapted from Olsen, *Speech*, and are used by permission of Peter Lang Publishing, Inc.

19. Karl Strecker, ed., *Waltharius*, in *Die lateinischen Dichter des deutschen Mittelalters*, Monumenta Germaniae Historica: Poetarum Latinorum Medii Aevi, vol. 6, fascicle 1 (Weimar: Hermann Böhlau, 1951), p. 81.

20. Elliott Van Kirk Dobbie, ed., "Waldere," in *The Anglo-Saxon Minor Poems*, vol. 6 of *The Anglo-Saxon Poetic Records* (New York: Columbia University Press, 1968), pp. 4–6; line references appear in the text.

21. Alain Renoir, "Eve's I. Q. Rating: Two Sexist Views of *Genesis B*," p. 263 in the present volume.

22. Jeff Opland, *Anglo-Saxon Oral Poetry: A Study of the Traditions* (New Haven: Yale University Press, 1980), p. 19.

23. Daniel G. Calder, *Cynewulf*, Twayne English Author Series, vol. 327 (Boston: G. K. Hall and Co., 1981), p. 111.

24. Helen Damico, "The Valkyrie Reflex in Old English Literature," *Allegorica* 5 (1980): 149–67; rpt., pp. 176 and 186 in the present volume. See also Damico's treatment of Elene in *Beowulf's Wealhtheow and the Valkyrie Tradition* (Madison: University of Wisconsin Press, 1984), pp. 25–39, 49–50, 68, 86, 179.

25. Damico, "Valkyrie Reflex," pp. 181 and 187 in the present volume.

26. Michael Murphy, "Vows, Boasts and Taunts, and the Role of Women in Some Medieval Literature," *English Studies* 66 (1985): 111, and Carol J. Clover, "Hildigunnr's Lament," in *Structure and Meaning in Old Norse Literature: New Approaches to Textual Analysis and Literary Criticism* (Odense: Odense University Press, 1986), p. 143.

27. Einar Ól. Sveinsson, ed., *Laxdœla Saga*, Íslenzk Fornrit, vol. 5 (Reykjavík: Hið Íslenzka Fornritafélag, 1934), pp. 164, 162.

28. Clover, "Hildigunnr's Lament," p. 145. Clover quotes "Bjargey . . . in *Hávarðar saga:* 'It is manly for those unfit for vigorous deeds to be unsparing in their use of the tongue in saying those things that may avail' " (144–45). I should like to thank Professor Clover for pointing out the relevance of this quotation to my argument.

29. Sveinsson, *Laxdæla Saga*, p. 164.

30. Gudbrand Vigfusson and F. York Powell, eds., "The Waking of Angantyr," in *Corpvs Poeticum Boreale: The Poetry of the Old Northern Tongue from the Earliest Times to the Thirteenth Century*, vol. 1: *Eddic Poetry* (Oxford: The Clarendon Press, 1883), p. 167.

31. Ursula Dronke, ed. and trans., *The Poetic Edda*, vol. 1: *The Heroic Poems* (Oxford: The Clarendon Press, 1969), p. 12.

32. Olsen, *Speech*, p. 53.

33. The following two paragraphs are adapted from Olsen, *Speech*, and are used by permission of Peter Lang Publishing, Inc.

34. Michael D. Cherniss, *Ingeld and Christ: Heroic Concepts and Values in Old English Christian Poetry* (The Hague: Mouton, 1972), p. 194.

35. Joyce Hill, "The Soldier of Christ in Old English Prose and Poetry," *Leeds Studies in English* 12 (1981): 69.

36. Damico, "Valkyrie Reflex," p. 185 in the present volume.

37. Ibid., p. 186.

38. Ibid., p. 181.

39. Sharon Elizabeth Butler, "Distribution and Rhetorical Function of Formulas in Cynewulf's Signed Poems," Diss., University of Ontario, 1976, p. 56.

40. Marie Nelson, "*The Battle of Maldon* and *Juliana:* The Language of Confrontation," in *Modes of Interpretation in Old English Literature: Essays in Honour of Stanley B. Greenfield*, ed. Phyllis Rugg Brown, Georgia Ronan Crampton, and Fred C. Robinson (Toronto: University of Toronto Press, 1986), pp. 142, 143–44.

41. Murphy, "Vows, Boasts and Taunts," p. 111; italics Murphy's.

42. Mombritius, *Passio*, p. 77.

43. Ibid., p. 77.

44. R. Barton Palmer, "Characterization in the Old English 'Juliana'," *South Atlantic Bulletin* 41 (1976): 13, 14.

45. Geoffrey Chaucer, *Works*, ed. F. N. Robinson, 2nd ed. (Boston: Houghton Mifflin Co., 1961), p. 39.

46. Elizabeth Petroff, "Eloquence and Heroic Virginity in Hrotsvit's Verse Legends," in *Hrotsvit of Gandersheim: Rara Avis in Saxonia?*, Medieval and Renaissance Monograph Series, vol. 7 (Ann Arbor: Marc Publishing Co., 1987), p. 229.

47. John Bugge, "*Virginitas*": *An Essay in the History of a Medieval Ideal* (The Hague: Martinus Nijhoff, 1975), p. 52.

48. Ibid., pp. 54, 55.

49. See, for example, Bjork, *Old English Verse Saints' Lives*, p. 47, and Palmer, "Characterization," p. 19.

50. Olsen, *Speech*, p. 98.

51. Claude Schneider, "Cynewulf's Devaluation of Heroic Tradition in *Juliana*," *Anglo-Saxon England* 7 (1978): 111.

52. Calder, *Cynewulf*, p. 79.

53. Palmer, "Characterization," p. 13.

54. Rudolph M. Bell, *Holy Anorexia* (Chicago: University of Chicago Press, 1985), p. 13.

55. Ibid., p. 17; italics mine.

56. Ibid., p. 20.

57. Ibid., p. 29; italics Bell's.

58. Ibid., p. 41.

59. Ibid., p. 53.

60. Murphy, "Vows, Boasts and Taunts," p. 111.

The "Deconstructed"
Stereotype

JOYCE HILL

"Þæt Wæs Geomuru Ides!"

A Female Stereotype Examined

15

In her recent book on the king's wife in the early Middle Ages, Pauline Stafford observes that "women have usually stood half hidden in the wings of the historical pageant."[1] For the period with which Stafford is concerned, A.D. 500 to the mid-eleventh century, the task of rescuing royal women from this sometimes unwarranted obscurity is made particularly difficult by the nature of the surviving historical record, which means that at times the activities of the men of the royal house are almost as obscure as those of the women. Even so, women consistently fare worse. To quote Stafford once again: "When the doings of the kings were retailed, the activities of their queens were normally considered unimportant" (p. 2), and when, for some reason, they did attract the attention of clerical chroniclers and biographers, the information recorded about them was subject to the distortions of anti-feminism and a political partisanship which often tended to make them scapegoats for the king's actions. The resulting historical stereotype can hinder our perception of the nature and significance of the woman's role within the royal circle almost as much as the straightforward lack of information. But the stereotypes are not totally unyielding, as a number of sensitive historical interpretations have recently shown,[2] with the result that a more rounded picture is now emerging which gives the royal women of this period the importance that they undoubtedly deserve.

As for history, so for heroic poetry. There too women stand half-hidden in the wings of the legendary pageant. On one level the comparison can be made directly, since many legend-cycles evolve from the events of history and all present themselves as the stories of kings, princes, and noble warriors. The aristocratic milieu within which the legendary events take place is thus, in social terms, equivalent to those most fully recorded in the annals and biographies of early medieval history, and if they, in various ways and for various complex reasons, underplay or distort the significance of the female role, so too does heroic legend, for reasons which are not dissimilar. Yet the comparison between history and heroic poetry is not a straightforward one, since heroic legend-cycles are history transformed into poetry or, in some cases, mythology or folktale re-presented as heroic legend. From the time when the majority of legend cycles originated, in the fourth, fifth, and sixth centuries, to the date of their surviving written form in late Anglo-Saxon manuscripts, a given narrative was subjected to the transforming effects first of oral and then of written transmission, which filtered it through the stylizing and stereotyping processes of mnemonic patterning and the formulaic structures of Germanic verse. Thus, on one level the new insights into the role of early medieval royal women can directly advance our understanding of the role of the aristocratic women in heroic legend, but on another they must be exploited indirectly, as a model of the historical reality from which the legendary stereotypes have emerged. Both kinds of comparison will be used in this paper, in an attempt to define how far the female figures in Old English heroic poetry are given roles which are plausible in historical terms, and to assess the effect upon their presentation of the transforming power of heroic legend. In the historical record of the early Middle Ages, the stereotyped images of royal women veered between "incarnation of evil or unattainable perfection, great ascetic or materfamilias, mistress of the household or Jewish warrior, seductress or virgin, Queen of Heaven or Byzantine empress,"[3] each, of course, developed and exploited for a particular purpose which is open to historical analysis and which, in turn, leads to an understanding of the reality behind the role. In heroic poetry, as will be shown, the dominant stereotype is that of the *geomuru ides*. The discussion of how and why it evolved leads into a discussion of its central importance in articulating the tragedy of heroic life.

The historical reality that is of fundamental importance in understanding the role of royal women, both in early medieval history and in heroic legend, is the fact that "the household was not only the center of government but a model for it."[4] That being so, no lines can be drawn within the royal family dividing public from private life; kings governed by personal rule and the consequence of this for royal women is that their domestic position in the royal court put them not on one side of dynastic politics, but at the heart of it. The sources of their power were, of course, informal, depending on their importance, as childbearers, for the maintenance of the dynastic line, their capacity to influence the king and those around him, their acquisition of privileged information, and their access to wealth, but the possibilities for exploitation were formidable and never more so than when the succession was at stake. As Stafford has reminded us: "The idea that royal blood in male veins carried claims to the throne died hard, and opened throneworthiness to a wide group,"[5] and, in a situation of such relative uncertainty, the queen could play the part of king-maker by using her informal but effective power-base to support one male claimant against all the rest. There were even times, if the dynasty were strong enough, when her support might ensure the acceptance of a minor as king with the queen holding power, to a greater or lesser extent, as regent, although it was always the case that "minorities were dangerous, even intolerable, at a date when kings ruled in more than name and especially if the need for military leadership was pressing."[6] The risks presented themselves as vividly to the imagination of the heroic poet as they did to the leaders of early medieval societies.

The exercise of power, particularly if it is through informal channels, is, of course, liable to abuse, and there were queens in history who were accused not only of incest and adultery but also of malevolence and murder. The one example of the wicked queen which Old English heroic poetry gives us is the problematic Modþryðo, or Þryðo, in *Beowulf*.[7] Against this, however, and despite all the political and ecclesiastical biases of chroniclers and biographers, there emerges a strongly delineated picture of royal women exercising power in an acceptable if "domestic" manner, contributing to dynastic stability, offering counsel, and upholding the dignity and status of the king through participation in the important practices of gift-exchange which cemented the system of personal rule.

Such was the power available to the queen temperamentally suited to make use of it. But not all women in the royal house had these possibilities, at least in the early years of their life. In an age when, as Andreas Fischer has recently reminded us, marriage was a contract between two men, guardian and suitor,[8] arranged marriages between ruling families often served the needs of dynastic policy and the woman became a pawn in the political game. The arrangement was often a success— aristocratic women did not, in any case, expect a free choice of husband for reasons of love—but where it was not a success, perhaps because the alliance that the marriage was meant to stabilize broke down, the woman might face repudiation or even death. The historian's observation that "when women sealed alliances made by the sword, they became forcible reminders of defeat"[9] is equally apt for heroic poetry.

Ealhhild in *Widsið* and Wealhþeow, Hygd, and Freawaru in *Beowulf* demonstrate how closely allied to historical reality as we now understand it heroic legend can sometimes be, although we have no certain knowledge that any of them as named is derived, unlike Eormanric, for example, from an actual historical figure.[10] The advantages of re-examining them in the light of modern assessments of the role of women in early medieval society as outlined above are that we are more alert to the implications of the often allusive details which are provided, and we can see that, despite the stylization of their presentation, they have a recognizable reality which, like the recognizable reality of the material objects of heroic poetry, establishes a relationship between the temporally imprecise world of legend and the world of the Anglo-Saxon audience.

Ealhhild, Wealhþeow, and Hygd all participate in the public ceremonies of gift-exchange which are so bound up, in heroic poetry as in early medieval history, with loyalty, status, and honour. In *Widsið* the *scop*, who is as much a preserver of the king's or hero's reputation as any warrior-*þegn*, portrays himself in his imagination as receiving from Eormanric a great torque, which he later surrenders to his own lord Eadgils, who gives him in return the land which is his patrimony. But he receives also, as part of the gift-exchange pattern, another torque from Ealhhild, which by implication he keeps. Her reward is that she is praised by him as a giver of gifts:

Hyre lof lengde   geond londa fela,
þonne ic be songe   secgan sceolde
hwær ic under swegle   selast wisse
goldhrodene cwen   giefe bryttian.
(Wds 99–102)

(Her praise lingered throughout many lands when I had to tell in song where I knew the best of gold-adorned queens dispensing gifts under the sky.)

The centrality of the act to the value-system of the heroic world is confirmed by the language and nature of the poet's response: *giefe bryttian* recalls the treasure-giver formulas (*beaga brytta* 'dispenser of rings', *sinces brytta* 'dispenser of treasure') which serve as kennings for the heroic king. In referring to the reputation that she (like kings) earns by treasure-giving, the poet uses *lof,* a word rich in connotations of male heroic glory; and the poet's reward, fame in poetic legends which will spread through many lands, is identical with that for the mighty kings and heroes. A similar pattern is found in *Beowulf.* The hero, rewarded with treasure by Hroðgar, surrenders that treasure to his own lord, Hygelac, in Geatland, and receives a sword, land, and rank in return, but a formal part of the same public ceremonies is Wealhþeow's gift of a neck-torque and horses to Beowulf and his presentation of them to Hygd. We recall Stafford's observations, based on the evidence of history, that "royal women in general and queens in particular cannot be divorced from ideas of wealth and status,"[11] and we set it alongside the approving comments of the *Beowulf*-poet that although Hygd was as yet a young queen:

> næs hio hnah swa þeah,
> ne to gneað gifa   Geata leodum,
> maþmgestreona.
>
> (Bwf 1929–31)

(nevertheless she was not mean, nor too niggardly of gifts, of precious treasures, to the people of the Geats.)

Hygd is also described as *wis welþungen* 'wise and accomplished' (1927), just as Wealhþeow, at the moment when she too is first introduced, is said to be *wisfæst wordum* 'wise in words' (626). The recurrence of the detail might well suggest that wisdom is a formal element in a stylized and idealized description and so, of course, on one level it is. But we have been made more aware recently of the practicalities that it points to: the participation of royal women in the exercise of personal rule, the frequency with which their advice influenced the course of events, and the acceptability of this kind of contribution to theorists such as Sedulius Scottus who, in his *Liber de rectoribus christianis,* commented on the appropriateness of kings plucking the fruits of their wives' good counsels.[12] Wealhþeow, realistically enough, offers advice to Hroðgar about his conduct as a treasure-dispensing king, about his response to Beowulf, and about the problems of succession, alluding obliquely in the process to the risks of rival claimants when primogeniture is not the exclusive hereditary principle (Bwf 1169–87). Her support of her own sons against the possibly older Hroþulf,[13] who could thus be seen by himself and others as a more promising candidate if Hroðgar's sons were still minors when he died, finds parallels in history, but the realities of history also help us understand the response of Hygd in passing over her own son when faced with the risks of minority rule in the face of external military threat. After Hygelac's death on the Frisian raid, she is in the position of many a queen dowager of history and takes direct action in arranging the succession, offering the throne to the elder and militarily more effective Beowulf, Hygelac's nephew, in an attempt to avoid the problems inherent in the succession of a child (Bwf 2369–72). Beowulf's refusal, which in any case has no historical foundation since he is a figure drawn into the Geatish dynasty from Germanic mythology,[14] makes sense in poetic rather than political terms.

In this survey of the correspondences between the royal women of history and the royal women of heroic legend, we turn finally to Freawaru, whose fate as a political pawn is graphically described by Beowulf (2024–69). It is clear from the outset that the marriage, to establish an alliance between the hostile tribes of Danes and Heathobards, is a matter of policy only. Hroðgar

> þæt ræd talað,
> þæt he mid ðy wife wælfæhða dæl,
> sæcca gesette.
> (Bwf 2027–29)

(considers it good counsel, that he should with the woman settle a part of his deadly feuds, of his battles.)

But it is a policy which, as Beowulf's immediately following aphorism makes clear, is carried out in the light of the universal perception that such an alliance is almost certain to fail:

> Oft seldan hwær
> æfter leodhryre lytle hwile
> bongar bugeð, þeah seo bryd duge!
> (Bwf 2029–31)

(Very rarely after the fall of a prince does the deadly spear remain quiet for a little while, although the bride may be of worth!)

Some kings in history felt uneasy about marrying their daughters far from the protection of their own kingroup, but marriages for purposes of allegiance were a political reality. On the one hand they point to the importance of women in dynastic matters, but on the other they highlight their vulnerability and their inferior status as formally defined. The poetic expression of this insignificance in Freawaru's case is the absence of any comment on her own reactions and her consequent reduction in the imagination to a mere cipher; for all her importance in the arrangement of the alliance, the initiative and action in the episode rest entirely with the men.

There is, then, a fundamental historical reality in the roles that are attributed to royal women in Old English heroic poetry. It is reflected, we notice, in the details of what they do and what is done to them which, as in history, show them to be central figures in royal government. But it is reflected also, again as in the historical record, in the imbalance between the attention given to them and the attention given to the men. In the gift-exchange ceremonies involving Eormanric, Eadgils, Widsið, and Ealhhild, the exchange with Ealhhild comes after the complete cycle of male gift-giving and receiving has been detailed, although admittedly, as we have seen, careful attention is paid to it. In *Beowulf* the gift-exchange involving the two queens is again subordinate to the male exchanges, both in its position in the narrative and in the noticeably small amount of space devoted to it. Wealhþeow's comments about the future of the Danish kingdom are clear but indirect and deferential, as if there are limits to a woman's public intervention; Hygd's momentous offer of the throne to Beowulf, even including the importuning of the people as a whole and Beowulf's refusal, is covered in eight lines; and the treatment of Freawaru, as noted above, puts her firmly on the sidelines, highlighting the difference between male and female roles. Women act or are acted upon within their blood or marriage family, and whilst this domestic focus is in no way demeaning, since family, dynasty, and rule are not separable, they are undeniably limited in their sphere of activity, operating through and on behalf of the royal men, whose power is initially won and then sustained on the battlefield.

The distinctions of role which constitute the historical ideal[15] and which were usually, if not always, observed, are sharpened by the processes of transformation which change history into heroic legend. I have examined elsewhere some of the patterns of transformation which occur insofar as they affect the development of the overall narrative and the presentation of the male heroes: the shedding of minor characters, the reassignment of events, the adjustments to chronology, and the blurring of the intrigues and manipulations of the sometimes unattractive political circumstances in which the original events were played out.[16] The resulting legends, which may be seen as stylizations of history, present us with a relatively uncomplicated and to some extent idealized view of male power, in which events are clearly shown to be motivated by the decision of individual heroes responding to immediate personal pressures and the demands of their own heroic code. It is far harder to specify how women are affected by these patterns of transformation, not least because the direct historical evidence for the start of the legend, which we sometimes have and which we can use in identifying patterns and developing analogies, gives little or no information about women. In a more general way, however, the recent work on the role of royal women in early medieval history provides a basis for some suggestions about what the nature and cause of the transformations might have been. If we now recognize that royal women in history often had considerable power, but that they exercised it through informal channels within the royal household by intrigue and personal influence, it follows that in any context where the warlike activity of men is emphasized and their political maneuverings played down, women will tend to appear less effective than the historical models lead us to expect. A polarization of this kind is a likely product of the circumstantial simplifications which are part and parcel of the transformation from history into legend: the highlighting and stereotyping of an idealized male heroism has as its counterpart the highlighting and stereotyping of female helplessness.

There are many examples of the stereotype in Old English heroic poetry, but the most developed is Hildeburh, who dominates the Finnsburh Episode in *Beowulf* (1063–1159). Parallels from history and from heroic poetry suggest that she might have been married to Finn as a *freoðuwebbe,* to cement an alliance between Danes and Frisians, but the poet does not tell us; the contrast with the presentation of Freawaru is striking. Instead Hildeburh is presented from the start as a stereotype of the sorrowing woman, the victim of a situation not of her own making, in which she is the inevitable loser as the Frisians and the Danes act against each other according to the dictates of their code of honor. They are the initiators, making and breaking oaths, giving and receiving treasure, concerning themselves with the formal symbols of public power and esteem in the temporary peace, and finally being galvanized into brutally destructive activity by the shame of being thought unwarlike and disloyal. She, on the other hand, gains in imaginative stature from her still dignity in mourning. The only initiatory act attributed to her is the command to place her brother and her sons shoulder to shoulder on the funeral pyre. But even this one act contrasts with the many acts of the male warriors, for it has only a backward-looking symbolic value in emphasizing the intertribal loyalties that could have been and which are now felt in a purely personal capacity by Hildeburh alone. The powerful but ultimately futile gesture highlights the polarization of male and female roles, which is further highlighted in the final scene, when the Danes, after the bloody massacre of Finn and his men, plunder the Frisian treasurehoards and carry Hildeburh back to Denmark as the supreme victim, reduced to the status of an object, as if she were part of the booty of war.

The poet, speaking with the voice of the *scop* in Heorot, knew that in Hildeburh he was presenting and defining a stereotype and signaled this fact by the curiously approving assessment *þæt wæs geomuru ides!* 'that was a sad lady!' (Bwf 1075), just as he established Scyld Scefing as the stereotypical king by the half-line *þæt wæs god cyning!* 'that was a good king!' (Bwf 11). Both stereotypes function in similar ways to serve the larger purposes of the poem: Scyld to define the essentials of kingliness and Hildeburh to define the essentials of heroic tragedy. The polarization is again apparent: the male figure being an opportunity to present in their ideal form concepts of success in war, decisive action, integration into a comitatus, the status-enhancing values of treasure, a loyalty that transcends death, and the refounding of an illustrious dynasty; the female being a figure of inaction and isolation, a victim of the destructive forces of "heroism," and a witness to the degradation of treasure—and of human (female) life—to the level of mere plunder. There is no difficulty in identifying in Hildeburh some of the ways in which the *geomuru ides* stereotype could be exploited by a poet responsive to the tragic implications of heroic life.[17]

Later, in underlining the epic scale of the hero's death, which brings a dynasty to an end and with it the security of the whole people, mourning women are used again. One, a *mægð scyne* 'beautiful maiden', figures in the Messenger's vivid prediction of Geatish exile. No longer will she wear a torque around her neck:

> ac sceal geomormod,   golde bereafod
> oft nalles æne   elland tredan,
> nu se herewisa   hleahtor alegde,
> gamen ond gleodream.
>
> (Bwf 3018–21)

> (but she will, sad-minded, deprived of gold, often, not once only, tread the foreign land, now the army leader has laid aside laughter, joy, and convivial mirth.)

The other, perhaps an older woman,[18] at Beowulf's funeral pyre:

(song) sorgcearig,   sæde geneahhe,
þæt hio hyre (hearmda)gas   hearde (ondre)de,
wælfylla worn,   (wigen)des egesan,
hy[n]ðo (ond) h(æftny)d.

(Bwf 3152–55)

(the sorrowful one sang, said often, that she feared for herself harsh days of harm, a great number of slaughters, terror of warriors, humiliation and captivity.)

Outside *Beowulf* the stereotype is exemplified by such figures as Beadohild and Mæðhild in *Deor* and by the women of *The Wife's Lament* and *Wulf and Eadwacer*. It is true that we cannot locate the anonymous women with any confidence, if at all, in known legend-cycles[19] and that the disputed attempts to identify Mæðhild take us only as far back as seventeenth-century Scandinavian ballads.[20] It is also true that Beadohild is a figure whose story, like that of Beowulf, is not history transformed into legend, but mythology re-presented in heroic form.[21] But none of these problems of origin and identification diminish the contribution that these female figures make to the perception that the stereotype of the woman-as-victim, as *geomuru ides,* was a dominant one in Old English and that it carried considerable emotional weight, akin to that of the exile, to which it is often close in circumstance and language.

In all these cases the stereotype is presented to us directly. Admittedly Deor, with the benefit of hindsight, knows that the troubles of Beadohild and Mæðhild passed away, but this statement stands apart from each allusion, just as the anticipation of the end of sorrow was beyond the power of either woman to conceive. The vignette captures each at the moment of helpless grief and makes its impact as much because we recognize the force of the image as because we know or can guess the story that surrounds it.

Recognition of the *geomuru ides* as the dominant female stereotype in Old English heroic poetry is also a factor in our response to the other women discussed earlier and, through them, a factor in our response to the heroic world at large. Of these, Freawaru is an obvious case in point, being in a position similar to that of Hildeburh. Her grief is not articulated, as we have seen, but the effectiveness of Beowulf's account depends in part on the extra-textual perceptions relating to the *geomuru ides* stereotype that we bring to bear upon the suggestive underplaying of her presentation. The circumstances by which Freawaru comes to be in this vulnerable position are all too clear and put none of the male figures in a good light. In the case of Wealhþeow, Hygd, and Ealhhild, the circumstances leading up to their marriages are unexplained, but again we have to admit that they are thereby made vulnerable and are thus drawn into the stereotypical pattern as potential victims.

Wealhþeow, despite her evident security when Beowulf visits Denmark, is likely to have been married to Hroðgar from another tribe, if her name "foreign slave" may be taken as an indicator that she was a captive in war. But even if we are inclined not to put much weight on extrapolation of this kind, we can still be in no doubt that her present happiness is precarious, since her comments on the succession cast a shadow over the celebrations by reminding us of the dynastic struggles which so thoroughly expose the woman's vulnerability. Hygd likewise anticipates trouble when Hygelac is dead if the young Heardred should succeed, which he does, and we know that the Geatish tragedy also is eventually played out. Heardred is killed by the Swedes, and although the end is postponed by Beowulf's rule, the dynasty ends with his death, when the conquest and exile of the Geats seems assured. Precisely how Hygd fares in all this we do not know, but she cannot escape being caught up in the destruction of the tribe. Like Wealhþeow, she can attempt to stave off trouble but, unlike the men, she cannot make the grand gesture of confronting fate directly and so achieve the freedom of heroic success that can be won either through victory or a glorious death.

Ealhhild is an altogether more problematic case. The most likely interpretation of the somewhat confusing information that we are given about her is that the *Widsið*-poet knew her in legend as the wife of Eormanric,[22] but there is little doubt that she is a woman married out of her own tribe and as a *freoþuwebbe* 'peace-weaver' (Wds 6), with all the risks that this entailed, both in legend and in life. If we go further and accept her identification with Eormanric's wife as known in Old Norse, where she is called Svanhildr, we can anticipate her later cruel death at the hands of her husband, a tyrannical figure who, for all his generosity, which is admitted in *Widsið* and in medieval German texts, has a well-deserved reputation for violence.[23] In any event, the predictable expectations are aroused by lines 5–9, when the stereotypes of female peace-weaver and oath-breaking king are brought together.[24]

What draws these women towards the model of the *geomuru ides,* then, is our recognition of patterns: our knowledge of the legends themselves, which exist outside the text as well as in it and which, in specific cases, may predict the woman's final sorrow; our perception of the general patterns of heroic narrative, in which there is always the risk, if not the realization, of tragedy; and the particular awareness, conditioned by the dominant stereotype, that the noble woman is, in the end, essentially helpless.

The patterns can be recognized even in the figure of *Hildegyð in *Waldere*.[25] She encourages the hero, she articulates as well as any male figure ever does the choice of absolutes that the hero must face, and she describes with great clarity the element of imprudence which impels the hero forward to fight on the enemy's terms. Alongside her

> [.ˑ.] is se dæg cumen
> þæt ðu scealt aninga oðer twega,
> life forleosan   oððe l . . gne dom
> agan mid eldum,   Ælfheres sunu
> (Wld I, 8–11)

(the day is come that you, son of Ælfhere, must do one of two things, lose your life or earn lasting glory among men)

we can place the *Maldon*-poet's:

> hi woldon þa ealle   oðer twega,
> lif forlætan   oððe leofne gewrecan
> (Mld 207–208)

(then they all wanted one of two things, to lose their lives or avenge their beloved one)

or the absolutes offered by Sigeferð in *The Battle of Finnsburh:*

> Ðe is gyt her witod
> swæþer ðu sylf to me   secean wylle.
>
> (Fnb 26–27)

(Furthermore, it is decreed for you here which of two things you will gain from me.)

And in Hildegyð's reference to Waldere's rash bravery (I, 12–19), we are reminded of the recurring pattern of heroic legend which dictates that the heroes seek out their opponents, fight on their ground, and in various ways allow the enemy to set the terms of the encounter.[26] In sum, her speech is as comprehensive an evocation of the determinants of male heroism as one could hope to find in so short a dramatic address. And yet, she speaks *as a woman* and her encouragements therefore—and I use therefore advisedly—contain within themselves the awareness that heroic risk, so often accepted as gloriously elevating, brings with it fear of loss:

> ðy ic ðe metod ondred,
> þæt ðu to fyrenlice   feohtan sohtest
> æt ðam ætstealle   oðres monnes,
> wigrædenne.
>
> (Wld I, 19–22)

(therefore I feared for your fate, in that you sought the fight too rashly at the other man's position, according to his plan of battle.)

If the outcome of the story is close to that in the Latin *Waltharius,*[27] as seems probable, it is, for once, a story with a happy ending, so that Hildegyð is not drawn towards the stereotype to the same extent as other participatory figures are, such as Wealhþeow, Hygd, or Ealhhild. But even Hildegyð does not stand completely outside it, for we recognize and accept the ambiguities in her speech because we recognize and accept that the woman is always potentially, if not actually, the victim.

To recognize this fact, to acknowledge the force of the stereotype, is not, however, to conclude that for women the patterns of heroic poetry are necessarily reductive. The heroic code puts a premium on action and physical aggression and takes as indicators of power success in war and the acquisition of treasure, often by brutal means. But in the Old English tradition the consequences of such a code also stand revealed and it is partly through the female figures that this revelation is achieved. If the processes which transform history into legend tend to marginalize the women of the heroic world, judged from the viewpoint of "story," the sophistication of certain Anglo-Saxon poets' responses to that legendary material give women a position of ethical and imaginative importance.

NOTES

1. Pauline Stafford, *Queens, Concubines and Dowagers: The King's Wife in the Early Middle Ages* (London: Batsford, 1983), p. 1.

2. There is a full bibliography in Stafford's *Queens, Concubines and Dowagers*, pp. 216–26. In my comments on the position of royal women in early medieval history I am particularly indebted to Stafford's book and, to a lesser extent, to her article "Sons and mothers: family politics in the early middle ages," in *Medieval Women*, ed. Derek Baker, Studies in Church History, Subsidia I (Oxford: Basil Blackwell, 1978), pp. 79–100, and to the articles by Christopher N. L. Brooke, " 'Both small and great beasts': an introductory study," and Janet L. Nelson, "Queens as Jezebels: the careers of Brunhild and Balthild in Merovingian history," on pp. 1–14 and 31–78 respectively of the same collection.

3. Stafford, *Queens, Concubines and Dowagers*, p. 31.

4. Ibid., p. 28.

5. Ibid., p. 152.

6. Ibid., pp. 153–54.

7. *Beowulf* 1931–62. For a summary of the textual problems, including the difficulty of determining the woman's name, see *Beowulf, with the Finnesburg Fragment*, ed. C. L. Wrenn, rev. W. F. Bolton (London: Harrap, 1973), p. 168. For a recent study of the episode, see Constance B. Hieatt, "Modþryðo and Heremod: Intertwined Threads in the *Beowulf*-poet's Web of Words," *Journal of English and Germanic Philology* 83 (1984): 173–82. The text of *Beowulf* which is cited throughout is that of *Beowulf and the Fight at Finnsburg*, ed. Fr. Klaeber, 3rd ed. (Boston: D. C. Heath and Co., 1950). For all other Old English poems the text cited is that of *The Anglo-Saxon Poetic Records*, ed. George Philip Krapp and Elliott Van Kirk Dobbie, 6 vols. (New York: Columbia University Press, 1931–42).

8. Andreas Fischer, *Engagement, Wedding and Marriage in Old English*, Anglistische Forschungen 176 (Heidelberg: C. Winter, 1986), p. 19.

9. Stafford, *Queens, Concubines and Dowagers*, p. 44.

10. For Ealhhild, see below n. 22 and 23. As for the women of *Beowulf* I am not, of course, suggesting that the Scandinavian kings did not have wives, merely that we do not have an historical record of them as named in the poem. There is no reason why we should: our historical evidence for the origin of legend cycles concerns only those leaders and tribes who were noticed by late antique historians and the Scandinavians were not, apart from the time when Hygelac made his raid on the Frisians, which was recorded by Gregory of Tours because it involved the Franks. In any case, the interaction between Wealhþeow and Beowulf and that between Hygd and Beowulf cannot have an historical basis, even though they are presented as "history," because Beowulf himself is unhistorical.

11. Stafford, *Queens, Concubines and Dowagers*, p. 109.

12. Sedulius Scottus, *Liber de rectoribus Christianis*, ed. S. Hellmann, Quellen und Untersuchungen zur lateinischen Philologie des Mittelalters (Munich: Beck, 1906), cap. V. An English version is available as *Sedulius Scottus: "On Christian Rulers" and "The Poems,"* translated with Introduction by Edward Gerard Doyle, Medieval and Renaissance Texts and Studies 17 (Binghamton: Medieval and Renaissance Texts and Studies, 1983).

13. Hroþulf is the son of Hroðgar's younger brother Halga. A possible scenario for the struggle for the throne, which includes the supposition that Hroþulf is older than Hroðgar's sons and is favored by Hroðgar more than his own offspring, is given by R. W. Chambers, *Beowulf: An Introduction to the Study of the Poem with a Discussion of the Stories of Offa and Finn*, 3rd ed. with supplement by C. L. Wrenn (Cambridge: Cambridge University Press, 1963), pp. 13–16. For a translation of the texts relating to Hroþulf, see G. N. Garmonsway and Jacqueline Simpson, *Beowulf and its Analogues* (London: J. M. Dent and Sons, 1968), pp. 155–206.

14. For the analogues to Beowulf's adventures, see Garmonsway and Simpson, *Beowulf and its Analogues*, pp. 301–39, and for a discussion of their mythological and folktale origins, see G. V. Smithers, *The Making of "Beowulf,"* Inaugural Lecture (Durham: Durham University Press, 1961). For further extensive discussion, including the theories about Beowulf's mythological origins which are not now generally accepted, see Chambers, *Introduction*, pp. 41–97. Beowulf's genealogical incorporation into the Scandinavian royal circle is discussed by R. T. Farrell, "Beowulf Swedes and Geats," *Saga Book of the Viking Society* 18

(1972): 225–86, and by Norman E. Eliason, "Beowulf, Wiglaf and the Wægmundings," *Anglo-Saxon England* 7 (1978): 95–105.

15. In addition to the ideal presented by Sedulius Scottus (for which, see note 12 above), there is, for example, the tract *De ordine palatii,* written by Archbishop Hincmar of Rheims, whose comments on the role of royal women are summarized by Stafford, *Queens, Concubines and Dowagers,* p. 99.

16. *Old English Minor Heroic Poems,* ed. Joyce Hill, Durham and St Andrews Medieval Texts 4 (Durham and St. Andrews, 1983), pp. 6–11, with further details in the Glossary of Proper Names, pp. 78–104. A valuable, broadly based study of the patterns of heroic legend is Jan de Vries, *Heroic Song and Heroic Legend,* trans. B. J. Timmer (London: Oxford University Press, 1963).

17. For a more extensive discussion of the relationship of this "digression" and others to the poem as a whole, see Adrien Bonjour, *The Digressions in "Beowulf,"* Medium Ævum Monographs 5 (Oxford: Blackwell, 1950).

18. The manuscript is in such a poor state at this point that much depends on editorial reconstruction, although the general situation is clear enough. Klaeber's edition, from which the quoted lines are taken, reconstructs line 3150b as *(s)io g(eo)meowle* 'the old woman/ wife', although this produces a *hapax legomenon* in *geomeowle.* Wrenn's edition as revised by Bolton reconstructs the quoted passage differently, although it is still a woman mourning, and makes *Geatisc meowle* '(a) Geatish maiden/woman', out of the scanty manuscript evidence for line 3150b.

19. An attempt was made by R. Imelmann, *Forschungen zur Altenglischen Poesie* (Berlin: Weidmann, 1920), pp. 1–38, to link *The Wife's Lament, Wulf and Eadwacer, The Husband's Message, The Wanderer,* and *The Seafarer* in an Odoacer legend. More recently A. C. Bouman, *Patterns in Old English and Old Icelandic Literature* (Leyden: Universitaire Pers, 1962), pp. 41–91, has proposed a connection between *The Wife's Lament* and the Sigurðr cycle. But such solutions to the enigmas of the "plot" are unsatisfactory and have met with little acceptance. Indeed, for *The Wife's Lament* arguments have been put forward that the speaker is the Church expressing her separation from and longing for Christ, the Synagogue, or a displaced pagan god, and even that the speaker is in fact a man. For one example of each approach, see respectively: M. J. Swanton, *"The Wife's Lament* and *The Husband's Message:* A Reconsideration," *Anglia* 82 (1964): 269–90; R. E. Kaske, "A Poem of the Cross in the Exeter Book: *Riddle 60* and *The Husband's Message,"* *Traditio* 23 (1967): 47–71 (p. 71); A. N. Doane, "Heathen Form and Christian Function in *The Wife's Lament,"* *Mediaeval Studies* 28 (1966): 77–91; Rudolph C. Bambas, "Another View of the Old English *Wife's Lament,"* *Journal of English and Germanic Philology* 62 (1963): 303–309. In the case of *Wulf and Eadwacer* a detailed argument has recently been put forward for returning to the idea that it is a poem about wolves: Peter Orton, "An Approach to *Wulf and Eadwacer,"* *Proceedings of the Irish Royal Academy* 85(C) (1985): 223–58. By far the most widely accepted reading of each, however, is that the speaker is a sorrowing woman, victimized by male-dominated social circumstances.

20. For the identification of Mæðhild, see *Deor,* ed. Kemp Malone (London: Methuen and Co., Ltd., 1933; 4th rev. ed., Exeter: University of Exeter, 1977), pp. 8–9. The serious difficulties with Malone's identification are pointed out by F. Norman, *"Deor:* A Criticism and an Interpretation," *Modern Language Review* 32 (1937): 374–81.

21. Beadohild, as daughter of Niðhad, is raped by the mythological smith, Welund, as part of his revenge against Niðhad. In the Eddic poem *Vǫlundarkviða,* the smith is already married to someone else, but in *Þiðreks saga* there is a happier ending: she marries Velent (Welund) and their son Viðga (the Wudga of *Widsið* 124, 130, and the Widia of *Waldere* II, 4, 9) is drawn into the legend cycles that grew up around Þeodric and Eormanric. For a summary, see my *Old English Minor Heroic Poems,* pp. 79, 95, 101–104, under the names Beadohild, Niðhad, Wada, Welund, Wudga.

22. For a summary of the problem, see my *Old English Minor Heroic Poems,* pp. 81–82.

23. The development of the Eormanric cycle is examined in detail by Caroline Brady, *The Legends of Ermanaric* (Berkeley: University of California Press, 1943). The traditions about Eormanric's wife and the possibility of identifying her with Ealhhild are discussed in *Widsith: A Study in Old English Heroic Legend,* ed. R. W. Chambers (Cambridge: Cambridge University Press, 1912), pp. 15–28.

24. *Fælre freoþuwebban* is used of Ealhhild in line 6 and *wraþes wærlogan* of Eormanric in line 9. In *Widsith,* ed. Malone, Anglistica 13 (Copenhagen: Rosenkilde and Bagger, 1962), pp. 29–35, the editor argues strongly for "hostile to treaty-breakers" as the interpretation of *wraþes wærlogan,* but this is a forced interpretation inspired by Malone's wish to rectify what he sees as being an otherwise inconsistent portrait. The effort is unwarranted, however, since the presentation of Eormanric in *Widsið* as both treacherous and generous is paralleled elsewhere. See my *Old English Minor Heroic Poems,* pp. 83–84.

25. The convention among critics is to assign the first speech in the *Waldere* fragment to Hildegyð although her name does not appear in the manuscript.

26. Beowulf goes *to* Denmark, *into* Grendel's mere, and *to* the dragon's lair. His initial proof of his heroic stature also observes this pattern since he fights the sea-monsters in the water, and it is very effectively exploited in lines 677–87, when Beowulf refuses to use a sword against Grendel. That this encounter is a wrestling match is integral to the given (mythological) plot, but in the Old English poem the hero had to be presented as conventionally armed. The common "pattern of imprudence" is used to explain, in heroic terms, how the hero comes to be in the position of fighting hand to hand. The same "pattern of imprudence" may be what justifies Byrhtnoð's heroic stature in *The Battle of Maldon.* For further discussion of this aspect of heroism, see N. F. Blake, "The Genesis of *The Battle of Maldon,*" *Anglo-Saxon England* 7 (1978): 119–29, and T. A. Shippey, "Boar and Badger: An Old English Heroic Antithesis?" *Leeds Studies in English* n.s. 16 (1985): 220–39. *Waldere* I, 12–19, presents some problems of interpretation, although the general sense is unmistakable. For a detailed discussion, see my *Old English Minor Heroic Poems,* pp. 44–45, and the further comment by Shippey.

27. Summarized in my *Old English Minor Heroic Poems,* pp. 20–23. For the whole text in translation, see H. M. Smyser and F. P. Magoun, Jr., *Survivals in Old Norwegian of Medieval English, French and German Literature, together with the Latin versions of the heroic legend of Walter of Acquitaine,* Connecticut College Monograph, vol. 1 (Baltimore: Waverly Press, Inc., 1941).

The Structural Unity
of *Beowulf*
The Problem of Grendel's Mother

16

The episode in *Beowulf* involving Grendel's Mother has been viewed as largely extraneous, a blot upon the thematic and structural unity of the poem. If the poem is regarded as two-part in structure, balancing contrasts between the hero's youth and old age, his rise as a retainer and his fall as a king, his battles with the Grendel family and his battle with the dragon, then her episode (which includes Hrothgar's sermon and Hygelac's welcoming court celebration with its recapitulation of earlier events) lengthens the first "half" focusing on his youth to two-thirds of the poem (lines 1–2199).[1] If the poem is regarded as three-part in structure, with each part centering on one of the three monsters or the three fights, then the brevity of her episode again mars the structural balance: her section, roughly 500 lines (1251–1784), is not as long as Grendel's, roughly 1100–1200 lines (86–1250), or the dragon's, 1000 lines (2200–3182).[2] Even if her episode is lengthened to a thousand lines (from line 1251 to 2199) so as to include Hrothgar's sermon and Hygelac's court celebration, still Grendel's Mother hardly dominates these events literally or symbolically as Grendel and the dragon dominate the events in their sections.

But her battle with Beowulf (and this middle section of the poem) is more than merely a "transition between two great crises," even though it is "linked with both the Grendel fight and the Dragon fight."[3] The key to her significance[4] may indeed derive from her links with the other two monsters in a way Bonjour did not envision when he made these statements.

Grendel and the dragon have been interpreted recently as monstrous projections of flaws in Germanic civilization portrayed by the poet as "Negative Men."[5] Grendel is introduced as a mock "hall-retainer" (*renweard*, 770; *healðegn*, 142) who envies the men of Heorot their joy of community; he subsequently attacks the hall in a raid that is described through the parodic hall ceremonies of feasting, ale-drinking, gift-receiving, and singing.[6] The dragon is introduced as a mock "gold-king" or *hord-*

weard (2293, 2303, 2554, 2593) who avariciously guards his barrow or "ring-hall" (*hringsele*, 3053),[7] and attacks Beowulf's kingdom after he discovers the loss of a single cup. The envy of the evil hall-retainer and the avarice of the evil gold-king antithesize the Germanic *comitatus* ideal first enunciated in Tacitus' *Germania* and pervading heroic and elegiac Anglo-Saxon literature: the *comitatus'* well-being depended upon the retainer's valor in battle and loyalty to his lord and the lord's protection and treasure-giving in return.[8]

Like these monsters, Grendel's Mother is also described in human and social terms. She is specifically called a *wīf unhȳre* 'a monstrous woman' (2120), and an *ides āglǣcwīf* 'a lady monster-woman' (1259). *Ides* elsewhere in *Beowulf* denotes "lady" and connotes either a queen or a woman of high social rank; outside *Beowulf*, primarily in Latin and Old English glosses, *ides* pairs with *virgo* to suggest maidenhood, as when *on idesan* equals *in virgunculam*.[9] In addition, as if the poet wished to stress her maternal role, she is characterized usually as Grendel's *mōdor* or kinswoman (*māge*, 1391), the former a word almost exclusively reserved for her, although other mothers appear in the poem.[10] It seems clear from these epithets that Grendel's Mother inverts the Germanic roles of the mother and queen, or lady. She has the form of a woman (*idese onlīcnes*, 1351) and is weaker than a man (1282ff) and more cowardly, for she flees in fear for her life when discovered in Heorot (1292–93). But unlike most mothers and queens, she fights her own battles. *Maxims* I testifies that, "Battle, war, must develop in the man, and the woman must flourish beloved among her people, must be light-hearted."[11]

Because the poet wishes to stress this specific inversion of the Anglo-Saxon ideal of woman as both monstrous and masculine he labels her domain a "battle-hall" (*nīðsele*, 1513; *gūðsele*, 2139).[12] (The dragon's barrow he describes equally appropriately, given the monster's avaricious symbolic nature, as a "ring-hall," as we saw previously.) In addition, he occasionally uses a masculine pronoun in referring to her (*sē þe* instead of *sēo þe* in 1260, 1497; *hē* instead of *hēo* in 1392, 1394). Such a change in pronoun occurs elsewhere in the poem only in reference to abstract feminine nouns used as personifications and to concrete feminine nouns used as synecdoches.[13] Other epithets applied to her are usually applied to male figures: warrior, *sinnige secg*, in 1379; destroyer, *mihtig mānscaða*, in 1339; and [male] guardian, *gryrelīcne grundhyrde*, in 2136. Indeed, in the phrase *ides āglǣcwīf* applied to Grendel's Mother as a "lady monster-woman" the *āglǣca* not only means "monster," as it does when directed at Grendel (159, 425, 433, 556, 592, 646, 732, 739, 816, 989, 1000, 1269) or the water monsters (1512), but also "fierce combatant" or "strong adversary," as when directed at Sigemund in line 893 and Beowulf and the dragon in line 2592.[14] Such a woman might be wretched or monstrous because she insists on arrogating the masculine role of the warrior or lord.

Her episode is thus appropriately divided like her monstrous but human nature and her female but male behavior into two parts to illustrate the various feminine roles—of the mother or kinswoman (*mōdor*) and queen or lady (*ides āglǣcwīf*)—she inverts. The poet constantly contrasts the unnatural behavior of Grendel's dam with that of the feminine ideal by presenting human examples as foils in each of the two parts. We turn first to an examination of the female ideal in *Beowulf,* then to a detailed analysis of the episode involving Grendel's Mother and its two parts, and finally to some conclusions regarding the structural unity of the entire poem.

I

The role of woman in *Beowulf* primarily depends upon "peace-making," either biologically through her marital ties with foreign kings as a peace-pledge or mother of sons, or socially and psychologically as a cup-passing and peace-weaving queen within a hall. Wealhtheow becomes a peace-pledge or *friðusibb folca* (2017) to unite the Danes and Helmings; Hildeburh similarly unites the Danes and Frisians through her marriage; and Freawaru at least intends to pledge peace between the Danes and Heathobards. Such a role is predicated upon the woman's ability to bear children, to create blood ties, bonds to weave a "peace kinship."

In addition, woman functions domestically within the nation as a cup-passer during hall festivities of peace (*freoþo*) and joy (*drēam*) after battle or contest. The mead-sharing ritual and the cup-passer herself come to symbolize peace-weaving and peace because they strengthen the societal and familial bonds between lord and retainers. First, the literal action of the *freoðuwebbe* 'peace-weaver' (1942) as she passes the cup from warrior to warrior weaves an invisible web of peace: the order in which each man is served, according to his social position, reveals each man's dependence upon and responsibility toward another. For example, after Wealhtheow gives the cup to Hrothgar, she bids him to be joyful at drinking as well as loving to his people (615ff). Then she offers it to the *duguð* 'old retainers', then to the *geoguð* 'young retainers', and finally to the guest Beowulf. Second, her peace-weaving also takes a verbal form: her speeches accompanying the mead-sharing stress the peace and joy contingent upon the fulfillment of each man's duty to his nation. At the joyous celebration after Grendel's defeat, Wealhtheow concludes her speeches with a tribute to the harmony of the present moment by reminding her tribe of its cause, that is, adherence to the *comitatus* ethic. Each man remains true to the other, each is loyal to the king, the nation is ready and alert, the drinking warriors attend to the ale-dispenser herself (1228–31). Yet minutes before she attempted to forestall future danger to her family and nation by preventive peace-weaving, she advised Hrothgar to leave his kingdom to his sons, and then, as if sensing the future, she reminded Hrothulf, his nephew, of his obligations to those sons (obligations he will later deny). Third, the peace-weaver herself emblematizes peace, for she appears in the poem with her mead-vessel only after a contest has been concluded. Thus Wealhtheow enters the hall only after the contest between Unferth and Beowulf (612); she does not appear again until after Beowulf has overcome Grendel, when the more elaborate feasting invites the peace-making speeches mentioned above. After Grendel's Mother is defeated the poet preserves the integrity of the pattern of feminine cup-passing after masculine contest by describing the homecoming banquet at Hygelac's court, where Hygd conveys the mead-vessel. This structural pattern to which we shall return simultaneously weaves together the Danish part of the poem with its Geatish part.

Most of the other female characters figure as well in this middle section so that the female monster's adventures are framed by descriptions of other women for ironic contrast. The role of mother highlights the first half of the middle section with the scop's mention of Hildeburh (1071ff) and the entrance of Wealhtheow, both of whom preface the first appearance of Grendel's dam (1258) in her role as avenging mother. Then the introduction of Hygd, Thryth, and Freawaru after the female monster's death (1590) stresses the role of queen as peace-weaver and cup-passer to preface Beowulf's final narration of the female monster's downfall (2143). The actual adventures of Grendel's Mother cluster then at the middle of the middle section of the poem.

11

In the first part of the female monster's section, the idea is stressed that a kinswoman or mother must passively accept and not actively avenge the loss of her son. The story of the mother Hildeburh is recited by the scop early on the evening Grendel's Mother will visit Heorot. The lay ends at line 1159; Grendel's Mother enters the poem a mere hundred lines later when she attacks the Danish hall, as the Frisian contingent attacked the hall lodging Hildeburh's Danish brother in the *Finns-burh Fragment*. The *Beowulf* poet alters the focus of the fragment: he stresses the consequences of the surprise attack rather than the attack itself in order to reveal Hildeburh's maternal reactions to them.

Hildeburh is unjustly (*unsynnum*, 1072) deprived of her Danish brother and Frisian son, but all she does, this sad woman (*geōmuru ides*, 1075), is to mourn her loss with dirges and stoically place her son on the pyre. In fact, she can do nothing, caught in the very web she has woven as peace-pledge: her husband's men have killed her brother, her brother's men have killed her son. Later the Danish Hengest will avenge the feud with her husband Finn, whether she approves or not, by overwhelming the Frisians and returning Hildeburh to her original tribe. The point remains: the peace-pledge must accept a passive role precisely because the ties she knots bind *her*—she *is* the knot, the pledge of peace. Her fate interlaces with that of her husband and brothers through her role as a mother bearing a son: thus Hildeburh appropriately mourns the loss of her symbolic tie at the pyre, the failure of herself as peace-pledge, the loss of her identity. Like Hildeburh Grendel's dam will also lose her identity as mother, never having had an identity as peace-pledge to lose.

As if reminded of her own role as mother by hearing of Hildeburh's plight, Wealhtheow demonstrates her maternal concern in an address to Hrothgar immediately after the scop sings this lay. In it she first alludes to Hrothgar's adoption of Beowulf as a son: apparently troubled by this, she insists that Hrothgar leave his kingdom only to his actual kinsmen or descendants when he dies (1178–79). Then she urges her foster "son" Hrothulf (actually a nephew) to remember his obligations to them so that he will "repay our sons with liberality" (1184–85). Finally, she moves to the mead-bench where the adopted Beowulf sits, rather symbolically, next to her sons Hrethric and Hrothmund (1188–91). The *past* helplessness of the first mother, Hildeburh, to requite the death of her son counterpoints the anxiously maternal Wealhtheow's attempts to weave the ties of kinship and obligation, thereby forestalling *future* danger to her sons. Later that night, Grendel's Mother intent on avenging the loss of her son in the *present* attacks Heorot, her masculine aggression contrasting with the feminine passivity of both Hildeburh and Wealhtheow. Indeed, she resembles a grieving human mother: like Hildeburh she is guiltless and *galgmōd* 'gloomy-minded' (1277); her journey to Heorot must be sorrowful (1278) for she "remembered her misery" (1259). But a woman's primary loyalty as peace-pledge was reserved for her husband, not her son, according to the Danish history of Saxo Grammaticus.[15] Perhaps for this reason Grendel's Mother is presented as husbandless and son-obsessed—to suggest to an Anglo-Saxon audience the dangers inherent in woman's function as *friðusibb* 'pledge of peace'.

However, her attempts to avenge her son's death could be justified if she were human and male, for no *wergild* 'man price' has been offered to her by the homicide Beowulf.[16] The role of the masculine avenger is emphasized throughout the passage (1255–78) in defining her motivation to attack: she performs the role of avenger (*wrecend*, 1256) "to avenge the death of her son" (1278). Whatever her maternal feelings, she actually fulfills the duty of the kinsman. Unlike Hildeburh, she cannot wait for a Hengest to resolve the feud in some way; unlike Freawaru, she cannot act as a peace-pledge to settle the feud. Tribeless, now kinless, forced to rely on her own might, she seizes and kills Aeschere, Hrothgar's most beloved retainer, in an appropriate retribution for the loss of her own most beloved "retainer" and "lord"—her son.

The monstrosity of her action is at first not evident. Hrothgar suspects she has carried the "feud" too far (1339–40). And from the Danish and human point of view she possesses no legal right to exact compensation for her kinsman's loss because Grendel is himself a homicide. However, Beowulf later implies that the two feuds must remain separate, as she desires her own "revenge for injury" (*gyrnwræcu*, 2118). Because she is legally justified in pursuing her own feud given the tribal duty of the retainer to avenge the death of his lord, regardless of the acts he has committed, she behaves monstrously then in only one way. For a mother to "avenge" her son (2121) as if she were a retainer, he were her lord, and avenging more important than peace-making, is monstrous. An analogy conveying her effect on the men in Heorot when she first appears suggests how unusual are her actions in human terms. Her horror 'is as much less as is the skill (strength) of maidens, the war-horror of a woman, in comparison to a (weaponed) man, when the bound sword shears the one standing opposite' (*Wæs se gryre læssa / efne swā micle, swa bið mægþa cræft, / wīggryre wīfes be wæpnedmen, / þonne heoru bunden . . . / . . . / . . . andweard scireð*, 1282–87). In their eyes recognizably female, she threatens them physically less than her son. But because female "peacemakers" do not wage war, the analogy implies, by litotes, that her unnatural behavior seems *more* horrible.

In the second part of her adventure she no longer behaves solely as an avenging monster, antitype of Hildeburh and Wealhtheow, who are both through marriage "visitors" to a hall like Grendel and his dam. Such hall-visitors contrast with the hall-rulers of this second part: the *merewīf* as queen or guardian (*grundhyrde*, 2136) protects her "battle-hall," the cave-like lair, from the visiting hero like the regal dragon guarding his ring-hall, and like King Beowulf his kingdom, in the last section of the poem. Accordingly, the stress on the relationship between mother and son delineated in the first part of her adventure changes to a stress on the relationship between host and guest.

As a tribeless queen or lady (*ides āglǣcwīf*) she rudely receives her "hall-guest" Beowulf (*selegyst*, 1545; *gist*, 1522) by "embracing" him and then "repaying him" for his valor not with treasure but with "grim grips" (*Hēo him eft hraþe andlean forgeald / grimman grāpum*, 1541–42) just as the dragon will "entertain" him in the future.[17] Indeed, the parody of the hall-ceremony of treasure-giving is complete when a "scop" (Beowulf's sword, acting as bard) sings a fierce "war song" off the side of her head (*hire on hafelan hringmǣl āgōl / grǣdig gūðlēoð*, 1521–22). It is interesting to note that this "hall-celebration" of the mock peace-weaver to welcome her valorous guest Beowulf following her attack on Heorot and her curiously listless "contest" with Aeschere duplicates the pattern of mead-sharing ceremonies involving peacemakers which follow masculine contests throughout the poem.

It is also interesting to note that the contest between this apparently lordless "queen" and her "guest" contrasts in its mock-sensual embracing and grasping with the other two major battles of the hero—the briefly described arm-wrestling between Grendel and Beowulf and the conventional sword-wielding of Beowulf against the fire-breathing dragon. Indeed, before Beowulf arrives at the "battle-hall" Hrothgar introduces the possibility of a Grendel's father in addition to the mother, even though they do not know of such a father (1355), and of possible additional progeny of such a father or even of Grendel himself (through an incestuous union with his mother?): *hwæþer him ǣnig wæs ǣr ācenned / dyrnra gāsta* (1356–57). His ostensible point is to warn Beowulf of additional monsters lurking nearby, but it serves as well to remind the reader that Grendel's Mother has an animal nature very different from that of a human lady. For during the passage describing their battle the poet exploits the basic resemblance between sexual intercourse and battle to emphasize the inversion of the feminine role of the queen or hall-ruler by Grendel's Mother. This is achieved in three steps: first, the emphasis upon clutching, grasping, and embracing while they fight; second, the contest for a dominant position astride the other; and third, the use of fingers, knife, or sword to penetrate clothing or the body, the latter always accompanied by the implied figurative kinship between the sword and the phallus and between decapitation and castration.

First, she welcomes him to the *mere* with an almost fatal embrace similar to the "embrace" (*fæðm*, 2128) to which Aeschere has succumbed. She "grasped then towards him" (1501), seizing him with "horrible grips" (1502–03) envisioned earlier by the hero as a "battle-grip" (1445) and a "malicious grasp" (1447). Second, inside the 'castle' (*hof*, 1507) where she has transported him, both grapple for a superior position over the other. After his sword fails him, for example, he "grasped her by the shoulder," hurling her to the ground. The poet, conscious of the monster's sex and Beowulf's definitely unchivalrous behavior, drily protests that in this case "the lord of the Battle-Geats did not at all lament the hostile act" (1537–38). Then, as "reward" for his valor, this lady "repaid" him with the treasure of her *grimman grāpum* 'fierce graspings', forcing him to stumble and fall (1541–44), after which she climbs, rather ludicrously, on top of her 'hall-guest' (*selegyst*, 1545), intent on stabbing him and thereby (again) avenging her only offspring (1546–47). Third, the battle culminates in very suggestive swordplay, and wordplay too. Earlier her "hostile fingers" (1505) tried to 'penetrate' (*ðurhfōn*, 1504) his locked coat-of-mail; now she tries unsuccessfully to pierce the woven breast-net with her knife. Previously Beowulf discovered his own weapon was impotent against the spell or charm of the "sword-greedy" woman (*heorogīfre*, 1498), who collects the swords of giants. Now the "sword-grim" hero substitutes one of these swords, an appropriate tool to quell such a woman. The "sword entirely penetrated (*ðurhwōd*) the doomed-to-die body" (1567–68). After this final "embrace" of the "grasping" of her neck, the sword *wæs swātig secg weorce gefeh* 'was bloody, the warrior rejoiced in the work' (1569). The alliteration links *sweord* with *secg,* to identify the bloody sword with the rejoicing, laboring 'man-sword' (*secg*); the "battle" appropriately evokes erotic undertones. The equation of the sword and warrior, with the subsequent sexual connotations, resembles the synedoche controlling Riddle Twenty, "The Sword," in which the sword becomes a retainer who serves his lord through celibacy, foregoing the "joy-game" of marriage and the "treasure" of children, and whose only unpleasant battle occurs with a woman, because he must overcome her desire while she voices her terror, claps her hands, rebukes him with words, and cries out *ungod* 'not good'.[18] Similarly in *Beowulf* once the sword finally penetrates the body its blade miraculously melts—like ice into water—either from the poison of Grendel's blood or of his mother's, the poem does not specify which (1601). And even the *mere* itself, approached through winding passageways, slopes, and paths, and in whose stirred-up and bloody waters sea monsters lurk and the strange battle-hall remains hidden, almost projects the mystery and danger of female sexuality run rampant.

Such erotic overtones in descriptions of battles between a male and a female adversary are not especially common in Anglo-Saxon literature but can be found in various saints' lives in the Old English *Martyrology* (ca. 850) and in Ælfric's *Lives of the Saints* (ca. 994–early eleventh century), and in another epic poem also contained in the same manuscript as *Beowulf, Judith.* In the saints' lives a large group of thirty-four portrays a physical conflict between a Christian woman and a pagan man wishing to seduce her physically or spiritually. The description of the torture the saint undergoes to preserve her chastity often veils with obvious sexual symbolism the act of intercourse, or else it lovingly lingers over the description of the virgin's rape (see, for example, the life of St. Lucia).[19] The reason for such descriptions should be clear to those acquainted with the *Canticum Canticorum* and its celebration of the love of the Sponsa for the Sponsus (of man's soul for God, of the Church for Christ), providing an analogous basis for the holy sacrament of marriage. The woman saint as a type of the soul longs to be joined, as in intercourse, with her spouse Christ; the threat of seduction by a human male must be read as an assault on the soul by the Devil.

In *Judith,* a work like *Beowulf* contained in MS Cotton Vitellius A.xv,[20] the fragmentary epic portrays similar sexual overtones in Judith's "battle" with Holofernes. As in *Beowulf* a warrior battles a monster: the blessed maiden grapples with the "drunken, vicious monster" (*se inwidda* 'the evil one', 28) Holofernes. However, the sexual role behaviour of *Beowulf* occurs in reverse in *Judith:* Holofernes parallels Grendel's dam, but whereas the *wīf* is aggressive and sword-greedy, Holofernes seems slightly effete (his bed enclosed by gold curtains, for example) and impotent from mead-drinking: "The lord fell, the powerful one so drunken, in the middle of his bed, as if he knew no reason in his mind" (67–69). These hypermetrical lines heighten the irony of his situation, for the warrior swoons on the very bed upon which he intended to rape the maiden. Having lost his head to drink in a double sense he himself is penetrated by the virgin's sharp sword, "hard in the storm of battle" (79), thereafter literally losing his head. But first Judith draws the sword from its sheath in her right hand, seizes him by the hair in a mock loving gesture (98–99), then 'with her hands pulls him toward her *shamefully*' (*teah hyne folmum wið hyre weard / bysmerlice*, 99b–100a). The "b" alliteration in line 100 (*bysmerlice, ond þone bealofullan*) draws attention to *bysmerlice*, which as a verb (*bysmrian*) elsewhere suggests the act of "defiling" (intercourse).[21] In this line what seems shameful is apparently her embrace of the warrior's body while she moves it to a supine position. As in *Beowulf*, the female assumes the superior position; she lays him down so that she may 'control' (*gewealdan*, 103) him more easily in cutting off his head. The ironic embrace and mock intercourse of this couple parallels that of Beowulf and the *ides āglǣcwīf:* the aggressive and sword-bearing "virgin" contrasts with the passive and swordless man (Holofernes, Aeschere, and even Beowulf are all momentarily or permanently swordless). The poet's point in each case is that a perversion of the sexual roles signals an equally perverse spiritual state. Holofernes' impotence is as unnatural in the male as the *wīf*'s aggression is unnatural in the female; so the battle with the heroine or hero in each case is described with erotic overtones to suggest the triumph of a right and natural sexual (and social and spiritual) order over the perverse and unnatural one. In the latter case Grendel's dam and her son pose a heathen threat to Germanic society (the macrocosm) and to the individual (Beowulf the microcosm) as Holofernes and the Assyrians pose a heathen threat to Israelite society (the macrocosm) and to the individual (Judith the microcosm).[22]

In this second part of her adventure, Hygd and Freawaru contrast with the *wīf* as queen or cup-passer as Hildeburh and Wealhtheow contrasted with Grendel's dam as mother in the first. Hygd, the first woman encountered after the defeat of Grendel's Mother, as truly fulfills the feminine ideal of *Maxims* I as does Wealhtheow. Her name, which means "Thought" or "Deliberation," contrasts her nature with that of the bellicose *wīf* and possibly that of the war-like Thryth, whose actions, if not her name, suggest "Strength" (only in the physical sense; the alternate form of her name, "Modthrytho" or "Mind-Force," implies in a more spiritual sense stubbornness or pride).[23] Although Hygd like the *wīf* and Thryth will be lordless after Hygelac's death, she does not desire to usurp the role of king for herself: doubting her son's ability to prevent tribal wars she offers the throne to Beowulf (2369ff). In addition, this gracious queen bestows treasure generously (1929–31), unlike the *wīf* and Thryth, the latter of whom dispense only "grim grips" and sword blows upon their "retainers."

The Thryth digression is inserted after Hygd enters to pass the cup upon Beowulf's return to Hygelac. Its structural position invites a comparison of this stubborn princess and the other two "queens," Hygd and the *wīf*. She appears to combine features of both: she begins as a type of the female monster, but upon marriage to Offa changes her nature and becomes a much-loved queen. According to the poet, Thryth commits a "terrible crime"; she condemns to death any retainer at court caught staring at her regal beauty. That she abrogates her responsibilities as a queen and as a woman the poet makes clear: 'Such a custom—that the peace-weaver after a pre-tended injury deprive the dear man of life—is not queenly for a woman to do, although she be beautiful' (*Ne bið swylc cwēnlīc þēaw / idese tō efnanne,   þēah ðe hīo ænlicu sȳ, / þætte freoðuwebbe   fēores onsǣce / æfter ligetorne lēofne mannan*, 1940b–43). The label 'peace-weaver' (*freoðuwebbe*) seems ironic in this context, es-pecially as she does not weave but instead severs the ties of kinship binding her to her people and the bonds of life tying the accused man to this world. That is, for any man caught looking at her 'the deadly bonds, hand-woven, were in store; after his arrest it was quickly determined that the sword, the damascened sword, must shear, make known death-bale' (*ac him wælbende   weotode tealde / handgewriþene;   hraþe seopðan wæs / æfter mundgripe   mēce geþinged, / þæt hit sceādenmǣl   scȳran mōste / cwealmbealu cȳðan*, 1936–40a). If she weaves at all then she weaves only "deadly hand-woven bonds" binding him to a grisly end. The "peace-weaver" cuts these bonds—imprisoning ropes—with a sword, simultaneously shearing the bonds of life to "make known death-bale." She resembles that other ironic peace-weaver, the *wīf*, who tried to penetrate the braided breast-net of Beowulf with her knife.

Both antitypes of the peace-weaving queen behave like kings, using the sword to rid their halls of intruders or unwanted "hall-guests." Unlike Thryth, the mon-strous *wīf* remains husbandless, having lost her son, "wife" only to the *mere* she inhabits both in life and in death. At this moment in the poem, both Thryth and Grendel's Mother belong to the past. If they represent *previous* inversions of the peace-weaver and cup-passer, and Hygd who is now passing the mead-cup to Beowulf's weary men in celebration signifies a *present* cup-passer, so the poet introduces a final queen, this time a cup-passer of the *future*, who will fail in her role as the first woman, Hildeburh, failed in hers.

Freawaru, like Hildeburh, seems innocent of any crime. She is envisioned by Beowulf as a queen married to Ingeld of the Heathobards in a digression (2032–69) immediately preceding his summary of the battles with Grendel and with his mother. She will fail in her role as peace-weaver because of an underlying hostility—an old Heathobard warrior's bitterness over ancient Heathobard treasure acquired through previous wars and worn by a young Danish man accompanying the new queen. The fragility of this role is heightened even further when, in the third section involving the dragon, Beowulf inhabits a queenless kingdom and when Wiglaf must become the cup-passer, pouring water from the "cup" of Beowulf's helmet in a futile attempt to revive his wounded lord.

Indeed, three women characters appear outside this middle section to convey dialectically the idea that woman cannot ensure peace in this world. First, Wealh-theow, unlike other female figures, appears in the first (or Grendel) section of the poem to pour mead after Grendel's challenge has been answered by the hero. This first entrance symbolizes the ideal role of Germanic woman as a personification of peace, as we have seen. In antithesis, Beowulf's account of the fall of the *wīf unhȳre* 'monstrous woman' appropriately ends the poem's second (Grendel's Mother) section which has centered on this role: the personification of discord, the antitype of the feminine ideal, has been destroyed. But in the poem's third section a synthesis emerges. The nameless and unidentified Geat woman who appears, like the other female characters, after a battle—this one between Beowulf and the dragon— mourns at the pyre. That is, the efforts of the peacemaker, while valuable in worldly and social terms, ultimately must fail because of the nature of this world. True peace exists not in woman's but in God's 'embrace' (*fæþm*, 188).

III

This idea is implied in Hrothgar's sermon (1700–84); like the court celebration of Hygelac, it is a part of the middle section belonging to Grendel's Mother but apparently unrelated to it. In it Hrothgar describes three Christian vices in distinctly Germanic terms. Impelled by envy like Grendel, Heremod kills his "table-companions" (1713–14). Next, the wealthy hall-ruler in his pride is attacked by the Adversary while his guardian conscience sleeps within the hall of his soul (1740–44). So the monster that specifically epitomizes pride in *Beowulf*, as in Genesis, is female—Grendel's Mother—thematically related to Thryth or Modthrytho, whose name (if it can be said to exist in manuscript in that form) means "pride." Grendel's Mother substitutes war-making for the peace-weaving of the queen out of a kind of selfish pride—if she were capable of recognizing it as such. Finally, this same hall-ruler 'covets angry-minded' (*gȳtsað gromhȳdig*, 1749) the ornamented treasures God had previously given him by refusing to dispense any to his warriors. So the mock gold-king dragon avariciously guards his treasure. Although the poet portrays the monsters as antitypes of Germanic ideals, his integument conceals a Christian idea. The city of man, whether located in a Germanic or Christian society, is always threatened by sin and failure.

Such sin alienates Christian man from self, neighbor, and God; it alienates Germanic man primarily from other men. Note that although in *Beowulf* each of the three monsters is described as guarding or possessing a hall, whether Heorot, a watery cavern, or a barrow, each remains isolated from humanity (and from each other—Grendel and his mother live together, but they never appear together in the poem until he is dead). Ideally when the retainer, the queen, and the gold-lord cooperate they constitute a viable nucleus of Germanic society: a retainer must have a gold-lord from whom to receive gold for his loyalty in battle; the peace-weaver must have a "loom"—the band of retainers and their lord, or two nations—upon which to weave peace.

Despite the poet's realization that these roles cannot be fulfilled in this world, this Germanic ideal provides structural and thematic unity for *Beowulf*. Grendel's Mother does occupy a transitional position in the poem: as a "retainer" attacking Heorot she resembles Grendel, but as an "attacked ruler" of her own "hall" she resembles the dragon. As a monstrous mother and queen she perverts a role more important socially and symbolically than that of Grendel, just as the queen as peace-pledge or peace-weaver ultimately becomes more valuable than the retainer but less valuable than the gold-giver himself.

If it seems ironic that a Germanic ideal that cannot exist in this world *can* exist in art, unifying the theme and structure of the poem, then Grendel's Mother, warring antitype of harmony and peace, must seem doubly ironic. The structural position of her episode in the poem, like woman's position as cup-passer among members of a nation, or as a peace-pledge between two nations, is similarly medial and transitional, but successfully so.

NOTES

1. This view of the structure as two-part has generally prevailed since its inception in J. R. R. Tolkien's "Beowulf: The Monsters and the Critics," in *Proceedings of the British Academy* 22 (1936): 245–95, rpt. in *An Anthology of Beowulf Criticism,* ed. Lewis E. Nicholson (Notre Dame: University of Notre Dame Press, 1963), pp. 51–104. The edition used throughout is Fr. Klaeber, *Beowulf and the Fight at Finnsburg,* 3rd ed. (Boston: D. C. Heath and Co., 1936, with supplements in 1941 and 1950).

2. This increasingly popular view of the structure as tripartite has been advanced by H. L. Rogers, "Beowulf's Three Great Fights," *Review of English Studies* 6 (1955): 339–55, rpt. in Nicholson, *Anthology,* pp. 233–56; John Gardner, "Fulgentius' *Expositio Vergiliana Continentia* and the Plan of *Beowulf:* Another Approach to the Poem's Style and Structure," *Papers in Language and Literature* 6 (1970): 227–62; and most recently, Kathryn Hume, "The Theme and Structure of *Beowulf,*" *Studies in Philology* 72 (1975): 1–27. Hume's fine analysis includes an extensive survey of the various approaches to and interpretations of structural and thematic unity in *Beowulf* (see pp. 2–5). She declares, p. 3, "That critics should disagree over whether the structure has two parts or three is hardly surprising. Those concentrating on the hero tend to see two, those on action usually prefer three. But neither camp has produced a structural analysis which does not, by implication, damn the poet for gross incompetence, or leave the critic with a logically awkward position." For example, William W. Ryding, *Structure in Medieval Narrative* (The Hague: Mouton, 1971), first regards the middle of *Beowulf* as "a point of maximum logical discontinuity," p. 40, and then, contradicting himself, as a more difficult, more intense, more exciting combat than the fight with Grendel, illustrating a "varied repetition" of the same narrative motif, therefore implying logical continuity (p. 88).

3. Adrien Bonjour, "Grendel's Dam and the Composition of *Beowulf,*" *English Studies* 30 (1949): 117. Other early *Beowulf* studies similarly ignored Grendel's Mother or treated her as a type of Grendel. See also Tolkien, "Monsters," in which he declares, "I shall confine myself mainly to the monsters—Grendel and the Dragon . . . ," in Nicholson, *Anthology,* p. 52. Similar treatments occur in T. M. Gang, "Approaches to *Beowulf,*" *Review of English Studies* 3 (1952): 1–12; Bonjour, "Monsters Crouching and Critics Rampant: or the *Beowulf* Dragon Debated," *Publications of the Modern Language Association* 68 (1953): 304–12; and even more recently, in Margaret Goldsmith, *The Mode and Meaning of Beowulf* (London: Athlone Press, 1970), e.g., p. 144; Alvin A. Lee, *The Guest-Hall of Eden* (New Haven: Yale University Press, 1972), pp. 171–223; and Daniel G. Calder, "Setting and Ethos: The Pattern of Measure and Limit in *Beowulf,*" *Studies in Philology* 69 (1972): 21–37.

4. Recently interpretations have stressed her significance in Germanic social terms, but without developing the implications of such insights: a Jungian analysis views her as symbolic of the "evil latent in woman's function, as Grendel symbolizes the destructive element hidden in Beowulf's *maegen.* . . . Grendel's Mother symbolizes the feud aspect of the web of peace. . . ." Further, as a destroyer she signifies "the obverse of the women we meet in the two banqueting scenes which precede Beowulf's descent into Grendelsmere," both of whom combine to form the dual mother image. See Jeffrey H erman, "*Beowulf:* The Archetype

Enters History," *ELH* 35 (1968), 12–13, 14. To other critics she represents vengeance (Nist, Irving, Hume), false loyalty (Gardner), revenge (Leyerle). See John A. Nist, *The Structure and Texture of Beowulf* (Línguia e Literature Inglése, vol. 1; São Paulo: Universidade de São Paulo, Faculdade de Filosofia, Ciências, e Letres, 1959), p. 21; Edward B. Irving, Jr., *A Reading of Beowulf* (New Haven: Yale University Press, 1968), p. 113, and *Introduction to Beowulf* (Englewood Cliffs, N.J.: Prentice-Hall, 1969), p. 57; Kathryn Hume, "The Theme and Structure of *Beowulf,*" p. 7; Gardner, "Fulgentius' *Expositio Vergiliana Continentia* and the Plan of *Beowulf,*" p. 255; and John Leyerle, "The Interlace Structure of *Beowulf,*" *University of Toronto Quarterly* 37 (1967–68): pp. 11–12.

Other recent interpretations have explored not only Jungian but also Scandinavian and Celtic mythic and legendary parallels, sources, or analogues of this figure: for the Scandinavian parallels, see Nora K. Chadwick, "The Monsters and *Beowulf,*" in *The Anglo-Saxons: Studies in Some Aspects of their History and Culture Presented to Bruce Dickins,* ed. Peter Clemoes (London: Bowes and Bowes, 1959), pp. 171–203, and Larry D. Benson, "The Originality of *Beowulf,*" in *The Interpretation of Narrative: Theory and Practice,* ed. Morton W. Bloomfield (Harvard English Studies, vol. 1; Cambridge, Mass.: Harvard University Press, 1970), pp. 1–43; for the Celtic parallels, see Martin Puhvel, "The Might of Grendel's Mother," *Folklore* 80 (1969): 81–88; and for amalgamated parallels—English, German, Latin, and Scandinavian—viewing Grendel and his mother as incubus and succubus, see Nicolas K. Kiessling, "Grendel: A New Aspect," *Modern Philology* 65 (1968): 191–201.

5. Groundwork for this interpretation of the monsters as enemies of man was first laid by Arthur E. Dubois, "The Unity of *Beowulf,*" *Publications of the Modern Language Association* 49 (1934): 391 (Grendel and his mother become "the Danes' liability to punishment" for the secular sins of weakness, pride, and treachery; the dragon, "a variation upon Grendel," is "internal discord"). More recently they have been understood as adversaries of both man and God: see Richard N. Ringler, *"Him Sēo Wēn Gelēah:* The Design for Irony in Grendel's Last Visit to Heorot," *Speculum* 41 (1966): 64, in which Grendel represents *ofermōd* or *fortrūwung,* "held suspect by both Germanic instinct and Christian doctrine." See also Lee, *Guest-Hall,* p. 186.

6. For this interpretation of Grendel, see especially Edward B. Irving, Jr., *"Ealuscerwen:* Wild Party at Heorot," *Tennessee Studies in Literature* 11 (1966): 161–68, and *A Reading,* p. 16; also William A. Chaney, "Grendel and the *Gifstol:* A Legal View of Monsters," *Publications of the Modern Language Association* 77 (1962): 513–20; Joseph L. Baird, "Grendel the Exile," *Neuphilologische Mitteilungen* 67 (1966): 375–81.

7. Irving, *A Reading,* p. 209; Lee, *Guest-Hall,* pp. 215–16.

8. Tacitus, *Germania,* ed. Rodney Potter Robinson (Philological Monographs, vol. 5; Middletown, Conn.: American Philological Association, 1935), p. 291 (cap. 14).

9. In *Beowulf:* in 620, 1168, and 1649 used of Wealhtheow, lady of the Helmings or Scyldings; in 1075 and 1117 of Hildeburh; in 1941 of Queen Thryth. Outside *Beowulf:* see "Kentish Glosses" (ca. ninth century) in Thomas Wright, *Anglo-Saxon and Old English Vocabularies,* ed. Richard Paul Wülcker, 2nd ed. (London: Trübner and Co., 1884), vol. 1, p. 88. For *on idesan* paired with *in virgunculam,* see *in iuuenculam* in the gloss on Aldhelm's *De Laudibus Virginitatis* 29.14, in *Old English Glosses,* ed. Arthur S. Napier (Oxford: Oxford University Press, 1900), p. 57; also for *ides* as *virguncula* see the gloss on Aldhelm's *De Laudibus Virginum* 191.7 and 194.14, pp. 181, 183.

10. Used of Grendel's Mother in 1258, 1276, 1282, 1538, 1683, 2118, and 2139. In 2932 *mōdor* refers to the mother of Onela and Ohthere.

11. George Philip Krapp and Elliott Van Kirk Dobbie, eds., *The Exeter Book,* vol. 3 of *The Anglo-Saxon Poetic Records* (New York: Columbia University Press, 1936), p. 159 (lines 83–85).

12. Bosworth-Toller's *Anglo-Saxon Dictionary* lists *hringsele* and *nīðsele* as compounds singular to *Beowulf,* underscoring the intentionality of the poet's irony.

13. Masculine pronouns refer to the feminine personifications of Old Age (1887) and Change or Death (2421), and to the feminine synecdoche "hand" (1344).

14. *Āglǣca* apparently means "fierce adversary" in *Juliana* 268 and 319 where the Devil in the garb of an angel brings tidings to the maiden; when she asks who sent him, *Hyre se aglǣca ageaf ondsware* 'The fierce adversary answered her' (319) in *The Exeter Book*, p. 122. Because he no longer appears to be a "wretch, monster, miscreant," the term *āglǣca* must denote "foe" in this passage. Indeed, Juliana addresses him in line 317 as *feond moncynnes* 'foe' or 'enemy of mankind'.

15. See the stories of the treacherous wife but loyal mother Urse in the twelfth-century *Saxonis Grammatici Gesta Danorum,* ed. Alfred Holder (Strassburg: K. J. Trübner, 1886), pp. 53–55; (*The First Nine Books of the Danish History of Saxo Grammaticus,* tr. Oliver Elton [London: D. Nutt, 1894], pp. 64–65 [II, 53–55]).

16. Dorothy Whitelock, *The Beginnings of English Society* (Baltimore: Penguin Books, 1952), p. 41; on duty to one's kin, see pp. 38–47; on duty to one's lord, see pp. 31ff. Duty to one's lord superseded duty to one's kin (p. 37). See also *Saxonis Grammatici Gesta Danorum,* p. 254 (VII), for the retainer's duty to lord; in cases of blood revenge the son remained most deeply obligated to his father, pp. 75, 96 (III), then to his brother or sister, pp. 53, 280 (II, VIII), finally to his grandfather, p. 301 (IX).

17. The poet uses similar wordplay in describing the "reception" of the guest Beowulf in the "hall" of the gold-lord dragon. First, Beowulf does not dare attack (or more figuratively, "approach") the gold-lord dragon in his ring-hall (*hringsele,* 2840, 3053); Wiglaf admits *hē ne grētte goldweard þone* 'he did not approach the guardian of the gold' (3081), literally because of the danger from fire, figuratively because of the dragon's avarice. Instead, *wyrd* 'fate' will dispense or distribute his "soul's hoard" for which Beowulf has paid with his life (*wyrd* will seek his *sāwle hord, sundur gedǣlan / līf wið līce* 'soul's hoard, separate his life from his body', 2422–23a; he "buys" the hoard with his life in 2799–800). After this "treasure-giving," the cup-passer—Wiglaf—pours water from the cup—Beowulf's helmet.

18. *The Exeter Book,* pp. 190–91. The sword declares:

                Ic wiþ bryde ne mot
hæmed habban,   ac me þæs hyhtplegan
geno wyrneð,   se mec geara on
bende legde;   forþon ic brucan sceal
on hagostealde   hæleþa gestreona.
Oft ic wirum dol   wife abelge,
wonie hyre willan;   heo me wom spreceð,
floceð hyre folmum,   firenaþ mec wordum,
ungod gæleð.   Ic ne gyme þæs compes.

(I may not have sexual intercourse with a bride, but he who formerly laid bonds on me denies me still the joy-game; therefore I must enjoy the treasures of heroes while living in my lord's house. Often I, foolish in ornaments, anger the woman, diminish her will; she speaks evil to me with words, cries out "not good." I do not care for the contest.)

Similarly erotic riddles include no. 21, "Plow"; no. 44, "Key"; no. 53, "Battering Ram"; no. 62, "Poker" or "Burning Arrow"; and no. 91, "Key."

19. When St. Lucia resists the advances of the pagan Paschasius and he condemns her to be 'defiled' (*bysmrian*) in a whorehouse as punishment, she retorts, 'To me intercourse with thy slave is not more pleasant than if an adder would hurt me' (*nis me þynes weales hæmed næfre þe leofre þe me nædre toslyte*). See *An Old English Martyrology,* ed. George Herzfeld (Early English Text Society, o.s., vol. 116; London: The Early English Text Society, 1900), p. 218.

20. Although the poems were written by different poets, *Beowulf* in the late seventh or eighth century and *Judith* in the middle or late tenth century, the second *Beowulf* scribe did transcribe all of the *Judith* fragment, probably in the late tenth century. All references to *Judith* derive from Elliott Van Kirk Dobbie, ed., *Beowulf and Judith,* vol. 4 of *The Anglo-Saxon Poetic Records* (New York: Columbia University Press, 1953).

21. See, for example, the life of St. Lucia in the *Martyrology,* p. 218.

22. For a discussion of these planes of correspondence in *Judith,* see James F. Double-day, "The Principle of Contrast in *Judith," Neuphilologische Mitteilungen* 72 (1971): 436–41.

23. See Klaeber's discussion of Thryth's possible prototypes, 1931–62nn. Thryth's name resembles that of Quendrida (Queen Thryth?) and that of the Scottish queen Her-mutrude, whose story is related in Saxo Grammaticus' *Danish History,* p. 124 (*Gesta Danorum,* pp. 101–102 [IV]). Hermutrude, loved by Amleth, remains unmarried because of her cruelty and arrogance, similar to Thryth's. Finally, note the similarity between the following descriptions and those in *Beowulf:* Offa murdered many without distinction, includ-ing King Ethelbert, "thereby being guilty of an *atrocious outrage* against the suitor of his daughter," in William of Malmesbury's *Chronicle of the Kings of England: From the Earliest Period to the Reign of King Stephen,* tr. J. A. Giles (London: H. G. Bohn, 1847), p. 238; in Latin "nefarium rem *in procum filiae operatus,"* from *Willemi Malmesbiriensis Monachi De Gestis Regum Anglorum Libri Quinque; Historiae Novellae Libri Tres,* ed. William Stubbs, 2 vols. (Rerum Britannicarum Medii Aevii Scriptores, vol. 90; London: Eyre and Spottiswoode, 1887), p. 262 (II, 210). Compare *Beowulf:* Modþrȳðo wæg, / fremu folces cwēn,   firen' ondrysne 'Modthrytho, the excellent queen of the people, carried on terrible wickedness' (1931–32). Did the *Beowulf* poet confuse the father of Modthrytho with the daughter herself?

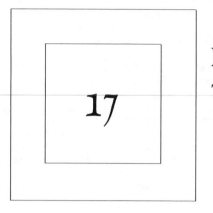

Eve's I.Q. Rating
Two Sexist Views of Genesis B

17

It is a fundamental dogma of the twentieth century that the Middle Ages had nothing but contempt for the intelligence of women. The assumption stands illustrated in the introduction to a translation of Andreas Capellanus' *De Amore* which has provided innumerable students with their only source of information on the subject and is the work of a reliable and deservedly respected mediaevalist:

> Outside of marriage, women might be used to alleviate concupiscence; and in the marriage state, recommended by St. Paul because it is better to marry than to burn, she had the additional function of being a childbearer and a housekeeper, hardly that of a companion with status equal to that of men. . . . Behind this medieval attitude towards women was a monastic tradition whose influence upon letters and institutions cannot be overestimated. The angry denunciation against the perennial Eve is a cry that is heard throughout the period: every woman is *Eva rediviva*. . . .[1]

What the passage means is that the intellectual Middle Ages thought all women as dumb as Eve, who had let herself be swindled out of her rightful portion of Paradise. One is reminded of the Wife of Bath's observation that "it is an impossible / That any clerk wol speke good of wyves. . . ." (688–89).[2]

Even though I am not unaware of Francis Lee Utley's argument that mediaeval misogyny was largely a discovery of the early Renaissance and that the early Renaissance itself produced more antifeminist satire than all the preceding periods put together,[3] and even though common sense tells me that most of the methodical research on the subject has hitherto been conducted either by men or by women trained by men and writing for a predominantly male audience, I know better than to question openly the joint verdict of modern scholarship and the Wife of Bath—especially since the epistolary dispute between Jean Gerson and Christine de Pisan seems to bear out that verdict, at least insofar as late mediaeval France is concerned. What nevertheless bothers me is that dictionaries tend to define the Middle Ages as "the period of European history . . . often dated from A.D. 476 . . . to A.D. 1453,"[4] and I am not totally convinced that such an attitude toward women as may have been prevalent among the Gothic warriors who followed Odoacer to Rome in the fifth century was necessarily the same as that of a major theologian in fifteenth-century Paris.

Yet, what readers find on the page usually resembles what they are looking for, and what they are looking for usually resembles what experience has taught them to expect;[5] and agreement with these propositions leads one to concur with Daniel Calder's reminder that "no subject entirely escapes its history."[6] The foregoing observations do not invalidate the views of the Wife of Bath and her scholarly followers, but they may help us place them within a context which we are otherwise too prone to disregard. As Charles Muscatine convincingly demonstrated years ago, Chaucer's literary context stems primarily "from the traditions originated and propagated, in the twelfth and thirteenth centuries, in France,"[7] and it is accordingly the same context which Christine de Pisan and Jean Gerson shared when they turned the *Roman de la Rose* into an excuse for arguing about the strengths and weaknesses of women. In an admittedly modified form, it is likewise the basis for the context within which scholars concerned with the literature of mediaeval England have shaped their expectations, for the study of Chaucer and his immediate followers forms a continuous line which goes back to the fifteenth century.[8] In contrast to Chaucer—and notwithstanding some occasional antiquarian interest during the sixteenth century as well as the pioneering philological efforts of such men as Franciscus Junius and Grímur Jónsson Thorkelin in the seventeenth and eighteenth or the critical forays of John Milton and George Hickes during the same period—the vernacular literature of England before the Norman Conquest did not become a normal concern of literary interpretation until the nineteenth century. It follows that the tradition behind the modern study of Old English literature reaches back to students who, even when they had attended German universities or were themselves German-born,[9] had been trained by mediaevalists wittingly or unwittingly accustomed to the French context in its Middle English incarnation.

Since the context in question reveals an underlying attitude toward the philosophical aptitudes of women which does not differ essentially from that expressed in the Latin monastic tradition mentioned in the citation at the outset of this essay and with which early students of Old English were presumably familiar,[10] it further follows that these students would have had excellent reasons for expecting to find the bulk of mediaeval thinking colored by the assumption that women had been created intellectually inferior to men. Approaching a previously neglected area of mediaeval literature with such an expectation, they would presumably have found what they were looking for, and they would naturally have passed on the resultant interpretation to their disciples, who might in turn have repeated the process from generation to generation. Nor can we assume that the process in question would have generated serious scrutiny on the part of the male scholars who occupied nearly all university chairs until recent times.

The scenario which I have worked out above is of course hypothetical, but, to illustrate the point, I should like to escape the French tradition momentarily in order to approach a passage of early mediaeval poetry in the light of my implied hypothesis that not every European who composed a line between 476 and 1453 was necessarily bent upon demonstrating the intellectual inferiority of women. For this purpose, I have chosen the account of the Temptation of Eve in the Old English *Genesis B*. Since Eve's behavior in Paradise is usually held responsible for the supposed mediaeval attitude toward women, this account is immediately relevant to my hypothesis.

The expected reaction of literary criticism toward the Eve of *Genesis B* is somewhat complicated by the recognized fact that the poet has portrayed her in an obviously sympathetic light and assures us that the fatal trespass was done with the best intentions in the world (708a–14b).[11] Recognition of this fact may make it difficult to see her as intrinsically evil, but it certainly would not stand in the way of calling her a well-meaning idiot; and professional students of Old English will recall how Humphrey Gurteen's influential study of the poem describes her: "She tastes of the Fruit, because she believes that it is verily God's command, and to shield her loved one [i.e., Adam] from any harm that might ensue from his supposed disobedience. . . . It is *his* welfare, and his alone, that dominates her will. She falls, but only in the hope of saving *him*. Even if she does bring 'woe' on all mankind, it is done with a noble motive, and Cædmon's Eve is the prototype of true Womanhood, selfless and self-sacrificing."[12] Even Rosemary Woolf's attempt at rescuing Eve from the kind of interpretation represented by Gurteen leaves things pretty much where they were in the first place, since it argues that she responded to the devil's temptation "with a willful credulity springing from nascent vanity."[13] The obvious lesson which one gets from the argument is that the poet has represented Eve as not terribly bright but decidedly equipped with the sin of pride and, in so doing, has helped vindicate the Wife of Bath's opinion of the clerical attitude toward women.

The assumption that *Genesis B* intentionally depicts Eve as intellectually inferior seems at first sight warranted by the narrative, which shows the Tempter turning to her only after coming a cropper with Adam. As she begins to show signs of weakening, the poet remarks parenthetically, *hæfde hire wacran hige / metod gemearcod* (590b–91a), and the way in which the remark has been construed by modern scholarship stands illustrated in Charles Kennedy's accurate and representative translation: "For God had fashioned for her a feebler mind."[14] In view of the Tempter's lamentable failure with Adam, the implication is that she scored decidedly lower than her husband on the Stanford-Binet test, and Kennedy's own discussion of the passage reinforces the point: "It is only after the temptation of Adam has failed that the fiend turns to Eve. . . . With tricks and lies . . . , he tempted the woman to sin until his counsel began to work within her—for God had fashioned her spirit the weaker. . . ."[15] The poem seems to clinch the case with another mention of the *wifes wac gepoht* 'the woman's weak mind' (649a) sixty lines later. Common sense tells me that Kathleen Dubs has a point when she observes that in fact "Adam is as blind to covert evil as is Eve,"[16] so that I ought at least to consider the possibility that a reader approaching the text without the benefit of the critical tradition which I have outlined above might conceivably find Eve intellectually *superior* to Adam.

In the first place, the way in which the Tempter conducts his business with Adam is so clumsy as to arouse his intended victim's suspicion from the start: Though disguised in the likeness of a snake, he presents himself as an angelic messenger of

God. We need not wonder, then, that Adam should be taken aback and exclaim, *þu gelic ne bist / ænegum his engla þe ic ær geseah* 'you don't look like any of His angels whom I have seen before' (538b–39b). Under the circumstances, his peremptory refusal to listen ought certainly not to be construed as a sign of superior intelligence. In fact, he sounds rather stupid when, after nineteen lines devoted essentially to repeating the circumstances under which he received God's original command (e.g., 523b–31a), voicing his own puzzlement at the present situation (e.g., 533b–35a), and stating his own but not exactly original conviction that snakes do not look like angels (538b–42a), he caps his argument with the simplistic conclusion, *ic þe hyran ne cann* 'I can't listen to you' (542b) and brings his discourse to an end with a mindless but very smug assertion of his faith in God: *Ic hæbbe me fæstne geleafan / up to þæm ælmihtegan gode þe me . . . worhte* 'as for me, I have unshakable faith in the Almighty God who created me' (543b–44b). The element of puzzlement in the middle of the passage is relevant to the outcome of the action since the Old English verb *cunnan* (Mod. Engl. *can*), with which Adam expresses his refusal—*ic . . . ne cann* (542b)—to listen to the Temptation, normally means *to know* or *to know how*. In other words, the textual evidence makes it tempting to imagine Adam as so puzzled by a situation which taxes the limits of his comprehension that his refusal to listen to the Tempter's argument may also be construed as an admission that he would not know how to listen to it if he wanted to.

In contrast, the Tempter—who has presumably derived a lesson from the experience—brilliantly puts Eve on the defensive from the start, so that she never gets around to questioning him about his identity. His ill-fated gambit with Adam had taken the form of a question bound to call the latter's attention to the facts of Heaven and thus generate doubts about the reptilian visitor's self-proclaimed identity:

> Langað þe awuht,
> Adam, up to gode? Ic eom on his ærende hider
> feorran gefered. . . .
>
> (496b–98a)

(Do you feel the least upward longing toward God, Adam? I have travelled hither on his errand from afar. . . .)

He uses no such potentially telltale question with Eve, whom he throws off balance with an initial assertion whose intrinsic shock capability is compounded by the dual form of the first indirect-object pronoun:

> Ic wat, *inc* waldend god
> abolgen wyrð, swa ic him þisne bodscipe
> selfa secge. . . .
>
> (551b–53a)

(I know that Almighty God will be furious at *both of you* when I personally tell him about this mission. . . .)

The unsettling message is that something unspecified has gone terribly wrong and that the speaker himself has access to the Almighty, whom he will inform accordingly and whose resultant wrath will be formidable. The dual object pronoun—*inc* rather than *Adam* or *you*—has the effect of implying that Eve will be assumed to have actively and intimately co-operated in the perpetration of a monstrous crime about which she presumably knows nothing. The terror normally attendant upon having to face an unspecified but potentially mortal threat needs no elaboration for readers of *Beowulf,* who will recall the pride which the youthful slayer of Grendel takes in the fact that he and his companions *frecne geneðdon / eafoð uncuþes* 'boldly dared the terror of the unknown' (959b–60a).[17] In *Genesis B,* this unnerving personal involvement with the unknown and with the unstated but nonetheless appalling consequences thereof hits Eve at the full with the Tempter's opening words. From the point of view of a Christian audience, the impact which this terrible revelation must be imagined to have on her can be nothing short of shattering. Since the Tempter goes on pushing his initial advantage with masterful rhetoric, her failure to question him about his identity ought not to be taken as incontrovertible proof of her intellectual inferiority to Adam.

In the second place, the most cursory examination of the text reveals that, whereas the Tempter gives up on Adam after only twenty-five and one-half lines (496b–521b) of straightforward and grossly materialistic entreaties, he devotes thirty-six and one-half lines (551b–87b) to a specious but superbly sophisticated and at times deeply moving[18] logical and moral argument in order to convince Eve that taking the fatal bite is the only logical course of action open to her. A glance at two of his rhetorical devices will illustrate the irresistible quality of his strategy.

The first device affects the position and nature of the injunction to bite into the Fruit. The injunction is preceded by several longish sentences in which the Tempter begins by complaining in general terms about the disregard of God's unspecified command and predicting an equally unspecified but inevitable punishment, and then goes on to suggest a remedy. Like an experienced teacher, he seems to know that students are more likely to act upon their own discoveries than upon the lessons of others, and he accordingly makes no mention of the Fruit until he has had time to explain to Eve that listening to his words will merely help her formulate her own solution to the problem facing her and Adam:

> Gif þu þeah minum wilt,
> wif willende,   wordum hyran
> þu meaht his þonne rume   ræd geþencan.
> (559b–61b)

(If you will freely listen to my words, O woman, then you will be able to think up some kind of plan.)

He continues with a two-line sentence (562a–63b) which admonishes her to think for herself—*Gehyge on þinum breostum.* . . . 'Consider within your own breast. . . .' (562a)—and only at the conclusion thereof does he utter the fateful injunction, which takes the form of a brief first hemistich: *Æt þisses ofetes!* 'Eat of this fruit!' (564a). The position, brevity, and directness of the injunction are important, not only because of the obvious contrast which they afford in regard to the length and indirectness of the immediately preceding statements, but especially because of the even more obvious contrast with the second hemistich, which is longer than average and ushers in three and one-half lines of uninterrupted depiction of the desirable results of eating the Fruit:

> þonne wurðað þin eagan swa leoht
> þæt þu meaht swa wide   ofer woruld ealle
> geseon siððan,   and selfes stol
> herran þines,   and habban his hyldo forð.
>
> (564b–67b)

(Then your eyes will become so clear that you will thenceforth be able to see far and wide over the entire world, to see the very throne of God and enjoy His good will for ever after.)

In short, the controversial injunction is introduced as nothing more than an innocuous statement intended to provide Eve with a point of departure for her own thinking, is pared down in size to the barest minimum, and is followed by a sales pitch much too long and too densely packed with enticing visions to allow her to utter a word until she has become so used to the Tempter's logic as to have lost whatever incentive to question his identity she might have had at the outset.

The second device is an expansion of the use of the dual pronoun to which I have already called attention in respect to the Tempter's opening words to Eve. The dual form occurs eight times in the course of his thirty-six and one-half lines of direct discourse, and seven of these occurrences link her with Adam in the manner already mentioned. In fact the exact message of the initial occurrence is repeated once in the very same words, *ðy ic wat þæt he inc abolgen wyrð* 'for I know that he will be furious at *both of you*' (558b), and once again, this time at the point when the Tempter urges Eve to share with Adam the Fruit which she seems about to taste, with one dual pronoun as a subject and another used to emphasize the fact that the mighty God about to become angry is lord over both Adam and Eve: *Span þu hine georne / . . . , þy læs gyt lað gode, / incrum wealdende,   weorðan þyrfen* 'Entice Adam earnestly, lest the *two of you* of necessity may become abhorrent to God, the Lord of *both of you*' (575b–77b). Three more instances reinforce the lesson by implication. The first of these occurs when the Tempter tells Eve that God will come in person to *demand* an answer from both her and Adam—*Nu sceal he sylf faran / to incre andsware* 'Now He shall come in person for an answer from the *two of you*' (556b–57a)—and thus implies that she and Adam will in fact have to stand trial together for the still mysterious crime on which the two of them have supposedly collaborated. Within this context, incidentally, the introductory adverb *nu* 'now' deserves mention insofar as it makes the subsequent statement sound as though the mysterious but heinous crime for which God will demand an explanation were in effect the latest installment in an unspecified series of equally heinous and mysterious crimes perpetrated jointly by Adam and Eve. The second instance occurs when the Tempter tells Eve that he merely wants to help her formulate her own plan to protect herself and Adam together from punishment—*. . . inc bam twam . . . / wite bewarigan* '. . . to protect *the two of you together* from punishment' (562b–63a)—and the mention of a yet unspecified punishment against which they ought to seek protection suggests by implication that they need such protection. The third instance occurs when the Tempter at long last offers to hide Adam's trespass and uses the dual pronoun in a way which, within the present context, once again suggests that Eve and Adam must be inextricably bound together in the eyes of divine justice: *forhele ic incrum her-ran . . .* 'I shall conceal from the Lord *of the two of you . . .*' (579a).

In all seven instances examined thus far, the dual pronoun serves to link Eve with Adam in respect to both the perpetration of a crime against God and the threatened punishment for it. In contrast, the remaining instance has the opposite effect, since it links Eve to the Tempter as he evokes the extremely attractive prospect of saving Adam through their joint efforts:

> he þone laðan strið,
> yfel andwyrde   an forlæteð
> on breostcofan,   swa *wit* him *bu tu*
> an sped sprecað.
>
> (572b–75a)

(within his breast he will give up the odious struggle, the evil reply, as *the two of us together* speak to him successfully.)

In other words, the cumulative effect of the eight instances of the dual pronoun is to bring home the never-stated argument that, just as association with Adam must be equated with a morally repugnant situation and emotionally terrifying prospects, so association with the Tempter must be equated with a morally attractive situation and emotionally reassuring prospects.

If we further keep in mind that the Tempter does not wait to be questioned before volunteering an accurate and convincing, though perfectly misleading, account of his familiarity with heavenly matters and of the length of his service with God (583a–87a), we need only put ourselves in Eve's place to realize that the argument thus advanced in favor of eating the Fruit seems absolutely impeccable. To be sure, the logic of that argument demands our disregarding the initial ban, but the annals of Christianity do not exactly bar the possibility of divine counterorders and are not noted for encouraging negative inquiry into directives from above. Nor should we forget that, however Biblical the story may be and however devoutly Christian the poet's intention may have been, the narrative tradition behind *Genesis B* is that of early Germanic verse, whose assumptions, themes, and formulas seem to have operated with a fair degree of independence from the Latin conventions of the monastery, even when the subject matter was drawn from the latter,[19] and the generally accepted date of composition before A.D. 900[20] rules out the influence of the French tradition as defined by Muscatine. Since one of the most clearly attested conventions of early Germanic verse is that a retainer is expected to risk everything in order to assist or avenge his lord,[21] since women do not seem to have been altogether exempt from this expectation,[22] and since Eve is so blatantly made to look up to Adam as her lord that she calls him *frea min* 'my lord' (655a), it is only fitting that she should obey an unexpected counterorder from above to save him from an unspecified but presumably terrible fate; and we need accordingly not be surprised at the poet's assertion that *Heo dyde hit þeah þurh holdne hyge* 'she acted through a loyal heart' (708a), which is precisely the way in which retainers and lords are expected to act toward one another.[23] Thus construed within the context of both the narrative tradition and the Tempter's line of argument, her decision betokens not only an admirable loyalty but also the intellectual ability to take the only logical action within her ken; and it also bears out Stanley B. Greenfield's view that the episode serves to remind us that "forces of destruction lurk behind human choices and actions, however good their motivations."[24]

I must repeat that the foregoing examination of the text has been conducted from the point of view of an unsophisticated reader. One may find it of interest that what the words on the page suggest is the possibility that Adam may have withstood temptation because he was too stupid to understand it, while Eve may have fallen because she was intelligent enough to follow a logical argument.

So far, so good. But what then of the statement that God had created Eve with a weaker mind? The answer, I suspect, may well be that the message is by no means that her mind was weaker than Adam's, and it is relevant to this possibility that what grammarians would call the standard of the comparison remains unexpressed and that Adam has been out of the picture for forty-four lines (547a–90b) by the time we come across the adjective *weaker*. In contradistinction to Adam, the Tempter has been specifically mentioned only two and one-half lines earlier within the same sentence, where we have learned that *Lædde . . . swa mid ligenum . . . / idese on þæt unriht* 'thus with lies he went on leading the woman into wrongdoing' (588a–89a), so that the proximity of the statement combines with the thrust of the sentence to make him the obvious standard of the comparison. This interpretation is grammatically sounder than that which would make Adam the standard of the comparison and certainly as sound as the alternative whereby the comparative would be understood as a mere intensifier ("rather weak"). Thus construed, what the text tells us is that Eve's mind was weaker than the Tempter's, and we could hardly expect anything else. Even though a lacuna in the manuscript makes it impossible to identify the Tempter beyond doubt, the remainder makes it possible to assume that he is an emissary entrusted by Satan himself with the task of implementing the Fall of Man. Since Satan was created *swa mihtigne on his modgeþohte* 'most mighty in his intellectual power' (253a) and *hehstne* 'next in importance' (254a) to God himself, we may reasonably assume that he would entrust such a delicate and all-important task to no one but the smartest demon available. In this light, Eve's superior but merely human intelligence must necessarily be outclassed by the Tempter's superhuman brain power and accordingly prove no match for his infernal arguments.

One may of course accept or reject the validity of the views advanced thus far. If one be willing to grant the paradigmatic quality of the passages examined, however, one must also grant at least some validity to the view that the rhetorical strategy with which the Tempter approaches Eve and conducts his business with her betokens more than a modicum of respect for his prospective victim's intellectual apparatus, since he could hardly be expected to waste such sophisticated logic on someone blatantly incapable of following it. In the light of my surmise that much of the common modern assumption concerning the mediaeval attitude toward the intelligence quotient of women may be traced back to a French tradition which could not have affected *Genesis B,* it may be worth glancing at a twelfth-century Norman version of the Fall for the sake of comparison. The version in question is a play usually printed under the title of *Le Mystère d'Adam,* and its treatment of the initial phase of the temptation of Eve should suffice to illustrate the vast difference between its underlying assumptions concerning her intelligence and those which I have assumed in *Genesis B.* In the French, Satan himself comes to Eve, who recognizes him, calls him by name, and urges him to begin talking as soon as he offers to tell her the secrets of Heaven: *Ore le comence, e jo l'orrai*[25] 'Now begin [your tale], and I'll listen to it' (212). Within the next four lines, she again promises to listen *bien* 'carefully' (213) and swears *par foi* 'by [her] faith' (215) to keep his confidence. In contrast to the corresponding moment in *Genesis B,* the initial phase of the actual temptation avoids any kind of serious problem and is totally devoid of any revelation likely to upset anyone in any way. The strategy would by no means seem out of place in one of those melodramas where the clever but morally depraved villain unctuously seduces the pretty but brainless young girl whom he has no intention of ever making his wife:

> Tu es fieblette e tendre chose,
> E es plus fresche que n'est rose;
> Tu es plus blanche que cristal,
> Que neif que chiet sor glace en val.
> (227–30)

(You are a helpless and tender thing, and you are fresher than a rose; you are whiter than crystal or than the snow falling on ice in the vale.)

Had the author of the Old English poem wanted to make his Eve seem as dumb as we assume her to be, he could have done no better than to present his account of the Temptation in a manner similar to that of the Old French play. Making the victim such an easy mark, however, would have deprived the poet of a good excuse for bringing the Temptation to an end with the Tempter laughing exultantly and applauding himself (724b) for his accomplishment; and it may be significant in this respect that the *Mystère d'Adam* includes no such display of pride in one's accomplishment and concludes the episode with the simple statement that *tunc recedat Diabolus ab Eva, et ibit ad infernum* 'at this point, the Devil leaves Eve and returns to Hell' (p. 54).

In view of the subject matter of *Genesis B,* one might find it amusing to consider that the simple-minded reading with which I have been playing may possibly prove theologically more appropriate than the conventional readings. Depending on one's point of view, the Fall may or may not be blessed, but I have been told that it was an expression of divine will, and the poet of *Genesis B* must have been told the same thing since he marvels at the fact that God *æfre wolde / . . . þolian* 'should ever have suffered' (596b–97a) it to happen. I accordingly doubt that he, or any other Christian poet, would want to tell us that divine will could triumph only because of the stupidity of the human beings affected by it; such a lesson would imply that, had God chanced upon someone with a slightly higher intelligence quotient, his will might have been thwarted right there, and this is not the kind of situation in which believers are wont to cast their God. I rather suspect that our poet would want to show that even the best possible human intelligence is necessarily helpless before Divine Will, and this is precisely the lesson which we get from the reading which I have suggested.

Whereas the conventional readings of the Temptation episode in *Genesis B* are obviously male sexist, the alternative which I have outlined is equally obviously female sexist. Nevertheless, the very fact that one can mount some kind of argument in defense of Eve's intelligence suggests a perfectly outrageous and futile hypothesis which I cannot refrain from formulating here: If mediaeval English studies had been initiated by female scholars nurtured on the Germanic tradition rather than by male scholars nurtured on the French and monastic traditions, our fundamental dogma today might conceivably be that the Middle Ages unexceptionally assumed the intellectual superiority of women.

NOTES

1. Frederick W. Locke, ed., "Introduction" to Andreas Capellanus' *The Art of Courtly Love* (New York: F. Unger Publishing Co., 1957), p. v.

2. All quotations from Chaucer are from *The Works of Geoffrey Chaucer*, ed. F. N. Robinson (Boston: Houghton Mifflin Co., 1957).

3. Francis Lee Utley, *The Crooked Rib* (Columbus: Ohio State University, 1944), pp. 3–4.

4. *The American Heritage Dictionary of the English Language* (Boston: Houghton Mifflin Co., 1976); definitions in other standard college dictionaries may differ by a few years but remain substantially the same.

5. The mechanics whereby readers find whatever they find in a given text have been studied in detail by, among others, Norman N. Holland, particularly in his *The Dynamics of Literary Response* (New York: Oxford University Press, 1968), e.g., pp. 1–30 and 90–91, and his *Poems in Persons* (New York: W. W. Norton, 1973), where he shows how a given reader "recreates a literary work" (p. 100) on the basis of expectations created by previous experience.

6. Daniel G. Calder, "The Study of Style in Old English Poetry: A Historical Introduction," in Calder, ed., *Old English Poetry: Essays on Style* (Berkeley: University of California Press, 1979), p. 2.

7. Charles Muscatine, *Chaucer and the French Tradition* (Berkeley: University of California Press, 1957), p. 5.

8. See Caroline F. E. Spurgeon, *Five Hundred Years of Chaucer Criticism and Allusions, 1357–1900* (Cambridge, England: The University Press, 1925; rpt. New York: Russell and Russell, 1961).

9. The most recent survey of the history of Old English scholarship is Carl T. Berkhout and Milton McC. Gatch eds., *Anglo-Saxon Scholarship: The First Three Centuries* (Boston: G. K. Hall, 1982); for observations pertinent to this study, see Eleanor N. Adams, *Old English Scholarship in England from 1566–1900*, Yale Studies in English, vol. 55 (New Haven: Yale University Press, 1917), pp. 12–33; Calder, "Study of Style," pp. 7–58, as well as John Petheram, *An Historical Sketch of the Progress and Present State of Anglo-Saxon Literature in England* (London: E. Lumley, 1840), esp. pp. 118–80. For an illustration of the influence of German scholars on English studies, in this case at Cambridge, see E. M. W. Tillyard, *The Muse Unchained* (London: Bowes and Bowes, 1958), p. 29.

10. See, e.g., Adams, *Old English Scholarship,* for illustrations of early Anglo-Saxonists studying Old English manuscripts "for ecclesiastical purposes" (p. 14). Though the ecclesiastical tradition of the monastery blames women for their ancestral part in the Fall, and the French tradition of courtly love praises them as objects of sexual desire while both assume their innate cleverness, neither stands out for suggesting anything but doubt concerning their generic aptitude for philosophical thinking.

11. All quotations from *Genesis B* are from the text in George P. Krapp, ed., *The Junius Manuscript,* vol. 1 of *The Anglo-Saxon Poetic Records* (New York: Columbia University Press, 1931).

12. S. Humphrey Gurteen, *The Epic of the Fall of Man* (New York: G. P. Putnam's Sons, 1896), pp. 215–16.

13. Rosemary Woolf, "The Fall of Man in *Genesis B* and the *Mystère d'Adam,*" in Stanley B. Greenfield, ed., *Studies in Old English Literature in Honor of Arthur G. Brodeur* (Eugene: University of Oregon, 1963), p. 196.

14. Charles W. Kennedy, trans., "The Temptation and the Fall of Man," in Kennedy, *An Anthology of Old English Poetry* (New York: Oxford University Press, 1960), p. 126.

15. Kennedy, *The Earliest English Poetry* (London: Oxford University Press, 1943), p. 168. This view represented by Kennedy's statement is one with which I used to be in agreement years ago, as illustrated in my "The Self-Deception of Temptation: Boethian Psychology in *Genesis B,*" in Robert P. Creed, ed., *Old English Poetry: Fifteen Essays* (Providence: Brown University Press, 1967), e.g., p. 58.

16. Kathleen E. Dubs, "*Genesis B:* A Study in Grace," *American Benedictine Review* 33 (1982): 59.

17. Quoted from the text in Elliott Van Kirk Dobbie, ed., *Beowulf and Judith,* vol. 4 of *The Anglo-Saxon Poetic Records* (New York: Columbia University Press, 1953).

18. I have discussed the moving aspect of the Tempter's rhetoric in my "Self-Deception of Temptation," pp. 60–61.

19. The way in which the tradition of early Germanic verse can function independently from a given Latin model stands illustrated in Alexandra Hennessey Olsen, "Guthlac on the Beach," *Neophilologus* 64 (1980): 290–95, and again in her *Guthlac of Croyland: A Study in Heroic Hagiography* (Washington, D.C.: University Press of America, 1981), e.g., pp. 25–47 and 142.

20. Stanley B. Greenfield and Daniel G. Calder, *A New Critical History of Old English Literature* (New York: New York University Press, 1986), points out that all four principal Old English poetic manuscripts were copied about A.D. 1000 and that most critics date the composition of the poems therein "from the seventh to the tenth" century (p. 130) although the exact dates "cannot be determined with precision" (p. 130).

21. One recalls, e.g., Wiglaf's reproach to the retainers who did not risk their lives for their lord, in *Beowulf,* 2864a–91b, or examples of unwillingness and willingness to die for one's lord in *The Battle of Maldon* (in George P. Krapp and Elliott Van Kirk Dobbie, eds., *The Exeter Book,* vol. 3 of *The Anglo-Saxon Poetic Records* [New York: Columbia University Press, 1936]), e.g., 185a–201b, 249a–54b, and 312a–19b.

22. One recalls, e.g., that it is Kriemhilt who shoulders the responsibility of avenging Sîvrit in the *Nibelungenlied* and that Guthrun does the same thing in several Old Norse texts, or that the *Hervarar Saga ok Heiðreks Konungs* attributes similar feelings to Hervǫr in respect to Angantýr, the Ongentheow of *Beowulf.*

23. For illustrations of this relationship, see, e.g. *Beowulf,* 375b–76b, or *Maldon,* 23a–24b; consult Jess B. Bessinger, Jr., and Philip H. Smith, Jr., *A Concordance to the Anglo-Saxon Poetic Records* (Ithaca: Cornell University Press, 1978) under the several forms of *hold* for additional instances.

24. Greenfield and Calder, *New Critical History,* p. 212.

25. *Le Mystère d'Adam,* ed. Henri Chamard (Paris: A. Colin, 1925); the line numbers cited in the text refer to this edition. As Woolf points out, it is impossible to tell on which side of the English Channel the play was composed ("Fall of Man," p. 188, n. 4), but the actual place of composition does not affect my argument. For the probable date of composition, see Gustave Cohen, trans. and ed., *Le Jeu d'Adam* (Paris: Delagrave, 1936), pp. 9–10.

Wulf and Eadwacer

The Adulterous Woman Reconsidered

18

I

The secular women of Old English poetry have marked the *Anglo-Saxon Poetic Records* with a virtual trail of tears. Alain Renoir, with appropriate *litotes,* has recently observed that these unhappy heroines "endure more than their rightful share of discomfort."[1] His essay, "A Reading Context for *The Wife's Lament,*" demonstrates in an unequivocal way just how imaginatively omnipotent and how poetically ubiquitous was this vision of women as full-fledged members of a sorrowing sorority. To be sure, as Renoir's essay notes, the *halgan heap* of virgins and martyrs are dispensed from the obligatory anguish that their secular sisters seem bound to endure. Mary, Juliana, Judith—all are prescriptively as "happy," "blessed," "famous," "glorious," and "triumphant" as any of their masculine counterparts, seeming to anticipate in their earthly careers the Pauline assertion that "in Heaven there is no male or female."

But for women who participate fully in the terrestrial, secular experience of the Anglo-Saxon world they inhabit, the universal refrain might well be *Ungelic is us* 'It is otherwise for us; our destiny different' (3a).[2] I shall return anon to this canon of the uncanonized, for it is here, I think, that we can best look for informative suggestions about the elusive text and context of *Wulf and Eadwacer,* a lyric traditionally read as a captive woman's lament for her absent husband and/or lover.

In this essay, I will review certain archeological and literary data connected to the poetic *topos* of the mother-grieving-for-her-son so frequently encountered in Old English poetry, and propose that an alternative reading of *Wulf and Eadwacer* in the light of this *topos* may throw new and suggestive light on one of the most obscure of Old English poems. In addition to extending the possible range of sensibility encountered in the poem, such a review raises the delicate but perennial question of intersecting pagan and Christian cultures evident in so much Old English poetry. It may also serve to focus certain questions about the *Totenklage* genre which have been recently raised by Renate Haas, who connects secular laments for the dead from antiquity to the *planctus Mariae* of early Middle English lyric.[3] More recently, Haas has ventured a provocative connection of the lament for the dead with the love complaint, suggesting that the several shared motifs of the two genres produced the peculiar blend of amorous and elegiac passion which characterizes some of Chaucer's early poetry.[4] It is just such a blurring of the elegiac and the amorous in the history of criticism on *Wulf and Eadwacer* that I believe we might profitably re-examine here, preparatory to relocating the poem in the elegiac category, where its passion would seem to be, rather than sexual and amorous, more maternal and religious in its motivation.

Whether the speaker of *Wulf and Eadwacer* is indeed one of those suffering Anglo-Saxon women discussed by Renoir—and critics have disagreed on this fundamental fact of life—there can be little doubt that, critically speaking, the poem has been a suffering text. Benjamin Thorpe transcribed the lines for inclusion in his 1842 edition of the *Codex Exoniensis,* but, with consummate honesty, he declined to attempt a translation, writing instead his now famous admission of non-comprehension: "Of this I can make no sense."[5] Thorpe guaranteed himself immortality as the scholar most invoked by all subsequent editors of Old English manuscripts; but in the process, *Wulf and Eadwacer,* the only poem in the entire *Exeter Book* to be left by Thorpe standing at the altar of unconsummated translation, was fated to be found obscure. Subsequent scholars attempted to supply a prior "life story" for the poem from the *Volsunga Saga,*[6] the *Wulfdietrich* story,[7] and the *Hildebrandslied.*[8] Consequently, *Wulf and Eadwacer* came to be perceived as a detached remnant of some larger poem, or as an attached lyrical pendant, relatively complete as transmitted, but dependent, in the words of Kemp Malone, ". . . on a tale familiar to the poet's audience but unknown to us."[9]

The poem also had its share of explicators who were predisposed by Thorpe's puzzlement to construe the text not as a specific personal utterance, but as a riddle, coming up with solutions that ranged from "a millstone"[10] to a "riddle"[11] to the name of Cynewulf himself.[12] In 1937 W. J. Sedgefield initiated a new era of textual speculation[13] with an essay that proposed the subject of the poem to be a literal bitch, this one dreaming of her wolf, an actual lupine specimen with whom she has had a forest fling; and at least one critic has suggested that the poem deals with "a little story of love and jealousy between two men Wulf and Eadwacer," a view which apparently gained at least limited critical acceptance.[14]

Alain Renoir's essay, titled *"Wulf and Eadwacer:* A Noninterpretation," marked a welcome watershed in criticism on this text.[15] Published in 1965, one hundred twenty-three years after Thorpe's admission of editorial puzzlement, it appeared for a time to have released *Wulf and Eadwacer* from further exegetical debate by focussing—not on some prior plot line that could never be proved nor disproved—but on the universal thematic components of hostility, suffering, union, and separation that inform the poem.

Following Renoir's compromise solution, a number of promising studies then undertook to attend to structural, syntactic, thematic, and metrical aspects of the poem.[16] But shades of Sedgefield have also reappeared, with new essays that reduce the mystery of this text to the level of a tumorous lump or "wen,"[17] and a scribal in-joke about a "misplaced manuscript."[18] Recently, Peter Baker has refreshed the debate with a new essay on "The Ambiguity of *Wulf and Eadwacer*,"[19] but Baker's careful essay represents an attempt to reduce the ambiguities and to re-credential Henry Bradley's 1888 interpretation of the poem as the lament of a captive woman torn between husband and lover, victimized by the outlawry of one, the tyranny of the other.[20]

Setting aside for the moment those commentaries that choose to dehumanize the subject or to alter the speaker's gender, every critic of the poem—whether he or she is generating an interpretation or a noninterpretation of the text—has made certain basic assumptions about the poetic situation, assumptions which I share. All agree that the speaker of the poem is female—a fact conveyed at the most basic interpreta-tive level by the grammar. All agree that she is in a present state of emotional extremity. All agree that her present anguish—conveyed with extraordinary poetic immediacy—derives from some grief-giving love relationship in the past with someone named Wulf. All agree that the poem peaks with the speaker's adjurative outcry to someone directly addressed—by name or epithet—as "Eadwacer." All agree that this passionate outburst includes reference to some offspring described as *uncerne earne [earme] hwelp* 'our wretched whelp' (16b). All agree that this moment of tumescent emotional delivery gives way to an intellectual contraction of the verse into riddling verbal forms of paradox and oxymoron, with explicit reference to something "easily severed that never was joined" (. . . *eaþe tosliteð þætte næfre gesomnad wæs*, 18a–b).

In the traditional text-world of the poem, occupied by an amorous woman torn between two men, certain interpretative variants, it is true, do abolish the *ménage à trois* and in its place enter a singular male—be he husband or lover—whose bad luck or bad habits have caused the speaker's present suffering.[21] Adultery or fornication, then—at the very least involuntary abstinence between consenting adults—has traditionally been assumed as the underlying crisis which energizes the utterance of *Wulf and Eadwacer*, with critical consensus-takers often debating the nominal iden-tity and marital status of the man or men in question, and the admissible or inadmissi-ble prior sexual history of the woman.[22] As I have already indicated, and will now discuss further, it is with this assumption that I take issue. To facilitate the following discussion, I include the complete text of the poem. My revisionist translation of it appears at the end of this chapter.

> Leodum is minum   swylce him mon lac gife;
> willað hy hine aþecgan,   gif he on þreat cymeð.
>   Ungelic is us.
> Wulf is on iege,   ic on oþerre.
> Fæst is þæt eglond,   fenne biworpen.
> Sindon wælreowe   weras þær on ige;
> willað hy hine aþecgan,   gif he on þreat cymeð.
>   Ungelice is us.
> Wulfes ic mines widlastum   wenum dogode;
> þonne hit wæs renig weder   ond ic reotugu sæt,

þonne mec se beaducafa   bogum bilegde,
wæs me wyn to þon,   wæs me hwæþre eac lað.
Wulf, min Wulf,   wena me þine
seoce gedydon,   þine seldcymas,
murnende mod,   nales meteliste.
Gehyrest þu, Eadwacer?   Uncerne earne hwelp
bireð wulf to wuda.
þæt mon eaþe tosliteð   þætte næfre gesomnad wæs,
uncer giedd geador.

II

Turning now to an overview of *Wulf and Eadwacer,* we may ask the poem to respond to the basic questions it raises. Who is Wulf? Who or what is Eadwacer? Who is the speaking woman? To whom is she talking? About what is she talking? What does her problematical past joy have to do with her present woe? The answers generated by the text and context of this lyric suggest to me the intriguing possibility that the cryptic poetic utterance of grief, separation, anxiety, and consummate anguish derives from the predicament of a mother lamenting a lost son. This ancient ritual of maternal grief, attested as early as Gilgamesh's lament for Enkidu ("Bitterly moaning like a woman mourning / . . . Like a mother mourning")[23] invites us to construe the often noted formalist anomaly of broken refrain and unfulfilled expectation of the obligatory verse pair in each concluding stanza of *Wulf and Eadwacer* as a technical device which conserves some sense of that ritual performance with peculiar emotional sufficiency.

In any event, it is interesting to note that the text, whose single manuscript transmission of course contained no "stanzaic" division, no punctuational refinements—a text whose very meaning has been in question from the day its editorial father first laid eyes on his baffling textual child—has nonetheless articulated itself so definitively that even those critics who find fault with the metrics, the structure, the formal irregularities in *Wulf and Eadwacer,* have almost universally expressed themselves unwilling to emend the anatomy of the poem.[24] They persist in this unwillingness even when they confess themselves unhappy with its apparent rudeness, much as Gargamelle, mother of Gargantua, expressed herself unwilling to perform certain suggested emendations upon her husband's intrinsic form, even though she, too, felt compelled to comment at length upon the difficulties she had thereby been caused.

My point here is not a frivolous one. I am suggesting that the poem is possessed of its own peculiar authority which it communicates most tellingly through the particulars of its received form, a form which I believe can be demonstrated as deeply rooted in traditions of elegiac memorial inscription. Furthermore, if we can put aside a century and a half of assumed amorous passion—no easy task, to be sure—and listen to the utterance of a mother lamenting a lost son, then content as well as form would seem to connect *Wulf and Eadwacer* to the mainstream of grieving mothers in Anglo-Saxon poetry. Read thus, the verses are no less moving, no less cryptic, but they are certainly far less idiosyncratic than they have generally been assumed to be.

We can also now begin to loosen certain textual and critical Gordian knots: to wit, the rather universally acknowledged fact that the "intense, romantic passion" of a sexually tormented woman is a theme which, in the words of David Daiches, speaking for generations of uncertain readers, is "quite uncharacteristic of Anglo-Saxon poetry as it has come down to us."[25] Moreover, if we return now to that "canon of the uncanonized" women mentioned at the beginning of this essay, we find that, in an overwhelming number of instances, their emotional and cultural problem involves variously adumbrated maternal anguishings over the present, past, or future fate of sons.

Thus, in *Beowulf*, we have Wealhþeow, wife of Hroðgar, complimenting the hero for having recently cleansed Heorot of its problems by killing the anti-social son of a monstrous mother; then, with typical poetic irony, the queen converts her elegant compliment into a veiled plea that Beowulf protect her two vulnerable young sons, Hreðric and Hroðmund, sitting to his left and his right, and champion them against the politically fated death that hangs a heavy doom over their innocent heads. Wealhþeow's phrase, *uncran eaferan* 'our sons' (1185a)[26] is close to the *uncerne earne hwelp* (16b) used by the woman speaker in *Wulf and Eadwacer*.

Likewise the grief of Hildeburh, wife of Finn and sister of Hnæf, celebrated in the song which *Hroðgares scop* performs at the victory banquet, is a grief that describes a woman who loses *bearnum ond bröðrum* 'son and brother' (1074a; not some pre-Lawrencian "sons and lovers"). When Hildeburh commits to Hnæf's funeral pyre *hire selfre sunu* 'her own son' (1115a), the psychological surrender is expressed in the text with two terse phrases: *ides gnornode* 'the woman mourned with sorrowing songs' (1117b) and *geōmrode giddum* 'lamented her *giddum*' (1118a). The dative plural noun literally means songs, stories, formal poetic laments. But here, as in the last phrase of *Wulf and Eadwacer—uncer giedd geador*—the *giedd* or *giddum* incorporate and memorialize the actual persons being lamented. In each case, there is a grieved-for son whose greatest hope of identity and survival now lies in the communicative success of the poem itself. The *Beowulf* poet, accustomed to observing the epitome of male expertise with the succinct phrase *þæt wæs gōd cyning*, now expresses his sense of the quintessentially female experience by observing *þæt wæs geōmuru ides!* 'that was a sad woman' (1075b). The catalog of sorrowing women includes the opening reference of *Widsið* to Ealhild, on her way to marry Ermanric, whose shady history includes the cruel possibility that among the many people he put to death, some were his own children.[27]

And there is the *geōmuru ides* of *Deor*, whose typical troubles with sons and brothers are not only entered into the poem, but also are ranked according to their priorities of grief, the maternal taking precedence over the fraternal problem:

Beadohilde ne wæs   hyre broþra deaþ
on sefan swa sar   swa hyre sylfre þing,
þæt heo gearolice   ongieten hæfde
þæt heo eacen wæs;   æfre ne meahte
þriste geþencan,   hu ymb þæt sceolde.

(8a–12b)

(Beadohild was not as heartsick over her brother's death as over her own affair [i.e., her pregnancy], a condition she had now unmistakably verified, that she was pregnant, and could not ever contemplate without having misgivings about the outcome.)[28]

The catalogue could be extended, perhaps not endlessly, but certainly further; here I simply note that of those three texts presumed by various early explicators of *Wulf and Eadwacer* to supply the "answer" to the so-called "riddle" of the poem, all have heroines whose emotional crux resides in the maternal rather than in the more narrowly erotic anguish. The *Vǫlsunga Saga's* Signy[29] literally harrows herself to death with episodes of infanticide and then incest with Sigmund, her brother, in order to conceive Sinfjotli, a son worthy enough to carry out the obligatory vengeance of the Wolfings on King Siggier. Hild, mother of Helgi-Wulf-Dietrich,[30] sees her child carried off to the woods by wolves shortly after his birth. The wife of Theodric in the *Hildebrandslied,* also hypothesized as the speaker of *Wulf and Eadwacer,*[31] is a "sad lady" left behind by her fleeing husband *barn unwahsan* 'with an ungrown son' (21b), a child who will eventually be killed by his own father.

Nor can we ignore here those moving verses that open the Old English *The Fortunes of Men:*[32]

Ful oft þæt gegongeð,   mid godes meahtum,
þætte wer ond wif   in woruld cennað
bearn mid gebyrdum   ond mid bleom gyrwað,
tennaþ ond tætaþ,   oþþæt seo tid cymeð,
gegæð gearrimum,   þæt þa geongan leomu,
liffæstan leoþu,   geloden weorþað.
Fergað swa ond feþað   fæder ond modor,
giefað ond gierwaþ.   God ana wat
hwæt him weaxendum   winter bringað!
    Sumum þæt gegongeð   on geoguðfeore
þæt se endestæf   earfeðmæcgum
wealic weorþeð.   Sceal hine wulf etan,
har hæðstapa;   hinsiþ þonne
modor bimurneð.

(1–14a)

(So often it happens, by the power of God, that a man and a wife bring forth in the world a newly born child, and they clothe him in colors, they tend and teach till the moment arrives, till the time comes to pass that the limbs of the youth, the quickening parts become sturdy and strong. So they fetch and they feed, the father and mother, they favor, they nurture. God alone knows what the seasons shall bring to the young growing boy! To one it shall happen, in the prime of his youth, that the end of his time for the most wretched man shall sorrowfully happen. The wolf shall devour him, the gray heathstepper; the mother shall mourn that sad going forth.)

This rather painful catalogue should support a signal point of my argument: the most typical lamentory predicament of an Old English woman tends to involve the negative fate of a male child rather than sexual longing for an absent husband and/or lover. Furthermore, the function of intertextuality in the generation of certain literatures, especially in elegiac verses, often involves a demonstrable technique of allusive quotation and poetic reference whereby a word, a phrase, a single cryptic statement is meant to summon forth an entire well of prior poetry and puts that font of deep emotional meaning at the service of the present text.[33] If I am at all right in my conjectures, what we have in *Wulf and Eadwacer* is a highly autonomous dramatic monologue simulating "the activity of a person imagined as virtually real,"[34] an imagined maternal speaker intimate with her own literary and funerary tradition, who is here uttering an elegiac lament for a lost son named Wulf. As in the manner of all successful dramatic monologues, the poem's disclosures are wrought through mimetic utterance involving a gradual appreciation by the audience of what the speaker has known from the outset.

III

It would be well to recall here, in an illustrative rather than an exhaustive way, the funerary tradition of elegiac inscription and poetic quotation that provides a helpful context for this re-reading of *Wulf and Eadwacer*. Sepulchral stones with carved runic inscriptions have survived in England from the late sixth and early seventh centuries, and seem to point to heathen as well as to unambiguously Christian interments.[35] But it is in the Scandinavian countries, where the revisions of Christianity were comparatively late in coming, that the common traditions inherited from Germanic antiquity have been most impressively preserved, qualitatively and quantitatively. Of Sweden's two to three thousand surviving stones bearing memorial inscriptions,[36] none are more impressive than the Östergötland Rök stone and the Västergötland Sparlösa stone. Both stones date from the ninth century and both offer important cognate evidence to certain aspects of form and content in *Wulf and Eadwacer*. They deserve our careful consideration here.

Kemp Malone, in his 1933 edition of the Old English *Deor,* has already noted the intimate connection of that poem's fourth section and the "East Geatish runic monument of the ninth century, the famous inscription of Rök."[37] The Old English poetic reference to Theodric's thirty-year reign over *Mæringa burg* 'the Mæring's stronghold' (19a) is mirrored in a complete poetic stanza carved on the Rök stone, a stanza which likewise refers to *ÞioðrikR . . . skati Mæringa* 'Theodric . . . protector of Mærings'.[38] Since there was "probably no great lapse of time between the inscription of the Rök stone and the composition of the Old English poem,"[39] and since we possess this indisputable evidence of a common poetic tradition, we might profitably examine other connections between parts of the Rök inscription and the lines of *Wulf and Eadwacer,* which text immediately follows *Deor* in the *Exeter Book,* and shares with *Deor* its unique poetic features of quasi-stanzaic verses and a repeated refrain.

We should note at the outset that the Rök stone, described as "the most impressive monument ever raised in Sweden to commemorate a dead kinsman,"[40] was, in fact, erected in honor of a lost son: *Aft Væmoð standa runaR þaR. Æn Varinn faði, faðiR aft faigian sunu* 'For Væmod stand these runes. And Varin wrote them, the father for his dead son'.[41] The commemorative inscription is followed by a series of highly allusive, highly compressed prose narratives, serving almost in the fashion of a catalogue of prose *incipits,* but whose mannered style, expressions, and word order clearly connect them "to the elevated language of poetry."[42] Each *incipit* begins with a formal phrase signaling ritual utterance: *Þat sagum . . . Sagum mogminni* 'I tell this . . . I tell the tale'. In each instance, there follows a cryptic reference to heroes and legends from antiquity, many now lost.[43] The complete stanza referring to Theodric is followed by a prose utterance: *Þat sagum tvalfta, hvar hæstR se GunnaR etu vettvangi an, kunungaR tvaiR tigiR svað a liggia* 'This I tell in the twelfth instance where the horse of the Valkyrie sees food on the battlefield, where twenty kings lie'. Now, "the horse of the Valkyrie" was a standard kenning in the poetry of the Vikings for the wolf, who typically roams the battlefield, "hungrily watchful for food," joining with the eagle and the raven who are "thirsting for the blood of the slain warriors."[44] This "twelfth instance" on the Rök stone can perhaps sensitize us to what was being summoned up for the poetically cultivated Old English audience of *Wulf and Eadwacer* when a lamenting woman was heard to cry out, *Uncerne earne hwelp / bireð wulf to wuda* 'the wolf bears our wretched whelp to the woods' (16b–17a). The possibility moves even closer toward probability when we recall the previously mentioned grieving mother in *The Fortunes of Men* whose son's fate is to die young and to be eaten by wolves. When we place these two poetic references into the context of the Old English formula of the beasts of battle, most familiar to us from *Beowulf, The Battle of Maldon,* and *The Battle of Brunanburh,*[45] we may assume a subtly variant form of the traditional theme, a variant which connects the formula to poignant maternal lament and invites us to construct the present re-reading of *Wulf and Eadwacer* as the grieving memorial utterance of a mother for a lost son whose name was Wulf.

Appropriation of a formulaic theme to the individualized needs of a poetic situation was of course one hallmark of a skillful poet. But here, with the *wælreowe weras* 'corpse-greedy warriors' (6a–b) found on the island—an island which may be either a burial site or a foreign land, but in either case a locale where the traditionally predatory wolf is imagined as bearing away the corpse of the slain Wulf—we may well have an instance of heretofore unnoticed ingenuity in manipulating the formulaic materials. The possibility needs to be considered in the context of a closer look at those perhaps overly familiar instances from *Beowulf, Maldon,* and *Brunanburh,* cited above. In *Brunanburh,* where the raven, the eagle, and the wolf do the postmortem honors of announcing and participating in the fact of death, the reference to the *græge deor / wulf on wealde* 'the gray beast, / the wolf in the wood' (64b–65a) is immediately followed by the reference to an ancient literary tradition that tells of "slaughter" on the "island" and shares the lexical referents of *wæl* and *eiglande* employed by the *Wulf and Eadwacer* poet.[46] In *Beowulf,* where the *wonna hrefn* meets with the *earne* and the *wulf* to do their post-mortem duties, the animals are mythically personified with great imaginative vitality as the raven discusses, in most grisly post-prandial fashion, *hū him æt æte spēow, / þenden hē wið wulf wæl rēafode* 'how he fared at the feasting, / when along with the wolf, he plundered the corpses' (3026b–27b). I suspect more than lexical coincidence in the fact that this reference to raven and wolf occurs in the narrative of slaughterous battle fought at "Ravenswood," where the Swedish king Ongenþeow is slain by two of Hygelac's retainers, brothers bearing the highly allusive names of "Eofor" and "Wulf." In *Maldon*, where the naturalistic references to eagle and raven are so obvious as to be scarcely worth comment—*hremmas wundon, / earn æses georn* 'ravens wheeled / the corpse-greedy eagle' (106b–107a)—we should observe that the traditional items are immediately preceded by an extremely subtle manipulation of the formulaic theme in the allusion to the Viking horde (*wicinga werod*, 97a) here described as *wælwulfas* 'slaughter-wolves' (96a). Indeed, there may be a grim oral/aural pun on Odin/Woden himself in the verb choice: *Wodon þa wælwufas*. . . . The suggestion is especially tantalizing when we recall the pagan tradition involved in Odin and his wolf-riding Valkyries. Byrhtnoð's famous death speech which directly follows the *wælwulfas* reference strengthens even further this possibility of a deliberate resonating of the pagan-wolf connection when the dying warrior prays for a safe journey for his soul to *þeoden engla* 'the Prince of Angels' (178b) and petitions that his spirit not be snatched off by the hellfiends (*þæt hi helsceaðan   hynan ne moton*, 180a–b).

It is interesting to note that this poetic theme of corpses as food for predatory animals occurs in a number of instances in the poetry inscribed on the runic monuments of Sweden, as well as in traditional Eddaic and scaldic verse that is closely connected to such inscription.[47] In this connection, too, it should be noted that the vast majority of the poetically inscribed rune-stones that survive were "made and inscribed as memorials to dead kinsmen," that a number of them record that they were commissioned by parents—often by mothers—for their dead sons, and that in numerous instances, the dead kinsmen are lamented as having fallen in battles fought in foreign lands, hence with no opportunity for burial in their homeland, among their own people.[48]

In *Wulf and Eadwacer*, then, the speaker's opening reference to "my people" (*Leodum is minum*, 1a), and to some veritable gift or sacrifice made in connection with them as a people (*swylce him mon lac gife*, 1b), can be read as the beginning of elegiac utterance which articulates the communal sense of loss before moving to more private and personal configurations of grief: To my people it (i.e., the death of the lamented one) is as if someone had offered a sacrifice for them. In the two half-lines that follow—verses which involve the lexically problematical *apecgan* 'to devour' or 'to feed' and *þreat* 'a troop, a company of people' or 'a need, a condition of necessity'—I would suggest that what we have is not some univocal reference which time has rendered semantically obscure, but rather that we may be audience to an exquisitely rendered poetic expression of that ambiguity, anxiety, and apprehension which the mother experiences on behalf of her son as he makes his second absolute journey away from her, passing from this world to whatever is next. Perhaps life ends in physical devourment by corpse-greedy *wælwulfas;* perhaps he will be fed at the pagan feast promised to the nobly slain as the wolf-riding messengers of Odin carry him over into the company of heroes; or perhaps those other divine messengers of the new Christian dispensation will conduct him into the communion of saints. Whatever the outcome, there is always that great gulf necessarily estranging the living from the dead which all elegy tries to articulate, and which *Wulf and Eadwacer* seems to me to iterate poignantly in its broken refrain: *Ungelic is us* 'It is otherwise for us (our destiny different)'.

Provisionally re-read this way as elegiac rather than as amorous lament, the speaker's description of herself and Wulf located on separate islands (*Wulf is on iege, ic on operre,* 4); Wulf's fen-surrounded island envisioned as populated by corpse-greedy warriors (*Fæst is þæt eglond, fenne biworpen. / Sindon wæl-reowe weras þær on ige,* 5a–6b); her final anguished outcry to someone called "Eadwacer" about the wolf bearing off their wretched whelp to the woods (*Gehyrest þu, Eadwacer? Uncerne earne hwelp / bireð wulf to wuda,* 16a–17a)—all of these admittedly cryptic poetic utterances can be construed as the sorrowful, traditionally allusive verses of a grieving mother at least as coherently, and perhaps more coherently, than as the complaints of a compromised wife.

Indeed, that section of reminiscence where she recalls that former season or time when some *beaducafa* 'battlebold man' (11a) "laid his arms about me," and the subsequent conversion of that former *wyn* 'joy', into her present woe, could well be what we would hear were the *wif* of *The Fortunes of Men,* cited above, to recitatively recall the beginning of her son's life, a reminiscence made more poignant by virtue of the fact that all personal and cultural expectations for that son have now been forfeited.

As the ensuing discussion will try to make clear, the cultural text of this grieving lyric is at least as important as the text of its personal elegiacisms, and the *renig weder* (10a) of the former days may involve much more than a mere meteorological reference to a former season in the speaker's life. We will return to that moment of former "rain/reign" shortly. First, however, it is necessary to attend to another lexical point in the text where philological possibility and the never univocal language of poetry need to be brought into more approximate alignment in order to approach their deeper poetic significance. The crucial item, of course, is *eadwacer* of line 16. My rendering of the term depends on the underlying tension between the heroic pagan past and the tenuous Christian present which characterizes much Old English poetry, and which in the present poem, I believe, significantly informs the final shaping of its emotional crux. The inherence of Christian/pagan consciousness in some form or another in virtually all surviving Old English poetry and the persistent ambiguity of interpretation generated thereby have always been, and will continue to be, something of a vexed question for subsequent criticism. Certainly, we should not deny the propriety of the question in this reconsideration of the meaning of *Wulf and Eadwacer.*

I V

When the humane Alcuin posed his now famous question to Bishop Hyge-bald—*Quid Hinieldus cum Christo?* 'What has Ingeld to do with Christ?'[49]—we should appreciate that he was probably not thundering some narrow exclusionary disapproval of the survival of the pagan gods and heroes under the newly built Christian roof. Rather, his question was the essential one of "accommodation" that centuries earlier Augustine had asked in Rome, and had answered with his theory of "Egyptian gold."[50] The radical iconoclasm of a Coifi as reported by Bede[51] was perhaps a shrewd political gesture, but it was far less psychologically informative than were the poignant uncertainties about the afterlife expressed by that same pagan priest's colleague in his incomparable metaphor of the sparrow in the meadhall. We need only recall the sophisticated response offered philosophically by Boethius, and artistically by the *Beowulf* poet, to remember that cultures in transition from paganism to Christianity often approach the central theological question with exquisite indirection. The poet of *Wulf and Eadwacer,* shaping an elegiac lamentation out of just such cultural materials, would have come up squarely against the question.

In many instances, the expressed attitudes were unambiguously Christian and certain runic inscriptions on memorial monuments attest the univocal conviction: "Valhalla is exchanged for the word *paradis,* Thor and mysterious magic charms are replaced by God and God's mother, Christ and Saint Michael."[52] From as early as 550 to 600 there survives in Brough, Westmorland, England, a monument whose "excessively old Double Cross," its palmbranch logo—"the earliest Christian symbol of triumph over death"—and the "still half-Scandian dialect in 12 lines of staverime verse" all "announce the overgang from heathendom."[53] Runically inscribed monuments survive in Denmark in large numbers, bearing the typical inscriptions that petition "Lord God and Saint Michael," "Christ and Saint Michael," "God and Saint Michael," to "help" or to "ease" the souls of the dead.[54] The Uppland runestone at Ängby, Knivsta parish, erected by a woman, Estrid, for Joar, her husband, concludes with the petition, *Mihel gætti and hans* 'Michael, take care of his soul'.[55] But such theological serenity, whether it comes early or late, cannot tell the entire story. There are other stones which illustrate the tension that must have been intrinsic to many interments when "the dead man was now to be buried in the consecrated ground of the churchyard, separated from his kin. He was no longer to lie in his grave on the slopes by the homestead where his ancestors lay."[56] Death far from home may have provided one version of poignancy; but deciding to have, or to forgo, burial in the new Christian cemetery was surely another typical, painful choice. That "venerable custom and family tradition were broken" often and that there was often deep cleavage "between old custom and new faith" can be inferred from the fact that the new burial rites finally needed to be articulated as obligations in the ecclesial sections of the provincial laws.[57] The Bogesund rune-stone gives us one testimony of parents who found the choice an impossible one and forged their own equivocal solution: "Gunne and Asa had this stone raised . . . in memory of . . . their son. He died at Ekerö. He is buried in the churchyard. Fastulv cut the runes." Here we have an instance—surely typical—where "a rune stone was evidently raised in the ancestral cemetery at home, while a more ecclesiastical monument was provided in the churchyard at Ekerö."[58]

From precisely such an entanglement of pagan past and Christian present, made especially acute by the crisis of death, I believe we can find the proper context for *Wulf and Eadwacer.* Likewise, in the widely attested petitions to angelic mediators at the moment of death, I believe we can look for a reasonable approximation of the elusive *eadwacer.*[59] The word has traditionally been taken as the proper name of a second man in that romantic triangle assumed to be the poem's situation. Some readings, it is true, have assumed that *eadwacer* is not a proper name but an epithetic reference—straightforward or ironic—referring to an absent or present husband or lover who is then addressed, in translations, as everything from "property-watcher" to "cradle-watcher."[60] But, assuming the lament for the lost son that I take to be the poem's more culturally logical and poetically probable situation, it seems eminently reasonable to construe the word as an epithetic compound, the *ead* cognate with the well-attested *eadig* which commonly refers to the blessed or happy who enjoy the treasure or possession of Heaven.[61] "Eadwacer," then, I would take to be some messenger or guide from the Christian spirit-world, appropriately addressed, as Michael the archangel frequently was, in the adjurative mode at the end of the poem's conclusion, as at the end of memorial epigraphy, with a petition concerning the conduct and reception of the soul into the midst of the heavenly company. This would be especially consonant with a prayer commending the soul of a dead kinsman into the cure of one who is, indeed, a "heaven-dweller" and who, in the most optimistic presumption, will "receive him, should he come into their midst" (*willað hy hine apecgan, gif he on þreat cymeð*, 2a–b)—perhaps a piece of wishful thinking to be placed beside the wistful urgencies of Wealhþeow as she utters her own poignantly hopeful prediction regarding her sons: *Ic mīnne can / glædne Hrōþulf, þæt hē þā geogoðe wile / ārum healdan, gyf þū ǣr þonne hē, / wine Scildinga, worold oflǣtest* 'I know my gracious Hrothulf that he will uphold the welfare of these youths if you, friend of the Scyldings, leave the world before him' (1180b–83b).

At the same time, underneath this Christian *eadwacer*, it is easy to imagine emotionally potent myths of shape-shifting warrior valkyries, those fierce, wolf-riding messengers of Odin who devoured corpses on the battlefield, but who also, in their own *eadwacer* guise, escorted into Valhalla those warriors who had died nobly, and "there welcomed them with horns of mead, as they are seen doing on many of the Gotland stones."[62] How, and if, and where, and by whom the dead kinsman will be received are excruciatingly problematic questions for the lamenting survivor. It is even possible that here we have an answer to the quasi-magical repetition of the question, *willað hy hine apecgan, gif he on þreat cymeð* (2a–b and 7a–b respectively), followed by the identically ritual refrain, *ungelic(e) is us,* question and refrain possibly representing in their doubled formality a powerful attempt to preserve both Christian and pagan options for the deceased, even as they express the inexpressible dilemma of cultural and religious uncertainty for the speaking survivor.

Even convinced Christian survivors could suffer ambivalence when burying their dead who may not have perfectly shared the convictions of those who were burying them. A number of rune-stones bear a prayer-formula that expresses just such problematic anxieties about the deceased: *Guð hialpi sal hans bætr þæn hann kunni til gærva* 'God help his soul better than he knew how to deserve it'; *Guð hialpi hans and ok salu bætr þæn hann gæroi til. Munu æigi mærki / mæRi verða, moðiR gærði æftiR sun sinn æiniga* 'May God help his spirit and soul better than he did toward it. No monuments / shall be better. The mother made it for her only son'; *Guð biargi sel hans bætr þæn hann hafR til gært* 'God save his soul better than he deserved'.[63] That even a deathbed conversion gave signal reassurance to such pious Christian survivors can be adduced from other inscriptions which announce that the deceased "died in white clothing" (*í hvítaváðum*), that is, in the "white clothes" or baptismal robes which "were worn by the convert at his baptism and for the week following."[64]

But for every convinced Christian survivor suffering anxiety about an unconverted kinsman, there must have been at least some who suffered from other versions of the same dilemma. Parents clinging to the old ways in faith or in fact might openly assert their belief in the continuing power of the pagan gods and their Valkyrie messengers over the fates of the dead: *Gehyrest þu, Eadwacer?   Uncerne earne hwelp / bireð wulf to wuda* (16a–17a). Or they may have mourned the *ragnarök*, the twilight of the old gods who were being supplanted by the new Christian deity, even as they questioned the adequacy of the Christian tutelary spirits to save their dead from the literal, or mythical, depredations of wolves.[65] Indeed, the uneasy ambivalence underlying the entire text of *Wulf and Eadwacer*, which nearly all responsible commentators upon the poem have noted, may locate its deepest core of meaning at this level of cultural statement, without which the power of the personal utterance cannot be fully appreciated.

Now we may usefully reconsider the meaning of that rather obscure tenth line— *þonne hit wæs renig weder*—usually translated "when it was rainy weather." This may indeed be a simple meteorological reference to a former season in the speaker's lifetime; nothing in the re-reading I am proposing would be unsettled by such a univocal interpretation. Nevertheless, recognizing the allusiveness and indirection of this poem which is intrinsic to its making, it is particularly intriguing to hypothesize that in the *renig weder* we may possess a rich lexical clue to the passing of the pagan era.

C. L. Wrenn, discussing diction and verse technique in *Beowulf*, points to the "very large number of the compound words found only in poetry" and explains that "doubtless the poet and his audience got connotations, associations, and subtle suggestions or memories from such compounds which we cannot recapture."[66] In detailing the inevitable process of obsolescence that attaches to such specialized poetic vocabulary, Wrenn notes a number of poetic compounds "which have a general meaning for the poet and his hearers, but have lost the precise significance of their first element, which has become archaic or obsolete."[67] To illustrate the phenomenon, Wrenn then cites the term *regn-heard* in l. 326 of *Beowulf* and glosses it

> in the general sense of 'marvellously strong': but its first element *regn* originally meant something like 'magic power' or 'divine power', and is etymologically related to the Gothic *raginōn*, 'to rule', and the Old Norse *regin*, 'gods', preserved in the term *ragnarök*. Doubtless the original meaning was 'tempered by the gods' or 'magically tempered': but with the obsolescence of the element *regn*, it has already in the time of the *Beowulf*-poet become identified with the ordinary prose term *regn*, 'rain', while the general sense of *regn-heard* remains intelligible as that of an established traditional poetic compound.[68]

Wrenn goes on to illustrate that just such a confusion has, in fact, taken place by citing the parallel use of the term *scur-heard* in l. 1033 of *Beowulf:* "if *regn-heard* meant 'rain-hardened' literally, why not 'shower-hardened'?"[69]

We can now make a final return to that famous Sparlösa stone, mentioned earlier in this essay, a memorial rune-stone which dates from the same period as that of Rök. In the partially obscure inscription on the Sparlösa stone, "the reader is invited to interpret *runaR þaR reginkundu,* 'the runes derived from the divine powers'." This same descriptive term applied to runes appears on the seventh-century Noleby stone in Västergotland, a stone "whose original site seems to have been inside a grave" and is hence even more certainly connected to magical powers and rites of great antiquity.[70] The same word, *reginkunnr,* appears in the Old Icelandic *Hávamál,* and again, it refers to the divine power of runes associated with the pagan past: *Þat er þá reynt / er þu at rúnum spyrr / inum reginkunnum / þeim er goðru ginnregin / ok faði fimbulþulr* . . . 'Then it is proved / when you ask about the runes / derived from the gods, / those which the mighty powers made / and the great word-master (=Odin) painted . . .'.[71] Finally, it should be noted that the cryptic inscription of "two stray lines" of poetry on the Swedish Skarpåker stone, raised "by Gunnar after Lydbjörn his son," are lines that closely resemble the "cataclysmic atmosphere of the doom of the gods" described by the poet of the *Vǫluspá,* and that each of these quotations involves "the image of a splitting of earth and heaven."[72] It is just possible that the final anguished reference in *Wulf and Eadwacer* to a tearing apart of what was never joined (. . . *eaþe tosliteð   þætte næfre gesomnad wæs*) involves an equally allusive, equally cryptic reference to the survival crisis of spirit over flesh, experienced and expressed at a time when pagan past and Christian present were themselves most uneasily conjoined.

To conclude, then, I suggest that *Wulf and Eadwacer* need not be read as the unambiguous lament of a sexually unsatisfied woman. It can be read coherently and far more consistently as the eloquent lament of a grieving mother reciting a formal *giedd* for her son whose death and/or burial may also have taken place on alien soil, adding to the already grievous separation imposed by death itself.[73] For a son whose name was Wulf, the very word that names him would summon up the coordinate image of animal predators carrying off the corpse. Such an image would resonate with literal and mythic poetic suggestion of the richest sort. The final anguished outcry to a guardian spirit—whether the speaker's point of view is explicitly Christian, or defiantly pagan, or something vacillating between the two—utters the truth of a complex cultural moment where pagan and Christian rites and their corresponding modes of consciousness are perceived as imperfectly fused or joined.[74] Out of these multiple and simultaneous dilemmas, the lyric speaks the particular, personal anguish of a woman whose son has lost his life, and consequently cannot fulfill the personal, cultural, and religious history of mother and son (*uncer giedd geador,* 19a). Re-reading the poem as a mother's lament, we can conserve the best philological and poetic insights of a century of commentators while making what I believe is a necessary adjustment of assumption about the speaker's basic predicament. Respecting the ironies and ambiguities that are a deliberate part of the poetry, I translate the text this way:[75]

> To my people it is as if someone offered a sacrifice for them.
>
> Will they $\left\{ \begin{array}{l} \text{receive him} \\ \text{devour him} \end{array} \right\}$ if he comes in their midst?
>
> $\left\{ \begin{array}{l} \text{It is otherwise for us:} \\ \text{Our destiny different.} \end{array} \right.$

Wulf is on one island; I on another.
Fast is that island, surrounded by fens.
There are corpse-greedy warriors there on that island;
Will they $\left\{ \begin{array}{l} \text{receive him} \\ \text{devour him} \end{array} \right\}$ if he comes in their midst?
$\left\{ \begin{array}{l} \text{It is otherwise for us:} \\ \text{Our destiny different.} \end{array} \right.$
I suffered from thoughts of my Wulf's journeyings.
When it was $\left\{ \begin{array}{l} \text{rainy weather} \\ \text{the olden days} \end{array} \right\}$ and I sat sighing,
When the battlebold man laid his arms about me,
What was a joy to me then was likewise my woe.
Wulf, my Wulf, thoughts about you
Have made me sick, your never-coming-back
Made me mournful of mind, it was not lack of provision.
Do you hear, Heavenwatcher? The wolf bears
Our wretched whelp away to the woods.
One can easily sever what never was joined:
$\left\{ \begin{array}{l} \text{Our tale together:} \\ \text{Our elegiac song.}^{76} \end{array} \right.$

NOTES

1. Alain Renoir, "A Reading Context for *The Wife's Lament,*" in *Anglo-Saxon Poetry: Essays in Appreciation,* ed. Lewis E. Nicholson and Dolores Warwick Frese (Notre Dame: University of Notre Dame Press, 1975), pp. 224–41.

2. All citations from *Wulf and Eadwacer* are from *The Exeter Book,* ed. George P. Krapp and Elliot Van Kirk Dobbie, vol. 3 of *The Anglo-Saxon Poetic Records* (New York: Columbia University Press, 1936), pp. 179–80 (cited hereafter as *ASPR*); all translations from Old English are mine.

3. See Renate Haas, *Die mittelenglische Totenklage* (Frankfurt: Lange, 1980); in her English Summary, pp. 353–55, Haas notes that "laments for the dead from different ages and even different cultures exhibit an astonishing degree of conformity" (p. 353), and attempts to work out a prototype in Chapter II. In Chapters III and IV, Haas traces the specific socio-cultural conditions of England in the high and late Middle Ages and the influence of Christian culture in shaping the *planctus Mariae* from the earlier traditions of passionate lament. Chapter IV studies the Middle English lament tradition as a continuation of preceding literatures, including those in Anglo-Saxon, where she notes that "the strict ethos of self-control as well as the marked community spirit of secular heroic poetry do not admit of spontaneous, egoistic wailing" (p. 354) in the manner of hair-tearing, garment-rending, self-lacerating swoons which were customary in France and Italy and had accordingly conditioned their tradition of literary lamentation.

4. Renate Haas, "Chaucer's Laments for the Dead," a paper delivered at Chaucer at Albany II, An International Congress in Honor, on his Retirement, of Rossell Hope Robbins (Albany: State University of New York at Albany, November 7, 1982). Professor Haas has very kindly shared the text of her paper with me.

5. Benjamin Thorpe, ed., *Codex Exoniensis* (London: Society of Antiquaries, 1842), p. 527.

6. W. H. Schofield, "Signy's Lament," *Publications of the Modern Language Association* 17 (1902): 262–95.

7. See P. J. Frankis, "*Deor* and *Wulf and Eadwacer:* Some Conjectures," *Medium Ævum* 31 (1962): 161–75; and L. L. Schücking, *Kleines angelsächsisches Dichterbuch* (Cöthen: O. Schulze, 1919), pp. 16ff.

8. Rudolf Imelmann, "Die altenglische Odoaker-Dichtung," in *Forschungen zur altenglischen Poesie* (Berlin: Weidmann, 1907), pp. 73ff.

9. Kemp Malone, "Two English *Frauenlieder*," in *Studies in Old English Literature in Honor of Arthur G. Brodeur*, ed. Stanley B. Greenfield (Eugene: University of Oregon Press, 1963), p. 108.

10. H. Patzig, "Zum ersten Rätsel des Exeter Buches," *Archiv* 145 (1923): 204ff.

11. Moritz Trautmann, "Cynewulf und die Rätsel," *Anglia* 6 (1883): 158ff.

12. See Frederick Tupper, "The Cynewulfian Runes of the First Riddle," *Modern Language Notes* 25 (1910): 235ff; see also Heinrich Leo's earlier "Quæ de se ipso Cynewulfus . . . tradiderit," on his interpretation of *Wulf and Eadwacer* published in the 1857 Halle program, cited in *ASPR*, vol. 3, p. lv, n. 2.

13. W. J. Sedgefield, "Old English Notes," *Modern Language Review* 36 (1931): 74.

14. See Schofield, "Signy's Lament": 262, n. 2.

15. Alain Renoir, "*Wulf and Eadwacer:* A Non-interpretation," in *Franciplegius: Medieval and Linguistic Studies in Honor of Francis Peabody Magoun, Jr.*, ed. Jess B. Bessinger, Jr., and Robert P. Creed (New York: New York University Press, 1965), pp. 147–63.

16. See Ruth P. M. Lehmann, "The Metrics and Structure of 'Wulf and Eadwacer'," *Philological Quarterly* 48 (1969): 151–65; Terrence Keough, "The Tension of Separation in *Wulf and Eadwacer*," *Neuphilologische Mitteilungen* 77 (1976): 552–60; Harry E. Kavros, "A Note on *Wulf and Eadwacer*," *English Language Notes* 15 (1977): 83–84.

17. Donald K. Fry, "*Wulf and Eadwacer:* A Wen Charm," *The Chaucer Review* 5 (1971): 247–63.

18. Norman E. Eliason, "On *Wulf and Eadwacer*," in *Old English Studies in Honor of John Collins Pope*, ed. Robert B. Burlin and Edward B. Irving, Jr. (Toronto: University of Toronto Press, 1974), pp. 225–34.

19. Peter S. Baker, "The Ambiguity of *Wulf and Eadwacer*," *Studies in Philology* 78 (1981): 39–51.

20. In a review of Henry Morley, *English Writers* II, *Academy* 33 (1888): 197–98, Henry Bradley suggests Wulf as the lover, and Eadwacer as the tyrant husband. Baker reverses the roles, but keeps the triangle. See Baker, "Ambiguity": 50.

21. See John F. Adams, " 'Wulf and Eadwacer': An Interpretation," *Modern Language Notes* 73 (1958): 1–5; see also Keough.

22. The best summary of varying surmises about the marital and affectional status of the persons known as "Wulf" and "Eadwacer" can be found in Renoir's "Noninterpretation," p. 161, n. 7 and n. 10.

23. *The Epic of Gilgamesh*, trans. N. K. Sandars (Harmondsworth: Penguin Books, Ltd., rev. ed. 1972), p. 94.

24. See, especially, Lehmann, "Metrics and Structure."

25. David Daiches, *A Critical History of English Literature*, vol. 1 (New York: Ronald Press Co., 1960), p. 20.

26. All citations from *Beowulf* are from *Beowulf and the Fight at Finnsburg*, ed. Fr. Klaeber, 3rd ed. with first and second supplements (Boston: D. C. Heath and Co., 1950), pp. 1–120.

27. For a discussion of Ealhild and Ermanric, see Kemp Malone, ed., *Widsith* (London: Methuen and Co., Ltd., 1936; rev. ed. Copenhagen: Rosenkilde and Bagger, 1962), pp. 140–42 and 146–49.

28. *ASPR*, vol. 3, p. 178; concerning that supremely tactful phrase, *hyra sylfre þing*, we might note that Beadohild was not exactly "doing her own thing" when she became pregnant as a victim of rape.

29. See Schofield, "Signy's Lament."

30. See Schücking, *Kleines angelsächsisches Dichterbuch;* and Frankis, "*Deor* and *Wulf and Eadwacer.*"

31. See Imelmann, "Die Odoaker-Dichtung": Theodric's persecutor was Odoacer, the Ostrogothic ruler of Italy whose name bore a suggestive phonic closeness to the elusive "eadwacer" addressed at the end of our poem.

32. *ASPR*, vol. 3, p. 154.

33. For a fuller description of the typical form, including the allusive use of *mogminni*—popular traditions encoded in concentrated narratives from mythical and heroic poetry—see the discussion of the Rök inscription included in the English "Summary" of Lis Jacobsen's *Rökstudier*, in *Arkiv för Nordisk Filologi* 76 (1961): 47–49.

34. Ralph Rader, "The Dramatic Monologue and Related Lyric Forms," *Critical Inquiry* 3 (1976): 150.

35. Ralph W. V. Elliott, *Runes, An Introduction* (Manchester: Manchester University Press, 1959; rpt. 1980), pp. 81–83; for an even earlier monument than those cited by Elliott, see Dr. George Stephens, *Handbook of the Old-Northern Runic Monuments of Scandinavia and England* (Edinburgh: Williams and Norgate, 1884), p. 116.

36. See Elliott, *Runes*, p. 26.

37. Kemp Malone, ed., *Deor* (London: Methuen and Co., 1933), p. 10.

38. Sven B. F. Jansson, *The Runes of Sweden*, trans. Peter G. Foote (New York: Bedminster Press, 1962), p. 14; here, and in all translations of runic inscriptions cited in Jansson's book, the translations are Foote's.

39. Jansson, *Runes*, p. 120.

40. Ibid., p. 11.

41. Ibid., pp. 13–14; the complete transcription and translation of the Rök inscription are found on pp. 14–15.

42. Ibid., p. 15.

43. Ibid., pp. 14–15.

44. Ibid., p. 43.

45. For *Beowulf*, see ll. 3024b–27b; for *Maldon*, see *ASPR*, vol. 6, p. 10, ll. 106b–7a; for *Brunanburh*, see *ASPR*, vol. 6, pp. 19–20, ll. 60a–65a.

46. *Ne wearð wæl mare* / *on þis eiglande   æfre gieta* / *folces gefylled   beforan þissum* / *sweordes ecgum,   þæs þe us secgað bec,* / *ealde uðwitan,   siþþan eastan hider* / *Engle and Seaxe   up becoman,* / *ofer brad brimu   Brytene sohtan,* / *wlance wigsmiþas,   Wealas ofercoman,* / *eorlas arhwate   eard begeatan* 'Nor was more slaughter wrought / on this island   ever yet, / a folk felled   before this / by sword's edge,   so the books tell us, / (and) the wise old bards,   since hither from the East / Angle and Saxon   came up / over the broad sea   sought the British, / proud warsmiths;   they whipped the Welsh, / fame-eager earls, begat (this) land', 65b–73b.

47. In addition to the Rök inscription discussed above, see, for example, the last stanza of the Gripsholm stone: *þæiR foru drængila* / *fiami at gulli* / *ok austarla* / *ærni gafu* 'They fared like men / far after gold / and in the east / gave the eagle food', Jansson, *Runes*, p. 41. See also the Sigtuna box with its curse/threat against thieves: *Fugl vælva slæit falvan* / *fann'k gauk a nas auka* 'The bird tore the pale thief. / I saw how the corpse-cuckoo swelled', Jansson, *Runes*, p. 123. See, too, Jansson's discussion of Eddaic and scaldic verse employing such phrases as "to gladden eagles" and "to give the eagle food," meaning "to kill enemies," *Runes*, pp. 43–44.

48. See Jansson, *Runes*, pp. 17–19, 22–23, 27, 30–35, 44, 60–65.

49. See Alcuin's letter to Hygebald, Bishop of Lindisfarne, *Monumenta Germaniæ Historica . . . Epistolarum, Tomus* 4, ed. E. Dümmler (Berolini: Weidmannos, 1895), p. 183.

50. Augustine, *Opera: De Doctrina Christiana*, Book 2, xl, in *Corpus christianorum Series Latina*, vol. 32, pp. 73–75.

51. Bede, *Opera Historica, Tomus Prior*, containing *Historiam Ecclesiasticam Gentis Anglorum*, ed. Charles Plummer (Oxford: Clarendon Press, 1896, rpt. 1946), pp. 111–13.

52. Jansson, *Runes*, p. 96.

53. See Stephens, cited in Elliott, *Runes*, p. 116.

54. See Lis Jacobsen and Erik Moltke, *The Runic Inscriptions of Denmark*, summary trans. Eva Nissen (Copenhagen: Ejnar Munksgaards Förlag, 1947), pp. 61–64.

55. Jansson, *Runes*, p. 96.

56. Ibid., p. 99.

57. "No one shall sacrifice to idols and no one shall put faith in groves or stones. All shall

honour the church, thither all shall go, the quick and the dead, those who come into the world and those who go from it." Quoted in Jansson, *Runes*, p. 99. Note that the Christian injunction to break with the pagan past focuses on memorial stones and interment customs.

58. Jansson, *Runes*, p. 100.

59. In addition to Byrhtnoð's dying petition to God as "prince of angels" who helps the souls of the dead in their journey to heaven (see *Maldon*, ll. 175–80, referred to earlier), we should also recall that angels were at the heart of the new Christian/national consciousness. Bede speaks of Pope Gregory's solicitude for "the salvation of our nation" when he records Gregory's famous pun on seeing the English slave boys in the Roman market and learning that they were called Angles: " 'Good,' he answered, " 'for they have an angelic face, and it is fitting for such as these to be co-inheritors of the angels in heaven' "(Bede, *Historia*, pp. 79–80). Translation mine.

60. See Adams, " 'Wulf and Eadwacer': An Interpretation."

61. See Joseph Bosworth and T. Northcote Toller, eds., *An Anglo-Saxon Dictionary* (London: Oxford University Press, 1882–98), p. 224, and Toller's *Supplement* (1921), p. 164.

62. H. R. Ellis Davidson, *Scandinavian Mythology* (London: Paul Hamlyn, 1969), p. 41.

63. Jansson, *Runes*, p. 97.

64. Ibid., pp. 92–94.

65. In support of this admittedly suppositious reconstruction, one can make tentative but provocative connections with all that material at the center of *Njál's Saga* which deals with the coming of Christianity to Iceland in A.D. 1000. Here I note, especially, those events narrated in chapters 100–107 which involve expressed Christian devotion to Michael as "guardian angel" of the new converts in *Njal's Saga* (trans. Magnus Magnusson and Hermann Pálsson [Baltimore: Penguin Books, Ltd., 1960; rpt. 1970], p. 218), and the making of competitive verses on the old and new religions where Christ and Thor are seen as duelling combatants (pp. 221–22), Odin is denigrated as "a dog," Freyja as "a bitch," and the new Christian religion as a "cowardly cur / that howls against our gods" (pp. 220–21). In tracing the *topos* of parent-and-child-in-religious-opposition, I note with particular interest Steinumm, the mother of Poet-Ref, who lectured Thangbrand, the Christian priest, "for a long time and tried unsuccessfully to convert him to paganism" (p. 221), and Mord Valgardsson who unsuccessfully urges his father to "take the new faith" since "you are an old man now," a suggestion which causes Valgard to break "all Mord's crosses and sacred symbols for him" after telling his son, "I would rather have you discard it [the Christian faith] and see what happens then" (p. 228). Throughout *Njál's Saga*, there are periodic visions of the coming of Christianity seen as coincident with the cataclysmic termination of the pagan era. The last such vision, which comes in the final pages, occurs on Good Friday and reveals twelve riders who disappear into a loom where men's heads serve as weights, men's intestines for warp and weft, a sword as the beater, and an arrow as shuttle. This vision engenders some of the saga's most powerful verses, uttered here to mark the final Christian reconciliation of Flosi and Kari, and the conclusion of the pagan order as the Valkyries "wind the web of war," sing of doom, and carry off corpses from the battlefield where "only the Valkyries / can choose the slain" (pp. 349–51). It is something of this anguished, apocalyptic awareness of physical and spiritual death-as-sundering that I would like to suggest lies in the poetic texture of *Wulf and Eadwacer*.

66. C. L. Wrenn, *Beowulf with the Finnesburg Fragment*, rev. ed. (London: George G. Harrap and Co., Ltd., 1958), pp. 80–81.

67. Ibid.

68. Ibid.

69. When W. F. Bolton revised Wrenn's edition (cited in note 66) in 1973, Bolton removed Wrenn's discussion of *regn* as "rain" and relocated this important etymological information in the glossary under *regn-heard* and *scur-heard*.

70. Jansson, *Runes*, pp. 15–16. The Noleby stone reads, "Runes, derived from the gods, I cut. . . ."

71. Quoted in Jansson, *Runes*, pp. 16–17.

72. The two lines on the Skarpåker stone read, *Jarð skal rifna / of upphiminn* 'Earth shall be riven / and the over-heaven' (Jansson, *Runes*, p. 132); the Vǫluspá lines are *Grjótbjorg gnata / . . . en himinn klofnar* 'Rock-cliffs crash / . . . and heaven is cleft' (Jansson, *Runes*, p. 134).

73. In suggesting the revised elegiac context, where the "other island" of Wulf's burial site may be either foreign soil or the traditional pagan grave site, I call particular attention to Elinor Lench's seminal essay, *"The Wife's Lament:* A Poem of the Living Dead," *Comitatus* I (December 1970): 1–23. The profound implications of Lench's suggestive insight—that the speaker of this elegy is imagined as a revenant communicating from beyond the pagan grave—becomes the subject of a subsequent essay by Raymond P. Tripp, Jr.; see his "The Narrator as Revenant: A Reconsideration of Three Old English Elegies," *Papers on Language and Literature* 8 (1972): 339–61. Tripp examines Lench's suggestion with great care, supplying a rich array of evidence from theological, literary, and anthropological sources to argue persuasively that we need, in this and in other Old English elegies, to re-negotiate the gap between earlier northern traditions of life-after-death and the superimposition upon them of later classical Mediterranean patterns of belief and their cognate cultural practices. The Wife's opening reference to the *giedd* she is singing or reciting on behalf of herself and her confinement *on wuda* 'in a wild overgrown spot' are both reminiscent of the funerary island and the painful *giedd* referred to by the woman speaker of *Wulf and Eadwacer*. In this connection, also see Jon Whitman, *Allegory: The Dynamics of an Ancient and Medieval Technique* (Cambridge: Harvard University Press, 1987), especially Appendices I and II, pp. 263–72, on the history of the terms 'Allegory' and 'Personification' where Whitman reminds us of the centrality of *prosopopoeia* to both, and connects Cicero's "Introduction of fictitious persons" (*personarum ficta inductio*) in *De Oratore* III, liii, 205, to Quintilian's *Institutio Oratoria* I, viii, 3; IV, i, 69; and XI, i, 41, where the Greek word is transliterated into Latin as *prosopopoeia* (*Institutio Oratoria* IX, ii, 29–37) which includes "the fashioning of conversations between ourselves and others, as well as the giving of speeches to the dead, to cities, or to abstractions ('formæ')," p. 269.

74. Note the heathenish observances of the Danes mentioned in *Beowulf*, 175a–86a. The ripeness of *Wulf and Eadwacer* for such fundamental re-interpretation is further attested by Marijane Osborn, "The Text and Context of *Wulf and Eadwacer*," in *The Old English Elegies: New Essays in Criticism and Research*, ed. Martin Green (London and Toronto: Associated University Press, Inc., 1983), pp. 174–89. This essay, like my own, claims a maternal anguish as the central preoccupation of the poem's speaker, though her particular path of meaning through the text diverges significantly from my own. Osborn's last footnote references an earlier version of my present essay, which appeared in *Notre Dame English Journal: A Journal of Religion in Literature* 15:1 (Winter 1983): 1–22, and came to her attention too late to be incorporated into her own argument. Stanley B. Greenfield's *"Wulf and Eadwacer:* all passion spent," *Anglo Saxon England* 15 (1986): 5–14, references both the Frese and Osborn essays.

75. I have tried to keep my translation as exact as possible while conserving at least a sense of the poem's poetic tone. Consequently, I have included two lexical possibilities for certain ambiguous passages, to reflect the lexical and poetic ambiguity that was possibly part of the original meaning.

76. I am grateful to Stanley B. Greenfield, Lewis E. Nicholson, and Alain Renoir for their generous reading of my manuscript in various stages of preparation and for suggesting important revisions.

ANITA R. RIEDINGER

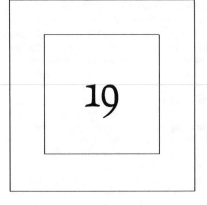

The Englishing of Arcestrate

Woman in Apollonius of Tyre

What images return
O my daughter.
—T. S. Eliot, "Marina," 1930

When the poet Venantius Fortunatus mourned his state of wandering exile in the sixth century, he likened himself to a fellow wanderer in sorrow, the shipwrecked Apollonius of Tyre.[1] If anyone ever found similar comfort in the trials of Arcestrate—of Pentapolis, Ephesus, and Antioch—we do not know about it. Yet hers was not an uneventful life: born a princess, she fell passionately in love with a penniless, shipwrecked musician, pursued him into marriage, and sailed off with him in anticipated wedded bliss, only to give birth to their daughter in the midst of violent seas. Mistaken for dead in childbirth, she was buried alive at sea, and then for three days floated across the waves in her coffin to the shores of Ephesus, where she was miraculously "restored" to life. Rather understandably, she then took a vow of chastity and sought refuge in the temple of Diana, where her career prospered: she rose to the position of *ealdor* 'chief' (36:1) and was even mistaken for the goddess Diana herself. Then, after more than fourteen years, she was reunited with her husband and for the first time met her daughter, Thasia—whose own young life had been complicated by attempted murder, pirates, and brothels. At the last, near the end of the tale, we are assured by the Old English translator that *æfter his earfoðnesse* 'after *his* hardships' (42:26)—a phrase that is an Old English addition to the Latin source[2]—*he leofode on stilnesse and on blisse ealle þa tid his lifes* 'he lived in peace and happiness all the rest of his life' (42:25–26). That is, Apollonius lived happily ever after.

It is, of course, the figure of Apollonius that unifies the tale, and we are told at the outset that the story is essentially his: *Her onginneð seo gerecednes . . . be Apollonige þam tiriscan* 'Here begins the story . . . about Apollonius the Tyrenian' (2:1–2). Women, however, are central to each of the hero's adventures, and in keeping with the purpose of *New Readings* this essay intends to discover the character of the nearly anonymous heroines of this earliest English romance—especially that of Arcestrate, his *wif* 'wife', whose progeny lived on into the twentieth century.

The Old English *Apollonius of Tyre* is remarkable in many respects. The story was extraordinarily popular all over Europe, yet of all the vernacular versions, the Old English is the oldest, probably dating from the late tenth or early eleventh century.[3] Further, it is an example of a genre commonly associated with the later Middle Ages and the pervasive influence of French writers, yet the Old English *Apollonius* stands as proof that the romance—and with it a taste for love stories nowhere else extant in Old English literature—entered England even before the Conquest. Finally, it is the only work of fiction to have been retold in Old, Middle, and Modern English. In spite of all these distinctions, however, the work has been curiously neglected. The reasons for this are probably threefold: deriving as it does from Greece via Rome, the work is not essentially Anglo-Saxon, or even Germanic; second, it is a translation, not an "original" work; and third, our Old English text is fragmentary, half of it missing.[4] To address the last point first: we are fortunate in the substance of the extant fragment. As Philip H. Goepp has observed, "It is the best part . . . it takes the tale as far as Apollonius' marriage, and thus forms a love-story complete in itself. The hero's subsequent misfortunes have little to do, artistically considered, with the first part of the story."[5] The extant text, then, affords us a nearly complete narrative line and, even more important for this study, a nearly complete portrait of Arcestrate. Still, it may be protested, she seems a stepchild of Old English literature, born in Greek romance and translated into Old English prose—but not transformed into a "true" Old English heroine, like Judith, Elene, or Juliana. Their apparent transformations from other cultures, of course, were largely effected by the prosody and formulaic character of the poetry in which their stories were retold. And our author works in prose. It has long been noted, however, that he is a skilled translator and a fine prose stylist. Peter Goolden demonstrates the ease with which he turns Latin constructions into idiomatic Old English, avoiding slavish adherence to his source (xxiii–v); and Stanley Greenfield commends the "smooth Old English prose," which he regards as "a taste of narrative style that might have been developed if William had lost at Hastings."[6] Clearly a writer and Latinist so talented as this was capable of altering his source and so transforming his characters when he wished or needed to—and he often did so, as I shall demonstrate below. This fact, in turn, makes his verbatim translations as important as his emendations, for both reveal what the author and his contemporary audience understood, applauded, condemned, or nonchalantly accepted in *Apollonius of Tyre*. This essay, then, will analyze both aspects of the translation, comparing it with Goolden's conflated Latin text, in order to determine specifically what kind of woman was acceptable to an Old English audience in the last years before the Conquest. The question is an important one, for Arcestrate represents a "new" type of heroine, one very unlike her Old English predecessors, yet one who was to be as long-lived as the genre of romance itself.[7]

In order to appreciate fully the expertise with which the translator adapts his text to his audience when he wishes to do so, let us first consider some obvious emendations in the work as a whole. For example, he identifies classical allusions. In Apollonius' anguished apostrophe to the sea, he cries out in the Latin, *O Neptune;* but the Old English translator adds an explanatory *sæ,* so that the phrase becomes, *eala þu sæ Neptune* (16:26). Similarly, an allusion to Apollo is amplified by *þara hæðenra God* (26:11). Epithets for the winds, Boreas and Affricus, are omitted altogether and become merely *eastnorðerne windas* and *suðwesterna wind* (16:20–21). Details of setting and custom are also sometimes changed. A *gebeorscipe* 'feast' is not held in a *triclinium* within a *domum* 'dining room' within a 'home' (27:7; 23:7 et passim), but merely in *ðare healle* (22:6; 26:12). And guests are not *discumbentes* 'reclining at tables', but more formally sitting, *ymbsittendan* (26:9 et passim). Perhaps, however, Old English feasts were more fun than the Roman, for the translator adds to his text that the guests *bliðe waeron* 'were happy' (22:13) and that not only were organs played, as in the original (39:14), but trumpets were blown, *biman geblawene* (38:15).

The translator freely modifies the character and behavior of the hero, as well. A major change is effected by deleting actions that might be deemed emotional or, less often, obsequious. For example, Apollonius treats King Arcestrates *officiose* 'deferentially' (21:14) in the Latin, but not in the Old English. And when the shipwrecked hero first saw a fisherman on shore, *Prostravit se illi ad pedes profusisque lacrimis ait . . .* 'He threw himself down at his feet and spoke with profuse tears' (19:4–5). But the Old English hero is far more stoic, and he does not weep; he merely *beseah and þus sarlice cwæð . . .* 'looked and spoke thus sorrowfully' (18:4–5). When he later sits at the king's feast, viewing all the luxury around him, one hero does so *dum flens cum dolore* 'while weeping with sorrow' (23:10); but the other just *sarlice sæt* 'sat sorrowfully' (22:17), again shunning tears. On one occasion Apollonius does weep: when, like Odysseus, he recalls past misfortunes (24:14). In this instance, however, the translator would have had difficulty had he deleted the tears, for they motivate the ensuing events. It is hard to imagine Beowulf, or the heroes of Maldon or Finnsburg, with tears in their eyes. The author's suppression of Apollonius' emotion seems a deliberate attempt to help him conform to Germanic heroic tradition. One other heroic emendation is particularly interesting to students of *Beowulf*: after his ship bursts in raging seas, *Apollonius ana becom mid sunde to Pentapolim* 'Apollonius alone came to Pentapolis, by swimming' (16:23–24). His Roman counterpart, on the other hand, was assisted *tabulae beneficio* 'with the aid of a plank' (17:18). The translator removes the plank; and like Beowulf, Apollonius performs an extraordinary swimming feat. Sometimes the author enhances the hero's character by additions to, rather than deletions from, the source. An already intelligent Apollonius is made more so by the added words *snotor* and *snotornesse* (4:31, 4:32). The fact that he is king is four times gratuitously introduced to the text (42:3, 42:12, 42:14, 42:21), and that he is a "famous" king—*se mæra cyngc*—is introduced twice (38:13; 42:3). Most conspicuous of all, however, is the repetition of the hero's name: in the one hundred ninety-one lines that constitute the "love story"—from Arcestrate's entrance to the imminent marriage at the end of the first fragment—Apollonius is named fifty-one times, eleven of which are the translator's additions to the Latin source. Meanwhile, the heroine is anonymous.

Arcestrate—heroine of the genre that was to supplant the heroic modes in which Elene, Judith, and Wealhtheow flourished—remains unnamed until almost the end. She enters the royal hall, greets the guests, sings, plays the harp, bestows gifts, falls in love, and chooses a husband—but she is never called "Arcestrate." Instead, she is called *dohtor* 'daughter' twenty-four times, *mæden* 'maiden' fifteen times, *cwen* 'queen' four times, *hlæfdige* 'lady' once, and *heo* or *hir* 'she' or 'her' uncounted times.[8] Only at the very end of the tale, at the climactic moment of recognition and reunion with Apollonius, is Arcestrate named, and then only twice:

Arcestrate soðlice, his wif, up aras and hine ymbclypte. . . . Heo ða micelre stæfne clipode and cwæð mid wope: "Ic eom Arcestrate, þin gemæcca, Arcestrates dohtor þæs cynges. . . . Hwær is min dohtor?" (38:4–11).

(Arcestrate, indeed his wife, rose up and embraced him. . . . She then called out in a mighty voice and spoke with weeping: "I am Arcestrate, your wife, daughter of Arcestrates the king. . . . Where is my daughter?")

For one brief moment, Arcestrate has a name; but she must further identify herself as wife, daughter, and—indirectly—mother. The latter role is barely alluded to again (38:29), and the proper name is never repeated. Instead, Arcestrate again recedes into anonymity, once more referred to only as *dohtor,* twice as *cwen* 'queen', and seven times as *gemæcca* or *wif* 'wife'. In each instance, the translator faithfully follows his source, but he tellingly does not choose to enhance the importance of Arcestrate by supplying her name where none is given, as he does so frequently for Apollonius.[9] This new Old English heroine, like her Roman prototype and unlike other Old English heroines, acquires her identity—indeed, even her name—solely from the male world around her.

Yet Arcestrate's first entrance into the hall proclaims her difference from all her predecessors. The timing of her entrance makes her almost a gift from heaven: King Arcestrates has just urged the despondent Apollonius to hope for better things from God—*gehiht on God þæt þu mote silf to ðam selran becuman* (22:24–25)—when Arcestrate enters:

ða færinga þær eode in ðæs cynges iunge dohtor and cyste hyre fæder and ða ymbsitten-dan. Þa heo becom to Apollonio. . . . (22:26–28).

(then suddenly the king's young daughter came in and kissed her father and those sitting about. Then she came to Apollonius. . . .)

When she finally speaks to him, she does so hesitatingly: *mid forwandigendre spræce* 'with faltering speech' (24:5). Though a princess, she is immediately subordinate to the hero. How changed from Wealhtheow's stately entrance into that earlier, Germanic hall: *Eode Wealhþeow forð* . . . 'Wealhtheow came forth' (Bwf 612b).[10] We are told Wealhtheow's name in the first verse, and we swiftly learn that she is both "noble" and "gold-adorned": *grette goldhroden guman on healle, / ond þa freolic wif ful gesealde* 'the gold-adorned one greeted the men in the hall, and the noble woman proffered the cup' (Bwf 614–15). Our anonymous heroine, on the other hand, is never "noble"; rarely, in fact, is Arcestrate described by any adjective other than *iunge*. Nor does the translator seem interested enough in her character to embellish it, as he does, for example, when he calls Apollonius *mære*. Furthermore, Arcestrate wears no gold, she proffers no cup—and her "greeting" is singular in Old English fiction: she kisses the guests. When she does so, however, she seems more restrained than does the original Arcestrate, for the Old English text uses the word *cyste* only once, while in the Latin, Arcestrate first gives her father a kiss—*dedit osculum patri*—and then explicitly goes on kissing one by one—*quae dum singulos oscularetur . . .* (23:18–19). A small change, one that merely deemphasizes a gesture—yet one of many efforts on the translator's part to mute customs and behavior that are atraditional, and perhaps not quite approved of. It is also one of the several means by which he reshapes the character of Arcestrate.

In *Medieval Romance,* John Stevens notes that the characters of romance lack "the comfortable, smudgy greys of ordinary life" and become instead merely "walkers and talkers who people the imaginary world. . . . White and black, good men and bad men, saints and devils." Stevens goes on to point out, however, that "not everyone in romance is a perfect knight or a perfect lady."[11] Thus, true to the genre, Arcestrate's character inevitably lacks subtle psychological complexity, and she is probably never intended to represent a complete portrait of a "perfect lady." Some of her qualities are so overtly applauded and emphasized, however, that they can be fairly taken, I believe, to represent attributes of an ideal woman. These "virtues" are primarily four: Arcestrate is kind, obedient, chaste, and—though not herself learned—she is a lover of learning. The value of both kindness and obedience is evident in the one brief scene, already noted, in which the translator allows Apollonius to weep. What was not noted earlier, however, was that Arcestrate is blamed for the tears. The king then chides her: *þu gesingodest. . . . ic bidde þe þæt þu gife him swa hwæt swa ðu wille* 'you have erred. . . . I command you to give him whatsoever you wish' (24:16, 18–19). When Arcestrate obeys, we then read one of the few direct statements ever made about her character: *se cyngc blissode on his dohtor welwillendnesse* 'the king rejoiced in his daughter's kindness (*benignitate*)' (24:23–24). It is interesting to note here that only when she has thus pleased both father and hero is Arcestrate said to be "kind." Her obedience is implicit throughout the text, as is the fact that she has no authority of her own. During the banquet scene, for example, she initiates no speech to the hero nor any other visible action without her father's express permission or command. We repeatedly hear her say such things as, *"nu ic mines fæder leafe habbe . . ."* or *"be mines fæder leafe"* (24:22; 26:27–28). It might be argued that this behavior is appropriate to one who is *iunge,* yet she is soon to wed Apollonius, who first becomes her tutor; thus the number of male authority figures in her life merely increases with time. Furthermore, Arcestrate's total compliance with authority seems to meet with the Old English translator's approval, for he further emphasizes it by adding to the Latin text, *Ða dide þæt mæden swa hyre beboden wæs* 'The maiden then did as she was bade' (28:17–18).

Even more overtly emphasized by both Latin and Old English texts is Arcestrate's role as "student." One of the few epithets that is accorded her is the hapax legomenon, *lærincg-mædene* 'learning-maiden', or 'pupil' (30:27). Another is *lare lufigend* 'lover of learning' (28:8).[12] This characteristic is insisted on throughout the tale, and even at the very end, she herself asserts: *þu eart Apollonius, min lareow, þe me lærdest; þu eart se forlidena man ðe ic lufode na for galnesse ac for wisdome* 'you are Apollonius, my teacher, who taught me; you are the shipwrecked man whom I loved not for lust, but for wisdom' (38:9–10). It has often been noted that Arcestrate is distinguished among Old English women because she sings and plays the harp, beautifully: *heo mid winsumum sange gemægnde þare hearpan sweg* (24:27–28). What has been less often noted, however, is that Apollonius does it better. When Arcestrate completes her song, all save one praise her *swegcræft* 'musical skill' (24:29): *Apollonius ana swigode* 'Apollonius alone was silent' (24:29). Chided by the king, the hero explains that *heo næfð hine na wel geleornod* 'she has not learned it well' (26:3). Apollonius then gives a stunning, superior performance on the harp; the description takes up thirteen lines (26:7–19). Arcestrate is merely a foil for the hero. This much is in the source. The superiority of Apollonius' learning to that of Arcestrate, however, is a theme that is embellished by the Old English translator. In both texts, Arcestrate is ordered to choose among suitors, who have made their proposals in writing. But in the Old English text alone, we are told that she is able to respond in writing solely because Apollonius has taught her how: *ðurh ða lare, þe þu æt me underfenge, þe silf on gewrite gecyðan* . . . 'you yourself make known in writing, through the learning that you have received from me' (32:4–5). Once again, the stature of the hero is enhanced, while that of the heroine is diminished.

This kind of change is not always effected by the juxtaposition of these two characters—that is, Apollonius' virtues are not always enlarged at Arcestrate's expense in particular. But the phenomena pervade the Old English translator's work: Apollonius grows more glorious, and Arcestrate grows slightly less able and important. I have already noted, for example, that the translator adds the words *snotor* and *snotornesse* to his initial portrait of Apollonius, who is already a scholar, abundantly lettered: *habundantia litterarum* (5:23). The scope of Arcestrate's knowledge, on the other hand, is specifically limited: when she wonders why Apollonius is sad, the king commands her to ask him directly, adding, *Decet enim te omnia nosse* 'Indeed, it is fitting that you know all things' (25:3). In the Old English, *omnia* 'all things' is silently dropped (24:4). Sometimes the textual changes seem to draw attention away from the person of Arcestrate. After her musical performance, for example, we learn that *tunc omnes laudare coeperunt* 'then all began to praise her', with the word "her" understood (25:23). The identical construction, *laudare coeperunt*, follows Apollonius' performance, as well (27:11), and the Old English translates it *hine heredon* 'they praised him' (26:16). The praise for Arcestrate, however, is deflected from her person to her musicianship when the translator adds the phrase *on hyre swegcræft* to the clause, *Ða ongunnon ealle þa men hi herian* 'Then all the men began to praise her' (24:29–30). Similarly, when she gives gifts to Apollonius, the Latin reads, *Laudant omnes liberalitatem puellae* 'all praised the girl's generosity' (29:3). But in the Old English, the attention is shifted from the fact of Arcestrate's generosity, to the gifts themselves: *and ealle þa men hire gife heredon* 'and all the men praised her gifts' (28:3–4). Perhaps, as Goolden suggests, this change is made as a concession to an Old English audience's traditional love of gifts and gift-giving (56); and perhaps it therefore also makes Arcestrate more like traditional Germanic gift-givers. But still there is a difference: Arcestrate gives only with the king's permission, and only with *his* gold (26:25). No other Old English gift-giver must first borrow the gift. This change, then, remains part of a larger pattern that detracts from the significance of the heroine. [13]

Another difference between Arcestrate and earlier Old English heroines has been often noted: she is the first woman in Old English literature to fall in love—*þa gefeol hyre mod on his lufe* (26:22).[14] But the translator, at least, does not seem to have regarded this innovation as a virtue; rather, it seems to have inspired some of his most industrious editorial work. In "Prudery in Old English Fiction," Morton Donner finds that the translator "reacts prudishly to both love and lust, to sexuality whether in thought or deed."[15] The suppression of Arcestrate's kissing when she first enters the hall foreshadows this reaction, but it grows much stronger than that. Donner notes, for example, that the Old English translator deletes a long passage in which the Latin heroine suffers a lovesickness so extreme that doctors are required (31:4–9). And as Donner also notes, one heroine explicitly *vidit amores suos* 'saw her love' (31:28); but her descendant merely *geseah Apollonium* 'saw Apollonius' (30:29). As the Old English translator continues to modify Arcestrate's love, he changes other aspects of her behavior as well, so that her whole demeanor grows more sedate. For example, the source says that she awoke at first light because she was unable to bear her love: *non sustinens amorem* (29:18). This causal phrase, too, is deleted in the Old English, although the motivation remains clear. Immediately thereafter, both the Latin and the Old English women seek the king to ask that Apollonius be made tutor; yet each enters the room very differently: the *puella* "burst in"—*irrupit in*—and affectionately cajoled her father with the epithet *carissime* 'dearest one' (29:18, 22). But the more reserved Old English heroine merely *eode* 'went' into the room, addressing her father simply as *ðe* (28:23, 27). She is just as successful as her predecessor, however, and the king agrees to make Apollonius her *lareow* 'teacher' or 'master'.

The latter scene illustrates more than Arcestrate's newly acquired decorum, however; it illustrates her capacity for dissembling. And this quality, in turn, is as new to women in Old English literature as is her love. In their comparison of Wealhtheow with a later romantic heroine, the thirteenth-century Rymenhild of *King Horn*, Cecily Clark and Elizabeth Williams make a distinction between the heroines of epic and romance. Regarding Wealhtheow's first speech in the hall, they note therein "nothing confidential or deceptive." They continue:

> In *King Horn*, on the other hand, open words and actions also act as a cover for something else, making us aware of a private scene going on inside the public one. . . . Rymenhild, in other words, has an inner emotional life as well as a public role. . . .[16]

This same characteristic of romance is already apparent in the character of Arcestrate: a "private scene" takes place within her that results in a kind of deception—one that the translator presumably finds acceptable, since he emends it not at all. At first it is only hinted at. When the king commands Arcestrate to give Apollonius gifts, we are told:

> Ða ða þæt mæden gehirde þæt hire wæs alyfed fram hire fæder þæt heo ær hyre silf gedon wolde . . . (24:19–20).

> (Then when the maiden heard that leave was granted her from her father to do what she herself had already wished. . . .)

Here we are merely told of Arcestrate's inner thoughts, thoughts of which no one else in the scene is aware. Shortly after, however, her actions are overtly and deliberately deceptive. Having fallen in love with the departing Apollonius, she has a new fear:

> Đa adred þæt mæden þæt heo næfre eft Apollonium ne gesawe swa raðe swa heo wolde, and eode þa to hire fæder and cwæð: "Ðu goda cyningc, licað ðe wel þæt Apollonius þe þurh us todæg gegodod is þus heonon fare, and cuman yfele men and bereafian hine?" (28:11–15).

> (Then the maiden feared that never afterwards would she see Apollonius as quickly as she wished, and she went to her father and said: "Good king, does it please you that Apollonius, who has been made rich by us today, should go away like this, and that evil men should come and rob him?")

The stratagem works, and the king commands her to arrange for Apollonius' stay. We smile at this harmless deception; yet it is a deception—and it clearly derives not only from a wish to disguise her love, but also from the fact that Arcestrate has no authority of her own. She has therefore learned to manipulate the male world around her, a feminine "talent" that is celebrated long after Arcestrate introduces it into English literature.

Once again, the differences between Arcestrate and earlier Old English heroines are striking: she cannot, like Elene or Judith, lead whole armies towards one grand goal, if only because this new heroine has no such power to command. And although she is as single-minded as they, her quest does not, like theirs, affect the fate of mankind, but is entirely personal: she wishes to marry Apollonius. When she is directed to choose a husband from a list of suitors and their *morgengife* 'marriage gifts' (30:22) and discovers that Apollonius' name is not among them, her moment of crisis comes.[17] The dissembling then ceases and she grows increasingly forthright, writing to her father:

> Þu goda cyngc and min se leofesta fæder, nu þin mildheortnesse me leafe sealde þæt ic silf moste ceosan hwilcne wer ic wolde, ic secge ðe to soðan þone forlidenan man ic wille, and gif ðu wundrige þæt swa scamfæst fæmne swa unforwandigendlice ðas word awrat, þonne wite þu þæt ic habbe þurh weax aboden, ðe nane scame ne can, þæt ic silf ðe for scame secgan ne mihte (32:11–17).

> (Thou good king and my dearest father, now that thy loving kindness has given me leave that I myself might choose which husband I would, I tell you in truth, I want the shipwrecked man, and if you wonder that so chaste a woman has so boldly written these words, then know that I have declared in wax, which knows no shame, that which I might not say for shame.)

Just as Arcestrate spoke hesitantly at the beginning—*mid forwandigendre spræce* 'with faltering speech'—she now speaks *unforwandigendlice* 'boldly'. She characterizes herself as a 'virgin'—*fæmne* (*virgo*)—and as 'chaste'—*scamfæst*—a word that dominates her portrait at the end of the story.[18] She is now very explicit: *Apollonium ic wille* 'I want Apollonius' (34:19). As she confronts her father, her weapons are several. She threatens: *and gif þu me him ne silst, þu forlætst ðine dohtor* 'and if you will not give him to me, you lose your daughter' (34:20). She prostrates herself: *ðæt mæden þa gefeol to hyre fæder fotum* 'the maiden then fell at her father's feet' (34:16). And with a winning stroke, she weeps: *Se cyng ða soðlice ne mihte aræfnian his dohtor tearas* 'The king truly could not endure his daughter's tears' (34:20–21).[19] Unlike all other Old English heroines, then, Arcestrate's final tactic in "battle" is what has become stereotypically feminine—her tears. Once again, these strategies are in the source: *Puella vero prostravit se pedibus patris sui. . . . Rex non sustinens filiae suae lacrimas . . .* (35:11–17). An Old English woman was apparently allowed to be more emotional than was a man, however, for it may be remembered that Apollonius' similar behavior was deleted from the text: *Prostravit se illi ad pedes profusisque lacrimis ait* became merely *he beseah and þus sarlice cwæð* 'he looked and spoke thus sorrowfully. . .' (19:4–5; 18:4–5).

We do see Apollonius bow down once, when near the end of the story he mistakes Arcestrate for the goddess Diana:

> he mid his aðume and mid his dohtor to hyre urnon and feollon ealle to hire fotum, and wendon þæt heo Diana wære seo giden . . . (36:9–11).

> (with his daughter and son-in-law he ran to her, and all fell at her feet, and thought that she was the goddess Diana. . . .)

The events leading up to this scene are lost from the Old English manuscript, but the Latin versions show that Arcestrate has given birth to a daughter, Thasia; been mistaken for dead; and become a priestess in the temple of Diana, where she has served for many years. Only at this moment, and in this place, does Arcestrate acquire stature. Among the women with whom she has served Diana, she is *ealdor* 'leader' or 'chief'—the only woman in Old English fiction to have earned that epithet. She has many followers: *micclum fæmnena [virginum] heape* 'a mighty band of virgins' (36:6). She is no longer powerless, for she has the authority to name her own successor: *heo gesette hyre gingran þe hire folgode to sacerde* 'she appointed her subordinate, who followed her, as priestess' (38:17). Further, Arcestrate is esteemed by all:

> Heo wæs soðlice þearle wlitig, and for ðare micclan lufe þare clænnesse hi sædon ealle þæt þar nære nan Dianan swa gecweme swa heo (36:7–9).

> (She was truly extremely beautiful, and because of her great love of chastity [*castitatis*] all said that there was none so pleasing to Diana as she.)

Now Arcestrate is said to be beautiful.[20] And she is openly praised, for her *clænnesse.*[21] Perhaps this is a characteristic that the Old English translator, too, can applaud, for his emendations finally enhance, rather than diminish, her portrait. When the source again says Arcestrate is beautiful, the translator adds *beorhtnesse* 'brightness' to her beauty: *hyre micclan beorhtnesse and wlite* 'her great brightness and beauty' (36:12). And when she prepares to receive Apollonius in the temple, the translator, not his source, crowns her in the finest Old English tradition, *mid golde:*

hire heafod mid golde and mid gimmon gelængde 'adorned her head with gold and with gems' (36:5). Shortly thereafter, as already noted, she can announce her identity: "*Ic eom Arcestrate . . .*" (38:7–8). Now she has name, status, and power.

The moment is brief, however, for when Arcestrate adds that she is *þin gemæcca, Arcestrates dohtor þæs cynges* 'your wife, daughter of King Arcestrates' (38:8), she swiftly recedes into the background. After more than fourteen years in Ephesus, where she has become a leader in a feminine society, she becomes once again an anonymous woman in a world ruled by men: she is reunited with her father, *Arcestrates þam cynge* (40:28), whose name and title are added to the text—*se cyning . . . Arcestrates* (40:30–42:1)—although he re-enters the tale for only six lines. When the king dies, he divides his lands between *Apollonio* and his unnamed *dohtor* (42:2). Arcestrate never rules over her inheritance, however, for Apollonius appoints his son *to cynge on Arcestrates cynerice his ealdefæder* 'as king in the kingdom of Arcestrates, his grandfather' (42:21–2). Further, she seems only peripherally instrumental even in the birth of her son: *Apollonius se cyngc sunu gestrynde be his gemæccan* 'Apollonius the king begot a son by his wife' (42:21); Apollonius' name and title here are textual additions. Finally, she participates in a long marriage: *And he sylfa welwillendlice mid his gemæccan seofon and hundseofonti geara and heold þæt cynerice* 'And he himself lived benevolently with his wife for seventy-seven years and ruled the kingdom . . .' (42:23–24). Presumably, Arcestrate got what she wanted—*Apollonium ic wille*—but she was thereby totally subsumed.

In the epilogue that the translator adds to his source, he—or perhaps a "she" who is as acquiescent to a masculine culture as Arcestrate—reasserts the subject matter of the narrative:

> Her endað ge wea ge wela Apollonius þæs tiriscan, ræde se þe wille.
>
> (Here ends both the grief and the happiness of Apollonius the Tyrenian, read he who will.)

The story is clearly meant to belong to Apollonius alone. Indeed, one must read closely to discern here also the tale of Arcestrate. But that fact itself is a significant part of her story, for she is perhaps as vividly defined by what she is not as by what she is. She seems, first of all, not of great interest to her translator—and therefore probably not to his audience—for he generally either diminishes her portrait or neglects it altogether, preferring instead to embellish that of the hero. Both approaches, however, effect the same change: Arcestrate is even more subordinate to Apollonius than was her Latin predecessor. She is less wise, less talented, less dignified, less important than he. She is also less conspicuous, for she moves anonymously through the story, in the shadows of Apollonius' masculine world. She is therefore also very unlike her Old English predecessors, for they were women of action, accustomed to power, subordinate to none. Wealhtheow, for example, can say of the warriors in the hall that they *doð swa ic bidde* 'do as I command' (Bwf 1231b). Elene makes Judas yield to her demands without subterfuge, tears, or subservient pleas, for she commands a whole army. Judith, too, moves on another plane: unlike the helpless daughter of King Antiochus, who is incestuously raped at the beginning of *Apollonius,* Judith beheads Holofernes before he can violate her. He, not she, is destroyed. And Juliana heroically defies both father and suitor, but she is suffused with a divine purpose larger than the power of the masculine society that would confine her. These heroines, however, were figures of epic, and of heroic saints' lives, while Arcestrate's role is circumscribed by the "new" world of romance, with its emphasis on love—a world in which battles and quests are often personal and only rarely affect the fate of nations. The stage is smaller now, the action private, and for Arcestrate, at least, it is essentially without conflict. She would not wish to defy either father or suitor, and even when she seems to do so, in her "battle" to win the husband of her choice, her victory has been smiled upon in advance by her father. She successfully fulfills the role defined for her by the patriarchy in which she lives, and she probably does so contentedly. Were she not content, she might have remained mute before Apollonius in the temple of Diana, never uttering the fatal words, "*Ic eom Arcestrate,*" returning instead to the world in which we glimpse her as *ealdor.* She might then have become heroine of an Old English epic, or saint's life, or elegy. But Arcestrate is the heroine of romance, and such a choice would never once have occurred to her.

As a result, perhaps, this newcomer to the Old English tradition has lived on longer than all the rest and is still occasionally recognizable today, both in art and in life: she is a gracious hostess, cordially greeting the guests at a dinner party, lightly kissing one or two, but not too effusively. She is politely accomplished: she plays at the harp, sings a little, and writes a bit. But not *too* well—and never so well that she outshines a man, particularly one she admires. She is reasonably compliant with her father's wishes, and though she marries a man she loves, he chances to meet with her father's approval: the man has, after all, a good background and a promising future (if he would give up sailing so much). She bears his children, and they are especially delighted when they finally have a son, and heir. When trials come, as they will to any life, she is forced to pursue a career for a time (and even discovers that she is rather good at it), but this distressing situation is only temporary: things sort themselves out and she returns home, where she belongs. Her husband can once again be responsible for their lives. She need not worry now about her recent inheritance, or politics, or travel plans, for example—her husband takes care of all that, as a man should. He is kind to her, too, as they grow old, and they live out their long lives together. He remains very active, travels a lot, is prominent in world affairs, and even begins work on his autobiography. We do not quite know what Arcestrate does, however, now that the children are gone. (Her son is away, running her father's business; and her daughter finally married, thank heavens, after some scandalous years abroad, and has a nice young man to take care of her.) Perhaps Arcestrate takes up the harp again—it has been years since she has touched it, and it used to please her father so. Or perhaps she writes letters to old suitors (her husband still thinks he taught her how, and she lets him). Perhaps she ponders the romance of her life. And perhaps she sometimes reads old books—or even recalls the song of some very old scop—telling tales of strange, heroic women of the past, who did not, as she did, live happily ever after.

NOTES

1. "Tristius erro nimis, patriis vagus exsul ab oris, / Quam sit Apollonius naufragus hospes aquis," *Miscellanea,* vi, ch. x, 5–6 in Migne, *Patrologiae,* T. 88. Quoted by Peter Goolden, ed., *The Old English Apollonius of Tyre* (London: Oxford University Press, 1958), p. xii. All quotations from *Apollonius* are from Goolden's edition. In his exhaustive study of *Historia Apollonii Regis Tyri,* G. A. A. Kortekaas dates the Fortunatus reference between 566 and 568 (Groningen: Bouma's Boekhuis, 1984), p. 98.

2. By "source" I mean Goolden's conflated Latin text. The original is no longer extant. In preparation of his conflation, however, Goolden consulted seventeen manuscripts, accepting Zupitza's identification of CCCC MS. 318 (denoted by Goolden as "*a*") as closest to the Old English version. With that manuscript as a base-text, Goolden emended his conflation (*G*) with readings from other mss. whenever they supplied words or omissions found in the Old English, but not in *a,* relying most heavily on those closest to the original *Historia,* which he designates *R1* and *R2* (xiv, xvii–xviii). For new editions of the latter two groups of mss., as well as a complete discussion of the many other Latin recensions, see Kortekaas, who cites Goolden's "experiment" appreciatively (139). To Goolden's comparisons of the Old English and Latin versions of *Apollonius* I have silently added my own, based on my own reading of the two texts. The interpretations of the causes of the variations are my own.

3. The Old English version is extant in CCCC MS. 201, which also contains a collection of Wulfstan's *Homilies,* all copied by a single scribe; *Apollonius* is therefore a copy of an earlier version no longer extant. Kortekaas (6) dates the ms. early in the eleventh century; in *A Study of Old English Literature* (New York: W. W. Norton, 1967), C. L. Wrenn dates the original to the late tenth century (255). In *The Lost Literature of Medieval England* (New York: Cooper Square, 1952), R. M. Wilson says that another version, now lost, probably existed also, for he finds " 'Apollonium, anglice' " entered in the catalogue (c. A.D. 1175) of the Benedictine Abbey at Burton-on-Trent (81). Many have remarked on the longevity of *Apollonius of Tyre.* Goolden notes its transmission from Old through Modern English, finding that it also "exerted a considerable influence on the medieval romances, French and English" (xiii). It was translated into nearly all the languages of Europe, and in English was popularized in a direct line of descent from Gower's *Confessio Amantis* (viii, 271–2008) to Shakespeare's *Pericles,* to Lillo's *Marina;* from *Pericles* came the inspiration for Eliot's "Marina." In addition to Goolden's Introduction, see especially Laura A. Hibbard, *Mediaeval Romance in England: A Study of the Sources and Analogues of the Non-Cyclic Metrical Romances* (New York: Oxford University Press, 1924), pp. 164–73, and Albert H. Smyth, *Shakespeare's Pericles and Apollonius of Tyre: A Study in Comparative Literature* (Philadelphia: MacCalla and Co., 1898), pp. 6–24, 47–59. Smyth also provides summaries of all the vernacular versions.

4. Kortekaas says that the first Greek version was "perhaps written in Syria" late in the second or early in the third century, adding: "Of this original Greek romance there is no trace to be found" (132). For the fragmentary nature of the Old English text, see Goolden, *Old English Apollonius,* p. 59.

5. "The Narrative Material of *Apollonius of Tyre,*" *English Literary History* 5 (1938): 170.

6. *A Critical History of Old English Literature* (New York: New York University Press, 1965), p. 63.

7. Feminist critics have often protested that it is not enough merely to call attention to a female character in a text. However, because Arcestrate (along with the whole text) has been so neglected in critical studies and because this Old English stepchild is so different from Elene or Judith or Wealhtheow—and from all the other Old English heroines who preceded her—an analysis of her character must be the first aim of this essay. For an excellent overview of types of critical approaches to women in Old English literature, see Alexandra Hennessey Olsen, "Women in *Beowulf,*" in *Approaches to Teaching Beowulf,* ed. Jess B. Bessinger, Jr., and Robert F. Yeager (New York: Modern Language Association, 1984), pp. 150–60.

8. The other women in the tale are similarly treated: King Antiochus' wife, daughter, and his daughter's *fostor-modor* (*nutrix*) are all unnamed. Arcestrate, like her daughter Thasia, is first named in the missing fragment. Thereafter, Thasia is named five times; however, she is referred to merely as Apollonius' *dohtor* nine times (and only twice as Arcestrate's), as *mæden* once, and as King Arcestrates' granddaughter (*nefan*) once. Thus, she, too, is essentially identified by her relationship to the men in the text. Only the villainous Dionysias is consistently, and immediately, identified by name. The men, on the other hand, are named immediately, however unimportant their status: Apollonius and Antiochus, in the Prologue; Thaliarcus the *dihtnere* 'steward' (8:4–5); the loyal Hellanicus (10:26–27); Stranguilio of Tarsus (12:25–26); even one of Arcestrate's three suitors—Ardalius—is named at his second entrance, although the name of the woman he would wed has still not been mentioned (32:21). Only the fisherman who shares his cloak with Apollonius goes unnamed. This fisherman is often associated with the story of St. Martin of Tours; perhaps his singular anonymity among men attests to such origins. Kortekaas, however, cautions that "the combination of a compassionate fisherman and a destitute castaway forms a stock prop of romance" (114).

9. Apollonius' name is added to the text another eleven times outside the passages already cited, bringing the total number of additions to twenty-two.

10. For a full discussion of woman as welcoming figure in Old English poetry, see Helen Damico, *Beowulf's Wealhtheow and the Valkyrie Tradition* (Madison: University of Wisconsin Press, 1984), esp. pp. 21–23. I quote *Beowulf* from Fr. Klaeber, ed., *Beowulf and the Fight at Finnsburg,* 3rd ed. with First and Second Supplements (Lexington, Mass.: D. C. Heath, 1950).

11. John Stevens, *Medieval Romance: Themes and Approaches* (New York: W. W. Norton, 1974), pp. 169–70.

12. This epithet is interesting, since Arcestrate is given this title by Apollonius before he becomes her *lareow* 'teacher'; she, in turn, twice calls him *lareow* (26:27; 28:1) before he has become her teacher (30:4–6). Thus epithets adhere to character rather than to context, a practice that William Whallon has shown to be true of Homeric verse, while finding the opposite to be true for Old English poetry. Perhaps this usage further attests to the Greek roots of *Apollonius*. See Whallon, *Formula, Character and Context: Studies in Homeric, Old English, and Old Testament Poetry* (Cambridge, Mass.: Harvard University Press, 1969).

13. Some other examples of such detraction are as follows: *magna* 'great' is deleted from the address to Arcestrate/Diana (37:21); *domina* 'lady' is deleted for both Thasia (41:8) and Arcestrate (29:13); and *domina mea regina* 'my lady the queen' is changed to *þu eadige cwen* 'thou happy [or 'fortunate'] queen' in Apollonius' address to Arcestrate (42:10). An opposite change is of particular interest because, as Damico points out, "There are no intimate relationships between females in Anglo-Saxon poetry, not even between mother and daughter" (*Beowulf's Wealhtheow,* p. 20). There is one such scene in this prose work, however: between Antiochus' daughter and her nurse, or *fostor-modor,* after the rape. The latter woman, who is warmly sympathetic to the younger and advises acquiescence because she fears her suicide, twice addresses her formally as *hlæfdige* 'lady'. In one instance this is a precise translation of *domina* (3:21), but in the other it is a change from the far more intimate *mea alumna* 'my foster-daughter' (3:18). They are thus distanced by what seems the Old English translator's sense of decorum.

14. This primacy is noted by Goolden, who also notes that the first man to do so is Antiochus (55).

15. Morton Donner, "Prudery in Old English Fiction" (*Comitatus* 3 [1972]: 95). Donner (93), however, uses Goolden's base text, CCCC MS. 318, rather than his conflated text. Since the latter supplies readings from other mss. whenever they accord with the Old English version, it seems likely to be closer to the lost original than is any single ms. Donner cites emendations at 28:21–22, 30:29, 31:4–9, and 32:8, as well as in the passages pertaining to the incestuous rape of Antiochus' daughter. The conflation, however, shows that the first of these citations is probably not an emendation, for a reading very close to the Old English is supplied by CCCC MS. 451: *verborum cantusque memor* (Goolden, 29). Donner (95) also finds that the

translator "prefers not to mention" the word "love"; however, I find the word mentioned five times in the early stages of the "love story" alone (26:22, 28:21, 32:7, 29, and 34:18).

16. "After 1066" in Christine Fell with Cecily Clark and Elizabeth Williams, (*Women in Anglo-Saxon England and the Impact of 1066* (Bloomington: Indiana University Press, 1984), pp. 172–73).

17. The marriage customs accord with the source, save for a slight difference regarding the phrase *hire morgengife,* which in the Latin reads *dotis quantitatem* 'the size of the marriage settlement' (31:22), without a reference to *hire.* This would be an important distinction for an Anglo-Saxon audience, for Christine Fell notes that the "morning-gift" is paid "not to the father or kin, but to the woman herself" (*Women in Anglo-Saxon England,* p. 57). The word *brydgifta* is used in the scene between Antiochus' daughter and her *fostor-modor* as a translation of *legitimum nuptiarum* 'lawful marriage' (2:27) and is added to the Old English text at 4:2. The shortened *gifta* translates *nuptiarum* (6:8) and *to giftelicre yldo* translates *ad nubilem aetatem* (2:7). Arcestrate's choosing among her suitors also accords with tenth- and eleventh-century documents described by Fell in which the woman's consent to a marriage is given or required (58).

18. The translator is very consistent in his translations of words for "woman." *Fæmne* means only "virgin" in this text. It is used first when he paraphrases Antiochus' violation of his daughter, making the act less vivid: for the Latin *virginitatis* 'of virginity' (3:16), he substitutes *fæmnan . . . ofercom* 'overcame . . . the virgin', or 'woman who is a virgin' (2:17). At the end of the story, *fæmnena* translates *virginum* (36:6, 37:5) and refers to the women who serve with Arcestrate in the temple of Diana. *Wif,* on the other hand, seems to mean not only "wife," but "woman who is not a virgin"; it does not mean merely "adult female." It is used as a translation of *coniunx* and *uxor,* both meaning "wife," as well as of *mulier* 'woman'. Dionysias, for example, is *wif* 'coniuge' and *wif* '*mulier*' (16:11, 17:8; 40:5, 11, 12 and 41:6, 11, 12). It has gone unnoted that in two of these instances, she is further an *yfel wif* 'evil woman' (*scelerata mulier, malae mulieri*), as is Arcestrate in the controversial phrase, *næs git yfel wif* (*nondum mulier mala,* 30:31, 31:30). This phrase is part of Apollonius' address to Arcestrate when he delivers the letters from her suitors. Goolden finds it "pointless and out of context" (57). In his article, "*Næs git yfel wif* in the Old English *Apollonius,*" *Journal of English and Germanic Philology* 30 (1931), Frederick Pottle translates it "there never was a wicked woman," adding, "That this makes very little sense in the context would not have bothered him [the translator] greatly" (23). Accepting Goolden's reading of *næs* as "not at all" (57), I translate the phrase, "not at all yet a bad woman," with "woman" implicitly including the idea of one who is sexually experienced. The point of the phrase is inherent in the meaning of the word *wif* and is not nonsensical: the translator has faithfully followed his source in a shift from *mæden (puella)* (30:29, 31:28) to *wif (mulier)* (30:31, 31:30). For this translator, in particular, just the change from "maiden" to "woman" is sufficient to justify the adjective "bad." Although he explains the phrase in yet another way, O. F. Emerson points out that "the classical story had been modified here and there by a Christian monk or cleric" and that the Latin author here was "influenced by his clerical conception of celibacy as the 'holy' state" ("The Old English *Apollonius of Tyre,*" *Modern Language Notes* 38 [1923]: 271). It seems probable that the same explanation applies to the Old English translator, a suggestion that is corroborated by his emendations: Donner has already noted that *amores suos* is changed to *Apollonium* (95) at the beginning of this scene (30:29); unnoted, however, is the fact that *cubiculum* 'to [my] bedchamber' (31:29) is deleted from the Old English altogether. Although the context is clearer in the source than in the bowdlerized Old English text, it seems to me consistent with both the translation and the invariably superior stance of the translator's hero that when Arcestrate wonders why he has come alone (30:30), Apollonius should chide, *Hlæfdige, næs git yfel wif. . . .* I believe that Arcestrate would have understood him, as would an Old English audience.

19. Even now, the true cause of the victory remains ambiguous, for the king adds, *Þu hafast gecoren þone wer þe me wel licað* 'you have chosen the husband who pleases me well' (34:23). Her wishes coincided with his.

20. Physical beauty is noted on only two, very antithetical occasions in the text: at this moment when Arcestrate is celebrated as goddess-like, and earlier, when Antiochus' daughter is debased (2:6, 4:22–23). This antithesis accords with Northrop Frye's analysis of the structure of *Apollonius* in *The Secular Scripture: A Study of Romance* (Cambridge, Mass.: Harvard University Press, 1976): "The story proceeds toward an end which echoes the beginning, but echoes it in a different world. The beginning is the demonic parody of the end . . ." (49).

21. In this respect, the Old English Arcestrate is very like the heroines of contemporary saints' lives, of whom Jane Chance says in *Woman as Hero in Old English Literature* (Syracuse, N.Y.: Syracuse University Press, 1986): "While many of these saints are not Anglo-Saxon and while their lives are translated into Old English from the Latin, nevertheless their popularity argues at least for strength of interest in them in this period: these women behave heroically by refusing to succumb to natural sexual desires conventionally associated with the female, because of their spiritual weapon of faith in God. As such they emulate the biblical and patristic models provided by the Virgin Mary, Judith, Juliana, and Elene" (55). This is the only way, however, in which I find Arcestrate to be like the latter "models."

Index